Realities of Canadian Nursing: Professional, Practice, and Power Issues

Marjorie McIntyre, RN, PhD
Faculty of Nursing
University of Calgary
Calgary, Alberta, Canada

and

Elizabeth Thomlinson, RN, PhD
Faculty of Nursing
University of Calgary
Calgary, Alberta, Canada

LIPPINCOTT WILLIAMS & WILKINS
A **Wolters Kluwer** Company

Philadelphia • Baltimore • New York • London
Buenos Aires • Hong Kong • Sydney • Tokyo

Senior Acquisitions Editor: Margaret Zuccarini
Developmental Editor: Deedie McMahon
Senior Editorial Coordinator: Helen Kogut
Production Editor: Diane Griffith
Senior Production Manager: Helen Ewan
Managing Editor/Production: Erika Kors
Design Coordinator: Brett MacNaughton
Manufacturing Manager: William Alberti
Compositor: Lippincott Williams & Wilkins
Printer: Maple/Binghamton

9 8 7 6 5 4 3 2 1

Library of Congress Cataloging-in-Publication Data

Realities of Canadian nursing : professional, practice, and power issues / Marjorie McIntyre and Elizabeth Thomlinson [editors].
      p. cm.
   Includes bibliographical references and index.
   ISBN 0-7817-3443-6 (alk. paper)
     1. Nursing—Canada. 2. Nurses—Canada. 3. Nursing—Social aspects—Canada. I. McIntyre, Marjorie, RN, PhD. II. Thomlinson, Elizabeth.

RT6.A1 .R435 2003
610.73'0971—dc21   2002031287

Care has been taken to confirm the accuracy of the information presented and to describe generally accepted practices. However, the authors, editors, and publisher are not responsible for errors or omissions or for any consequences from application of the information in this book and make no warranty, express or implied, with respect to the content of the publication.

The authors, editors, and publisher have exerted every effort to ensure that drug selection and dosage set forth in this text are in accordance with the current recommendations and practice at the time of publication. However, in view of ongoing research, changes in government regulations, and the constant flow of information relating to drug therapy and drug reactions, the reader is urged to check the package insert for each drug for any change in indications and dosage and for added warnings and precautions. This is particularly important when the recommended agent is a new or infrequently employed drug.

Some drugs and medical devices presented in this publication have Food and Drug Administration (FDA) clearance for limited use in restricted research settings. It is the responsibility of the health care provider to ascertain the FDA status of each drug or device planned for use in his or her clinical practice.

LWW.com

ABOUT THE AUTHORS

Marjorie Ruth McIntyre, RN, PhD, attended the Royal Alexandra School of Nursing in Edmonton and practised both in acute care and community settings. She earned a BN at The University of Victoria, an MSN at the University of British Columbia, and a PhD at the University of Colorado in Denver. As an associate professor, she currently teaches at the University of Calgary, where her interests include critical feminist philosophy, hermeneutics, and issues in nursing and health care.

Elizabeth Helen Thomlinson, RN, PhD, attended the Winnipeg General Hospital School of Nursing and practised in rural and northern settings in Manitoba. She earned her BN and MN at the University of Manitoba and her doctoral degree from the University of Minnesota in Minneapolis. She is currently an associate professor at the University of Calgary. Among her areas of expertise are rural and remote health care and nursing, family violence and violence against women, and nursing education.

CONTRIBUTORS

Geertje Boschma, RN, PhD
Assistant Professor
Faculty of Nursing
University of Calgary
Calgary, Alberta, Canada
Chapter 6

Isobel I. Boyle, RN, MN
Family Health Manager
Wellington, Dufferin, Guelph Health Unit
Fergus, Ontario, Canada
Chapter 20

Laurel Brunke, RN, MSN
Executive Director
Registered Nurses Association of British
    Columbia
Vancouver, British Columbia, Canada
Chapter 8

Barbara L. Brush, RNC, PhD, FAAN
Associate Professor
School of Nursing
Boston College
Chestnut Hill, Massachusetts
Chapter 6

W. Dean Care, RN, EdD
Academic Assistant to the Dean
Faculty of Nursing
University of Manitoba
Winnipeg, Manitoba, Canada
Chapter 13

Tracy Jean Carr, BN, MSc, PhD(c)
Assistant Professor
Department of Nursing
University of New Brunswick
Saint John, New Brunswick, Canada
Chapter 25

Christine Ceci, RN, MN, PhD (candidate)
Doctoral Student
Faculty of Nursing
University of Calgary
Calgary, Alberta, Canada
Chapters 2 and 23

Wanda M. Chernomas, RN, PhD
Assistant Professor and Associate Dean,
    Undergraduate Programs
Faculty of Nursing
University of Manitoba
Winnipeg, Manitoba, Canada
Chapter 13

Heather F. Clarke, RN, PhD
Health and Nursing Policy, Research and
    Evaluation Consulting
Vancouver, British Columbia, Canada
Chapter 4

C.E. Cragg, RN, EdD
Professor
Director, School of Nursing, Associate Dean
    of Health Sciences
University of Ottawa
Ottawa, Ontario, Canada
Chapter 10

Diana Davidson Dick, RN, MEd
Dean, Nursing Division
Saskatchewan Institute of Applied Science
    and Technology
Saskatoon, Saskatchewan, Canada
Chapter 10

David Gregory, RN, BScN, MN, PhD
Professor and Dean
Faculty of Nursing
University of Manitoba
Winnipeg, Manitoba, Canada
Chapter 13

Laurie Hardingham, RN, BN, MA
Senior Fellow in Clinical Ethics
The Toronto Rehabilitation Institute
University of Toronto Joint Centre for Bioethics
Toronto, Ontario, Canada
Chapter 18

Fjola Hart-Wasekeesikaw, RN, BN, MN
Lecturer
Faculty of Nursing
University of Manitoba
Norway House, Cree Nation Site, Manitoba,
   Canada
Chapter 24

Carol I. McDonald, RN, BN, PhD (candidate)
Doctoral Student
Faculty of Nursing
University of Calgary
Calgary, Alberta, Canada
Chapters 15, 17, and 19

Sioban Nelson, RN, BA, PhD
Associate Professor
School of Postgraduate Nursing
University of Melbourne
Melbourne, Australia
Chapter 12

Dorothy Pringle, RN, BScN, MS, PhD, DSc(hon)
Faculty of Nursing
University of Toronto
Toronto, Ontario, Canada
Chapter 14

Mary Ellen Purkis, RN, PhD
Associate Professor
School of Nursing
University of Victoria
Victoria, British Columbia, Canada
Chapter 12

Sandra M. Reilly, RN, EdD
Associate Professor
Faculty of Nursing
University of Calgary
Calgary, Alberta, Canada
Chapter 26

Ginette Lemire Rodger, RN, PhD
Chief of Nursing
The Ottawa Hospital
Ottawa, Ontario, Canada
Chapter 7

Judith Shamian, RN, PhD
Executive Director
Office of Nursing Policy
Health Canada
Ottawa, Canada
Professor
Faculty of Nursing
University of Toronto
Toronto, Canada
Chapter 5

Judith Skelton-Green, RN, PhD,
President, TRANSITIONS: HOD Consultants
   Inc.
Ottawa, Canada
Chapter 5

Janet Storch, RN, PhD
Professor
School of Nursing
University of Victoria
Victoria, British Columbia, Canada
Chapter 3

Meryn Stuart, RN, PhD
Associate Professor
School of Nursing
University of Ottawa
Ottawa, Ontario, Canada
Chapter 6

Deborah Tamlyn, RN, PhD
Professor and Dean
Faculty of Nursing
University of Calgary
Calgary, Alberta, Canada
Chapter 26

Sally Thorne, RN, PhD
Professor
School of Nursing
University of British Columbia
Vancouver, British Columbia, Canada
Chapter 11

Hanneke M. Th. Van Maanen, DrNSc
Professor
Faculty of Health and Human Services,
   Department of Nursing Science
University of Bremen
Bremen, Germany
Chapter 9

Michael Villeneuve, RN, MSc
Senior Nursing Policy Consultant
Office of Nursing Policy
Health Canada
Chapter 5

Christina B. Whittaker, RN, BN, MN Student
Sessional Lecturer and Research Assistant
University of Manitoba
Winnipeg, Manitoba, Canada
Chapter 13

REVIEWERS

Sheryl Boblin, RN, PhD
Assistant Professor
McMaster University
Hamilton, Ontario

Madeline Buck, MSc(A)N
Professor
McGill University
School of Nursing
Montreal, Quebec

Stephanie Buckingham, RN, CD, MA
Faculty
Malaspina University College
Nanaimo, British Columbia

Kathleen Carlin, RN, MSc, PhD(c)
Instructor
Ryerson University
Toronto, Ontario

Tracy Carr, BN, MSc, PhD(c)
Assistant Professor
University of New Brunswick, Department of
    Nursing
Saint John, New Brunswick

Marilyn Chapman, RN, BScN, MAdEd
Chair, Baccalaureate Nursing Program
Malaspina University College
Nanaimo, British Columbia

C. Roberta Clark, RN, MN
Associate Professor
University of New Brunswick at Saint John
Saint John, New Brunswick

Gail J. Donner, RN, PhD
Professor and Dean
Faculty of Nursing
University of Toronto
Toronto, Ontario

Margaret Earle, BN, MScN
Nursing Consultant, Communications and
    Health Policy
Association of Registered Nurses
    of Newfoundland and Labrador
St. John's, Newfoundland

Lynne Esson, RN, BSN
Lecturer
University of British Columbia
School of Nursing
Vancouver, British Columbia

Mae Gallant, RN, MN
Nurse Manager, Intensive and
    Coronary Units
Queen Elizabeth Hospital
Charlottetown, Prince Edward Island

Sandy Gessler, BN, MPA
Lecturer-Course Leader
University of Manitoba
Faculty of Nursing
Winnipeg, Manitoba

Angela Gillis, PhD
Professor and Chair
St. Francis Xavier University
Antigonish, Nova Scotia

Genevieve Gray, RN, RM, DipEd,
Dip Adv Nsg St, MSC, FCN
Dean and Professor
Faculty of Nursing
University of Alberta
Edmonton, Alberta

Sandra Hirst, RN, PhD
Associate Professor
University of Calgary
Faculty of Nursing
Calgary, Alberta

Karen Kennedy, RN, MEd
Centre for Nursing Studies
St. John's, Newfoundland

Rennetta Loewen, RN, MN
Faculty, Nursing Education Program
SIAST Kelsey Campus
Saskatoon, Saskatchewan

Heather McAlpine, RN, PhD
Associate Professor
University of New Brunswick
St. John, New Brunswick

Edna M. McKim, BScN, MN
Associate Professor
Memorial University School of Nursing
St. John's, Newfoundland

Ivy O'Flynn, RN, MSN
Instructor
BCIT
Vancouver, British Columbia

Aroha Page, BA, BSN
Assistant Professor
University of New Brunswick
Faculty of Nursing
Fredericton, New Brunswick

Mary Ellen Purkis, RN, PhD
Associate Professor
University of Victoria, School of Nursing
Victoria, British Columbia

Mary Reidy, RN, BN, MSc, PhD (candidate)
Professor Titulaire
Faculte de sciences infirmieres
Universite de Montreal
Montreal, Quebec

Marlene Reimer, RN, PhD, CNN(C)
Faculty of Nursing Professor
University of Calgary
Calgary, Alberta

Sharon Richardson, RN, PhD
Associate Professor
University of Alberta
and President of Alberta Association of
    Registered Nurses
Edmonton, Alberta

Joan Sawatzky, RN, MCEd
Professor
University of Saskatchewan
College of Nursing
Saskatoon, Saskatchewan

Sharon Simpson, RN, MSc
Assistant Professor
University-College of the Cariboo
Kamloops, British Columbia

**Donna Lynn Smith, RN,
MEd C Psych CHE**
Associate Professor
University of Alberta
Edmonton, Alberta

Marie-France Thiboudeau, MScN
Retired Professor Emeritus
Universite de Montreal
Faculte des sciences infirmieres
St. Laurent, Quebec

Patricia Valentine, RN, PhD
Associate Professor
University of Alberta
Edmonton, Alberta

Virginia A. Vandall-Walker, RN, MN, PhD (C)
Assistant Professor and Chair of Research
    Ethics Board
Athabasca University
St. Albert, Alberta

Karen Webber, MN, RN
Associate Professor
Memorial University of Newfoundland
School of Nursing
St. John's, Newfoundland

Donna M. Wilson, RN, PhD
Associate Professor
University of Alberta
Edmonton, Alberta

Patricia Winans, RN, MN
Senior Nursing Instructor
University of New Brunswick
Moncton, New Brunswick

Lynne Young, RN, PhD
Assistant Professor
University of Victoria
School of Nursing
Langara College
Vancouver, British Columbia

PREFACE

The idea for *Realities of Canadian Nursing: Professional, Practice, and Power Issues* emerged from conversations about our work. In co-teaching an undergraduate course in nursing issues, we began to articulate a vision of how nursing issues might be addressed differently. We were drawn together by our shared valuing of nurses' work and by the idea that a political and critical feminist analysis would provide the genesis for a book on Canadian nursing issues. Many of the questions we were struggling with in teaching nursing issues were playing themselves out daily in the news and in journal publications. Attendance at the Canadian Association of University Schools of Nursing Conference, Vancouver, 2000, provided us with the opportunity for conversations with Margaret Zuccarini, the senior acquisitions editor at Lippincott Williams & Wilkins, and a subsequent invitation to write a proposal, the outcome of which is this book.

Books are written for many reasons and *Realities of Canadian Nursing: Professional, Practice, and Power Issues* is no exception. At first glance, it might seem that the decision to edit a book on nursing issues was a simple one. On one level, we convinced ourselves that a new and different book for teaching nursing issues was needed. On another level, we were looking for a book that would do more than provide the material needed to understand issues. We wanted to prepare and inspire students to participate in political action alongside the generations of nurses who have already taken the lead in political action. We imagined a book that would engage readers in such a way that they would be prepared to work with others in addressing the longstanding barriers to many of the issues that confront nurses and people who seek the services of nurses. We further speculated that, in addressing these issues, nurses who understood the barriers to resolving these issues were in the best position to make a significant contribution to resolving them. We wanted to dispel the many cultural myths that question the need for nurses to be political and the notion that others will act on our behalf. This book is unapologetically feminist, shows respect for our history, and is deeply invested in our future.

We hope that *Realities of Canadian Nursing: Professional, Practice, and Power Issues* will not only influence students to engage with nursing issues in new ways, but that the chapters in this volume will stimulate new writing amongst Canadian scholars on nursing issues. An additional goal of this book is to disrupt the notion that changes to nursing and health care will happen without informed political action on the part of nurses. We hope to instill in nurses the obligation to use their regulatory power, collectively and individually, to influence decision making in professional associations, collective bargaining units, government, and work places.

The decision for a distinctly Canadian book was to create space amongst other texts to highlight the issues faced by Canadian nurses. As well as informing Canadian students of the relevant issues in this country, this volume deliberately creates space to situate Canadian nursing in the international community. It takes its place among a number of previously published books addressing nursing issues. We would like to respectfully acknowledge the contributions of Betsy LaSor, Alice Baumgart and Jennice Larsen, and Janet Kerr and Jannetta MacPhail, from whom the Canadian nursing community has already benefited. This text both builds on and extends the work of these previously accomplished writers and the other authors within their texts. Although the focus of *Realities of Canadian Nursing: Professional, Practice, and Power Issues* is Canadian issues, its scope crosses regional, provincial, and national boundaries. In addition to chapters on ICN, CNA, and provincial associations, contributions from international scholars enhance and extend our understanding of Canadian issues.

The unique intention of *Realities of Canadian Nursing: Professional, Practice, and Power Issues* is to provide the reader with a critical analysis of the tensions and contradictions that exist between nurses' legislated authority to self-regulate and the changing nature and realities of nurses' work. The organizing framework is the changing conditions of nurses' workplaces, the changing settings and contexts of nurses' work, and the realities of contemporary society that daily challenge nurses' practice.

This volume highlights the centrality of nurses' work and its contribution to the health of Canadians. The subject matter of earlier publications on professional regulation, health care systems, leadership, education, research, ethics, and legal issues is also included. Drawing on feminist and other forms of critical analysis, writers in this volume offer strategic points of resistance to dominant discourses by attributing significance to that too often considered insignificant, the underlying experiences and unheard concerns of nurses. Thoughtful exploration of these issues calls us all, nurses and non-nurses, to reflect on the ways in which we disrupt and maintain complicity in dominant discourses and on how we can deliberately use our knowledge to resolve barriers and act strategically in issue resolution.

The audience for the proposed primary course textbook is nursing students taking issues courses offered at the third and fourth years of an undergraduate program. The text will also serve as a resource for related courses and as a reference text for practicing nurses and graduate students.

Our ambition is to engage students in relevant issues in health, health care, and the nursing profession. Students will be prepared to identify, articulate, critically analyse, and generate possible solutions to relevant issues for nursing. The subject matter of *Realities of Canadian Nursing: Professional, Practice, and Power Issues* will be the comprehensive exploration of nursing issues with subfields in the Canadian Health Care System, Professional Associations, Nursing Research and Education, Nursing Ethics, and Societal Issues on current practice. The approach to the material is intended to both restate what is already known in the field of nursing issues and to expand on this knowledge through reconceptualising issues for the purpose of generating new understandings for resolution. A pragmatic approach to developing and evaluating strategies for resolution is also employed.

Although reviewers are without question central to the creation of such a text, it would be remiss not to add that for this text the reviewers were exceptional in taking themselves and their contributions seriously. We are indebted to these nurses for the time and dedication they have shown in the review process, beginning with those who reviewed and made suggestions on the original prospectus. Despite the invisibility of the work of reviewers, those of us with the insider's view see and appreciate the significant contributions they have made to this book. More than once when we or one of our chapter contributors were challenged by a reviewer's comments, we managed to read them one more time and the text that you now see is all the better for it.

We would like to thank all of the contributors for their commitment to this project. *Realities of Canadian Nursing: Professional, Practice, and Power Issues* brings together an exciting group of chapters, all peer reviewed and previously unpublished. One of the most exciting, and likely the most challenging, parts of editing this book was in the selection of the contributors to write the chapters and in the negotiating and renegotiating of due dates for work to be received. Editing this book provided us the opportunity to get to know and increase our respect for nurses across the nation. Editing this book brought us in contact with a wide variety of nurses who surprised, thrilled, and dismayed us all at once. Most of the angst created in the editing process can be traced to our own naiveté. Yet in the end when the reviews went out and the revised chapters came in, working with the nurses who wrote these chapters was the most satisfying part of the editing experience. New relationships developed and existing relationships were enhanced. We were repeatedly impressed with how writers took up our tentatively articulated vision and returned to us, in countless and creative ways, how such a vision could be realized.

As co-authors of *Realities of Canadian Nursing: Professional, Practice, and Power Issues*, we are grateful for the support and encouragement of family and friends who have accompanied us on this maiden journey. For Marjorie, this special group of people includes Carol McDonald, Brent Clark, Astrid and Jeff Clark, Mary McDonald, Murray McIntyre, Yvonne Oliver, and Verna Kershaw. Elizabeth recognizes the support she got from Tanya and David, Monica and Michael, Debra and Mark, and Eugene and Ebony Thomlinson. For a break from writing or editing, cuddles from William, Maia, Devin, Benjamin, and Aidan helped. Cathy Hopfner raised questions and challenged the writing of one of Elizabeth's chapters.

Our collegial relationships with faculty and graduate and undergraduate students have inspired and sustained this work. Special thanks to Dr. Beverly Anderson, Christine Ceci, Meg McDonagh, Julianne Sanguins, and Kathryn Crooks. We must acknowledge the invaluable support of a University of Calgary Killam Resident Fellowship to Elizabeth that provided a semester in which she was able to write, edit, and contact authors.

The staff at Lippincott Williams & Wilkins with whom we worked has been incredibly helpful, encouraging, and understanding. They include Margaret Zuccarini; Deedie McMahon, who is an editor without equal; Helen Kogut, who kept track of the contracts and many iterations of each chapter; and Barry Wight, who believed in the need and value of a Canadian text on nursing issues. They have survived many e-mails and conference and individual telephone calls, and throughout the past 2 years have been a strong support.

Finally we would like to dedicate *Realities of Canadian Nursing: Professional, Practice, and Power Issues* to nurses everywhere struggling to create space for the concerns of nursing to be heard in a way that will influence the health of Canadians. The intent is to close the gap between university teaching and the scholarly and work lives of practicing nurses.

CONTENTS

Chapter 8,

PART **III** *Nursing Knowledge: How We Come to Know What We Know 181*

15   *Issues Arising From the Nature of Nurses' Work*   288
      Marjorie McIntyre and Carol McDonald

      The Nature of Nurses' Work   289
      The Significance of Nurses' Work Issues   289
      Issues Arising From the Nature of Nurses' Work   290
      Incongruities Between Nurses' Work as Taught and Practised   292
      Lack of Control Over the Work   293
      Framing and Analysing Issues Arising From the Nature of Nurses' Work   295
      Critical Feminist Analysis   297
      Ethical Analysis   297
      Barriers to Resolving Issues Arising in Nurses' Work   297
      Strategies for Resolving Issues Arising in Nurses' Work   299

16   *The Workplace Environment*   304
      Marjorie McIntyre

      The Nature of Nurses' Workplaces   305
      Workplace Issues   306
      Framing and Analysing Work Environment Issues   312
      Barriers to Resolution   316
      Strategies for Resolution   317

17   *Unionisation: Collective Bargaining in Nursing*   322
      Marjorie McIntyre and Carol McDonald

      Collective Bargaining   323
      Framework for Analysing Collective Bargaining Issues   330
      Barriers to Resolution   333
      Strategies for Resolution   334

18   *Ethical and Legal Issues in Nursing*   339
      Laurie Hardingham

      Story: The Winnipeg Nurses   340
      What Is Ethics?   341
      Recognising Ethical Issues   341
      Identifying and Articulating Ethical Issues   341
      Ethical or Legal Issue? Alike but Different   344
      Issues of Moral Integrity   347
      Barriers to Resolving Ethical and Legal Issues   351
      Strategies for Resolution of Ethical and Legal Issues   353

PART I

Nurses, Nursing, and the Health Care System

CHAPTER 1

Introduction to Nursing Issues: Implications for the Nursing Profession

Marjorie McIntyre ■ Elizabeth Thomlinson

Chapter Objectives

At the completion of this chapter, you will be able to:

1. Understand the importance of political action for nurses.
2. Differentiate among issues, problems, and trends.
3. Know how to use a framework for articulation and analysis of an issue.
4. Select and defend a particular stance on an issue.
5. Identify barriers to issue resolution.
6. Discuss a variety of strategies for issue resolution.

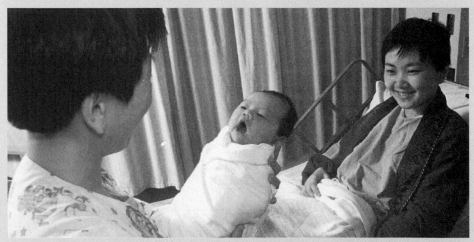

Photograph by Larry Arbour. Used with permission of Faculty of Nursing, University of Calgary.

This chapter introduces the reader to nursing issues and provides an overview of issue articulation and its significance to nursing. Specifically, readers are provided with a framework to explore and articulate, analyse, and generate possibilities for increased understanding and, when feasible, resolution of nursing issues. Examples of barriers to issue resolution and specific strategies to generate possibilities for resolution are also discussed.

RECOGNISING AND ARTICULATING AN ISSUE

Issues, as discussed in this chapter, can be understood in different ways:

- As a concern on a topic of widespread interest to the general public
- As a question or a matter that is in dispute, the decision of which is of special importance

The chapter discussion includes those concerns that arise in and are related to nurses' practise (including the nature and conditions of nurses' work), the nursing profession (including nursing education and nursing research), and the health care system (including health care reform and thereby the health of Canadians).

Particular events in nursing history have not always been explicitly articulated and analysed as issues. However, from its inception, nursing has been faced with complex issues related to power, knowledge, and societal beliefs about women's work that remain unresolved today. In addition to providing a framework by which to articulate and analyse issues, this chapter addresses the significance of clear articulation of issues for nurses, the nursing profession, the health of Canadians, and health care reform.

Understanding Issues as Political

It is important for nurses to question the ways in which issues are conceptualised because how a situation in nursing is understood by nurses and other decision makers will have implications for how it is likely to be addressed. The many issues affecting nurses, the profession, and the health care system can be understood and articulated as political issues in that they ultimately involve influencing others for the purpose of quality patient care.

SIGNIFICANCE FOR NURSES

Understanding something as political requires one to ask particular questions—political questions, such as the following:

- Who benefits from this situation?
- At what cost?
- Who pays the cost?
- Who suffers? Or who does not benefit—who or what is left behind?
- Whose purpose is served by the situation remaining unchanged?

By posing political questions, nurses can make central and visible the idea of nurses' work. Drawing on historical, political, economic, social and cultural, and critical feminist analysis, nurses can offer strategic points of resistance to dominant discourses. Such an analysis attributes significance to a concern that too often is considered insignificant: the underlying experiences and unheard concerns of nurses.

Thoughtful exploration of these political questions calls us all, nurses and non-nurses, to reflect on that which constrains—and enables—the ways we can communicate and think about nursing. When nurses find themselves unable to nurse as they had envisioned, as they believe they can or should, or when their interpretations of what is occurring in health care are excluded from policy discussions, a sense of being incorrect, in some essential sense, in their understanding of themselves and their work, comes into play. A profound dissonance emerges between what one believes one is called on to be and do and what the world, and one's relationship to it, allows. This distress deepens when it remains unheard, when what is of concern to nurses remains stubbornly invisible to others (Ceci & McIntyre, 2000).

Political questions highlight nurses' work and make it visible. Recent popular literature (Buresh & Gordon, 2000; Picard, 2000) has emphasised the need for nurses to communicate the following to the public:

- Their clinical knowledge and competence
- Their professional identity
- Their expertise and equal membership on the health care team

In a recent article in the *Canadian Nurse* (2000), the editors talk about nursing as a political act: "Generally identifying something as a political issue involves noticing common problems affecting your clients have broader implications for a whole group of people" (p. 10). Later in the same article, the editors conclude that "our history, both recent and remote, is filled with examples of nurses who have understood the inherent political nature of nursing. It is not difficult to see how acting on a political level is a natural extension of the essence of nursing—caring. Heath care privatisation, increasing global 'corporationisation,' increasing poverty, and environmental destruction all have clear repercussions for health. We [nurses] have a proud tradition of advocacy, both individual and systemic—and centuries of evidence that nursing is, indeed, a political act" (p. 12).

In discussing the importance of political awareness in nursing, Kerr (1991) suggested that nurses tend to be more aware of the "political factors in the development of policy than in working or other everyday situations. Where service is the primary activity the politics of patient care may be less visible, but . . . important and essential to good care" (p. 210). It seems to be easier for nurses to recognise the political nature of policy development than to recognise that every nursing act is a political act. For example, it is in nurses' day-to-day work with patients, families, and communities that the public's image of nursing is developed.

SIGNIFICANCE FOR THE NURSING PROFESSION

The significance of clear articulation of issues for the profession goes beyond the individual nurse to include the organisation of nurses and their ideas into a larger collective. To be effective in supporting political action within the profession, nurses need to speak in unison on issues and organise themselves to act provincially/territorially, nationally, and internationally.

In 1977, Mussallem claimed what is still true today: In the context of state-provided health care, the link between health care and political action is inseparable. The *raison d'etre* of nursing is health care. The quality of health care depends to a large extent on the nature of the nursing component determined by four elements:

- Standards of education and preparation for those entering the profession
- Quality of care provided by the practitioner—a quality closely associated with education and preparation

- Number of nurses available—a determination considered in modern times largely by the social and economic status the profession offers its members
- Milieu in which care is offered

If nurses are concerned about health care, they must accept responsibility for safeguarding these four dynamic elements of nursing practise. This can be achieved only by the participation of nurses in political action (p. 156).

In addition, the Canadian Nurses Association (CNA) *Code of Ethics* mandates that nurses represent nursing interests and perspectives before legislature, employers, other disciplines, and the media (Banks, 1988, p. 31). Particular issues around which professional organisations have pledged their support include the following:

- Patient advocacy
- Speaking out on issues that directly affect the health status of Canadians
- Lobbying for positive changes in health policy
- Improving the image of nursing

SIGNIFICANCE FOR CANADIAN HEALTH CARE

According to the CNA, there were 254,964 registered nurses in Canada in 1998. The CNA is the largest association of health professionals in Canada. In terms of numbers, nurses are the most important group of health care workers. In addition, nurses' work situates nurses close to people and their health care problems and gives them "privileged access" (Ceci, 1999) to the health care needs of the community.

The *Code of Ethics* (CNA, 1997) mandates that the purpose and goals of nursing can be advanced most effectively through involvement in political action.

In advocating change, Andre Picard, a journalist for the *Globe and Mail* and author of a newly released book on Canadian nurses, reported that many of the nurses he spoke to talked about "how powerful nurses in Canada could be if only they were united. With a quarter of a million registered nurses in Canada, the potential for influence is there. But it is untapped potential" (Picard, 2000, p. 211). Because of their privileged access to health care experiences, these many nurses have a tremendous opportunity to affect the health of Canadians through political action. The ability to articulate and act on issues is one of the means of preparing nurses for political action. Box 1.1 presents a health care issue identified by nurses.

Distinguishing Issues From Trends and Problems

Although a number of nursing textbooks have been published under titles including terms such as issues, transitions, and trends, the distinction in the use of these terms is not clearly apparent. Assumptions on the differences among these terms and the importance of explicating these differences follow (Table 1.1).

TRENDS

According to LaSor and Elliot, "nursing education generally acquaints students with a history of their profession and with significant facts about nursing and professional behaviour" (1977, p. xiii) in courses on trends and perspectives. However, "because nursing has seen such rapid growth in its history, dilemmas have taken on a quality that is much more than a trend. What we are seeing is the development of pertinent issues that must be disputed, agreed upon and established. This exercise stresses the

BOX 1.1

Health Care Issue: Political Action Results in Screening Program

Four community nurses working with homeless persons suspected there was an increase in tuberculosis (TB) based on several cases of active TB and an increase in positive skin tests among their patients. However, when they approached the public health department, they were informed that the statistics did not indicate an increase. Although the nurses asked that TB screening be conducted in homeless shelters and drop-in centres, the health department refused.

The nurses believed that TB was increasing and therefore decided to press the health department to initiate a screening program. They proceeded with the following steps:

- Calling a meeting with other health care workers, shelter and drop-in staff, and homeless people
- Forming an action group
- Educating group members about TB
- Researching the experiences of other cities
- Making representations to health departments
- Offering to assist with screenings

These efforts resulted in a major screening program that demonstrated the increased numbers of people with TB. The group then expanded its focus to include other issues.

From *Canadian Nurse*, (2000). C.N.A. Today, *10*(2), 11, with permission.

need to collect material about nursing that has both historical and contemporary significance in today's society" (p. xiii).

Given that the words of LaSor and Elliot are now more than two decades old, it is amazing that nursing education has continued using models that are still largely those of trends and transitions without the needed political analysis of these trends and their implications for nursing. Inherent in the way that nurses study and practise nursing is the opportunity for a more politically active role in nursing.

PROBLEMS

Although problem identification and problem solving relate in a very central way to the articulation and resolution of issues, they are different. Both the relationship between problems and issues and the way in which they are different from each other are important to understand. The problem of the nursing shortage is a relevant example to illustrate this. Viewed as a problem of numbers, the nursing shortage could be resolved by producing more nurses. The recognition that there is a much larger issue behind the shortage opens the issue up to be understood differently and to generate more possibilities for resolution.

Some problems are clear-cut, and resolving them is straightforward and does not require the lengthy analysis that is required for issues. For example, if more funds are

Table 1.1 Comparing Issues, Problems, and Trends

ISSUE	PROBLEM	TREND
Requires analysis	Benefits from analysis	Analysis not required
Multiple dimensions	One dimension	Signifies a direction
Multiple possibilities	Solution is apparent Usually response based Numerically measurable	Does not involve a solution
Multiple barriers to resolution		
Persists over time	Can be resolved immediately	

needed for research and they are provided, one can assume the problem is solved. If, on the other hand, funds are more available for some problems than others, or for some professionals than others, there is a situation of power imbalance that would benefit from exploration as an issue. Problems that persist over time, such as the exclusion of nurses from important decisions in health care, are more likely to be adequately addressed as issues.

How, then, are issues understood in this textbook? Issues as understood in this text are related to problems and trends in nursing in that they highlight concerns held by nurses about their practise, the nursing profession, the health care system, and the health of Canadians over time. Issues are different from problems and trends in nursing in that in articulating issues one assumes nursing is a political act and that nurses can function in activist roles. The chapter raises the following questions:

- In what sense is nursing a political act?
- In what sense can professional nurses be activists?
- How is political analysis and activism important for issue clarification and resolution?

Framing and Analysing an Issue

To begin examining and acting on an issue, one identifies the topic of interest and from this selects a particular issue and expresses—articulates—it clearly. An issue can be expressed as a dilemma, conundrum, question or series of questions, or simple statement. Once the issue is articulated clearly, the analysis may proceed as outlined in the following section.

Some issues call for a particular framework or approach to analysis. Most issues benefit from more than one approach to analysis. However, it is unlikely that all approaches to analysis would be undertaken with every issue. Some categories of analysis or frameworks are discussed later and constructed as guidelines. They are intended to generate rather than limit possibilities for discussion. You may generate other questions as you work. The purpose of asking these questions is to increase understanding of all aspects of the issue and to move the discussion towards resolution. In Chapter 2, The Nursing Shortage, the framework for analysis presented here is explicitly used to articulate and analyse the issues arising from the nursing shortage.

Before beginning the analysis, you need to make explicit your own beliefs and assumptions about the issue. All of us operate from day to day under assumptions. An assumption is an idea that is held to be true without any support or substantiation.

NATURE OF THE ISSUE

Some questions to ask when analysing what you assume to be a nursing issue follow:

- What makes this issue a nursing issue?
- In what ways are nurses involved in the issue?
- Who are the other participants and what is their involvement in the issue?
- Who first became concerned with the subject?
- Who began to raise the subject as an issue and why?

HISTORICAL ANALYSIS OF THE ISSUE

- When did the issue originate?
- What are the conditions that led to the development of the issue?
- How have these conditions changed over time?
- What has contributed to the stance taken by participants in the issue?
- What have been the barriers to resolution along the way?
- What strategies for resolution have already been tried?

ETHICAL AND LEGAL ANALYSIS OF THE ISSUE

- What are the laws that influence this issue?
- What professional codes or legislative acts mandate participants' responses to this issue?
- What professional, organisational, and governmental (municipal, provincial/territorial, and national) documents inform, constrain, or influence the issue? Possibilities include the CNA *Code of Ethics*, provincial/territorial standards of practise, British North America Act, Health Professions Act, and Canada Health Act.

SOCIAL AND CULTURAL ANALYSIS

All issues develop in a societal context that shapes the issue and influences the possibilities for resolution.

- What contexts shape this particular issue?
- What are the prevailing attitudes in society about this issue?
- What values and priorities of the dominant culture influence this issue? In what ways, if any, do these values and priorities privilege the dominant culture over other members of society?

POLITICAL ANALYSIS

- Who benefits from this issue being resolved?
- Who benefits from things staying the same?
- What is the relationship between knowledge and power in this situation?
- How do ageist, sexist, racist, and ablest ideologies influence our understanding of this issue?

CRITICAL FEMINIST ANALYSIS

- Are there errors or myths about women's abilities or realities contained in this issue?
- Is this issue influenced by the power inequities or the hierarchic or patriarchal structures of institutions over nurses or patients?
- In this situation, is expert power given authority over personal power and the right to be the subject of one's own life?

ECONOMIC ANALYSIS

In what ways are the forces of supply and demand at work in this issue?

Box 1.2 summarises the steps used in articulating and analysing an issue.

BARRIERS TO RESOLUTION

One of the most important strategies for moving an issue towards resolution is identifying barriers that may impede the resolution process. Once the barriers are identified, there may be an increased opportunity for resolution through mediation, collaboration, or negotiation. The following are some potential barriers to resolution of nursing issues:

- Limited accessibility to resources, such as human and financial resources, knowledge, or expertise, may obstruct resolution.
- Issues are not clearly understood or understood in a limited way. For example, a barrier to the resolution of issues of the nursing shortage is conceptualising the issue as only a problem of numbers of nurses entering the profession.
- Irresolvable differences or competing interests between participants may block the resolution of issues.
- Circumstances in which some participants benefit from the issue remaining unresolved limit the opportunity for resolution.
- Power inequities between parties invested in the issue can contribute to resistance to resolution.
- Participants in the issue may experience unconscious resistance to change.
- Key stakeholders in the issue may lack tolerance for multiple viewpoints.
- Stakeholders may ascribe to differing underlying assumptions or beliefs that influence the way that the issue is understood and the way that resolution is undertaken.

BOX 1.2

Articulation and Analysis of an Issue

1. Identify the topic of interest.
2. Select a particular issue and articulate it clearly. Define your own beliefs and assumptions about the issue.
3. Proceed with the analysis by addressing appropriate frameworks.
4. Identify barriers to resolution.
5. Explore strategies for issue resolution.

- Alienation from coworkers, hostility from bureaucratic and administrative officials, and fear of job loss may isolate nurses from the supports needed for resolution.
- Lack of time, energy, role models, and mentors seriously undermines possibilities for effective resolution.

DEVISING STRATEGIES FOR RESOLUTION

After an issue relevant to the profession of nursing or health care is articulated and analysed, multiple strategies can be implemented to address and resolve the issue. Essential to the success of any effort is the communication of a well-developed plan of action. Strategies for resolution include, but are not limited to, the following:

- Formation of lobby groups
- Preparation of resolutions for presentation to agencies, associations, and organisations
- Establishment of a letter-writing campaign
- Involvement of the news media through letters to the editor and articles that solicit public support

The use of any of these strategies is dependent upon the following:

- People affected by the issue
- Interest that is generated
- Time available
- Human and financial resources available

To generate the maximum amount of support, it is important to enlist the assistance of as many people as possible who are affected by the issue. A greater response and resolution can be anticipated if the affected parties are unified in their efforts to address the specific issue. The following sections of the text include specific detailed examples of strategies that have been employed by individuals from multiple segments of the population in their efforts to create change and to address an issue of relevance to them.

Lobbying Strategies

Although lobby groups are usually associated with influencing elected officials to persuade them to vote a certain way on an issue or to carry an issue forward for debate, change within an organisation can be promoted by lobbying of key individuals. Regardless of whether the issue is of national or international importance, or whether the issue affects nurses and health care on a particular unit or agency, the same techniques are available and applicable.

Lobbying may occur through direct contact with people who are in positions to address the issue and through indirect methods by which others influence the officials (Hood, 1998). Table 1.2 provides a comparison of direct and indirect strategies.

Nurses must keep several key points in mind when initiating a lobby and planning meetings with key officials, including the following:

Table 1.2   Comparing Direct and Indirect Lobbying Strategies

DIRECT STRATEGIES	INDIRECT STRATEGIES
Engaging in letter, phone call, and e-mail campaigns to elected officials or others in power	Writing reports, articles, books
Meeting with key persons professionally	Enlisting the support of key persons
Taking opportunities to meet key persons socially	Using the media through news announcements on radio and television, newspaper and magazine columns, and advertisements
Submitting resolutions to professional organisations and unions	

- Become informed about the issue by reading newspapers, documents, and reports; watching television, listening to radio; and knowing the professional association's position.
- Use simple statistics and avoid percentages. The clearer the statistics, the more attention they will generate. Then apply the numbers in human terms, and illustrate the statistics with personal stories.
- Be sure to articulate clearly why the issue is an issue and identify its importance.
- Know what other people are saying about the issue.
- Keep in mind that the more people supporting the issue, the more effective the lobby.
- If you are lobbying government officials or bodies, remember to include members of the opposition parties.
- Follow meetings with written submissions that are accurate and succinct.

LETTERS TO OFFICIALS

One popular and well-used lobbying strategy is writing letters. Prepare the letter so that it outlines a selected issue and the possibilities for resolution. Send the letter to a public official such as the dean of your school or faculty, the unit manager in your facility or organisation, a city councillor, members of the legislature (MLA) of your provincial government, or members of parliament (MP) of the government of Canada. Consider sending a copy of the letter to other stakeholders and interested parties, and keep a copy of letters for your own files. See Box 1.3 for an example of a lobbying letter. See Appendix for additional samples of written documents.

LETTERS TO THE EDITOR

To be published, letters to the editor should comment on a public issue, and they usually are a response to a particular article or editorial published in newspapers. An example of a response may be one to an editorial discussing the next federal budget, which is expected to be a "health budget." Keeping the letter short and punchy will

BOX 1.3

Lobbying and Letter Writing: An Example

Whether you are writing to your MP or to the Minister of Health or Finance, adapt these letters to fit your own situation. Personalised letters have more impact. The sample letter presented here is to the Minister of Health.

The Honourable _____, P.C., M.P. Minister of Health

House of Commons Ottawa, Ontario K1A 0A6

Dear Minister,

At the CNA Biennial Convention in Ottawa, in June, you noted that "since Jeanne Mance set foot in this land, nurses have been caring for this country, and now, more than ever, it is time for Canada to show how much it cares for nurses." I thank you for these words and am writing you today to encourage you to demonstrate your willingness to invest in the nursing profession.

Canadians are worried about the state of the health care system and associate the declining quality of care with the decreasing availability of nurses. *(Note: add a personal example from your own area as appropriate.)* As you are aware, Canada faces a severe shortage of nurses with the knowledge and skills to meet the future health needs of Canadians. Care is becoming increasingly complex and technologically advanced. As you work to create an integrated continuum of care, Canadians will require highly qualified nurses to plan and deliver that care.

As the federal government examines its fiscal priorities and resources for the coming year, the nurses of Canada urge you to take a leadership role in making sustainable investments in the health care system, including:

- Increasing federal transfer payments
- Expanding the continuum of care to include accessible home and community care
- Making a modest investment of $200 million over 5 years to support nursing recruitment, retention, research, and the dissemination and uptake of evidence to provide the best patient care

The nurses of Canada are looking to the federal government to demonstrate the strength of your commitment to ensure that all Canadians continue to enjoy ready access to the best health care system in the world.

Sincerely,

(Your name & address)

From *The Quiet Crisis in Health Care. Lobby Kit.* Canadian Nurses Association. September 1998, with permission.

enhance its chances of being published. Remember to sign the letter and add a day-time telephone number in case the editor wants to verify or obtain more information from you. Information on where to send letters is usually found in the letters section of the newspaper.

NEWS RELEASES

A news release is much like a letter but does not have a salutation. Information should include relevant facts—the who, what, when, where, why, and how of the issue that you want to highlight. The release should also include the name and telephone number of a person whom the media could contact for further comments or to arrange for an interview. The following example of a news release may be adapted to fit various needs:

> In (*name of region*), registered nurses will be meeting with politicians and holding events, such as news conferences, to build support for the nursing investment. A meeting with (*name of politician*) will be held (*insert date*) at (*insert place*). A photo opportunity and brief statement by the nursing group will follow at (*time and place*). The event is scheduled in response to a public meeting held (*insert when and where*) when nurses joined their voices with the growing number of Canadian nurses calling for a federal investment in health care. Canadian nurses are warning the government that Canadians will soon be deprived of care if action is not taken to avert a massive nursing shortage.

"Nurses make up 75% of health professionals. Without registered nurses at the bedside, who will care for Canadians?" asked (*insert name*). "You can't open beds in hospitals or deliver quality home care if there are no nurses," she said.

Earlier, in Ottawa, in meetings with members of parliament and government officials, the Canadian Nurses Association (CNA) called on the federal government to support recruitment and retention of registered nurses, nursing research, and the dissemination and uptake of evidence. CNA estimates the federal government investment should be $40 million a year over the next 5 years. "Our support of this is essential. We know firsthand the impact of the nursing shortage on patient care," said (*insert name*).

RESOLUTIONS

Prepare a written resolution for presentation at a professional organisation's annual general meeting, such as a provincial association or college of nursing or the CNA. To be most effective, resolutions should be submitted in writing before an annual meeting date. Check deadlines. Resolutions received after the deadline date may not be able to be considered by the Resolutions Committee. Although resolutions may usually be presented from the floor of the meeting, this means that time for consideration and discussion may be limited. You will be most effective if you allow participants time to formulate their own responses and opinions on the topic.

A resolution is an original main motion written with great formality. The resolution may have two parts: a preamble (optional) and the resolution.

The preamble states the reasons for making the resolution and is the equivalent to debating the question before it is on the floor. Each paragraph begins with the word *whereas*. Each paragraph in the preamble closes with a semicolon. There is no limit to the number of *whereas*'s used. All proposed resolutions must include supporting documentation, including the financial implications relevant to the proposal.

The resolution is introduced with the word *resolved*. *Resolved* must be underscored or in italics and is followed by a comma. The word following *resolved* begins with a capital letter (i.e., That). There may be more than one resolved sentence. It is helpful if the proposed resolution includes an implementation date. An example follows:

Whereas, The biennial meeting will be held in Vancouver; and
Whereas, There will be business, education sessions, and special awards; therefore
Resolved, That all the members of the Canadian Nurses Association be encouraged to attend the 2000 Biennial Meeting from June 19 to 23, 2000.

Each resolution must be moved and seconded.

Questions or assistance requests regarding preparation of a resolution can usually be answered by contacting the association office to which you will be submitting the resolution. Box 1.4 summarises the resolution process. See Appendix for an example of a complete resolution.

Additional Resources and Political Action

Nurses seeking resources to assist with political action can obtain information from their national and provincial nursing associations. The use of electronic media has made resources available to nurses across the country. Each of the associations may be accessed through the web sites.

Other sources of information include the nursing unions. The web sites and e-mail addresses for the nursing unions may be found in Chapter 17.

SUMMARY

This chapter addressed the significance of nurses understanding the inherently political nature of nursing and being able to articulate clearly the relevant issues in nursing, in health care, and in advocating for the health of Canadians. Issues, as discussed in this text, are understood to be a concern of widespread interest to the general public, a question or a matter that is in dispute, the decision of which is of special inter-

---

BOX 1.4

What to Ask About Resolutions

1. Do the *Whereas*'s support the resolution?
2. Does the resolution conflict with the act under which the association is legislated?
3. Have you indicated who will carry out the action (e.g., a taskforce of members, a staff person)?
4. Have you projected the cost of the resolution (e.g., will the resolution for a lobby be limited to one letter from the Association to a minister or will the campaign be expanded to a major letter-writing campaign involving all members [10,000 × 0.48 = 4,800] for mail plus paper, envelopes, staff time, and phone for a total of 6,000)?
5. Have you included supporting documentation for the resolution, if appropriate?
6. Have you indicated a deadline date for completion?
7. If the action requires reporting back, have you identified to whom and when?
8. Have you considered the intended effect of your resolution, political implications, and so forth?

est. Issues are differentiated from problems and trends by the need for analysis, the multiple dimensions of an issue, and the multiple possibilities for movement towards resolution.

Articulation of an issue involves selecting the particular issue from a topic of interest. The nature of the issue is articulated by asking questions such as, Who are the participants in the issue? What makes this a nursing issue? Who first raised this as an issue and why?

After articulation of the issue, the reader is introduced to the idea of beliefs and assumptions that inform an understanding of the issue and the importance of articulating these assumptions as the first step of issue analysis.

A framework for the analysis of issues includes raising questions of a historical, ethical-legal, social and cultural, political, critical feminist, and economic nature. The purpose of asking these questions is to increase understanding of all aspects of the issue and to move the discussion towards resolution. The categories of analysis are, however, not intended to be exclusive; pertinent questions may arise during the analysis process.

The identification of barriers to resolution of an issue is an important step in moving the issue towards resolution. Potential barriers to resolution include inaccessibility of resources, irresolvable differences or competing interests between participants, and differing underlying assumptions on the part of key stakeholders.

Essential to the success of any effort in issue resolution is the communication of a well-developed plan of action. Strategies for resolution include, but are not limited to, formation of lobby groups; establishment of a letter-writing campaign; involvement of the news media through letters to the editor; submission of news releases which solicit public support to print, radio, and television media; and preparation of resolutions for presentation to agencies, associations, and organisations.

Reflections on the Chapter

1. From your practise experience, identify examples of nursing as political action.
2. There is evidence to suggest that nurses take a variety of stances in relation to using their knowledge and influence to address relevant issues in their practise. How might you account for these differences?
3. Identify at least one issue in your practise experience. Using the questions highlighted in the chapter, begin to explore the nature of this issue and possibilities for why it has remained an issue. Identify your own assumptions and beliefs that would influence your interpretation of this issue.
4. What are the barriers to this issue being resolved?
5. Review the strategies for issue resolution offered at the end of the chapter and discuss the advantages and limitations of each for the issue you have selected.

REFERENCES

Banks, P. (1988). Lobbying: A legitimate, critical nursing intervention. *RNABC News, 12*(5), 31–32.

Buresh, B., & Gordon, S. (2000). From silence to voice: What nurses know and must communicate to the public. Ottawa: Canadian Nurses Association.

Canadian Nurses Association. (2000). Canadian nurse. (2000). *CNA Today 10*(2), 11.

Canadian Nurses Association. (1997). *Code of ethics.* Ottawa: Author.

Canadian Nurses Association. (1998). *Lobby kit.* Ottawa: Author.

Canadian Nurses Association. (1998). *A quiet crisis in nursing: A position paper.* Ottawa: Author.

Ceci, C., & McIntyre, M. (2001). A "quiet" crisis in health care: Developing our capacity to hear. *Nursing Philosophy, 2*(2), 122–130.

Ceci, C. (1999). *Woman: mother: poverty: Lived meanings, material realities.* Unpublished masters thesis. Calgary, AB: University of Calgary.

Hood, L. (1998). The professional nurse's role in public policy. In S. Leddy (Ed.). *Conceptual bases of professional nursing* (4th ed., pp. 275–298). Philadelphia: Lippincott Williams & Wilkins.

Kerr, J. (1991). Political awareness in nursing. In J. Kerr & J. McPhail (Eds.). *Canadian nursing: Issues and perspectives* (pp. 208–215). St. Louis: CV Mosby.

LaSor B, & Elliott R. (Eds.). (1977). *Issues in Canadian nursing.* Ontario: Prentice Hall.

Manitoba Association of Registered Nurses. (1997). *Directions for a pharmaceutical policy in Canada.* Report prepared for the National Forum on Health. Winnipeg: Author.

Manitoba Association of Registered Nurses. (1989). Resolutions to the 1990 annual meeting. *Nurscene, 14*(5), 25–26.

Mussallem, H. (1977). Nurses and political action. In B. LaSor & R. Elliott (Eds.). *Issues in Canadian nursing.* Ontario: Prentice Hall.

Picard, A. (2000). *Critical care: Canadian nurses speak for change.* Ontario: Harper Collins.

CHAPTER 2

The Nursing Shortage: Historical Links and Current Understandings

Marjorie McIntyre ▪ Christine Ceci

Chapter Objectives

At the completion of this chapter, you will be able to:

1. Identify relevant issues in relation to the nursing shortage.

2. Articulate selected frameworks for analysing issues arising from the nursing shortage.

3. Analyse selected strategies to address these issues.

4. Understand different interpretations of the current and past nursing shortages.

(continued)

Nurses in Saskatchewan took very public steps to communicate their response to nursing cutbacks and other work environment issues that "invalidate their concerns, fragment their practices, and disallow their understandings." They marched and left their shoes as a calling card, inviting officials and others to "run a mile in [a nurse's] shoes." (Photo: Larry Lemoal, Saskatchewan Union of Nurses. Used with permission of *Canadian Nurse.*)

5. Make explicit assumptions underlying different conceptualisations of the shortage.

6. Identify past and current barriers to resolution of the nursing shortage.

7. Discuss strategies for resolution of the nursing shortage.

This chapter challenges existing assumptions about the nursing shortage in order to generate new ways of understanding it and new possibilities for resolving it. At the outset, it is assumed that the recurrence of nursing shortages relates directly to an inability to see beyond the immediate problem of not enough nurses to the larger issues that have sustained and perpetuated shortages. The chapter then challenges the acceptance of the inevitability of recurrent shortages and the ethos of nurses as expendable, interchangeable, and easily replaced. Finally, questions are raised about the relationship between recurrent shortages and the conceptualisation of nurses' work, women's work, and nursing knowledge. The arguments proposed on these pages resist the notion that the predicted scarcity of nurses is a problem that can be solved by providing resources or superficial changes in working conditions. Instead, different perspectives on the issue are presented in an effort to generate new possibilities for its resolution.

NATURE OF THE NURSING SHORTAGE

In addition to the confusion around the idea of shortage itself, there are signs that what is currently occurring in nursing involves something other than—or at least in addition to—a problem of numbers of nurses.

Ceci & McIntyre, 2001

The Canadian Nurses Association (CNA) has highlighted an impending shortage of nurses who have the skills and knowledge to meet the health care needs of the Canadian population, a shortage, according to the CNA, that has been unequaled in past decades (1998, 2000). Historically, nursing shortages have alternated with periods when too many nurses were available for the positions offered by employers. The question that arises, then, is what, if anything, is different now? Before answering the question, we must consider how the complexity of the issue precludes finding quick solutions, such as hiring more nurses, recruiting more students, or paying higher wages.

Hospital administrators, board members, leaders in professional nursing organisations, collective bargaining groups, and all people involved in staffing nursing positions have been and continue to be concerned with the numbers of nurses available for work. When the inability to fill vacant positions is conceptualised simply in terms of shortage, as a temporary and easily corrected mismatch of supply and demand, mainly instrumental or quick-fix solutions suggest themselves. The concern with these quick-fix solutions is that there is an element of distress which remains unaccounted for, suggesting perhaps that nurses suffering and exodus from the workforce "may arise not only from the conditions of their work but also more existentially, from having one's way of understanding the world unacknowledged" (Ceci & McIntyre, 2001, p. 123).

Although analyses of shortages with predictions of a future shortfall of nurses have been done, to date there is little evidence that these studies have influenced policy development and long-term planning in health care (CNA, 1998). It is not clear from the literature whether the failure to take these studies into account relates to the limitations of the studies themselves or to the attitudes and understandings of policy developers and decision makers toward nurses, their work, and their contributions to health care (Baumann et al., 2001).

The issue of nursing shortages will ultimately be discussed many times in this book in relation to many other topics. This chapter, for example, provides a critical analysis of the way in which the nursing shortage has been conceptualised and of the strategies aimed at its resolution.

FRAMING AND ANALYSING THE ISSUE

Like other complex issues, the nursing shortage can be best understood as multiple problems—all raising issues for nurses, health care providers, and Canadians seeking health care. Viewed simply as a problem of numbers, the nursing shortage could be resolved by producing more nurses. Viewed as a problem of working conditions, the issue could be resolved by mobilising resources to improve working conditions. Viewed as problem of work satisfaction, the issue could be resolved by addressing nurses' concerns about salaries and other contractual issues. Studies on work satisfaction for nurses have identified alleviating work pressures, security and workplace safety, support of managers and colleagues, opportunities for education, professional identity, control over practise, scheduling, and leadership as elements that are as important to nurses as remuneration (Baumann et al., 2001).

Clearly, more than the temporary provision of resources or superficial changes in nurses' working conditions is at stake in this issue. Each of these elements—numbers, working conditions, and work satisfaction—incorporates underlying and unexamined assumptions about the nature of nurses' work, nursing knowledge, and the relationship of each to power structures in health care and society. What follows is a discussion of different frameworks for analysis and the possibilities they generate for understanding the nursing shortage, its recurrence, and its resolution.

Historical Analysis of the Nursing Shortage

The point is to write about and render historical what has hitherto been hidden from history.

Joan Scott, 1992

The purpose of an historical analysis is to show how a particular issue has evolved and how it has been, and continues to be, analysed in relation to different points of view. If we draw on the work of feminist historians, such as Joan Scott (1992), we quickly realise that histories are written from different perspectives. Historical analysis helps us to understand the views we currently hold or could hold about an issue. It may also provide insights into how we have come to hold them.

WHAT CONSTITUTES A SHORTAGE OF NURSES?

Some questions to answer through historical analysis include the following: What exactly constitutes a shortage? Who decides that a shortage is a shortage? To begin these discussions, consider the following comments that appeared in a 1943 issue of the *Canadian Nurse:* "How would you answer the age old imponderable—Is there a shortage of nurses? A study made not long ago showed that on November 20, 1942, there were 986 vacancies for nurses reported in Canada. A statement from all registries revealed the fact that 1133 nurses were on call that same day. We do not know what a statistician would make of these figures . . . but, so long as these conditions persist, we must say there is a shortage of nurses in certain vital services" (Kathleen Ellis, p. 269).

Sound familiar? What makes these words written more than 60 years ago so relevant today is that there is still no consensus about what constitutes a shortage and the relationship between persistent vacancies and the apparent availability of nurses to fill them. Despite the confusion about whether or not there is a shortage, Ellis feels bound to say there is a shortage as long as there are vacancies in particular areas. What has continued since, and likely preceded, Ellis' clear conceptualisation of the confusion about what constitutes a shortage is this: Until we know better what is going on when faced with vacancies in nursing positions, we will continue to talk about the situation as a shortage. To support what Ellis brings into question, it is not just that the shortage is expressed in numbers that must be challenged but that the number often reflects vacant positions as opposed to nurses available.

WHO IS THE AUTHORITY ON WHAT COUNTS AS A SHORTAGE?

The literature contains ample evidence that shortages are recurrent in nursing history. What is less clear and never really made explicit is whose and what authority defines a shortage? Does what we mean by a shortage depend to some extent on the authority of the speaker? That is, does what actually counts as a shortage in nursing rely less on what is happening at a particular moment in history and depend more on "who" claims that a shortage exists? You may ask, for example, if one nurse is doing the work that to be done competently should be done by two, is there a shortage? Or, if nurses are mandated to work past their 12-hour shift, on days off or holidays, is there a shortage? Or, if nurses on a particular unit are overworked, but there are no vacant positions for nurses, is there a shortage? Whether these situations represent a problem of numbers or a problem of management is unclear.

In many instances, nurses are excluded from important decisions about the number of nurses needed, how nursing positions are best managed to provide care, or even what constitutes adequate care. In situations in which well-qualified nurse managers are present, the best-planned staffing can be undermined by so-called cost-containment strategies. Thus, it is not always clear to others or even to nurses what it is that we are short of when we talk of shortages (Ceci & McIntyre, 2001).

HOW ARE NURSING SHORTAGES CREATED?

In considering how shortages come about in the first place, we need to take into account how strategies for dealing with shortages, such as unfilled registered nurse (RN) positions, are frequently based on the assumption that not enough nurses are being produced or maintained in the system. In some ways, this is true. In other ways, it is a limited understanding of how shortages are created. In many ways, shortages are linked to an increased demand for what it is that professional nurses are thought to provide—nursing care. These questions confound the issue: What creates an identified need, and is this need linked to a clearly articulated need for nursing care? Nurse positions are created for many reasons—which are not always clearly linked to the need for nursing service.

Aiken and Mullinex (1987) reported that the versatility of RNs in performing a wide range of other functions "including those assigned at other times to secretarial and clerical personnel, laboratory technicians, pharmacists, physical therapists and social workers" and the ability of RNs to "substitute for physicians" and "assume management roles after regular hours" made it advantageous for hospitals to create nurse positions rather than other positions. This is so because RNs "require little supervision and can assume responsibility for a wide range of duties" (p. 646). Aiken and Mullinex link the increased demand for nurses who for "relatively low wages" (1987, p. 646) can do much more than provide nursing care to a created demand for, and therefore a shortage of, nurses.

This and other studies do not mention the effects of hospitals taking advantage of nurses' presumed versatility on nursing practise. That it is unimaginable that a pharmacist, physiotherapist, or physician would be asked to take on a role usually assigned to others suggests that nurses are viewed differently than their contemporaries in practise. Other professionals clearly have the same ability to assume responsibility with minimal supervision for a wide range of duties outside their own practise fields, and yet no one would consider this possibility, making it clear that nurses' work is viewed differently from the work of other professionals.

Another way to illuminate the picture of how shortages come about is to consider the relationship between shortages and surpluses. For example, the nursing shortages of the 1980s can be linked to the development of new technologies leading to increasing demand for medical services. The expansion of services and increased use of medical technologies increased the demand for nurses, who were now needed to administer and monitor the new technologies. Given that nurses could also take on the care provided by other nursing personnel, the numbers of licensed practical nurses and orderlies decreased. These shortages, created by demand for more nurses to incorporate the advances in technology into patient care, became, in the context of health care restructuring and government cost-containment strategies, the nursing surplus of the 1990s (Donner et al.,1994).

What is important to grasp here is that there was no significant change in the number of nurses available. More often, what changed was the demand for nurses, not a decline in the supply of nurses. Increased medical services increased the number of RN positions needed. Later, the reduced funding available for structures that provided nursing positions, such as hospitals and health units, created the impression that a surplus of nurses existed where once there was a shortage. In reality, the number of nurses available for work had scarcely changed.

What is even more important to understand from the past, and what remains important today, is that structural changes seldom mean improved health care services. Many would argue and produce substantial evidence to support the claim that these changes have decreased the quality and availability of health care services (Taft & Steward, 2000).

Across Canada, the past decade of restructuring and downsizing has had profound effects. Without a plan of how care would be provided or concern for the welfare of nurses whose positions were cut, or those nurses who remained in a system decimated by the cuts, extensive layoffs of nursing positions took place. Nurses struggled and continue to struggle to provide care in environments characterised by heightened patient acuity, intensified workloads, and limited resources. Experienced RNs and new graduates were abandoned by the system they had prepared themselves to serve through advanced education and years of clinical service. Recurrent shortages and surpluses continue to be viewed in relation to numbers of nursing positions left vacant. What remains unacknowledged are the underlying conditions that created the surplus and the conditions—now about a decade later—that have led to a predicted nurse shortage of crisis proportions. What also remains unacknowledged are the effects of all this on nurses. The problem for nurses who make these claims and who continue to gather data to support these claims is that the predictions, however compelling, were not and are not accompanied by authority to act. The concerns of nurses have not been heard (Ceci & McIntyre, 2001).

Another issue that remains unacknowledged and unaccounted for is the weak link between the creating and cutting of nursing positions and the health of Canadians. American studies of magnet hospitals have shown lower mortality rates, suggesting that the "organisation of nursing care" can be linked to improved care outcomes (Aitken et al., 1994). Although a shortage of nurses to provide care undoubtedly puts the health of all Canadians at risk, the biggest and often overlooked risk is to the health of Canadian nurses. Recent Canadian studies show that the nature and conditions of nurses' work (increased workloads, work overload, patient acuity, and the complexity of care) increasingly affect the health and well-being of nurses themselves (Baumann et al., 2001).

Social and Cultural Analysis of the Nursing Shortage

Cultural ideas about gender are inherent in claims about what constitutes skill or what counts as knowledge, and these often unexamined assumptions create boundaries shaping what we are able to see and perhaps more importantly, what we don't see when we look to understand nursing.

Steinberg, 1990

The purpose of social and cultural analysis is to provide the background to how particular issues develop in particular contexts that influence both the way the issue is understood by others and its possibilities for resolution. Important questions to guide social and cultural analysis include, but are not limited to, the following:

- What are the prevailing attitudes in society about this issue?
- What values and priorities of the dominant culture influence this issue?
- In what ways, if any, do these values and priorities privilege the dominant culture over other members of society?

Stuart (1993), a nurse historian, makes social and cultural analysis central to her discussion of recruitment and retention in nursing. According to Stuart, lessons can be learned from the early 20th century by examining patterns that continue "to threaten the recruitment and retention of nurses today" (p. 19). A social and cultural analysis can "provide us with clues to patterns and themes that recurred throughout our history" (p. 19). Stuart offers the following themes: cultural myths about the nature of women's character and their work; social class and family strategies about daughters' educational career choices; and the sexual division of labor in the patriarchal health care system (p. 19). To support Stuart's claims, according to a report released by CNA in 1998, nursing is not replenishing itself; that is, fewer potential students are choosing nursing, nurses are leaving nursing, and the nurse population is aging. See Tables 2.1, 2.2, and 2.3 for more information.

There is little doubt what these indicators mean from a numbers viewpoint: we need to increase our recruitment and retention strategies. A closer look at these indicators, however, leads us to consider questions about nursing itself, our own understanding of nursing, and the way nursing is understood by others.

In a recent study, Sibbald (1998) reported, "Statistics Canada predicts that by 2011, Canada's population will grow 23 per cent, and the largest portion of the population will be 45 years or older. Older populations tend to have the highest utilization of health services. Rates of utilization of hospital days indicate the demand for RN services will grow by 46 per cent between 1993 and 2011" (p. 22). Sibbald also claims that "in the face of this increased demand, the supply of RNs will be diminished due to an aging workforce, inadequate retention, and declining enrollment" (p. 22).

The knowledge that Canadians seeking care and the nurses providing that care are aging and that aging will affect the number of nurses needed has been part of professional nursing platforms for decades. In the wake of the "BSN by the year 2000" agenda, nurses across Canada were lobbying provincial governments for baccalaureate education decades before such changes were needed. Meetings between provincial/territorial professional organisations and their governments have been, and continue to be, strategically and thoughtfully undertaken to inform governments about the predicted need for more nurses and nurses with various levels of preparation. However, there was and continues to be very little recognition of these predictions or actions taken to address them. A baccalaureate education—the level of education needed to address the increasing complexity of nursing care and predicted to make nursing more competitive and challenging to potential students—was and is the very thing governments most strongly resist.

Table 2.1 Projected Number of Registered Nurses in 2011, by Age

AGE IN 2011	RETAINED FROM 1995	NEW ADDITIONS SINCE 1995	TOTAL	PERCENTAGE
≤24	—	3,438	3,438	1.5
25–29	—	18,112	18,112	7.9
30–34	—	21,996	21,996	9.5
35–39	2,824	24,715	27,539	11.9
40–44	18,642	14,133	32,775	14.2
45–49	30,314	7,856	38,170	16.6
50–54	32,242	4,759	37,001	16.0
55–59	30,855	2,253	33,108	14.4
60–64	14,475	940	15,415	6.7
Total	**132,361**	**98,217**	**230,578**	**100**

Source: Canadian Nurses Association. Used with permission.

Table 2.2 Employment Prospects for Nurses in 2011: Three Scenarios

BETWEEN 1993 AND 2011, NO. OF NURSES MUST INCREASE	LOW GROWTH 23%	MEDIUM GROWTH 34.5%	HIGH GROWTH 46%
No. of RNs employed 1993	235,630	235,630	235,630
No. of RNs employed 1996	227,830	227,830	227,830
Projected No. of RNs required 2011	290,000	317,000	344,000
Additional RNs required 2011	62,000	89,000	116,000
Projected No. of RNs available 2011	231,000	231,000	231,000
Projected Shortage of RNs	**59,000**	**86,000**	**113,000**

Source: Canadian Nurses Association. Used with permission.

In the end it was not so much what was decided or what might have been decided differently that really counted. The major difficulty was that someone other than nurses made the decisions that nurses were in the best position to decide. Nurses were and are making their points, but for the most part, it would appear that nurses are not being heard. Nurses were lobbying for changes that would address not only current and future shortages but also other health care concerns over the long term, whereas politicians were making and continue to make decisions over the short term—usually to address immediate concerns.

Table 2.3 Nurse Staffing Levels by Province

PROVINCE	1992	1997	% CHANGE
Newfoundland	5,064	5,210	2.9
Prince Edward Island	1,246	1,281	2.8
Nova Scotia	9,128	8,587	−5.9
New Brunswick	7,349	5,858	−20.3
Quebec	57,330	59,160	3.2
Ontario	86,413	78,067	−9.7
Manitoba	10,251	10,510	2.5
Saskatchewan	8,698	8,456	−2.8
Alberta	21,461	21,428	−0.2
British Columbia	26,969	28,974	8.5
Yukon	N/A	252	—
Northwest Territory	492	476	−3.3
Canada	**234,128**	**228,259**	**−2.5**

Source: Canadian Nurses Association. Used with permission.

The disparity between what society believes it means to be a nurse—a belief that draws many students into nursing—and the reality of the nature and conditions of nurses' work continues to grow. Although the nature and conditions of nurses' work have not changed significantly over time, the attitudes toward the nature of work, the conditions of nurses' work and the availability of other possibilities for work have changed.

Economic Analysis of the Nursing Shortage

And now, as we experience a "reinvestment" in health services, the system claims it is about to be once more "short" of nurses.

Ceci & McIntyre, 2001

An economic analysis can highlight how the forces of supply and demand work in a particular issue. What some call a nursing "shortage" may manifest itself principally as a "problem" of numbers, which in turn can be most effectively addressed by managing or rebalancing supply and demand. Put another way, nurses are viewed as "an application of technology, as objects to be controlled, managed and understood primarily in practical instrumental ways" (Ceci & McIntyre, 2001, p. 123).

For example, the view of the current situation in nursing as principally an imbalance of supply and demand is considered to be so self-evident by some health care planners that it is seldom discussed as merely a point of view. Yet for others, particularly those who have either lived or read the history of the shortage, this focus inadequately accounts for what is happening. This suggests that more convincing interpretations are now necessary. For some, though, it is difficult to move past the idea that, the nursing "shortage," be it current or forecasted, is a problem with obvious solutions: "We need more nurses and we need them faster," is a view that has shown itself to be short-sighted, failing to address the concerns of actual nurses in its preoccupation with providing sufficient "cover" or pairs of hands (Davies, 1995).

Although understanding the economic elements of any issue is important, this point of view has limitations. Its effects have created problems for nursing—particularly in relation to nursing shortages. What makes an economic analysis so useful are not just what the numbers are telling us but what they do not tell us. For example, vacancy rates are frequently cited as evidence of a shortage of nurses. However, vacancies only indicate "the inability to recruit people or retain them in a particular position" (Ross, 1996, p. 201). There is no analysis of how the numbers of needed nursing positions are determined or of who determines this. New RN positions can be created for many reasons. Ideally, positions are created or added in response to an identified need for the knowledge and skills an RN provides. What is notable is that numbers tell us very little about the different knowledge, skills, and experience that the new positions require. In addition, what an analysis of numbers of nurses or numbers of positions may overlook is the hidden and nonnursing work incorporated in what many positions involve.

In her analysis of why the number of employed RNs increased in the 1970s and 1980s, Ross cited four factors: increase in RN employment opportunities; reduction in the RN-to-patient ratio; reduced number of non-RN assistants; and an increase in the number of part-time RN positions (1996, pp. 197–200). Ross's analysis draws on Meltz and Marzetti's 1988 analysis of labour market context to provide examples of both the strength and limitations of such analyses. The strength of this work is what it can tell us about where employed nurses are working and how these numbers have changed compared with other selected occupations. For example, how are the decisions to create new nursing positions or to cut back on the number of nurses made? Who makes these decisions? It is not so much that a good economic analysis is not useful in making these decisions, but rather, how are other perspectives taken into account? How much influence do nurse leaders have in challenging purely cost-containment strategies when the health of Canadians is thought to be at risk? Influence is discussed further in the following section on political analysis.

Political Analysis of the Nursing Shortage

Starting one's inquiries from the perspective of nurses' experiences is simply to concede that nurses, by virtue of their positioning, not only see and experience the world in particular ways but in ways that may be substantively different from more dominant views.

Ceci & McIntyre, 2001

Politics is often talked about as the art of influencing another person. When individuals and groups with disparate values enter into decision-making processes, politics shapes the content of what is discussed and the decision-making process itself. Although some nurses claim they are not political, others insist there is no escaping politics. A political analysis can be useful in highlighting the relationship between knowledge and power. To be able to persuade others that nurses working to their full capacity will produce different outcomes, that practise could be restructured to maximise nurses' skills and knowledge, and that nurses are a scarce resource that cannot be spared to do nonnursing tasks is to have power. Put another way, knowledge is power and may be nurses' greatest source of power. Although many nurses have recognised the importance of developing political skills, using their knowledge to influence health and nursing policy has not been that easy. What structures keep nurses from using what they know to influence others?

Ideologies are the voices of power and of authority within a culture. Ideologies are how we come to know who we are, what we are to think, and how we are to behave. Ideologies are ways through which we come to understand ourselves. The power of ideologies lies in the authority they have to define many of our social arrangements as obvious or natural (Althusser, 1971). How do dominant ideologies keep a nurse from accepting one's own ideas or the ideas of one's leader over those imposed by other authorities? The concept of power is not generally associated with nursing. The concept usually refers to the power of major corporations, politicians, trade unions, medical associations, and male-dominated organisations. Despite nurses' numbers and roles in health care, it is not that common for the nursing profession and nurses to be considered powerful.

A political analysis points to the conditions that influence us to act or not on that which we know. What follows are examples of changing conditions that have enabled nurses to use knowledge to pursue or influence decision-making and policy development. In many provinces, nurses have, through changing legislation, acquired legal powers that legitimise various nurse roles. In several provinces, roles such as the nurse practitioner and clinical nurse specialist have been created, accepted by the public, and integrated into the health care system In addition to the clinical expertise nurses in these roles provide, these advanced practitioners also contribute to the larger system. Through serving on advisory boards and acting as preceptors, these nurses are able to monitor and influence course content in schools of nursing. Through their involvement in research, evidence-based practise, and quality assurance, these nurses have opportunities to monitor activities and facilitate change in service settings. Most importantly, through these changing conditions, nurses' power base is expanded. Nurses have begun to encourage and support nurse candidates for political office and are increasingly involved in professional organisations' lobbying efforts.

Critical Feminist Analysis of the Nursing Shortage

That nursing is typically work undertaken by women is not the problem; that this work is understood in particular ways because it is ordinarily performed by women is, and it is this that requires us to be willing to challenge and raise questions about those discourses and ways of thinking, in the world or in us, which diminish nursing and act to constrain our understanding.

Ceci & McIntyre, 2001

A feminist analysis looks beyond the experiences of a particular nurse—man or woman—to the structures and ideologies that influence these experiences. Although one could use many different approaches to guide feminist analysis, the questions selected for this chapter are the following:

- What are the structures and ideologies in our world that contribute to errors or myths about a nurse's abilities or realities?
- Is this issue influenced by the power inequities or the hierarchic or patriarchal structures of institutions over patients?
- In this situation, is expert power given authority over the right to be the subject of one's life?

A feminist analysis helps us to understand the views and the effects of the views that others hold about nurse's abilities and realities. It also makes us more aware of how we as nurses—most of us women—participate in perpetuating these views. Put another way, feminist analysis helps us to understand our own complicity in sustaining structures and ideologies that foster misinterpretation of women's and nurses' experiences. A feminist analysis of a nursing issue is useful because it increases our knowledge and awareness of relevant power structures and thereby positions us effectively to participate in changing them. The discourses which define nursing are more than merely "ways of thinking"; they are also the ways of constituting the knowledge, practises, subjectivities, and relations of power which together make up the meanings of nursing (Weedon, 1999). The term *discourse* as it is used here pertains to the "social practices, values and cultural beliefs that prevail in a given culture or subculture at a specified historical moment, and shape the collective sense of what is right, proper, worthwhile or valuable" (Thorne et al., 1995, p. 2).

STATUS OF NURSING KNOWLEDGE

Despite our significance in health care settings, nurses are thought by many to be "marginal players, and this marginality affects our sense of ourselves and our possibilities for practice" (Ceci & McIntyre, 2001, p. 128). Although the marginal position of nurses can be linked to the "subordinate status of women" and the value of what is commonly thought of as "women's work, nursing marginality is also specifically related to the subordinate status of nursing knowledge" (p. 128). Despite the significant contributions of nurses to health and health care, the question of whether or not nursing is "a practice that requires a substantive knowledge base" is still asked and particularly by those outside of nursing (p. 128). As Rafferty (1996) has suggested, this anti-intellectual prejudice attaches to women's work in general. For nurses this becomes a prejudice that contributes to their social and intellectual subordination.

Nowhere is this more apparent than in discussions of how to address the current so-called nursing shortage. Discussions of shortage are all too easily transformed into arguments concerning what constitutes an adequate nursing education. Shortages are and have always been accompanied by discussions of how to shorten the time needed, assuming that "skilled and intelligent nursing care may be accomplished in the absence of a broad and substantive knowledge base. Not only does it seem that anyone can be a nurse but that any nurse is better than no nurse—again a claim hard to argue with but one that merely reinforces the intellectual subordination of nurses" (Ceci & McIntyre, 2001, p. 128).

STATUS OF NURSE'S WORK

Although the nursing literature and other human care literature highlight the importance of relationship accompanied by an ethic of care in the work of nursing, there is still an unquestioned assumption that implicitly or explicitly nursing is an expression of women's natural capacities, a view that effectively erases the knowledge required by nurses to comprehend and respond to the needs of another (Ceci & McIntyre, 2001, p. 128). Still "other discourses obscure or slide over the emotional labor and stress involved in nurses' work and instead emphasize the instrumentality [of nurses' work], the tasks that need to be done and [the] pairs of hands" (p. 128) needed to perform them. It is not that difficult to see how "these ideas about women, about women's work and how it does or does not require significant knowledge, responsibility and skill are embedded in nursing and become part of nursing's taken for granted reality" (p. 128).

IDENTIFYING BARRIERS TO RESOLUTION OF THE NURSING SHORTAGE

That nurses are considered expendable as evidenced by the recent cost cutting (1993–1996) was in no sense inevitable but rather the result of values, beliefs, and choices among possibilities. An outcome of these choices that seems not yet to be appreciated by the public or by policymakers, at least not in any deep sense, is the way in which these actions and policies have precipitated a certain suffering among nurses, a suffering which needs to be understood as now contributing to both a scarcity of nurses and a deficiency of nursing care (Ceci & McIntyre, 2001). One of the most important strategies for moving an issue toward resolution is identifying barriers that may impede the resolution process. Once the barriers are identified, chances for resolution through mediation, collaboration, or negotiation increase. What makes identifying barriers so useful in issue resolution is that we may lack awareness of the taken-for-granted assumptions that sustain an issue and obstruct its resolution. Nowhere is this truer than for the nursing shortage.

The biggest barrier to resolving what has been called a nursing shortage is the way this issue has been conceptualised and understood. Typically, shortages have been viewed as short-term problems solved temporarily either by educating more nurses or by recruiting nurses internationally. Although it can be argued that a focus on the recruitment and retention of student and graduate nurses would go a long way in addressing the current shortage, history has shown that it does not effectively address many of the underlying issues that sustain and perpetuate the ongoing cycle of surplus and shortage.

A second barrier that follows from the first is viewing nurses as temporary workers created to fill a gap in services. In this view, the gap is thought to be easily addressed by accelerating training, increasing head counts, and adding full-time equivalent positions, actions that undermine attempts at long-term recruitment and retention (Brush, 1992).

A third barrier to resolving the nursing shortage is the incongruity between the complex nature of nursing practise and the status of nurses' work and nurses' knowledge. In nursing history and today in practise, it is disturbing how "significant knowledge, insight, and experience that nurses require in their practices can be so effortlessly rendered invisible. How does this trivialization of the knowledge of nursing work itself contribute to what is called a nursing shortage?" (Ceci & McIntyre, 2001, p. 124). This failure to acknowledge the skilled knowledge required for nursing practise keeps the focus on numbers of nurses needed to fill vacant positions.

A fourth barrier is government's failure to consider the long-term ramifications of cost cutting on health care and of the nurses who are central to its provision.

One cannot overlook the possibility that the negative impacts on health and wellbeing of nurses contribute to nurses leaving the profession, nurses not being available for work, or nurses not being able to contribute effectively at work. We should consider the possibility that nurses are refusing to tolerate work environments that "invalidate their concerns, which fragment their practices, and disallow their understandings" (Ceci & McIntyre, 2001, p. 126). At least some part of the current situation in nursing has to do with how these conditions of practise conflict with "nurses' beliefs about what is necessary in terms of care. Nurses, it seems, are refusing to accept such unreasonableness as part of what it means to be a nurse" (p. 126).

A final and important barrier is that the concerns of nurses are all too often dismissed as groundless complaints, even though the well established pattern of these complaints suggests to us that there is something here worth paying attention to.

DEVISING STRATEGIES TO RESOLVE SELECTED ISSUES

If we intend to disrupt those understandings of the current situation in nursing which presume to already know what the present "problem" is, we could probably do no better than to begin by taking seriously the dilemmas and distress that arise for nurses because they are, paradoxically, unable to get on with the work of nursing, or at least the work of nursing as they understand it.

Ceci & McIntyre, 2001

Following the articulation, analysis, and discussion of barriers to resolution of a nursing issue, strategies for resolution must be generated. Although there are a wide variety of effective strategies to choose from, complex issues such as the nursing shortage call for particular strategies for resolution. As the analysis of the nursing shortage in this chapter clearly shows, long-term strategies are most important in moving this issue toward resolution. Also, given that the focus on numbers and instrumental solutions has been conceptualised as part of the problem, the strategies section deliberately highlights other possibilities for resolution. Finally, given the concern that nurses have been left out of many of the discussions involving the nursing shortage, emphasis is placed on the contributions that nurses have to make in its resolution. Strategies that nurses can carry out are central, beginning with what nurses must change to move the nursing shortage issue to resolution.

A first and likely a pivotal strategy is to acknowledge that nurses' concerns have been largely ignored in the past decades. There is no point in continuing strategies that history clearly shows have not worked. Concerns about the knowledge and skills needed for entry to practise, predicted shortages due to an aging workforce and declining enrollments, and the restructuring of the health care system in the 1990s have been articulated clearly by nurses and supported with research. Professional organisations have lobbied all levels of government on behalf of nurses, the health of Canadians, and the health care system. History tells us that nurses have not been heard.

Specifically, the strategy proposed here is this: Rather than discounting nurses' experiences or interpreting nurses' differing viewpoints as simply wrong, we might profitably ask why it is that we as nurses interpret our experience of the health care system and its workings differently from others. In taking up this point, Ceci and McIntyre (2001) suggest, "difference may be most productively interpreted not as mere diversity but as difference in experience and perspective which both reflects and establishes differences of power" (p. 127). The point these authors stress is that "nurses have a different experience of health care systems . . . this difference holds ethical and political meanings and implications for nurses and for our practices" and this "difference always plays itself out in a material world" (p. 127).

The specific action that would follow from this strategy would be to challenge ourselves and others to hear what nurses have to say as significant. Put another way, we need to insist that concerns which are sometimes dismissed as groundless complaints be seen as the "beginnings of a critique . . . of the dominant modes of thinking that organize the work of health care" (Ceci & McIntyre, 2001, p. 126).

The term *critique*, as used here, is not to suggest that nurses are right and that dominant modes of thinking are somehow misinformed. Rather, the point is to suggest that there is room in the discussion of health care concerns for the different perspective that nurses can bring. To sum up this first strategy then, nurses are well positioned by their knowledge and experience of the health care system to critique dominant ways of thinking that inform health care decisions. The point is not that dominant ways of thinking are wrong, but that they are simply insufficient to handle important issues in the Canadian health care system, of which the nursing shortage is one example.

Emanating from this first strategy of listening to what nurses have to say and hearing their views as significant among others' views is the second strategy of developing issues to put forward for consideration. First, nurses, nurse educators, and nurse researchers can draw on a feminist analysis to raise questions about assumptions and beliefs about the nature and value of women that obscure or distort the realities of nursing from those outside of nursing. Second, we must become critically aware of how nurses and women may be implicated in self-invalidation. It is essential that we explore our own complicity in ways of thinking that diminish nursing.

A third strategy is to look to understanding nursing contexts as involving and expressing questions that provide the foreground to the relations of power inherent in the hierarchies of gender, the ideologies of knowledge, and the dominant institutional realities that constitute our practises. By addressing these three dimensions, our understanding, including self-understanding, can change how we understand what we, as nurses, are meant to do and be in our practises.

A fourth strategy is to challenge those viewpoints that position nursing and nurses as simply incorrect. Such viewpoints must be taken up as meaningful, "not as natural or inevitable but as pointing to social structures and ways of thinking which privilege some perspectives and exclude others" (Ceci & McIntyre, 2001, p. 122). There is little doubt that some views of nurses "hold greater authority than others but what may be more consequential is that, even among nurses, nurses' own understandings of themselves and their work are not necessarily among those thought most legitimate" (Ceci & McIntyre, 2001, p. 122).

SUMMARY

The point is not only that nurses have a different experience of health care systems but also that this difference holds ethical and political meanings and implications for nurses and our practise.

(Ceci & McIntyre, 2001)

Those who understand nurses as something more than a pair of hands or more than technical support for the real work of medicine will recognise the need and necessity for opening the current situation in nursing as discussed in this chapter to questioning. By being thoughtful about the questions that arise in situations in which nurses find themselves, we can generate new possibilities for extending or deepening the overall understanding of the current context of nurses' work and nurses' practise.

As we have discussed in numerous ways throughout this chapter, nurses' views of the world are both overshadowed and undermined by more dominant views that define who nurses are, the work they do, and in many cases the knowledge and skill needed to do this work. The difficulty nurses currently face and have always faced is that nurses are often left to express their concerns about health care in terms and forums which are not necessarily their own.

Nurses' complaints and frustrations, their distress, though not in itself constitutive of critique, conveys clearly the position that nurses' knowledge and experience is somehow not covered or accounted for in the dominant discourses that define, describe, and enact health care.

Until we can move beyond thinking of recurrent nursing shortages as inevitable, of the ethos of nurses as expendable, interchangeable, and easily replaced, and of the immediate problem of not enough nurses to the larger issues that have sustained and perpetuated shortages, the current situation is unlikely to change. Questions raised about the relationship between recurrent shortages and the conceptualisation of nurses' work, women's work, and nursing knowledge must be addressed. In our discussions, we must resist the notion that the predicted scarcity of nurses is a problem that can be solved by providing resources or superficial changes in working conditions.

We can be concerned with the invalidation of nurses and of women because the suffering of nurses disturbs us, or we can be concerned because of the ways that such invalidation directly obstructs care. In either case, however, we should recognise that we are involved in political struggles over how to see and interpret our worlds, remembering that seeing is not passive but rather is an activity of selection and interpretation.

(Ceci & McIntyre, 2001)

(O) Online RESOURCES

Add to your knowledge of this issue:

Canadian Nurses Association	**www.cna-nurses.ca**
Federal government's primary site	**www.gc.ca**
Canadian Parliament	**www.parl.gc.ca**
Health Canada	**www.hc-sc.gc.ca**
Links to provincial and territorial sites	**www.gc/othergov/prov/html**
Canadian Health Services Research Foundation	**www.chsrf.ca**
Center for health services and policy research	**www.chspr.ubc.ca**

Reflections on the Chapter

1. From your practise experience, identify the different ways the shortage of nurses has been talked about and the reasons given for the shortage.

2. This chapter presents evidence of the different ways of understanding why a shortage of nurses is thought to exist and what has contributed to it. How would you account for these differences?

3. Identify the assumptions and beliefs you hold that contribute to a particular way of understanding a shortage of nurses. Identify the assumptions and beliefs held by others that support other ways of understanding a shortage of nurses.

4. In addition to those barriers to resolution of the shortage already provided in the chapter, what other obstructions to resolution can you identify?

5. Of the strategies offered in this chapter for resolving the nursing shortage, which have you seen implemented in practise? What are your views on the strengths and limitations of each of the strategies presented in the chapter or that you have seen utilised in a practise setting?

6. What other strategies can you offer for resolving nursing shortage issue?

7. What other readings or resources have assisted you in understanding this complex issue?

8. How would you describe the stand of your professional organisation (provincial or territorial) on this issue? How would you account for this stand?

REFERENCES

Aiken, L., Mullix, C. (1987). Special report: The nursing shortage—myth or reality. *New England Journal of Medicine, 317*(10), 641–646.

Althusser, L. (1971). Ideology and ideological state apparatuses. In L. Althusser (Ed.). B. Brewster (Trans). *Lenin and philosophy and other essays* (pp. 123–173). London: New Left Books.

Baumgart, A., Wheeler, M. (1992). The nursing workforce in Canada. In A. Baumgart & J. Larsen (Eds.). *Canadian nursing faces the future* (2nd ed.). Toronto: Mosby.

Baumann, A., O'Brien-Pallas, L., Armstrong-Strassen, M., Blythe, J., Bourbonnais, R., Cameron, S.,

Doran, D., Kerr, M., Gillis-Hall, L., Vezina, M., Butt, M., & Ryan, L. (2001). *Commitment and care—the benefits of a healthy workplace for nurses, their patients and the system: A policy synthesis.* Ottawa: Canadian Health Services Research Foundation.

Brush, B. (1992). Shortage as shorthand for the crisis in caring. *Nursing & Health Care, 13*(9), 480–486.

Campbell, M. (1987). Productivity in Canadian nursing: Administering cuts. In Darcy, Torrence, & New (Eds.), *Health and Canadian society: Sociological perspectives* (pp. 463–475). Markham: Fitzthenry & Whiteside.

Canadian Nurses Association. (1998). *The quiet crisis in health care: A submission to the House of Commons Standing Committee on Finance and the Minister of Finance.* Ottawa: Author.

Center for Health Services and Policy Research. (2000). *Nursing Workforce Study: The supply of nursing personnel in Canada* (Vol. II). University of British Columbia, Vancouver: Author.

Ceci, C., & McIntyre, M. (2001). A quiet crisis in health care: Developing our capacity to hear. *Nursing Journal of Nursing Philosophy, 2*(2), 122–130.

Davies, C. (1995). *Gender and the professional predicament in nursing.* Philadelphia: Open University Press.

Donner, G., Semogas, D., & Blythe, J. (1994). *Towards an understanding of nurses' lives: Gender, power and control.* Toronto: Quality of Nursing Work Life Research Unit Monograph Series.

Ellis, K. (1943). Some pertinent questions. *Canadian Nurse 39*(4), 268–271.

Meltz, N., & Marzatti, J. (1988). *The shortage of registered nurses: An analysis in labour market context.* Toronto: Registered Nurses Association of Ontario.

Rafferty, A. (1996). *The politics of nursing knowledge.* New York: Routledge.

Ross, E. (1996). From shortage to oversupply: The nursing workforce pendulum. In J. Kerr & J. McPhail (Eds.), *Canadian Nursing: Issues and Perspectives* (pp. 196–207). St. Louis: Mosby.

Shamian, J. (2000). Re-energizing hospital care. *Reflections on Nursing Leadership*, First Quarter.

Scott, J (1992). Experience. In J. Butler & J. Scott (Eds.), *Feminists Theorize the Political.* London: Routledge.

Sibbald, B. (1998). The future supply of registered nurses in Canada. *The Canadian Nurse, 94*(2), 22–23.

Steinberg, R. (1990). Social construction of skill: Gender, power and comparable worth. *Work and Occupations, 17*(4), 449–482.

Stuart, M. (1993). Nursing: The endangered profession. *The Canadian Nurse, 89*(4), 19–22.

Taft, K., & Steward, G. (2000). *Clear answers: The economics and politics of for-profit medicine.* Edmonton: Duval House Publishing.

Thorne, S., McCormick, J., and Carty, E. (1996). Deconstructing the gender neutrality of chronic illness and disability. *Health Care for Women International* 18(1), 1–16.

Weedon, C. (1999). *Feminism, theory and the politics of difference.* London: Blackwell.

White, J. (1999). Changing labour process and the nursing crisis in Canadian hospitals. In P. Armstrong & M. P. Connelly (Eds.), *Feminism, political economy and the state: Contested terrain* (pp. 57–90). Toronto: Canadian Scholars' Press.

3

The Canadian Health Care System and Canadian Nurses

Janet Storch

The Canadian Nurses Association recommendations in favor of health promotion and disease prevention are as important as they were when presented to the second Hall Commission 25 years ago. Today's Canadian nurses are well-positioned to educate young citizens and their older counterparts about healthful life choices and ways to prevent disease. (Photograph by Larry Arbour. Used with permission of University of Calgary.)

At the completion of this chapter, you will be able to:

1. Understand how and why Canada's health care system differs from other systems of health care.

2. Recognise the history in our current challenges in health care.

3. Understand the system's impact on Canadian nursing and individual nurse's work.

4. Recognise the need for nursing leadership in maintaining all that is good about health care and making changes to correct deficiencies.

5. Identify future possibilities for nurses in the health care system.

Nurses' practise is influenced by social, cultural, and historical realities worldwide, and Canadian nursing practise is no exception to this. These influences underlie the context within nurses' practise, a context which affects their everyday lives as nurses.

Therefore, nurses need to understand how social, cultural, and historical influences, along with economic and political forces, have shaped Canadian health services and the systems in which nurses work. Such understanding includes the philosophical framework for Canadian health care, the values that underlie a mainly public health insurance system, and key policy decisions that established the national programmes. By gaining greater awareness of how social and cultural values influenced the development, financing, and delivery of health care, nurses can appreciate the nature of the value conflicts that underlie current health care debates. Further, through such understanding, nurses can better understand their practise environments and take an informed political advocacy role to continue shaping health care for the benefit of patients.

This chapter aims to provide nurses with an understanding of the health care system in which they work to equip them for the challenges involved in preserving the best of the system while making changes and improvements to health care. Specifically, the chapter invites nurses to focus on how the system affects the nursing profession and how nurses have attempted to influence the system and their own work. The reader is encouraged to consider nursing's involvement in the health care system (past and present) and the nursing leadership needed to make a difference in this complex system.

HEALTH CARE IN THE GLOBAL CONTEXT

Considering Canada's approach to health care in comparison with other countries is important in establishing its context and in assessing the challenges and potentials of our collective approach to health care. How and why health care systems differ is a function of multiple influences, which may include societal values and beliefs, sociocultural climate, the state of the economy, political realities, geographic density, international influences, historical accident, established practises and programmes, and other factors. As we consider how Canada's system developed, it is clear that several of these factors were at play at different points in time. The same is true for countries around the world.

One way to think about system differences is to consider that all Western countries provide for health care in a variety of ways, all of which involve variable combinations of private or public funding of services and private or public delivery of services (Health Canada, 2001). In the typologies noted below, the degree of public involvement in financing health services and the essential role envisioned for the health care system are shown (Najman & Western, 1984) (Table 3.1).

In the first type (type I) of health care system, private approaches to health services predominate, wherein both physician or other caregiver (such as midwife) and patient have maximum autonomy. This means that those who can afford private health insurance, or who simply can pay for their health care directly, chose their care providers and receive health services. Those who cannot pay do not have choice or benefit. In the pure form of type I, there would be no option other than to pay for service. In reality, most countries have adopted a mix of system types. For example, although the United States has mainly a private pay system of health care, there are some publicly funded programmes to assist elderly and poor people. Even with these programmes, it is estimated that 42 million Americans have no health insurance and, therefore, are limited in their ability to access health care.

The polar opposite of type I described above is type IV. This type of health care system focusses on keeping people healthy so that they can contribute to society and the economy. Health care is considered an essential service, not necessarily driven by compassionate motives for those who are ill as much as by motives of productivity. Physicians are considered agents of the state who work to keep others working efficiently. In Canada, the military establishment runs a similar system, as do most hockey teams and other sports teams. Physicians are hired to ensure that players in the "game of life" do their part.

Between the two extreme types are two different types of health care systems. Type III is a health care system funded and operated by the government. This would have been typical of the health care system in Great Britain some years ago. There, the state-

Table 3.1   Types of Health Care Systems in the Western World

TYPE I	TYPE II	TYPE III	TYPE IV
Private health insurance	National health insurance	National health service	Socialized health system
Primary goal: preserve autonomy	Primary goal: egalitarian	Primary goal: egalitarian	Primary goal: essential service
Secondary effect: acceptance of social differences	Secondary effect: preserve autonomy	Secondary effect: public management	Secondary effect: physicians as state employees

From Najman J. M., & Western, J. S. (1984). A comparative analysis of Australian health policy in the 1970s. *Social Science and Medicine, 18*(1), 949-958, with permission.

operated and state-funded health services were based on an egalitarian value. Public management of each service was considered key to efficient and effective operation.

Finally, type II is a hybrid of systems shown as type I and type III, wherein egalitarian values are high while autonomy of practitioner and patient are preserved to the maximum extent possible, thereby reconciling the two often-conflicting values. Type II health care systems use tax dollars to pay for health services through health insurance available from a nonprofit agency (e.g., government), whereas each health service is operated more or less autonomously by others: municipalities, citizen groups, and physicians or physiotherapists in private offices, group practises, or other modes. All services rendered to patients are then paid from the central pool of health insurance funds created through taxation. This distinctly Canadian approach embodies collective sharing of burdens and benefits while allowing a degree of autonomy in delivery (Storch, 1996).

Before leaving this brief section, it is important to underscore several qualifying points. First, the term *health care system* is a misnomer. In Canada, health services are far from being integrated systems of care, yet the ideal of an integrated and coordinated system of health services is important. Second, the four types noted exclude a group of Third World countries that cannot afford the type of health care enjoyed in Canada. Yet many of these countries have developed primary care systems that are not as institution dependent as those in Canada. Primary care includes preventive health care as well as first point of contact and continuing care. In some cases, these preventive systems have been undermined by the influence of Western countries promoting high technology and institutionalisation. Finally, even within the countries that finance health insurance through tax dollars, there are variations in services provided, for example, some fund home care whereas others do not; some provide coverage for prescription drugs and others do not.

To appreciate how Canada's health care policies and modes of delivery influence nursing, one needs to consider how the health care system developed. As you reflect on the origins and development of Canada's health care system, identify the multiple factors influencing development and how that development led to patterns of care that are commendable and others that are less than ideal.

HISTORY AND BACKGROUND: CANADA'S HEALTH CARE SYSTEM

For some, history can be a tedious subject. With that in mind, the following focusses the key historical necessities for understanding Canada's health care system and its legacy on a set of players, that is, people who took leadership at particular points in history to create, sustain, reform, or challenge the health care services system as we know it today. Here is the cast: a lay nurse and hospital administrator named Jeanne Mance, a group of leaders known as the Fathers of Confederation, a visionary physician named J. W. McIntosh, an ambitious graduate student named Leonard Marsh and a bored politician named Ian MacKenzie, a young boy stricken with osteomyelitis named Tommy Douglas, a Prime Minister from Saskatchewan named John Diefenbaker, a French Canadian Health Minister named Monique Begin, two provincial premiers by the names of Ralph Klein and Mike Harris, and an actress named Shirley Douglas. Not all are top stars in the production, but they are characters that can remind us of particular events around which health care took shape. They provide mental images of real people who influenced health care.

Jeanne Mance and the Period Before Confederation

In the late 1600s and up until the late 1800s, the new territory eventually named Canada was being settled. It was a time characterised by very limited government involvement in any social or health services. The Colony was largely a rural society, and the limited collective health efforts needed centred on communicable diseases, epidemics, and other difficulties (such as insanity or leprosy) that were beyond the helping capacity of neighbor or lay workers. Historical accounts, for example, focus on the need for better care for the mentally ill, referring to the need for "lunatic asylums" or "institutions for the feeble-minded," noting that these facilities were badly overcrowded and that preventive work was underdeveloped (Cassidy, 1947). Charitable organisations and religious orders, the latter particularly in Quebec, were essential in providing care.

Jeanne Mance was the first lay nurse in North America and the first to arrive in Canada. Her task of building the first hospital in Mont Royal (Montreal) and her negotiation with benefactors in France to bring more nurses to Canada (Ross Kerr, 1996) was a mark of her commitment to the new Colony. Following her lead, the Grey Nuns of Montreal, a "uniquely Canadian order of nuns," formed. They were visiting nurses as well, and the order was instrumental in serving pioneers in western Canada (Ross Kerr, 1996). Ross Kerr notes the importance of the French influence in early Canadian nursing because this influence allowed Canada to escape some of the effects of the regressive period of nursing rampant in the United Kingdom at the time. As the Colony that was to become Canada approached confederation in 1867, there were isolated actions involving government regulation (e.g., for the sale of meat, for managing epidemics), but for the most part, this was generally a time of benign neglect.

The Fathers of Confederation

The Fathers of Confederation, our next set of players, are notable mainly for what they did not know about health care needs and what they could not have known. When these leaders set out the terms of the British North America (BNA) Act of 1867—an Act which continues to form a part of our current Constitution Act—they had no idea how trends in industrialisation and urbanisation would affect health care needs (Wallace, 1950; Cassidy, 1947; Hastings & Mosley, 1980). Thus, they wrote of what they knew and outlined very basic responsibilities of the federal government, leaving wide room for the provinces to be the key players in the provision of health care with the conviction that individuals could and should be self-reliant.

The federal responsibilities were seen as follows:

> Sec. 91—taking of the census, . . . collecting statistics (birth, marriage, death), establishing quarantine regulations and hospitals for those in quarantine, and taking responsibility for Canada's native peoples (Van Loon & Whittington, 1976).

For the provinces, a clause was developed in the Act that proved to be inclusive of almost all types of health services:

> Sec. 92 (7)—The Establishment, Maintenance and Management of Hospitals, Asylums, Charities, and Eleemosynary Institutions in and for the Province, other than Marine Hospitals (Van Loon & Whittington, 1976)

This division of federal and provincial responsibilities continues to have the effect of creating permanent tension between the federal government, who collected most of the taxes, and the provincial governments, who saw their mandate for the provision of health services growing each year (Lindenfield, 1959).

Before being too critical of the Fathers of Confederation, however, one must note that the philosophical basis of the Canadian constitution they developed establishes that the federal government is responsible for making " . . . Laws for the Peace, Order and good Government of Canada" (Van Loon & Whittington, 1976, p. 480). In contrast to our U.S. neighbors, whose constitution centres on individual liberties and freedoms, the stage was set for enacting legislation emphasising the common good (or the collective good).

A Visionary Thinker

Between the signing of the BNA Act in 1867 and World War II, the young country of Canada underwent profound change. Immediately after Confederation, a number of charities were formed to address growing unmet needs. These charities included several that involved Canadian nurses to a substantial degree. They included the Red Cross, the Victorian Order of Nurses, the Canadian Mental Health Organization, and several other such organisations (Meilicke & Storch, 1980). Canada was urbanising as well. With the series of economic depressions that befell the new country, it became evident that reliance on self and family were insufficient for many. There were growing needs for social assistance and health services (both prevention and curative services). Because there were no federal structures to facilitate the development of health services and no provincial structures yet in place, local municipalities were forced to take significant responsibilities in providing health care (Cassidy, 1947). They had limited resources available to them to do so. The unmet health needs of Canadians were never more apparent than when many of Canada's young men volunteered to fight in World War I and were found unfit for combat because of poor health.

Just before World War I, the president of the Vancouver Medical Society, J. W. McIntosh (1914), delivered a paper at the Royal Sanitary Conference in Vancouver on the topic of the interrelationship of physician, citizen, and state to public health. He provided a conceptual framework to describe the disabilities affecting many Canadians, classifying them as hereditary, personal or self-imposed, or environmental—"the gift of our neighbors and surroundings." Years later, his framework would resonate with the writing of a federal civil servant named Laframboise (1973) in an article which was the basis of a prominent Canadian report known as the Lalonde report (1974), named after the Minister of Health under whose tenure this report was released. The Lalonde report, entitled *A New Perspective on the Health of Canadians*, marked Canada as a leader in formulating a four-point policy framework that considered heredity, environment, lifestyle, and health services as critical to health. Although McIntosh was visionary in his views, his ideas for implementation may have been traditional, as reflected in the concluding comments of his speech: "Of good omen is the welcome announcement from Ottawa, that shortly, the government will create a Public Health Department and appoint a member of the Cabinet—a trained medical man—as Minister of Public Health" (McIntosh, 1914, p. 454).

Between World War I and World War II, public health activities increased significantly in an attempt to address deficiencies in health services, and public health nursing expanded (Hastings & Mosley, 1980, pp. 149–150). This growth of public health nursing was considered a threat by many physicians because " . . . these nurses worked semi-independently in the community" (Coburn, 1988, p. 443). Physician concern about nursing independence continues to be prevalent in Canadian nursing today. Yet, it must also be recognised that there was a degree of support and cooperation between the two professions. Further, even as many nurses attempted to gain professional recognition, there was division within nursing ranks about whether nursing should pursue this independence as an important goal, just as there was division within medical ranks about nursing aspirations (Kinnear, 1994). This same diversity of opinion characterises nursing and medical–nursing relationships in the 21st century.

A Bored Politician and an Ambitious Graduate Student

By the time Canada entered World War II, health care needs continued to exceed the supply of any type of comprehensive health care. Infant and maternal mortality rates were high, and morbidity and mortality from communicable diseases were of grave concern (Taylor, 1987). One third of the men who were examined for military service were unfit for service, with one third of that group rejected because of "psychiatric disorders" (Cassidy, 1947, p. 51).

As World War II began, a young politician by the name of Ian MacKenzie was Minister of Defense. The demands of his position were not seen as particularly challenging until the time for real engagement in the war action began. At that point, his boss, Prime Minister Mackenzie King, moved Ian MacKenzie from the Department of Defense to what was considered a less demanding role in the Department of Pensions and National Health. Despite being excluded from the main focus of government attention and action (i.e., the war), Ian MacKenzie was not content to remain idle. In 1939, he wrote to Prime Minister King "urging that unemployment and health insurance be introduced as war measures," suggesting that the demand for a national health system was inevitable (Taylor, 1987, p. 16). Over time, he managed to present a convincing case by suggesting that Canada owed such services to its returning troops, noting that other countries were developing these types of programmes as well and thereby heightening his moral persuasion.

Meanwhile, a young graduate student in economics at London University, Leonard Marsh, participated in research for British lord Sir William Beveridge (Bliss, 1975; Taylor, 1987), author of the famous Beveridge report which advocated social insurance in Great Britain. Leonard Marsh subsequently relocated to Canada and became Director for Social Research at McGill University. There, he directed a programme of research on employment and produced several major studies on Canadian social conditions. In this and later posts, he was a consultant to the federal government and gradually became involved with the Committee on Postwar Reconstruction in 1944–45. Meanwhile, Ian MacKenzie commissioned the Director of Public Health Services, Dr. J. J. Heagerty, to develop proposals for health insurance. In doing so, he urged Dr. Heagerty to consult with provincial counterparts and establish an Inter-Departmental Advisory Committee on Health Insurance. This Heagerty did, and he produced a massive report at the same time Marsh was completing his Report on Social Security for Canada. Marsh's report is now regarded as the single most important document in the historical development of the welfare state in Canada and a key document in the development of postwar social security programmes, the equivalent in Canada to the Beveridge report. Marsh's report included a comprehensive package of social programmes for Canadians (Rice & Prince, 2000). It recognised that all are deserving of adequate social supports for living.

The reports of Marsh and Heagerty in 1943 became a key part of the documentation for discussions on postwar reconstruction, and they were tabled together at the Postwar Reconstruction Conference by Ian MacKenzie on August 6, 1945. They reflected a postwar idealism fostered by international influences, such as the freedoms outlined in the Atlantic Charter (Taylor, 1973; Marsh, 1975). As told so dramatically by Malcolm Taylor, these reports and proposals were comprehensive, and the agenda for the meeting at which they were to be discussed was hailed by Prime Minister Mackenzie King as likely the "most important Canadian conference since Confederation" (Taylor, 1987, p. 50). But a hiatus in proceedings occurred when news of the bombing of Hiroshima was received at the meeting. The adjournment and rescheduling of the meeting left room for those considering economic priorities, rather than those holding philosophical and humanitarian commitments, to triumph in defeating the introduction of this comprehensive plan for health and social security. (Note that this type of tension in world views is not dissimilar from current opposing positions in health care today.) Nevertheless, over the next 20 years, the plans set out by Marsh and Heagerty served as something of a blueprint for the development of health insurance and social insurance in Canada.

A Young Boy From Saskatchewan

Much of the difficulty encountered in the acceptance of the Proposals for Postwar Reconstruction was also related to who had the legal authority for health care. The BNA Act's division of federal and provincial responsibilities was high in the minds of those proposing less federal interference and more provincial autonomy—a theme that continues to dominate debates in Canadian health care. However, in the province of Saskatchewan, a different mentality was at play. In many respects, the rural and isolated population in this prairie province did not mind as much who offered the programmes to combat, in the words of Lord Beveridge, "Want, Disease, Ignorance, Squalor, and Idleness" (Taylor, 1987, p. 34) as that programmes be available to all.

Saskatchewan had a long history of working collectively to solve practical problems of everyday living. And when it came to health care, the province united in a significant step of using public tax dollars to pay a physician a retainer to ensure medical care could be available to all in the municipality. This scheme, called the Municipal Doctor System, was implemented in 1916 and was followed shortly thereafter by collective action to develop hospitals through pooling municipal monies to do so (Gelber, 1966).

In 1945, Saskatchewan was, therefore, positioned to benefit from whatever federally funded programmes the government would offer. When the federal government's decision to move ahead with the recommended programmes was aborted, Saskatchewan determined that it would go ahead on its own. Because of the hospital construction planned and underway, this province was ready for the federal programme for funding hospital construction, a programme the federal government was able to salvage from the aborted proposals of 1945 (Taylor, 1987). In addition, with these matched funds, Saskatchewan was also ready to introduce a hospital insurance programme in 1947, at least 10 years before the introduction of hospital insurance in most of the other provinces. Key architects of this planning and development were members of the Canadian Cooperative Federation (CCF), a predecessor of the National Democratic Party (NDP). And a leader in the move to health insurance programmes was the young boy, now young man, destined to lead the CCF party, Tommy Douglas.

Having suffered with disease and disability as a child, Tommy Douglas understood the importance of good health care covered by health insurance and the need to make it available to all (Margoshes, 1999). Mr. Douglas became both premier and health minister at one point in his party leadership to bring about his vision of a comprehensive health insurance programme. Other provinces in Canada had also engaged in various programs and strategies to make "insurance against sickness" a reality (including the British Columbia Legislative Assembly's resolution of 1922 to urge the federal government to "give early consideration to legislation providing for an adequate system of insurance against sickness" and Alberta's adoption of initiatives similar to those in Saskatchewan). Saskatchewan's leadership became a model for the rest of Canada (Gelber, 1966). In fact, Saskatchewan, under Tommy Douglas, became the "laboratory" of pilot projects for what eventually became national health insurance programmes involving hospital insurance and medical insurance. Table 3.2 outlines this history.

Although hospital insurance was greeted by almost all with appreciation and relief when it was introduced in Saskatchewan in 1946–47, the same could not be said about medical care insurance when it was introduced in 1961–62. The introduction of the medicare programme was radically opposed by physicians, who took strike action to protest what they regarded as a slip into socialised medicine. Their relative pleasure with hospital insurance is understandable. After World War I, but particularly in the period after World War II, many of the new medical technologies discovered and advanced during the war years were introduced in North America. The average physician could not afford the new diagnostic and treatment technologies for the individual office. Therefore, hospitals became the logical place for doctors to have access to these new tools of their trade. As early as the 1920s, medical and surgical procedures previously performed at home had moved to hospitals. Hospital holdings of x-ray machines and laboratory equipment increased dramatically in the 20-year period following. By the early 1950s, hospitals had been transformed (Hastings & Mosley, 1980; Torrance, 1987).

The effect on nurses and nursing was equally dramatic. No longer were most nurses working relatively independently caring for patients in homes. By 1948, about 65% of nurses were working in hospitals or nursing schools, as compared with 25% in 1930 (Coburn, 1988). This change in service venue created a significant shift in how nursing was practised and how it was valued. Stinson (1969), in describing and comparing the model nurse of the 1920s with the model nurse of the 1960s in terms of professionalisation and deprofessionalisation, observed that the private duty nurse of the 1920s was a "near-paragon of solo practice" (p. 333). She was not supervised by

Table 3.2   Saskatchewan as a Laboratory for Federal Programs: Key Legislation

YEAR	PROVINCE OF SASKATCHEWAN	GOVERNMENT OF CANADA
1916	Rural Municipality Act; Union Hospital Act	
1944		The Department of National Health and Welfare Act
1947	Hospital Insurance Act	Provincial grants, including public health grants and a grant for hospital construction
1956-57		Hospital Insurance and Diagnostic Services Act, with provision for in-patient insurance and testing
1962	Medical Care Insurance Act	
1967-68		Medical Care Act

other nurses and rarely by physicians and was quite autonomous. However, she had little authority over anyone but herself and to some extent the patient and the family. Stinson noted that the nurse of the 1960s had far more responsibility but less autonomy in her hospital-based and technology-laced practise. Further, this 1960s nurse had many "masters," including the doctor, the hospital administrator, the nursing supervisors, and possibly the patient and family (Stinson, 1969).

A Prime Minister From Saskatchewan

The final plank of Canada's health care system, a national medicare programme, was put in place in the mid-1960s. It would seem natural that the battle for medicare fought in Saskatchewan would pave the way for a relatively easy introduction of a similar programme in Canada. However, such was not the case. Many provinces had already established systems of private medical insurance they believed were superior to any national plan. At least three provinces, for example, paid all or part of the costs of health insurance for those considered poor risks, while leaving the majority of the population who could afford voluntary insurance to the private sector (Taylor, 1987).

With the popularity of private medical insurance plans (particularly in the eyes of physicians and business leaders), and with hospitals now available for use, Prime Minister Diefenbaker, as leader of the Progressive Conservative government, was reluctant to hurry to introduce the long-promised medicare programme. Instead, he chose to take the advice of the Canadian Medical Association (CMA) to appoint a Royal Commission on Health Services (1964, 1965) to study the matter. This commission was chaired by Justice Emmett Hall, and neither the prime minister nor the CMA would have believed that this commission would strongly recommend a national medicare programme. Yet, when the commissioners considered the total package of health care services needed by a Canadian family, they rejected the extra costs of creating a means test for eligibility for these services and recommended that it was cost-effective to subsidise the 10 health insurance programmes in Canada (Taylor, 1973).

Further, public support for a comprehensive health insurance system was evident. By the time this programme came into being, a new government had been formed under the leadership of Prime Minister Lester B. Pearson, who could at last fulfill the longstanding Liberal election promise, the introduction of medicare. As in Saskatchewan, this national programme was controversial and politically costly. However, it served to complete the general blueprint proposed in the Marsh and Heagerty documents even though the final programmes were not nearly as comprehensive nor as farsighted as the 1945 proposals.

So how did the federal government manage to succeed in introducing these federal programmes when the BNA Act gave primary responsibility for health care to the provinces? This is a particularly germane question, given that in the late 1930s, another Royal Commission had been appointed to examine the matter of federal–provincial responsibility (Lindenfield, 1959). The commission's findings reaffirmed the provincial authority for health care as established in the BNA Act. The breakdown of the Postwar Reconstruction Conference reinforced the federal government's powerlessness to establish national programmes. Yet the federal government was able to overcome these obstacles to develop national programmes. How?

First, they compromised some of the blueprint for federal programmes by developing a single payer (the public) system utilising tax base to pay (health insurance) for health services that would be supplied by autonomous or semiautonomous "private" providers (e.g., physicians, hospitals) (Fuller, 1998).

Next, ingenious ways were found to influence national standards in health care, approaches which continue to be the vehicle for such federal interventions today. One way was to amend the BNA Act. This was rarely used and only once for social security reasons—to introduce old age pensions. The provinces welcomed this without controversy. Another way was to give the provinces specific grants: nothing could stop one government *giving* to another. The cost of taking the grant was that "rules" prescribed the way in which each specific grant (e.g., a grant for venereal disease control, for tuberculosis control, for hospital construction) had to be used. In fact, the federal government offered numerous grants to the provinces, with a particular emphasis on public health, thereby establishing priorities and setting standards. These conditional grants offered in 1946–47 formed the basis of public health departments and programmes within the provinces for many years (Defries, 1962), thereby fulfilling the objectives of the federal government without breaching constitutional mandates.

A third way to influence national standards in health care was to establish cost-shared programmes, whereby the federal government would give any province roughly 50% of the cost of a programme if that province paid the other 50% and agreed to a set of principles. The principles of medicare were, for example, that the programmes be universally available, comprehensive in coverage of services, portable across the provinces, and operated on a nonprofit basis. This particular strategy for developing national programmes was used for the introduction of hospital insurance and diagnostic services in the late 1950s and again for the introduction of medicare in the late 1960s. It frequently took several years before all provinces bought into either programme, but most could not afford to forego the 50% funding offered. Both programmes were difficult for the Quebec government to accept, with the consequence that citizens of Quebec were late beneficiaries of these programmes. In Quebec, the longstanding tradition of Catholic charity (Cassidy, 1947), ties to the "Old World," a commitment to maintaining an identity, and a lag in industrial development (Lindenfield, 1959) were some of the barriers that precluded easy adoption of these and other federal programmes.

Once these major federal-provincial programmes were in place, both federal and provincial governments conducted extensive studies to determine the effectiveness of the established system. A theme of many of these studies was that costs were rising and out of control. Yet, consumers and politicians alike begged the question, how much is too much? In every country, there was tension in the allocation of resources regarding the share of resources that should go to the health care system versus the rest of society because all countries were facing rising health care cost (Evans, 1984).

One federal study in the late 1970s was the second Hall Commission which examined the existing system to determine its effectiveness (Hall, 1980). The Canadian Nurses Association (CNA) was quick to respond to the request for input to this Commission. Their submission to the Health Services Review of '79 was entitled, "Putting Health Back into Health Care" (CNA, 1980). This document is noteworthy because it represents positions nurses have continued to take up with the federal government. The recommendations of CNA included the following:

- That the existing legislation underlying the hospital and medical insurance programmes be revised to allow the emergence of a health insurance programme which would stimulate the development of primary health services, permit the introduction of new entry points, and promote the appropriate utilisation of qualified health personnel

- That provincial legislation be revised to enable qualified nurses and other prepared health personnel to undertake activities currently defined as medical acts
- That remuneration of all health personnel be by salary
- That Health Services Review '79 strongly support the initiation of better preventive, diagnostic, and ambulatory care programmes through various community-based points of entry
- That the federal and provincial governments, together with relevant nongovernmental organisations, develop criteria to ensure that the underlying principles of the Canadian health insurance system are being upheld
- That a health sciences research council be established to focus on the study of health services, the system of delivery, and its effectiveness
- That the federal government be requested to reinstitute a national health survey which would provide the necessary information on which to build and evaluate a health care system to meet the needs of the people
- That all governments and health profession organisations be urged by Health Services Review '79 to adopt, as a priority, better and broader health education programmes to sensitise consumers to the cost of acute care services

Not surprisingly, the second Hall report, "A Commitment for Renewal: Health Services Review '79," was strongly supportive of the health programmes implemented, and it was open to recommendations, such as those offered by CNA. This overall support of the health care system strengthened the federal government's conviction about the need to maintain these programmes. Yet even with that conviction, both the federal government and the provinces have been reluctant to tackle longstanding traditions in health care, such as moving physicians towards salary or capitation payment and away from fee-for-service payment, and implementing the types of recommendations for primary health care put forward by Canadian nurses. Such care includes care provided in an accessible health care system focussed on health promotion and illness prevention with public participation, appropriate use of technology, and intersectoral cooperation (CNA, 2000a).

Enter Health Minister Monique Begin

The various government reports published between the mid-1960s and mid-1970s, in particular, indicated grave concern about rising costs of medical care; indeed, costs did rise in the first few years of medicare's introduction. Payments to doctors increased because doctors were now being paid to care for patients they had previously served without pay when those patients could not afford payment. Suddenly, reimbursement was available to physicians. But those mounting costs soon settled to a reasonable level before rising again as a function of a growing medical technology and changing demographics. During this time as well, the federal and provincial governments renegotiated the cost-sharing arrangements for health care and postsecondary education. Rather than continue on the roughly 50–50 basis of cost sharing, which left the federal government with a serious problem of predicting health care expenditures, the federal government transferred taxation points to the provinces in exchange for payment of a lower cash transfer to the provinces (Van Loon, 1978). At the time, the provinces were delighted. The country's economy was good, and they stood to benefit from the additional taxation power. Yet, the political opposition to these federally sponsored programmes continued.

Alarms about rising costs, concerns about socialised medicine interfering with doctor–patient relationships, and any number of reasons were put forward for the need to increase the private operation of health services. In Alberta in particular, physicians moved to bill patients extra for the care they received based on the premise that limited medicare funds restricted their right to adequate compensation for services. This practise, known as *extra billing* or *balance billing,* set the stage for a national drama as the federal health minister, Monique Begin, took a highly public stance against the Alberta government on this issue. With the transfer of tax points to the provinces, the federal government had lost some leverage in its insistence on adherence to the national standards for medicare. The outcome of this drama was the passage of a new federal act as a means to enforce the principles of medicare.

Thus, the Canada Health Act was introduced in 1984 to affirm the principles of medicare, adding to the four previous principles the principle of "access to care" (Table 3.3). The Act also replaced the Hospital Insurance and Diagnostic Services Act and the Medical Care Act, and it banned extra billing (Rice & Prince, 2000). The penalties for provinces that allowed extra billing were accomplished by withholding cash transfer

Table 3.3   Canada Health Act (1984): Principles of "Medicare"

PRINCIPLE/ CRITERION/ CONDITION	DEFINITION
Public administration	The provinces health care insurance plan must be administered and operated by a public authority accountable to the provincial government. Provincial governments determine the amount spent.
Comprehensiveness	The plan must insure all medically necessary services, i.e., services "for purposes of maintaining health, preventing disease, or diagnosing or treating an illness or injury, or disability" must be covered.
Accessibility	The plan must provide for all Canadians to have reasonable access to insured hospital and physician services without barriers. Additional charges to insured patients for insured services are not allowed. No one can be discriminated against on the basis of income, age, health status, etc.
Universality	The plan must entitle 100% of the insured population (i.e., eligible residents) to insured health services on uniform terms and conditions. This also means that Canadians do not have to pay an insurance premium in order to be covered through provincial health insurance programs.
Portability	The plan must ensure that Canadians are covered by their provincial plan when they move from province to province, or when they travel within Canada or abroad. There may be some limits on coverage for services provided outside Canada, and prior approval for nonemergency out-of-province services may be required.

From Health Canada (2002). *Canada's health care system.* Health Canada web site and Canadian Nurses Association (2000b) fact sheet on "The Canada Health Act," also on the CNA web site, with permission.

payments, dollar for dollar, to those provinces. The residual effect of this action on the provinces has been strained relationships with the federal government and continual accusations of reduced funding. Although this reduced funding is a reality, what is seldom acknowledged by the provinces is the provincial benefit of the tax point transfer agreed to in 1977. This tax money too, now collected by the provinces, was intended to be used for health services. Where these funds are now being directed is not always clear to the public.

The Klein and Harris Governments (Alberta and Ontario)

By the late 1980s, the economic downturn began to threaten seriously Canada's federal-provincial health care programmes. The political climate of the Western world was strongly influenced by the dominant neoconservative ideology of political leaders in England, the United States, and Canada (Prime Minister Brian Mulroney). The development of large corporations, a concentration of wealth, and free trade were outcomes of this ideology, which included adopting a business model for health care delivery, identifying people as deserving and undeserving, and growing attempts of governments to withdraw from involvement in comprehensive public programmes and to promote private sector providers. In Alberta, Premier Ralph Klein took the lead in downsizing health care through sudden and severe budgetary cutbacks. For those who were involved in Premier Klein's health care round tables, it was not difficult to see parallels between a book published in New Zealand called *Unfinished Business* and the tactics employed by the Premier. Although participants in his round tables urged Mr. Klein to implement changes over a period of several years to preserve the best of the systems in place, he was determined to act quickly. His use of the phrase that he "would not blink" seemed a sure sign that *Unfinished Business* had become his bible for health care reform. The strategy for health care reform promoted in New Zealand included 10 "principles" that seemed in effect in Alberta and later in Ontario when Premier Mike Harris followed Alberta's lead. These included recommendations to implement reform in quantum leaps; to regard speed as essential because it is almost impossible to go too fast; to ensure that momentum once started does not stop rolling; to strive for consistency and credibility to create confidence; and to remember "not to blink" because public confidence rests on your composure (Douglas, 1993).

Thus began massive layoffs of hospital workers—particularly nurses. Although layoffs were occurring in other Canadian provinces as well, Klein's confidence in the rightness of the government's actions and the support he was enjoying from prominent business leaders gave impetus to the continued and often merciless dismissals of staff nurses and senior nurse leaders. Included in these cutbacks was the removal of one or two levels of nurse managers from the system. The effects of these actions are most evident today in the serious nursing shortages, the low morale in nursing, and the absence of clinical nurse leaders to mentor and support nurses entering practise and those changing practise settings (Shamian & LeClair, 2000; Broughton, 2001).

Part of the downsizing strategy included a push toward health care reform that promoted health care as just another "business" and promoted the regionalisation of health services. Regionalisation involved the rationalisation of services with some potential for good outcomes. However, when this approach was put in place too rapidly, limited attention was given to preserving the good elements of the system. The result has been that, in many areas, regionalisation has been more destructive than constructive. Further, there has rarely been good evidence to explain how the effect of hospital closures would improve services (or even save money). In regionalisation, the downsizing of the provincial health departments was also a consequence because centralised policies and services are no longer needed. The loss of intellectual ability, experience, and wisdom in public sector management and in health care policy development cannot be measured.

Although there is no question that some of these changes may have led to improved services, the cost to the morale of the health professionals, most of whom were excluded from decision making, has been monumental (Shamian & LeClair, 2000). And although considerable restructuring has occurred, actual health reform is not readily apparent.

Many regions also implemented programme management, an approach adopted from the business world that is built on product-line management strategies. The goal in programme management is the integration of care through "seamless systems" that would be devoted to one similar focus of care, such as heart health, to include the spectrum from prevention to tertiary care (Leatt et al., 1994). Further, adopting this business way of thinking overlooks the unique aspects of health care, including the fact that patients, for example, do not fit into neat categories like product lines, such as shoes or cars. This might be described as the "false simplification of human life" (Saul, 1995). Although there is a cry for evidence-based practise, a worthwhile goal in many respects, the evidence to support removing many systems that were put in place to promote high-quality care is lacking.

In the midst of this conundrum, some parts of the health policy framework suggested by J. W. McIntosh (1914), Laframboise (1973), and Marc Lalonde (1974) and by the CNA's response to the second Hall Commission Report (1979) began to resurface. In September 1994, the Meeting of Health Ministers received a report entitled *Strategies for Population Health: Reinvesting in the Health of Canadians*. This report called for governments to address the entire range of factors that determine health rather than focus on risks and clinical factors related to particular diseases. The report also urged a focus on collective health rather than on individual health only. The framework for action included attention to the social and economic environment, the physical environment, personal health practises, individual capacity and coping skills, and health services. Embedded in all of these strategies was healthy child development. As with the Lalonde report released in 1974, there was considerable discussion about the sensibility of such an approach with limited action taken. This was followed by a rapidly decreasing level of interest by provincial governments, who likely could see only an expanded mandate in health care when their key desire was for a reduced mandate.

In 1994, the federal government established a National Forum on Health Care to make recommendations about the "crisis in health care." This eight-member committee studied various aspects of health care and came out in strong support of the merits of current Canadian health programmes, adding to them the need to enhance home care services as well as improve coverage of pharmaceutical costs. Most of the Forum's recommendations have yet to be implemented as other political agendas shift the emphasis in health care reform. Many Canadians doubt that the promise of regionalisation has been fulfilled. Many see it instead as a way for provincial governments to shed their responsibility to regional boards, who lack the funding to effect needed changes in service offerings but who will take the blame for service deficiencies.

In 1999, the federal and provincial governments signed an agreement called the Social Union Agreement. Its purpose was to define the principles "for the design and development of social policies and programs" (CNA, 2000b). The principles include citizen engagement and accountability, and the Agreement reconfirmed the conditions (principles) of the Canada Health Act of 1984.

Yet, regional variations in availability and calibre of services remain problematic within each province. Further, data released by the Canadian Institutes for Health Information indicate mounting evidence of wide gaps in health care benefits across the provinces. In May 2001, for example, the press reported on a survey suggesting that the likelihood of surviving a heart attack varied from 9% mortality during a hospital stay in Alberta to 18% in Newfoundland. A further infraction to the principle of portability in the Canada Health Act is apparent in the way each province covers services. For example, the experience of those attempting to coordinate benefit programmes for employees of nationally based voluntary organisations leads one to conclude that variations in health services covered in each province are increasingly detrimental to a comprehensive national health insurance programme which has portability as one of its principles.

Enter Shirley Douglas, Actress and Advocate

In the fall of 2000, Alberta's Premier Klein chose to use his political power to assert provincial responsibility for health care. He made clear his plan to make legal provision in Alberta for the increasing involvement of private for-profit health services delivery. This he did by developing Bill 11, a bill that made provision for using public health care funds to subsidise private for-profit acute care hospitals, private imaging clinics, and other private for-profit services (Alberta Association of Registered Nurses [AARN], 2000).

The AARN was among the groups most active in opposition to this bill. In other provinces, as well, there were protests about Alberta's Bill 11 by those who regarded the bill as destructive to Canada's health programmes. In British Columbia, many nurses joined the march to protest Alberta's Bill 11. These protest marches were led by Shirley Douglas, actress, advocate for medicare, and daughter of the late Tommy Douglas.

RECURRING POLITICAL AND ECONOMIC THEMES IN HEALTH CARE: IMPACT ON NURSING

For more than two decades, Evans (1984) and his colleagues in health economics provided sound evidence to show the effect of rising costs when public and private for-profit systems coexist. They found that duplicate administrative costs and for-profit practises increase cost without an accompanying increase in quality health care. They also found that socially and economically disadvantaged patients' access to health care is affected by for-profit health services delivery. Further, they highlighted the lack of evidence to support the claim that introducing competition into health care with private for-profit systems will provide better and less expensive care.

John Ralston Saul (1995) spoke about the corporatist society, urging that people be alert and react to false consciousness, stating " . . . we live in a corporatist society with soft pretensions to democracy. More power is slipping every day over to groups [sic, corporations]. That is the meaning of the marketplace ideology and of our passive acceptance of whatever form globalization happens to take" (pp. 34–35). Andre Picard (1999) added a note of caution to this matter in stating that free trade may be boosting corporate profits, but it is systematically undermining public health measures and leading to poorer health for Canadians.

Canada does, in fact, have a mix of public and private for-profit care, but the private for-profit element is normally linked to certain sectors of care. Roughly 70% of total health expenditures in Canada are paid by public sector funding, with 30%

financed privately through supplementary insurance, employer-sponsored benefits, or direct out-of-pocket expenditures (Health Canada, 2002). For example, dental and orthodontic care falls outside the publicly funded health services in most provinces. There are also numerous private for-profit nursing homes because these fall outside the acute care and medically oriented emphasis of Canada's health programmes; and complementary medicine is not normally covered.

What is different about initiatives in Alberta, Ontario, and some other provinces is that private for-profit care, subsidised by government, would be offered as a service competing with the publicly funded service. What does this do to integration and coordination of care? Will this eventually lead to patients with better finances routinely jumping waiting lists to pay for their surgeries and other services, thereby creating even longer waiting times for those unable to purchase a place at the top of the queue? Might it lead to a competition for health professionals if a for-profit service offers significantly better salaries and benefits to doctors and nurses, thereby creating a two-class system of care?

In June 2001, the Organization for Economic Cooperation and Development reported that 29.4% of Canada's health care spending is in the private sector, which is twice the rate of the United Kingdom and Sweden, and that Canada's health care ranking has dropped (National Post, 2001). This 29.4% estimate stands in sharp contrast to Evans' estimate of 15% as the for-profit share of health care expenditures in the early 1980s (1984, p. 209).

To address these types of external pressures on Canada's health care programmes, several additional government reports were commissioned. In Saskatchewan, the province that gave birth to medicare, Premier Roy Romanow commissioned Ken Fyke to conduct a study. The title of the Fyke report (2001), "Caring for medicare: Sustaining a Quality System," made clear a continued support for the health insurance programs in Canada. Before the Fyke report had been delivered, Roy Romanow stepped down as Premier and was commissioned by the federal government to conduct a study of Canadian health care. Romanow faced increasing pressure from businesses and some provincial governments to open the door to private for-profit health insurance and health delivery.

PAST AND CURRENT IMPLICATIONS

In reflecting on the way health services unfolded in Canada, it can be helpful to think about all the "what-ifs." How would the current situation be different if different choices had been made?

The What-ifs of Health Care

What if we had paid more attention to socioeconomic and environmental influences on health in the early 1900s? What if that emphasis had continued to be strong throughout the decades? What if nurses had been able to continue to take a greater role in public health services and in institutional care, similar to their more independent role between the 1920s and the 1940s? What if medical care insurance had been introduced before the building of hospitals and before the passage of the Hospital Insurance and Diagnostic Services Act? What if Klein in Alberta, and Harris in Ontario, had proceeded more slowly with their health reforms and had involved health professionals in thinking through how to move towards goals of integration and coordination of care? What if CNA's (1980) recommendations to the second Hall Commission had been implemented when they were offered? Why, despite some visionary thinkers and planners dating as far back as the early 1900s, power dynamics within the health care system seem so little changed?

Our Heritage in Health Care

Despite all its flaws, Canada's system of health care is well worth saving. While respecting its limitation, one can make a few general statements about the system's virtues. People in Canada do not have to be as fearful about their access to care nor about the devastating costs of an illness or surgery as do many of our neighbors in the United States. And Canadian patients have considerably more choice in the selection of their doctor—and even their hospital—than many of their neighbors to the south. Many managed care plans in the United States, for example, offer extremely limited choices to the consumer of the plan, with considerable choice reserved for the managers of the plan whose goal it is to purchase the most cost-efficient services for their patient group.

Physicians in Canada have freedom to choose their practise location without restriction, and they can set their work pace and manage their scheduling. Canadian national programmes have also allowed for an enviable collection of data about hospital stays, patients conditions, and physician services. And the programmes still have the support of the majority of the public.

The serious pressures on the system in the 21st century need to be carefully considered both in relation to our historical legacy and in relation to the wider context of international capital in which our health care system and other countries' health care systems are embedded (Coburn & Rappolt, 1999). Problems arising from this legacy are our failure to develop a comprehensive system of care and our failure to recreate, reenergise, and renew our systems based on known evidence. These problems also represent our failure to change traditional practises, to move to primary health care, and to utilise all health professionals well. All of these problems might well be included in what Coburn (1999) describes as the "logic of medicare."

So what has our history (our heritage) told us about our current situation in health care and the need and potential for change?

1. We continue to operate under the terms of the BNA Act provisions (now incorporated into the Constitution Act) for determining federal and provincial responsibilities in health care. This means that we operate with the same division of federal and provincial responsibilities in health care as seemed timely in 1867. Such a division of responsibility leaves room for provinces to assert their authority when it suits their particular situation, and it forces the federal government to work through three main alternate approaches to influence health care. More importantly, it leaves room for each level of government to blame the other for failure to take action (e.g., in areas such as pollution or home care) and to leave the public waiting (and often lobbying) for the impasse to be overcome.
2. We continue to talk about social determinants of health but have yet to deal with those determinants in a comprehensive and committed way. Governments and the public are both responsible for the lack of attention to these matters, yet conditions like full employment, a guaranteed annual income, stamping out poverty, and other such fundamental health-related conditions could have a significant effect on improving the health status of all and decreasing expenditures on tertiary health care.

3. Medicare continues to enjoy a high level of public support, although that level is slipping as corporate claims of better, more efficient care by for-profit medicine woo the public to their way of thinking. This is often accomplished by "scare tactics" which distort the "facts" about current and projected public health care spending. As a prominent U.S. medical ethicist stated some years ago, "Today's exigencies are created less by scarcity of resources than by a disinclination to share them" (Pellegrino, 1975).

4. As our history shows, in implementing federal and provincial programmes, we have continued to compromise on what should be included and how the systems should operate. In the mid-1940s, we did not adopt a comprehensive approach to health and social security as had been suggested by Marsh and Heagerty. Instead, we chose to implement publicly appealing programmes selectively (Armstrong et al., 2000). This had the effect of setting us up for rising costs because many of these programmes were oriented towards high-technology medicine (e.g., the hospital insurance and diagnostic services programme) and took the focus away from holistic patient care. Further, these programmes excluded funding for many programmes, such as nursing homes, home care, and pharmaceutical coverage, many of which differentially disadvantaged elderly and poor people. Later during the introduction of medicare, Saskatchewan first and the federal government second abandoned the concept of all-on-a-salary and gave in to doctors' demands for fee-for-service payments instead. This also paved the way for cost increases for health care and closed the door to a more level playing field in power relationships among physicians, nurses, and other health professionals. This has had a serious effect on women and on nursing.

5. The majority of nurses work in hospitals or other institutions where their autonomy is more limited than that of their counterparts working in the community. Relationships between physicians and nurses are not ideal. This does not create the best environment for high-quality care.

6. The promise of health reform has *yet to be* realised; in fact, reforms such as regionalisation may have added to the shortfall in comprehensive care as different regions make different decisions about what services they are prepared to offer.

7. Canada has failed to manage the growth of medical technology in a rational way. We have been unable to set limits to professional desires and public expectations.

8. The CNA's recommendations to the second Hall Commission continue to be as necessary today as they were in 1980; the need to develop primary health care services, to make legislative provision for new entry points to the system, and to promote better use of qualified health personnel have yet to implemented. Health promotion and disease prevention are key recommendations critical to current population needs.

WHAT CONSTRAINS FUNDAMENTAL CHANGES IN THE HEALTH CARE SYSTEM?

Many health care policy experts agree that fundamental health care system problems have either not been addressed or have been dealt with marginally, often by throwing money at them. Leatt and colleagues (2000) noted that "in comparison to other countries, Canada has a relatively static healthcare system. Many providers are organized and paid in the same ways as when medicare was implemented in the 1960s" (p. 32).

Many policymakers past and present continue to identify concerns and offer worthwhile suggestions, but they may still constrain their perception of what could be by thinking "within the box" of health care. There is a pressing need to think "outside the box."

To think outside the box, for example, would be to question whose interests are being served in keeping the system relatively unchanged since the 1960s. To ask what effect free trade and increased moves to globalisation have had on maintaining a system characterised by medical dominance, an emphasis on technology without limits, unequal access to care, and marginalisation of many health professionals and many patient groups. It is also to ask what effect ideologies of individualism and egalitarianism have had on our inability to see the socioeconomic barriers that prevent patients from taking personal responsibility for their health (Anderson & Reimer-Kirkham, 1998).

Joan Anderson, a nursing professor at the University of British Columbia (UBC), and her colleagues from various academic disciplines have engaged in thinking outside the box. They suggest that the rhetoric that emerges from assumptions of individuals' equal opportunity to maintain good health, for example, are embedded in some of the finest government policies about health promotion. This rhetoric blinds us to the actual barriers to health care (e.g., clinic hours from 9 to 5, uncomfortable waiting rooms, inadequate financial assistance for healthful diets). They stress the importance of understanding and acknowledging assumptions in our health institutions today so that we can move towards fundamental changes in the health care system. Recognising the context of our "medical-industrial system," they believe, would allow us to see that the capitalist world system drives the economic realities of health care (Anderson & Reimer-Kirkham, 1998).

This thinking is like that of John Ralston Saul (1995) and others who urge us to not be complacent and accepting of the way things are. Saul suggests that readily agreeing that health care costs are out of control and unaffordable is a false consciousness. As noted previously, there is no question about the need to work towards greater coordination and efficiencies in health care, as in any line of work. But at the end of the day, the question remains: Where else is the money going? What other corporate demands are driving health care? Who is profiting by maintaining the status quo in health care?

Within health care, recent media attention has, once again, been directed at the extremely high and rising costs the pharmaceutical companies are imposing on the health care dollar and the government dollars the Canadian government is investing in these private firms. The promised return on this investment has been job creation in Canada. Yet, according to media sources (Robinson, 2001), there is minuscule job creation as a result, and generic drug companies are limited in their ability to reduce the cost of drugs by recent federal legislation.

WHAT WILL DRIVE THE HEALTH CARE SYSTEM IN THE 21ST CENTURY?

Several analysts (Coburn & Rappolt, 1999; Armstrong et al., 2000) provide insights for understanding the context of health care today and prospects for tomorrow. They suggest that the gradual rise in medical dominance over the past decades in Canada and the implementation of medicare by the governments in Canada were the last keys in the welfare state. In their analysis, they see this as representing the triumph for labour and for the state (the government). However, they suggest that the gradual decline of medical dominance in health care and a decline in government involvement in health care has occurred as a result of a " . . . major transformation of national and international political economies towards the internationalization of capital" (p. 142). This has led to an increase in business power and a decrease in the relative autonomy of the state.

Coburn and Rappolt (1999) suggest that the " . . . welfare state, and particularly anything to do with labour market policy, is brought under fierce attack from a newly united right and its international and national agents in the business community, in neoliberal international institutions such as the International Monetary Fund, in national neoconservative policy institutions and think tanks, as well as the conservatively skewed media" (p. 152). Labelling this relatively recent phenomena as the "internationalization of capital" or "global capitalism," Coburn notes how the International Monetary Fund, the World Bank, and the new ideological unity between large and small business have had substantial influence on domestic business interests. This has enhanced the power of business with Canadian governments (both federal and provincial) and has particularly strengthened the hand of American influences on governments. Thus, free trade agreements are viewed as inevitable costs of keeping Canada competitive, even though they have the potential to undermine Canadian social programmes.

The potential scenario here is that governments' gradual undermining of social programmes causes the public to see these programmes as inadequate or outdated for 21st-century needs. One has only to cut costs to particular services for so long before the public comes to believe that there must be no more money and, therefore, there is "no choice" except to welcome private for-profit health care services. The effect has been one of transformation with new " . . . structures of class, state, welfare state, health care, health profession interaction [taking] one form under the particular dynamics of monopoly capitalism and [assuming] a new form under the somewhat different structure of global capitalism" (Coburn & Rappolt, 1999, p. 160). The overall impact has been designed " . . . to produce powerlessness . . . making citizens powerless within their own countries" (p. 160).

Yet, when Coburn and Rappolt (1999) examine how global globalisation really is, they point out that within the three major trading blocs in the world, the greatest influence on Canada is from the United States. The effect in health care is that we are harmonising downward toward this partner (Coburn & Rappolt, p. 161). (This strong U.S. influence has become even more apparent since the September 11, 2001, terrorist attacks on the World Trade Center in New York, as many cherished Canadian policies in areas outside of health care, such as border guards carrying firearms in Canada, changed because of U.S. demands.) By altering the balance of power in Canada, the Free Trade Agreement (the agreement between the United States and Canada for free trade) and NAFTA (the North American Free Trade Agreement that includes Mexico) have far-ranging consequences for Canada's social fabric and its social policies (p. 161). But even Coburn argues that there are " . . . degrees of freedom and openings for resistance to neoliberal doctrines" (p. 160). To suggest that there is no choice left and that we cannot expect our social programmes to continue is to adopt a fatalistic view that flies in the face of the power of individual and collective action to make a difference.

NURSES LEADING TO INFLUENCE CHANGE

If nurses are to be effective leaders in influencing change, both individually and through collective action, some homework is needed. They need to understand the history and structures of the health care system in Canada, to educate themselves to the needs of their patients, and to set goals and work together to achieve those goals.

What Nurses Need to Know

Individually, there is a need for nurses to know about the history of Canadian health care, at least to be aware of basic programmes and structures that have been put in place over time. This includes some understanding of the historical ideologic debates and how those same debates continue to play out in health care today. This knowledge and understanding should not only give nurses confidence in stating their case but also ensure that they are not susceptible to being silenced by other's rhetoric. Additionally, nurses must be clear about some of the international and national pressures on the health care system and be ready to push against the perceived inevitability of a business orientation that diminishes the effectiveness of health care delivery.

Second, nurses need to keep abreast of good information. This includes keeping up to date with public debates in the media and elsewhere, and also digging deeper to uncover reliable facts and other viewpoints. Professional nursing associations, educational institutions, public libraries, and the Internet can be helpful resources for nurses.

Other knowledge and information needed by nurses include keeping abreast of the influence of trade agreements on health care and professional practise as well as on basic needs for the public's health, such as an adequate supply of clean water, clean air, security, and other essentials of life. Nurses also need to know about their professional associations, including the freedom and responsibilities of self-regulation and the importance of collective action.

What Nurses Need to Be

Above all, nurses need to be well educated, good listeners and sensitive caregivers. Nurses need to see and respond to the many people who are marginalised in society—aboriginal peoples, immigrants, different ethnic groupings, women and particularly single mothers and their children living in poverty, poor elderly people, and so forth. We also need to see and critically think about the dominant players in health care and seek to understand their views as well as directing attention towards ways to broaden and influence their thinking. Despite the difficulties nursing faces today in regards to being valued, we need to keep on caring without regard for race, color, creed, religious persuasion, or political alignments. In short, we need to continue to be role models of caring practises.

What Nurses Need to Do

Collectively, nurses need to be willing to work together to reach good outcomes for their patients and for themselves. Canada has fine examples of nurses involved in collective action to make a difference. The push towards Direct Access to Care in Alberta, led by the AARN in the early 1990s, is one example of such collective action to influence the types of issues nurses continue to strive for (AARN, 1993). Similar activities are part of other provincial nursing association agendas, including specific foci during provincial and federal elections, as for example, the Registered Nurses Association of Ontario (RNAO, 1999), and in the activities of individual nurses (e.g., Wilson, 1996).

Nurses also need to use the knowledge gained through nursing education and nurse–patient relationships to focus attention on the determinants of health. Frank and Mustard (1994), and many before them, demonstrated the relationships between illness and socioeconomic factors. In addition to noting how the job hierarchy influences health, these authors suggested that " . . . an individual's sense of achievement, self-esteem, and control over his or her work and life appears to affect health and well-being" (p. 9). As nurses come to know their patients, they see the effects of these variables on patient well-being and on their own health. That is important knowledge to be utilised in dialogue with politicians or bureaucrats.

Working collectively towards the goal of primary health care for all is also critical work for nurses today (Rodger, 1993). The evidence is in! Nurses in advanced nursing practise make a difference to patient care and can improve the health system overall. Unfortunately, attempts to implement advanced nursing practise are often thwarted by physician, government, or business interests, who see a loss of power for their own interests if they collaborate with nurses in practise or support nurses' independence to practise. Such is the case of the nurse practitioner movement in Ontario, wherein family health networks failed to use the full range of services nurse practitioners could offer (Mackie, 2001). However, the persistence of nurses in moving towards these patient-centred goals continues to make a difference within specific areas which have a spillover effect over time.

Individually, nurses can also be ready to speak, to question, and to spread hope (Broughton, 2001). As nurses, we may not have all the answers, but we do know most of the questions. With regard to information about the political economy discussed earlier in this text, an individual nurse may not have complete knowledge but can ask politicians, government bureaucrats, as well as other civil servants, neighbors, friends, and colleagues questions to make them think and potentially to influence their actions however large or small they may be. This is to move against a place of powerlessness.

The history and current status of Canadian health care makes it clear that many of the important ideas and services in health care came about through struggle and persistence. A commitment to change is a commitment to engage in a political struggle which accompanies the change (Anderson & Reimer-Kirkham, 1998).

SUMMARY

Nurses need to clarify what drives today's health care system, particularly in regard to the underpinnings of medicare, the international economic manipulation of resources available for health care, and related disempowerment of health care professionals.

The same value conflicts that we see today were inherent in the development of Canadian policies and programmes since their inception. These include the tension between a focus on individual responsibility and self-reliance versus collective responsibility, the tension between a free market system versus more socially oriented collective policies and programmes in health care (the privatisation debate), the tension between an emphasis on scientific discovery and technologic imperatives versus humanism and care for the disadvantaged, and the tensions between those who believe that all have equal opportunities to health care versus the reality that gender, race, and class differences affect the way in which health care is delivered.

These are some of the influences that keep Canada's health care system focussed on primary care as opposed to primary health care: *Primary care* is a medical concept referring to a situation wherein the physician provides diagnosis, treatment, and follow-up for a specific disease or problem" (CNA, 2000a). *Primary health* care, as adopted by the World Health Organization in 1978 as the basis for the delivery of health services, most effectively involves both "a philosophy and an approach" to the way health services are delivered. It includes health promotion, disease prevention, curative services, rehabilitative care, and supportive or palliative care (CNA, 2000a). Primary health care involves a shift from traditional practises and power dynamics in health care to a system in which all health professionals are utilised to their maximum potential to effect good patient outcomes in care. Nurse practitioners, advanced practise nurses, and staff nurses alike are able to practise to their full scope of practise in this model.

This is the model of care Canadian nurses have sought for almost three decades, and it continues to be a model worth pursing. In fact, it is one of the CNA's two key goals in the new millennium, the other goal being improved quality of work environments for nurses.

Nurses can influence change by attending to the history, current status, and future projections for health care; by being listening and caring caregivers; and by taking action individually and collectively to influence greater attention to social determinants of health and better health care provision for their patients.

As nurses, we need to be clear about our own values and opinions and able to stand by them. If we are not prepared to do so, nursing and nurses will have little to say in the health care system of tomorrow.

ACKNOWLEDGEMENTS

The helpful contributions of Bernadette Pauly and an anonymous reviewer, for their assistance in bringing greater clarity to several sections of this chapter, are acknowledged with gratitude.

Online RESOURCES

Add to your knowledge of this issue:

Canadian Nurses Association	www.cna-nurses.ca
Health Canada	wwwnfh.hc.sc.gc/publicat/public/canada.htm

Reflections on the Chapter

1. In what ways do you think the Canadian Health Care System would have been different and less subject to political influence if the Fathers of Confederation had chosen to assign principle responsibility for health care and education to the federal government rather than to the provinces?

2. If medical care insurance had been introduced before the introduction of hospital insurance, what differences might we see in the formation of health facilities? What contributions do you think this might have made in controlling the costs of technology? Would primary health care likely have become the norm?

3. Do you believe that health care costs are out of control? Why or why not?

4. In reflecting on what you know about nurses' individual or collective actions to influence better health care, what types of knowledge have they utilised to influence change?

5. To what degree have you felt powerless or powerful against business interests in health care? Why have you felt that way?

REFERENCES

AARN (Alberta Association of Nurses). (2000). AARN action on Bill 11. The health care protection act (HCPA). *Alberta RN, 56*(5), 6.

AARN (Alberta Association of Registered Nurses). (1993). Direct access to services provided by registered nurses: A nursing perspective. *AARN Newsletter, 49*(1), 15–17.

Anderson, J., & Reimer-Kirkham, S. (1998). Constructing nation: The gendering and racializing of the Canadian health care system. In V. Strong-Boag, S. Grace, A. Eisenberg, & J. Anderson (Eds.), *Painting the maple: Essays on race, gender, and the construction of Canada* (pp. 242–261). Vancouver: UBC Press.

Armstrong, P., Armstrong, H., Bourgeault, I., Choiniere, J., Mykhalovskiy, E., & White, J.P. (2000). *"Heal thyself": Managing health care reform.* Aurora, Ontario: Garamond Press.

Bliss, M. (1975). A preface. In L. Marsh, *Report on social security for Canada.* Toronto: University of Toronto Press.

Broughton, H. (2001). *Nursing leadership: Unleashing the power.* Ottawa: Canadian Nurses Association.

Callahan, D. (1990). *What kind of life: The limits to medical progress.* New York: Simon & Schuster.

Canadian Nurses Association (2000a). *The primary health care approach.* Fact sheet. Ottawa: Author.

Canadian Nurses Association (2000b). *The Canada Health Act.* Ottawa: Author.

Canadian Nurses Association (1980). *Putting "health" back into health care:* Submission to the Health Services Review '79. Ottawa: Author.

Cassidy, H. M. (1947). The Canadian social services. *The Annals of the Academy of Political and Social Sciences, 253* (September), 190–201.

Cassidy, H. M. (1945). *Public health and welfare organi-* zation: The post-war problem in the Canadian provinces. Toronto: Ryerson Press.

Coburn, D., & Rappolt, S. (1999). The `logic of medicare': Variants of capitalism and medical dominance. Contextualizing profession-state relationships. In D. Coburn, S. Rappolt, I. Bourgeault, & J. Angus (Eds.), *Medicine, nursing and the state* (pp. 139–167). Aurora, Ont.: Garamond Press Ltd.

Coburn, D. (1988). The development of Canadian nursing: Professionalization and proletarianization. *International Journal of Health Services, 18*(3), 437–456.

Defries, R. D. (1962). *The federal and provincial health services in Canada* (2nd ed.). Toronto: Canadian Public Health Association.

Douglas, R. (1993). *Unfinished business.* Auckland, New Zealand: Random House.

Evans, R. (1984). *Strained mercy: The economics of Canadian health care.* Toronto: Butterworths.

Frank, J. W., & Mustard, J. F. (1994). The determinants of health from a historical perspective. *Daedalus,* (Fall), 1–19.

Fuller, C. (1998). *Caring for profit: How corporations are taking over Canada's health care system.* Vancouver: New Star Books.

Fyke, K. J. (2001). *Caring for medicare: Sustaining a quality system.* Regina: Saskatchewan Health.

Gelber, S. M. (1966). The path to health insurance. *Canadian Public Administration, 9* (June), 156–165.

Hall, E. M. (1980). *Canada's national-provincial health program for the 1980s: A commitment for renewal.* Justice E. M. Hall, Special Commissioner. Ottawa: Department of National Health and Welfare.

Hastings, J. E. F., & Mosley, W. (1980). Introduction: The evolution of organized community health services in Canada. In C. A. Meilicke & J. L. Storch

(Eds.), *Perspectives on Canadian health and social services policy: History and emerging trends* (pp. 145–155). Ann Arbor, Michigan: Health Administration Press.

Health Canada (2002). *Canada's health care system.* Ottawa: web site [http://www.hc-sc.gc.ca/datapcb/iad/hcsystem-e.htm].

Kinnear, J. L. (1994). The professionalization of Canadian nursing, 1924–1932: Views in the CN and the CMAJ. *CBMH/BCHM, 11,* 153–174.

Laframboise, H. L. (1973). Health policy: Breaking the problem down into more manageable segments. *Canadian Medical Association Journal,* 108 (February), 388–393.

Lalonde, M. (1974). *A new perspective on the health of Canadians.* Ottawa: Information Canada.

Leatt, P., Pink, G. H., & Guerriere, M. (2000). Towards a Canadian model of integrated healthcare. *Healthcare Papers, 1*(2), 13–35.

Leatt, P., Lemieux-Charles, L., & Aird, C. (1994). *Program management and beyond: Management innovations in Ontario hospitals.* Ottawa: Canadian College of Health Service Executives.

Lindenfield, R. (1959). Hospital insurance in Canada: An example in federal-provincial relations. *Social Services Review, 33,* 148–160.

Mackie, R. (2001). Project not helping ease MD shortage. *The Globe and Mail.* July 9, A7.

Margoshes, D. (1999). *Tommy Douglas: Building the new society.* Montreal: XYZ Publishing.

Marsh, L. (1975). *Report on social security for Canada 1943.* Toronto: University of Toronto.

McIntosh, J. W. (1914). Inter-relation of physician, citizen and state to public health. *The Public Health Journal, 5* (July 14), 451–455.

Meilicke, C. A., & Storch, J. L. (Eds.) (1980). *Perspectives on Canadian health and social service policy: History and emerging trends.* Ann Arbor, Michigan: Health Administration Press.

Morgan, J. S. (1980). Social welfare services in Canada. In C. A. Meilicke & J. L. Storch (Eds.), *Perspectives on Canadian health and social services policy: History and emerging trends* (pp. 83–113). Ann Arbor, Michigan: Health Administration Press.

Najman, J. M., & Western, J. S. (1984). A comparative analysis of Australian health policy in the 1970s. *Social Science and Medicine, 18*(1), 949–958.

National Forum on Health Care (1997). *Canada health action: Building the legacy.* Ottawa: Health Canada.

National Health Forum (1997). *The public and private financing of Canada's health system.* Ottawa: Author.

National Post. (2001). 29% of our health care private. June 29.

Pellegrino, E. (1975). The Catholic hospitals: Options for survival. *Hospital Progress, 56*(2), 49.

Picard, A. (1999). Free trade agreement no boon to health care, U.S. conference told. *The Globe and Mail.* November 9.

PMO's Health Fact Sheet (2001). Budget 2001 New Investments in Health Initiatives. Ottawa.

Registered Nurses Association of Ontario (RNAO) (1999). *Putting nurses back into health care: Who will respond?* Toronto: Registered Nurses Association of Ontario.

Rice, J. J., & Prince, M. J. (2000). *Changing politics of Canadian social policy.* Toronto: University of Toronto Press.

Robinson, J. (2001). Prescription for high prices. *National Post,* April 27.

Rodger, G. L. (1993). Success and nurses: Its influence on society. *AARN Newsletter, 49*(1), 17–18.

Ross Kerr, J. (1996). Nursing in Canada from 1760 to the present: The transition to modern nursing. In J. Ross Kerr & J. MacPhail (Eds.), *Canadian nursing: Issues and Perspectives* (3rd ed.) (pp. 11–22). Toronto: Mosby.

Royal Commission on Health Service (Vols. I, II). (1964, 1965). Justice E. Hall, Commission Chair. Ottawa: Queen's Printer.

Saul, J.R. (1995). *The Unconscious civilization.* Concord, Ontario: Anansis.

Shamian, J., & LeClair, S. J. (2000). Integrated delivery systems now or … ? *Healthcare Papers, 1*(2), 66–75.

Stinson, S. M. (1969). *Deprofessionalization in nursing.* Columbia University, Health Sciences, Unpublished dissertation.

Storch, J. L. (1996). Foundational values in Canadian health care. In M. Stingl & D. Wilson (Eds.), *Efficiency vs. equality: Health reform in Canada.* Halifax: Fernwood Publishing Co. Ltd.

Strategies for population health: Investing in the health of Canadians. (1994). Prepared by the Federal, Provincial and Territorial Advisory Committee on Population Health for the Meeting of the Ministers of Health, September 14–15.

Taylor, M. G. (1987). *Health insurance and Canadian public policy* (2nd ed.). Montreal: McGill Queens University Press.

Taylor, M. G. (1973). The Canadian health insurance program. *Public Administration Review, 33* (January-February), 31—39.

Torrance, G. M. (1987). Hospitals as health factories. In D. Coburn, C. D'Arcy, G. M. Torrance, & P. New (Eds.), *Health and Canadian society* (2nd ed.). Markham, Ontario: Fitzhenry & Whiteside.

Van Loon, R. J. (1978). From shared cost to block funding and beyond: The politics of health insurance in Canada. *Journal of Health Politics, Policy and Law, 2* (Winter), 454–478.

Van Loon, R. J., & Whittington, M. S. (1976). *The Canadian political system: Environment, structure and process* (2nd ed.). Toronto: McGraw-Hill Ryerson Ltd.

Wallace, E. (1950). The origins of the social welfare state in Canada, 1867–1900. *Canadian Journal of Economics and Political Science, 16,* 383–393.

Wilson, D. (1996). Where do we go from here? The 72 billion dollar question. In M. Stingl & D. Wilson (Eds.), *Efficiency vs. equality: Health reform in Canada.* Halifax: Fernwood Publishing Co. Ltd.

CHAPTER 4

Health and Nursing Policy: A Matter of Politics, Power, and Professionalism

Heather F. Clarke

Chapter Objectives

At the completion of this chapter, you will be able to:

1. Appreciate the real and potential contributions of nurses to health and nursing policy.
2. Understand types of policy.
3. Understand the policy process and the significance of contextual factors.
4. Identify roles, responsibilities, and opportunities for nurses in the policy process.
5. Identify challenges to nurses' involvement.
6. Determine strategies required for successful involvement.

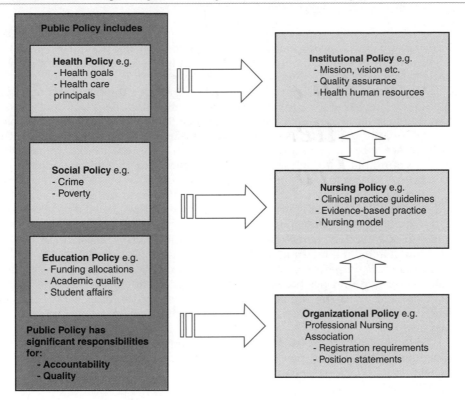

Public policy forms a basis for emerging institutional, nursing, and organisational policies.

Health and nursing policy and nurses' responsibilities and roles within the policy process are discussed in this chapter. Policy is introduced as a process and as a product as well as an instrument. Relevant contextual and infrastructure requirements for nurses' involvement in policy are also discussed and illustrated with examples of nurses' influence in health and nursing policy.

The importance of nurses understanding policy—its development, implementation, and evaluation—cannot be overemphasised. Public policy decisions directly affect the health care of everyone as well as the practise of nursing. Nurses can and should become more involved with the policy-making process to ensure that decisions benefit the public at local, provincial/territorial, and national levels. Nursing leadership in the public policy arena will give nurses the best opportunities for putting forth agendas that will accomplish health goals that are in the public's interest.

POLICY, POLITICS, POWER, AND PROFESSIONALISM

Health policy, nursing policy, and institutional policy are all significant types of public policies that call for nursing involvement. A *policy*—a broad goal statement—has been defined as "the principles that govern action directed towards given ends" (Titmus, 1974, p. 23).

Policy

Public policy is whatever governments choose to do or not to do (Dye, 1978). It is a conscious choice of action directed towards an end. It is based on a commonly held value, and it gives direction for action (e.g., rules, laws).

Health policy, one aspect of public policy, includes the directives and goals for promoting the health of the public. Health policy may include policy related to population health goals, for example, provincial health goals (see http://www.healthplanning.gov. bc.ca/pho/hlthgoals.html); health care system principles, such as the Canada Health Act (see http://laws.justice.gc.ca/en/C-6/index.html); and service priorities and accountabilities, such as B.C. Liberal New Era document, outcomes indicators (see http://www.cihi.ca/eindex.htm).

Nursing policy may be an aspect of, and influenced by, public policy (e.g., provincial and territorial nursing acts, free trade agreements) as well as a component of institutional policy (e.g., clinical practise guidelines, care maps, and critical paths). Nursing policy also includes organisational policy of the nursing association (e.g., policy and position statements, nursing practise and education standards).

Organisational policies, such as those of professional nursing associations, are the rules governing and positions taken by the organisation. Some organisational policies may be determined by public policy (e.g., registered nursing acts, scope of practise), whereas others are association specific (e.g., education standards, registration requirements).

Institutional policies, such as those of a hospital or health care agency, comprise the rules governing workplaces. Some institutional policies may be grounded in public policies (e.g., policies governing responsibility and accountability of health authorities), whereas others, such as mission, vision, and core value statements, are institution specific.

The difference between public policies, such as health policy, and institutional, nursing, and organisational policies is that government does not necessarily have the policy responsibility for the latter types. The responsibility belongs to the professional regulatory body, governance board of an agency, or managerial staff of a department. However, there is interplay and influences between these types of policies. Each type of policy is shaped by politics and power.

Distinguishing Policy From Politics

In determining how to participate in shaping any type of policy, one needs first to distinguish between political strategies and policy agendas. *Policy* deals with *shoulds* and *oughts*. *Politics* deals with *conditions* and sometimes impedes or accelerates the policy process. Politics involves using power to influence, persuade, or otherwise change—it is the art of understanding relationships between groups in society and using that understanding to achieve particular outcomes. As a phenomenon, politics is often reactive. Policy, on the other hand, is based in values, goals, or principles, even when those values may represent idiosyncratic biases (Table 4.1). Policy is more proactive, involving give-and-take in negotiation (Solomon & Roe, 1986).

Policy development is a value-laden process, beginning with what problems become policy issues and concluding with who decides how a policy will be evaluated. When values are in conflict, as they often are in the health and nursing policy arenas, politics necessarily comes in to play. When individuals and groups with disparate values enter into the policy process, politics, a major determinant of health policy, shapes the content and process of policy development (Mason et al., 1993).

Table 4.1   Policy and Politics: Some Comparisons

POLICY	POLITICS
Deals with shoulds and oughts	Focuses on conditions
Based on values, goals, and principles	Uses power to persuade and influence
Frequently proactive—negotiable	Primarily reactive—nonnegotiable
Stages of development from formation of the problem, through adoption of the policy, implementation, and evaluation	Political process is the way policy is developed—requires identification of true issues and stakeholders and their goals and interests.
Objective is to be evidence based (e.g., using research, epidemiology, databases in health information, surveys)	Foundation is philosophical—party oriented (e.g., liberal, conservative, socialist)
The chosen theoretical perspective with its values and principles determines details of the policy process	Shapes the content for the policy and the policy process

People perceive politics in different ways. For some, the term evokes images of smoke-filled rooms, devious dealings, or power in the hands of a few. For others, the images have a different and more generic meaning (Ross Kerr & MacPhail, 1996). Whatever the perception, politics can be viewed as the art of influencing another person. There is no escaping politics in any arena. Many nurses recognise the importance of developing political skills, realising that these skills are as important on the nursing unit as they are in other spheres of social activity where decisions must be made. In both the policy and political processes, skills needed include the following:

- Analytical thinking
- Visionary perspective—future and goal oriented
- Force of commitment
- Communication of goals
- Personal qualities of reliability and integrity

Power

The concept of power is not generally associated with nursing. The media, public at large, and other opinion makers refer to the power of major corporations, politicians, trade unions, medical associations, and male-dominated organisations; seldom are the nursing profession and nurses considered powerful (Ferguson, 1993). However, today's idea of empowerment replaces yesterday's notion of power (Barnum & Kerfoot, 1995), and nurses are demonstrating significant empowerment in all contexts of practise. Instead of the capacity one has to influence others to accomplish something they would not normally accomplish, empowerment is authority purposefully shared with others to increase the total amount of nurses' influence in the organisation. Nurses, like anyone else, fulfill their mission better when they are empowered to work to their full capacity. Sources of empowerment include the following:

- Expanded expertise and restructured practise that aim to use each nurse's skills and knowledge level

- Where nurses are valued as scarce resources, knowledgeable workers who cannot be spared to do lower-level tasks
- New legal powers that legitimise various nurse roles, such as nurse practitioner, and public acceptance of these roles integrated into the health care system
- New roles, such as clinical nurse specialist, that provide clinical expertise as well as contribute to system-level responsibilities, such as quality assurance, research, and evidence-based practise
- Changed self-perception—accepting one's own ideas or the ideas of one's leader over those imposed by others who would create limitations (Barnum & Kerfoot, 1995)

Why should nurses pay attention to power and empowerment? Ferguson (1985) notes that:

- Nurses must be able to get things done on behalf of the people they serve—they are advocates.
- Nurse educators and nurse administrators need to make course content in schools of nursing and activities in service settings of interest and applicable to students of nursing and other disciplines.
- Nurses' power base is expanded as nurses encourage and support nurse candidates for political office and professional organisation lobbying efforts.
- Knowledge is power. As such, it confers authority upon the possessor. Knowledge then may be nurses' greatest source of power.

Nurses find that a number of strategies and skills increase their ability to influence policy (Loveridge & Cummings, 1996; Grohar-Murray & DiCroce, 1997). These include the following:

- Enhanced skills and knowledge—being well-informed and current—are the basis for attaining credibility.
- Good working relationships with all coworkers are essential and include the use of networking and consultation.
- The ability to convince others of the appropriateness of one's views is based on providing logical arguments and proposing positive solutions.
- Being visible and in a position to speak with groups and individuals is the basis for influencing those groups and individuals.

Professionalism

The *raison d'etre* of any profession is the contribution it makes to society. The nursing profession contributes to the delivery of care and health status of the population. The ultimate reason for enhancing nurses' political influence and empowerment, be it in the workplace, community, government, or professional organisation, is to improve the health care received by patients—individuals, families, groups, communities, and populations who require nursing expertise (Mason & McCarthy, 1985). Nurses and their knowledge are pivotal to advocating for and ensuring that health and nursing policies promote quality patient care through professional nursing practise in clinical, administrative, educational, and research domains—wherever nurses practise. Policy, politics, and power (empowerment) are essential components of professional nursing practise, just as the professional practise of nursing must inform public policy. Therefore, we need to clarify the roles and responsibilities of nurses in policy development, implementation, and evaluation.

HISTORY AND BACKGROUND: PERSPECTIVES ON POLICY

Historically, nurses have influenced, and indeed initiated, public policy related to health and nursing. However, until recently, the study of health and nursing policy has not been part of formal nursing education. The science of policy as a domain of nursing practise has received little attention in nursing literature. There is minimal research related to nurses' involvement, the roles and responsibilities for nurses' participation, and competencies required for various contexts of policy making. Thus, this chapter highlights anecdotal accounts of some significant nurse involvement in policy and theoretical underpinnings from a public policy perspective.

Historical Perspective

Nurse leaders, past and current, have clearly demonstrated an ability to mobilise nurses' political strength to influence health and nursing policy to change a woefully inadequate system. Florence Nightingale was a consummate politician who recognised the value of data in influencing policy (Mason et al., 1993). Her fame was widespread in the 1860s as the heroine of the Crimean War, a foremost sanitarian and social reformer, and an authority on the management of hospitals and training of nurses (Allemang, 2000). Dock states, "As a reformer and political activist she [Nightingale] helped establish a new attitude toward the contributions of nurses in a military environment and the education of women" (cited in Kramptiz, 1985, p. 10).

EDUCATIONAL ACHIEVEMENTS

In Canada, after the successful founding in 1874 of the first training school, based on Nightingale's work at the General and Marine Hospital in St. Catherines, Ontario, nursing schools became an essential part of the organisation of large and small hospitals. Graduates became superintendents of the schools and hospitals where they influenced policy development and implementation for nursing and health (Allemang, 2000). Later in the decade, Lady Aberdeen, wife of the Governor General of Canada, facilitated the development of a visiting nurse component to health care and repatriated Charlotte Macleod, a Canadian from New Brunswick, as the first superintendent of the Victorian Order of Nurses (VON) for Canada (Pringle & Roe, 1992). Macleod's experience as superintendent of the Waltham Training Home for District Nurses in Massachusetts was critical to the development of the Canadian VON.

SPECIALISATION

In 1913, Mary Ard MacKenzie, national superintendent of the VON and president of the Canadian National Association of Trained Nurses, brought to national attention the inadequacy of nurses' training. A national committee of nurses and two university presidents subsequently recommended that nursing schools or colleges be connected with the educational system and offer a general course and an honours course with specialisation options, for example, district and public health nursing (Allemang, 2000). By 1920, nurses such as E. Kathleen Russell, Director of the Department of Public Health Nursing at the University of Toronto, Margaret Moad, District Supervisor with VON, and Jean I. Gunn, Director of Nurses at the Toronto General Hospital successfully influenced policy to fund public health nursing certificate programmes at six Canadian universities: Toronto, Western Ontario, McGill, Dalhousie, Alberta, and British Columbia (Allamang, 2000).

LEGISLATION ENACTED

In British Columbia, just before this educational policy advance, the Vancouver Graduate Nurses Association lobbied arduously for registered status so that nurses would have the legal right to set standards and establish training requirements. The *Nurses Registration Act* became law in 1918 (Brown, 2000). Although weakened from its original form, the Act formed a basis for professional legitimacy and won over opposing arguments that if nursing standards were too high, nursing service would not be affordable. Additionally, the legislation would shift control of nursing from the male-dominated medical profession, who thought it should have a greater say in decisions about the nursing profession, into the hands of graduate nurses who were, with few exceptions, women (Brown, 2000). Urged on by nurses, other provinces eventually passed similar legislation. In the last quarter of the 1900s, nurses lobbied for and got revisions to provincial and territorial nurse registration acts that gave them greater control of and accountability for standards of nursing practise, education, and continuing competency as well as protection of the use of the titles *nurse* and *RN*.

LEADERSHIP AND NATIONAL INFLUENCE

Since the early 20th century, nurses in Canada have influenced federal and provincial/territorial health and nursing policy. Some nurses have held official positions, such as "nurse advisor" or "chief nursing officer." Others have supported their professional association's policy advocacy efforts, and others have acted in advisory and consultative roles to government. Of particular national significance was the Canadian Nurses Association (CNA) submission, *Putting "Health" Back Into Health Care,* to the federal government's commission for the review of the national and provincial health programmes (CNA, 1980). The recommendations served as the basis for the major 1984 lobbying efforts of nurses across Canada to influence amendments to the Canada Health Act (Rodger & Gallagher, 2000). For more information, see Box 4.1.

The new enabling legislation allowed nurses and health professionals other than physicians to be fully used in a reformed health care system inspired by primary health care. The primary health care approach is both a philosophy of health care and an approach to providing services (World Health Organization [WHO], 1978; WHO, 1986). Primary health care embraces five types of care: promotive, preventive, curative, rehabilitative, and supportive/palliative, based on principles of accessibility, public participation, appropriate technology and intersectoral cooperation. Since then, the national, provincial, and territorial professional nursing associations have been clarifying their positions on primary health care, a major thrust of nursing, and recommending strategies to attain health for all (Rodger & Gallagher, 2000).

Primary health care demonstration projects (e.g., Comox Valley Nursing Centre in British Columbia, Saskatchewan's Beechy Collaborative Practice Pilot Project, Nova Scotia's Cheticamp Primary Health Care Project), position statements, briefs, and meetings with politicians and bureaucrats have been developed and implemented by nurses since mid-1980. The CNA states that "the goal of nursing practice is to improve the health of clients. In working to that goal, nurses must apply the five principles of the primary health care approach. This is true for nurses involved in direct care, in education, in research, in administration, or in policy roles" (CNA, 2000a).

BOX 4.1

Nurse-Influenced Amendments to the Canada Health Act

Lobbying efforts of nurses nationwide in 1984 led to amendments to the Canada Health Act (RS. 1985 c.C-6). Amendments included the following:

1. A definition of health care practitioner that expanded the recognition of those providing health services beyond physicians and dentists:

   "Health care practitioner means a person lawfully entitled under the law of a province to provide health services in the place in which the services are provided by that person."

2. Inclusion of health care practitioners in one of the five criteria for federal funding to provinces and territories:

   "9. In order to satisfy the criterion respecting comprehensiveness, the health care insurance plan of a province must insure all insured health services provided by hospitals, medical practitioners, or dentists, and where the law of the province so permits, similar or additional services rendered by other health care practitioners."

Department of Justice Canada, Canada Health Act. Retrieved July 20, 2002. http://laws.justice.gc.ca/en/C-6/16506.htm section#2

Today, the policy work of nurses is more important than ever. Federal, provincial, and territorial governments are recognising the need to have senior nurses at the policy table. In creating the Office of Nursing Policy, federal health minister Alan Rock stated, "the new position is a positive step towards finding ways to better utilize the remarkable knowledge and expertise of nurses in strengthening the health of all Canadians" (cited in Shamian, 2000). Several provincial governments have also instituted an office for nursing policy and strategic planning. Others are in the process of doing so. The proactive work of professional nursing associations and unions is increasingly recognised as an important component of public policy work.

HISTORICAL SIGNIFICANCE OF POLICY

Policies determine the context in which nurses provide and patients receive care, whether it is in an institutional or community setting, whether care is privately or publicly funded, which individuals and groups are entitled to receive care, and which resources are allocated to fund services. Policies influence nurses' roles at a number of levels: provincial/territorial, professional associations, health care organisations, units within organisations, and individuals. Although nurses are generally knowledgeable about policies that guide specific nursing practises (e.g., use of restraints, incident reporting), they have less understanding of public policy (e.g., health and nursing) and its relationship to their work (i.e., practise and work environment). Yet, the relationship between nursing practise and public policy is crucial when we consider that nurses' daily working lives and patients' daily lives are defined and controlled by this policy.

The CNA states that "Nursing is a political act . . . a natural extension of the essence of nursing—of caring" (CNA, 2000b, p.4). Health care privatisation, increasing poverty, environmental pollution and destruction, and escalating violence all have clear repercussions for health and nursing.

Regardless of the policy context—government, association, workplace—involvement of all nurses is needed to address health and nursing policy and strategic planning priorities, which include the following:

- Nursing human resource planning and deployment
- Safe, healthy, and professionally supportive work environments
- Scope and models of nursing practise grounded in primary health care principles
- The continuum of health care—the bigger picture, including the primary determinants of health
- Nursing data requirements in clinical and administration health information systems
- Nursing as a career choice, with sufficient educational facility and financial support

Theoretical Perspective

Conventional wisdom holds that elected governments make health policy; that federal and provincial cabinets approve programmes and policies on the advice of their Minister of Health; that Ministers of Health are advised by professional public servants working in their departments; and that Canada's parliament and provincial legislatures then formally make health policy by passing laws governing the health system (Decter, 2001). This conventional wisdom also applies with respect to nursing policy at government, association, or local levels. In reality, the policy process is more complex and messy and is shaped and influenced by public strategies, media reports, interest groups and stakeholders, academics, and policy consultants. The policy process is not always the same or as rational and linear as logic and democratic beliefs suggest (Brooks, 1998).

Several theories, or theoretical perspectives, have been developed, however, in an attempt to bring logic and understanding to the policy process. A theory offers an explanation of why things happen the way they do. With respect to the policy process, theories, or theoretical perspectives, provide a map that directs our attention to particular features of the world or issue. Depending on the theoretical perspective, our attention focusses on different features of the situation we seek to understand, different stakeholders and players who will be involved, different priorities to be set, and different goals identified (Brooks, 1998). Major theoretical models include the pluralistic, public choice, and Marxist models.

PLURALISTIC MODEL

A pluralistic model of policy making in democratic societies views the process as a competition among elites. Powerful groups influence policymakers to have their wishes become applied to all (Brooks, 1998). Such groups as physicians, unions, and policy consultants have influenced health policy in the past. More recently, professional nursing associations and consumer groups have become more powerful and influential in the process, advocating for issues-related health promotion (e.g., tobacco legislation) and injury and disease prevention (e.g., bicycling helmet regulations).

PUBLIC CHOICE MODEL

The public choice model, concerned with economics and individual positions, grounds the policy process in strategic behaviours of individuals. Individual politicians and bureaucrats act on the basis of rational self-interest, often under conditions of imperfect knowledge (Brooks, 1998). Politicians, and board members, seek to be elected and, once elected, to maintain themselves in power. Bureaucrats, and staff, seek promotion and more control of their work environment (Brooks, 1998). Policy influence is primarily at the individual-to-individual level. Thus, new government chief nurse positions are important for exerting influence on a one-to-one basis as well as within groups, bringing forward nursing issues and perspectives.

MARXIST MODEL

The Marxist model is based on the belief that antagonistic relationships exist between different social and economic classes of people. This antagonism is the central factor of politics and policies (Brooks, 1998). The capitalist class, considered supreme, is the determinant of public policy decisions. The private versus public health care system policy debate exemplifies the Marxist model. Influencing this policy process perspective may be difficult if the issue is not framed as a social or economic class issue.

Understanding the Complexity of Policy

No one theoretical perspective is consistently taken in the policy process. The perspective differs depending on a variety of factors, including the specific policy issue, timeframe for resolution, politics, and power. What is important for nurses to understand and learn is how to become part of the process and use their knowledge and expertise to enlighten and influence specific policy processes, regardless of the theoretical perspective taken.

All types of policy involve a conscious choice that leads to deliberate action or inaction. The conscious choice of selecting a particular goal requires a plan of action—or the means for achieving the goal—to be developed and put into effect. Policy goals may be actualised in such products or instruments as laws, regulations, policy or position statements, briefs, taxes, or fines.

Spheres of Nurse Involvement

"Our challenge is to exercise our power and influence and use the political process to help bring about a major change in the delivery of nursing services to society" (Rodger, 1993, p. 25). Professional nursing holds some plausible solutions to current crises in health care.

Nursing leaders are increasingly aware that all health issues, no matter how seemingly remote from nursing itself, will have an impact on the direction of health policy and thus eventually on nursing. For example, today's nursing shortage is the result of policy decisions made in the mid-1990s to reduce the number of hospital beds and at the same time reduce the number of students accepted into nursing schools. Other policy decisions, such as regionalisation, reduction in funds for certain services, scopes of practise, and decreased funding for equipment, have direct effects on nurses' professional practise in direct care, education, administration, and research.

WORKPLACE: THE HEALTH CARE INSTITUTION

At an institutional level, evidence-based policy is required not only to address management and financial issues (e.g., health and human resource deployment, health information systems) but also to make critical interdisciplinary clinical decisions (e.g., practise guidelines for prevention and treatment of pressure ulcers, care maps) and develop work environments supportive of quality care and professional nursing practise. Clinical practise is a political endeavour because nurses influence the allocation of scarce resources, collaborate in evidence-based clinical decision making, work in the interest of other parties (e.g., patients or patients' families), and facilitate development of health resources and supports for groups and communities. Nurses in clinical and administrative practise frequently lead interdisciplinary care teams in development, implementation, and evaluation of evidence- and outcome-based clinical practise guidelines and critical care paths. Involvement in policy may be in the development and implementation of clinical practise guidelines for nursing care, care maps and critical paths for interdisciplinary care, or quality assurance initiatives, for example. It may also be in advocating for practise environments supportive of quality nursing care. The international study on hospital characteristics and patient and nurse outcomes has contributed to our understanding of critical relationships between the work environment and outcomes and suggests areas where changes in policy are required (Clarke et al., 2001.). In addition to adequate resources, nursing leadership at middle management and executive levels is crucial to improving patient and nurse outcomes.

A health care agency or institution's mission, vision, and core values are the foundations for operational policy and decision making as well as strategic planning. Nurses have a responsibility to contribute to the development of their institution's policy foundations and to the philosophy of nursing and patient care at both institutional and unit levels. It is the role of nurse leaders and senior executive nurses to ensure that a process is in place to facilitate nurses carrying out this responsibility. Nursing practise councils are one structure that has been used to encourage and support nurses' participation in these institutional policies.

Nurses also need to be aware of their institution's key policies: the organisational chart with its lines of communication and responsibility (i.e., power); mission statement, goals, and objectives (i.e., organisational culture); and policy and procedure manuals (i.e., expectations). Additionally, all health care institutions and agencies have an informal life not bound by a formal chain of command, board of directors, or committee structure. Nurses who want to influence an institution should take stock of the informal structure and processes. Those with formal titles usually have power and authority; however, others who do not have important titles can also wield power and influence. It is important for nurses to know where the sources of power and influence lie.

Policies in health care institutions are profoundly influenced by policies and politics of government as well as by changes in the workforce and patient populations and by economic and social changes within communities and professional organisations. In turn, workplace policies influence learning experiences for students, new employees, and nurses with new or different responsibilities. Important opportunities, such as mentoring, preceptoring, orientation, and professional development, are directly affected by clinical and institutional policies. Empowered nurses and students can influence such policies and their implementation.

GOVERNMENT

An understanding of political, demographic, and other forces shaping health care now and in the future is necessary if nurses are to ensure that workplace policies promote the health of the public and foster a supportive environment in which health care is provided—health care that spans the continuum of care from health promotion and illness and injury prevention to rehabilitative and palliative care. One of the most pressing policy issues facing all societies today is the nurse shortage and how to plan for and maintain relevant health resources, with appropriate mix and optimal utilisation of these scarce resources.

Although nursing is a self-regulating and self-governing profession, government provides society with a legal definition of nursing and what is within its scope of practise. Nursing associations and individual nurses advocate with government to ensure that nursing legislation and subsequent rules are in the best interest of the public—that they facilitate and support the full participation of nursing practise to achieve the goal of safe and appropriate health care.

Government also determines who will get what kind or level of health care (e.g., needle exchange sites, medications). Canadian nurses have been influential, locally and globally, in advocating for health care policy that promotes health and prevents illness in addition to curing disease, rehabilitating, and providing palliative care. Canadian nurses have also exerted influence to ensure that quality care is accessible, universal, and equitable and is supported by qualified, professional health care providers who are publicly accountable. The CNA's advocacy role in federal policy and politics has been increasingly evident at the turn of the century, as has its involvement of individual members and provincial and territorial nursing regulatory associations (Box 4.2).

In recent years, governments have once again recognised the need to provide infrastructure aimed at increasing nurses' input into the health and nursing policy process. At both federal and provincial levels, positions and offices are once again being created for senior nurse executives. The first federal Principal Nursing Officer, Verna Huffman Splane, was appointed in 1968 (Splane & Splane, 1994), and Laura Holland was the first appointed nurse advisory to the British Columbia Ministry of Health in 1938 (Paulson et al., 2000). Multiple-stakeholder federal, provincial, and territorial nursing committees are also being instituted to be advisory to government ministers and senior staff. It is absolutely critical that nurses support both these current initiatives by contributing their expertise to the policy work to be undertaken.

Through its funding priorities, government influences which health problems will be researched and targeted for government funding and support. Without nurses' unfaltering involvement in research policy and sharing their nursing knowledge and evidence, research-funding agencies would not recognise the value of supporting nursing research. In turn, nurses would not be able to make significant contributions of knowledge to improve the health of the public. The recently established Nursing Research Fund within the Canadian Health Services Research Foundation is the result of lobbying by Canadian nurses and demonstration of the power of nursing knowledge (Box 4.3).

BOX 4.2

Strengthening the Voice: The Ninth Decade of the Canadian Nurses Association

Looking back throughout each decade in its history, the Canadian Nurses Association (CNA) has made a significant impact on the advancement of the nursing profession and the promotion of quality, accessible health care for Canadians. The document identified below by its online address is a retrospective of the period 1990 to 1999, the ninth decade since the creation of the CNA.

Canadian Nurses Association. Retrieved July 20, 2002.
http://206.191.29.104/_frames/aboutcna/aboutusframe.html

BOX 4.3

The Nursing Research Fund

The Nursing Research Fund was created as an answer to concerns raised by nursing organisations and others representing nursing interests. The CNA and other major nursing voices lobbied the federal government extensively for funding to develop nursing researchers and to support research on nursing recruitment, retention, management, and the issues emerging from health-system restructuring. In 1999, the federal government responded by providing the foundation with enough funds to support research personnel, research dissemination, and research projects on nursing management, organisation, and policy at a level of $2.5 million per year for 10 years. The fund supports the production of research with health-system decision makers in mind, as well as training and personnel support. Nursing leadership, organisation, and policy are themes of the open grants competition.

Canadian Health Services Research Foundation, Nursing Research Fund. Retrieved July 20, 2002, from http//www.chsrf.ca/nrf/index_e.shtml

PROFESSIONAL ORGANISATIONS AND UNIONS

Professions exist at the pleasure of society and address a specific human need (Joel, 1993). Out of respect for the complex and learned nature of its work, the public allows a high degree of internal regulation by the profession itself. The public recognises the complexity of professional practise and looks to the profession as a collective to define its standards of safety and competence. Until the 1973 Supreme Court decision, *Service Employees International Union v. Saskatchewan Registered Nurses Association* (SRNA), collective bargaining was a function of the professional association. The Supreme Court decision agreed with the union's contention that the SRNA could not legally represent staff nurses in Saskatchewan because of management domination. Since then, there has been a separation of professional associations and unions (Rosswell, 1982).

Today's professional organisations' decision-making bodies develop policy to meet their public mandate, move a strategic plan, direct the association's resources, and guide implementation. It is important for their policy to target both nursing and health issues and provide clarity about the point beyond which there is no compromise. The professional associations of Canadian nurses have the potential to influence the nursing profession, health policy, and patient care.

Professional nursing organisations are instrumental in shaping nursing practise. They develop standards for nursing practise, education, ethical conduct, and continuing competence. They lobby for progressive changes in the scope of nurses' practise and play a role in collective action in influencing workplace policies. Whether the issue of concern is primarily nursing or health care, nurses have responsibilities to use their political skill and nursing expertise to contribute to their association's leadership role in public policy development—policy that aims to improve the health of communities and ensure the provision of high-quality nursing care.

Unions representing nursing are primarily concerned with the development of legally binding agreements that regulate staff nurses' salaries, working conditions, and other negotiable benefits. However, unions also advocate for health and nursing policy related to other issues (e.g., scope of nursing practise, primary health care). Nurses may be involved in union policy work—its development and implementation as well as monitoring contractual agreements. Such involvement is essential to the promotion of work environments supportive of nurses' practise and their health.

Professional organisations and unions have some common goals, including the welfare of members and improvement of their working conditions. They share a concern for professional ethics, although it is the professional organisation that is responsible for ensuring that the standard of professional conduct reflected in the code of ethics is practised. Although they do have common interests, professional organisations and unions are also different in many ways, with different responsibilities and perspectives on public policy, including that related to health and nursing. When relevant, professional nursing organisations and unions work together to influence policy affecting the professional practise of nursing and health of the population. Such collaboration was evident in identification of workplace issues affecting nurse retention and recruitment, enabling employment of student nurses outside their educational requirements, and addressing mentor–preceptor issues.

EDUCATIONAL INSTITUTIONS

Both faculty and students have opportunities and responsibilities for involvement in public education policy. Such involvement may be with government-level policy (e.g., initiatives with respect to legislation, funding, scholarships and bursaries, quality of education); within the institution level (e.g., with respect to mission, vision, curriculum, learning opportunities); and with associations (e.g., Canadian University Schools of Nursing, Canadian Nursing Student Association, professional association) and their policies, positions, standards, and the like (Box 4.4).

COMMUNITY

As members of a community, nurses have a responsibility to promote the welfare of the community and its members. The community's resources can be invaluable assets for health promotion and health care delivery. Nurses' contributions through community development and participation in community initiatives provide another credible and trusted voice in the policy process. Outcomes of nurses' contributions can be witnessed in the sustainability of demonstration and pilot projects, such as nursing and community health centres in a number of Canadian provinces and territories.

BOX 4.4

Professional Nursing Educational Associations: CAUSN and CNSA

The Canadian Association of University Schools of Nursing (CAUSN) was formed to promote desirable standards of education and research and to support the development of future university schools of nursing. CAUSN, the official accrediting agency for university nursing programs in Canada, is a voluntary association representing all universities and colleges which offer undergraduate and graduate programs in nursing. CAUSN participates in a national network for discussion of issues in higher education.

http://www.causn.org/new/causn/causn.htm

The Canadian Nursing Students' Association (CNSA) is the national voice of Canadian nursing students in diploma and baccalaureate registered nursing programs. The aim is to increase the legal, ethical, professional, and educational aspects that are an integral part of nursing. The Association is dedicated to an active and positive promotion of nurses and the nursing profession as a whole.

http://www.cnsa.ca/

Nurses working with First Nations communities are especially aware of the need to work with the community to incorporate aboriginal values, beliefs, and practises into health care and nursing policies. Reaching community health goals can only be achieved with true partnerships, with nurses contributing their expertise while at the same listening to and understanding First Nations people's priorities and preferences. The Nuu-chah-nulth Community and Human Services Community Health Nurses on Vancouver Island received the Advocacy for Health Award from the Registered Nurses Association of British Columbia for their advocacy in providing culturally sensitive nursing care to the people of the communities (Moore, 2001). The community health nurses developed a nursing framework that defines their relationship with their patients, setting the parameters of a health partnership that recognises Nuu-chah-nulth traditions and values.

CONCEPTUALISING THE POLICY DESIGN PROCESS

Policy making, a dynamic and cyclical process, can be conceptualised as a model of systematic and functional activities (Anderson, 1990) aimed at exploring the causal links between problems and solutions. Although it is useful to use such a model, one must also remember that policy making is messy, often with iterations of some of the stages. There are also power differentials to take into consideration in the policy process. Some current powerful influencers of policy include characteristics of the economy and society and the recent globalisation of information availability. The latter has both competition and cooperation potential because of unequal access to information technology within the country. As well, there are differential power relationships between governments (e.g., federal and provincial governments regarding federal contributions to provincial health care funding) as well as between governors and the governed (e.g., the professional regulatory organisation and its members regarding continuing competency requirements for registration). These differences bring with them opportunities for negotiation and revisions to a proposed or existing policy.

Identifying Issues

Policy problems are identified through situations that produce needs or dissatisfaction for which relief is sought (Anderson, 1990). Policy problems must be brought to the policymakers' attention. Once there, the policy issues and theoretical perspective to policy making are influenced by many factors (Brooks, 1998). The strengths of political and cultural influences are often determined by geographic location (e.g., rural, urban), language (e.g., English, French), ethnicity (e.g., majority, minority), and values and principles (e.g., public, private). Problem definition develops as values, beliefs, and social attitudes towards a concern are delineated and policy approaches considered.

Setting Priorities: The Policy Agenda

Ideally, policy making involves interested parties coming together to formulate ideas and solutions to given circumstances or problems. In reality, however, struggles for power are, and always have been, principal factors in motivating change (Hart, 1994). At provincial and federal levels, commissions have been formed to help identify policy issues, priorities, and strategies. In recent years, many provincial governments have also established health care commissions to address health care system and health profession issues. More recently, the 2001 federal Commission on the Future of Health Care in Canada has been commissioned to make recommendations on sustaining a publicly funded health system that balances investments in prevention and health maintenance with those directed to care and treatment. Although such commissions provide information for decision making and priority setting, they are frequently linked to politics and the political party of the time. Thus, findings and recommendations are often not acted on because of change in government or political priorities.

Policy issues and priorities may also arise from research. However, historically, there has been a gap between research and policy—having the evidence available for policymakers when it is required, researching issues of current interest to policymakers, and having policymakers focus on evidence in decision making. More recently, attention has been given to encouraging a closer link between policymakers and researchers. Granting agencies, such as the Canadian Health Services Research Foundation, promote and fund management and policy research in health services and nursing to increase the quality, relevance, and usefulness of this research for health system policymakers and managers and work with health system decision makers to support and enhance their use of research evidence when addressing health management and policy challenges.

Besides gaps between researchers and policymakers and reexamination of issues through commissions, challenges to nurses' consistent and meaningful involvement in setting policy agendas are related to the following:

- Dominance of the medical profession
- Culture, values, and structures of predecessor health care systems
- Invisibility of nursing
- Stability of the "iron triangle" of civil servant (bureaucrat), politician, and physician (Hart, 1994)

Uncovering the Evidence

Discovering reasons for policy involves discovering the data on which policies are based (Solomon & Roe, 1986). However, sometimes there are no data, just someone's idea of what should be. Although this situation can be found at the level of public policy as politics, it is also evident at the clinical level, where many practises have become policy for less than rational reasons.

Ideally, policy depends on data—data gathered from existing information and summarised and synthesised with a particular question in mind. Existing sources of data used in the policy process include published and unpublished reports, briefs, and research as well as public, stakeholder, or member communication. Thus, it is critical for nurses to pay attention to the development of data-gathering systems (e.g., health information systems, nursing workload and classification systems) and to learn how to make clinical knowledge and wisdom accessible and meaningful to the policy process.

During data analysis—a systematic description and explanation of causes and consequences of action and inaction—conversation among researchers and scientists and among politicians and stakeholders or advocates should be maintained (Anderson, 1990). The role of nurses in data analysis is part expert advisor and part advocate in providing their unique professional nursing perspective for policy decisions.

Choosing Instruments for Policy Formulation

The successful attainment of policy goals depends on the choice of instruments for achieving them (Brooks, 1998) and is influenced by values and the theoretical perspective taken (e.g., pluralist, public choice, Marxist). Instruments may include passage of a law or regulation, the expenditure of money, an official speech, or some other observable act. In general, carrots (incentives) are less intrusive than sticks (commands and prohibitions) and are more likely to be preferred by those decision makers predisposed towards smaller governance structures and greater scope for individual choice. In deciding how best to accomplish a policy goal (or set of related goals), policymakers consider a number of factors, such as the following:

- Political considerations
- Past experiences
- Bureaucratic or staff preferences
- Random factors, like personal values of key decision makers
- Measures most likely to achieve the goals
- How the goals can be accomplished at the least cost

Some of the policy instruments or products particularly relevant to nurses, but also used in other public policies, are the following:

- Endorsed positions (e.g., CNA *Code of Ethics for Registered Nurses* by other nursing jurisdictions)
- Briefs, position statements, official messages (e.g., CNA response to the Health Services on Health Care in Canada *Putting "Health" Back Into Health Care* [CNA, 1980])
- Strategic policy (e.g., mission, vision, core values, priorities)
- Procedures (e.g., clinical practise guidelines)
- Standards (e.g., practise standards, care and accreditation standards)
- Rules and regulations (e.g., communicable disease control)
- Legislation (e.g., nurse registration acts)

Adopting and Implementing the Policy

Adoption of the policy, or enactment of legislation, occurs before implementing the policy. Consideration must be given to ensuring that stakeholders are aware of the policy. For example, most professional nursing organisations publish new or revised position and policy statements, practise expectations, and standards in a form that all members receive. Although it is the responsibility of the policymaker to communicate the policy, it is the responsibility of those affected, the stakeholders, to recognise and take note of the new policy and its enactment.

Implementation is about doing: accomplishing a task, achieving a goal. Policy implementation is the process of transforming the goals associated with policy into results (Brooks, 1998). However, goals established by policymakers may be extremely vague, relying on words whose meanings are ambiguous and open to interpretation. Policymakers do not always know exactly what they want; consequently, their instructions are sometimes imprecise or even conflicting (Brooks, 1998). Thus, goals must be set, well articulated, and understood and translated in programmes with budget and funding appropriations. Programmes are vehicles by which policies are implemented and ideally have input from those who have a stake in the issue—policymakers, interest groups, professional associations, and appropriate others (Anderson, 1990). Once a legitimate authority approves the programme, it can be implemented.

Implementation involves such activities as applying the rules, interpreting regulations, enforcing laws, and delivering services. Ideally at this time, evaluation criteria are set for determining whether a programme meets policy goals and objectives. Programme development and implementation are usually the responsibility of staff of an organisation or government.

Communicating the Policy

Communication, a vital link between goals and implementation, has tremendous importance. Without clear and concise communication about the policy—what it means and how it is to be implemented—policy goals will never be accomplished. Furthermore, implementation and communication problems may be related to coordination within and between organisations. Virtually all programmes depend on some level of joint action. As the number of separate decisions that must be made increases, the likelihood of successful implementation decreases (Brooks, 1998).

Recognising Barriers to Implementation

Other issues confound the implementation of policy. These include the following:

- Attitudes and beliefs of programme administrators
- Territorialism and reluctance to give up that which is considered to be one's own
- External stakeholders' interests
- Political culture

Evaluating the Outcome

A feedback or monitoring process should be included from the beginning of any policy programme development. Planned evaluation should be carried out at specified intervals throughout the process to monitor the impact of the policy (outcomes evaluation) and to be certain that the policy deals with the identified needs, issues, and goals (Glass & Hicks, 2000). How do we know when a programme works or whether or not the policy has achieved its goal? How can we be sure that the results achieved have been accomplished as efficiently as possible? Although difficult, evaluation is an important part of policy and its implementation. Some of the difficulties include the following:

- Quantity does not mean quality.
- Policy goals may be nebulous, such as "promoting, protecting, improving" something.
- Some politicians have an interest in hard numbers, and others have an interest in ambiguous, or soft, data.

Revising the Policy

Findings from the evaluation phase should identify whether a programme has satisfactorily met the original concerns and should be continued. Segments of the original policy goals may remain unmet, or new issues may surface, indicating that the policy process cycle needs to start again with further clarification of the policy problem.

Given the complexity and barriers within the policy process, it is not unreasonable that nurses and others are skeptical about the actualisation of policy intents or goals. However, this only emphasises the need for nurses to be involved in all stages of the policy process. Whether one is a student, new graduate, seasoned expert, or leader, all nurses can play important roles in the policy process.

IMPACT ON NURSING: THE RELEVANCE
OF A NURSING PERSPECTIVE

A policy perspective for nurses must be one that assumes professional nurses pay attention to what patients need and deliver that service (Solomon & Roe, 1986). That means health and nursing policy are part of the practise of nursing. Nurses need to shape policy in a variety of ways and in a variety of places, not the least of which are the places where they work (Mason et al., 1993). Nursing perspective and expertise are required in government and professional association policy work. Nurses who understand the institution in which they work, the professional association they belong to, their community organisation, and the government structure are more likely to be able to participate in the policy process effectively.

Professional associations need the energy, expertise, and vision of all nurses, from students to renowned leaders. Support and influence for professional nursing organisation's own policy and involvement in public policy can be expressed in many ways, including the following:

- Active membership
- Submission of resolutions
- Membership on task forces or committees
- Identification of issues
- Candidacy for or membership on board of directors
- Membership or leadership in a professional interest group
- Support of lobbying efforts with letters, telephone calls, networking, and the like

FUTURE IMPLICATIONS: CHALLENGES AND STRATEGIES

What is often thought of as a challenge frequently takes on the characteristics of an opportunity requiring particular strategies. Changing one's perspective from challenge to opportunity requires a vision and a belief in one's self and the nursing profession. Thus, the challenges outlined below can be thought as nothing more than opportunities to change what existed in the past and what can exist in the future.

Challenges

Nurses often have the experience of not being listened to or not finding a suitable channel by which their voices will be heard and their contributions to policy valued. Thus, change occurs, and that change is to the detriment of nurses who have not known what the full consequences of change would be. Change also occurs when nurses feel powerless, when they feel that any resistance or any attempts to effect change on a specific issue would be hopeless. This most often occurs when nurses lack the empirical evidence upon which to make their case.

Yet, the clinical knowledge and expertise of nurses is their greatest asset in the policy process. Expert power is actualised in the increasing number of well-educated and degreed nurses. There is also recognition of nursing as a learned profession with the capacity for independent as well as collaborative practise and all the attendant and inherent rights, responsibilities, and accountabilities that go along with that status.

Nurses need to feel empowered with the authority commensurate with this knowledge and expertise as caregivers closest to patients and proportionate to their numbers. They need power to ensure their ability to provide competent, humanistic, and affordable care to people, power to help shape health policy and alter the disproportionate leverage of physicians, and power to ensure that nursing is an attractive career option for women and men who expect to influence and improve nursing, health care, and health policy (Ferguson, 1993).

The fundamental source of empowerment is self-confidence—the projection of a powerful image that emanates from a sturdy self-image. The key to acquiring this lies, to a great extent, in the hands of nursing leaders and managers in decision-making roles who actualise nurses' legitimate power and the authority to bring about change (Ferguson, 1985). The role of the governing structures in institutions and government is important in establishing and maintaining organisational and professional arrangements by which nurses control their practise and professional affairs. The workplace must be committed to ensuring that nurses have accountability for decisions affecting nursing.

Some groups are more adept at exploiting the policy process and better placed to do so. This can affect the interest not only of one occupational group against another, but also of individuals within a particular group, such as nursing. An example of this can be found in the increased number of hospital nurses at a time when primary health care policies and directions dictate that more resources and nursing personnel should be directed into community nursing. "There can be little doubt that one of the primary problems facing nurses is actually identifying what their best interests are and then arriving at strategies for advancing them" (Hart, 1994, p. 184). Not being a homogeneous group endlessly complicates the policy-influencing process, as does nurses' general position in the health care system pecking order. The closer nurses in all contexts of practise work together to advance policies that will improve the health of the public, and the more collaboration there is between nursing professional associations and unions, the greater will be the voice and influence of nursing in the policy process.

Strategies for Involvement

Nurses need to be sensitive to the political process. Experience shows that positive results are most often obtained by working with the system, not against it (Glass & Hicks, 2000). Working with the system requires an understanding of the political process, the global perspective of the health system, and issues in the local community. It is essential for nurses to be knowledgeable about current policy directions, to be aware of the expected outcomes of the programmes, and to participate in the development of policy in the many sectors influencing health and nursing.

Some strategic guidelines for influencing the policy process include the following:

- Educate yourself about the issue, the decision makers, and other stakeholders.
- Vote for policymakers who support humanistic policies. Get to know your representatives personally at various levels—local, provincial, territorial, federal.
- Participate in your professional nursing association's work. This communicates your message to the appropriate people. Hold an office. Be on a committee.
- Join a professional organisation with goals and philosophies you can identify with and support in working to shape nursing and health care.
- Work with colleagues to transform the places in which health care is provided or nursing is taught.
- Involve those directly affected by the issue in planning and carrying out strategies.

- Enlist allies; mobilise a group of colleagues to address a policy issue in government.
- Participate in improving neighbourhoods, schools, and communities.
- Speak from your experience as a nurse; learn how to communicate your ideas effectively using examples, analogies, and history.
- Create public support for an issue; develop the important socialisation and networking skills to convey your points to the policymakers.
- Use the media (local newspaper, association newsletter); cultivate relationships with media personnel you believe you will be sympathetic to your issue.
- Learn the arts of compromise and tact; sometimes, it is more advantageous to reach half your goal than lose the entire fight. See others' points of view so that you understand where the opposition is coming from. Plan your strategy and reach compromise without sacrificing your beliefs.
- Volunteer to serve as a member of a local health or nursing advisory committee (Mason et al., 1993; Vance, 1993; Ross Kerr & MacPhail, 1996; CNA, 2000b).

"Walking the corridor," meeting with departmental heads in informal ways, and contributing to policy making and decisions through telephone calls and conversations are approaches to policy influence that need to be better developed and more readily available to nurses (Hart, 1994). Nurses are beginning to learn the benefits of collective action, mutual support, and interdependence (Beck, 1982), not just in labour issues but also in other issues that affect their ability to provide safe and effective care. Individual nurses increase the power of all nurses when they acknowledge their own expertise and that of their peers. Nurses who participate in interdisciplinary groups with consumers of health care services and in organisations, associations, and boards beyond nursing achieve personal growth and help others understand nurses and nursing better.

Knowledge is a strategic resource that confers authority on its possessor. Nurses who view themselves as lifelong learners will have a more potent effect on deliberations and the ultimate decision-making process than nurses who fail to devote time to their formal and informal continuing education.

In a dynamic environment, where conditions change rapidly and power and influence take on new forms, the continued acquisition of knowledge and skills is essential. Power and empowerment are gained, maintained, and expanded as nurses give sustained attention to perfection of practise, education for practise, research to improve practise, and administrative activity to enable practise (Ferguson, 1993). As nurses compete for increased participation in management, governance, planning, and policy development in the health care system, they must value scholarship and continually apply it as nursing is practised.

SUMMARY

Reconceptualising nursing and the nursing role as a political act will promote a new understanding of the role and its relationship with policy. Such reconceptualising will need to defend and expand knowledge in the fields of clinical practise, management, education, research, and policy and challenge the power structures that seek to devalue nurses' roles.

Nurses have gradually gained understanding of the processes and skills involved in influencing others, thereby becoming more powerful and exercising more control of the factors that influence their working lives. The nursing profession's history of political action and policy influence is something of which every nurse can be proud. Yet, there are many more challenges in the 21st century that require the policy expertise of nurses—expertise that requires political savvy and power.

Nursing and policy, with its adjuncts of politics and empowerment, are as congruent to nursing practise as are diagnosis and intervention—both require acute problem-solving and decision-making skills. Nurses are part of the policy solution to health care and public health problems. Nursing's history, both recent and remote, is filled with examples of nurses who have understood the inherent political and policy nature of nursing. Our challenge is to continue that legacy.

Reflections on the Chapter

1. Policy roles and responsibilities of nurses may vary throughout one's career. As a senior student or new graduate, identify opportunities for you to enact a policy role in clinical practise, student affairs, or professional association involvement. Discuss ways in which you could fulfill the responsibilities of that policy role.

2. One of the major challenges to nurses influencing the policy process is the invisibility of nursing as a political force. How might individual nurses and the profession of nursing address this challenge?

3. Identify a public policy—health or nursing—that has been developed at a government or professional association level. Determine how the policy process unfolded from issue identification to outcome evaluation.

4. From your clinical or educational experience, identify and select an issue that concerns you and that you consider requires a new or revised policy. Compose a letter to an appropriate decision maker to propose a policy change.

5. Review resolutions submitted to the recent annual meeting of your professional association. For one of the resolutions, critique the background, rationale, and recommendations for policy implications and the feasibility of developing a policy.

6. Consider ways in which you have been influenced by a health or nursing policy—whether as a citizen, student nurse, or graduate nurse. Determine where in the policy process you could have been influential and what strategies you could have used to be influential.

REFERENCES

Alberta Registered Nurses Association. (2000). RNs value AARN role as advocate for health care policy, say survey results. *Registered Nurse, 56*, 6, 8–9.

Allemang, M. M. (2000). Development of community health nursing in Canada. In M. J. Stewart (Ed.). *Community nursing: Promoting Canadian's health.* (2nd ed., pp. 4–32). Toronto: W. B. Saunders.

Anderson, J. E. (1990). *Public policymaking.* Boston: Houghton Mifflin.

Barnum, B. S., & Kerfoot, K. M. (1995). *The nurse as executive* (4th ed.). Gaithersburg, MD: Aspen.

Beck, C. T. (1982). The conceptualization of power. *Advances in Nursing Science, 8*, 1–2.

Brooks, S. (1998). *Public policy in Canada: An introduction.* Toronto: Oxford University Press.

Brown, D. J. (2000). *The challenge of caring: A history of women and health care in British Columbia.* British Columbia: Ministry of Health and Ministry Responsible for Seniors, Women's Health Bureau.

Canadian Nurses (2000). Nursing policy: making the talk matter. Interview with Judith Shamian. *Canadian Nurse, 96*(10), 16–20.

Canadian Nurses Association (1980). *Putting "health" back into health care*: Submission to the Health Services Review '79. Ottawa: Author.

Canadian Nurses Association (2000a). Primary health care approach. *Fact sheet* [On-line]. Available: http://206.191.29.104/_frames/policies/policies-mainframe.htm.

Canadian Nurses Association (2000b). Nursing is a political act: the bigger picture. *Nursing Now: Issues and Trends in Canadian Nursing, 8*, 1–5

[On-line]. Available: http://206.191.29.104/_frames/issuestrends/issuestrendsframe.htm.

Clarke, H. F., Lashinger, H. S., Giovannett, P., Shamian, J., Thomson, D., & Tourangeau, A. (2001). Nursing shortages: Workplace environments are essential to the solution. *Hospital Quarterly, 4*(4), 50–57.

Decter, M. (2001). Who makes health policy? *Health Policy Forum, 3*(3), 2.

Dye T. (1978). *Understanding public policy* (3rd ed.). Englewood Cliffs, NJ: Prentice-Hall.

Ferguson, V. D. (1985). Power, politics and policy in nursing. In R.R. Wieczorek (Ed.), *Power, politics, and policy in nursing* (pp. 5–15). New York: Springer.

Ferguson, V. D. (1993). Perspectives on power. In D. J. Mason, S. W. Talbott & J. K. Leavitt (Eds.), *Policy and politics for nurses* (2nd ed., pp. 118–125). Philadelphia: W. B. Saunders.

Glass, H., & Hicks, S. (2000). Healthy public policy in health system reform. In M. J. Stewart. (Ed.), *Community nursing: Promoting Canadians' health* (2nd ed., pp. 156–170). Toronto: W.B. Saunders.

Grohar-Murray, M. E., & DiCroce, H. R. (1997). *Leadership and management in nursing.* Stamford, CT: Appleton & Lange.

Hart, C. (1994). *Behind the mask: Nurses, their unions and nursing policy.* London: Bailliere Tindall.

Joel L. A. (1993). Contemporary issues in nursing organisations. In D. J. Mason & S. W. Talbott (Eds.), *Policy and politics for nursing* (2nd ed., pp. 539–548). Menlo Park, CA: Addison-Wesley.

Krampitz, S. D. (1985). Historical overview of nursing and politics. In D. J. Mason and S. W. Talbott (Eds.), *Political action handbook for nurses* (pp. 10–22). Menlo Park, CA: Addison-Wesley.

Loveridge, C. E., & Cummings, S. H. (1996). *Nursing management in the new paradigm.* Gaithersburg, MD: Aspen.

Maslin, A. (2001). Serving the underserved: An international imperative. *Reflections on Nursing Leadership, 27,* 2, 8–9, 45.

Mason, D. J., & McCarthy, A. M. (1985). Politics of patient care. In D. J. Mason & S. W. Talbott (Eds.), *Political action handbook for nurses* (pp. 38–52). Menlo Park, CA: Addison-Wesley.

Mason, D. J., McEachen, I., & Kovner, C. T. (1985). Contemporary issues in the workplace. In D. J. Mason & S. W. Talbott (Eds.), *Political action handbook for nurses* (pp. 223–240). Menlo Park, CA: Addison-Wesley.

Mason, D. J., Talbott, S. W., & Leavitt J. K. (1993). *Policy and politics for nurses* (2nd ed). Philadelphia: W. B. Saunders.

Moore, G. (2001). Advocates for culture, advocates for health. *Nursing BC, 33*(4), 18–22.

Paulson, E., Zilm, G., & Warbinek, E. (2000). Pioneer Government Advisor: Laura Holland, RN, RRc, CBE, LLD (1883–1956). *Canadian Journal of Nursing Leadership, 13*(3), 36–39.

Pringle, D. M., & Roe, D. I. (1992). Voluntary community agencies: VON Canada as example. In A. J. Baumgart & J. Larsen (Eds.), *Canadian nursing faces the future* (2nd ed., pp. 611–626). St. Louis: Mosby Year Book.

Rodger, L. M. (1993). Nurses and the political process. *AARN Newsletter, 49*(2), 24–25.

Rodger G. L., & Gallagher S. M. (2000). The move toward Primary Health Care in Canada: Community health nursing from 1985 to 2000. In M. J. Stewart (Ed)., *Community nursing: Promoting Canadian's health* (2nd ed., pp. 33–55). Toronto: W. B. Saunders.

Ross Kerr, J., & MacPhail, J. (1996). Political awareness in nursing. In J. Ross Kerr & J. MacPhail (Eds.), *Canadian nursing issues and perspectives* (pp. 208–215). St. Louis: Mosby.

Rowsell, G. (1982). Changing trends in labour relations: effects on collecting bargaining for nurses. *International Nursing Review, 29*(5), 141–145.

Shamian, J. (2000). Office of Nursing Policy Comes to Ottawa. *Registered Nurse, 12*(5), 5–6.

Solomon S. B., & Roe S. C. (1986). *Integrating public policy into the curriculum.* New York: National League for Nursing.

Splane, R. B., & Splane, V. H. (1994). *Chief Nursing Officer positions in national ministries of health: Focal points for nursing leadership.* California: The Regents, University of California.

Talbott, S. W. (1985). Political analysis: structure and process. In D. J. Mason & S. W. Talbott (Eds.), *Political action handbook for nurses* (pp. 129–148). Menlo Park, CA: Addison-Wesley.

Titmus, R. M. (1974). *Social policy: An introduction* (p. 23). New York: Pantheon Books.

Vance, C. (1993). Politics: A humanistic process. In Mason, D. J., Talbott, S. W., & Leavitt J. K. *Policy and politics for nurses* (2nd ed., pp. 104–117). Philadelphia: W. B. Saunders.

World Health Organization. (1978). *Declaration of Alma-Ata* International Conference on Primary Health Care, Alma-Ata, USSR, 6–12 September [On-line]. Available: http://www.who.int/hpr/archive/docs/almaata.html.

World Health Organization. (1986). *Ottawa Charter for Health Promotion: An International Conference on health Promotion.* November 17–21, 1986. Retrieved July 20, 2000. Health Canada, Population Health Approach. http://www.hc-sc.gc.ca/hppb/phdd/docs/charter/.

CHAPTER 5

Policy Is the Lever for Effecting Change

Judith Shamian ▪ Judith Skelton-Green ▪ Michael Villeneuve

Chapter Objectives

At the completion of this chapter, you will be able to:

1. Describe the relationship between research and policy.
2. Explain why quality research is—in and of itself—insufficient to effect policy change.
3. Identify and explain the key components of effective research–policy linkages.
4. Apply a basic change formula to analyse and plan for change.
5. Identify the steps in the policy cycle and give examples of how the various steps might play out with a real-world issue of nursing concern.

(continued)

Policy sets
the direction
for *action*

6. Describe the connection between political acumen and policy influence.

7. Identify ways in which political acumen may be leveraged in the advancement of nursing policy.

Policy "involves the application of reason and evidence to problem solving, whether in public or private settings. It connects basic scientific knowledge to practice. . . . Policy incorporates both a process of decision-making and the product of that process" (Helms et al., Anderson & Hanson, 1996, p. 32). In *Health Policy and Politics: A Nurse's Guide,* public policy is defined as the "directives that document government decisions . . . the process of taking problems to government agents and obtaining a decision or reply in the form of a program, law, or regulation" (Milstead, 1999, p. 1). Health policy has been defined as "the principles, plans and strategies for action guiding the behaviour of organizations, institutions and professions involved in the field of health, as well as their consequences for the health-care system" (West & Scott, 2000, p. 818).

Policies exist as part of the everyday practise of nursing. They are found in many forms:

- Governmental laws and regulations
- Organisational policies
- Union contracts
- Nursing unit procedures

Policies guide "the way things are done around here," particularly when they are explicitly stated. Policies are often equated with rules. And policies may even be found limiting, as in "You can't do that for your patient because it is the policy here that we don't allow." Indeed, Cheek and Gibson (1997) caution that unrestrained generation of policy—particularly at the organisational level—can actually serve to limit and control negatively the practise of nursing.

Why should nurses be concerned with health policy? Clinical care can be improved either by focussing on the work of individual nurses or by focussing on the systems in which they work. The organisation of health care services, the culture of health care organisations, and the quality of work life of staff are as important to quality patient care as are direct nurse–patient encounters (West & Scott, 2000). Health policy is an important vehicle for influencing and changing the environments in which nurses work. As limiting as policy can be at times, it is certain that if something does not become policy, it won't happen.

This chapter illustrates the reasons that compelling research findings—often demonstrating clearly what nurses want and need in their work environments to optimise their contributions to society—do not always result in the changes in nursing practise environments that are needed. The chapter also proposes ways to overcome such barriers by recognising that effective influence of policy occurs when five levers are utilised:

- Good evidence or research
- Effective research–policy linkages
- An understanding of change management
- An understanding of the policy cycle
- Political acumen

Ultimately, the chapter aims to help the reader understand and use each lever, to provide examples of how others have done so, to examine lessons learned, and to encourage every nurse to think about and become involved, in some way, in influencing health policy.

THE CHALLENGE: AVOIDING CRITICAL SITUATIONS

North America is entering a period of a very serious nursing shortage. Given all of the studies of nursing workplace satisfiers that occurred in the 1980s and 1990s, it seems reasonable to expect that we would have learned lessons to help us avoid yet another critical situation. This hasn't happened for several reasons.

Shortages

First, the actions taken to address our historical cycles of nursing shortage and surplus have too often been short sighted, providing interim relief but long-term residue. During the 1980s shortage, many organisations introduced unregulated health care workers to provide some aspects of patient care. Research now shows that patient care outcomes may have been negatively affected by this decision (McGillis Hall et al., 2001). Alternately in Canada, during the period of fiscal restraint and health care system restructuring in the mid-1990s, thousands of nurses across the country were laid off or accepted the offers of early retirement. Thousands more underwent job changes in the bumping that followed. In Quebec, the Clair Commission recently concluded that these departures and changes contributed to weakening the level of expertise within the system and negatively affected the team environment (Commission d'étude sur les services de santé et les services sociaux, 2000). The short-term solutions in both of these circumstances had long-range consequences that were not anticipated and might have been avoided.

It is not a sufficient excuse that nurses did not, or could not, know what the long-term consequences of these decisions might be. Research on the correlation between levels of registered nurse (RN) staffing and patient morbidity and mortality had been published before the introduction of unregulated workers (Aiken et al., 1994; Knaus et al., 1986; Hartz et al., 1989; Prescott, 1993).

Second, nurses have done a poor job of translating what is known from research into the actions that need to be taken. Despite increasingly robust research defining what nurses want and need to optimise the effectiveness of their work and working lives, nurses have not been very effective at influencing those who make the decisions that affect nursing practise.

Kimball and O'Neil (2001) suggest that several major developments have contributed to the unique and overwhelming nature of the current nursing crisis: a changing demography, a changing health care system, changing social values, and an alteration in the nature of work. They indicate that the size and complexity of these changes is so significant that strategies to deal with past nursing shortages will be inadequate for today's crisis.

Actions to Ameliorate Shortage

Kimball and O'Neil (2001) describe a continuum of the kinds of actions needed to address the challenges in the nursing workforce. And they make a convincing case that for long-lasting positive impact, solutions that use and respect the nurse as a valued asset and professional partner will be most effective. The four kinds, or stages, of actions follow.

STAGE 1. SCRAMBLE

In the early stage of a workforce shortage, there is a "scramble"—a flurry of short-term actions that are unilaterally initiated by providers of care. Examples include colourful recruitment brochures, international headhunting visits, sign-on bonuses, accelerated placement on the wage scale, and other activities focussed on monetary incentives. These kinds of actions treat the nurse as a commodity that will respond to traditional market incentives. In the scramble stage, little attention is paid to changing nursing education, the nature of work, or the structure of the profession.

STAGE 2. IMPROVE

Once the reality and the seriousness of the shortage is clear, employers begin to recognise that nurses have particular wants and needs, after which the employers begin to approach nurses as customers. Interventions focus on increasing choice, reducing stress, and improving safety. Examples of improve-stage responses are improved clinical experiences in nursing programmes, scholarships and loans, Internet-based distance learning, flexible benefits and scheduling, and preceptorship and mentorship programmes—activities designed to make longer-term investments in people to cultivate their loyalty. In this stage, there is still minimal structural change to the professional aspects of nursing.

STAGE 3. REINVENT

As the challenge of providing high-quality care with fewer professional nurses continues to mount, it becomes clear that there is a need to rethink the ways professional nurses are recruited and trained, how they are integrated into the system, and how they are challenged and rewarded. In the reinvent stage, new roles are developed that blur the traditional boundaries between nursing roles. Examples of reinvent-stage responses include shared governance models, specialty internships, the adoption of magnet hospital values, and incentive rewards for sustained clinical outcomes improvement. The role of the professional nurse in the delivery of high-quality, patient-centred care is not only recognised but also leveraged by the employer as a valued asset. The employer, in turn, is rewarded with improved patient clinical outcomes and satisfaction.

STAGE 4. START OVER

At the far end of the response continuum are interventions in which nurses are viewed as professional partners, practising at the upper limits of their professional licences, and respected by consumers as patient advocates, information resources, and teachers and supporters of self-care. Examples of start-over actions include new systems of care delivery and professional practise that cross traditional care boundaries, such as an academic nursing school's establishment of community-based, primary-care clinics staffed by nurse practitioners.

The key question is this: How can nursing recruitment and retention be managed in a more predictable, thoughtful, stable fashion than in the past? In particular, how can nurses move beyond short-term, knee-jerk scramble and improve strategies to longer-term reinvent and start-over strategies?

This shift will require more deliberate and more carefully managed approaches to the problem, with policy being the key that unlocks the door to these higher-level solutions. For it is only with the introduction of significant, broad-based policy change that substantive solutions will have staying power. If nurses want to influence successfully the formulation of appropriate and relevant policy, they must learn to utilise a number of levers, including the following:

- Robust evidence or research
- Effective research—policy linkages
- Understanding of change management
- Understanding of the policy cycle
- Political acumen

GOOD EVIDENCE

Evidence-based decision making has become a growing expectation in health care since the 1990s, not only for clinical medicine but also for management and policy formulation. Along with this expectation, nursing research funding and initiatives have increased dramatically.

Essentially, two basic kinds of information or evidence are needed to make meaningful changes in nursing recruitment, retention, and role optimisation:

1. *Information about nurses themselves.* What are the demographics of today's nurses? What will attract good candidates into the profession? What it is that nurses want and need to perform their work most effectively? What is required to keep them in the workforce?
2. *Information about the context within which nursing is practised.* What are the health and health care needs of our population? What are the most significant determinants of health? What changes are occurring and anticipated in the Canadian health care system? What can be learned from what is happening elsewhere in the world? What are the plans, initiatives, and political agendas of those in power?

Progress is being made in both areas of research. The information to answer the first set of questions is becoming more plentiful and more robust. Provincial nurse registries now track the demographics of their members on a number of key dimensions. Numerous studies have been published that clearly point out the conditions that will attract, retain, and satisfy nurses. These studies have been cited in other parts of this chapter and in other chapters in this book. In late 2001, the Canadian Institute for Health Information (CIHI) released a paper summarising what we know and what we do not know about factors affecting the supply, demand, education, health, and work lives of the members of health care providers in Canada (CIHI, 2001b). Much of the information to answer the second set of questions is also available, although the data are somewhat more elusive and certainly less well known and accessed by nurses.

If the necessary evidence regarding nursing practise is growing, why is it that those in decision-making positions are not acting on the information? First, the timing may not be right. Policy windows open and close at their own pace, having more to do with election cycles, public opinion, and fiscal years than with the release of research findings. Even when a study has been directly commissioned and competently performed, it may have to compete for attention with other priorities and influences at the time that it is completed.

Second, although the data may be in, the facts are not always clear. Jonathon Lomas, Executive Director of the Canadian Health Services Research Foundation (CHSRF), cautions us that with recent increases in research funding come risks. Rather than research supporting and informing practise changes, a gap may emerge between researchers and decision makers (Lomas, 2000). On the one hand, researchers' bias for methodologic purity can limit the practical utility of their findings; on the other hand, managers' push for speed and output can compromise the quality of the research. The CHSRF has developed a unique linkage-and-exchange approach to its work, which it hopes will offset both risks. This approach is in keeping with Davis and Howden-Chapman's (1996) conclusions that research is more likely to be translated into policy if researchers, policy analysts, managers, and politicians negotiate the language and frame of reference before research is undertaken.

Finally, although the evidence is growing, it is growing more quickly than our knowledge of how to use research findings to influence policy. Chunharas (2001) suggests that although good-quality research on policy-relevant issues, with well-packaged and well-targeted products, may succeed in informing decision-making processes, the linkages between policy and research will only be optimised through an understanding of the key components of their interface.

EFFECTIVE RESEARCH–POLICY LINKAGES

Chunharas (2001) identifies five key components of effective research–policy linkages:

- Interface between the dual processes of research and policy development
- Sensitivity to the context in which they both operate
- Appreciation for the attitudes of the stakeholders involved
- Astute use of the research outputs
- Role of mediators

Interface Between Research and Policy Development

Chunharas (2001) emphasises the importance of building linkages between all steps of the research and decision-making processes, from the definition of research questions and policy priorities to the dissemination of research results and policy or programme implementation. He argues that both processes will be richer for the interaction.

Sensitivity to Context

By *context*, Chunharas means the social, political, and economic environment surrounding the research and decision-making processes. He emphasises the need to consider deep-seated values, practises, and traditions as well as prevailing decision-making climates and mechanisms and the influence of mass media.

Appreciation for Stakeholders' Attitudes

Chunharas identifies three main stakeholders in the research–policy interface: researchers, decision makers, and members of the community. He suggests that decision makers would be more likely to use research results if researchers involved them in formulating questions and problems. Researchers, on the other hand, may be more interested in conducting needed research if they were consulted about the appropriate approach and methodology, Finally, members of the community—the putative subjects and targets of research and decision-making—who are often intimidated by both researchers and decision makers and forgotten in the processes, can contribute much to both the issues that need investigating and the appropriate application of results.

Astute Use of Research Outputs

One of the critical requirements in using research outputs effectively is the ability to tease out from complex research methods and findings a limited number of clear, concise, and relevant messages.

West and Scott (2000) suggest that research ideas (and, we would suggest, messages) related to the "great themes of our times," and those that offer solutions to current problems, are more likely to be taken up and implemented than ideas that are not currently high on the political agenda. This assertion emphasises the importance of knowing the popular themes and priorities as well as the importance of making the connection between "our findings" and "their priorities." West and Scott also suggest publishing summaries of scientific papers in journals that policymakers are likely to read and including "health policy" as key words in academic publications, as concrete means to ensure that important research comes to the attention of policymakers.

Even more basic is the fact that the key policy-relevant messages in research papers are often difficult to locate. From their study of what got the attention of policymakers in presentations by tobacco control advocates, Montini and Bero (2001) advise that advocates present science in a format that is well organised and easily absorbed. Gebbie and associates (2000), in a study of 27 American nurses currently active in health policy, suggest that researchers write findings in a style that can help policymakers draw conclusions and include in every study (including clinical studies) a clear and deliberate discussion of policy ramifications.

Role of Mediators

The differences between the priorities, time constraints, languages, and cultures of researchers and policy decision makers have been acknowledged, described, and likened to the existence of two communities that prohibit successful communication. A number of authorities (CIHI, 2001a; Crosswaite & Curtice, 1994; Feldman et al., 2001) argue the case for skilled mediators or research-knowledge brokers who can bridge the gaps. Research brokers have been described as individual specialists with effective communication skills, the ability to educate and report, and familiarity with differing approaches and research methods—a hybrid of journalist, teacher, and researcher (Crosswaite & Curtice, 1994).

Although Chunharas (2001) recognises that the mediator role can be critically important, he also emphasises that researchers themselves must develop skills of communication and advocacy as well as an understanding of how decision makers make resource allocation decisions and how policymakers develop, implement, and monitor policies.

Nurses may argue that nurses and the nursing profession can act in a brokering role, strengthening the linkages among research, decision making, and policy formulation.

CHANGE MANAGEMENT

In a recent presentation to policymakers, Gina Browne (2001), founder and director of the System-Linked Research Unit on Health and Social Service Utilization, stated, "I don't think we should ever fund another study on the efficacy of nurse practitioners. Every piece of research for 30 years has shown the effectiveness of the role. Why have we not been able to translate all those robust findings into action?" Browne went on to answer her own question this way: "I really don't think any more that we have a serious knowledge development problem. We have a serious research dissemination and transfer problem." In other words, nurses aren't very good at making and managing change.

Dannemiller and Jacobs (1992) describe a basic change formula that is very useful, both for diagnosing a situation and for developing interventions in change situations. The formula is as follows:

$$D \times V \times F > R$$

Dannemiller and Jacobs state that change can and will only occur when the product of discomfort or dissatisfaction (D) with the present situation, a vision (V) of what is possible or desired, and the concrete first steps (F) toward reaching the vision are greater than the resistance (R) to the change. It is important to understand that it is the product of the factors on the left side of the equation with which one must be concerned. If any one of these variables (D, V, or F) is zero, or near zero, the product of the three will also be zero, or near zero, and the resistance cannot and will not be overcome.

Consider this example. Many hospitals have attempted to implement self-scheduling on their nursing units. The appeal (vision, V) of nurses managing their own schedules is clear, and it fits with their ideals of nursing autonomy and work–life balance (let's give the V 1 out of 1). The steps needed to implement self-scheduling are carefully thought out and put into place (first step, F, gets 0.8 out of 1). About a third of the staff is quite unhappy with the current scheduling system and keen to try the new system along with the manager. Some staff members are indifferent, and some are reluctant (let's say dissatisfaction, D, is initially 0.4, and resistance, R, is 0.2). At the outset of the change effort, the formula looks favourable, if not overwhelmingly so: D (0.4) $\times$ V (1.0) $\times$ F (0.8) = 0.32; whereas R is only 0.2.

However, implementing the new scheduling practises proves awkward; it creates tensions among staff members, and some individuals do not get as many of the "preferred" shifts as they had hoped. Grumbling breaks out, along with accusations of favouritism or breaking the rules. Some of the original proponents even become disillusioned (resistance, R, grows to 0.5; dissatisfaction, D, falls to 0.2). Eventually, those responsible to see that the ward is adequately staffed (whether front-line staff volunteers or the manager) become discouraged, and the staff votes to discontinue the plan. This can be explained by the fact that the change equation has shifted, and now looks like this: D (0.2) $\times$ V (1.0) $\times$ F (0.8) = 0.16; whereas R = 0.5.

What was missing in this change situation was that not enough staff members were unhappy enough with the old schedule to carry the change momentum through the difficult adjustment period. Spending more time at the outset getting people "on board" and really wanting to replace the "old, unsatisfactory" scheduling practises with new ones could have enhanced the likelihood of success.

The applications to the research–policy links are clear. One can think of examples of situations in which research data have been the primary driver of health policy change—for instance, seatbelt and bicycle helmet legislation. In these cases, one might argue that the resistance to the policy change was low, and thus the dissatisfaction quotient did not play out as a large factor. On the other hand, there are other situations—like tobacco and gun control in the United States—in which organised resistance has been strong, and the absence of strong dissatisfaction with the status quo has hindered necessary policy change.

In summary, good research may provide the data for a vision of a better world for nurses. A robust and detailed plan may even be proposed to act on the research. However, if there is not sufficient dissatisfaction with the status quo to overcome any resistance that may be encountered, the desired policy changes may not occur.

POLICY CYCLE

Milstead (1999) elaborates on four major stages of the policy process: agenda setting, legislation and regulation programme implementation, and programme evaluation. Agenda setting is concerned with identifying a problem and bringing it to the attention of government; legislation and regulation are the formal responses to the problem; programme implementation is the execution of programmes designed to enact the legislation; and programme evaluation is the appraisal of the programme's performance. Milstead emphasises that "the policy process is not necessarily sequential or logical. The definition of a problem, which usually occurs in the agenda-setting phase, may change during legislation. Program design may be altered significantly during implementation. Evaluation of a policy or program (often considered the last phase of the process) may propel onto the national agenda (often considered the first phase of the process) a problem that differs from the original" (Milstead, 1999, p. 21).

Of particular concern in this chapter are the first two of Milstead's four stages. The federal Office of Nursing Policy (ONP) has promoted understanding of a conceptual framework (adapted from Tarlov, 2000) that explains the way in which nurses can move matters onto the policy agenda, and how they can move that agenda forward into action. Figure 5.1 illustrates the eight-step policy cycle of (1) values and cultural beliefs, (2) emergence of problems or issues, (3) knowledge and development of research, (4) public awareness, (5) political engagement, (6) interest group activation, (7) public policy deliberation and adoption, and (8) regulation, experience, and revision.

The actions taken by the ONP to move the issues surrounding nurses' health and nursing workplaces onto the country's policy tables illustrate how the cycle works. The policy cycle has two distinct phases, each of which is anchored by a particular step in the cycle. The first phase, Getting to the Policy Agenda, is anchored by beliefs and values. If society and its representative structures do not value and believe in the issues that are put forth in the policy arena, the issues will have no oxygen to feed them and will die on the floor.

The second half-cycle, Moving into Action, is anchored by political engagement. To advance an issue to policy and then to action, political engagement is required. Without the engagement of political sponsors, policy issues can be "out there," and acknowledged by various stakeholders, but they will not result in policy change.

Values and Cultural Beliefs

Action on any policy issue must be firmly grounded in a supportable set of values and cultural beliefs. In the case of the Healthy Nurses, Healthy Workplaces agenda, four basic—yet powerful—beliefs or values were dominant:

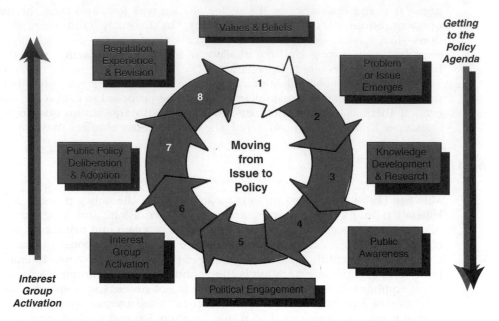

FIGURE 5.1.   The Policy Cycle (Adapted from Tarlov, A., 1999, 2000).

- Canadians are firmly in support of the principles of the Canada Health Act.
- Nurses are an essential part of the health care delivery system.
- To offer both access and quality, the health care system needs nurses.
- The public trusts nurses.

Identification, validation, and articulation of these basic values were important not only at the outset of the initiative (to ensure that the agenda was value based) but also in moving forward (to connect others who share those values).

Emergence of Problem or Issue

Kingdon (1995) makes the point that an issue can come from anywhere and that in some ways its source or origin does not matter. Rather, it is essential that the issue lands on fertile soil and is nurtured. That is to say, it is not sufficient for an issue just to exist; it must have some urgency. It must be a problem that is visible and important to others, not just to those affected. Kingdon also points out that "policy windows open infrequently and do not stay open long" (Kingdon, 1995, p. 167). It is important, therefore, for those who wish to advance policy initiatives, to be alert to opportunities as they present themselves.

For years, nurses complained that aspects of their workplaces were negatively affecting not only their productivity and performance but also their personal health. More recently, they were vocal in articulating the effects of organisational downsizing and restructuring on their workloads. They related that the situation was becoming intolerable and that it was leading to increased absenteeism, increasing job dissatisfaction and low morale, and high illness rates. In 2000, the frustration boiled over, with highly emotional and visible job action surrounding labour contract negotiations in many provinces.

Knowledge and Development of Research

Once the issues are clear and pressing, one must ask whether solid evidence and research exists to support the perceptions. Fortunately, in the case of nurses' health, the answer is a resounding "yes." Data from the Statistics Canada Labour Force Survey (Akyeampong, 1999) showed that in 1998, the average nurse was off work 15.75 days per year. That figure translates to 8.4% of nurses being absent from work each week.

More recent evidence compiled for the Canadian Nursing Advisory Committee suggests little change in that situation. Statistics were not available for licensed practical nurses (LPNs) or registered psychiatric nurses (RPNs), but "compared to 47 broad categories of occupations, nursing supervisors and RNs have a higher rate of temporary absences due to illness and injury than any other group" (Canadian Labour and Business Centre, 2002, p. 3). The impact of this situation—not only on costs to the health care system but on quality of patient care—is undeniable.

The relationship between nursing and patient outcomes has also been well established, through, for example, the magnet hospital studies (Aiken et al., 1994) and the International Study of Nurse Staffing and Patient Outcomes (Aiken et al., 1998).

And finally, multiple studies and reports—from the late 1970s (Slavitt et al., 1978), 1980s (Price & Mueller, 1981; Blegan & Mueller, 1987), and 1990s (Irvine & Evans, 1992), more than two decades of magnet hospital research (Scott et al., 1999), through to the most recent studies of the Ontario Nursing Effectiveness, Outcomes and Utilization Unit (Clarke et al., 2001; O'Brien-Pallas et al., 2001) and Commitment and Care, a synthesis paper commissioned by the Canadian Health Services Research Foundation (Baumann et al., 2001)—have clearly, consistently, and repeatedly described the conditions that make a difference to nurses' satisfaction with the quality of their workplaces.

Although additional research might prove valuable, it was more important to make the messages about the existing results accessible and compelling. The ONP set out to do just that, creating tight, succinct, emotionally engaging messages (based on facts such as absenteeism statistics) that could be easily articulated, easily repeated, and easily reported. Speaking engagements for the executive director were used as opportunities to present these messages. The many sources supporting the key messages were cited, to add emphasis and credibility to the case.

Public Awareness

The next phase in the policy cycle is the creation of broad-based awareness—both of the issue and of the solution or strategy for addressing it, as identified in the research. In this quest, it is important to identify as many potential supportive audiences as possible and to customise the message for each audience. When customising the message, one needs to think as the target group thinks, identifying how they would benefit from change. The various publics targeted by the ONP for the Healthy Nurses, Healthy Workplaces message included nurses and nursing organisations, other care providers, employers, unions, politicians (both government and opposition), and the general public. Of course, it was also important to include both the broadcast and print media. Radio, television, newspapers, and magazines such as *Chatelaine* and *Macleans* picked up articles about the health of nurses and the impact of healthy workplaces.

Political Engagement

Kingdon (1995) says that for an issue to be placed on a political agenda, it must have been "softened up." The softening-up process refers to the fact that people have to get used to the idea, so that support and acceptance for the proposed solution or strategy can be built. This process of political engagement should be designed to initiate a ripple effect that can grow into a wave of support for the proposed strategy. In planning for political engagement, it is critically important to accomplish the following:

- Know the government structure, committees, caucus, and key members of Parliament (those in power, those in opposition, and the nonelected players who have informal power).
- Target individuals with interest, information, passion, or influence regarding your topic.
- Utilise carefully considered person-to-person contacts.
- Customise the message for each contact person.
- Keep these individuals regularly updated regarding your activities, your progress, and your specific needs for ongoing support.

Milstead (1999) emphasises the importance of personal stories, gained from professional nurses' experiences. These stories provide real-world anchors for altruistic conversations and forge an emotional link that is important in connecting the targets with the proposed strategies. In building support, it is also wise to encourage complementary initiatives that might be undertaken by other individuals or organisations.

Interest Group Activation

Once public awareness and political engagement have been sparked, it is important to exploit deliberately every opportunity to repeat the message, to build the ripples of interest into a wave, if possible, a tidal wave. Actions taken by the ONP to engage other interest groups in the agenda included the following:

- Direct mail from the office ("Here is the basic message; please spread and respond; please send input regarding any activities happening on the ground in your locale")
- Publications (the ONP electronic newsletter and editorials and columns in other nursing and health publications—both regular and by special request)
- Word of mouth (speeches, regional visits, interviews, and formal and informal gatherings and meetings)
- Bringing key people together (e.g., a National Stakeholder Consultation Meeting was hosted by the ONP in Toronto in the fall of 2000, and the proceedings of the meeting were widely shared)
- Direct dialogue with nursing organisations (e.g., the Canadian Nurses Association, the Canadian Practical Nurses Association, Registered Psychiatric Nurses groups, and the Canadian Federation of Nurses Unions)

Public Policy Deliberation and Adoption

When the wave of interest and support is great enough, the agenda needs to be deliberately moved to the tables where it can be debated and policy formulated. Kingdon (1995) says that once an issue is on the political agenda, it must meet five criteria if it is going to survive: technical feasibility, value acceptability within the policy community, tolerable cost, anticipated public agreement, and a reasonable chance for elected officials to be receptive to it.

At the time this chapter was written, the policy cycle for the Healthy Nurses, Healthy Workplaces agenda had progressed to this stage. The issue had appeared on public and government agendas, including the First Ministers' Meeting (September 11, 2000) and the Clair, Kirby, Fyke, and Romanow Commissions—the latter still to be completed. (Commission d'étude sur les services de santé et les services sociaux, 2000; Commission on Medicare, 2001; Standing Committee on Social Affairs, Science and Technology, 2001). A number of public documents have been initiated or are underway to address the matter, for example, the Advisory Committee on Health Human Resources Nursing Strategy for Canada (2000) new quality workplace indicators being developed by standards by the Canadian Council on Health Services Accreditation.

Still ahead lie the challenges of monitoring the health status of nurses. Mechanisms should be put in place to provide accurate, ongoing information to update the nursing and policy communities and to supplement—in greater detail—the Labour Force Survey. The establishment of a national Canadian Nursing Advisory Committee (CNAC)—first recommendation of the Nursing Strategy for Canada—represents an important step forward in the policy cycle. The CNAC has a mandate to make recommendations to improve quality of nursing work life, further strengthening the positioning of nurses and nursing in the health and human resources policy agenda.

Regulation, Experience, and Revision

In the final stage of the policy cycle, the proposed action becomes a formal policy, law, or regulation. This, in turn, becomes a new value or norm in the culture, which is routinely experienced and revised until the next issue comes along. During this phase, programme implementation and programme evaluation take place, and these processes may in turn generate new information to continue the cycle.

POLITICAL ACUMEN: THE DRIVE BEHIND POLICY MAKING

It is important to keep in mind that policymaking is not always—in fact, it is seldom—the rational, step-by-step process portrayed in the previous discussion. It is rarely driven by factual data or logical process. Rather, it is more often a value-driven, dynamic, and at times chaotic cascade of influence and decision-making behaviour. It is a process of social influence involving activities of persuasion, attitudinal change, decision making, and compromise (Mittelmark, 1999; Taylor, 1997). This is why the final requisite for influencing policy is political acumen.

Florence Nightingale stands out as the ultimate role model for nurses' use of political skill to influence policy for the benefit of patients. Milstead (1999) traces the current recognition of the importance of the links among nursing, politics, and policy to the 1960s and 1970s, when the explosion of social programmes and the raising of social consciousness alerted nurses to the value of political activity. Since that time, increasing numbers of nurses have realised that to control practise and to move the nursing profession forward as a major player in the health care arena, nursing and nurses need to become politically involved in influencing and formulating policy. Nursing colleagues in the United States have historically been more organised and more deliberate about this initiative than have Canadian nurses. For example, in 1992, the American Nurses Association (ANA) realised that decisions that affected nurses and their patients were made in Washington, DC, so it moved its national headquarters to that city. The ANA also accomplished the following:

- Created political action committees that developed processes for endorsing public officials
- Created a department of governmental affairs that employed registered lobbyists who developed ongoing relationships with elected and appointed officials and their staffs and undertook significant fundraising to support these activities
- Educated nurses about the political process through continuing education programmes
- Created senate and congressional district coordinators—nurses who volunteered to create relationships with their senators and representatives in order to serve as liaisons between legislators and organised nursing
- Created the Nurses Strategic Action Team (N-STAT), a grassroots network of nurses throughout the country who were informed when immediate action was needed and who responded quickly to their legislative representatives
- Promoted political appointments of nurses to key positions in government (Milstead 1999)

The Canadian Nurses Association (CNA) has undertaken similar, targeted political activities through the 1990s, including *Action 301*, aimed at ensuring that across Canada, nurses are actively engaging politicians on issues in each federal riding. Groups such as the CPNA and CFNU have also widened their activities to include more education of their members around policy and politics. In other words, evidence suggests that nurses and nurse leaders are rapidly awakening to the notion that the message and the timing really are as important as the content. According to Haylock, "for nurses to gain acceptance in health policy arenas, individual nurses and groups of nurses must become expert in assessing the environment, the interpretation of cues, and the development and implementation of realistic strategies targeting priority health policy and legislative issues" (2000, p. 76). To these suggested areas of expertise may be added the use of social networks, rhetoric, and the media. This section of this chapter discusses these means to enhance nursing's political acumen.

Helms and coauthors (1996) emphasise the need to understand how the *environment of policymaking shapes both the substance of policy change and the strategies needed for political adoption.* They advise that both the health care sector and the health care policy agenda are large, complex, and profoundly affected by current organisational behaviour. They offer a number of tips for nurses and nurse leaders to increase their chances of successfully influencing policy in this environment, three of which are offered here:

- Become "insiders" within the halls of policy formulation, so that you can identify and capitalise on opportunities of timing and design.
- Learn to formulate policy options with greater potential for adoption within the range of available resources and controllable variables. Understand what can be done, not just what should be done.
- Do not try to formulate specific policy objectives too broadly. Rather, strive to nudge policy forward in smaller ways that can incrementally improve the health of the population and the role of nurses.

West and Scott (2000) highlight the importance of social relationships in the policymaking process. They describe *policy networks* as formal or informal groups of politicians, civil servants, policy analysts, experts, and professionals that use their relationships to influence the formation and implementation of policy. Boundaries around the policy networks create "insider" and "outsider" roles, wherein insiders are needed by government for advice or cooperation in order to advance an item on the policy agenda. Nurses must maneuver to be included in policy networks as insiders; they can be successful in achieving this status on the basis either of their specialised knowledge or their ability to promote or thwart the aims and objectives of the policy-makers.

Hewison (1999) argues that if nurses become skilled in the art of rhetoric and combine this with a thorough understanding of the policy process, they can be more effective in shaping policy. *Rhetoric* is defined as communication with the objective of persuading or identifying with an audience to influence attitudes and behaviour. Hewison points out that language does more than simply reflect that which it attempts to describe; the act of labelling something plays a significant role in how that thing is acted towards. Therefore, if nurses become skilled at using rhetoric, they will become more effective in influencing and modifying policy that never makes it onto the policy tables, even though there are people who feel and speak passionately about them. Rather, there exists a complex agenda-setting process, which is an ongoing competition among the proponents of a set of issues, to gain the attention of media professionals, the public, and policymakers. Problems, these authors suggest, require exposure—coverage in the mass media—before they will be considered public issues and thus of sufficient importance to be addressed through policy. The Centre for Advancement of Health at the University of Calgary (2001) suggests the following tips for researchers in interacting with the media:

- Get the attention of media (be strategic!).
- Write an engaging news release.
- Think like a reporter.
- Prepare for and conduct successful interviews.

The CNA has published several useful documents for nurses wishing to enhance their knowledge and skills in the political arena, for example, *Getting Started: A Political Action Guide for Canada's Registered Nurses* (1997) and *Nursing is a Political Act: The Bigger Picture* (2000). Similar publications are available from a number of provincial RN and LPN associations as well as unions and other bodies. A good example is the Alberta Association of Registered Nurses' (AARN's) MLA Mentorship Program, which encourages registered nurses to engage and interact with elected representatives to promote understanding of AARN's positions and increase the individual nurse's understanding of ways that nurses can influence public health policy.

In 1996, several Centres of Excellence for Women's Health (CEWH) were established across Canada, with the goal to improve women's health. The Summer 2001 Research Bulletin of CEWH investigates the influence that the Centres have had on policy. Several of the articles describe mechanisms to "get the word out" and to ensure that research findings become part of policy debates. Processes used include media events, research symposia, websites, policy road shows, a dedicated research chair, and women's health awards. For example, the Montreal Centre hosted a symposium with caregivers' associations from various parts of the province of Quebec, and then took this information, along with 5 years of research experience on women caregivers and a coalition of interested groups, into public consultations to change policy at the local community-health level.

OVERCOMING BARRIERS: LESSONS FROM THOSE WHO HAVE WALKED BEFORE

In countless situations, nurses have been involved with change in general and the policy cycle in particular. Examples that illustrate many of the points made in this chapter follow.

Success Abroad

Aitken and co-workers (2001) describe the successful creation of a bill to fund a nurse home visitation programme for high-risk mothers in Arkansas. In summarising what allowed them to be successful in this policy initiative, the authors noted six factors:

1. Realistic time commitment
2. Community needs assessment, data assimilation, and review of existing resources
3. Identification and incorporation of stakeholders
4. Narrow focus on the area of greatest need
5. Backing of political partners
6. Favourable opportunities to advance child health issues

Valentine shares policymaking and political lessons learned in the course of a partially successful crusade to upgrade the chief nurse position in the U.S. Veterans Health Administration (VHA). Her insights and words of advice include the following:

1. Advocacy for a decision-making role in an organisation requires stamina and commitment and takes time, effort, and passion.
2. Changing organisational culture takes time and requires the involvement of senior-level champions.
3. Never underestimate the value of nonnurse advocates.
4. Never underestimate the value of turnover among one's adversaries.
5. Nurses are right most of the time, but not all of the time—we need to listen to criticisms more carefully.
6. Benchmarking is important, but may not be sufficient to call the question.
7. There is no such thing as overnight success. The key is hard work and never giving up (2000, pp. 45–46).

Success at Home

Nurses do not have to look south of the border for examples. Professional nurses and nursing organisations across Canada have been successful in influencing policy change in several different venues. Take the following examples:

1. As of mid-2002, Alberta was in the final stages of making adjustments to its Public Health Act to provide increased opportunities for nurse practitioners (NPs). Currently able to practise only in underserviced areas, the new legislation will permit Regional Health Authorities to engage the services of NPs wherever there is felt to be a need. The realisation of this project reflects the culmination of a careful, collaborative process spearheaded by the Alberta Association of Registered Nurses (AARN) but involving multiple partners. The project was given life within an environment of growing advocacy for primary health care—specifi-

cally, one in which the NP role in primary health care delivery was recognised as perhaps the most important initiative in health reform. In this case, the AARN recognised the opportunity and timing and led the policy lobby, governments worked collaboratively and enabled legislative changes, employers agreed to provide the actual employment and contractual arrangements, and nurse educators implemented the requisite NP programmes—all serving as a prime example of nurse-led policy change that took perfect advantage of timing, stakeholder interest, and political will.

2. In Quebec, the Ordre des Infirmiéres et infirmiers du Québec (2000) actively used its political clout to obtain government adoption of a regulation enabling second-year nursing students to be hired as "externs" for summer and holiday season vacation relief work. This regulation, which benefits both the nursing students and employers, resulted in nearly 1,200 students being hired by 50 institutions in its second year of operation.

3. In the late 1980s, in response to research and lobbying by nursing associations for nurses to have greater participation in the decisions that affected them, the Ontario Minister of Health introduced a new regulation to the Public Hospitals Act, mandating the seating of elected staff nurses and (s)elected nurse managers on all hospital committees dealing with administrative, financial, operational, and planning matters (Skelton-Green, 1996).

4. In Saskatchewan, the "Band Aid" campaign, led by student nurses and supported by the Saskatchewan Registered Nurses Association (SRNA), was significantly influential in forcing the provincial government to backtrack on an announced policy change that would have caused nursing education to revert from the baccalaureate degree to the diploma. In January 2000, the provincial government had said it could not support the SRNA's position on baccalaureate education as entry to practise for RNs and was going to look again at diploma programmes. Backed by SRNA, the student nurses sent postcards to every member of the legislative assembly as well as the Premier—as well as appearing in person on the steps of the legislature—asserting that reverting to diploma education was a "Band Aid" solution that would do nothing for nursing recruitment and retention in the long term. Eventually, the government dropped its plan and has since supported the SRNA in its position on minimal education for RNs.

5. In 1998, a Nursing Task Force was established to address concerns regarding the future supply and retention of registered nurses and registered practical nurses in Ontario. In 1999, in response to one of the two key recommendations of the taskforce, the Minister of Health and Long-Term Care created a $375 million Nursing Enhancement Fund (NEF). Over the next 2 years, the NEF supported more than 12,000 new nursing positions in the province (Joint Provincial Nursing Committee, 2001).

6. At the federal level, it was the successful lobbying of nurses, nursing organisations (such as the CNA), and individual nurse leaders that led to creation of the ONP and revival of the notion of a Chief Nurse for the country; the same holds true for jurisdictions as diverse as Nova Scotia, British Columbia, and New Brunswick.

These are just a few of dozens of success stories that were provided to the Office of Nursing Policy in response to a request for instances where nurses have influenced policy change. Clearly, nurses can make a difference!

OVERCOMING BARRIERS AND INITIATING ACTION

Nurses and the nursing profession are at the centre of public health issues that are of tremendous and long-lasting importance—issues such as who has access to what providers and what makes a difference in quality and cost-effectiveness of care. There are also issues crucial to the future of the nursing profession, such as who will be the gatekeeper in primary care, and what is the appropriate scope of practise for RNs, LPNs, and RPNs across various service sectors. As Milstead (1999) says in *Health Policy and Politics: A Nurse's Guide*:

> Nurses are articulate experts who can address both the rational shaping of policy and the emotional aspects of the process. Nurses cannot afford to limit their actions to monitoring bills; they must seize the initiative and use their considerable collective and individual influence to ensure the health, welfare, and protection of the public and health care professionals (p. 23).

She goes on to say,

> The opportunity to sustain an ongoing, meaningful dialogue with those who represent [us] . . . and those who administer public programs is ours to initiate. Nurses must become indispensable to elected and appointed officials (p. xi).

Milstead contends that nurses who have been reluctant to become "political" cannot afford to do so any longer. She emphasises that "each nurse counts, and collectively, nursing is a major actor in the effort to ensure the country's healthy future" (Milstead 1999, p. 34). Gebbie and coauthors (2000) suggest several strategies that individual nurses can use to influence policy formulation:

- Cultivate and maintain relationships with knowledgeable and influential people.
- Become knowledgeable about current developments on policy-relevant issues.
- Join professional nursing organisations.
- Develop network strategies to mentor political neophytes.
- Share the "how to" success stories of individual nurses and nursing organisations in the policy arena.
- Create linkages between nursing research and political and policy-related activity.
- Develop clear, well-informed, jargon-free communication when interacting with policymakers.
- Capitalise on the positive views that communities have of the nursing profession by being visible at forums and other community meetings.

If individual nurses can do this much, organised nursing groups can accomplish even more. For example, Gebbie and coauthors (2000) suggest that representatives from nursing organisations could develop an annual national institute for policy to bring nurse's best research into the policy arena. Professional nursing organisations could set aside time at national meetings to allow nurses to converse about health policy strategies and activities and include planned discussions of ways nurses can effectively influence health policy at individual and organisational levels. Individuals in these organisations should become experts in interacting with the media and positioning their work to draw media attention.

There are several reasons that it is essential for nurses to be involved in influencing policy. "Together, RNs, LPNs and RPNs account for more than a third" of the health workforce (CIHI, 2001b, p. 10) and provide some 75% of the paid care delivered in the system. Nurses are the best-educated and largest group of professional women in the world. Nurses know about health and health care; indeed, nurses are the health care system in many countries. Nurses know about communities and people. And finally, surveys repeatedly show that nurses are highly respected by the public (Pollara Canada, 1998). Only in the wake of the events of September 11, 2001, have fire fighters threatened to overtake nurses in that top position. There is no group in a better position than nurses to make a difference. And so, this chapter concludes with a challenge to all nurses to think about ways in which they can positively influence health policy, both individually and collectively and wherever they practise.

SUMMARY

Effective policy is best linked with research findings. In health care, an example of what happens when policy does not factor in research is the recurrent cycle of nursing shortages.

Research indicates what nurses want and need in their work environments to optimise their contributions to health care, but these findings went unheeded when policymakers implemented workforce cutbacks.

A variety of levers can be used to effect change and influence health care policy. They include good research, effective links between research and policy, understanding how to initiate and manage change, and understanding the policy cycle and political savvy.

Research is more likely to be translated into policy if researchers, policy analysts, managers, and politicians negotiate the language and frame of reference before research is undertaken.

Keys to effecting change are appreciation and understanding of the policy cycle, which includes agenda setting, legislation and regulation, programme implementation, and programme evaluation. Behind the development of policy are values and cultural beliefs from which certain problems or issues emerge. Ideally, interested parties then build knowledge and research related to the problems or issues; they bring the knowledge to the attention of the public, become politically active in various arenas, and participate in the activation of interest groups. Public deliberation and adoption of policy related to the issues ensues, and ongoing regulation, revision, and refinement of the policy follow. A component of most successful policies is political acumen, a process of social influence involving activities of persuasion, attitudinal change, decision making, and compromise.

Valuable tools and tactics for successful policymaking include ongoing positive relationships with knowledgeable and influential people; interest in and understanding of current developments in policy-relevant issues; activity in professional nursing organisations; networking and mentoring; sharing success stories and promoting previously successful strategies; creating links between nursing research and political and policy-related activity; communicating clearly and intelligently with policymakers; and capitalising on nursing's positive aspects and image in the community.

Online RESOURCES

Add to your knowledge of this issue:

Canadian Council on Health Services Accreditation	**www.cchsa.ca**
Canadian Federation of Nurses Unions	**www.cfnu.ca**
Canadian Health Services Research Foundation	**www.chsrf.ca**
Canadian Institutes of Health Research	**www.cihr.ca**
Canadian Nurses Association	**www.cna.ca**
Canadian Nursing Students Association	**www.cnsa.ca**
Canadian Practical Nurses Association	**www.cpna.ca**
Canadian Women's Health Network	**www.cwhn.ca**
Commission on the Future of Health Care in Canada	**www.healthcarecommission.ca**
Health Canada	**www.hc-sc.gc.ca**

Reflections on the Chapter

1. Think of an existing health care policy that you consider successful. What kind of research, if any, do you think is linked to this policy? What factors do you think make the policy successful?

2. Alone or with a group of classmates, select a problem or an issue that you have encountered in your own experience as a nursing student or in related situations. What kind of action plan do you think would be effective in building a policy to address the issue(s).

REFERENCES

Advisory Committee on Health Human Resources (ACHHR) (2000). *The nursing strategy for Canada.* Ottawa, ON: Health Canada Publications.

Aiken, L. H., Smith, H. L., & Lake, E. T. (1994). Lower Medicare mortality among a set of hospitals known for good nursing care. *Medical Care, 32*(8), 771–787.

Aiken, L. H., Salmon, M., Shamian, J., Giovannetti, P., Muller-Mundt, G., & Hunt J. (1998). *An international study of the effects of the organization and staffing of hospitals on patient outcomes.* Presentation at Outcomes/Indicators April 1998 Session, WHO, CCNM, Korea.

Aitken, M. E., Rowlands, L. A., & Wheeler, J. G. (2001). Advocating for children's health at the state level: Lessons learned. *Archives of Pediatrics and Adolescent Medicine, 155*(8), 877–880.

Akyeampong, E. B. (1999). Missing work in 1998: Industry differences. In *Perspectives on labour and income.* Statistics Canada, Cat. No. 75-001-XPE.11(3):30–36.

Baumann, A., O'Brien Pallas, L., Armstrong-Stassen, M., Blythe, J., Bourbonnais, R., Cameron, S., Doran, D., Kerr, M., McGillis Hall, L., Vezina, M., Butt, M., & Ryan, L. (2001). *Commitment and care: The benefits of a healthy workplace for nurses, their patients and the system. A policy synthesis.* Ottawa: Canadian Health Services Research Foundation & the Change Foundation.

Blegen, M. A., & Mueller, C. W. (1987). Nurses' job satisfaction: A longitudinal analysis. *Nursing and Health, 10,* 227–237.

Browne, G. (2001). *Key findings from the System-Linked Research Unit on Health and Social Service Utilization.* Presented to the Advisory Committee on Health Human Resources' Working Group on Nursing & Unregulated Healthcare Workers. Ottawa, ON. October 24, 2001.

Canadian Institute for Health Information. (2001a). An environmental scan of research transfer strategies. *Canadian Population Health Initiative,* February. Ottawa, ON: Canadian Institute for Health Information.

Canadian Institute for Health Information. (2001b). *Canada's health care providers*. Ottawa, ON: Canadian Institute for Health Information.

Canadian Labour and Business Centre (2002). *Full-time equivalents and financial costs associated with absenteeism, overtime, and involuntary part-time employment in the nursing profession: A report prepared for the Canadian Nursing Advisory Committee*. Ottawa ON: Author.

Canadian Nurses Association. (1997). *Getting started: A political action guide for Canada's Registered Nurses*. Ottawa, ON: Author.

Canadian Nurses Association. (2000). Nursing is a political act: The bigger picture. *Nursing Now. Issues and Trends in Canadian Nursing*, Issue #8. Ottawa, ON: Author.

Centre for the Advancement of Health (2001). *Communicating health behaviour science in the media: Tips for researchers*. Washington DC: Author.

Centres of Excellence for Women's Health (2001). *Research Bulletin 2*(1), Summer edition.

Cheek, J., & Gibson, T. (1997). Policy matters: Critical policy analysis and nursing. *Journal of Advanced Nursing, 25*(4), 668–672.

Chunharas, S. (2001). Linking research to policy and action. In Neufeld N., & Johnson, N. (eds.) *Forging links for health research: Perspectives from the Council on Health Research for Development*. Ottawa, ON: International Development Research Centre.

Clarke, H., Giovannetti, P., & Shamian, J. (1998). *Outcomes of hospital staffing: A cross-national study*. Presentation at Canadian Nurses Association Biennial Convention, June 1998, Ottawa, Ontario.

Clarke, H. F., Lashinger, H. S., Giovannetti, P., Shamian, J., Thomson, D., & Tourangeau, A. (2001). Nursing shortages: Workplace environments are essential to the solution. *Hospital Quarterly 4*(3), 50–55.

Commission d'étude sur les services de santé et les services sociaux. (2000). *Les solutions émergentes: Rapport et recommandations*. Québec, QC. Gouvernement du Québec. ISBN 2-550-36958-0.

Commission on Medicare (2001). *Caring for Medicare: Sustaining a quality system*. Regina, SK: Government of Saskatchewan. ISBN 0-9687942-1-1.

Crosswaite, C., & Curtice, L. (1994). Disseminating research results: The challenge of bridging the gap between health research and health action. *Health Promotion International, 9*(4): 289–296.

Dannemiller, K. D., & Jacobs, R. W. (1992). Changing the way organizations change: A revolution of common sense. *Journal of Applied Behavioral Science, 28*(4) 480–498.

Davis, P., & Howden-Chapman, P. (1996). Translating research findings into health policy. *Social Science and Medicine, 43*, 865–872.

Dearing, J. W., & Rogers, E. M. (1996). *Agenda-setting*. Thousand Oaks, CA: Sage Publications.

Feldman, P. H., Nadash, P., & Gursen, M. (2001). Improving communication between researchers and policy makers in long-term care: Or, Researchers are from Mars; policy makers are from Venus. *The Gerontologist, 41*(3): 312–321.

Gebbie, K. M., Wakefield, M., & Kerfoot, K. (2000). Nursing and health policy. *Journal of Nursing Scholarship, 32*(3), 307–315.

Hartz, A. J., Krakauer, H., Kuhn, E. M., Young, M., Jacobson, S. J., Gay, G., Muenz, L., Katzoff, M., Bailey, R. C., & Romm, A. A. (1989). Hospital characteristics and mortality rates. *New England Journal of Medicine, 321*, 1720–1725.

Haylock, P. J. (2000). Health policy and legislation: Impact on cancer nursing and care. *Seminars in Oncology Nursing, 16*(1), 76–84.

Helms, L. B., Anderson, M. A., & Hanson, K. (1996). "Doin' politics": linking policy and politics in nursing. *Nursing Administration Quarterly, 20*(3), 32–41.

Hewison, A. (1999). The new public management and the new nursing: Related by rhetoric. Some reflections on the policy process and nursing. *Journal of Advanced Nursing, 29*(6), 1377–1384.

Irvine, D., & Evans, M. (1992). *Job satisfaction and turnover among nurses: A review and meta-analysis*. Toronto, ON: Quality of Worklife Research Unit, University of Toronto.

Joint Provincial Nursing Committee (JPNC) (2001). *Good nursing, good health: A good investment. First progress report on The Nursing Task Force recommendations*. Toronto, ON: Ministry of Health and Long-Term Care.

Kimball, B., & O'Neil, E. (2001). The evolution of a crisis: Nursing in America. *Policy, Politics & Nursing Practice 2*(3), 180–186.

Kingdon, J. W. (1995). *Agendas, alternatives, and public policies*. New York, NY: HarperCollins College Publishers.

Knaus, W. A., Draper, E. A., Wagner, D. P., & Zimmerman, J. E. (1986). An evaluation of outcome from intensive care in major medical centers. *Annals of Internal Medicine, 104*, 410–418.

Lomas, J. (2000). Using 'linkage and exchange' to move research into policy at a Canadian foundation. *Health Affairs (Chevy Chase), 19*(3), 236–240.

McGillis Hall, L., Irvine Doran, D., Baker, G. R., Pink, G. H., Sidani, S., O'Brien-Pallas, L., & Donner, G. J. (2001). *A study of the impact of nursing staff mix models and organizational change strategies on patient, system and nurse outcomes*. Toronto, ON: University of Toronto.

Milstead, J. A. (1999). *Health policy and politics: A nurse's guide*. Gaithersburg, MD: Aspen.

Mittelmark, M. B. (2001). The psychology of social influence and healthy public policy. *Preventive Medicine, 29*(6 Pt. 2), S24–S29.

Montini, T., & Bero, L. A. (2001). Policy makers' perspectives on tobacco control advocates' roles in regulation development. *Tobacco Control, 10*(3), 218–224.

O'Brien-Pallas, L., Thomson, D., Alksnis, C., & Bruce, S. (2001). The economic impact of nurse staffing decisions: Time to turn down another road? *Hospital Quarterly 4*(2),42—50.

Ordre des infirmiéres et infirmiers du Québec. (2000). *Le financement et l'organisation des services de santé et des services sociaux.* Mémoire présenté á la Commission d'étude sur les services de santé et les services sociaux. Montréal, QC: Author.

Pollara Canada (1998). Perspectives Canada Poll. Quarter 2.

Prescott, P. A. (1993). Nursing: An important component of hospital survival under a reformed health care system. *Nursing Economics, 11,* 192–199.

Price, J. L., & Mueller, C. W. (1981). A causal model of turnover for nurses. *Academy of Management Journal, 24*(3), 543–565.

Scott, J. G., Sochalski, J., & Aiken, L. (1999). Review of magnet hospital research. *JONA, 29*(1), 9–19.

Shamian, J., & Chalmers, B. (1996). *Nurse effectiveness: Health and cost-effective nursing services.* Review of literature and policy and organizational recommendations. The Global Network of WHO Collaborating Centres for Nursing/Midwifery Development. Toronto, Ontario.

Skelton-Green, J. M. (1996). The perceived impact of committee participation on the job satisfaction and retention of staff nurses. *Canadian Journal of Nursing Administration, 9*(2), 7–35.

Slavitt, B. B., Stamps, P. L., Piedmont, E. G., & Haase, A. M. (1978). Nurses' satisfaction with their work situation. *Nursing Research, 27,* 114–120.

Standing Committee on Social Affairs, Science and Technology (2001). *The Health of Canadians: The federal role (interim report).* Ottawa, ON. Government of Canada.

Tarlov, A. (1999). Public policy frameworks for improving population health. *Annals of the New York Academy of Sciences, 896,* 281–293.

Tarlov, A. (2000). *The future of health in Canada: "The art of the possible."* Proceedings of the 69th Annual Couchiching Summer Conference, August 10–13, 2000, Geneva Park, Orillia, Ontario.

Taylor, C. (1997). The ACIDD test: A framework for policy planning and decision-making. *Optimum, The Journal of Public Sector Management, 27*(4), 53–62.

Valentine, N. M. (2000). The evolving role of the chief nurse executive in the Veterans Health Administration: Policy and leadership lessons. *Policy, Politics, and Nursing Practice, 1*(1), 36–46.

West, E., & Scott, C. (2000). Nursing in the public sphere: Breaching the boundary between research and policy. *Journal of Advanced Nursing, 32*(4), 817–824.

PART II

Regulatory Power

CHAPTER 6

International Council of Nurses

Geertje Boschma ▪ Barbara Brush ▪ Meryn Stuart

Chapter Objectives

At the completion of this chapter, you will be able to:

1. Reflect on the history of the ICN.
2. Identify selected roles and objectives of the ICN.
3. Understand ICN's relationship to world health.
4. Discuss some of the current issues facing the ICN.
5. Analyse selected ICN strategies to address these issues.

Delegates register at the 1997 ICN Congress held in Vancouver, BC, Canada (with permission from the Lynaugh Collection, Bryn Mawr, PA; In Brush, B. L., Lynaugh, J. E., Boschma, G., Rafferty, A. M., Stuart, M., & Tomes, N. J. [1999]. *Nurses of all nations: A history of the International Council of Nurses, 1899–1999*. Philadelphia: Lippincott Williams & Wilkins).

This chapter presents an historical perspective of the development of the International Council of Nurses (ICN) and discusses its current objectives in the broader historical context of the evolution of organized nursing. Specifically, the chapter reviews the history of the ICN in relationship to its contributions to world health and its initiatives to support national regulation of the nursing profession within ICN membership countries. Some examples of current issues facing the ICN and ICN responses to them are also discussed.

THE ICN: AN HISTORICAL PERSPECTIVE

In 1999, at the ICN Centennial Conference in London, England, the ICN celebrated its 100 years of existence as an international organisation for nurses. For more than a century, the ICN has sustained its place as an important and meaningful organisation for nurses from around the world. The overall goal of the ICN is to unite nurses world wide by forming a confederation of national nursing organizations. The ICN supports national nursing organizations in their effort to influence national health and nursing policy. Motivation, commitment, and enthusiasm banded nurses together despite turbulent social and economic changes, hardships of war, and profound cultural differences. Currently the ICN represents national nursing organisations of more than 120 countries with more than 1 million members. Yet, the ICN started out as a small organisation in the broader context of the women's movement. It was founded in 1899, upon the initiative of the British nurse and suffragist Ethel Gordon Manson, later Mrs. Bedford Fenwick, a prominent leader of the British Nurses Association (BNA).

Early Goals

From the outset, the professional welfare of nurses, the interests of women and the improvement of the people's health were intertwined goals for the founders of the ICN. A small group consisting primarily of British, American, Canadian, Scandinavian and German nurses, the ICN intended to unite nurses worldwide through an international organisation. Nursing as a respected, paid professional occupation for women from the middle class was a new phenomenon at the end of the 19th century.

Health care profoundly changed as a result of industrialization and urbanization. Hospital reform and modern hospital developments in the new world were important goals throughout Europe and North America at the time. The foundation of hospital schools for the professional training of nurses followed in its wake. The women's movement sprung in part from the desire of middle class women to make themselves more socially useful and carve out respectable work opportunities in areas deemed appropriate for women, thereby extending women's traditional roles in the family, such as care of the sick, teaching, and social work. The founding members of the ICN were part of the growing number of women who were active in social and health care reform and who simultaneously sought to improve women's social position and obtain the right to vote.

On July 1, 1899, Fenwick attended the Annual Conference of the Matron's Council of Great Britain and Ireland in London, where 200 women and nurses from around the world had gathered. At this meeting, she proposed organizing an international council of nurses, modeled after the International Council of Women (ICW). The next day, she

FIGURE 6.1.   Founder and charter members of the ICN (left to right): founding President Ethel Gordon Fenwick (Britain), Secretary Lavinia L. Dock (USA), and Treasurer Agnes Snively. (Photos of Ethel Gordon Fenwick reproduced with permission from Dock, L. L. *History of nursing* (Vol. 3) (1912); of Lavinia Dock, from Lynaugh Collection, Bryn Mawr, PA; of Agnes Snively, from Bridges (1967) *History of the International Council of Nurses;* in Brush, B. L., Lynaugh, J. E., Boschma, G., Rafferty, A. M., Stuart, M., & Tomes, N. J. (1999). *Nurses of all nations: A history of the International Council of Nurses, 1899–1999.* Philadelphia: Lippincott Williams & Wilkins.)

instituted a provisional committee to draft a constitution. Among the founders were Lavinia L. Dock, a nurse and activist in the women's movement from the USA and Agnes Snively, an influential Canadian nurse, as well as various representatives from Australia, Denmark, the Netherlands, New Zealand and the Union of South Africa. A year later the constitution was approved, with Fenwick elected president, Lavinia L. Dock secretary, and Canadian Agnes Snively treasurer (Fig. 6.1).

The ICN held its first meeting in 1901 in Buffalo, New York (USA), at the Pan American Exposition and met again 3 years later in Berlin in conjunction with the Congress of the ICW. This time, German nurses, inspired by nurse leader Agnes Karll joined the group as well.

Very much aware of the need to establish their independence as a predominantly female professional group and to run their own affairs free from hospital, medical or state control, the early leaders envisioned the ICN as a federation of national nurses' organisation, headed by a nurse, representing nurses only. However, at that time, nurses in most countries had not organized on a national level. At the 1904 meeting only Germany, Great Britain, and the USA were ready for confederation.

The ICN requirement that only self-regulated bodies of nurses could join the ICN in many ways stimulated the formation of independent national nursing organisations. For example, Canadian nurse leaders were organized jointly with their United States colleagues until that time. After the Berlin meeting, however, Agnes Snively, who served as director of the influential Toronto General Hospital School of Nursing from 1884 until 1910, helped form the Canadian National Association of Trained Nurses, later the Canadian Nurses Association (Canadian Nurses Association, 1968). Canada joined the ICN at the next ICN Congress in 1909, held again in London, with nursing associations from the Netherlands, Finland, and Denmark.

As nurses organized, their commitment to creating an international body of nurses became evident. Indeed, influenced by their involvement in the women's movement, the founding leaders believed that an international organisation of nurses would improve their professional standing and unite their efforts to develop a firm basis for nursing education and practise. They argued that if nursing practise met universal standards and was protected by state regulation, nurses, as women, could make a crucial contribution to social progress and the improvement of people's health. The examples of professional nursing already developed in North American or Western Europe inspired the founding leaders. In a sense, their ideas reflected Western cultural dominance typical of international politics at the time. The early ICN leaders—all from American and Western European backgrounds—were strongly committed to spreading the international idea of nursing.

Early Impact of Organised Nursing: Developments in German Nursing

The establishment of the German Nurses Association (*Berufsorganisations der Krankenpflegerinnen Deutschlands*), and its involvement with the ICN during the early decades, exemplifies the significance of international relationships for the development of nursing within diverse national contexts (Boschma, 1996). Agnes Karll (1868–1927), the influential president of the German Nurses Association, energetically sought to change contemporary conditions of nursing by creating opportunities for a respected, independent paid career for German nurses. The situation of the German nurses illustrates the wider social and political impact on nursing during the World War I period.

The work opportunities and social position for German nurses changed profoundly at the turn of the 20th century as a result of rapid population growth, industrialization, changing health needs in the population, and in response, a changing role for women. By 1900 Germany was one of the largest industrial powers of Europe. Religious and charitable nursing orders provided most nursing care to the sick in Germany. The situation in Germany at that time was comparable to the situation in Canada, where the Grey Nuns were among the leaders in establishing modern nursing (Paul, 1994). Roman Catholic orders had flourished in Germany since the early decades of the 19th century. Eventually, Protestants followed the Catholic example by reviving the function of the deaconess. The most famous deaconess institute was in Kaiserswerth, established by Theodor Fliedner in 1836. Organized in a motherhouse structure, the institute enabled deaconesses to pursue a socially accepted public role. However, in the rapidly changing social context of the early 20th century, the motherhouse system was unable to meet the increasing demand for nurses. Especially in the cities, many nurses separated themselves from motherhouses and began to work either in private duty or in municipal hospitals. A new generation of nurses sought economic independence and an autonomous life. Yet, the "free" nurses, as those who had separated themselves from motherhouses were called, risked their reputations and remained vulnerable, since they were largely unprotected and prone to exploitation. Moreover, in the urban hospitals, work conditions were harsh. Many nurses experienced poor physical or mental health at early ages (Lungershausen, 1964; Bischoff, 1984).

With the founding of the German Nurses Association in 1903, Agnes Karll sought to change the situation of the independent nurses. She had obtained training in nursing at the Clementinen House in Hannover, a Red Cross motherhouse, and then worked in private duty nursing in Berlin. Yet, by 1901, the hard work had weakened her physical condition and at the age of 33, she was forced to abandon private duty. Thereafter, Karll devoted herself to the betterment of nurses' social conditions. Through her connections with the women's movement, she gradually came to envision an avenue towards self-organisation for nurses and arranged for the founding meeting of the German Nurses Association in Berlin. One of the German Nurses Association's key functions was to create an employment bureau to actively protect and mediate the placement of nurses in private duty.

Karll's efforts attracted the interest of the ICN leaders and led to the German Nurses Association's acceptance into the ICN at the Berlin meeting in 1904. The connection with international colleagues was a valuable resource for Karll. She perceived the accomplishments of American and British colleagues as a model for German nurses. She corresponded regularly with Lavinia L. Dock, the ICN secretary, to discuss German nursing affairs.

In 1909, at the second quinquennial ICN Congress in London, England, Agnes Karll was elected president. The Congress strongly supported women's suffrage and recommended that each national group advocate for state regulation of nursing practise. Although the ICN did not retain a regulatory function itself, it supported the establishment of state regulation through its member national nursing organisations. Upon an invitation by the German nurses, the ICN held its next congress in Cologne, Germany, in 1912. There, the urgency of improving nurses' social welfare and working conditions was widely debated. In particular, the keynote speech addressed the effects of physical strain and fatigue on nurses' health. In addition, the objectives of suffrage, nurses' expanding role in social progress and public health, and improving nurses' work conditions preoccupied the minds of the ICN delegates. Delegates also discussed the need for common standards of nursing and for clear criteria to join the ICN.

Finding common working ground and bridging the diverse national contexts of nursing took considerable effort by ICN members (Brush & Stuart, 1994). Despite the enthusiasm for the nursing cause, stability within the ICN was threatened by unstable international politics prior to the beginning of the First World War. In Cologne, delegates elected American Annie Goodrich, inspector of nurse training schools in New York, as the fourth president and decided to have their next meeting in San Francisco in 1915. However, growing political tension soon disrupted this plan.

The Interwar Years

World War I abruptly interrupted the innovative initiatives of the ICN. Because of the devastating war situation with many nurses mobilized for war service, the 1915 Congress never happened. With members suddenly divided on opposite sites of the world conflict, the ICN's deliberate neutral stand toward national politics was compromised. At a much smaller business meeting in 1915, delegates elected Henny Tscherning from war-neutral Denmark as the new president, forming the beginning of a more prominent northern European presence among the ICN leadership in the interwar years. Tscherning, a founding member and president of the Danish Council of Nurses, was instrumental in connecting nurses in the Northern European countries. In 1920, she co-founded the Northern Nurses Federation (Wingender, 1995). Tscherning and the Scandinavian national organisations provided continuity in turbulent times and kept the ICN idea going.

ICN members did not meet again until 1922 when the Fourth Regular ICN Meeting was held in Copenhagen, Denmark. Tscherning's leadership facilitated a gradual shift away from the strong dominance of Anglo-American leadership in the ICN. The unity of the Nordic nurses probably strengthened the role of Northern European leaders. In Copenhagen, another Scandinavian nurse, Sophie Mannerheim of Finland, was elected president. She was one of the early presidents of the Finnish national nurses' association, founded in 1898. She played a central role in international nursing activities for more than 25 years. The eminent Christiane Reimann from Denmark became secretary, replacing Lavinia L. Dock, who had been in the position for 22 years.

In assuming this role, Reimann also became the first paid ICN secretary. She travelled frequently to facilitate the establishment of national nursing councils and often contributed from personal funds to maintain ICN activities and publication of the *ICN Bulletin*. What started as a small newsletter, regularly sent to all members, gradually evolved into a professional international nursing journal. Today, the *International Nursing Review* is the official journal of the ICN and is published six times per year.

In 1922, the ICN now represented 15 countries, including India, New Zealand, Belgium, China, Italy, Norway and South Africa. Prior contact with Anglo-European nursing influence and direction was a key feature in many countries' successful linkage with the ICN. Russia, unlike China, for example, never joined the ICN. However, Western powers controlled China at the time and facilitated the establishment of a Western health care system, even though traditional Chinese medicine did not disappear (Chen, 1996). Along with the creation of Western hospitals, training schools for nurses were opened in China and were often directed by American or European nurses. In 1914, a Chinese national nurses organisation was founded; it joined the ICN in 1922.

Sophie Mannerheim turned out to be the right leader to navigate the ICN through complex post-World War One nursing politics. Revolutions spread over Europe at that time and intense nationalism characterized international politics. Economic malaise and political unrest created complex problems. Tuberculosis and high infant mortality threatened public health. The Red Cross established many new schools of nursing in Eastern European countries to meet the pressing demand for qualified nurses. Many times, British or North American nurses headed these schools and formed linkages with the ICN. Red Cross standards of nurse training, however, did not necessarily match ICN ideals and created considerable debate within the ICN. To meet demands for military nursing, the Red Cross had instituted many short training programmes, which exacerbated tension over standardization of nurse training and legal regulation of nursing practise. At that time, various European countries that were not ICN members founded the European Council of Nursing Education (ECNE), whose perspective on nursing education also varied from that of the ICN. The various organisations maintained competing ideas over nursing education and work, differing substantially from the ICN's proposed standardization of a 3-year nurse training period. Mannerheim, participating in both the Red Cross and the ICN, was an excellent mediator in these politics and ensured the role of the ICN in international health affairs.

Effect of Worldwide Depression on Nursing

By the time the ICN reached some stability in the 1930s, the worldwide economic depression impacted nursing. Unemployment of nurses was high on the agenda of the ICN Paris–Brussels Congress in 1933, and debates on dues and monetary exchange rates also reflected difficult financial times. At that meeting Austrian Princess Anna Schwarzenberg became the new executive secretary and Alicia Lloyd Still from Great Britain was elected president. The ICN counted 30 member countries, growing increasingly diverse in cultural and political backgrounds, which gradually confuted the dominance of Western countries in ICN affairs. Soon however, threat of war once again determined ICN's leaders' action. The rise of National Socialism in Germany ended the independence of the German Nurses Association, which dissolved into the Reich's Union of German Nurses and Nursing Assistants in 1939. In that same year, the World War II broke out as Hitler overran Poland.

Effie Taylor, elected ICN president in 1937 in London, made sure that ICN records and office materials, which just had been moved to new headquarters in London, were transported to the United States. She temporarily established an ICN office at her own workplace at Yale University in New Haven, Connecticut (USA). The London ICN offices were destroyed by bombs in 1941; all ICN meetings had to be postponed.

ROLES, OBJECTIVES, AND SCOPE OF THE ICN AFTER WORLD WAR II

In 1947, the ICN was able to again meet in Atlantic City, New Jersey (USA) for the ninth ICN Congress. More than 40 countries participated and Gerda Hojer from Sweden was elected president. Delegates decided to return ICN headquarters to London, and within 2 months ICN opened new offices at the site of the British College of Nurses at 19 Queens Gate—a building undergoing repairs because of war damage. By 1948, Daisy Bridges, former president of the National Council of Nurses of Great Britain and Northern Ireland, was appointed as executive secretary, serving the ICN for the next 13 years and moving the work of the ICN increasingly into the international field.

Alice Sher, former president of the International Nurses Screening Board, became ICN's assistant general secretary. Sher's prior role was to oversee the Displaced Persons (Nurses) Register which the ICN had taken over from the International Relief Organisation. The board of this organisation determined the professional status of nurses who had lost their credentials during the war. Sher was ultimately instrumental in helping thousands of displaced nurse refugees to continue their professional careers.

The disruption, destruction, and political realignments of the two world wars resulted in profound social change and ultimately changed the postwar identity of the ICN. The organisation struggled to regain normalcy as many member associations had changed, others no longer existed, and some rejoined under new circumstances. However, still inspired by its commitment, the ICN regrouped and set a new, ambitious agenda at the 1947 meeting. Two years later the ICN celebrated its 50th anniversary at a conference in Stockholm. Three member associations whose activities had been suspended during the war years—Australia, Germany, and Japan—were reinstated. Five new national organisations joined—Haiti, Italy, Korea, South Rhodesia, and Turkey.

In the 1950s, the ICN assumed a more activist role, linking with other international organisations, such as the United Nations and the World Health Organisation (WHO). To carry out its many new international responsibilities, ICN raised its dues and staff members undertook a series of visits to national organisations to strengthen international ties. In response to postwar changes, the initial voluntary approach to international organisation gave way to a professional way of running ICN affairs. Gradually the ICN's board put in place more adequate staff and facilities, hiring professionally trained and qualified staff to carry out its growing number of programmes and activities, and reflecting a more prosperous situation.

ICN Vision Affirmed

Some issues, on the agenda since the beginning of the ICN, remained: educational standards of professional nurses; the meaning of national nursing respresentation; and financial matters. On the definition of nursing, a certain consensus was reached. The powerful statement on the unique function of the nurse formulated by Virginia Henderson (Fig. 6.2) became the basis for the ICN's vision statement on nursing. Henderson's influence was largely due to her leadership status in U.S. nursing. A longtime faculty member of the Department of Nursing at Teachers' College, Columbia University (New York, USA), Henderson moved away from detailed descriptions of separate

FIGURE 6.2. Virginia Henderson (with permission from American Journal of Nursing Collection; In Brush, B. L., Lynaugh, J. E., Boschma, G., Rafferty, A. M., Stuart, M., & Tomes, N. J. (1999). *Nurses of all nations: A history of the International Council of Nurses, 1899–1999.* Philadelphia: Lippincott Williams & Wilkins).

nursing tasks to a comprehensive perspective on the goals of nursing: "The unique function of the nurse is to assist the individual, sick or well, in the performance of those activities contributing to health or its recovery (or to a peaceful death) that he would perform unaided if he had the necessary strength, will or knowledge" (Lynaugh & Brush, 1999).

Later ICN definitions of nursing and restatements of its vision would remain faithful to this early work. At the occasion of its 60th anniversary, at the ICN meeting in Helsinki in 1959, the ICN Board approved Virginia Henderson's publication *Basic Principles of Nursing Care* as a core publication on behalf of the ICN Nursing Service Division. Within 5 years, the booklet had been translated into 12 languages. Eventually it would become a classic nursing text translated into more than 30 languages.

A new internationalism in the 1950s gradually displayed a shift in ICN leadership away from Anglo-European control. Much of this shift coincided with the introduction of new member associations from a broader contingency of nations. Better economic circumstances and conditions for women's work, for example, enhanced nurses' ability to create organisations in Africa, Asia, South America, and Latin America. In 1957, more than 3,000 nurses from 57 countries attended the congress in Rome. The national nurses associations of Barbados, Colombia, Ethiopia, Iran, Liberia, Malaysia, Panama and Uruguay were admitted, while Yugoslavia rejoined and Israel's membership was also confirmed. Cold War barriers, however, prevented membership in Eastern European countries, Russia, and China (Fig. 6.3).

Increasing Activism: Position Statements

The increasingly activist role of the ICN impacted its political course. At the international meetings, the ICN began to adopt *position statements* that publicly articulated the membership's point of view related on nursing and health matters such as "the nurse's role in family planning," or "smoking and health." Also, more political statements were accepted on topics such as "activities of war and their influence on person-

FIGURE 6.3. More and more nurses from more and more nations joined the delegates arriving at INC congress of 1965 held in Frankfurt (with permission from American Journal of Nursing Collection; in Brush, B.L., Lynaugh, J. E.,Boschma, G., Rafferty, A. M., Stuart, M., Tomes, N. J. (1999). *Nurses of all nations: A history of the International Council of Nurses, 1899–1999.* Philadelphia: Lippincott Williams & Wilkins).

ality development of children and adolescents" (International Council of Nurses, 2001a). Position statements had political implications. The aim was that national nursing organisations would strive towards implementing the suggestions made in the statements within their country. In doing this, nurses at the national level would have to influence national health policy and to develop strategies for nursing action.

However, an increasing political course created new dilemmas. While the ICN claimed neutrality in the national affairs of its member countries, a profound internal conflict arose within the ICN over the membership of South Africa. The South African Nurses Association (SANA) adhered to its country's apartheid directives, inhibiting nonwhite membership into the organisation. Faithful to the ICN standpoint on racial matters, some member organisations insisted that SANA open up membership to all nurses irrespective of racial background or national law. Eventually the Dutch and Swedish national organisations moved that the ICN accept a resolution to expel South Africa from membership; the resolution was passed in 1974. By declaring itself against racism, the ICN also disapproved of the internal politics of one of its member associations. As a consequence the ICN lost one of its earliest members (Rafferty & Brush, 1995). Today a newly integrated South African national nursing organisation (DENOSA) is an active ICN member (Box 6.1).

The ICN's scope widened after World War II. By 1985, the ICN represented 97 countries. National nurses association's paid dues based on the number of individual members of its association. In the 1980s "ICN membership grew 18% between 1980 and 1985, from 862,123 to 1,056,066 members" (Brush et al, 1999, p. 169). Despite ICN's increasing diversity, however, 11 ICN countries (Japan, United States, Canada,

---

BOX 6.1

ABCs of Who's Who

The following list identifies various nursing and other organisations referred to by acronyms or abbreviations in this chapter.

ANA	American Nurses Association
BNA	British Nurses Association
CNA	Canadian Nurses Association
CNR	Council of National Representatives
ECNE	European Council of Nursing Education
FNIF	Florence Nightingale International Fund
ICN	International Council of Nurses
ICW	International Council of Women
ILO	International Labour Organization
NNA	National Nurse Associations
NNF	Northern Nurses Federation
RCRCS	Red Cross and Red Crescent Societies
SANA	South African Nurses Association
UNESCO	United Nations Educational, Scientific, and Cultural Organization
UNICEF	United Nations International Children's Emergency Fund
WHO	World Health Organization

United Kingdom, Sweden, Denmark, Australia, Spain, Finland, Norway and Switzerland) accounted for 86% of the ICN members. The agenda of industrialized countries importantly influences policy directions within the ICN. However, the political point of view of the ICN has changed from the past, representing a multinational vision. During the 1970s and 1980s, the ICN clearly spoke out against violation of human rights and political suppression. The ICN considered health a basic human right for all.

ICN and World Health

From the time of its founding, the ICN was strongly committed to the improvement of world health. In the early decades of the 20th century, contagious diseases and high infant mortality had a devastating impact in the industrializing Western world. The ICN's initial dedication to furthering social progress and public health assumed new meaning in the aftermath of the World War I. Wartime devastation prompted the expansion of public health services, especially in child welfare and tuberculosis care, and set a new public health agenda. The Red Cross and the League of Nations facilitated the preparation of qualified nurses for public health activities, but philanthropic foundations, such as the Rockefeller Foundation also funded the training of public health nurses.

The Rockefeller Foundation considered nurses essential for postwar public health service. Through their International Health Commission, the Rockefeller Foundation supported public health programmes throughout the world, either by founding or by cooperating with existing medical and nursing schools. Foundational support often involved and facilitated linkages with the ICN, because of the leadership of American and European nurses in most Foundation projects. The Rockefeller Foundation profoundly influenced tuberculosis control in France, for example, and financed the establishment of training schools for nurses and health visitors in several French cities. In the process, the Foundation initiated establishing the French Central Nursing Bureau in 1925. In that same year, France joined the ICN under the leadership of Leonie Chaptal, a long-standing leader in French public health nursing and the founder of an independent professional organisation for French nurses (Boschma & Stuart, 1999).

At the ICN meeting in Helsinki, in 1925, Bulgaria, Cuba, France, Irish Free State, and Poland became part of the confederation, increasing membership countries to 20. American Nina Gage, representing the Chinese nursing association, was elected president. Meanwhile, the ICN board members decided to move ICN headquarters to Geneva, Switzerland. Viewed as politically neutral and stable, Geneva was also becoming the centre of an increasing number of international organisations.

During the 1929 ICN meeting in Montreal, French Leonie Chaptal was elected ICN president. The massive changes in public health nursing dominated the agenda. Acceptable standards and conditions for general and public health nursing education provoked much debate. The Nursing Education Committee, headed by Isabel Stewart from Teacher's College of Columbia University (New York, USA), presented its report on nursing education. The powerful presence of Teacher's College graduates in the ICN, influenced the ICN's thinking that science and research in nursing should be promoted as a way to strengthen the nursing profession. For most membership countries, however, this novel idea had limited immediate relevance, although the issue would not disappear from the ICN agenda again.

After World War II, international initiatives to make health care accessible for all gained momentum. The powerful advent of antibiotics and medical technology on a wider scale generally increased confidence that world health could be improved and should be considered a basic human right. In 1948, the newly established WHO declared that "Health is a state of complete physical, mental and social well-being and not merely the absence of disease or infirmity" (Howard-Jones, 1981, p. 472).

In many ways, the ICN conference in Stockholm in 1949 marked the ICN's voice — and thus nurses' voice — among other international players all working towards the common goal of world health. Gradually, the ICN carved out the right to speak for nursing in an ever-wider sphere of influence. Linking with the United Nations and WHO, the ICN implemented a new, more global agenda, addressing economic, racial, religious, and gender issues that continued to complicate the professional development of nursing in many countries.

International Voice of Nursing Validated

ICN's "official relationship" status with WHO gave ICN new privileges and responsibilities. ICN was also on the mailing list of UNESCO, the Economic and Social Council, and UNICEF. These developments furthered recognition of the ICN as the international voice of nursing. In 1949, Olive Baggallay, formerly the secretary of the Florence Nightingale International Fund (FNIF), became the first nursing consultant to WHO. In the early 1950s, the ICN strengthened its relationship with the International Labour Organisation (ILO) and began to officially represent nurses on employment issues. During this time, the ICN developed the International Code of Nursing Ethics, translated into numerous languages, and again updated in 1973 (International Council of Nurses, 1973). It provides national nursing associations with a valuable resource to address ethical nursing issues. Up until the 1980s, the Canadian Nurses Association, for example, relied on the ICN ethical standards for its own Code of Ethics.

In 1966, ICN relocated its headquarters again to Geneva, reflecting the importance of ICN's growing external relationships. At that time, Canadian Alice Girard (Fig. 6.4) was president of the ICN (1965–69). She was the founding Dean of the Faculty of Nursing Education at the Université de Montreal and the first bilingual president of the Canadian Nurses Association (1958–60). In the 1980s, the ICN and the League of Red Cross and Red Crescent Societies (RCRCS) collaborated in preparing a teaching kit on human rights and the Geneva Convention, and continued to work with the WHO, UNICEF, and the ILO towards world health.

CURRENT THINKING: ISSUES FOR THE ICN AND THE INTERNATIONAL COMMUNITY*

Many concerns facing ICN in the 1990s had been issues throughout the organisation's history, including professional service issues, economic stability, international relations and global nurse representation. In the 1990s the ICN sought new ways to

---

*This section is adapted from Brush, B. L. Leading nurses to a new century: ICN during the 1990s. *International Nursing Review 46* (5), 1999, 151–155, with permission

FIGURE 6.4. Canadian nurse Alice Girard *(left)* was president of ICN from 1965 to 1969. Here she takes time for tea and talk with colleague Helen Nussbaum, who was the ICN's general secretary from 1961 to 1967. (Photo courtesy of ICN Collection; In Brush, B. L., Lynaugh, J. E., Boschma, G., Rafferty, A. M., Suart, M., & Tomes, N. J. (1999). *Nurses of all nations: A history of the International Council of Nurses, 1899–1999.* Philadelphia: Lippincott Willliams & Wilkins.)

address these familiar problems. As the century drew to a close, more than 4,500 nurses from every region of the world gathered with joy and pride at the ICN Centennial Conference in London, where they accepted a new vision to lead ICN and nursing into the 21st century.

Regulating Nursing

With the many new national nursing associations joining ICN in the 1970s and 1980s, regulation of nursing again became an agenda of the ICN. Many national associations, facing difficult legal and cultural circumstances, often called on the ICN for help in dealing with these complex matters. Between 1988 and 1991, the ICN held six "Nursing Regulation: Moving Ahead" project workshops. The intent of the workshops was to assist leaders of national nurse associations (NNAs) to develop and implement universal national nursing regulatory systems. Through this project the ICN helped prepare 161 nurses from 99 NNAs and 62 governments to take an active role in assessing and revising regulations and laws controlling nursing practise and care delivery in their countries. At its 1995 meeting, the Council of National Representatives (CNR) approved continued examination of international nurse regulation. The W.K. Kellogg Foundation provided funding to appoint nurse consultant Fadwa Affara to head a 3-year nursing regulation study for the ICN.

Korean Mo-Im Kim, elected ICN president in 1989, played an essential role in increasing political activities regarding nursing regulation. Kim, who had previously served as the president of the Korean Nurses Association and as a member of the Korean Parliament (1981–85), was keenly aware of the urgency for all nurses to become more politically involved in defining nursing's place in their country's healthcare system. Without an official position on international regulation of nursing practise, she argued, the ICN and its member associations were vulnerable to the *ad hoc* decisions of local government officials. Nurse education and practise varied widely among nations, which enhanced opportunities for politicians to create nurse practise acts based on their own political agendas rather than on professional nursing standards.

Standardisation and Credentialing

Following these initiatives, in 1999, at the Centennial Conference, the CNR proposed to expand nursing's role in professional standard setting and quality assurance in health care. The CNR felt that it was timely to develop a framework and criteria for international standardisation and credentialing procedures for nursing and health care as a way to assure recipients of health care of the educational practise competence of nurses and other health professionals.

Regulation became one of the key programme areas of the ICN, in addition to professional practise issues and socioeconomic welfare of nurses. ICN's long-standing goal to enforce standards for nursing education and practise provoked a renewed effort to develop universal guidelines for basic and specialty practise. In this way, ICN seeks to assist nurses associations dealing with expanding roles of nurses, new educational standards and the evolution of nursing specialties. After World War II, membership countries faced the increased use of auxiliary and unlicenced personnel in a rapidly expanding health care system, making clear definitions and explication of boundaries of nursing practise all the more urgent. The recent plans of the ICN to become involved in credentialing of nursing competence is part of the strategy to respond to changing practise demands. ICN's position on these issues and its effort to collect reliable data on nursing helped nursing associations to effectively represent nursing within national health policy debates and governmental politics (International Council of Nurses, 2001b).

Global Shortage of Nurses

The urgency of addressing issues related to regulation and classification of nursing care in the 1990s, indeed provoked immediate efforts to regulate nursing practise and education. However, critical nursing shortages around the world compromised these initiatives at the same time.

In its 1989 report to the 42nd World Health Assembly, ICN urged WHO member states to develop strategies to:

- Recruit, retain, and educate nurses and midwives
- Elevate nurses to senior leadership and management positions
- Support nursing research
- Adopt policies to include nurses in primary care activities

Factors that influence decreasing nurse supply in many industrialised nations included declining lengths of hospital stay; increased nursing workloads through the use of technology and higher patient acuity; shift work; and attrition through marriage and childbirth. Low wages and layoffs also play a role. Canada for example, facing severe budget cuts in health care in the early 1990s, and consequently layoffs in nursing, saw many of its qualified nurses cross the borders to better paying nations. Simultaneously, however, nurses from developing countries are attracted to Canada. To balance their own demand for nurses, many developed nations recruit nurses from developing countries. Higher salaries and better working conditions, coupled with high-powered recruitment strategies, attracted nurses to the United States, Canada, Great Britain, Australia, Israel and other industrialized nations. A case in point is the situation in the Philippines, which faced a severe "brain drain" of its qualified nurses in the 1980s. In 1989, about 65% of the country's 13,000 new nurse graduates emigrated abroad, mostly to the United States and Middle Eastern countries, leaving many of the health care facilities in the Philippines short of staff (Brush, 1999b).

In the face of a rapidly spreading AIDS epidemic in Africa, African nations suffered severe shortages of nurses because of the increased demand for nursing and preventive care. In 1991, in sub-Saharan Africa, 7 million individuals were reported to be infected with HIV/AIDS. Despite widespread need for nursing care, only an estimated 2.5 nurses per 10,000 individuals were available in this area. In Europe, reports on nursing shortages varied. The Nordic countries had the highest nurse-to-population ratio in the world at approximately 85 to 87 nurses per 10,000 individuals. Other members of the European community, however, such as Italy, Germany, Britain, and the Netherlands, reported increasing national shortage of nurses. The United States and Canada reported similar problems of shortages. Nurse migration compromised local and international efforts to improve short-term nurse recruitment and retention, and long-term personnel planning. The ICN sought to assist member associations to study nursing personnel needs and resources, share information pertaining to nursing's worldwide employment status, and continue discussion of the international impact of nurse shortages (Brush, 1999b).

Furthering Nursing Practise

A key problem with global nurse regulation is the dearth of data about *what* constitutes nurses' work and *how* it is shaped by health care service payments. In response, in 1989 the American Nurses Association (ANA) proposed a council resolution urging national nurses associations to develop nation-specific classification systems for nursing care. The initiative may have been triggered by a difficult situation the ANA was confronted with when the American Medical Association proposed to introduce a new health care worker in the United States. The ANA, which had successfully lobbied against such a decision, argued that the nursing profession must name its distinct contribution to health care to be recognized in worldwide health care planning and financing. The ANA proposed to collect, document, and share data on nursing practise across countries, clinical settings, and patient populations to assist national associations in planning types and amounts of nursing needed, determining skill mixes for various care settings and patient groups, and evaluating clinical efficacy and cost.

Responding to the ANA resolution in 1990, the ICN Board of Directors invited June Clark (UK) and Norma Lang (USA) to develop a feasibility study for an International Classification for Nursing Practice (ICNP). Margretta Madden Styles, chair of the Professional Services Committee and elected ICN President in 1993, nurse consultant Fadwa Affara, and Denmark's Randi Mortenson and Gunnar Nelson completed the team. From 1990 to 1997, they consulted with nurses and classification experts to collect, group, and rank nursing phenomena, interventions, and outcomes, with the ultimate goal of creating a universal nursing language.

Another pertinent issue that arose in the 1990s was advancing nursing practise to respond to expanding primary health care demands and changing conditions of specialty nursing care. The ICN established an International Nurse Practitioner/Advanced Practice Nursing Network with the view to provide international resources for nurses practicing in these roles and elude policymakers and health planners to the essential function of these roles in enhancing healthcare services. Again, ICN saw it as a major responsibility to provide relevant data and support nurses and countries in the process of expanding nurses' roles (ICN, 2001c).

FUTURE IMPLICATIONS: THE ICN IN THE 21ST CENTURY*

At the 1993 CNR meeting in Madrid, Spain, the ICN adopted "Toward the 21st Century: A Strategic Plan, 1994–1999." The plan addressed the issues ICN considered crucial to health planning for the new century, including formulating health and social policy; establishing professional standardization and socioeconomic equity; collaborating with other international bodies; disseminating nursing knowledge; and developing frameworks for identifying and measuring nurses' work. The strategic plan clearly laid out ICN goals for the future, which realistically could be accomplished considering available resources.

The ICN further endorsed several key position statements, emphasizing its expansionist agenda, at the 1995 CNR meeting in Harare, Zimbabwe. Revisiting its 1981 Resolution of Female Excision, Circumcision and Mutilation, ICN resolved to work with local, national and international groups opposed to the practise. Position statements related to psychiatric mental health nursing and to the costs and value of nursing were also endorsed. Other resolutions specifically addressed issues of nurse titling, health policy participation, nursing school accreditation, and nursing students' roles in NNAs (International Council of Nurses, 2001a).

In 1997, Canadian Judith Oulton, formerly Executive Director of the CNA, assumed the post of ICN Chief Executive Officer. She brought her belief that it is critical for nurses in all countries to participate in shaping health policy and to have their work backed up by accurate data showing nursing's contributions to health outcomes. During that year, some 5,000 nurses from 120 countries convened in Vancouver, Canada, to "Share the Health Challenge" at ICN's 21st Quadrennial Congress. It was the second time Canada hosted an ICN congress, since the first one held in Montreal in 1929.

At many of the sessions, participants were repeatedly told that nurses must become more influential. "We must raise our social status as a profession to our level of social contribution and our influence to the level of our strength," said outgoing ICN President Dr. Styles, "We must raise the intensity of our politics to the intensity of our ethics" (Brush, 1999b, p.155).

At the 1999 Centennial Conference in London, England, issues discussed included nurses' role in safeguarding children against exploitation, the Hague Appeal for Peace to abolish global armed conflict, and zero tolerance in workplace violence. To commemorate the century of nurses caring and contribution to world health and welfare, the CNR adopted the "white heart" as ICN's symbol of humanity. ICN President Kirsten Stallknecht, addressed the audience at the opening ceremony of the conference, urging nurses to "forge a renewed vision for nurses and nursing" that emphasized "high-touch" over "high-tech." At the end of her speech, she unveiled ICN's vision statement for the 21st century, which opens as follows: "United within ICN, the nurses of all nations speak with one voice. We speak as advocates for all those we serve and for all the unserved, insisting that prevention, care, and cure be the right of every human being" (Brush, 1999b, p.155).

---

*This section is adapted from Brush, B. L. Leading nurses to a new century: ICN during the 1990s. *International Nursing Review 46* (5), 1999, 151–155, with permission.

SUMMARY

The ICN vision for nursing in the 21st century reflects the organisation's century-long involvement in the politics of health care.

The new century will undoubtedly present many challenges and opportunities, including the internationalisation of markets, which may create an unknown effect on the process of reworking and redefining nursing.

Tensions between generations of nurses and philosophical differences among ICN member associations also may pose new challenges to ICN in the 21st century. However, throughout the past 100 years, the ICN has proven its ability to respond to change, making it the more likely that the ICN will maintain its enduring meaning for many nurses around the world in the new century.

Online RESOURCES

Add to your knowledge of this issue:

Allemang Centre on Nursing History	**www.allemang.on.ca**
Canadian Nurses Association	**http://www.cna-nurses.ca**
Canadian Association for the History of Nursing	**www.ualberta.ca/~}** **jhibberd/CAHN _ ACHN**
International Council of Nurses	**www.icn.ch**
World Health Organization	**http://who.int**

Reflections on the Chapter

1. Discuss in your group the impact of organized international nursing on changing health care demands and world health. Identify three political strategies nurses developed to change health care and health.

2. Identify three important issues that the ICN has faced throughout its history and discuss strategies developed in response.

3. What role had the ICN over time in issues of regulation of nursing practise?

4. Select one ICN position statement from the ICN web page (www.icn.ch) and discuss its potential impact on health policy. How could the position statement contribute to the issues resolution at the local level or in your nursing practise?

ACKNOWLEDGEMENTS

This chapter is largely based on research conducted by Barbara L. Brush, Joan E. Lynaugh, Geertje Boschma, Anne Marie Rafferty, Meryn Stuart, and Nancy J. Tomes for *Nurses of All Nations: A History of the International Council of Nurses, 1899–1999*

(Philadelphia: Lippincott Williams & Wilkins, 1999), used in this chapter with permission from the publisher. Appreciation is acknowledged for the support and cooperation of the International Council of Nurses in developing this book. For more detailed references, please refer to this book. A series of articles on the history of the ICN, published by the authors of this chapter in the 1999 issue of the *International Nursing Review*, nos. 1, 2, 3, and 5 have also been used with permission. They include Lynaugh, J. E. & Brush, B. (1999). The ICN story 1899–1999. *International Nursing Review*, *46*(1), 3–8; Boschma, G., & Stuart, M. (1999). ICN During Wartime: 1912–1947. *International Nursing Review*, *46*(2), 41–46; Brush, B. L. (1999). Turmoil and transformation: ICN during the postwar years. *International Nursing Review*, *46*(3), 75–79; and Brush, B. L. (1999). Leading nurses to a new century: ICN during the 1990s. *International Nursing Review*, *46*(5), 151–155.

REFERENCES

Bischoff, C. (1984). *Frauen in der Krankenpflege. Zur Entwicklung von Frauenrolle und Frauenberufstätigkeit in 19. und 20. Jahrhundert*. Frankfurt am Main: Campus Verlag.

Boschma, G. (1996). Agnes Karll and the creation of an independent german nurses association, 1900–1927. *Nursing History Review*, *4*, 151–168.

Boschma, G., & Stuart, M. (1999). ICN during wartime: 1912–1947. *International Nursing Review*, *46*(2), 41–46.

Brush, B. L. (1999a). Turmoil and transformation: ICN during the postwar years. *International Nursing Review*, *46*(3), 75–79.

Brush, B. L. (1999b). Leading nurses to a new century: ICN during the 1990s. *International Nursing Review*, *46*(5), 151–155.

Brush, B. L., Lynaugh, J. E., Boschma, G., Rafferty, A. M., Stuart, M., & Tomes, N. J. (1999). *Nurses of all nations: A history of the International Council of Nurses, 1899–1999*. Philadelphia: Lippincott Williams & Wilkins.

Brush, B., & Stuart, M. (1994). Unity amidst difference: The ICN project and writing international nursing history. *Nursing History Review*, *2*, 191–204.

Canadian Nurses Association. (1968). *The leaf and the lamp*. Ottawa, Canada: Author.

Chen, K. (1996). Missionaries and the early development of nursing in China. *Nursing History Review*, *4*, 129–150.

Howard-Jones, N. (1981). The World Health Organization in historical perspective. *Perspectives in Biology and Medicine*, *24*(3), 467–482.

International Council of Nurses. (1973). *ICN code for nurses: Ethical concepts applied to nursing*. Geneva: Author.

International Council of Nurses. (2001a). ICN position statements [On-line]. Available: http://www.icn.ch/policy.htm.

International Council of Nurses. (2001b). Regulation: Regulation programme area overview [On-line]. Available: http://www.icn.ch/regulation.htm.

International Council of Nurses. (2001c). Nurse practitioner/advanced practice network [On-line]. Available: http://www.icn.ch/networks_ap.htm.

Lynaugh, J. E., & Brush, B. L. (1999). The ICN story 1899–1999. *International Nursing Review*, *46*(1), 3–8.

Lungershausen, M. (1964). *Agnes Karll, Ihr Leben, Werk und Erbe*. Hannover, Germany: Elwin Staude Verlag.

Paul, P. (1994). The Contribution of the Grey Nuns to the development of nursing in Canada: Historiographical issues. *Canadian Bulletin of Medical History*, *11*, 207–218.

Rafferty, A. M., & Brush, B. L. (1995). Conflict and consensus: The International Council of Nurses and international nursing. *International History of Nursing Journal*, *1*, 4–16.

Wingender, N. B. (1995). *The Northern Nurses Federation, 1920–1995: An English summary*. Aarhuus, Denmark: Stiftsbogtrykkerie.

7

Canadian Nurses Association

Ginette Lemire Rodger

The power of representation is illustrated in political action. Here, nurses confer with Ginette Lemire Rodger (center), President of C.N.A., to begin the process for change that will protect the health of Canadians and the nursing profession. Photo by Tony Fouhse. Used with permission of the Canadian Nursing Association.

1. Understand the roles of professional organisations and identify Canadian nursing organisations that are fulfilling these roles.

2. Describe areas in which the power of representation of the Canadian Nurses Association (CNA) has brought about significant social change.

3. Differentiate the elements of the CNA structure and governance process, and describe some of its partnerships.

4. Identify current CNA priorities and challenges at both the national and international levels.

5. Discuss some of the expected challenges ahead.

This chapter provides an overview of the role of the Canadian Nurses Association (CNA) and the context in which it exercises its role and functions. Various examples highlight the complexity of the issues, including the tensions or contradictions inherent in bringing about social change and success. The structure and the governance process of CNA are described, the current priorities and challenges are discussed, and the areas of representation and self-regulation are featured as well.

ROLE OF PROFESSIONAL ORGANISATIONS

The role of professional organisations is derived from the need of professions to interface with society. This social reality can be described either generically or specifically, for the profession of nursing.

Professional Organisation: Characteristics of Professions

Many people have offered definitions of a professional association or professional organisation. Several of the definitions are conditioned by the context in which the professional organisation exists. For example, Dalton and colleagues (1994) would focus on the role of professional association in two parts: one related to educational standards and licensing fulfilled by the Boards of Nursing in the United States, and one related to influence and focus on protection of the public and improvement of practise fulfilled by the state associations which are nursing unions. Dollinger (2000) would focus on the role of the professional association in speaking to the public on behalf of nursing and exerting political influence as a moral duty of professionals. These roles are related to the protection of the public; they include development of standards of practise, granting licenses to practise, setting educational standards, acting as nursing advocates, and protecting the nurse, which involves negotiating and collective agreements and advocacy in the workplace.

In his seminal work, Merton (1958) focussed on the nature of the professional association. "The professional association is an organization of practitioners who judge one another as professionally competent and who have banded together to perform social functions which they cannot perform in their separate capacity as individuals" (p. 50). Each individual professional cannot speak on behalf of his or her profession unless mandated by the collective to represent the profession. Paradoxically, the behaviours of individual professionals reflect on their professions and contribute to the public image of a profession. A profession is recognised by several characteristics that have evolved over the years. The characteristics that are most frequently noted include the following:

- Specialised body of knowledge
- Code of ethics
- Competent application of knowledge
- Standards of practice
- Self-regulation
- Tradition of public service
- Autonomy
- Accountability
- Professional association (Hawthorne & Yurkovich, 1994; Registered Nurses Association of British Columbia [RNABC], 1999; Styles, 1983).

Of the various characteristics, one is the existence of a professional association. Merton (1958) recognised that despite diversity, associations essentially perform functions that are related to the individual practitioners, the profession as a whole, or society in general. These functions are not mutually exclusive. For example, a specific professional association or organisation like a nursing union would exist to ensure the protection of the individual nurse by negotiating contracts, promoting healthy workplaces, advocating for patient safety, providing educational support, and speaking out about the health care system. Similarly, a professional association or college would exist to ensure the protection of the public by establishing standards of practise and education, determining competencies and licensure requirements, monitoring the quality of the workplace environment, and advocating for patient–nurse safety and social changes that impact the public.

As you can see, some of the functions overlap, but the main purpose of each organisation is grounded in its social role. These could be conceptualised as protecting the nurse or the individual practitioner (union), protecting the public or society (association or a college), and speaking on behalf of the profession—a service that can be fulfilled either by an organisation that exists to protect the nurse or the public or by an association that exists exclusively for this purpose.

Role of Canadian Nursing Organisations

The International Council of Nurses (ICN) is a federation that represents different types of national nursing associations internationally. In 1997, the ICN conducted a survey to identify the nature of its national nursing associations. A total of 62% of national nursing associations identified their major role as representing the profession. They did not have a specific role concerning protection of the public (i.e., regulatory role) or protection of the nurse (i.e., a union role or a socioeconomic mandate). A total of 31%

of national nursing associations are unions that negotiate for nurses; only 7% have a regulatory mandate to protect the public (ICN, 2001b).

In Canada, the CNA is a federation of provincial/territorial associations that have the mandate to protect the public and speak on behalf of the profession. The federation includes the Association of Registered Nurses of Newfoundland and Labrador, Association of Nurses of Prince Edward Island, College of Registered Nurses of Nova Scotia, Nurses Association of New Brunswick, Registered Nurses Association of Ontario, College of Registered Nurses of Manitoba, Saskatchewan Registered Nurses Association, Alberta Association of Registered Nurses, Registered Nursing Association of British Columbia, Northwest Territories Registered Nurses Association, and Yukon Registered Nurses Association. The exception among the grouping is the Registered Nurses Association of Ontario (RNAO). RNAO represents the profession in Ontario without a public protection mandate. The protection role is fulfilled by the College of Nurses of Ontario.

In Canada, the provincial/territorial governments have delegated the right to self-regulation to the nursing profession. These rights have been delegated to many other health professions as well.

Nationally, the Canadian Federation of Nurses Unions is another nursing federation that represents provincial nurses' unions that have the mandate to protect the nurse and speak on behalf of the profession in the realm of their competencies. Many other national nursing organisations exist that represent nursing's interest in a specific area of competence, in particular, specialty groups, areas of work groups, and the like.

Influence of Professional Organisations

Convergence of action, complementarity of roles, and collaboration among the diverse organisations within a profession increase the power and influence they have to fulfill their social obligations. *Power* is defined as the degree of influence the profession has (Shiflett & McFarland, 1978). Versteeg (1979) identifies five characteristics that affect the power of a group in society:

- Size
- Information of the members
- Expertise
- Available resources
- Personal attributes of the group's spokesperson

In regard to size (of the group that is represented and the percentage it represents of the total group), CNA speaks for 113,120 registered nurses in Canada (CNA, 2000a). This number includes almost all nurses in eight provinces and three territories. The exceptions are Ontario and Quebec. In Ontario, the RNAO, which is not a regulatory association, represents 14,366 (CNA, 2000a) of 81,679 registered nurses (Canadian Institute of Health Information [CIHI], 2001). In Quebec, the Order des Infirmiéres et Infirmiers du Québec (OIIQ) withdrew from the CNA in 1985 at the height of the separatism movement. Today, Quebec has 58,750 registered nurses (CIHI, 2001). In 2001, the number of practicing registered nurses in Canada totaled about 232,412 (CIHI, 2001). CNA has been recognised as the voice of professional nursing in Canada by governments both nationally and provincially as well as by other professional organisations.

THE CANADIAN NURSES ASSOCIATION: NATIONAL VOICE OF NURSING SINCE 1908

In 1908, the first national nurses' association was formed so that nurses could exercise their professional responsibilities on behalf of the Canadian public and provide them with a vehicle to join the ICN (CNA, 1968). This first association was known as the Canadian National Association of Trained Nurses (CNATN) before it changed its name to the Canadian Nurses Association in 1924.

Since then, the CNA has been the voice of nursing in Canada, influencing public policies, articulating the viewpoints of nurses on health and nursing issues, and playing a key role in the Canadian political process and in the development of nursing in Canada (CNA, 1958, 1968; MacPhail, 1996; Meilicke & Larsen, 1988). In the past 2 decades, the role of the CNA has expanded considerably both in the area of representative power and self-regulation.

Power of Representation

Since Florence Nightingale's time, nursing leaders have been politically active on behalf of those they represented. Throughout history, many social changes were spearheaded by nursing leaders, although most nurses did not consider their role to be political activism, either individually or collectively as professionals. One of the first Canadian articles on the topic of grass roots political action by nurses was published in 1974 (RNABC, 1974). The power of representation is exercised most of the time through *political action,* meaning "a systematic series of actions directed toward influencing others into conformity with a pursued goal" (Lemire Rodger, 1999, p. 281). Nationally, since the early 1980s, CNA has promoted political action by nurses as a means of exercising the power of representation.

CHANGES IN HEALTH CARE: CANADA HEALTH ACT

Nationally, the turning point for representation was in 1985, with the proclamation of the Canada Health Act. Many nurses participated for the first time in political lobbying from coast to coast to coast and influenced changes in national legislation. These changes represented their values and beliefs about the future of the health care system. These beliefs were presented in a brief entitled "Putting Health Into Health Care" (CNA, 1980), which has guided pursuant changes by CNA since its publication.

The advocated changes are based on the principles of *primary health care.* The principles include health promotion and prevention of disease and injury, accessibility, public participation, multidisciplinary and intersectoral collaboration, and appropriate technology (World Health Organization [WHO], 1978). The changes also incorporate the principles of the Canada Health Act, including universality, portability, accessibility, comprehensiveness, and public administration (Canada Health Act, 1984). These principles are central in the national debate about needed changes in health care.

The CNA's power of representation has had an impact on legislative changes to the Canada Health Act (1984) and has ensured that the national and provincial plans for the future of the health care system are guided by the principles of primary health care and the Canada Health Act (Mhatre & Deber, 1992). The nursing voice was part of the review of the Canadian health care system by the National Health Forum in 1997, when Madeleine Doyon Stout, Margaret Rose McDonald, and Dr. Judith Ritchie, past president of CNA, participated for the nursing profession. The nursing voice was also evident in 2001 at the Romanov Commission, whose purposes are similar to those of the National Health Forum. The Commission seeks and entertains close communication with CNA (communication through private meeting, information before major events, invitation to official events of CNA).

RESEARCH AGENDA

Another example of the power of representation can be seen in the overall progress and development of nursing research both nationally and provincially. Nursing has been recognised only recently as a discipline in Canada. In fact, most of the debate about the legitimacy of doctoral programmes in nursing related to recognising nursing as a discipline. Only in the 1980s did the Medical Research Council of Canada and some universities, such as McGill University and University of Alberta, considered academic approval of doctoral programmes in nursing and support for the research infrastructure.

CNA developed a national plan for the development of nursing research in Canada (CNA, 1984) and has lobbied government, universities, and foundations over the past 2 decades. The power of representation of CNA was effective even if some of the gains were not sustained (MacPhail, 1996). They include nursing representation at the policy level of the Medical Research Council of Canada in the 1980s and 1990s, and leadership at the National Health Research and Development Program (NHRDP) of the Health Promotion Directorate of Health Welfare Canada (Dr. Mary Ellen Jeans, a nurse, completed her mandate as Executive Director in 1995.)

For the first time, national career awards were instituted for individual nursing researchers (three) at the beginning of the 1990s, and five national nursing research chairs were allocated at the end of the decade (CHSRF, 2000).

In 1999, for the first time in history, the federal budget included specific funds for nursing research (Orthoscope, 1999). The first funded nursing doctoral programme at the University of Alberta was approved in 1991 (Lemire Rodger, 1991), and today, nine doctoral programmes in nursing are preparing scholars in the discipline. These programmes are sponsored by the University of Alberta, University of British Columbia, University of Toronto, McGill University, Université de Montréal, University of Calgary, McMaster University, Université de Sherbrooke, and University of Victoria by special arrangement (Wendy McBride, Executive Director CAUSN, personal communication).

NURSING WORKPLACE AND HUMAN RESOURCES

The power of representation was exercised with great determination by CNA in recent years because issues related to the environment in which nursing is practised have always been part of the CNA mandate under the category of socioeconomic welfare. Issues such as working conditions and contracts negotiated for nurses, human resources statistics, and standards in nursing administration were addressed. The socioeconomic environment of nurses was greatly transformed by the events of the 1990s when major cutbacks in health care funding had a devastating effect on the nursing workforce and the workplace. Thousands of nurses lost their positions when hospital and community services were curtailed by provincial governments across the country. In the workplace, there was a loss of nursing leadership positions, an increase in the number of patients cared for by one nurse, and a loss of support structures for education and research.

The CNA commissioned the Ryten Report in 1997, on the future supply of registered nurses in Canada. The report predicted a serious shortage of nurses by 2011 if no strategic action was undertaken immediately. CNA made several presentations to convince federal and provincial governments and associations of employers (CNA,

1998, 1999a, 2000b, 2001b) to act immediately. Recently, further reports (Canadian Council of Social Development, 2001; CIHI, 2001) validated the projections, and further attempts were made to convince the governments that the situation was serious and that a lack of action would undermine the sustainability of the Canadian health care system. A concerted effort with the provincial jurisdictions and other nursing and health associations (including the Canadian Association of University Schools of Nursing [CAUSN], the Canadian Federation of Nursing Unions [CFNU], Canadian Health Care Association, and Canadian Medical Association, to name a few) was also needed to persuade governments and employers that action was needed now. The issues of recruitment and retention were addressed in these representations, and the issues of retention and the quality of the professional practise environment became a priority for CNA (see End 3 in Box 7.1).

The power of representation helped create a national/provincial/territorial agenda on nursing health resources with the reintroduction of nursing advisor positions in many governments, including the Office of Nursing Policy within Health Canada, that is, the federal government and the following provincial/territorial governments: Nova Scotia, Ontario, Saskatchewan, and British Columbia (Office of Nursing Policy, Health Canada, personal communication).

Representation also helped create a national/provincial/territorial agenda on the development of a nursing strategy for Canada (Advisory Committee on Health Human Resources, 2000) and the creation of a Canadian Nursing Advisory Committee with equivalent committees in provinces and territories to implement the national strategy. Several provincial government plans of action were developed (Newfoundland, Prince Edward Island, Nova Scotia, New Brunswick, Ontario, Manitoba, and Saskatchewan [personal survey, June 2001]). In addition, the topic of nursing recruitment and retention was established as a regular item on the federal/provincial policy agenda for the health ministers and even on the First Minister's Agenda in 2002. Provincial/territorial premiers meet periodically with or without the Prime Minister of Canada to discuss issues of importance for them, and nursing is now one of their issues. The power of representation was effective in creating a national agenda so that the issues in this area could be addressed.

Self-Regulation

One area that has experienced exponential growth in the past 2 decades has been regulation. The CNA always played a supportive role in regulation; for example, the CNA developed a testing service in 1969 to prepare and administer the National Registration Examination. CNA also played a leadership role in determining the educational requirement for entry into the profession.

NURSING EDUCATION

In 1982, CNA members took the position that the entry-level competencies to the profession would be at a baccalaureate level. Today, because of the power of representation of CNA, provincial and territorial nursing associations, and other partners, such as CAUSN, the provinces of Newfoundland and Labrador, Prince Edward Island, Nova Scotia, New Brunswick, and Saskatchewan and the territory of Nunavut, have established baccalaureate education as a requirement for entry to the profession. Manitoba, which had attained the same educational entry level, rolled back their progress by opening one diploma school of nursing in 2000 as a perceived solution to nursing shortage. As for Alberta and British Columbia, most education is provided in collabo-

BOX 7.1

Canadian Nurses Association Ends

End 1 is the vision, and the missions under End 1 become Ends 2, 3, 4, and 5. In the main document, the ends are not numbered, but they are numbered here for greater clarity.

END 1

The vision of the Canadian Nurses Association is:

Registered nurses collectively contributing to the health of Canadians and the advancement of nursing.

In pursuit of that vision, CNA's mission is that:

- Public policy incorporates the determinants of health and the principles of primary health care and expands the application of the principles of the Canada Health Act across the health care continuum.
- Public trust in nurses is maintained.
- The nursing profession achieves its full potential.
- The Canadian nursing profession contributes to the advancement of global health and equity.

END 2

The end, "Public policy incorporates the determinants of health and the principles of primary health care and expands the application of the principles of the Canada Health Act across the health care continuum," is further interpreted to include, but is not limited to:

1. Policymakers are knowledgeable about the relevant issues.
2. Public is supportive of the nursing position on the issues.
3. Nurses are leaders in public policy development.
4. Nurses are an entry point to the health care system.
5. Nurses understand and operationalise primary health care in their day-to-day practises.
6. A national framework for a primary health care-focussed system is operationalised.
7. A national nursing strategy exists to discourage the use of publicly funded, private, for-profit delivery of necessary health care.

END 3

The end, "Public trust in nurses is maintained," is further interpreted to include, but is not limited to:

1. A coordinated framework for national nursing issues
   1.1 A coordinated regulatory framework.
      1.1.1. A valid and reliable Canadian registered nurse examination that ensures that entry-level registered nurses demonstrate the competencies required to practise safely and effectively in Canada.
      1.1.2. Relevant coordinated regulatory frameworks that support provincial/territorial nursing regulatory bodies in maintaining quality and consistent regulatory practises.

(continued)

BOX 7.1

Canadian Nurses Association Ends (Continued)

1.1.3. An assessment instrument to assist and facilitate individual foreign nurses to make informed decisions about their readiness to become registered nurses in Canada.

1.2 A coordinated national approach to nursing resource planning.

1.3 An up-to-date, relevant code of ethics for registered nurses that gives guidance for decision making concerning ethical matters.

2. Nurses present an informed view of national nursing and health care issues.

3. Nursing self-regulation is maintained or attained.

3.1 Entry- and advanced-level competencies required for nursing practice are established by nursing regulatory bodies.

END 4

The end, "The nursing profession achieves its full potential," is further interpreted to include, but is not limited to:

1. Nursing practice* demonstrates integration of current knowledge.

2. The history of the nursing profession is preserved.

3. Competency and knowledge base for nurses is enhanced.

3.1. Registered nurses work to their full scopes of practice.

4. Nursing is central to health care delivery.

4.1. Registered nurses play a leadership role in the identification, development, implementation, and evaluation of best practices and innovations in health care.

4.2. Practice environments support nurse leadership at all levels.

4.3. The voice of nursing is influential in health policy and within health services.

4.4. Adequate numbers of well-prepared nurse leaders are in management roles.

5. Practice environments are conducive to quality nursing care, attracting and retaining registered nurses, and enabling excellence in professional practice.

5.1. A national nursing strategy exists to direct and support the development of practice environments that enable excellence in professional practice.

6. Canadian standards of excellence in professional practice.

END 5

The end, "The Canadian nursing profession contributes to the advancement of global health and equity," is further interpreted to include, but is not limited to:

1. CNA has a leadership role in ICN.

2. CNA has a leadership role in fostering national and international networks for Canadian nurses and international health interest groups.

3. CNA's International Bureau maintains an overseas development program that strengthens nursing's capacity to support nursing excellence globally.

---

*To include all domains—clinical practice, education, research, administration, etc.

Source: Board of Directors, November 2001. Printed with permission from the Canadian Nurses Association.

rative programmes in which graduates can exit after earning a diploma. Most students, however, exit after earning a baccalaureate degree. In the year 2000, a total of 131 students graduated with a diploma, whereas 707 students graduated with a baccalaureate degree (RNABC, undated). Ontario has identified the year 2005 for the baccalaureate degree as the requirement for entry into practise.

Educational preparation of registered nurses still encounters opposition from some provincial governments and some nurses; therefore, political action is still needed. The changes in nursing education were also accompanied by major legislative changes. These changes are varied; significant changes relate to the scope of nurses' practise and to the mandate of the association.

LEGISLATIVE CHANGES

Most nursing legislation in the provinces and territories has been substantially amended since 1980, as follows: Newfoundland and Labrador, 2001; Prince Edward Island, 1997; Nova Scotia, 2002; New Brunswick, 1984; Ontario, 1997; Manitoba, 2001; Saskatchewan, 1988; and British Columbia, 1988 (personal communication with executive directors of provincial or territorial associations).

All provincial and territorial nursing associations or colleges regulate the profession and approve the educational programme. In Alberta, the approval of educational programmes is granted to the University Coordinating Council (UCC). UCC can delegate this approval to the regulatory bodies, and the Alberta Association of Registered Nurses (AARN) has requested that the delegation be to the Nursing Education Program Approval Board (Tricia Mark, Nursing Consultant Practise, personal communication). This is an indication of the importance of legislative reform in health and in the Health Professions Act. In the 1980s, CNA started developing certification exams, and to date, there are 11 nursing specialty certification programmes and more than 10,000 registered nurses are certified (CNA, 2002). The changing legislative environment and the free-trade movement within Canada, North America, and the world have increased the need to have a strong national and international voice.

In 1996, CNA revised its constitution to include a new objective that focusses on supporting nursing regulation (CNA, 2001a) and added this area as one of the goals (or *ends*) to be pursued more actively by the Association (see Box 7.1). In addition, a new Division of Regulation was created within the staff structure to focus the work in this area.

Internationally, a new forum has been created. The forum regroups national nursing associations that are involved in regulation. As a participant, CNA influences the agenda. To date, an international framework for the development of credentialing (ICN, 2001c) and a registry for credentialing research have been developed to guide the evolution of credentialing in nursing (ICN, 2001d). In 2002, CNA will host the third forum which will focus on credentialing in clinical practise. Credentialing indicates that an individual, programme, institution, or product has met established standards. The standard may be minimal and mandatory or above the minimum and voluntary (ICN, 2001c).

THE CANADIAN NURSES ASSOCIATION: THE CONTEMPORARY ORGANISATION

In light of all the social, health, and nursing changes, CNA reviewed and revised its structure and processes several times over the years.

Structure and Representation

The current structure was adopted by the membership in 1998. Some elements of the previous structure were maintained. For example, each registered nurse continues to be an individual member of CNA through his or her respective jurisdiction, the jurisdictional members being the nursing body approved in membership, that is, provincial/territorial associations or colleges and the associate members. Changes to the structure included a smaller board of directors and a different representation on the board. Representation was reduced in the domains of practise (i.e., clinical, management, education, research, and socioeconomic domains), whereas provincial/territorial and public representations were maintained. New areas of representation were created through an associate member's representative and corporate portfolios chosen by the Board in line with the Board's priorities. The Board is composed of 20 members or directors: a president, president-elect, 11 provincial/territorial representatives, 4 public representatives, 2 corporate members, and 1 associate members' representative chosen by associate and affiliate members of CNA.

The first priorities chosen for the corporate directors were relations with Ontario and Quebec nurses in hopes of finding a way to increase membership in these provinces. This strategy was not successful. Since 2000, the corporate portfolios are quality workplace and primary health care; these reflect current priorities.

The staff structure complements the policy structure and is organised on the same model as the major goals of the Board of Directors (see Ends, Box 7.1). CNA is represented officially by two spokespersons: the president and the executive director or their delegates (Box 7.2). This representation role calls for attendance at nursing meetings across the country, media relations, governmental relations, and linkage with other strategic organisations. The CNA maintains structures and processes which

---

BOX 7.2

Canadian Nurses Association Presidents and Executive Directors, 1980-2001

CNA PRESIDENTS

Dr. Shirley Stinson, 1980-1982

Dr. Helen Glass, 1982-1984

Lorrine Bessel, 1984-1986

Helen Evans, 1986-1988

Dr. Judith Ritchie, 1988-1990

Dr. Alice Baumgart, 1990-1992

Fernande Harrison, 1992-1994

Eleanor Ross, 1994-1996

Rachel Bard, 1996-1998

Lynda Kushnir Perkul, 1998-2000

Dr. Ginette Lemire Rodger, 2000-2002

CNA EXECUTIVE DIRECTORS

Dr. Helen K. Mussallem, 1963-1981

Ginette Lemire Rodger, 1981-1989

Judith Oulton, 1989-1995

Dr. Mary Ellen Jeans, 1995-2001

Lucille Auffrey, 2001-

include a lobbying network to ensure that CNA is represented at the policy table in health and in nursing at the national and international levels. Regular meetings with the Federal Health Minister and specific meetings with other ministers are part of the structure of representation.

Governance

Once a year, delegates from each jurisdiction meet at the Annual General Meeting to fulfill their fiduciary responsibilities, such as electing a president-elect, choosing an auditor, changing bylaws, and giving guidance to the Board of Directors through voting on resolutions regarding the policy areas that they feel should be pursued. Even though the Board of Directors is not bound by the resolutions on policy directives, a review of annual reports submitted to membership confirms that almost all resolutions have guided the CNA and have been implemented.

The Board of Directors is the governing body of CNA and has provided national and international leadership for nursing in Canada in the areas of standards of practise, educational research, administration, and health issues in the public interest (CNA, 2001c). The Board decides on policy options, priorities, and resources. The Board also ensures that strategies are implemented satisfactorily by staff. The Board appoints an executive director who has the authority and responsibility to implement the Board policies, provide services to members, develop an appropriate network to fulfill the mandate, manage a team of staff members, and ensure linkage with subsidiary (e.g., Assessment Strategies, Inc.) and parallel organisations (e.g., Canadian Nurses Foundation and Canadian Nurses Protective Society). The Board reports back to the membership at the Annual General Meeting.

Partnership

Nurses have always worked in partnership, but in recent years, more and larger partnerships have developed to increase the influence of nurses and other health providers. Two large partnerships are the National Nursing Forum (NNF) and the Health Action Lobby (HEAL).

The NNF was initiated in 1996 by CNA following a review of its strategic directions. "The purpose of the Forum is to provide an opportunity to bring together a broad range of nursing organizations, including the provincial/territorial nursing associations, regulatory bodies, unions, educators, students, and specialty nursing associations. The forum is a venue to discuss issues of concern to the nursing community and to develop strategies to address these issues" (CNA, 1999b). About 50 nursing organisations attend these meetings annually.

Another partnership that has been successful has been Health Action Lobby (HEAL), a coalition of national health and consumer organisations dedicated to protecting and strengthening Canada's health care system. CNA was a founding member in 1991 and co-chaired the coalition with the Canadian Health Care Association (CHCA). The regroupment counts 33 organisations and represents more that 500,000 providers and consumers of health care (HEAL, 1992).

Several multiorganisation partnerships have also evolved around specific issues, such as the need to have a strategy focussed on health care human resources. In this context, the CNA, the Canadian Medical Association (CMA), and CHCA have met with the federal minister and federal/provincial ministers of health.

Patient safety is another important issue. The representatives of several health professional associations, regulatory bodies, protective societies, and legal scholars, to name a few, are developing a national strategy to reduce errors and omissions in health care. Many other partnerships were developed or reinitiated, such as bilateral executive meetings to discuss issues and plan joint actions with CFNU, CMA, CHCA, and several others organisations.

Internationally, the bilateral meetings with the American Nurses Association are ongoing, as are strategic meetings with some other national nursing associations. Even ICN changed its structure to encourage national networking and collaboration among the diverse groups of nurses in the country (ICN, 2001b). It is an era in which networking and partnerships are major assets in moving any agenda ahead.

CURRENT PRIORITIES AND CHALLENGES FOR CANADIAN NURSING

The national vision for nursing in Canada is that nurses, as a collective, contribute to the health of Canadians and the advancement of nursing. Over the years, CNA has expressed its commitment to contribute to the health of the public and to the development of the profession, in that order. This vision has been reiterated in corporate objectives and in diverse briefs to governments, health committees, and various commissions. The document on CNA ends (see Box 7.1) summarises, in a policy format, the majors issues or goals that are current priorities for Canadian nursing.

National Priorities

These goals do not represent all the current issues that a national association has to address, but they focus the policy work and the resources of CNA. The CNA Board further focusses its work after scanning the environment. The scanning exercise is a survey of national provincial and territorial organisations to identify major trends and issues as well as emerging issues that can affect the CNA agenda. The scanning exercise is essential for taking advantage of opportunities and for keeping an eye on emerging issues in nursing and health. The Board of Directors has selected two issues as urgent priorities. They are primary health care and quality practise and leadership.

PRIMARY HEALTH CARE

When the federal government announced that it intended to spend $800 million on primary health care in the 2001 budget, it was an opportunity for CNA to influence once again national and provincial/territorial policy decisions.

The definition of *primary health care* that was approved at the 1978 WHO conference follows:

> Primary health care is essential health care based on practical, scientifically sound and socially acceptable methods and technology made universally accessible to individuals and families in the community through their full participation and at a cost that the community and country can afford to maintain at every stage of their development in the spirit of self-reliance and self-determination. It forms an integral part both of the country's health system, of which it is the central function and main focus, and of the overall social and economic development of the community. It is the first level of contact of individuals, the family, and community with the national health system bringing

health care as close as possible to where the people live and work, and constitutes the first element of a continuing health care process. (WHO, 1978, p. 21)

For the past 2 decades, CNA has been promoting primary health care as a favoured strategy to guide reform of the Canadian health care system. In early 1990, when every province/territory assembled advisory committees and commissions to determine the orientation of the health care reform required, they all included the elements of primary health care (Mhatre & Deber, 1992). The CNA influence was evident since it was the only national health association that was advocating primary health care. Unfortunately, the reform fell short of the direction advocated by the committees and commissions. "Despite the evident political will, the barriers created by the dominant paradigm of the hospital/medical model in most Western industrialised countries, which is antithetical to the principles of a primary health care model, remain a significant challenge for the Canadian nursing profession" (Lemire Rodger & Gallagher, 1995, p. 6).

Today, the current dilemma is that the cutbacks in health care funding do not help redirect the system. Community services are as affected as the hospital sector. Funding for primary health care is not integrated in the regular funding but favours a project approach that can be curtailed at will. As a result, CNA is increasing its efforts to influence future directions. Recently, CNA developed a primary health care framework that incorporates the principles of primary health care, the determinants of health, and the principles of the Canada Health Act to guide a national strategy. CNA is also increasing its coordinated lobbying efforts to make a difference for the health of Canadians (CNA, 2001c).

QUALITY PRACTISE ENVIRONMENT AND LEADERSHIP

The other priority is also directly related to the effects of the cutbacks in health care funding and the so-called reform that started in some parts of the country, such as Alberta, in the early 1990s, and in other parts of the country, such as Ontario, during the later part of the 1990s. The infrastructure that supported nursing in the workplace was in great part eliminated by the introduction of programme management. In programme management, generic managers, rather than health professionals, conduct the programmes and services. Even though the intent of programme management was to increase the collaboration of the multidisciplinary team for the benefit of patients, it eliminated direct supports to each discipline, such as mentorship, educational support, research development, and follow-up on standards of practise, to name a few.

Similar changes were implemented in the United States, with nurses becoming generic executives and less visible to their profession. Fagin (1996) calls the phenomenon a crisis of national discipline leadership in health care and stated, "our institutions can boast of superb leaders in nursing responding to current political and managerial challenges. However, there seems to be an absence of the visionary, transforming nursing leaders who not only respond to their institutional challenges but also speak for their professions and for the public they serve" (p. 30).

Today, there is evidence that practise environments that do not support nurses have adverse effects on patient outcomes, nurse satisfaction, and organisational impact (Baumann et al., 2001; Aiken et al., 2001). In a time when recruitment and retention of nurses is critical, governments are having difficulty effecting changes in the workplace. The role of the federal government has been mostly through funding. The role of provincial/territorial governments has been through funding and directives, for the most part, without any accountability mechanism to ensure that required changes are implemented. In response, CNA has built on previous work and developed a position statement based on the current evidence: "Quality Professional Practice Environments for Registered Nurses" (CNA, 2001c). This position statement will guide a coordinated effort by nurses and other groups to be more effective in bringing about the needed change. The support for further research and the multiple strategies mentioned in the previous section, Nursing Workplace and Human Resources, are part of the national strategy.

National Challenges

There is no doubt that two of the great challenges facing the nursing associations are the complexity of issues and the ability of the profession to be heard.

COMPLEXITY OF ISSUES

The transition from the Industrial Age to the Information Age has brought with it an increased visibility of the complexity of issues. The complexity, the speed, and the force of change we are experiencing simultaneously is described by Toffler (1980) in his book *The Third Wave* as a social upheaval. These changes are mirrored not only in society and in a federal provincial/territorial context but also in health care and nursing. The nursing agenda plays out against this backdrop.

Professional organisations face complexities of their own. An association that is proactive is sensitive to the members it represents and the issues they and the profession are likely to face in the future. The futuristic nature of an effective association is likely to create some tensions within the membership that live in the "here and now." So, "some" member discontent is a positive indicator of an organisation fulfilling its role for the public, the profession, and the members. Too much discontent makes an organisation dysfunctional and paralyses action.

A proactive nursing organisation also seeks opportunities in the sociopolitical environment to pursue its objectives and takes advantage of these opportunities to put forth a nursing agenda. The ability to mobilise quickly is very important. At the same time, the finite resources, the challenge of information in a vast country, the membership base represented, and the effectiveness of the spokepersons are part and parcel of this complexity and the association's ability to influence.

POLITICAL VOICE

The ability to influence and bring about change is one of the powerful tools professional associations like CNA use. In a complex environment, with many agendas competing for attention, it is a very challenging endeavour, and nurses have been preparing themselves for these challenges. The themes of political action, power and influence, strategies, managing change, and leadership are among the most popular themes of conferences and meetings of provincial/territorial, national, and international specialty groups. The topic of political action is also becoming increasingly more visible in the curriculum of many nursing education programmes.

CNA's influence is recognised in such changes in the Canada Health Act, the federal budget for nursing research, and entry-level nursing education. As we begin a new century, nursing has never had more attention from governments than it has now. Nursing is explicitly on the political agenda of all provincial/territorial and federal governments. Paradoxically, major issues to be resolved, such as rebuilding professional practise environments, workloads for nurses, and changes to enrollment in nursing education programmes, are not being addressed adequately. Instead, governments that need a strong nursing profession to ensure sustainability of the Canadian health care system are challenging nursing education, scope of practise, and workloads, among other issues. To have an effective political voice and to manage changes in a very complex environment are major challenges for CNA.

International Priorities

The national priorities and challenges are reflected at the international level. Among ICN priorities, the nursing workforce and credentialing are directly related to CNA's goals.

NURSING WORKFORCE

In the mid–1990s, many countries of the world, in particular the industrialised countries, experienced so-called health care reform or at least cutbacks in health care funding. The impact on the nursing workforce worldwide became evident and of grave concern for the organised profession. In 1996, ICN developed a forum for discussion around nursing workforce issues facing industrialised countries, including Canada, Denmark, Germany, Iceland, Ireland, Japan, New Zealand, Norway, Sweden, the United Kingdom, and the United States. CNA has been an active participant in this forum since its inception. Key issues and trends discussed include working conditions, aging workforce, salary, migration of nurses, industrial action, and work hours. The forum also collaborated on joint positions, such as unethical recruiting in the developing countries (ICN, 2001a).

CREDENTIALING

Another forum was created in 2000 when ICN noticed that governments' focus was increasing on professional self-regulation and that free trade discussions would impact regulation of the profession. Internationally, standard setting was also on the increase, with standards for distance learning, international standards for telenursing, and international competencies for generalist nurses.

The forum is composed of countries who are actively involved in credentialing activities or who have well-advanced plans to become involved. They are Canada, Denmark, Ireland, Jamaica, Japan, New Zealand, Spain, Taiwan, the United Kingdom, and the United States. CNA was again a founding member and contributed to the development of an ICN credentialing framework and ICN credentialing research registry. A few of the key issues and trends discussed include terminology, gaining and maintaining competencies, cross-border assessments, and evidence of impact on patient outcomes (ICN, 2001a). These forums are means to leverage international partnerships for the benefit of the profession and the public.

International Challenge

One international challenge that has direct ramifications for CNA is the need for ICN to increase its membership and to be more inclusive. With the proliferation of nursing groups representing diverse facets of the profession in most countries, the need to find ways to unite the voice of nurses becomes a serious challenge.

ICN and its national nursing associations must face the fact that this relationship alone is no longer sufficient to maintain a strong organisation. Change is needed—change that will build on diversity and facilitate four outcomes:

- United voice
- Enhanced national and global recognition
- International connection
- Flexibility and choice (ICN, 2001a, p.8).

CNA supported the proposal for a new membership model in ICN and explored for Canada a model of collaboration with other national nursing partners. This new model will increase the power of representation of Canadian nursing on the international scene.

THE ROAD AHEAD

The issues are complex, the power of representation more challenging than ever, and the voice of nursing must be strong and united. Within that context, the representation power of CNA is important. The road ahead for CNA will need to include an increased representation base in Quebec and Ontario. Another key element for the future of the profession is how the profession will deal with the issue of leadership. Within the priority of quality practise environments, this issue needs to be addressed very strategically. After the dismantling of the professional infrastructure in health care in the late 1990s, it would be shortsighted to recreate and to count only on positional leadership. The profession needs to move toward a model of leadership and influence by all professionals so that nursing values can be present in all disciplinary and multidisciplinary networks in health care. In an ideal model,

- Clinical nurses lead the clinical decisions.
- Nurse managers lead decisions about structure, processes, resources, and the environment in which care is provided.
- Nurse educators lead the educational decisions.
- Nurse researchers lead the knowledge discovery, dissemination, and application decisions.
- Horizontal leadership creates new relationships among nurses for a stronger profession.

The road ahead will also include phenomenal growth not only at the provincial/territorial level but also at the national level in the areas of credentialing and regulation. The ICN framework will guide the need to pursue credentialing of individuals, programmes, and products. In Canada, credentialing mechanisms have been developed for individuals in regard to registration for entry to practise and certification in a specialty. We have credentialing for some programmes, such as accreditation of a school of nursing or nursing services, but we have not developed credentialing for our products. A lot needs to be done, and CNA must find its role in this new environment. These are a few of the issues Canadian nursing and CNA will face within the profession on the road ahead.

SUMMARY

This chapter addresses the major roles, priorities, and challenges for CNA. In Canada, CNA's role is to protect the public and speak on behalf of the profession and its professionals.

Some of the characteristics required to increase the influence of a professional association are a specialised body of knowledge and competent application of that knowledge, a code of ethics, standards of practise, autonomy and self-regulation, a tradition of public service, accountability, and professional association.

CNA is the national voice of nursing. As such, it focusses on the power of representation and self-regulation. The work of CNA in self-regulation is reflected in the educational field and in the evolution of credentialing in nursing.

Examples of the power of representation include the CNA's influence on the initial Canada Health Act and subsequent legislative changes, nursing research and education, and conditions of nurses' workplaces.

Current national priorities for CNA are primary health care and quality practise environments and leadership. Current and national challenges for CNA include the complexity of health care and professional issues and an effective political voice. Future challenges for Canadian nursing are a strong and united voice with increased representation in Quebec and Ontario; development of appropriate leadership models to promote nursing values in all disciplinary and multidisciplinary health care networks; and growth and influence in the areas of credentialing and regulation.

Reflections on the Chapter

1. Describe a professional association you are familiar with and explain what role it fulfills in society.

2. In the past 20 years, what issues have been affected by the power of representation of CNA? Select one and describe how the influence of CNA changed the course of action.

3. Identify the types of members of CNA and discuss the role they play in the formulation of policy.

4. What are the two current priorities for CNA? Discuss one priority and its progress at both the national and international levels.

5. What are the challenges facing Canadian nursing, now and in the future?

REFERENCES

Advisory Committee on Health Human Resources. (2000). *The nursing strategy for Canada.* Ottawa, ON: Author.

Aiken, L., Clarke, S. P., Sloane, D. M., Sochalski, J. A., Busse, R., Clarke, H., Giovanetti, P., Hunt, J., Rafferty, A. M., & Shamian, J. (2001). Nurses report on hospital care in five countries. *Health Affairs, 20*(3), 43–53.

Baumann, A., O'Brien-Pallas, L., Armstrong-Stassen, M., Blythe, J., Bourbonnias, R., Cameron, S., Irvine Doran, D., Kerr, M., McGillis Hall, L., Vezina, M., Butt, M., & Ryan, L. (2001). *Commitment and care: The benefits of a healthy workplace for nurse, the patient and their system.* Ottawa, ON: Canadian Health Services Research Foundation.

Baumgart, A. J., & Larsen, J. (1988). *Canadian nursing faces the future development and change.* St Louis, MI: CV Mosby.

Canadian Council on Social Development. (2000).

Report on the labour market integration of nursing graduates in Canada, 1986–1997. Ottawa, ON: Canadian Nurses Association.

Canada Health Act of 1984—Bill C-3. (1984). Ottawa: House of Commons, Government of Canada.

Canadian Health Services Research Foundation. (2001). *CHSRF/CIHR Chair Awards.* [On-line]. Available http://www.chsrf.ca/programs/cadre/chairs/awarded_e.shtml.

Canadian Institute of Health Information. (2001). *Registered nurses database, supply & distribution of registered nurses in Canada 2000.* Ottawa, ON: Author.

Canadian Nurses Association. (1958). *The first fifty years.* Ottawa, ON: Author.

Canadian Nurses Association. (1968). *The leaf and the lamp.* Ottawa, ON: Author.

Canadian Nurses Association. (1980). *Putting health*

into health care: Submission to the Health Services Review. Ottawa, ON: Author.

Canadian Nurses Association. (1984). *The research imperative for nursing in Canada: A 5 year plan towards the year 2000.* Ottawa, ON: Author.

Canadian Nurses Association. (1998). *The quiet crisis in health care.* Ottawa, ON: Author.

Canadian Nurses Association. (1999a). *Repair, realign, and resource health care.* Ottawa, ON: Author.

Canadian Nurses Association. (1999b). *Report on the 3rd National Nursing Forum "Positioning nursing for the next millennium."* Ottawa, ON: Author.

Canadian Nurses Association. (2000a). *CNA membership 2000—Finance & Administration Division.* Ottawa, ON: Author.

Canadian Nurses Association. (2000b). *Rebuilding Canada's health system starts with renewing the nursing workforce.* Ottawa, ON: Author.

Canadian Nurses Association. (2001a). *Letters patent, bylaws, rules and regulation.* Ottawa, ON: Author.

Canadian Nurses Association. (2001b). *Revitalizing the nursing workforce and strengthening medicare.* Ottawa, ON: Author.

Canadian Nurses Association. (2001c). *Board of Directors Minutes, November 2–3, 2001.* Ottawa, ON: Author.

Canadian Nurses Association. (2002). Certification. Retrieved from www.cna-nurses.ca/pages/certification /certification_frame.html. September, 2002.

Dalton, J., Speakman, H., Duffey, M., Carson, J. (1994). The evolution of a profession. Where do boards of nursing fit in? *Journal of Professional Nursing, 10*(5), 319–325.

Dollinger, M., (2000). Professional Associations: Ethics, duty and power. *Journal of the New York State Nurses Association, 31*(2), 28–30.

Fagin, C. M. (1996). Executive leadership: Improving nursing practice, education, and research. *Journal of Nursing Administration, 26*(30), 30–37.

Hawthorne, D., & Yurkovich, N. (1994). Caring: The raison d'être of the professional nurse. *CJNOA, 7*(4), 35–55.

Health Action Lobby. (1992). *Medicare: A value worth keeping.* Ottawa, ON: HEAL.

International Council of Nurses. (2001a). *Council of National Representatives Meeting, Copenhagen, Denmark, June 2001.* Geneva, Switzerland: Author.

International Council of Nurses. (2001b). *From vision to action: ICN in the 21st century* (revised February 2001). Geneva, Switzerland: Author.

International Council of Nurses. (2001c). *The ICN credentialing framework Unpublished manuscript.* Geneva, Switzerland: Author.

International Council of Nurses. (2001d). *The ICN credentialing research registry—Draft 1.* Unpublished manuscript. Geneva, Switzerland: Author.

Kerr, J. R., & MacPhail, J. (1996). *Canadian nursing issues and perspectives* (3rd ed.). St. Louis: Mosby.

Lemire Rodger, G. (1991). Canadian nurses succeed again! The launch of Canada's first doctoral degree in nursing. *Journal of Advanced Nursing, 16*(12), 1395–1396.

Lemire Rodger, G. (1985). The move toward primary health care in Canada: Community health nursing from 1985 to 1995. In M. J. Stewart (Ed.), *Community nursing: Promoting Canadians' health* (pp. 37–58). Toronto: W. B. Saunders.

Lemire Rodger, G. (1999). Intraorganizational politics. In J.M. Hibberd & D.L. Smith (Eds.), *Nursing Management in Canada* (2nd ed.) (pp. 279–295).

MacPhail, J. (1996). The role of the Canadian Nurses Association in the development of nursing in Canada. In J. Ross Kerr & J. MacPhail (Eds.), *Canadian nursing issues and perspectives* (3rd ed.) (pp. 31–54). St. Louis: Mosby.

Meilicke, D., Larsen, J. (1988). Leadership and the leaders of the Canadian Nurses Association. In A. J. Baumgart & J. Larsen (Eds.), *Canadian nursing faces the future* (pp. 421–459). St. Louis: Mosby.

Merton, R. K. (1958). The functions of the professional association. *AJN, 58*(1), 50–54.

Mhatre, S. L., & Deber, R. (1992). From equal access to health care to equitable access to health: Review of Canadian provincial commissions and reports. *International Journal of Health Services, 22*(4), 645–668.

National Forum on Health. (1997). *Canada health action: Building on the legacy.* Vol. 1. Ottawa, ON: Author.

Orthoscope. (1999). CNA corner. Nursing research fund created in 1999 federal budget. *Orthoscope, 5*(2), 6.

Registered Nurses Association of British Columbia. (1974). Political action influenced health legislation in Quebec. *RNABC News, 6*(1), 11–12.

Registered Nurses Association of British Columbia. (1999). *Nursing self-regulation: Nurses govern nursing in the public interest.* Vancouver, BC: Author.

Registered Nurses Association of British Columbia. (undated). *Education requirements for future nurses.* Vancouver, BC: Author.

Ryten, E. (1997). *A statistical picture of the past, present, and future of registered nurses in Canada.* Ottawa, ON: Canadian Nurses Association.

Shiflett, N., & McFarland, D. E. (1978). Power and the nursing administrator. *Journal of Nursing Administration, 7*(3), 19–23.

Styles, M. M. (1983). The anatomy of a profession. *AORN, 38*(3), 484–498.

Toffler, A. (1980). *The third wave.* New York: William Morrow.

Versteeg, D. F. (1979). The political process or the power and glory. In: D. E. McFarland & N. Shiflett (Eds.), *Nursing dimensions, 7*(2), p. 20–27.

World Health Organization. (1978). *Primary health care: Report on the International Conference on Primary Health Care,* Alma Ata, USSR, 6–12 September 1978. Geneva, Switzerland: Author.

CHAPTER 8

Canadian Provincial and Territorial Professional Associations and Colleges

Laurel Brunke

Chapter Objectives

At the completion of this chapter, you will be able to:

1. Describe the evolution of nursing regulation in Canada.
2. Recognise how differences in legislation have resulted in different approaches to nursing regulation.
3. Identify differences in the roles and responsibilities of provincial and territorial associations and colleges.

(continued)

Nurses attending this conference discuss rural health, policy, and research. Photography by Meg McDonogh.

2) what is CNO

1) Evolution of regulatory — what are they
how benefit. Public
Those
what is Regulatory

Chapter Objectives *(Continued)*

4. Understand issues associated with registration mobility and trends in regulation.

5. Discuss potential implications of current issues facing provincial and territorial colleges and associations.

This chapter will assist the reader to understand and appreciate the value of nursing self-regulation. To achieve this, the evolution of nursing regulation in Canada is described, as are differences in regulatory approaches across jurisdictions, issues associated with these differences, and considerations for the future of the regulation of nursing by provincial/territorial nursing associations and colleges.

REGULATION

The purpose of regulating the nursing profession is straightforward: protection of the public, which makes regulation itself a most complex issue.

The What and Why of Regulation

What is regulation? Regulation is simply the "forms and processes whereby order, consistency, and control are brought to an occupation and its practises" (International Council of Nurses, 1985, p. 7). The International Council of Nurses (ICN) states the following goals of regulation:

- Define the profession and its members.
- Determine the scope of practise.
- Set standards of education and competent and ethical practise.
- Establish systems of accountability and credentialing processes (Styles and Affara, 1997).

Finocchio and colleagues, with the Taskforce on Health Care Workforce Regulation (1995), take a broader view of regulation. They believe that regulation of the health care workforce best serves the public's interest if it promotes effective health outcomes and protects the public from harm; ensures accountability to the public; respects consumers' rights to choose their health care providers from a range of safe options; encourages a health care system that is flexible, rational, and cost-effective and that facilitates effective working relationships among health care providers; and provides for professional and geographic mobility of competent providers.

Evolution of Regulation

Regulation of the professions really began with the formation of crafts and guilds. There was, and always has been, competition among trades people in relation to the goods they sold and the services they provided. The crafts and guilds were made up of the people who were known to provide quality products and services, in part because they developed standards for these products and services. Of course, with increased quality came increased costs and, in some circumstances, a monopoly on the products and services the guilds were providing. From these guilds and crafts arose licensing laws intended to protect the public and ensure that only members of the crafts or guilds could provide the specified services and products (Cutshall, 1998). These traditional licensing laws provided for exclusive scope of practise, or what is sometimes referred to as *turf protection*. Today, there is a shift away from this approach to regulation (discussed later in the chapter).

The nature of regulation has changed in other ways over the years. Historically, professional regulation focussed essentially on "gate-keeping," that is, setting the requirements for those who can enter the profession and disciplining those who fail to meet the standards of the profession. Finocchio and colleagues (1995) have said, in relation to health care workforce regulation in the United States, "though it has served us well in the past, health care regulation is out of step with today's health care needs and expectations" (p. vii); however, nursing regulatory bodies in Canada have for some time embraced a more contemporary approach to regulation. This approach recognises that there is more to regulation than gate-keeping.

The Canadian Nurses Association (CNA) (2001a) "believes that the public interest is best served when regulatory bodies adopt a framework that strengthens clinical practise and leadership; provides supports to correct and improve practise; and focuses not only on individual nurses, but also on promoting quality practise environments" (p. 1). The Registered Nurses Association of British Columbia (RNABC) and others have adopted a regulatory framework of promoting good practise, preventing poor practise, and intervening when practise is unacceptable. The benefits of promotion and prevention strategies—the quality improvement approach—means that intervention with unacceptable practise can be kept at a minimum (RNABC, 2000).

REGULATION OF NURSING

Many nurses take it for granted that nursing is a profession and that, like other professions, nurses are entitled to collective professional autonomy, that is, the self-regulation of the profession as a whole. Professional autonomy means that, with appropriate public input, professional groups govern themselves. Canada has a tradition that communities of people within society take responsibility for meeting their obligations, both to themselves and the community at large. They do this by managing their affairs in a way that respects and furthers the good of society while recognising the legitimate interests of their members. This is the essence of self-regulation (RNABC, 2000). However, self-regulation is a privilege of a profession, not a right. In Canada self-regulation of nursing is less than a century old.

History of Nursing Regulation in Canada

The move to obtain registration for nurses began in 1893 with the formation of the American Society of Superintendents of Training Schools for Nursing of the United States and Canada. This was followed by the development of the Associated Alumnae of the United States and Canada in 1896. Securing legislation to "differentiate the trained from the untrained" (CNA, 1968, p. 35) was the purpose of the Associated Alumnae. When it was recognised that the fight for the nursing legislation had to be fought separately in each country, the Canadian and American groups separated. Consequently, the Canadian Society of Superintendents of Training Schools for Nurses was formed in 1907, with formation of the Provisional Society of the Canadian Nurses Association of Trained Nurses following in 1908 (CNA, 1968).

The development of provincial graduate nurses' associations was due in large part to the increase in the number of nursing personnel that occurred at the end of the 19th century. Competition between trained professional nurses and nurses with little or no professional training was evident in the areas of wages and status. Moreover, no mechanisms for ensuring uniformity in nursing service standards were in place (CNA, 1968). Kerr (1996) identified two powerful social forces that affected the pursuit of legislation for the registration of nurses: first, consciousness raising regarding women's rights that was part of the effort to obtain the vote for women; and second, the increased valuing of nurses and nurses' services that occurred during World War I. Kerr speculated that these factors, as well as a general recognition that a mechanism was needed to ensure that nurses were qualified, led to the passage of legislation in all provinces over a 12-year period—a relatively brief time.

In 1910, the nurses of Nova Scotia became the first to have nursing legislation. Registration was voluntary, and nongraduate nurses could still practise. The Registered Nurses Act, which incorporated the Graduate Nurses Association of Nova Scotia, set out, among other things, the powers of the Association and the duty of officers, admission of nurses as members, discipline of members, and appointment of examiners. Legislation proclaimed in Manitoba in 1913 was more in keeping with current legislation as it set out minimum standards for admission, curriculum in schools of nursing, and the registration and discipline of practicing nurses. By 1914, all provinces except Prince Edward Island had a provincial nurses' association.

Work to achieve legislation was not easy, as can be seen in the following example from British Columbia, where efforts to achieve legislation began in 1912. In 1914, the government decided that the nurses' Bill could not be accepted as a government measure, and the Association was advised to have the Bill presented as a public measure introduced by a private member.

When the Bill was reintroduced in 1916, it was suggested that the President and Secretary of the College of Physicians and Surgeons should be members of the Council of the Nurses' Association and that the orders, regulations, fees, and bylaws should be subject to the approval of the College of Physicians and Surgeons. The Nurses' Association decided to withdraw the Bill rather than include these amendments. A letter was sent to the College of Physicians and Surgeons asking if these amendments met with their approval and if they wished to have graduate nurses under their control. This was unanimously opposed by the College. A revised Bill was passed in 1918, and interestingly enough, the first council was named by the College of Physicians and Surgeons (Kerr, 1944).

Ontario was the last province to achieve legislation for nursing because of objections from nurses who felt they could not meet the qualifications and lobbying by hospitals whose administrators feared that education standards for schools could not be met. However, by 1922, all nine provinces had some form of nurse registration.

The first act concerning nursing in Newfoundland came into effect in 1931, and the Newfoundland Graduate Nurses' Association was incorporated in 1935. Newfoundland formed as a province in 1949 and enacted legislation for nurses, with mandatory registration, in 1953. Legislation regulating nurses in the Yukon and Northwest Territories was enacted in 1994 and 1988, respectively. Membership in the Northwest Territories Registered Nurses Association, formed in 1975, was initially voluntary. Before the legislation being enacted in 1994 in the Yukon, registered nurses working in the Yukon had to be registered in another Canadian jurisdiction.

Mandatory Registration

Initial legislation for nursing varied across provinces, and in some instances, aspects of the legislation were inconsistent with the primary purpose of the regulation of the profession, (i.e., protection of the public). Initially, not all nurses had to be registered to practise nursing. In some jurisdictions, these nonregistered individuals were permitted to use the title registered nurse even if they did not meet the requirements for entry to the profession or uphold the professions' standards. In 1922, the Nova Scotia Act was amended to the effect that a register be kept "in which shall be entered the name of every member of the Association" and "only those persons whose names are entered in the register shall be deemed qualified to hold themselves out to the public as registered nurses" (S. Farouse, personal communication). Although not the same as mandatory registration, it was a first step toward this important mechanism for public protection.

Quebec was the first province to have mandatory licensing with the passing of the Quebec Nurses' Act in 1946 (CNA, 1968). The achievement of mandatory registration took considerably longer in other provinces, with British Columbia and Saskatchewan being the last to make this change to existing legislation. Mandatory registration was a requirement in the first acts for nursing enacted in the Yukon and Northwest Territories.

Authority of Nursing Regulatory Bodies

In Canada, authority to regulate the profession comes from legislation enacted by provincial and territorial governments. The nature of the legislation varies across Canada, although there is an increasing interest from governments in enacting uniform legislation for all professions in a province or territory. Regardless of the form of the legislation, nursing regulatory bodies in Canada generally have authority for the following:

- Standards of education and qualifications for members
- Standards of practise and professional ethics
- Use of title
- Scope of practise
- Professional discipline
- Approval of education programmes for entry to the profession
- Continuing competence requirements for members

With the exception of Ontario, responsibility for regulation of registered nursing rests with the provincial/territorial professional association. In Ontario, this authority rests with the College of Nurses of Ontario, which also has responsibility for regulating registered practical nurses. In other provinces, this group of professionals, also known as licensed practical nurses or certified nursing assistants, are regulated by separate organisations. Ontario is the only jurisdiction in Canada to have both a regulatory organisation and professional association, the Registered Nurses Association of Ontario (RNAO). The RNAO's mission is to promote excellence in nursing practise and to advocate for the role of nursing in empowering the people of Ontario to achieve and maintain their optimal health and to provide membership-centred services.

Contrast this with the mission of the College of Nurses of Ontario to protect the public's right to quality nursing services by providing leadership to the nursing profession in self-regulation. Risk (1992) identifies that the uniqueness in Ontario "is based on the philosophical premise that there is an inherent conflict (real or perceived) between professional self-interest and public interest, and that regulatory decisions must be separate from professional advancement" (p. 368). At the heart of this issue is the question of whether an association that has as one of its goals the promotion of the profession can do this in a way that does not interfere with meeting its public interest mandate. There is no evidence to suggest that this combined role has affected the ability of the other Canadian nursing regulatory bodies to meet their public protection mandate. Perhaps that is why the Ontario model is unique, not only in Canada but in many other countries as well.

Other differences between jurisdictional authority relate to approval of nursing education programmes, requirements for continuing competence for registration renewal, requirements for reentry into practise, language requirements for registration, and approaches to regulation of nurse practitioners.

APPROVAL OF NURSING EDUCATION PROGRAMMES

Of particular interest is the authority for approval of nursing education programmes for entry to the profession. This authority typically includes establishing the criteria for approval of the nursing education programme as well as actually approving the programme. Essentially, this gives the profession the authority to establish the education, that is, the competency requirements for entry to the profession. In most instances, approval is limited to education programmes for entry to the profession. However, the Association of Registered Nurses of Newfoundland and Labrador has authority to approve the education programme for nurse practitioners. Until recently, the responsibility and authority for approving nursing education programmes has resided with the nursing regulatory body, except in Ontario, Alberta, and Quebec. The 1999 agreement in Alberta to establish the Nursing Education Program Approval Board (NEPAB) transfers the authority from the Universities' Coordinating Council to this board, which is composed of representatives from regional health authorities, educational institutions, the nursing profession, and the public (Way, 2001). Although the Alberta Association of Registered Nurses (AARN) provides funds for NEPAB support staff, space, and expenses, AARN has no direct influence on the NEPAB. Until recently in Ontario, authority for approval and monitoring of university programmes was vested in the Council of University Programs in Nursing and the university senate or governing council. Recent changes to the regulations under the Ontario Nursing Act provide for baccalaureate programmes in nursing to be approved by a body or bodies designated by the Council or by the Council itself. This is a very significant change because before this, the College of Nurses of Ontario (CNO) had no formal role in the approval of schools. CNO has selected the Canadian Association of University Schools of Nursing (CAUSN) as the agency to conduct the approval process. In Quebec, the Ministry of Education has responsibility for monitoring diploma programmes. The Ordre des Infirmieres et Infirmiers du Quebec (OIIQ) was invited to participate, for the first time in 2002, in the consultation process for nursing curriculum.

REGULATION OF NURSE PRACTITIONERS

Another area of notable difference among jurisdictions is in the current or intended approaches to the regulation of nurse practitioners. Registered nurses have been working in extended or expanded roles, predominantly in rural or remote settings, for many years. Although these roles are considered by some to parallel those of the nurse practitioner, authority to carry out functions such as diagnosing, prescribing, and managing labour and delivery comes through delegated medical acts rather than legislation that authorises registered nurses to carry out these functions autonomously. Pressures related to physician shortages, particularly in underserviced areas, and increasing pressures on health budgets have resulted in renewed interest in implementing the nurse practitioner role. The current status of nurse practitioners across Canada can be seen in Table 8.1, which demonstrates that use of nurse practitioners varies considerably across the country, as does the way in which the role is enacted. In some jurisdictions, collaborative relationships with physicians are mandated; in others, they are not. In some jurisdictions, such as Newfoundland, the title nurse practitioner is, or will be, protected. In many others, there are no plans to protect the title; and in some provinces, these nurses are identified in different ways. In Ontario, for example, they are registered as RN/Extended Class.

This raises questions as to how the public can be easily informed about which registered nurses have authority for some of the functions commonly associated with the nurse practitioner role. Another significant difference is that, in some jurisdictions, the nurse practitioner has authority for a "package" of functions, such as in Ontario and

Table 8.1 Regulation of Nurse Practitioners in Canada

JURISDICTION	STATUS OF NURSE PRACTITIONER LEGISLATION
Alberta	• Authority under the Public Health Act to provide extended health care services in primary health care settings (the community must be designated by the Minister of Health and Wellness and includes some urban settings, such as the inner city in Calgary). • Nurses are registered on an extended-practise register and are authorised to provide the following extended health services: diagnosis and treatment of common disorders affecting the health of adults and children; referral; and emergency services. • Limits on practise, including prescriptive authority, are defined at the regional level. • In response to the 2002 report of the Premier's Advisory Committee on Health (the Mazankowski report), legislation and regulations to provide for nurse practitioners to practise independently will be finalized in July 2002.
British Columbia	• In 2000, the B.C. government announced its intention to educate, regulate, and deploy nurse practitioners by 2002.
Manitoba	• Registered nurses with the required competencies will have the authority to include one or more of the following in their practise: ordering/receiving reports of screening and diagnostic tests designated in regulation; prescribing drugs designated in regulation; and performing minor surgical and invasive procedures designated in regulation. These nurses will have their names entered on a separate register.
New Brunswick	• In 2001, government announced its intention to introduce nurse practitioner legislation in the fall as well as remove legislative barriers that prevent registered nurses from practising to full scope. • The Nurses Association of New Brunswick approved bylaws in 2001 that provide for the regulation of nurse practitioners.

(continued)

Table 8.1   Regulation of Nurse Practitioners in Canada (*Continued*)

JURISDICTION	STATUS OF NURSE PRACTITIONER LEGISLATION
Newfoundland and Labrador	• Advanced practise nurse practitioner (primary health care) implemented in 1998 and advanced practise nurse practitioner (specialty practise) implemented in 2001. • Primary health care nurse practitioner must establish and document a collaborative working relationship with a physician. Regulations outline circumstances in which consultation is required. • Regulations set out the diagnostic tests and drugs nurse practitioners can order.
Northwest Territories/ Nunuvat	• 60% of nurses work in expanded roles in primary health care settings. • Legislative changes of 2002 included prescriptive authority for nurse practitioners.
Nova Scotia	• The Registered Nurses Act authorizes nurse practitioners (both primary care and specialty), working in collaborative arrangements with a physician or group of physicians anywhere in Nova Scotia, to make diagnoses of diseases, disorders, or conditions and communicate those diagnoses to patients; order and interpret selected screening and diagnostic tests; select, recommend, prescribe, and monitor the effectiveness of certain drugs and treatments; and perform other procedures that are outlined in collaborative practise agreements. • A three-party committee, made up of representatives from the regulatory bodies for nursing, medicine, and pharmacy, will establish guidelines for expectations for diagnosing, ordering diagnostic tests, and prescribing drugs. • Nurse practitioners in both primary health care and speciality practise will be expected to establish a practise agreement locally with a physician colleague to specify their accountabilities, consultation, and referral processes with respect to patient care.
Ontario	• Primary health care nurse practitioner implemented in 1998. • No plans to regulate specialty nurse practitioners. • Primary health care nurse practitioners can communicate a diagnosis of a disease or disorder; order diagnostic ultrasonography and some forms of x-ray tests; and prescribe and administer drugs listed in regulations.
Prince Edward Island	• There are no provisions for nurse practitioners. Initial consultation is underway with members of the Association of Nurses of Prince Edward Island.
Quebec	• Registered nurses work in expanded-scope roles primarily in primary health care in remote and isolated settings and in demonstration projects in neonatal intensive care. • The Ordre des Infirmieres et Infirmiers du Quebec has proposed the regulation of primary care and specialist nurse practitioners with authority to, under certain conditions, diagnose health problems; order and interpret diagnostic tests; and prescribe, dispense, and adjust medication.

Table 8.1 Regulation of Nurse Practitioners in Canada *(Continued)*	
JURISDICTION	**STATUS OF NURSE PRACTITIONER LEGISLATION**
Saskatchewan	• Amendments to the Registered Nurses Act in 2001 enable the Saskatchewan Registered Nurses Association to regulate nurse practitioners.
	• Registered nurses whose practises overlap significantly with medical or pharmaceutical roles will require advanced practise regulation.
	• Areas for which special regulation will be required are advanced nursing/medical diagnosis; ordering and interpreting diagnostic tests; prescribing and distributing medications; and minor surgical procedures.
Yukon	• 20% of nurses work in nurse practitioner-type roles in rural communities.
	• Existing legislation governing all registered nurses is broad and provides authority for this practise.
	• Registered nurses will not make full use of their authority to prescribe until related competencies and criteria are established, but legislative changes are not required.

Newfoundland, whereas in others, such as Manitoba, authority will be given for each individual function.

The evolution of the regulation of nurse practitioners provides a good example of how differences in regulatory approaches can have implications for the consumer of health care. Consider how much easier it would be for consumers and other health care providers to understand the role and the responsibilities of nurse practitioners if the regulatory framework was the same in all jurisdictions. It also provides an example of how differing approaches to regulation can affect the mobility of nurses across the country because the requirements for recognition as a nurse practitioner are beginning to vary across jurisdictions.

ISSUES IN REGULATION

As demonstrated in earlier sections of the chapter, there is a need for regulation to evolve to respond to the changing world and needs of the health care system. Emerging issues in regulation are related to a variety of factors.

Impact of Globalisation

Globalisation of the economy presents significant challenges to countries to remain competitive in world markets. In this context, we are seeing the adoption of policies favouring deregulation, decentralisation, and, in some instances, a reduced role for government. Advances in technology are already affecting how health care is delivered, with increasing use of video and data communications. At the same time, trade agreements, such as the General Agreement on Trade in Services, the North American Free Trade Agreement, and the Treaty on European Union, are facilitating the movement of goods, people, and services across national boundaries. These agreements have significant implications for regulated professions because they promote uniform standards and reduce bureaucratic and regulatory barriers to mobility.

MOBILITY IN CANADA

In Canada, the Agreement on Internal Trade (AIT) requires governments to recognise mutually the occupational qualifications of workers who are qualified in any other province or territory and to reconcile differences in occupational standards. Standards, criteria, and indicators to support the registration process are developed by jurisdictions to ensure that practitioners are able to provide safe, competent, ethical nursing care. Registered nurse regulatory bodies are committed to registration processes that are efficient, transparent, and fair and guided by the following principles:

1. Public interest—nursing is regulated in the public interest. The purpose of regulation is to protect the public from incompetent or unethical practitioners; promote efficient and high-quality provision of services; and strike a balance between the rights and responsibilities of members and those of the public.
2. Flexibility—processes must evolve to allow for growth, change, and innovation.
3. Fairness and equity—demonstration of fairness and equity in all regulatory processes is essential to maintaining the public's trust that the profession should retain the privilege of self-regulation.
4. Administrative efficiency—the interests of the public, members, and applicants are best served when regulatory bodies operate in a cost-effective and efficient manner.
5. Mobility—mobility of nurses means that nurses wishing to register in another Canadian jurisdiction encounter only those registration processes necessary to ensure that quality care for the public is not compromised. (Canadian Registered Nurse Endorsement Document, 2001).

Work to achieve registration by endorsement in Canada began in the early 1980s with a series of resolutions passed at the Canadian Nurses Association's annual meeting. Initially, discussions centred on developing standards for reciprocity of registration, which implied that a nurse registered in one Canadian jurisdiction could become registered in another jurisdiction simply by showing his or her registration card. Because of concerns that reciprocity, interpreted in this way, did not allow for jurisdictional differences in legislation and might not fully protect the public, it was agreed to work toward endorsement as the mechanism to support mobility.

Endorsement means that once a nurse has established registration in a Canadian province/territory, that nurse should be granted registration on the basis of having been registered in another Canadian province/territory, provided that the nurse's registration is in good standing and that the nurse has met the requirements regarding current practise in the province in which she or he is making application. Standards and criteria, with indicators for each criterion, are used as the basis for endorsement and the identification of differences in requirements between jurisdictions. Four concepts form the basis for the standards: initial competence; continuing competence and capacity to practise; satisfactory professional conduct and character; and confirmed identity (Box 8.1). These standards form the basis of the Mutual Recognition Agreement developed by Canadian registered nurse regulatory bodies in response to the

BOX 8.1

Standards for Endorsement of Registration

Standard 1: The applicant has acquired the competencies (knowledge, skills, attitudes, abilities, and judgement) required for entry to practise as a registered nurse in a Canadian jurisdiction.

Standard 2: The applicant has met the continuing competence requirements imposed by the jurisdiction in which the nurse is registered/licensed or was most recently registered to practise.

Standard 3: The applicant demonstrates the capacity to practise as a registered nurse.

Standard 4: The applicant demonstrates the good character and ethical professional conduct necessary to practise as a registered nurse.

Standard 5: The applicant establishes and confirms identity for entry on the register.

requirements of the Agreement on Internal Trade (AIT). By the fall of 2001, most jurisdictions had signed the agreement. In some jurisdictions, changes in legislation are required before the regulatory body can meet the requirements under AIT.

COMPETENCIES OR CREDENTIALS AS THE BASIS FOR REGISTRATION

Because of agreements such as AIT, there is increasing emphasis on competencies rather than credentials as the basis for registration. The challenge is twofold. First, how to achieve consensus across Canada regarding the competences required for registered nurses' practise. Second, how to develop an efficient, affordable approach to competence assessment.

Consensus on the competencies required for entry-level practise in 1996 and projected for 2001 for registered nurses, registered psychiatric nurses, and licensed/registered practical nurses was reached in 1997 through the National Nursing Competency Project (NNCP) (CNA, 1997). In addition, the project identified contexts for entry-level practise in 1996 and 2001 for these three nursing groups as well as entry-level competencies that are shared and those that are unique for 1996 and 2001. The competency statements developed were intended to provide information for decision making regarding registration of new graduates, equivalence of out-of-province graduates, requirements for entry examinations, and curricula for basic nursing education programmes. It was cautioned that the competency statements would need to be considered in the context of a health care system characterised by constant and rapid change. The report further cautioned that the competency statements are not at a level of specificity which would be required for measurement or assessment and further work would be required to refine the results (CNA, 1997).

Since the project's completion, several jurisdictional regulatory bodies have engaged in various processes to validate and further refine the competencies for their registrants. Of note is that assessment of the competencies further identified by jurisdictions demonstrates significant consistency between jurisdictions. The competencies for the Canadian Registered Nurse Examination (CRNE) draw on the NNCP competencies and the entry-level competencies used in the provinces and territories. The revised CRNE exam is one significant means of reducing barriers to mobility of the nursing workforce across Canada as required by AIT.

The 1998 decision by the OIIQ to discontinue using the Canadian Nurses Association's Nurse Registration/Licensure Examination and develop its own examination has added another dimension to the issue of mobility. At the time the OIIQ exam was implemented in January 2000, no validation and comparison studies had been conducted to compare it and the CRNE. Because successful completion of the CRNE is a requirement for registration in all jurisdictions and for endorsement of registration, OIIQ proposed that for a transition period of at least 2 years, OIIQ would recognise nurses from other jurisdictions who passed the CRNE if those jurisdictions would recognise OIIQ members who passed the OIIQ Professional Examination (H. Rajotte, personal communication, December 23, 1999). Response to this request from jurisdictions has varied, with several not agreeing to this request for accommodation until the validation and comparison studies have been completed. This situation provides another example of how differing approaches to regulation at the jurisdictional level can have a negative impact on the mobility of nurses.

Development of an efficient, affordable approach to competence assessment presents considerable challenge. The reality is that affordable assessment technology is not readily available. If competence assessment is to substitute for credentials as a mechanism for ensuring assessment for practise, the tools must be valid and reliable, and development of these takes both time and money. For example, estimates of the individual cost for assessment of competencies required for certification as a nurse practitioner range as high as $4,000, not including developmental costs for the process. The question is, who should pay—the practitioner, the profession through the regulatory body, or the governments driving this change? This is a significant question because competence assessment processes must evolve as practise evolves and therefore do not represent a one-time cost.

REGISTRATION ACROSS BORDERS

As technology increases, the geographic borders of practise begin to disappear. Registered nurses working in call centres, as well as those providing consultation or education services over the Internet, may be providing services to patients in other provinces, territories, or even countries. Canadian nursing regulatory bodies have agreed in principle that when the nurse and the patient are in two different jurisdictions, the nurse is considered to be practising in the jurisdiction in which he or she is located. As such, the expectation is that registered nurses provide these services in a manner consistent with the code of ethics, standards for nursing practise, practise guidelines, and relevant legal authority of the province or territory in which they are registered and practising. Under this model, registered nurses must ensure that patients are aware of the nurse's name, professional designation, provincial or territorial regulatory body, and place of work to ensure that the patient has the information required to make a complaint regarding the nurse's practise, if needed (Canadian Nurses Association, 2001b).

This approach differs from that being implemented in the United States, where the National Council of State Boards of Nursing agreed to establish a model for multistate recognition of the basic entry-level nursing license for registered nurses and licensed practical nurses. The model, based on the driver's license model, provides for one license only to be issued by the state of the nurse's residence and allows the nurse to practise in other states (remote states) under the authority of the state of residence but the practise requirements of the remote states. Individual states will be required to enter into interstate compacts that supersede state laws and may be amended by all party states agreeing and then changing individual state laws. As of early 2002, 15 states had enacted the Nurse Licensure Compact.

Advantages of the one license concept include reducing barriers to interstate practise, improving tracking for professional conduct purposes, and facilitating interstate commerce (National Council of State Boards of Nursing, 1996–2001). Nurses will be held accountable to the nursing practise laws and other regulations in the state in which the patient is located at the time care is given.

Remaining to be seen are what differences, if any, emerge in implementing the Canadian versus the U.S. model. Of more relevance is that these models signal that regulation must continue to evolve in response to globalisation and increased use of technology in health care. "End Provincial Lock on Professional Licenses" was the title of an editorial printed in a large Canadian newspaper in 2001 (*Vancouver Sun*, 2001). This editorial maintained that national licensing is the only way to ensure that skilled professionals do not have to jump through hoops when they wish to practise their profession in another province or territory. It further suggested that provincial licensing is a waste of time and money. The system of provincial licensing evolved because health, under the Canadian constitution, is a provincial/territorial responsibility and we continue to see the federal, provincial, and territorial governments struggle with this issue. Is it likely that registered nursing in Canada will move to a national registration system? Perhaps. Is it also likely that the day will come when there will be agreement for nurses to move between countries with licensure or registration only from their home country? If so, care must be taken to ensure that regulatory responsibilities for activities such as monitoring the competence and conduct of members is not diluted.

Changing Approaches to Regulation

Governments across Canada have been exploring and, in some jurisdictions, implementing new approaches to the regulation of health professions. Driving these changes to legislative frameworks are concerns regarding accountability of professions to the public, turf protection, creation of economic monopolies by self-interested occupational groups, and lack of uniformity in legislation regulating health professions causing confusion for consumers.

SCOPE OF PRACTISE LEGISLATION

Traditional licensing laws provide for exclusive scope of practise or what is sometimes referred to as turf protection. As identified earlier in the chapter, governments are beginning to move away from this approach to regulation and toward a model that is the same for all regulated health professions in the jurisdiction. This model includes a broad nonexclusive scope of practise statement describing what the profession does, the list of reserved acts (also called *controlled acts* or *restricted acts*) which practitioners are authorised to carry out, and protected titles.

Use of broad nonexclusive scope of practise statements is intended to break down unnecessary practise monopolies that limit the consumer's right to choose a health provider, inhibit access to health care through limiting consumer choice, and increase the cost of health care. Although some may consider that this approach serves the interests of powerful groups such as physicians, employers, and government because of the overlapping roles and the potential to use health professionals differently, others argue that this approach will result in new and exciting roles for registered nurses.

An example of a nonexclusive scope statement comes from the Ontario Nursing Act in which the practise of nursing is established as "the promotion of health and the assessment of, the provision of care for and the treatment of health conditions by supportive, preventive, therapeutic, palliative and rehabilitative means in order to attain or maintain optimal function."

The Ontario Nursing Act does not differentiate the scope of practise of registered nurses and registered licensed practical nurses. Scope of practise statements proposed for registered nurses, registered psychiatric nurses, and licensed practical nurses in British Columbia by the Health Professions Council are virtually identical (Box 8.2). In other jurisdictions, the scope of practise of these three nursing groups differ significantly, which poses the following question: Is there one scope of practise for the profession of nursing, or is the scope different for each of the three nursing groups?

Within the new regulatory framework being implemented, differentiation of practise occurs primarily through the reserved acts that practitioners are authorised to carry out. Reserved acts are tasks or services performed by a health professional that carry such a significant risk for harm to the health, safety, or well-being of the public that they should be reserved to a particular profession, or shared among qualified professions (Health Professions Council, 2001). The intended outcome of reserving only those acts which present a significant risk for harm is to ensure that the focus of professional regulation remains public protection and not the enhancement of profes-

BOX 8.2

Proposed Scope of Practise Statements for Nurses in British Columbia

LICENSED PRACTICAL NURSING

The practise of nursing by licensed practical nurses is the provision of health care for the promotion, maintenance, and restoration of health and for the prevention, treatment, and palliation of illness and injury, including assessment of health status and implementation of interventions.

REGISTERED NURSING

The practise of nursing by registered nurses is the provision of health care for the promotion, maintenance, and restoration of health; the prevention, treatment, and palliation of illness and injury, primarily by assessment of health status, planning, and implementation of interventions; and coordination of health services.

REGISTERED PSYCHIATRIC NURSING

The practise of nursing by registered psychiatric nurses is the provision of health care for the promotion, maintenance, restoration and palliation, primarily of mental and emotional health and associated physical conditions, by assessment of mental and physical health, planning, and implementation of interventions and coordination of health services.

sional status or control. The Manitoba Law Reform Commission (1994) identified three factors to evaluate in considering the seriousness of a threatened harm:

- Likelihood of its occurrence
- Significance of its consequences on individual victims
- Number of people it threatens

Examples of controlled acts that registered nurses in Ontario are authorised to carry out include performing a prescribed procedure below the dermis or a mucous membrane; administering a substance by injection or inhalation; and putting an instrument, hand, or finger beyond the external ear canal, beyond the point in the nasal passages where they normally narrow, and beyond the larynx.

Procedures below the dermis include cleansing, soaking, irrigating, probing, débriding, packing, dressing, and performing venipuncture to establish peripheral intravenous access and maintain patency of the vessel using a solution of normal saline (0.9%), in circumstances in which the individual requires medical attention and delaying venipuncture is likely to be harmful to the individual.

Regulations under the Ontario Nursing Act set out the conditions under which registered nurses may initiate and carry out these acts. Legislation in British Columbia and Alberta is similar in its specificity. Important questions for consideration are: What impact will this specificity have for the ability of registered nurses to practise to the full scope of their competence? Can regulations be revised with sufficient frequency to reflect changes in practise? Does legislation such as this reduce nursing to a list of tasks and procedures? Will this approach to regulation ensure public safety while enhancing consumer choice? These questions remain unanswered.

UMBRELLA LEGISLATION

The changing regulatory approach brings with it a changing legislative framework. Historically, every profession has had its own act that developed over time in response to the needs of the profession and the public it served. The British Columbia Royal Commission on Health Care and Costs (1991) concluded that in British Columbia, lack of consistency in professional acts contributes to insufficient accountability to the public and that lack of uniformity in the structure, organisation, and language of statutes results in confusion for the public. The same conclusions can be drawn from a review of health professions legislation across Canada. For example, in some jurisdictions, some regulatory bodies are called colleges and others are called associations. Processes related to managing complaints from the public vary among professions, as do the legislated responsibilities of regulatory bodies.

Umbrella legislation, seen by some as a mechanism to address these issues, has been implemented in Ontario and British Columbia. In Alberta, the Health Professions Act was passed in the legislature and will come into force as regulations for each profession are developed and approved. Different approaches to umbrella legislation range from one act for all professions to individual acts for each profession with parallel legislative language. The Ontario model relies on the Regulated Health Professions Act to set out the overall guidelines for the health professions, with each profession having its own satellite act. In British Columbia and Alberta, there is no provision for satellite acts. Instead, the requirements unique to each profession are set out in regulations under the act. It remains to be seen what differences in regulatory outcomes, if any, emerge from these differing models. On one hand, there may be more consistency in public policy as it relates to governance of health professions, and the public may be better able to understand how to get assistance with problems. On the other hand, the one-size-fits-all approach may be ineffective in addressing the differing issues of new and established professions and considering how differences in clinical practise should be reflected in regulation of the professions.

PUBLIC PARTICIPATION IN REGULATION

It should come as no surprise that the public wants to play an increasingly active role in the regulation of health professions. Consumers feel that their complaints about the health care system are not heard, and the increased focus on "customers" in the private sector is beginning to spill over into the government and not-for-profit sector. In the 1970s, the RNABC became one of the first to appoint public representatives to its board of directors. Today, most nursing regulatory bodies have, on their boards or councils, public representatives appointed by government. In Ontario, public representatives make up just under 50% of board members.

Public representation on the boards of regulatory bodies is an important public accountability mechanism as well as a means of ensuring that the public interest is served by the boards' decisions. For a profession to be truly self-regulating, public representatives should not exceed 50% of the membership of the board of directors. Even in this situation, an issue that polarises the nurse representatives on the board can result in the public representatives being the decision makers on a significant nursing practise policy issue. In March 2001, the Ontario Health Professions Regulatory Advisory Committee (HPRAC) completed a review of the Regulated Health Professions Act and concluded that self-governance should be maintained by keeping professional members on boards in the majority. The HPRAC maintained that increased accountability for governing professions in the public interest "can be achieved through methods other than changing the mix of elected and appointed members and moving away from self-regulation" (Health Professions Regulatory Advisory Committee, p. 45).

Essential to the success of public representation is that public representatives can meaningfully articulate the public perspective. Of concern is the practise noted in some jurisdictions of board appointments being based on political affiliation rather than criteria such as knowledge, abilities, and commitment to fulfill the public role as well as criteria that will ensure geographic, cultural, and demographic diversity. Also of concern is the orientation received by public representatives. Typically, the regulatory bodies assume responsibility for orientation. Although the regulatory bodies are best positioned to do this in relation to regulatory and profession specific issues, government must play a role in ensuring that public representatives are knowledgeable about their roles on boards and have access to information and other supports.

Challenges to Regulatory Authority

Challenges to the authority of regulatory bodies come from many sources. At the time of labour strife, governments and the public may question whether leaving decisions regarding the standards for entry to the profession has implications for the potential size of the labour pool and hence the wages that can be demanded. Others suggest that allowing regulatory bodies to establish education requirements can result in "credential creep" which serves only to improve the status of the profession and has no direct impact on the outcome of care service provided by the profession. Credential creep refers to increasing the academic credential required for entry to a profession. Some suggest that regulatory bodies entrench barriers to registration to ensure the required need for the regulatory body itself. The truth is that regulation does pose barriers—barriers that are intended to protect the public served by the regulatory body. The question that must always be asked is whether the regulatory body has achieved the appropriate balance in safeguarding the interests of the public and those of the profession.

SUMMARY

This chapter addresses the purpose and issues associated with the regulation of nursing in Canada. Nursing regulation has evolved significantly since first set in motion in the early 1900s. The impact of globalisation, evolving regulatory frameworks, and new roles for registered nurses will ensure that regulation in nursing is dynamic in meeting the health care needs of Canadians. The great unknown is how regulation will evolve and whether in its evolution it will serve to not only protect the public interest but also contribute to the advancement of the profession.

Online RESOURCES

Add to your knowledge of this issue:

The International Council of Nurses	www.icn.ch/
The Canadian Nurses Association	www.cna-nurses.ca/

Provincial and Territorial Organisations

Registered Nurses Association of British Columbia	www.rnabc.bc.ca/
Alberta Association of Registered Nurses	www.nurses.ab.ca/
Saskatchewan Registered Nurses Association	www.srna.org/
College of Registered Nurses of Manitoba	www.marn.mb.ca/
Registered Nurses Association of Ontario	www.rnao.org/
College of Nurses of Ontario	www.cno.org/
Ordre des Infirmieres et Infirmiers du Quebec	www.oiiq.org
Nurses Association of New Brunswick	www.nanb.nb.ca/
College of Registered Nurses of Nova Scotia	www.rnans.ns.ca/about.html
Association of Registered Nurses of Newfoundland and Labrador	www.arnn.nf.ca
Association of Nurses of Prince Edward Island	www.iwpei.com/nurses
Northwest Territories Registered Nurses Association	www.nwtrna.com
Yukon Registered Nurses Association by e-mail	yrna@yknet.ca

Reflections on the Chapter

1. Examine the legislation that regulates nursing practise and education in your province or territory and highlight the similarities and differences you note with other provinces and territories.
2. Identify at least one issue in nursing practise that you would describe as a regulatory issue. What strategies would you formulate to address this issue?
3. What are some of the viewpoints you have heard from practising nurses regarding regulation? What is your analysis of the differences in opinions?
4. What are the advantages and disadvantages of regulation of nursing practise and the registration of nurses?
5. How does the regulation of nursing practise compare to the regulation of health care professionals and other professionals?
6. Formulate and support a stance regarding the use of umbrella legislation to regulate health professions.

REFERENCES

British Columbia Royal Commission on Health Care and Costs. (1991). *Closer to home.* Victoria, Canada: Province of British Columbia.

Canadian Nurses Association. (1968). *The leaf and the lamp.* Ottawa, Canada: Author.

Canadian Nurses Association. (1997). *National nursing competency project.* Ottawa, Canada: Author.

Canadian Nurses Association. (2001a). *Position statement: Nursing professional regulatory framework.* Ottawa, Canada: Author.

Canadian Nurses Association. (2001b). *Position statement: The role of the nurse in telepractice.* Ottawa, Canada: Author.

Canadian registered nurse endorsement document. (2001). Vancouver, Canada: Registered Nurses Association of British Columbia.

Cutshall, P. (1998). Regulating nursing: A new chapter begins. *Nursing BC, 30*(3), 35–38.

Finocchio, L. J., Dower, C. M., McMahon, T., Gragnola, C. M., & the Taskforce on Health Care Workforce Regulation. (1995). *Reforming health care workforce regulation: Policy considerations for the 21st century.* San Francisco: Pew Health Professions Commission.

Health Professions Council. (2001). Shared scope of practice working paper [On-line]. Available: http://www.hlth.gov.bc.ca/leg/hpc/review/shascope.html.

Health Professions Regulatory Advisory Committee. (2001). Adjusting the balance: A review of the Regulated Health Professions Act [On-line]. Available: http://www.hprac.org/downloads/fyr/RHPAReport.pdf.

International Council of Nurses. (1985). *Report on the regulation of nursing: A report on the present, a position for the future.* Geneva, Switzerland: Author.

Kerr, J. R. (1996). Credentialing in nursing. In J. R. Kerr & J. MacPhail (Eds.), *Canadian nursing: Issues and perspectives* (3rd ed.) (pp. 363–372). New York: Mosby.

Kerr, M. (1944). *Brief history of the Registered Nurses' Association of British Columbia.* Vancouver, Canada: Author.

Manitoba Law Reform Commission. (1994). *Regulating professions and occupations.* Winnipeg: Canada: Author.

National Council of State Boards of Nursing. (1996–2001). Nursing regulation: Mutual recognition: FAQ [On-line]. Available: http://www.ncsbn.org/public/regulation/mutual_regulation_faq.htm.

Registered Nurses Association of British Columbia. (2000). *The regulation of nursing: Statement of principles.* Vancouver, Canada: Author.

Risk, M. (1992). Regulatory issues. In A. J. Baumgart & J. Larsen (Eds.), *Canadian nursing faces the future* (2nd ed.) (pp. 365–379). Toronto, Canada: Mosby.

Styles, M. M., & Affara, A. A. (1997). *ICN on regulation: Towards 21st century model.* Geneva, Switzerland: International Council of Nurses.

End provincial lock on professional licenses. (2001, January 18). *The Vancouver Sun,* p. A14.

Way, L. (2001). Nursing education program approval board: an update. *Alberta RN, 57*(4), 15.

CHAPTER 9

International Regulation: Nursing in Germany and the Netherlands

Hanneke M. van Maanen

Chapter Objectives

At the completion of this chapter, you will be able to:

1. Discuss international regulation using the exemplars of Germany and the Netherlands.
2. Explore the effects of regulation or its absence on the advancement of nursing.
3. Describe the influence of government legislation on the regulation of nursing.
4. Account for the evolution of nursing "professionalism."
5. Understand how history, politics, and culture influence the education and regulation of nurses.

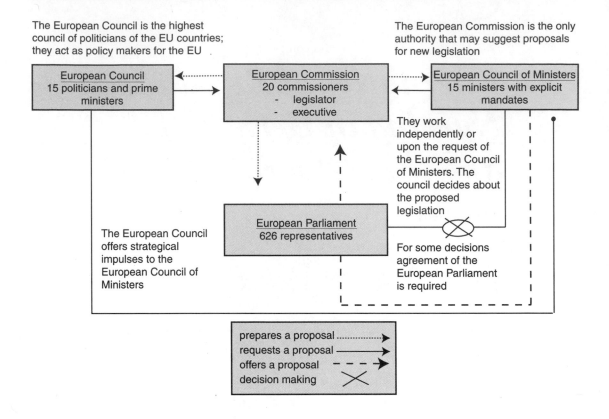

This chapter addresses the meaning of nursing regulation internationally and the issues that arise from the way that regulation is influenced by politics and culture. This begins with an understanding of what regulation means, how it is applied in Canada, and how it has been taken up or interpreted in other countries. Specifically, this chapter uses nursing in Germany and the Netherlands as exemplars to illustrate international nursing regulation. These two countries have been chosen to demonstrate the ways in which the political and cultural histories of a country have influenced the regulation of nursing in the country. There are similarities and differences between the histories of these European countries that have resulted in radical differences in the ways in which the nursing profession has evolved in them. To provide an understanding of the context within which nursing in both countries developed, the chapter is structured around common frameworks for analysis, including historical, cultural, and political influences.

INTERNATIONAL PERSPECTIVES ON REGULATION

According to the International Council of Nurses (ICN), regulation is the "forms and processes whereby order, consistency and control are brought to an organisation and its practices" (Styles & Affara, 1997). The ICN has identified the following goals to address regulation of the nursing profession:

1. Define the profession and its members.
2. Determine the scope of practise.
3. Set standards of education and competent ethical practise.
4. Establish systems of accountability and credentialing processes (Styles & Affara, 1997).

Although the central purpose of regulation has always been the protection of the public, a recent Taskforce on Health Care Workforce Regulation (1995) has recommended extending this to include the following: the promotion of effective health outcomes, respect for consumer rights to choose among safe options for care, and a flexible, rational, cost-effective system. Regulatory processes can also address effective working conditions and provide professional and geographic mobility for competent members (Finocchio et al., 1995).

Regulation is closely linked to legislation. Legislation, as it is used in this chapter, refers to the laws and rules established through the authoritative power of government. In Canada, the authority to regulate the nursing profession comes from legislation enacted by provincial and territorial governments. Nursing regulatory bodies in Canada generally have the authority to determine the following:

- Use of the title
- Scope of practise
- Professional discipline
- Standards of education
- Standards of practise and continuing competence

The goals of the ICN for international regulation and an understanding of the way in which nursing is regulated in Canada form a basis for the discussion of international regulation.

ICN Influences on International Regulations

In a landmark study on the regulation of nursing, the ICN examined the regulatory practises and policies of the nursing discipline worldwide (Styles, 1985). Because the findings of the study indicated a wide variety of definitions of nursing (i.e., basic and specialised nursing education programmes) and identified inconsistent regulatory guidelines, the ICN developed practical and concrete guidelines for the development of national nursing regulatory models.

Whereas in the past ICN referred to nurses in terms of first- and second-level nurses, it later recommended referring to nurses in terms of *nurse* and *nursing auxiliary*. By doing so, the ICN clarified the professional role of the nurse and acknowledged that a broader range of nursing personnel may deliver nursing services.

Specifically, the ICN recommended mandatory licensure for nurses in accordance with each country's regulation of its professions. It was recommended that the entry into professional education and the preparation for nursing practise be comparable to the education and preparation of other professionals. This recommendation indicated that future nurses should meet the same entry criteria into educational institutions as other professionals and stipulated that the academic and clinical preparation of the nurse should be firmly grounded in the sciences and humanities in order to deal with the increasing complexity of nursing practise (Styles, 1985). In addition to providing a clear definition of nursing, the ICN study addressed nursing specialisation and recommended a regulatory framework with standards and operational guidelines. This landmark study can be regarded as one of the first efforts to clarify the complex variations of nursing regulation around the world. The Styles study attempts to make clear, through systematisation and definitive terminology, what nursing is about and what infrastructure is required to deliver safe practise.

Under the auspices of international trade agreements, European countries formed the European Community in 1957. This group of nations has since become known as the European Union. An international council was formed to identify commonalities in basic nursing curricula and to make recommendations about the instruction and education of nurses throughout the European Union. The advantage of this mandate was that nursing diplomas awarded by European Union member countries would be recognised throughout the European Union. The mandate clarifies the educational terms under which this recognition will be granted (Cutshall, 2000). As a consequence of these directives, the Advisory Committee on Training in Nursing (ACTN) was established in 1977.

In recent years, the ACTN, as well as the ICN and World Health Organization for Europe (WHO/EURO), have issued reports of recommendations for nursing competency in the European region. In 1998, the ACTN released a report with recommended entry-level competencies, a step toward evidence-based nursing practises. Parallel to this work, the ICN and WHO/EURO initiated the establishment of expert groups to discuss the functions and roles of the general nurse and the family health nurse (van Maanen, 2001). In the past, qualifications were described in terms of knowledge and experience to be gained during basic nursing education. Today, the scope of education appears to have shifted to clinical judgement and clinical decision making competencies that enable the nurse to handle complex nursing situations.

It is remarkable, that despite collaboration among ICN, World Health Organization (WHO) and WHO/EURO in generating recommendations of the scope of nursing practise, the recommendations of these reports appear to have limited impact. For example, a WHO report in 1986 of nursing and midwifery services in 25 countries showed that legislation was in fact restricting women's access to nursing, midwifery services, and education.

A WHO study group convened to examine laws and regulations governing nursing education and practise in Geneva (1983) stated: "Nursing practice and education are governed by legislation that is often archaic, determined by persons from other disciplines, detrimental to the status of the nurse, and not in tune with the needs of society. The primary health strategy involved the re-evaluation of the old policies and this must certainly include nursing legislation" (WHO, 1983 p. 31). These recommendations emphasise that the scope of nursing practise has expanded dramatically in a few countries but is restricted in other countries by legal and social barriers (WHO, 1986). The WHO study group advised initiating a reorientation of basic nursing education and evaluation of educational programmes with respect to the countries' health needs instead of the desires and demands of health care professionals (WHO, 1986).

NURSING REGULATION IN GERMANY

German nurses frequently ask why the course of events in nursing developed so differently in their nation as compared with other industrialised European countries. The cultures of European countries vary from highly industrialised and affluent to predominately rural and less prosperous. Regions may share the same values, but conditions of employment, health, and living differ considerably (Salvage & Heijnen, 1997; WHO/EURO, 1999).

Over and above these cultural and geographic differences, nurses questions regarding the pace of the advancement of nursing need to be understood as arising in a particular society. It is within this same society that German medical (technical) care has been recognised as one of the leading systems in the world. Barriers to the advancement of nursing in Germany can be understood as issues arising from the societal values with regard to a woman's role and women's work, the history and heritage of the nation with the prominent role of the churches, the (denominational) development of nursing education programmes, and the influence of political ideologies on nursing. The term *ideologies* as it is used here refers to a powerful and authoritative voice in society that tells us who we are and how we are to behave (Althusser, 1971).

Culture as a Framework for Analysis

German society is deeply rooted in family values. The family is regarded as the cornerstone of the society. Within the family unit, the mother plays a central role as the facilitator and organiser of family life in the upbringing of the children and the support of the spouse. Outside the family, the mother has social responsibilities within the (church) community. A German statement relates to the role of the woman as determined by "Kinder, Kuche, Kirche" that translated means children, kitchen, church. A mother, *plegt,* is a term synonymous to nursing (Kruse, 1987). Because nursing, by tradition, has been a predominantly female profession, the perception of the nurse tends to be one of a woman who cares for other people in health and sickness. Caring in the sense of *plegt* is traditionally strongly intertwined with the image of *caritas* (a Latin word for charity) in which laypeople as well as professional workers are involved.

History as a Framework for Analysis

German nursing developed along the same trajectory as nursing in other European countries during the early 20th century. The strong commitment to delivering quality patient care and the proper education of the nurse is reflected in early documentation. This development was interrupted by the world wars (World War I, 1914 to 1918 and World War II, 1940 to 1945) and the years preceding World War II, a situation that affected the nursing discipline in every facet of its practise (Brush et al., 1999). Although the world wars affected the advancement of nursing worldwide, the effects of war on nurses and nursing in Germany is of particular importance. The advancement of nursing was disrupted by both the involvement of Germany in war and the influence of the political ideologies of the times. One should not underestimate the effects of prewar, wartime, and postwar conditions on the advancement of nursing in Germany.

Only since the late 1980s has there been a systematic recording of advancements in the nursing profession. These advancements have been credited to the financial impetus of grants for advanced nursing education and innovative practise (Stiftung, 1992/93, 1993b, 1996, 2000). Questions that guide the following discussion of the historical analysis include the following: How have the role of the church, the existence of Red Cross Sororities, and the effects of political ideologies influenced nursing history in Germany?

ROLE OF THE CHURCHES

The Evangelical and Roman Catholic churches, both state churches, affect social life of the German people in many respects. Their influence reaches far beyond religion and church-related activities and embodies many aspects of social life. The churches have strongly influenced the development of nursing in the initiation, implementation, and supervision of nursing education and practise. Nursing was carried out in church-owned facilities, such as hospitals, nursing homes, homes for the aged, and community nursing services. Religious orders were instrumental in framing nursing education within the context of church and society, and Christian values are reflected in basic nursing curricula of hospital schools of nursing. Advanced nursing education is to a large extent organised by church-related institutions. According to both Roman Catholic and Protestant perspectives, nursing is a charitable occupation deeply rooted in the religious tradition of the New Testament from which the role of the woman is interpreted as enabling, facilitating, and caring (Kruse, 1987). The core of nursing was described as *mein Lohn ist, daf ich darf* which translates to mean my reward is that I may serve others. This perspective is still reflected in the functions and roles of Protestant Deaconesses and Sisters of Roman Catholic orders today (Kruse, 1987).

ROLE OF THE RED CROSS

In the middle of the 19th century, the Red Cross Sororities grew out of the women's organisations. Their origins date from the times of war when women took care of wounded soldiers, which required nurses to have formal training. Included in the Geneva Convention in 1864 was support for the idea that capable women, often belonging to the nobility of the country, could be educated as professional nurses (Kruse, 1987). As early as 1902, the Red Cross established an official curriculum for the nurses of their Sororities. Within the Red Cross Sororities to date, nurses make a voluntary commitment to provide professional nursing services based on the latest developments within the discipline. Although the Red Cross nurse is free to establish a family, she or he, like her or his Salvation Army counterparts, must be prepared to serve the Red Cross Sorority in those places where help is required. Today, all the German Orders and Sororities are integrated in to one organisation, *Arbeitsgemeinschaft der Deutschen Schwesterngemeinschaften* (ADS), which is the speaking voice of the nominational (or denominational) nursing communities in Germany.

INFLUENCES OF POLITICAL IDEOLOGIES ON NURSING

German nursing had a rich tradition of community and public health nursing until the early 1930s (Kruse, 1987). However, in the early 1930s before WW II, professional nursing began to stagnate in terms of the scholarly advancement of the discipline (Steppe, 1990). This stagnation can be linked, in part, to the emerging political ideologies of the time.

In examining historical documents, one can see how nursing education and practise were gradually incorporated into the ideology of National Socialism. Nurses who intended to follow a career path were forced to comply with the National Socialist principles of German heritage and racial segregation. Nursing was provided with the "power" to assess the destiny of people with impaired health and handicaps, in particular people who had been identified as having mental and physical disabilities. It is important to note that this so-called power did not emerge from professional advancement of nursing but rather was mandated by law supported by political ideologies. Nursing aims were subordinated to the National Socialist system. For example, public health and community nurses in the National Socialist system became the uniformed representatives of the political authorities. They were expected to select patients for admission to "special" treatment centres, from which most never returned (Historical Museum, Krankenhaus Bremen-Ost; study trip, Poland 1997). It is not surprising that

BOX 9.1

Nursing Under National Socialism

Nursing under National Socialism (NS) in Germany was an occupation that could be characterized as:

- *Diffuse and unclear in its aims.* Nurses worked in dependence of medicine; they indicated that their aims were different but had problems in describing the distinction between nursing and medicine.
- *A woman's occupation.* Nurses were expected to act in an extended role of mothers, caring for and serving others.
- *Determined by law.* Nurses were placed in an assisting role to physicians (*Hilfsberuf*).
- *Unorganised.* The fragmented nursing associations were organised according to religious and social orientation and operated without common goals.
- *Victimised by professional hostility.* The rights and responsibilities of nurses that were granted under the Weimar Republic were not rooted in professional development, but embedded in a political structure that would gradually dictate to nurses what was considered law and order under the system. Nurses were not recognised as professionals, but employed as instruments of a war (Steppe, 1990).

the war imposed a severe setback of public health and community nursing and that even today German people are resentful of government interference with their privacy. This resentment raises questions about how this image of nurses interfaces with a cultural ideal of nurses as nurturing and protective (Box 9.1).

RECONSTRUCTION OF NURSING EDUCATION, 1950 TO 2000

In collaboration with the ICN, links to the international nursing community that had been disrupted by the war years were reestablished in 1949 (Brush et al., 1999; Quinn, 1989). The changing political ideologies and the effects of World War II were to influence significantly the reorganisation of nursing in Germany into the present century.

United efforts during the 1950s to reconstruct nursing saw competition among hospitals to provide educational programmes. A nursing law passed in 1957 that allowed nursing education programmes to be operated under the jurisdiction of labour law prompted criticism from church-related health care institutions. They expressed concern that the control of nursing education and practise would erode as soon as nurses were educated under the jurisdiction of the labour law. Within this restructuring, a controversy was provoked by asking whether educated nurses were really wanted: "German nursing should not be endangered by academically prepared nurses" (Spiegel, 1957, in Steppe, 1990, p. 13). According to Steppe (1990), nursing remained dominated by a moral perspective that focussed on women's virtues.

In the 1960s, with the rapid advancement of medical technology, technical specialisation in nursing became a trajectory of career planning. Although nurses still emphasised the importance of the person-to-person relationships, medical technology started to prevail over comprehensive nursing care. To solve the acute shortage of nurses, practical nurses were introduced into the health care system. Nursing education, now 3 years in duration, was described in terms of basic nursing (*Grundpflege*) and therapeutic nursing (*Behundlungspflege*). The emphasis was on procedures rather than processes of nursing intervention.

During these years, the nursing process, the logical analysis of nursing care activities, was introduced and the recording of patient care systematised in a patient care record. Through postbasic education, nurses gained the competence to develop innovative strategies and empower themselves as professionals.

In the late 1970s, German nurses became involved in a health-focussed perspective on nursing. Health promotion, prevention, and rehabilitation became key concepts to those who supported change and advancement. During this period, Germany hosted several WHO/EURO meetings to facilitate the development and analysis of multicultural action research. An interest in the study and application of foreign nursing theories developed. In the late 1980s, projects were initiated to test and implement these foreign models into some clinical settings.

Professionalisation of Nursing

The historical development as described by Steppe (1990, 1996) reflects the highlights of the German nursing scene. In a country with 80 million people and 475,000 nurses, change and development take place gradually. New initiatives may take years before they are regarded as common knowledge, based on professional consensus, and supported by the members of the nursing discipline. An example is the introduction of the nursing process, *Pflegeplanung und Dokumentation,* into nursing practise, which, according to Steppe (1990), started as early as the 1970s, when it was systematically introduced. However, because nurses in Germany continued to be trained in hospital schools of nursing and were expected to function in rigid health care structures, the real transition toward professional nursing as a collective effort was not substantial until the early 1990s.

According to nurse-educators, the first signs and signals of nursing-focussed guidelines for nursing education were reflected when a new 1985 nursing law was passed (Kurtenbach et al., 1994). In this law, the statement that the inclusion of the nursing process is a compulsory component in the education of nurses provided some distancing from medicine (Box 9.2). However, the theoretical education strongly

---

BOX 9.2

The Professional Nurse and the Nursing Process

The responsibilities and expertise of the professional nurse were described in terms of the nursing process approach when a new nursing law was passed. By law, the nurse:

- Can systematically assess and analyse the nursing needs of the patient, group of patients, or patient population.
- Can formulate an individual nursing plan or plan nursing interventions, as far as possible, with the agreement of and in collaboration with the patient or group of patients.
- Can perform these nursing interventions in a skilled way or delegate the practise and coordination of these interventions.
- Is able, when appropriate, to consult with or refer to a colleague.
- Reassesses and evaluates the nursing plan and implementation, in relationship to assessed needs (National *Raad voor de Volksgezondheid,* 1988, p. 27; 1992, p. 27).

remains a reflection of medical thinking, with emphasis on the preparation for the extended role of nurses within the medical domain. Nursing theory and research are not included in the 1985 nursing law.

Whereas nursing, as a typical women's profession, was not part of the regular educational structure of the German *Bildungssystem* until 1995, nursing in its professional practise remained vulnerable and outside the mainstream of legislative accreditation and legal protection. However, two decrees (of 1995 and 1997) represent important steps toward change. Through the 1995 decree, nursing education was integrated into the formal German *Bildungssystem,* with all the rights, responsibilities and perspectives granted to a registered profession. The 1997 decree recommended that in the future, the education of nurse-educators should be embedded into higher education (Bals et al., 1997; Bundesausschuss, 2000; Sekretariat der Ständigen Konferenz et al., 1995, 1997). These two decrees are significant for the development of nursing education. To prepare German nursing for the 21st century, the next move should be to transfer basic nursing education from hospital schools of nursing into colleges (*Berufsschulen*), the polytechnics' equivalent institutions of higher education.

Legislation and Regulation

Positioned as a typical women's occupation in Germany, nursing was not registered as a *Beruf* (profession) within the educational structure of the Federal Republic until 1995. This societal position, of course, delayed the educational advances of the discipline (Krüger, 1996; Krüger et al., 1993), which meant that nursing could be taught and learned by any person with a caring attitude and that the quality of nursing education depended on the vision and competence of the nurses responsible for the nursing curricula and practise.

Whereas the (male) *Berufsbildung* (vocational education) in Germany is embedded in a well-organised, comprehensive educational system, provided by highly qualified teachers and practitioners (*Meister Fachleute*), the traditional women's occupations did not follow this track. Although the nursing discipline undertook several efforts to improve the position of nursing education, changes in the regulation of nursing were required before the discipline could advance as a profession.

The Nurse Practise Act of 1985 is a federal act that describes nursing as an auxiliary occupation to medicine and regulates nursing education under the jurisdiction of the medical profession (Kruse, 1987; Kurtenbach et al., 1994). This legislative framework has delayed the development of nursing as a discipline. Nursing education and practise have been advanced along the core of medicine, with emphasis on medical technology and the treatment of diseases. This perspective is reflected in the nursing curricula by a priority setting in the natural sciences. Nursing students at the University of Bremen (personal communication, 2001) argue that during their nursing training, they have been inadequately prepared in the social sciences and humanities, which would enable them to deal better with the complexity of holistic, comprehensive nursing.

Compared with nursing in other northern and western European countries, German nursing has taken a different trajectory of development. Several initiatives to strengthen the professional role of nurses have been taken over the years. For political reasons, however, these initiatives have had little impact on the anticipated change and development in nursing. As early as 1963, a landmark project in German nursing was the first university-based nurse-teachers programme at the Free University of Berlin (Mischo-Kelling & Witneben, 1995). Because of political interventions, this project did not survive; however, the seeds were laid for other initiatives.

In a collaborative effort beginning in the late 1980s, nurse leaders in Germany started to develop educational and research programmes aimed at more efficiency and effectiveness in the advancement of nursing. These initiatives were financially supported through grants and bursaries. Experienced, hospital-trained nurses were able to study nursing in other western European countries and gain degrees in nursing sciences. Other nurses took on academic studies in Germany in health-related fields and qualified in the social sciences and humanities. It is through this first generation of academically prepared nurses that the upgrading of nursing management and education into polytechnics and universities has become a reality. To date, 33 programmes of nursing, nursing management, and nursing education have been established in German polytechnic institutes, whereas six degree programmes in nursing science and nursing pedagogies have developed within the universities.

Nurses anticipate that the professional nursing movement will accelerate in the coming years and that with constructive collaboration among nurse leaders, postbasic nursing programmes will increase in quality and depth. With the establishment of programmes into the tertiary system, nursing education is, like other practise disciplines, framed within the educational system of the country. Whereas nursing research will primarily be promoted through university departments of nursing science and education, applied nursing studies have become the mandate of polytechnics.

NURSING REGULATION IN THE NETHERLANDS

The Netherlands is a small coastal country situated next to Germany, with a high-density population of nearly 16 million people. Nursing in the Netherlands has a long tradition, developing in a similar way as nursing in neighboring western European countries.

In the Netherlands, the Nursing Law of 1921 regulated the education, examination, and registration of nurses. The Law protected the diploma and title of the nurse but did not provide substantial direction for the nursing education or nursing practise performed under this jurisdiction (Van der Kooij, 1990; Sindram 1993, 2001). With the advancement of the biomedical sciences, nursing followed in the footpath of medicine and developed an interest in the technical methods underlying the assessment of diagnosis and treatment of patients. The introduction of the human and social sciences in the health care services of the late 1960s and the 1970s forced nursing to reevaluate its purpose and aims.

The 1970s may be regarded as a phase of professional reflection, an "awakening time" of nursing, characterised by a growing interest in the nature of nursing and its scientific potential. In 1972, the first undergraduate academic programme for nurses was established at a polytechnic level, soon followed by an increase of other higher professional education programmes for nurses (Nationale Raad voor de Volksgezondheid, 1992).

The 1980s saw rapid development with the establishment of the first university degree programme for experienced, postbasic, hospital-trained diploma nurses at the State University of Maastricht. This contributed to a growing cohort of highly qualified nurses. At the same time, the health care institutions became involved in innovations and change, such as team and primary nursing, quality appraisal programmes, and nursing audits. The upgrading of nursing education into polytechnics and the state university stimulated interest in the scientific foundation of the discipline.

The 1990s were characterised by a desire to use nursing theory and research as an underpinning for clinical practise. The change of the century sees us focussing on the establishment of clinical nurse specialists, named "nurse practitioners" in the Netherlands. (Grypdonck, 2000; Raatgever, 2000; Roodbol & van de Bunt, 2000; Spijker & Niehuis, 2000). It appears that the nursing profession is restructuring itself, and the legislation of the BIG Law, also known and referred to in this chapter as the Health Professions Act of 1997, provided the impetus for nursing to develop an infrastructure for the licensure and control of professional conduct (NU '91, 2000; Vlaskamp, 2000).

Culture as a Framework for Analysis

The Netherlands is rich in tradition and has strong family values. In the past, the single-family income was seen as the yardstick of socioeconomic well-being. Until the 1960s, the Netherlands had the smallest percentage of working married women in the world (16%). The situation has slowly changed during the past 20 years, with women gradually catching up within the workforce, now representing about 65%. Because most women have part-time jobs, this percentage camouflages the actual employment situation as well as the limited opportunities for career building.

Although the family unit is still regarded as a cornerstone of the society, the Netherlands is among the progressive countries that have accepted alternative ways of partnership and regulated these through legislation. Gradually, the single wage earner (male) employed in the family was replaced by the employment of both partners leading to a significant change in the traditional family structure. The once prominent role of the Protestant and Roman Catholic churches, which dominated public life until the second part of the 20th century, gradually eroded, and church-related organisations changed into nondenominational institutions.

Nursing was originally considered to be subservient to medicine. With the changes in societal attitudes towards women and work and the upgrading of nursing education, the discipline has taken on a role more complementary to medicine, a view strongly advocated by the current Minister of Health Dr. (med.) Els Borst (Van der Pasch, 2000; Koopman, 2000; Van der Veen, 2000).

History as a Framework for Analysis

In reviewing the history of nursing in the Netherlands, one can see that responsibility for caring for the sick, which originally belonged in the family domain, gradually moved into society at large (Van der Kooij, 1990). Many health services emerged from a private initiative and, once well established in the society, were retrospectively brought under the legislation of the Dutch health care system.

In the Netherlands, organised nursing care dates back to 1870. The publication of a nursing journal occurred in 1890, and the first Dutch Society for Nursing (NNA) was established in 1893. The Netherlands joined the ICN in 1909 and has been an active member of international nursing and health organisations since that time. The first trained nurses received a diploma, awarded by the White Cross, a community-based public health organisation in the province of North Holland between 1879 and 1883 (Van der Kooij, 1990). However, the registration of a nursing diploma was not possible until the Nursing Law of 1921 was adopted.

In the Netherlands, as in Germany, the influence of Protestant and Roman Catholic churches significantly influenced the development of nursing as a charitable occupation. Hospital nursing schools with religious affiliation educated Deaconesses and religious Sisters as well as "lay" nurses. Since the 1960s, most of these institutions have been integrated with nondenominational, intercultural health services and educational institutions. Although the Red Cross used to possess a few health care institutions with nursing school annexes, its influence was geared primarily towards its international mission in time of war and disaster.

Legislation and Regulation

Nursing regulation in the Netherlands was landmarked by the Nursing Law of 1921 and the Health Professions Law of 1997, under which jurisdiction the nursing profession has been classified. Between 1921 and 1997, several attempts were made to update the legislation to the actual level of nursing practise. The major changes in the intervening decades related to the following:

- Biomedical advances in health care with immediate repercussions for nursing practise
- Upward mobility of nursing education from primarily hospital-based training programmes to comprehensive, generic nursing education as offered in polytechnic institutions and universities
- Increased complexity of the nursing process to be managed under frequently restricted resources and time constraints
- Demand for more in the effectiveness and efficiency of health care delivery

EDUCATIONAL PERSPECTIVES

With regard to nursing regulation, a major point of consideration has been the upward mobility of nursing education. In the Netherlands, as in most countries, this upward mobility from vocational training to professional education is planned in various phases. The first phase is to detach the traditional nursing school from the hospital and establish an independent institution for generic professional education, preferably in collaboration with other schools of nursing. Such a programme can be offered at a medium or higher level of professional education. Depending on the educational structure within a country, the higher level of education can be identical to the teaching within a polytechnic institution and lead toward a baccalaureate of nursing science degree or diploma. The next step within the tertiary educational system is the university degree programme.

INTERNATIONAL MODELS OF TERTIARY NURSING EDUCATION

Since the 1960s, the Netherlands and other countries in the European Region have been discussing which model of advanced education would serve nursing best in its move towards professionalisation. Some suggested selecting experienced clinical nurses to start the process, with or without university entry qualifications, offering them a "bridge" postbasic degree programme tailored to the needs of this special cohort. The advantage of this approach would be that these graduates could return to the workplace and be reintegrated in their nursing positions, where they were respected as nurses before attending the university. The disadvantage could be that adult learners with long experience in the workplace would be "set in their ways" and might encounter difficulty with the role transition and academic challenges such as the change from intuitive to problem-oriented reasoning.

The second model suggests encouraging young high school graduates, who are qualified, to enter a nursing degree programme at the university and to stimulate a postgraduate degree enrollment soon after graduation to prepare the nurse for an academic career path. This model is similar to the scientific trajectory followed by graduates of the natural, human, and social sciences. The advantage would be academic socialisation at a relatively young age and the realistic prospect of a university career. Such a graduate could be disadvantaged, however, upon entering the clinical nursing arena without the expected practical experience. The question arises whether nursing's prime responsibilities as a practise discipline lie in the scientific advancement of nursing, in the clinical conduct of science-based nursing, or in a combination of both.

The preferred model in northern and western European countries has been to educate a selected group of experienced clinical nurses who, upon graduation with a post-basic degree, could act as a bridge generation of scholars in preparing the workplace for the changes to come and assisting the next generation of academically prepared nurses to familiarise themselves with the challenges of nursing practise.

DUTCH SOCIAL POLICY STATEMENT ON NURSING

Based on the increasing demands for health care of the Dutch population and the trends of nursing developments in other nations, the nursing discipline accepted the mandate to design an educational structure that could meet the expectations for health care of the next century. In 1988, the National Council for Public Health (Nationale Raad voor de Volksgezondheid, 1988) and the Nursing Commission developed a position paper. This paper encompassed an educational structure for nursing and differentiated the various levels of nursing personnel according to the required levels of competencies and accountability. The preparation of vocational auxiliary nurses or short-term trained personnel has never been an option in the Netherlands and, therefore, has not been part of health care personnel planning.

The polytechnic programmes that developed between 1972 and 1988 were well established and had demonstrated the usability of professionally educated nurses. University education, started under the jurisdiction of nonnursing disciplines in 1980, was gradually taking shape and gaining definition when the first professor of nursing science was appointed at the state university in 1988. At the start, the university offered an academic programme in health sciences with a major in nursing science only, excluding the clinical component that would qualify its graduates as licensed, registered nurses. Therefore, high school graduates who were awarded this degree had difficulty finding employment. This was not the case for registered nurses whose clinical experience was expanded by university study that offered surplus value to their position. To integrate the graduates without nursing background into the health care system, a bridge programme was established that enabled them to be clinically prepared as nurses. From a regulation point of view, this was a political move. Because the formal licensure to practise nursing remained at a polytechnic level, the nurse was placed at a different level from other academically prepared health professionals.

To establish clarity at a competency level, the National Council for Public Health and the Nursing Commission designed a structure that was congruent with the decisions about nursing education and service as agreed on by expert panels. This structure accepted the premises that the nurse was expected to be competent in certain ways (Box 9.3). In 1992, the Council also described the responsibilities of the second-level, or technical, nurse (Box 9.4).

IMPACT OF THE HEALTH PROFESSIONS ACT ON REGISTRATION

Aside from nursing, the Health Professions Act passed in 1997 registered the following health disciplines: medicine, dentistry, pharmacy, clinical psychology, psychotherapy,

BOX 9.3

Nursing Competencies

The structure designed by the National Council for Public Health, the Nursing Commission, expected nurses to exhibit competence in the following:

- Psychosocial aspects of professional practise
- Mastery of instrumental and technical skills for professional practise
- Application of professional knowledge to enable judgement of (complex) nursing situations and to form an independent opinion

Competency requirements were based on the common goals of health care:

- Promotion and maintenance of health
- Prevention and postponement of illness and disability
- Contribution to curing and rehabilitation
- Alleviation of suffering and discomfort (palliative care)

physiotherapy, and midwifery. In the near future, nurses registered under this health professions law will be subject to a licensure system that articulates the conditions for nurses to practise: it will embody the criteria for safe nursing care. Advanced nursing education will no longer be pursued on a voluntary basis, but it will become mandatory to update nurses' competencies on a continuing basis.

The Health Professions Act expands the accountability of nurses (Table 9.1). The title of nurse remains protected. Further, the nurse becomes subject to disciplinary jurisdiction. By government decree, the nurse will be given functional independence with regard to situation-related (authorised) procedures. The register is placed under the jurisdiction of the Inspection for Health Care. Unlike Canada, the Netherlands does not position the register under the authority of the nursing discipline. One reason for this larger jurisdiction is that the Health Professions Act embodies many health disciplines, and its application is to be coordinated by a recognised authority with legisla-

BOX 9.4

The Technical Nurse

In regard to role and competency, the technical nurse:

- Assists in systematic assessment and analysis of the nursing needs of the patient
- Is able to assist in formulating an individual nursing plan as far as possible with the agreement and collaboration of the patient
- Can perform delegated nursing activities in a skillful way
- Is able to consult with a nursing colleague or members of other disciplines
- Participates in the evaluation and implementation of the nursing plan, in relation to the assessed needs

(*Note:* The verbs assist, delegate(d), consult, and participate indicate that the vocational nurse is expected to work in close collaboration with the professional nurse.)

Table 9.1 Health Professions Act (1997) as Applied to Nursing Practice

ACCOUNTABILITIES	NURSES: PROFESSIONAL	NURSES: VOCATIONAL
Title protection	Yes	Yes
Registration leading to . . . (constitutional registration)	Yes	No
Regulation of specialisation	Yes	No
Competence not independent	Yes	Yes
Possibility of providing authority to function independently by Government Decree	Yes	No
Disciplinary jurisdiction	Yes	No
Measures in case of incompetence	Yes	No
Cause of harm or injury to another person	Not liable to punishment within the domain of professional nursing competence	Not liable to punishment within the domain of vocational nursing competence

tive power. A second reason could be that the nursing profession in transition needs time to prepare for encroaching changes in the organisation of its practise. The framework for professional practise is designed, but the consequences of this legislation are in the process of review and development.

The operationalisation of the project "renewed registration of nurses" through the Health Professions Acts planned by two leading organisations in nursing: the General Council for Professional and Vocational Nurses, and the National Center for Professional and Vocational Nursing. In these two organisations, all the professional nursing associations are integrated, irrespective of nurses' educational background and nursing specialty. These nursing organisations are important discussion partners of the Ministry of Health and contribute to those health care platforms in which the professional and employment conditions for nursing personnel are discussed (Van der Pasch, 2000). The Health Professions Act has also intensified the dialogue between nursing and medical professions and resulted in several consensual decisions about modes of collaboration in health care delivery (NU '91, 1997).

Professionalisation of Nursing

Implementing the recommendations of the position paper was a first step in developing an educational structure that would ultimately differentiate professional and vocational nursing into five competency levels. In this structure, nurses are educated at three levels (Box 9.5).

Whereas the previous career path of nurses was mainly facilitated through programmes of nursing management services and nursing education, nurses in the late

---

BOX 9.5

Three Levels of Nursing Education

- Nursing colleges that offer generic programs and appear to be a combination of the old system and enriched with current trends in nursing education
- Polytechnic institutions (HBO-V) regarded to be the core preparation for professional nursing
- University level, with emphasis placed on science and research as well as clinical specialization

---

1990s demonstrated a growing interest in the possibility of clinical specialisation. This trend was most likely influenced by the career patterns in Canada and the United States. Professionals still propose arguments about which educational programme will serve the patient population most effectively. The prime interest of the nursing profession is in the advancement of quality care and the perspective of a career that enables the nurse to pursue her or his interests and enrich both knowledge and experience.

The Ministry of Health has also expressed an interest in the differentiation of nursing positions, but from another perspective. The Ministry would support the position that nurses be authorised to perform routine medical procedures and, by doing so, relieve the burden on medicine. Delegated medical interventions could then be performed at a cost-effective level and help to control the steady rising costs of health care.

In expressing their concern about the government's perspective, nurses indicate that they are not interested in becoming second-class physicians or physician's assistants. Their response has been that measures should be taken to relieve workloads and improve employment conditions. The attrition rate of nursing personnel is supported by the following data: nurses doing other work (33%), no perspective of personal development (19%), no job satisfaction (19%), the burden of the workload (15%), the family situation (15%), and the financial reward (14%) (Sikking, 2001a).

The waning interest in pursuing a nursing career, combined with the steadily decreasing enrollment in nursing education, is leading to an acute nursing shortage that is not solved by rerouting nurses' responsibilities into medicine. Reports from the higher education programmes for nurses relate decreased enrollments of 25% in 2000 and 20% in 2001 (Sikking, 2001b). Nursing vacancies in 2000 were assessed at a 1% to 4% level, particularly in highly specialised nursing areas. In 2001, the shortage of nurses was projected to be at 10% for 2002 (Bruinsma, 2001).

SUMMARY

This chapter addresses the progress and challenges of international nursing regulation and legislation, particularly in Germany and the Netherlands, and the roles of various international organisations, such as ICN, WHO, and WHO/EURO, in that regulation and legislation.

The history of German nursing helps explain not only its origin and tradition but also the infrastructure leading to current laws and decrees that regulate nursing.

With regard to Germany, nursing science has accelerated at an advanced pace since the late 1980s. The result is the establishment of nursing management, nursing education, and nursing science programmes within polytechnic institutions and universities. A first generation of well-educated nurses is gradually being integrated into the health care system, although it is still too early to evaluate the effect of their contribution.

In the Netherlands, the upgrading of nursing education has had a significant impact on the development of the nursing discipline. A corps of well-educated nurses has been integrated into the health care scene and started to influence patient care services, nursing management, nursing education, and the scientific advancement of the profession.

The Nursing Law of 1921 was finally replaced by the Health Professions Law of 1997 that included nursing as one of eight health disciplines. The consequences of this law require the nursing profession to register under more stringent conditions for professional practise. The transition process will take a number of years, and the development of regulatory conditions for nursing practise and continuing education are in progress.

The introduction of the Health Professions Act has also revitalised discussions about the nursing specialist, that is, the nurse practitioner with extended accountability. From the perspective of the Ministry of Health, the nurse should be authorised to take over some routine medical procedures. Nurses emphasise that their extended role should focus more strongly on the delivery of comprehensive patient care.

Nursing regulation is the key to the advancement of nursing; it offers the infrastructure for authorised development and change. Nurses in Germany and the Netherlands are actively engaged in building infrastructures that enable them to participate in the establishment of health service delivery, a challenge for which they are prepared.

Online RESOURCES

Add to your knowledge of this issue:

International Council of Nurses (ICN) Regulation	***www.ich.ch/regulation.htm***
ICN	***www.icn.ch***
ICN Regulation Network	***www.icn.ch/regnet.htm***
World Health Organization (WHO)	***www.who.int***
WHO Nursing and Midwifery Services	***www.int/health-services-delivery/nursing***
Nursing Regulation in Europe	***www.clearq.org/europe.html***

Reflections on the Chapter

1. How is regulation talked about in this chapter? How does this compare with our discussion of regulation elsewhere in the text?

2. How does regulation differ in Germany and the Netherlands? In what ways does the interpretation of regulation in these countries resemble or differ from regulation in Canada? What issues do these differences raise for the professional advancement of nursing?

3. How would you account for the differences in the advancement of nursing between Germany and the Netherlands? Are there similarities with the advancement of nursing in Canada?

4. Discuss issues that arise out of the relationship between "women's work" and "nurses' work" in each of these countries. Compare these with issues that Canadian nurses and the profession face in Canada.

5. What stand has the ICN taken on international regulation?

6. What government structures and legislated policies influence regulation in each country: Germany, the Netherlands, and Canada?

7. What issues are raised by the statement, "mandatory licensure in accordance with the customs of a country, in the licensure of its professions"?

8. Discuss the difference between "power" gained by nursing through professional advancement and that mandated by law. What issues does this raise for nursing regulation nationally or internationally?

REFERENCES

Althusser, L. (1971). Ideology and ideological state apparatuses. In B. Brewster (Trans). L. Althusser (Ed.).*Lenin and philosophy and other essays* (pp. 123–173). London: New Left Books.

Bals, T., Beikirch-Korporal, E., Bischoff-Wanner, C., et al. (1997). *Bundesausschuss der Länderarbeitsgemeinschaften der Lehrerinnen und Lehrer für Pflegeberufe. Bildung und Pflege.* Stuttgart: Thieme Verlag.

Bruinsma (2001).

Brush, B. L., Lynaugh, J. E., Boschma, G., Rafferty, A., Stuart, M., Tomes, N. (1999). Nurses of all nations: A history of the International Council of Nurses 1899–1999. New York: Lippincott Williams & Wilkins.

Bundesausschuss der Lehrerinnen und Lehrer für Pflegeberufe e.V. (2000). Structural changes in health- and social care: A challenge for nurse-educators [German taext]. In *Bildung und Pflege: Die Europäische Dimension* (pp. 62–75). Conference proceedings, Potsdam, May 2000.

Cutshall, P. (2000). *Understanding cross border professional regulation: What nurses and other professionals need to know.* Geneva: International Council of Nurses.

Deutscher Berufsverband für Krankenpflege (DBfK) (1989). *Nursing research for professional practice.* Workgroup of European Nurse Researchers (WENR). 12th Workgroup Meeting and International Nursing Research Conference. Frankfurt am Main: Verlag "Krankenpflege."

Finocchio, L., Dower, C., McMahon, T., & Gragnola, C. (1995). *Reforming health care work force regulation: Policy considerations for the 21st century.* San Francisco: Pew Health Professions Commission.

Grauhan, A. (1989). Development of nursing research and academic nursing education in W. Germany. *In Nursing research for professional practice* (pp. 12–21). 12th Workgroup Meeting and International Nursing Research Conference. Workgroup of European Nurse Researchers. Frankfurt am Main: Deutscher Berufsverband für Krankenpflege (DBfK).

Grypdonck, M. (2000). De nurse practitioner: Meer dan een nieuwe hype in de Nederlandse verpleegkunde? *Tijdschrift voor Verpleegkunde TVZ, 110*(10), 299–301. HIVMJNEUR 82.2 p. 13.

International Council of Nurses. (1953, 1973, 1997). Code of Ethics. In *ICN Statements.* Geneva: Author.

Koopman, P. (2000). De vierde Dinsdag in September: Minister opent bestuurlijk overleg met verpleegkundigen en verzorgenden. *Tijdschrift voor Verpleegkundigen TVZ, 110*(19), 574–575.

Krüger, H. (1996). Pflege zwischen besetzten Stühlen? Die Neuordnung der Ausbildung vor dem Hintergrund der Anforderungen neuer pflegerischer Handlungsfelder. In *Bundesausschuss der Länderarbeitsgemeinschaften der Lehrerinnen und Lehrer für Pflegeberufe: Conference Proceedings* (pp. 67–76). Fürth/Bayern, Mai 1996.

Krüger, H., Rabe-Kleberg, U., Mischo-Kelling, M. (1993). *Pflegewissenschaft als berufliche Bildung: ein Weg aus der Sackgasse: Entwicklung und Erprobung eines Studiengangs mit berufspädagogischem Fachrichtungsprofil für Lehrkräfte in der Alten—und Kranken/Kinderpflege.* Berufliche Erstausbildung und Lehramtstudium als biografische Bausteine. Werkstattberichte des Forschungsschwerpunktes Arbeit und Bildung der Universität Bremen. Bd. 24. Universität Bremen.

Kruse, A.P. (1987). Berufskunde 11: Die Krankenpflegeausbildung seit der Mitte des 19. Jahrhunderts. Kohlhammer Studienbücher. Berlin: W. Kohlhammer.

Kurtenbach, H., Golombek, G., & Siebers, H. (1994). *Krankenpflegegesetz und Ausbildungs—und Prüfungsverordnung für die Berufe in der Krankenpflege. 4. Auflage.* Krankenhausrecht Köln: Verlag W. Kohlhammer GmbH.

Mischo-Kelling, M., & Witneben, K. (1995). *Pflegebildung und Pflegetheorien.* München: Urban & Schwarzenberg.

Nationale Raad voor de Volksgezondheid (1988). *Verpleegkundig Beroepsprofiel.* Zoetermeer: Author (National Council for Public Health).

Nationale Raad voor de Volksgezondheid (1992). *Dutch social statement on the nursing profession.* Zoetermeer: Author.

NU '91 & Koninklijke Nederlandsche Maatschappij tot B evordering der Geneeskunst (1997). *Voorbehouden handelingen in de praktijk: Richtlijnen voor de samen-*

werking tussen artsen, verpleegkundigen en zieken-verzorgenden. Utrecht: Authors.

NU '91 (2000). *Evaluatie Wet BIG*. Document National Nurses Association of the Netherlands—Fax of the Ministry of Welfare, Health and Culture +31-71-5253782, Research 17/01/2000.

Quinn, S. (1989). *ICN past and present*. ICN: Scutari Press.

Raatgever, M. (2000). Een nurse-practitioner op de mammapolikliniek. *Tijdschrift voor Verpleegkundigen TVZ, 100*(17), 524–527.

Roodbol, P., & van de Bunt, C. (2000). De "Nurse Practitioner voegt inderdaad iets toe!" Is de kritiek van Professor Grypdonck terecht? *Tijdschrift voor Verpleegkundigen TVZ, 110*(14), 437–438.

Salvage, J., & Heijnen, S. (1997). *Nursing in Europe: A resource for better health*. WHO Regional Publications, European Series, No. 74. Copenhagen: WHO/EURO.

Sekretariat der Ständigen Konferenz der Kultusminister der Länder in der Bundesrepublik Deutschland (1995). *Rahmenvereinbarung über die Ausbildung und Prüfung für ein Lehramt der Sekundarstufe II (berufliche Fächer) oder für die beruflichen Schulen*. Beschluß der Kultusministerkonferenz vom 12.05.1995. be165bls. Bonn: Author.

Sekretariat der Ständigen Konferenz der Kulturminister der Länder in der Bundesrepublik Deutschland (1997). *Bericht der Gemeinsamen Arbeitsgruppe KMK/GMK/ASMK "Studiengänge im Tätigkeitsfeld Gesundheitswesen."* Bonn 24.04.1997 A/Br23-04.Kö. Bonn: Author.

Sikking, I. (2001a). Zorg aan bed komt in gevaar: Drastische afname van aantal studenten verpleegkunde. *Algemeen Dagblad, 31*(8), 1.

Sikking, I. (2001b). Zorg om de zorg. *Algemeen Dagblad Diagnose, 31*(8), 26. Statistical Data LCVV, research Primant en HBO-raad.

Sindram, I. P. C. (1993). *BIG in zicht: De wet op de beroepen in de individuele gezondheidszorg*. Verplegenden en verzorgenden onder de wet BIG. Utrecht: Nieuwe Unie '91.

Sindram, I. P. C. (2001). *BIG: De wet op de beroepen in de individuale gezondheidszorg—Inzichtelijk*. Verpleegkundigen en verzorgenden IG onder de wet BIG. Uitgave van de Nieuwe Unie '91: Beroepsorganisatie van de verpleging. Venlo: van Grinsven Drukkers.

Spijker, T., & Niehuis, M. (2000). De positionering van de verpleegkundig specialist. *Tijdschrift voor Verpleegkundigen TVZ, 110*(7), 203–204.

Steppe, H. (1990). Krankenpflege im Wandel 1939–1989: von der Berufung zum Beruf–vom Dienen zur Dienstleistung. *Krankenpflege, 1*(90), S.11–15.

Steppe, H. (Hrsg.) (1996). *Krankenpflege im Nationalsozialismus. 8. Auflage*. (1. Auflage unter dem Titel: Geschichte der Krankenpflege: Versuch einer kritischen Aufarbeitung, 1984). Frankfurt am Main: Marbuse-Verlag GmbH.

Stiftung, R. B. (Hrsg.) (1992, 1993). Pflege braucht

Eliten. *Denkschrift zur Hochschulausbildung für Lehr—und Leitungskräfte in der Pflege* (3rd ed.). Beiträge zur Gesundheitsökonomie 28. Gesundheitspflege. Gerlinger: Bleicher Verlag.

Stiftung, R. B. (Hrsg.) (1993b). *Pflegeförderung: zur Situation in der Bundesrepublik Deutschland*. Materialien und Berichte, Band 39. Gerlingen: Bleicher Verlag.

Stiftung, R. B. (Hrsg.) (1996). *Pflegewissenschaft: Grundlegung für Lehre, Forschung Und Praxis*. Denkschrift. Materialien und Berichte 46. Stuttgart: Bleicher Verlag.

Stiftung, R. B. (2000). *Pflege neu denken: Zur Zukunft der Pflegeausbildung*. Stuttgart: Schattauer.

Styles, M. (1985). *Report on the Regulation of Nursing. Report on the present: A position for the future*. International Council of Nurses, Professional Services Committee. Geneva: ICN.

Styles, M., & Affara, Λ. (1997). *ICN on regulation: Towards a 21st century model*. Geneva: ICN.

Van der Kooij, C. H. (1990). 1980–1990: De vermaatschappelijking van de zorg. In: A. H. M. van den Bergh-Braam, C. H. von der Kooij, & A. E. W. M. van de Pasch (Eds.), *Honderd jaar verplegen* (pp. 13–64). Lochem: Uitgeversmaatschappij De Tijdstroom.

Van der Pasch, T. (2000). "We betrekken verpleegkundigen nog onvoldoende bij de beleidsontwikkeling": Minister Borst over versterking positie verpleegkundigen [Interview]. *Tijdschrift voor Verpleegkundigen, TVZ, 110*(14), 434–436.

Van der Veen, A. (2000). Gezondheidszorgberoepen in beweging: Stel een platform in voor beleidsadvisering van de minister. *Tijdschrift voor Verpleegkundigen TVZ, 110*(17), 530–531.

Van Maanen, H. (1998). *Two decades WENR: Did history write nursing research or did nursing research write history?* Keynote address, 20th Anniversary Workgroup of European Nurse Researchers (WENR) and 9th Open Conference of the WENR. Helsinki 5–8 July, 1998.

Van Maanen, H. (2001). *The family health nurse: An old concept in a renewed appearance*. The German experience with community nursing care. Paper presented at International Council of Nurses ICN 22nd Quadrennial Congress, Copenhagen, 10–15 June, 2001.

Vlaskamp, L. (2000). Verpleegkundige beroepsuitoefening en tuchtrecht. *Tijdschrift voor Verpleegkundigen TVZ, 110*(7), 212–215.

World Health Organization. (1954). *Expert Committee on Nursing: Third report*. World Health Organization Technical Report Series No. 91. Geneva: Author.

World Health Organization. (1966). *Expert Committee on Nursing: Fifth report*. World Health Organization Technical Report Series No. 347. Geneva: Author.

World Health Organization. (1977). *Criteria for the evaluation of learning objectives in the education of health personnel*. Report of a WHO Study Group. Technical Report Series No.608. Geneva: Author.

World Health Organization. (1983). *New approaches to health education in primary health care*. Report of a

WHO Expert Committee. Technical Report Series No.690. Geneva: Author.

World Health Organization. (1984). *Education and training of nurse-teachers and managers with special regard to primary health care.* Report of a WHO Expert Committee. Technical Report Series 708. Geneva: Author.

World Health Organization. (1986). *Regulatory mechanisms for nursing training and practice: Meeting primary health care needs.* Report of a WHO Study Group. Technical Report Series 738. Geneva: Author.

World Health Organization. (1988). *From Alma Ata to the year 2000: Reflections at the midpoint.* Geneva: Author.

World Health Organization Regional Office for Europe. (1970). *Trends in European nursing services.* Report on a Working Group, Bern, 1970. Copenhagen: Author.

World Health Organization Regional Office for Europe. (1972). *Higher education in nursing.* Report on a Symposium, The Hague, 1972. Copenhagen: Author.

World Health Organization Regional Office for Europe. (1984). *Postbasic and graduate education for nurses.* Report on a WHO meeting. EURO Reports and Studies 99. Copenhagen: Author.

World Health Organization Regional Office for Europe. (1999). *Health 21: Health for all in the 21st century.* European Publications "Health For All," No 6. Copenhagen: Author.

III

Nursing Knowledge: How We Come to Know What We Know

10

Undergraduate Education: Development and Politics

Diana Davidson Dick ■ Betty Cragg

Students unite, participating in the democratic process by influencing policy as knowledgeable workers, caregivers, and stakeholders.

For more than 100 years, undergraduate education has been a major focus of the political and policy initiatives of organised nursing in Canada. The preparation of the next generation of registered nurses (RNs) determines the viability of the profession and its ability to influence the health care system and the health of society. In advocating for changes in undergraduate education, leaders in nursing education and practise have struggled for recognition of their knowledge base and their capacity to determine their own standards. Initiatives to change undergraduate education provide examples of the barriers, innovations, and successes nurses have experienced in their efforts to affect policy and influence legislation to improve the health care of Canadians. Educational changes, for example, baccalaureate entry to practise, also demonstrate how nurses have been able to mobilise the members of their profession, members of the larger society, and governments to achieve the objectives of contributing to a higher standard of care, improving patient outcomes through improving undergraduate education.

OVERVIEW OF CURRENT ISSUES IN NURSING EDUCATION

This chapter views the contemporary realities and expectations of Canadian undergraduate education not only from a conceptual, informational, and historical perspective but also within the framework of political processes. Two major undergraduate educational issues and concerns are addressed:

- Achievement of baccalaureate education as the entry standard for practise as an RN
- Application of the model of the integration of the political and the nursing processes in educating undergraduate students in a clinical experience

Both issues are examples of the visibility, breadth, and scope of nursing practise and political action.

Influence of Nursing and Political Processes

The political process is parallel and integral to the nursing process. Both are problem-solving processes. The nursing process is applied to issues of care and service, and the political process is applied to issues of power and influence. Although both include similar key steps, both are intertwined and nonlinear. Nursing process includes data collection and analysis, diagnosis or problem identification, nursing orders with projected outcomes and dates, implementation, and evaluation. The political process includes the steps of data collection and analysis and the identification of issues, goals or objectives, strategies with projected outcomes, dates and key players, implementation, and evaluation (Box 10.1).

The nursing process and the political process include similar fundamental elements, which are also processes in themselves. These elements include the following:

- Developing and maintaining relationships
- Identifying and understanding the key players or stakeholders
- Planning and organising
- Collecting, analysing, and disseminating information
- Educating and communicating
- Taking advantage of opportunity and acting with persistence

One tends to think of the political process as the application of politics, which has been described as the authoritative allocation of resources—or who gets what, when, and how (Lasswell, 1958). From this definition, one can see that politics is a part of everyone's daily life. Although the word often has negative connotations, one can also see that "politics" as a concept or an entity is value neutral, neither good nor bad; rather, it exists. *How we use* politics and the political process determines whether the process is good or bad, just as how we use the communication process determines

---

BOX 10.1

Comparing the Nursing Process and the Political Process: The Interrelationships

THE NURSING PROCESS

Goal: Care and service provision

Steps: Diagnosis/problem identification, expected outcomes/dates, nursing orders, evaluation

THE POLITICAL PROCESS

Goal: Power and influence

Steps: Issue/goal/objectives identification, desired outcomes/dates, strategies, implementation, evaluation

COMMON ELEMENTS

Opportunity: recognising or creating it, then seizing it

Relationships: development and maintenance

Identification of key players

Planning and organisation

Information and education

Communication

Persistence

whether the process is good or bad, effective or ineffective. It is important that we are aware of politics and the political process and, like other processes, that we learn how to use them constructively and effectively (Dick, 1985).

The political process involves the exercise of power which goes on in words—written or spoken (Smith, 1981). Being visible, writing, being read, speaking, being heard, and communicating effectively are requirements for the exercise of power and for the advancement of health and the practise of nursing. Examples of nurses who used the political process to achieve desired education levels and of a clinical group of students and their educator who used political processes to achieve desired results for a patient are presented in this chapter. These examples show that power can be viewed as a health issue. In this context, if you have power, you feel well, or better; if you do not have power, you feel unwell, or less well. The acquisition of power in this context is a worthy goal towards growth, healing, and well-being, and the exercise of power through the political and nursing processes can be seen as an act of caring. It is worthwhile to note that these are principles that a good clinician encourages for his or her patients.

Patricia Benner, nurse leader and researcher, speaks about the "full appreciation for the power that nurses acquire when they articulate the skill and knowledge that is embedded in their practise" (2000, p. ix). Benner continues:

> We have found that discerning and describing the knowledge, competence, and skill that goes into day-to-day nursing work allows nurses themselves to comprehend their work in a more empowering way. It increases nurses' mastery and appreciation of their own work and, by extension, nurses' ability to better care for patients. The articulation of nursing work [or visibility] can not only spur hospital management, politicians and policy makers to value and reward nursing as well as contribute to nurses valuing themselves and each other. (Benner, 2000, p. ix; bracketed material added)

This approach to nursing takes the view that nursing is the application of competencies that include a combination of knowledge, judgements, and skills by an individual nurse, or a group of nurses, to make a positive health difference. Competencies are "the knowledge, skills, attitudes and judgment expected of practitioners" (Canadian Nurses Association [CNA], 1997, p.42). Nursing, which is informed by a large body of theoretical and clinical knowledge, relies on and involves knowledge-based caring and decision making that makes a difference to health.

As well, nursing education, legislation and regulation of nursing practise, social movements, and political processes have a long history of tension and interreliance. This history makes evident the need for Canadian nurses to be involved in the systems, policies, and legislation that have an impact on their capacity to provide safe, effective care and service to the Canadian public. One role of undergraduate education is to convey this background and framework to those who are entering the profession: Canadian undergraduate nursing students.

Key Policy and Political Issues

Policy and political issues about nursing education in the 20th century included the need for registration to recognise nurses who met educational standards, thus protecting the public from those with inadequate nursing preparation. Another issue was which kind of institution (service or educational) should educate undergraduate nurses. A consequential issue is the level at which nurses needed to be educated to meet the competencies required by the bodies that regulate nursing practise and register beginning practitioners.

Since their earliest days, Canadian nursing organisations have made recommendations about undergraduate nursing education designed to ensure that graduates have the competencies to meet the needs of the patient, or population, and to meet the increasingly complex demands of health care systems. Implementation of such recommendations usually depended on legislation and funding. As a result, these organisations have had to influence governments to achieve the most profound and desired changes. Nurses have mobilised and used political processes to create political will. Frequently, in seeking changes for the profession to meet the changing needs of the health care system and the needs of the public, nurses have met opposition from governments, other health professions, other professions, and other nurses.

HISTORY OF WOMEN'S PLACE AND NURSING EDUCATION

Formal nursing education in Canada started at a time when women had few rights in Canadian society and were, therefore, disadvantaged politically. Before the 1880s, women could not vote; they could not own property in many places; they were not accepted as full participants in postsecondary education (Errington, 1990). Early in the 20th century, predominantly male professions, such as medicine and law, moved from an apprenticeship model to an educational model and became established in universities. Until the early 21st century, nursing remained a predominantly female occupation, with educational preparation for nursing established mainly in hospitals or at community colleges. As a predominantly women's profession, nursing has reflected many of the problems of women in society. Despite its educational base of science, clinical, and professional skills, knowledge, and judgement, the history of nursing education has reflected a social perception that nursing is "women's work," which, therefore, requires little knowledge and preparation, or remuneration (Reverby, 1987).

Nursing has also been seen as a calling, as evidenced by the importance of religious orders of nurses in establishing and providing health care in French Canada. Those with a vocation do the job for love, with little consideration for their own needs or those of the profession. With the influence of Florence Nightingale in the English-speaking world in the last half of the 19th century, nursing became a respectable way for middle-class laywomen to earn a living and display altruism (McPherson, 1996). Nightingale and her followers demonstrated that nurses needed particular skills and knowledge. It was not generally recognised until the second half of the 20th century, however, that nursing comprises a unique body of knowledge and skills (Rogers, 1970, p. xii). The development of nursing theories and research has provided the evidence to justify nursing judgements, decisions, plans, and actions. In some jurisdictions, governments have recently accepted the need, identified by the profession, for specifying competencies nurses must have to function safely and effectively in the current and future health care system. Most regulatory bodies of nursing across the country have concluded that the competencies identified for new RNs require the content of a baccalaureate education programme.

Nursing Education in New France

Nursing has a long history in Canada, starting with the founding of hospitals in Quebec City and Montreal in New France by members of religious orders in the 17th century. Jeanne Mance, who founded the Hotel Dieu hospital in Montreal in 1642, has been recognised as the first lay nurse in Canada (The History of Nursing Society, 1929). The

Roman Catholic nursing orders sent nuns who had been taught religious observance and care of the sick in their convents in France (Nelson, 1999). Later in the 17th century and in the 18th century, especially after Quebec became a British colony in 1759, which cut off most contacts with France, nursing orders prepared local women to provide care (Gibbon & Mathewson, 1947). A system of hospital-based nursing care developed, and the Grey Nuns under Marguerite d'Youville also started home care in Montreal in 1738. Catholic nursing orders provided early health care to westward-moving pioneers. By the end of the 19th century, these orders had founded hospitals and nursing training schools in various parts of Canada (Ross-Kerr, 1998). Such initiatives reinforced the perception of nursing as a religious vocation and made the provision of nursing care respectable in the cultural context of French Canada. Nuns could exert considerable power and influence within their own settings, controlling the management of hospitals they founded and ensuring that students' educational needs were considered in a way that proved impossible in secular hospitals controlled by boards (Paul, 1998). In a broader social context, religious orders were controlled by the hierarchy of the church and exerted relatively little political influence in secular society.

Nursing Education in English-Speaking Canada

In English-speaking Canada, the religious tradition of nursing was less important. It was not until the influence of Florence Nightingale after the Crimean war in the 1850s that nursing became a respectable occupation for middle-class women and a source of upward mobility for girls from poor homes and farm regions (McPherson, 1996). In the late 19th and early 20th centuries, there was a rapid development of hospitals throughout North America. Nursing schools were founded to train the required nurses and provide staffing for the new hospitals. The founders of new schools of nursing frequently cited Nightingale's principles. However, one of her key principles, the financial autonomy of the nursing school from the hospital, did not occur. Schools in English Canada were usually governed by hospital boards. Therefore, the service needs of the hospital were considered more important than the educational needs of student nurses.

Modern undergraduate nursing education began in Canada in 1874 with the opening of the Mack Training School in St. Catharines, Ontario. The founder was Dr. Theophilis Mack, a physician, who wanted to ensure competent care in hospitals. He believed that middle-class patients would choose modern, scientific hospital treatment if they were assured that they would receive professional nursing care (Gibbons & Mathewson, 1947). Thus began the linkage of nursing education in Canada with the needs of hospitals—and the practise of subservience of nursing to the demands of medicine. It is notable that the motto of the Mack School of Nursing was "I see and am silent" (Coburn, 1981). This contrasts sharply with current professional obligations, responsibility, and accountability to advocate for patients, to question and challenge decisions and approaches to care, and to act and speak to protect patients from harm. From the 1880s to the 1960s, nursing care in Canadian hospitals was provided mostly by nursing students. Graduate nurses worked mainly in homes as private duty nurses or followed the tradition of leaving the workforce upon marriage.

Life and Education in Hospital Nursing Schools

In hospital schools, students lived regimented lives, passing uniform inspections, working long hours, and being required to live in residence under strict rules. In the early 20th century, a time of poor working conditions for most workers, students were expected to work 12-hour shifts, with only one-half day off per week (Paul, 1998). In return for their labour, they received free tuition, room, and board. In some cases, they also received a stipend in recognition of the service they provided.

The very restrictive environment of the nursing school perpetuated the notion of the nurse as the physician's handmaiden and discouraged expression of independent thinking or action. Nurses, especially students, were supposed to stand when physicians entered the nursing station, to defer to medical opinions, and to follow doctor's orders for patients. In the hospital schools in the first half of the 20th century, there were few educational or curriculum standards, and the few instructional hours were mainly doctor's lectures, taken by students on off time or in the middle of split shifts (Weir, 1932). Hospitals hired few graduate nurses; therefore, the main practical instruction came from fellow students with only months more experience. As one writer commented, it was an apprenticeship system that had no masters to supervise the apprentices (Paul, 1998). With the exception of a few supervisors who were graduate nurses, hospitals in Canada were staffed and run by student nurses. On evenings and nights, senior students were in charge of wards, supervising the work of their juniors.

Despite the many problems, the hospital training system had advantages for the students as well as the hospitals. It was a source of affordable postsecondary education and an entrance to a respected occupation. Students and graduates felt a strong loyalty to their institution and its patients and often went beyond even the extreme demands of their training for the sake of patient care. For example, student nurses volunteered for literally life-threatening assignments during epidemics of diseases such as smallpox and polio (Garey & Hott, 1988). Living together in residence, students were able to support each other in dealing with the intense demands of life-and-death situations. Much informal debriefing and learning occurred after hours in the residence. There was no teaching–service dichotomy; therefore, students were integrated into the life of the institution. Even when hospital schools became more educationally focussed, the teachers, as employees of the hospital, were an integral part of the unit where they taught. They and their students were not treated as guests but as full participants who were expected to contribute to the quality of the care provided. Boards, administrators, and physicians who wielded power and control within hospitals were motivated to respond to calls for reform within hospital nursing schools because having a nursing school with a good reputation was a source of pride to everyone associated with the institution.

Nursing Programmes in the University

The first university nursing programme in Canada was founded by Ethel Johns at the University of British Columbia in 1919, providing preparation for nursing in what became known as the "sandwich" model: training in a hospital school sandwiched between first and final years at a university (Mussallem, 1965). After World War I, the need for improved public health and for nurses with university-based public health preparation led the Red Cross to provide seed funding for programmes to upgrade diploma-prepared nurses at five additional Canadian universities. The pattern of university education for the next 30 years was created.

Most universities offered post-RN programmes that prepared RNs for public health positions or educated those employed in hospitals for leadership positions as nurse educators or administrators. Those who wanted a university degree as their initial preparation for nursing could take the sandwich programmes. By incorporating time at the university before and after traditional hospital nursing training, these programmes ensured that the students had the general education for which many reformers had called. However, when learning nursing, the students were not required to apply their general education to the situations they were encountering in hospitals. The university had no control over the content or teaching of their nursing courses (King, 1970).

In 1942, Kathleen Russell pioneered an integrated nursing programme at the University of Toronto (Carpenter, 1970). A similar programme followed shortly thereafter at McMaster University in Hamilton. In integrated programmes, the university controlled the nursing as well as the general education portions of the programme and therefore could ensure that clinical applications and connections were made with the various theory courses the students were taking. The university could also ensure that clinical experiences met students' learning needs and were sequenced in accord with educational principles. Only after Mussallem (1965) studied nursing education in Canada for the 1965 Royal Commission on Health Services were clear recommendations made about the superiority of integrated nursing education. The recommendations led the majority of university schools in the country to move to this model. Entry-level integrated programmes began to flourish, but post-RN diploma education also remained a major focus of university education. Many diploma-prepared nurses—who still constituted the majority of the graduates and working nurses—wanted a stronger educational background to satisfy their personal aspirations and increase their career options. Currently, generic baccalaureate education, offered in collaboration with colleges, is becoming the norm. Post-RN diploma baccalaureate degrees will eventually decline, and more emphasis will be placed on graduate education and research within the universities.

STRATEGIES TO IMPROVE NURSING EDUCATION

By the middle of the 20th century, educational leaders in nursing were able to persuade their hospital boards that students needed adequate theoretical preparation as well as the practical learning that occurred on the wards. Initial probationary periods with intensive learning of basic sciences and practise laboratories, as well as block scheduling with class times segregated from ward work, represented attempts to ensure more and better-quality nursing education within hospital schools (Paul, 1998). However, projects such as the demonstration school at the Metropolitan hospital in Windsor in the 1950s (Lord, cited in Mussallem, 1965), and the Nightingale school in Toronto in the 1960s demonstrated that students could reach the same outcomes in 2 years rather than 3, if they were not required to meet the service needs of the hospital.

Concerns about the quality of nursing education led nurses to gather data from external, and therefore presumably more objective, experts to demonstrate that changes were needed. In 1929, the CNA and the Canadian Medical Association commissioned George Weir, a professor of education at the University of British Columbia, to study the current state of nursing education. His report, published in 1932, included scathing indictments of some of the exploitative practises in the hospital nursing system. Among other things, he discovered schools of nursing that accepted students who had Grade 7 education and schools that had hired no instructors to teach students. He identified that a great deal of students' time was spent on what he called "maid's work." Weir commented:

[T]here is abroad in Canada today a certain school of opinion that would single out the nurse from the procession of social progress and ask her to revert to the good old days of apprenticeship and rule-of-thumb standards! A nineteenth century nursing education in a twentieth century world, with its more exacting and specialised demands on intelligence, knowledge, ingenuity, resourcefulness and social adaptability, is sometimes the solution recommended for our nursing problems. Such a strange position is difficult to understand unless it be that these critics believe that nurses should hold membership in a cult of intellectual serfdom. . . . (Weir, 1932, pp. 380–381).

Weir made many recommendations for improving students' conditions and education. He recognised the need for nurses to have general as well as practical education and recommended that to meet the needs of the public universities should, "in the judgment of the Survey, award degrees in Nursing as in Arts, Law, Engineering, Pharmacy, Agriculture, Medicine, or any other field of learning" (Weir, 1932, p. 393). It was almost 60 years before his recommendation was taken seriously outside the nursing profession.

The Royal Commission on Health Services in 1965 provided another case of external recommendations for nursing education that reflected and supported the position of nursing leaders. The commission was influential in the movement of nursing education to postsecondary educational institutions and development of integrated generic baccalaureate programmes. In the 1990s, the approach used by leaders seeking educational change was to focus on required entry-level competencies. The competencies led in turn to identification of the educational level required to meet these standards—a university degree in nursing.

CURRENT ISSUES IN UNDERGRADUATE EDUCATION IN CANADA

The considerable changes that have occurred in nursing in the past century often have been led by nurses concerned with educational issues. Among these have been registration, the move to postsecondary educational institutions, and the baccalaureate as the required educational level for entry to the practise of nursing, known as the baccalaureate entry to practise.

Registration as Recognition of Education

With the establishment of hospital nursing schools at the turn of the 20th century came concerns that nurses who had graduated from formal programmes of nursing received no more recognition than women who had picked up whatever skills they might have informally. Therefore, one of the first policy concerns of the nursing organisations in Canada was registration for trained nurses. It is indicative of the importance of entry-level education that one of the first nursing organisations in Canada was the Canadian Society of Superintendents of Training Schools, a precursor, with societies of graduate nurses, of the CNA. As discussed in Chapter 8, they wanted registration as recognition that there should be legislated standards for people who provided nursing care. Registration recognised the value of nursing education from programmes that met the standards established by the professional regulatory bodies under provincial legislation. Registration provided the public with an expectation of standards of knowledge, skill, and care from RNs.

Educational Standards

Because the motivation of many hospitals in opening schools of nursing was access to a cheap labor force, another early and continuing concern for nursing organisations was the establishment of educational standards. Could hospitals with fewer than 50 or 75 beds provide enough diversity of experiences to prepare students adequately to provide safe, competent care as graduates? How could specialised hospitals, such as psychiatric institutions, provide students with enough general nursing experience? Did nurses not need more general educational background than could be provided in the limitations of an institution devoted to educating only one type of graduate? Standardised curricula were developed by educators and other nursing leaders in the United States and Canada, but they were not made mandatory during this period. However, many schools used these models voluntarily to guide programme development.

The Move From Hospitals to Postsecondary Educational Institutions

Those who sought reform and improvement of nursing education advocated transferring nurse education responsibilities from the hospital schools to postsecondary educational institutions (Mussallem, 1965). Moving nursing students from the control of hospital boards would reduce exploitation based on the inherent conflict of interest between the hospitals' need for patient care and students' need for purely educational classes and clinical experiences. There was also recognition that nurses needed general education in the arts, social sciences, and sciences in addition to the more focussed learning related to nursing skills and decision making they received in hospitals. Student nurses should not have watered down summaries of anatomy, psychology, and pharmacology "for nurses." Rather, they need to meet the same standards as other postsecondary students. Change from the hospital sector to the educational sector also required political will because it involved a change in provincial responsibility from ministries of health to the ministries responsible for postsecondary education. It also involved the mechanisms for funding nursing education.

In the 1960s, as community colleges were founded across Canada, several provinces, notably Quebec, Ontario, and Saskatchewan, moved nursing education completely out of hospitals. In Alberta, British Columbia, Manitoba, and Nova Scotia, some hospital schools remained in existence until the mid-1990s, although most schools went to the new colleges.

Hospitals were no longer responsible for the education of nurses. New graduates, many of whom would have clinical experiences in a number of hospitals and community agencies, needed orientation as new employees. This change led to some tensions between educational and service institutions. Employers and others in service agencies have expressed views that nursing graduates are not prepared for the real world, that they are book smart but do not appreciate reality, that they have no loyalty, and that their instructors, whether from the college or university, live in ivory towers and do not appreciate the needs of the workplace.

As Kramer pointed out in the United States in 1974, students graduating from nursing schools suffered "reality shock" in the world of work because the ideals they had been taught in school were not played out in their workplaces. Nearly 30 years later, this phenomenon is still evident in new graduates (Boychuk Duchscher, 2001). Competition for educational clinical placements in health service institutions has become a problem, especially in big cities. Health care agencies, stressed by funding cutbacks and restructuring of the 1990s resulting in nursing position layoffs, the disappearance of senior nursing leadership and management positions, bed closures, shorter lengths of stay, higher patient acuity, and a nursing shortage, are more selective about how many and what level of students they will accept on any given unit and at any time. At the same time, employers and others in the service setting comment that the new graduate has strong skills of problem solving and critical thinking and a strong theoretical base. The recognition that the aim of both education and service is to ensure the safe, quality, knowledge-based nursing care for the patient has led to greater dialogue among service agencies and education programmes.

Entry to Practise

Educational qualifications for entry level RNs have been a policy issue from the early days of organised nursing. The superintendents of nursing and graduates in the early years of the 20th century wanted to ensure that entry to practise as an RN was restricted to those who had completed approved nursing education programmes. In the final years of the century, most nursing organisations in the country were working to achieve the bachelor's degree as the new minimum qualification to become an RN. This policy position became known as "baccalaureate as entry to practise." In 1982, the CNA endorsed a resolution calling for the baccalaureate degree as entry to practise by the year 2000.

By 1989, all provincial professional associations had passed similar resolutions (Bajnok, 1992). However, there was resistance from many provincial governments, from members of other professions, and from a number of nurses. The need for increased education of nurses was questioned on the grounds that existing nurses were adequately prepared, concerns that baccalaureate-prepared nurses would be more expensive to educate and hire, and an implied fear that more educated nurses would be less compliant. Concerns on the part of diploma-prepared nurses that they would lose their jobs if the entry standard were changed have been reduced by grandparenting provisions in all provinces and by the realities of a nursing shortage. Leaders were careful to emphasise that diploma graduates continued their learning in nursing practise as they, like other new graduates, moved along the continuum that Benner (1984) identified as being from novice to expert.

Under the authority of legislation, nursing regulatory bodies in each province or territory establish the educational standards and mechanisms to approve curricula, thereby ensuring that graduates will be educationally prepared to meet the minimum competencies required to begin or enter the practise of nursing. Nursing, like law, medicine, and engineering, for example, is a self-regulating profession. For many years, registration as an RN has been based on graduation from an approved school of nursing and success on standardised national registration examinations.

Nursing organisations recognised that nursing competencies for beginning practitioners needed to be clearly identified. The CNA initiated a national initiative to identify entry-level competencies (CNA, 1997). Regulatory bodies are responsible for protecting the public from harm and for the regulation of nursing practise and education. Because nursing is a self-regulating profession, the regulatory bodies determine the minimum educational requirements. Across the country, they have moved to use the competencies as their requirements of entering or beginning RNs to meet standards of nursing practise. To receive provincial approval for their programmes from the nursing regulatory body, schools of nursing must prepare graduates who meet these competency requirements. It became evident that the curriculum offered in baccalaureate programmes most closely matched the competency and standard requirements. The regulators of nursing concluded, therefore, that to provide nursing care to meet the needs of the Canadian public, educational standards for entry to practise would have to change. In some provinces, no changes in legislation or regulation were required. In others, persuading provincial governments to make the required changes to legislation or regulations, despite the strong evidence for the need for change, has proved to be a major challenge.

Many governments have been slow to support the new entry-level requirement and, in some cases, such as Saskatchewan and Manitoba, have attempted to move away from baccalaureate as entry to practise after it was established as public policy. A key question to ask is whether these governments would consider reversing support of educational requirements viewed as necessary by the members of the profession for any profession other than nursing. Political action by nurses, nursing students, and other health care providers has been pivotal in persuading provincial governments that nurses do indeed need the content of the baccalaureate curriculum (Buresh & Gordon, 2000).

Canadian Approach to Achieving the Degree for Entry to Practise

The baccalaureate entry-to-practise policy position of the profession of RNs has led to cooperation among nursing schools. Now community colleges, institutions, and universities throughout Canada are collaborating to offer nursing degree programmes together. Collaboration among colleges and universities in most provinces and territories has been the route chosen to capitalise on the strengths of both types of institutions. This approach maximises the range of faculty expertise and combines available resources to achieve quality nursing education programmes.

COLLABORATION

Although more complex to administer than stand-alone programmes, the commitment of nursing educators to the baccalaureate degree for entry to practise has been reflected in the work of nursing educators to maintain collaborative efforts. Many collaborations were initiated well in advance of the common deadline set by nursing regulatory bodies (in most cases, the year 2000), or before the passage of any legislation. Nurse educators from diploma and baccalaureate programmes in several parts of the country got together to create collaborative, joint, or partnership programmes that would reflect the best of college and university programmes. In some cases, for example in Ontario, these bottom-up collaborative initiatives initially failed because of the reluctance of the provincial government to finance them. However, when the Ontario government adopted the policy of the College of Nurses of Ontario (the regulatory body) that the baccalaureate degree should be the criterion for entry to practise, relationships had been formed and much of the groundwork was in place.

In provinces such as British Columbia and Alberta, collaborative programmes were funded but were required to retain a diploma exit after 3 years. The numbers of students who could proceed to the degree were restricted. In other provinces, such as New Brunswick and Nova Scotia, diploma schools have been closed, and the human and physical resources have been allocated to the universities.

APPLICATION OF POLITICAL PROCESSES: SASKATCHEWAN

Policy implementation is well underway across Canada after many decades of lobbying by nurses and nursing organisations through effective successful use of political processes. It is useful to explore the example of the achievement of the baccalaureate as entry to practise in one Canadian jurisdiction using the framework of the political process. In 1984, the Saskatchewan Registered Nurses Association (SRNA), the regulatory and professional association, formally adopted the policy position of the baccalaureate as entry to practise by the year 2000. The Nursing Education Program of Saskatchewan (NEPS), a collaborative programme of the Saskatchewan Institute of Applied Science and Technology (SIAST) and the University of Saskatchewan, which accepted its first students in 1996, was set to have the convocation of its first graduates in the spring of 2000.

On January 21, 2000, the Minister of Health announced that the government did not support the degree as the sole entry to practise but would also recognise a diploma as entry to practise. There were a number of pressures that gave rise to the announcement, one of which was the growing realisation of the existing and expected nursing shortage. The SRNA objected to the government's announcement. Its position was that in keeping with the fact that nursing is a self-regulating profession, the responsibility for regulation of nursing practise and entry-to-practise educational requirements was legitimately that of the SRNA, through legislation and through expertise.

On the day of the announcement, government representatives made presentations to the students and faculty at both collaborative partner programme sites in Regina and Saskatoon. With faculty providing powerful models of leadership, nursing students from all 4 years of the programme demonstrated their skills in organisation, education, information sharing, and communication—and their understanding of the importance of respectful relationships throughout the process. They advanced their strong position in support of their education programme and of the degree as the requirement for entry to practise, backed by evidence. Their position, like that of the SRNA, was for the need for an undergraduate education that would prepare them for an increasingly complex health care system and increasingly complex patient health problems. They advocated for their own education and also for the quality of education of those students who would follow them. They met with politicians, senior public servants, and the media. They planned effective rallies at the legislature in Regina, and during one rally, brought their suitcases as a symbol of their intent to leave the province if they were unable to convince the government of the need for the full content of the nursing degree programme.

The SRNA reactivated their previously established Political Action Committee, which had already laid solid groundwork on the issue, by having met with all members of the legislative assembly. SRNA officials met with the Minister of Health, public servants, editorial boards of major media, columnists, and reporters. The deans of nursing at SIAST and the University of Saskatchewan developed two policy option briefing notes for the Minister and her staff outlining first, broad options and second, educational options to address the nursing shortage. The Minister of Health met with the deans, faculty, students and other stakeholders and agreed that there could be a different approach. At a March 13, 2000 meeting, the issue was resolved when the minister, the president of the SRNA, and the deans of nursing signed a Memorandum of Understanding that was based on the policy option briefing notes. The student representative made a significant contribution to the meeting.

This experience helped students to understand the role of politics and the political process in establishing policy and influencing decisions that directly affected them, their future, their profession, and the public (Box 10.2). This experience was also notable with respect to the actions of the Minister of Health who had taken a firm and public policy position on January 21, 2000. In the ensuing days and weeks, the Minis-

BOX 10.2

Reflecting on the Saskatchewan Experience

The processes and outcomes represented in the Saskatchewan experience show how sound policy, leadership, hard work, commitment to an evidence-based position, and collaboration, as well as careful, respectful participation in the political process, can achieve desired results. Identify the elements inherent in the implementation of the political process. Here are some activities to guide your reflection on the processes:

- Identify the policy issue. Comment on the opportunity.
- Identify the steps of the political process as they were used in this situation.
- Speculate on the powerful or powerless feeling of the students with respect to the future of the programme in which they were enrolled and the future of the profession of nursing from the day of the announcement (January 29, 2000) until receiving news of the signing of the memorandum of understanding (March 13, 2000).
- Speculate on the range of feelings of the students with respect to esteem, confidence, and health, in the time period from the announcement by the Minister to the resolution of the policy.
- Identify the role of visibility and how it was operationalised.
- Identify the key stakeholders and how they exercised their power and influence.
- Identify the role of collaboration and innovation.
- Imagine yourself a student leader in this situation; then develop a political action plan.
- How would you evaluate the use of the political process and the elements of the process in this situation? What are the ways in which you could define success, had the government not supported the policy?
- What suggestions would you recommend to acknowledge the Minister of Health for her leadership and courage in accepting a policy that she did not initially support?

ter was open to reviewing policy options presented by the deans and to hearing the evidence that was presented by many groups and individuals. She is to be commended for having the courage and wisdom to get cabinet support for publicly changing her position, based on sound information. This is a fine example of democracy in action.

Although this situation had a successful outcome, there have been different outcomes in other provinces, such as Manitoba. As of Spring 2002, the issue of an undergraduate university nursing degree as the educational requirement for beginning RNs had not been consistently resolved across Canada.

ORGANISATIONS FOCUSSING ON UNDERGRADUATE NURSING ISSUES

Although the first university programmes began shortly after World War I, it was not until 1942, in the middle of World War II, that the leaders of Canada's university nursing programmes got together to find what became the Canadian Association of University Schools of Nursing (CAUSN). The shortage of nurses precipitated by the war created opportunities from which the association could benefit (Kirkwood & Bouchard,

1992). The CNA facilitated the first meeting, and in the early days, there was much debate about whether this organisation should be affiliated with the CNA. Eventually, the deans and directors of the university-based programmes decided that they had unique concerns that could best be articulated by a separate organisation. With improvements in communications and a clearer vision of the future of undergraduate nursing education, CAUSN became one of the first voices encouraging other nursing organisations to endorse baccalaureate preparation as the entry to practise requirement.

CAUSN also recognised a need for developing and implementing accreditation of university schools of nursing. Provincial nursing regulatory bodies had standards for schools of nursing that had to be met for students to be eligible for registration. These standards were applied both to diploma and to university schools and were minimum requirements for entry to practise. As a result, the standards did not reflect excellence in academic nursing education. Accreditation was implemented to assess and monitor baccalaureate programmes using criteria of excellence in relevance, accountability, relatedness, and uniqueness (CAUSN, 1995).

In 1985, the first accreditation review was completed (Kirkwood & Bouchard, 1992). Since then, most university schools have undergone the peer-review process that helps schools to recognise their strengths and identify areas for improvement. In Ontario, when the educational standard became baccalaureate entry to practise by 2005, the College of Nurses of Ontario—the regulatory body in that province—designated CAUSN accreditation as the requirement for approval.

Students in universities formed their own organisation, the Canadian University Nursing Students Association (CUNSA), in 1971. CUNSA initially represented only university nursing students. It provided opportunities for exchange of ideas and solidarity among students across the country. CUNSA regional and national conventions have been sources of inspiration and professional pride for nursing students. The organisation decided in 1992 to change its name to the Canadian Nursing Students Association (CNSA) to be more inclusive and consistent with the partnership innovations in nursing education programmes in many parts of Canada. With collaboration among universities and colleges, the concerns of all nursing students could be better served by one organisation. Students have taken the lead in recognising similarities of issues and the strength of one national nursing student organisation. The organisation provides important opportunities for networking, communication, learning, and leadership to its members (Therrian, 1992) and has produced an impressive videotape designed for recruitment to the profession of nursing.

FUTURE CHALLENGES IN UNDERGRADUATE EDUCATION

Undergraduate nursing education still faces a number of challenges that must be addressed, including curricula, recruitment, and relationships with clinical agencies.

Curriculum

To prepare nurses to meet the requirements of a rapidly changing health care system today and in the future, schools of nursing continually update and modify curricula. The competencies identified by nursing regulatory bodies are the foundation on which curricula are developed and have a fundamental influence on what is taught to nursing students. However, programmes differed in their approaches to organising and delivering curricula. For example, the caring curriculum, primary health care and population health, and particular theories have provided the philosophical organisers for different programmes.

RESEARCH

In recent years, there has been increasing emphasis on research findings to ensure that nursing practise decisions are based on evidence (this is sometimes referred to as *research utilisation* or *knowledge transfer*). There has also been an increased emphasis on the theoretical underpinnings of nursing practise and decision making.

Most curricula for entry-level RNs are designed to educate clinical generalists who can function at a beginning level in a wide variety of health care situations. New graduates need background to function in workplaces ranging from the community to acute care and to demonstrate an understanding of primary health care principles. Most hospital units are highly specialised, with a high level of patient acuity, early discharge, and high patient turnover. Because of these factors, along with a nursing shortage, there is often a tension between employers who would like job-ready employees and educators whose responsibility is to meet the educational needs of students whose future careers are likely to involve work in a variety of settings.

A paradox of employer expectations is that, although there is a desire for nurses who have specialised skills, there is often an assumption in their work assignment patterns that any nurse can work in any setting (i.e., "a nurse is a nurse is a nurse"). The hiring of new graduates in casual positions to float throughout the organisation is an example of this approach, which exacerbates the difficulties faced by new graduates adapting to the work place.

Realising that health care and the demands for nursing skills are changing and will continue to change rapidly, nursing educators have chosen to concentrate on teaching students skills that will help them to adapt over a working lifetime. Rapid changes in technology and social expectations mean that specific skills or procedures may not be relevant by the time today's students are established in their careers. Students require basic clinical knowledge and skills, along with skills of analysis and critical thinking, communication and relationships, self-directed learning, problem solving and decision making, and patient teaching. They also need to learn to apply theory and use research-based evidence to inform their care.

TECHNOLOGY

One particular knowledge area for which students must be prepared is the use of technology. As the machinery of acute care and the communications of the Internet and intranets become more sophisticated and are used more broadly in community care, students need the basic skills of informatics to be able to use present technology and adapt to new developments (Hebert, 2001). Students also need the critical skills to assess the benefits and threats that technology may pose to quality of life, collection of data for evidence-based decisions, access to information, and patient confidentiality. They will need the preparation to make informed and ethical decisions about incorporating technologic initiatives into their practise.

SYSTEMS

Because nurses need skills to influence their work places and to help shape the health care system, there is an ethical and practical imperative to include courses on the political process and systems theory in undergraduate programmes. Students need a sound knowledge and understanding about how systems are designed, how they work or fail, and how to influence them. They need this knowledge to function effectively as clinicians for their patients and to survive and thrive as employees and as team members and leaders. Such knowledge can be as important in a nurse's career as the science base and clinical competence; it is enhanced when programmes include student representatives in policy development activities.

APPLICATION OF POLITICAL AND NURSING PROCESSES IN UNDERGRADUATE EDUCATION

The earlier review of how nurses applied the political process to a major public policy issue—the baccalaureate degree as entry to practise—is replicated by the equally important and effective application of the political process integrated with the nursing process in an undergraduate student patient care situation.

A first-year nursing student was one of eight classmates who had an extended clinical experience in a convalescent rehabilitation care setting. Her patient was a young, developmentally delayed woman who required extensive personal care. As a consequence, the nursing student developed an understanding of the character and personality of the patient as well as of her needs and problems. During the course of the clinical experience, the attending physician sought a psychiatric consultation. The student read the consult notes and disagreed with the conclusions the psychiatrist had reached. The adoption of the view of the psychiatrist would have a profound impact on the life of the patient in a particular and limiting direction. The adoption of the view of the nursing student would have an equally profound influence on the life of the patient, but in a more positive and growth-supporting direction that the patient had identified as important to her.

The identification of the issue was based on a clinical assignment. The teacher had asked each of the students to identify with their patient, when possible, one issue that was important to the patient and that would have an impact on the patient's life. The students were to present that issue in the multidisciplinary weekly team conference. The teacher asked the students to use the framework of politics (who gets what, when, and how) and the political process (the problem-solving process applied to issues of power and influence) along with the nursing process (the problem-solving process applied to issues of care and service).

The student discussed the situation with the teacher, and using the elements of the political process, together they approached the unit manager and then the social worker. In each instance, they presented the findings of the student and her rationale for her position and asked for their support in the weekly rounds, if they agreed with her position. The student was a novice in the situation and was not a confident participant in this new and rather intimidating situation. She practised the presentation of her case in private with classmates, and when the time came, though very nervous, she presented all of her well-developed case, the analysis and the conclusions, before the large group of professionals. The unit manager spoke up with her support, followed by the social worker, and the student's position was endorsed at the meeting. Her use of politics and the political process were particularly meaningful in this case because the young woman could not speak effectively in her own interests.

This was only one of the achievements of the eight students who implemented politics and the political process in representing the interests of their patients at that team conference that day. They each gained an understanding of the relationship of power and health, the interrelatedness of the nursing and political processes, and the key elements of each (Box 10.3).

BOX 10.3

Reflecting on Nursing Process, Politics, and Education in Action

Just as the Saskatchewan nurses applied the political process to achieve baccalaureate education for entry to practise, so did a student and her colleagues use the political process to advocate for a patient. Here are some thoughts and exercises to consider in relation to that situation:

- State the issue that the student identified.
- Identify the steps of the nursing and political processes as they were used in this situation.
- Identify the elements inherent in the implementation of the political process.
- Speculate on the student's feelings of powerfulness or powerlessness.
- Speculate on the range of feelings of the student with respect to courage, esteem, confidence, and health in the situation.
- Identify how this student's actions made her or his role in knowledge-based caring and decision making more visible.
- Identify the key stakeholders. Identify the role of collaboration and innovation.
- Imagine yourself the student leader in a similar situation; develop the nursing process and political process plan.
- Imagine that the multidisciplinary team had not supported the perspective of the student. What process would the student need to use to achieve the best result for the patient?

In contemporary society, nursing students also need an understanding of the social, cultural, economic, and environmental contexts that affect health and the requirements for nursing care. These vary depending on regions, communities, cultures, and the variables that determine health of populations. As graduates, nurses then take these understandings to inform their efforts to influence health and social policy.

Recruitment and Retention

With an aging population that will require more health care, the impending nursing shortage, and the aging of qualified faculty to teach in nursing programmes (Canadian Institute for Health Information [CIHI], 2001), recruiting qualified students, faculty, and academic leaders is a pressing concern for nursing educators. There is a global skills shortage, and nowhere is it more pronounced than in nursing and nursing education.

SUFFICIENT STUDENTS, EDUCATORS, AND ADMINISTRATORS

During the 1990s, as part of dramatic downsizing and restructuring of the health care system across Canada, thousands of RNs lost jobs, and nursing positions at all levels of service organisations were deleted. Although other groups of employees were affected, nursing was by far the hardest hit. The federal government's financial transfers to provinces for health care and education were decreased from $18.5 billion to $12.5 billion between 1996 and 1999 alone (CNA, 1998). At the same time, some provincial governments decreased funding for nursing education seats. These events had a domino effect, creating a shortage of nurses in practise and education. In some jurisdictions, there has been a shortage of qualified applicants to nursing schools because people made career plans based on the reality of news stories about nursing position cuts and lack of availability of jobs in the health care workplace. Equally serious and significant were the deletion of senior nursing leadership and management positions. This was an international phenomenon and one of the most stunning examples of policy decisions being made and implemented without adequate research or evidence.

There has been a pattern since the 1960s of nursing shortages followed by oversupply. Governments, administrators, and educators have made decisions that have long-term consequences without adequate data for human resource forecasting. In some cases, these decisions reflect a lack of vision about the future of health care or a lack of agreement on the vision. Because there is a lag time of about 5 years between application and graduation from a baccalaureate nursing programme, the education system has often been out of step with the numbers of employees needed by the workplace. Reactive rather than proactive planning for future needs has meant that undergraduate nursing programmes have been unable to satisfy demands even when they have been able to predict trends. Policies producing cutbacks, followed by reinstatement of nursing positions, have had impacts throughout the system, including reduction in applications to nursing programmes in some geographic areas. The number of new graduates is thus reduced, and the long-term impact on health care will be felt for many years. Bed closures and budget cuts in community health and home care and throughout the system have meant that there are fewer clinical placements available for student learning, increased workload, and a stressful work environment along with fewer nurses to serve as mentors to novice nurses.

Nurses in all areas are aging. The Nursing Strategy for Canada (Advisory Committee on Health and Human Resources, 2000) recommended that governments increase student enrollment by 10% to allow for replacement of the nurses older than 40 years of age who can be anticipated to retire as the baby-boom generation reaches senior citizen status. The mean age of faculty is about 6 years older than the mean age of staff nurses (43.3 years and 48.8 years, respectively) (CIHI, 2001). There will be a crisis in the capacity to prepare new nurses unless effective strategies to ensure replacement of nursing educators are implemented immediately.

DIVERSITY

As well as ensuring adequate numbers of new nurses and the faculty to teach them, it is important that the nurses and those who educate them reflect the diversity of Canada's population. Cultural issues are included in curricula of schools of nursing largely because Canadian RNs can expect to care for and provide service to an increasingly culturally diverse patient base—individuals, families, groups, and communities (CNA, 2000). Although the principles of cultural diversity theory provide the framework for this area of competence, examples and application differ according to regional differences across the country. For example, in Saskatchewan and northern British Columbia, where there is a high aboriginal population, emphasis would be on understanding the culture and health practises of native peoples, whereas the focus in Vancouver or Toronto would reflect the cultural diversity of immigrant populations in those locations.

In contrast to the past when Weir (1932) reported that 84% of the Anglophone student nurses who responded to his questionnaires gave their ethic origin as English, Scottish, or Irish, the RN student population is become increasingly diverse. There was a time when the great majority of students entered nursing schools directly from high school and nursing studies were their major responsibility. Although students continue to come from high school, large numbers enter programmes with degrees, diplomas, or other credentials in other disciplines, from other occupations and careers, and many have many roles and responsibilities in addition to those of student. They may be parents, be caregivers for elderly relatives, and have full- or part-time jobs.

Despite this diversity, most nursing students in many schools of nursing continue to be white and female. Faculty who teach, coach, and guide and administrators and managers of nursing programmes (deans, directors, programme heads) are even less culturally diverse. This is a concern on a number of levels. People of color, men, and those whose culture and race is not reflected in their school or profession lack role models. They rarely see themselves and their particular concerns reflected in their peers, faculty, and nursing education administration or in the practise settings. The Canadian government developed and has proudly championed cultural diversity through public policy promoting and celebrating multiculturalism, and Canada's population has become increasingly culturally diverse.

In light of these factors, it is increasingly important that the population of working nurses, and hence the nursing student population, should be proportionally culturally representative of the general population of a province, territory, or region. For example, a number of initiatives are underway to recruit and retain aboriginal nursing students (see Chapter 24). There are solid examples of this in nursing education programmes across the country.

Changing Relationships Among Educational and Service Agencies

As they face the challenges of dealing with recruitment issues and shortages of nurses, nurses working in educational and service institutions are developing new relationships and new models for educating nurses. Programmes that allow student nurses to work and gain some credit; demonstration projects where educators, unit nurses, and students work together to break down some of the barriers within health care (Horsburgh et al., 1998); and new ways of preceptoring, mentoring, and supervising student practise are being proposed and tested. Thirty years after most hospital schools of nursing closed, the time may have come to examine ways to regain some of the advantages students experienced in hospitals and other service settings, while avoiding the exploitation to which hospital-based students were vulnerable. Changing public expectations, with growing emphasis on accountability, transparency, and disclosure, influence curricula and nursing practise.

The next few years will show challenging and demanding new initiatives that will continue to change the face of undergraduate nursing education to meet rapid changes in health care and an increasing demand for new approaches to the provision of nursing care and services with stronger links among education, practise, research, and administration. As the move to reverse some of the negative outcomes of restructuring and programme management continues, one result is likely to be that nursing leaders in management positions in education and service come together to support an environment for evidence-based or research-based nursing practise and the conduct of applied research in the clinical or service setting.

SUMMARY

Since the first modern nursing schools opened more than 100 years ago, undergraduate nursing education in Canada has been influenced by policies of nursing organisations, health service agencies, educational institutions, and governments. The health care system throughout Canada is highly political, and it is one of the most highly valued publicly funded social programmes. Its maintenance is a profound concern of the Canadian public and a number of stakeholders. It is a system with many subsystems, such as rural, remote, northern, community, acute, and home care, with a range of disease-based specialties and approaches to health such as population health and primary health care. An understanding of the intertwining of relationships, systems, and nursing and political processes is needed by students and graduates to be effective clinicians and participants in decision making. This understanding is needed to achieve positive outcomes for patients and the effective functioning at many levels of the systems in which patients receive care and service. All of these factors have current and future implications for the curriculum and for student learning, and they play a role in job satisfaction.

Nursing educators have a responsibility to be proactive in identifying and researching improvements in curricula and teaching–learning strategies and also to be open to responding to initiatives and recommendations of others. Research is one of the mandates of university faculty. With the establishment of educational programmes based on partnerships of colleges and universities, coupled with a pressing need to make the most efficient use of resources, there will be increased emphasis on collaborative research among university and college faculty and students. One of the challenges facing nursing education is the need for increased emphasis on asking the questions and collecting the evidence upon which sound educational policies can be based and for developing a stronger research base in the area of effective teaching–learning strategies in undergraduate education.

Nursing has identified four domains: practise, education, research, and administration. There is an urgent need to increase the domains to six, with the addition of leadership and policy. Leadership and policy need to be integrated into the curricula of undergraduate nursing education.

Reflections on the Chapter

1. What strategies would you use to attract men and members of underrepresented groups into nursing?

2. How could educational and service organisations work together to improve the clinical education of undergraduate students? What policies would need to be in place for students and for faculty? Would there be an effect on patients?

3. What is the regulatory body in your province or territory? Has the policy of the baccalaureate as the minimum educational requirement for entry to practise been implemented?

4. Discuss the established domains of nursing (practise, education, research, and administration). What would the likely impact be of adding leadership and policy as two additional domains of nursing?

REFERENCES

Advisory Committee on Health Human Resources (2000). *The nursing strategy for Canada* [On-line]. Ottawa: Health Canada. Available: http://www.hc-gc.ca/English/nursing/nursing.pdf.

Bajnok, I. (1992). Entry-level educational preparation for nursing. In A. J. Baumgart & J. Larsen, (Eds.), *Canadian nursing faces the future* (2nd ed., pp. 401–419). Toronto: Mosby Year Book.

Benner, P. (1984). *From novice to expert: Excellence and power in clinical nursing practice.* Menlo Park, CA: Addison-Wesley.

Benner, P. (2000). Forward. In B. Buresh & S. Gordon. *From silence to voice* (p. ix). Ottawa: Canadian Nurses Association.

Boychuk Duchscher, J. E. (2001). Out in the real world: newly graduated nurses in acute-care speak out. *Journal of Nursing Administration, 31*(9), 426–438.

Buresh, B., & Gordon, S. (2000). *From silence to voice: What nurses know and must communicate to the public.* Ottawa: Canadian Nurses Association.

Canada, Royal Commission on Health Services, & Hall, E. (1965). *Royal commission on health services: Report.* Ottawa: Queen's Printer.

Canadian Association of University Schools of Nursing. (1995). *Accreditation guidelines.* Ottawa: Author.

Canadian Institute for Health Information. (2001). *Canadian Institute for Health Information reports moderate rise in registered nurses workforce, fewer RNs working on casual basis, more working full-time* [Executive Summary, On-line]. Available: http://www.cihi.ca/medrls/23may2001.shtml.

Canadian Nurses Association. (1997). *National nursing competency project final report.* Ottawa: Author.

Canadian Nurses Association. (1998). The quiet crisis in health care: A proposal for a federal government investment in quality health care [Brief, On-line]. Available: http://www.cna-nurses.ca/pages/qcrisis/frames/qcframe.htm.

Canadian Nurses Association. (2000). Cultural diversity: Changes and challenges. *Nursing Now, 7*, 1–4.

Carpenter, H. M. (1970). The University of Toronto School of Nursing: An agent of change. In M.Q. Innis (Ed.), *Nursing education in a changing society* (pp. 86–108). Toronto: University of Toronto Press.

Coburn, J. (1981). "I see and am silent": A short history of nursing in Ontario. In D. Coburn, C. D'Arcy, P. New, & G. Torrance (Eds.), *Health and Canadian society* (pp. 182–201). Toronto: Fitzhenry & Whiteside.

Dick, D. D. (1985). *Politics, power and the political process.* Tel Aviv, Israel: ICN Quadrennial Congress.

Errington, J. (1990). Pioneers and suffragists. In S. Burt, L. Code, & L. Dorey (Eds.), *Changing patterns: Women in Canada* (pp. 51–78). Toronto: McClelland & Stewart.

Garey, D., & Hott, L. R. (Producers). (1988). Sentimental women need not apply: A history of the American nurse [videorecording by Florentine Films]. Willowdale, ON: McNabb & Connolly.

Gibbon, J. M., & Mathewson, M. S. (1947). *Three centuries of Canadian nursing.* Toronto: MacMillan.

Government of Canada. (1964–1965). Royal commission on health services [E. Hall, Chairman]. Ottawa: Queen's Printer.

Growe, S. J. (1991). *Who cares?: The crisis in Canadian nursing.* Toronto, ON: McClelland & Stewart.

Hebert, M. (2000). A national education strategy to develop nursing informatics competencies. *Canadian Journal of Nursing Leadership, 13*(2), 11–14.

The History of Nursing Society, School for Graduate Nurses, McGill University. *Pioneers of nursing in Canada.* Montreal: Canadian Nurses Association.

Horsburgh, M. E., Stamler, L. L., Snowdon, A. W., Foster, M., McCracken, S., Fox, S., Gagnon, J., Grondin, S., Passador, D., Klinck, S., Purushotham, D., Merrit, D., & Dickson, R. (1998, July). Paper: The role of the professional nurse mentor and staff nurse outcomes in the clinical education unit. In *Proceedings* (Vol. 1, pp. 342–348). The Workgroup of European Nurse Researchers, 9th Biennial Conference, Helsinki, Finland.

King, M. K. (1970). The development of university nursing education. In M. Q. Innis (Ed.). *Nursing education in a changing society* (pp. 67–85). Toronto: University of Toronto Press.

Kirkwood, R. A., & Bouchard, J. L. (1992). *Take counsel with one another: A beginning history of the Canadian Association of University Schools of Nursing, 1942–1992.* Ottawa: Canadian Association of University Schools of Nursing.

Kramer, M. (1974). *Reality shock: Why nurses leave nursing.* St. Louis, MO: Mosby.

Lasswell, H. D. (1958). *Politics: Who gets what, when, how.* New York: World Publishing.

McPherson K. (1996). *Bedside matters: The transformation of Canadian nursing 1900–1990.* Toronto: Oxford University Press.

Mussallem, H. K. (1965). *Nursing education in Canada* [Submission to Royal Commission on Health Services]. Ottawa: Queen's Printer.

Nelson, S. (1999). Entering the professional domain: The making of the modern nurse in 17th century France. *Nursing History Review, 7*, 171–187.

Paul, P. (1998). Nursing education becomes synonymous with nursing service. In J. C. Ross-Kerr (1998). *Prepared to care: Nurses and nursing in Alberta 1859–1996* (pp. 129–153). Edmonton: University of Alberta Press.

Reverby, S. (1987). A caring dilemma: Womanhood and nursing in historical perspective. *Nursing Research, 36,* 5–11.

Rogers, M. E. (1970). *An introduction to the theoretical basis of nursing.* Philadelphia: F. A. Davis.

Ross-Kerr, J. C. (1998). *Prepared to care: nurses and nursing in Alberta, 1859 to 1996.* Edmonton: University of Alberta Press.

Saskatchewan Registered Nurses Association (SRNA). (2000).

Smith, D. (1981). Lecture notes. Toronto, ON: Ontario

Institute for Studies in Education.

Therrien, L. (1992). *CUNSA & CNSA: A beginning history* [On-line]. Available: http://www.cnsa.ca/publications/history/.

Weir, G. M. (1932). *Survey of nursing education in Canada.* Toronto: University of Toronto Press.

World Health Organization. (1978). *Primary health care.* Report of the international conference on primary health care at Alma-Ata, Kazakhstan, September 6–12. Geneva: Author.

World Health Organization. (1986*). Ottawa charter for health promotion.* International conference on health promotion: The move towards a new public health, November 17–21. Ottawa: Author.

11
Graduate Education

Sally Thorne

Chapter Objectives

At the completion of this chapter, you will be able to:

1. Understand the implications of the historical context associated with graduate nursing education in Canada.

2. Identify specific challenges faced in Canada by nurses with graduate preparation at various levels.

(continued)

Among the primary focuses of graduate education, be it the master's or doctoral level, is the development of leaders for nursing practice, administration, education, and research. Graduate level programs with explicit research development resources (such as programs of research or research units) make it possible for nurses to conduct research that is applicable not only to education and administration, but also to practice. Photography by Beverly Anderson.

3. Recognise the impact of various social, historical, economic, and political forces on the practise realities of Canadian nurses who have graduate degrees.

4. Interpret major issues and controversies associated with graduate nursing education in Canada.

5. Examine current social, political, and economic trends as they shape current graduate nursing education.

6. Identify opportunities by which the profession of nursing in Canada can direct its future through strategic advancement of graduate education.

This chapter focusses on the contributions made to the health care system by nurses educated at the graduate level. A special emphasis is placed on the contributions of nurses prepared at the master's level, whose focus is *advanced practise*, and those prepared at the doctoral and postdoctoral levels, whose focus is *research*.

Building on an historical overview of the evolution within graduate education in Canada, this chapter examines the impact of graduate education in general as well as some of the specific contributions made by Canadian nurses with graduate level education. Within this discussion, the reader will find a further exploration of some of the realities of graduate-prepared nurses in their places of work, the issues that arise for these nurses in practise, and the barriers that need to be addressed if the full potential of these nurses is to be realised.

HISTORY OF GRADUATE NURSING EDUCATION IN CANADA

The second half of the 20th century brought graduate nursing education into the mainstream for the profession in Canada. In 1959, the first master's programme in the country was launched at the University of Western Ontario, followed quickly by the inauguration of three more within the next decade, at McGill, Montréal, and the University of British Columbia (UBC). With a handful of new programmes becoming available each decade, 18 universities were offering master's degrees in nursing by the end of the century (Association of Universities and Colleges in Canada [AUCC], 2001). The first doctoral programme in the country, at the University of Alberta, admitted students in 1991, and within the next decade, the country boasted six established doctoral programmes in nursing (AUCC, 2001). The history of the evolution of graduate programmes in this country explains something of the shape that graduate nursing education has taken in comparison to that of other jurisdictions and provides a foundation for understanding some of the issues that face nurses with graduate preparation in the current academic, scientific, and social context.

Evolution of Master's Degree Programmes

Although graduate degrees in other disciplines have been available to nurses for a much longer time, the history of master's programming in the country is one of only 40 years. As can be seen in Table 11.1, there has been a relatively stable proliferation of

Table 11.1   Proliferation of Graduate Nursing Programs in Canada

UNIVERSITY	MASTER'S PROGRAM	DOCTORAL PROGRAM
Dalhousie University	1975	
L'université de Laval	1991	
L'université de Moncton	1997	
L'université de Montréal	1965	1993
McGill University	1961	1993
McMaster University	1994	1994
Memorial University	1982	
Queens University	1994	
University of Alberta	1975	1991
University of British Columbia	1968	1991
University of Calgary	1981	1999
University of Manitoba	1979	
University of New Brunswick	1995	
University of Ottawa	1993	
University of Saskatchewan	1986	
University of Toronto	1970	1993
University of Western Ontario	1959	
University of Windsor	1994	

Note: Not tabulated in the list above are master's programs leading to a degree other than nursing, including:

- Athabasca University (Master of Health Sciences)
- University of Northern British Columbia (Master of Science in Community Health)
- University of Victoria (Master of Arts—Studies in Policy and Practice in Health and Social Services Program). University of Victoria's Master of Nursing Program has been approved and will start admitting students in September 2002.

Also not listed are universities in which doctoral nursing degrees are outside of the context of an approved program but occur by special case or special arrangement, including the University of Victoria.

new master's degree programmes in nursing every decade throughout the latter part of the century. However, graduate programmes designated as *nursing* degree programmes still compete with a range of other options open to nurses in Canada, and nursing programmes remain only one of several routes by which Canadian nurses obtain graduate education.

Before the local availability of master's nursing programmes in Canada, many nurses obtained their graduate preparation in other countries, particularly in the United States. Others undertook graduate work at Canadian universities in such fields as public health, education, medical science, social science, or business administration (Field et al., 1992). Although some of these degree programmes drew nurses away from the main focus of their discipline for much of their academic development, others were quite sensitive to the special needs of nurse leaders and produced graduates with specialisation in the study of problems directly relevant to their profession. In some instances, nursing faculty members with cross-appointments augmented the learning opportunities for nurses in those disciplines. In other instances, some nurses managed to retain their disciplinary focus within academic environments that were not entirely supportive.

For reasons of proximity and preference, many Canadian nurses continue to obtain graduate education outside of the discipline, and for the most part, the profession has enjoyed the healthy skill-set mix that can derive from an interdisciplinary perspective. In the early years, however, nurses tended to be less confident that their discipline would produce the highest-quality graduate level preparation for their advancement within such fields as nursing education and health administration (Beaton, 1990; Field et al., 1992); hence, consciousness raising about the relevance of graduate preparation within nursing has been an ongoing challenge.

A continuing complication has been the availability of graduate programmes designed specifically with nurses in mind but located somewhat outside of the disciplinary core, such as Master of Health Science programmes. In some universities, these programmes have evolved collaboratively with the involvement of other disciplines as an evolutionary step towards more comprehensive nursing master's degree offerings (McBride, 1995).

In recognition of the urgent need for augmented graduate educational opportunities for nurses to advance the general academic level of professional nursing in Canada (Mussalem, 1965), nursing leaders creatively pursued a variety of strategies and mechanisms in developing master's programmes. Among the strongest supporters of this initiative was the Kellogg Foundation. This foundation was a major presence in Canadian nursing education from 1949 through 1981 (Kerr, 1995). The foundation's fellowships to individual nurses helped Canadians obtain graduate degrees elsewhere, and its development grants helped many Canadian universities to support initial programmes in their early phases. Approvals to deliver graduate programmes were accomplished individually by each university's senate and in most instances were explicitly built on a foundational history of high-quality undergraduate programming (McBride, 1995).

Within the Canadian nursing master's programmes as they evolved over time, the initial focus was primarily on filling the articulated needs within nursing education or nursing administration (McBride, 1995). Since the mid-1970s, that focus has shifted from these functional areas towards clinical specialisation and leadership (Allen, 1986; McBride, 1995). Although nursing theory and science are still integral to the curriculum, the primary role of master's degree programmes in preparing nurse researchers has gradually shifted since the 1980s as more Canadian nurses have had access to doctoral programmes. Although rigorous research preparation was the standard within Canadian nursing master's programmes until the advent of doctoral programmes in 1991 (Kerr & McPhail, 1996), the master's thesis has become increasingly controversial since then. Some master's programmes in nursing continue to require a research-based thesis or include a thesis option; others no longer provide direct research training at this level (Gein, 1994; Kerr & McPhail, 1996; McBride, 1995).

Over its 40-year history, master's education in Canadian nursing has also experienced the effects of other trends and innovations. The rate of admission into graduate programmes has not yet attained a sufficient level to meet the profession's projected need to fill senior practise, education, and administrative positions (Kerr & McPhail, 1996). Because Canada's geography makes proximity to learning experiences a significant barrier for many nurses, and because the dominantly female constitution of the profession implies multiple demands upon learners, accessibility and flexibility of graduate education have been important aspects of the ongoing discussion (Broughton & Hoot, 1995; Kerr, 1988). Over the years, a number of innovations in distance learning have been noted (Kerr, 1988), and some components of many of the existing programmes are currently available by distance delivery or web-based format. Beyond the three master's programmes now delivered entirely by distance format (Canadian Nurses Association [CNA], 2001), alternative format master's programmes are likely to proliferate across the country as the technology becomes available to ensure high-quality interactive learning experiences. Two early innovations in the formatting of master's degree programmes were the clinical training master's programme available at the Family Nursing Unit in Calgary (Wright et al., 1985), and the generic master's programme at McGill (Ezer et al., 1991). Although the dominant language of master's instruction in the country has remained English (with 15 English language and 3 French language programmes currently available), the University of Ottawa was the first to offer a bilingual programme in 1993 (Kerr & McPhail, 1996).

Although master's programmes have rapidly proliferated and produced a generation of leaders for nursing practise, administration, education, and research, this evolution has not resolved the leadership shortage, let alone addressed the projected future demand at this point in our history (Kerr & McPhail, 1996). It is well recognised, in the early 21st century, that Canada has insufficient numbers of adequately prepared nurse educators (Beaton, 1990; Ford & Wertenberger, 1993) and that a significant percentage of the current cadre of nurse educators is within sight of retirement age (Nursing Education Council of British Columbia, 2001; May, 2000). In addition, consensus remains elusive as to what constitutes graduate education in nursing, how it ought to be funded and delivered, and whether academic or professional jurisdictions ought to take the lead in shaping the direction of future developments in master's preparation for Canadian nurses (Beaton, 1990).

Evolution of Doctoral Degree Programmes

The evolutionary process for doctoral nursing education in Canada has been much more recent and strategic than the development of master's degree programmes. In 1978, the CNA sponsored a national seminar in which nursing leaders endorsed the value of working towards making doctoral nursing education possible in the Canadian context (Zilm et al., 1979). From that, the Canadian Nurses Foundation (CNF) and the Canadian Association of University Schools of Nursing (CAUSN) developed a proposal dubbed Operation Bootstrap to obtain funding for the infrastructure upon which doctoral programmes in nursing might be established (Kerr & McPhail, 1996). Although that proposal was never funded, the cooperative efforts involved in its development stimulated nursing educational leaders across the country to engage in sufficient strategic dialogue to create the basis upon which explicit programme proposals became successful a decade later. Through this process, Canadian nursing leaders developed a consensus with regard to the general conditions under which doctoral programmes ought to be established, including the following:

- Universities with a successful track record in undergraduate and master's programming in nursing
- Close proximity to a full range of interdisciplinary doctoral/medical degree programmes
- Sufficient number of doctorally prepared faculty members
- Explicit research development resources (such as programmes of research or research units)
- Sufficient levels of research funding and a high degree of scholarly productivity shared among a range of faculty members (Field et al., 1992)

Although the first Canadian nurse to obtain a doctoral degree was Sister Denise Lefebre, SQM, PhD (Docteur de Pédagogie) from l'université de Montréal in 1955, the first to graduate with a doctoral degree in nursing on a special-case basis was Francine Ducharme from McGill in 1990 (Banning, 1990). Such special arrangement programmes, allowing nurses to obtain doctoral degrees with a substantial nursing component, developed in a number of universities before the launching of actual nursing doctoral programmes (Field et al., 1992; Kerr, 1995) and have continued in some universities to the present. They differ from interdisciplinary doctoral degrees or degrees taken in another discipline in their explicitly nursing focus but lack the programmatic core disciplinary component that the established nursing programmes offer (Kerr & McPhail, 1996).

In 1991, University of Alberta was the first in the country to launch a fully funded doctoral programme in nursing, and its first graduate was Joan Bottorff in 1992, having begun her studies as a special-case student. The political negotiating involved in obtaining funding for that programme and admitting the first group of students attracted considerable excitement across the country and was recognised as a landmark achievement (Brink, 1991; Field et al., 1992; Godkin & Bottorff, 1991; Rodger, 1991; Trojan et al., 1996). A second programme, at UBC, admitted its first students later that same year (1991), and in rapid succession, programmes were launched at the University of Toronto and by collaborative arrangement at McGill and Montréal in 1993, and at McMaster a year later (Kerr & McPhail, 1996).

Because of the commitment to dialogue and strategic planning throughout the developmental phase of advancing graduate education for the country, the character and shape of the Canadian doctoral nursing programmes evolved in a somewhat distinct manner from those in other parts of the globe. A forum on doctoral education in Canada, held in late 1990 in Edmonton, just before launching the country's first programmes, compared the history of doctoral nursing education in the United Kingdom, United States, and Europe and took advice from such international leaders as Rozella Schlotfeldt and Lisbeth Hocky. By unanimous agreement, the Canadian leaders who were present concluded that doctoral preparation in Canada should lead to a doctorate of philosophy in nursing, and not to a professional doctorate (Jeans, 1990).

A second invitational conference held in Toronto in April 1995 brought together student and faculty representatives from the five doctoral programmes in existence at that time, as well as from universities in which special-case opportunities were available for doctoral degrees in nursing, to examine the substantive context of Canadian Ph.D. nursing programmes as they were evolving and developing (Wood, 1997). It was noted that the Canadian programmes all had a rather similar structure, requiring an average of four or five courses in core disciplinary knowledge. Upon that foundation, both coursework and research training were individualised in conjunction with a carefully matched faculty supervisor for each student. Led by Ada Sue Hinshaw, who drew upon American examples to point out the quality and resource challenges that a rapid proliferation of doctoral programmes could create, participants at that meeting also grappled with such challenging questions as how many doctoral programmes Canada ought to support.

As doctoral programmes took hold within the profession's national consciousness, it became apparent that they provide nursing not only with high-quality research training but also, and perhaps more importantly, with the following:

- The capacity to study the clinical phenomena pertinent to the discipline
- The conceptual leadership to direct the development of scholarly practise

- The grounded analytic skills to design systems of nursing practise and health care delivery (Field et al., 1992)

In so doing, these programmes create a body of future leaders with expertise in both the art and science of nursing.

However, the development of doctoral nursing education in Canada is not without its ongoing challenges. Among the most pressing has been the difficulty in obtaining funding to support nurses pursuing doctoral education. In contrast to the more traditional academic model in which doctoral degrees are pursued before the establishment of family and professional responsibilities, most Canadian nursing doctoral students to date have been mid-career professional women, for whom full-time study is often problematic and expensive. Financial support exclusive to nursing has been scarce, with the CNF able to provide only small numbers of graduate fellowships (Kerr, 1995). Further, the kinds of substantive problems relative to nursing care delivery and its outcomes that nurses want to investigate have seldom been viewed competitively within the clinical (medical) and social science funding arenas (Field et al., 1992). The CNA has called on partners within government, health care agencies, universities, and nursing associations to plan cooperatively and share resources to support doctoral education for nurses (CNA, 1977).

With the advent of the Canadian Institutes of Health Research in 2000, many nursing leaders became actively involved in trying to shift the traditionally narrow direction of research support beyond basic and clinical (biomedical) science to include such concerns as the social determinants of health, the psychosocial experience of illness, and the impact of the caring sciences. On the basis of this effort, there is considerable optimism that the profession will continue to make progress in the funding of doctoral nursing education. Without doubt, the exceptional quality and productivity of Canada's early nursing doctoral programme graduates bodes well for the profession's continuing success in this regard.

PRACTICE REALITIES AND CHALLENGES FOR GRADUATE-PREPARED NURSES

In the early years of graduate nursing education in Canada, advanced preparation was generally understood to be a route away from the bedside and into teaching or administration. However, as the percentage of Canadian nurses prepared at the master's level has risen, it has become increasingly apparent that a significant proportion of nursing's professional leadership and scholarship ought to be in the clinical practise arena. Although all aspects of nursing scholarship play a significant role in advancing nursing knowledge and influence, the unique contribution of the discipline to the Canadian health care system inherently depends on the application of knowledge in the practise arena.

Thus, from the early 1980s onward, a number of master's programmes have explicitly shifted their emphasis to professional and clinical leadership as a primary objective. Moreover, they have expanded the opportunities for a range of clinical leadership learning options. Similarly, when doctoral programmes came on board in the 1990s, most nurses assumed that their primary goal would be to produce the next generation of academic nurse researchers. Although many graduates have gone on to faculty positions, the potential for developing clinical scholarship leaders at that level has also been recognised. Thus, the practise reality for nurses with graduate preparation in the discipline is a moving target, in keeping with the rapid changes in the population, the health care system, and knowledge proliferation within society.

Among the more subtle but challenging practise realities for nurses at a graduate level has been the general level of skepticism and distrust within the mainstream nursing population for the value that advanced education brings to the profession. In preparing this chapter, a wide range of students and recent graduates were interviewed for the purpose of clarifying the issues that might be included in the discussion. Many of them pointed out that, although attitudes are slowly shifting, it is not uncommon for nurses "coming back to do their master's work" to report the absence of endorsement or support from their colleagues. Even those who remain active in their clinical roles for the duration of their studies may find it an ongoing challenge to convince their colleagues that the university has anything relevant to provide to the practise setting.

Where expertise and professional leadership is clearly evident within the practise setting, it is often attributed to the special qualities of an individual nurse rather than to knowledge and skills that graduate education can bring to the effectiveness of nursing practise.*

Perhaps because nurses have had longstanding debates about entry-to-practise levels and scope of responsibility, some remain reluctant to recognise the value of diversifying to achieve collective aims. Pressures from union ideologies, an inherent democratising ideal, and a reluctance for self-promotion have made nurses more comfortable with the general notion that "a nurse is a nurse is a nurse" than with the ramifications of leveling and specialising nursing contributions. By packing extreme amounts of content and experience into tightly crafted curricula, and by sending new graduates out into a health care system that is exceedingly complex and strained, nurses sometimes feel that their educational programmes have set them up for failure (Griffiths, 2000). This pressure may be felt particularly strongly by diploma-level graduates in the context of the current climate of health reform and instability.

Sadly, however, nurses have not always provided one another with a mechanism for understanding how their practise reality is shaped by the prominent forces of the day. Many simply fail to appreciate that the profession is advantaged, not disadvantaged, by an increasingly educated majority. Thus, nurses as a group have not always been supportive of the continuing educational advancement of their peers, and may interpret "going back to school" as abandonment, rather than as adding ammunition for the collective battles. Certainly, an emphasis on increasing social awareness and political analysis among the mainstream of practicing nurses will continue to be an important element in the general experience of graduate education and the practise reality of nurses prepared with graduate degrees.

A somewhat similar climate of misunderstanding can occur for doctorally prepared nurses with primary appointments in a clinical practise setting. Although the profession has had a generally high level of collective comfort with the traditional model of the academic researcher-educator, it seems much less comfortable with how to apply the skills of doctorally prepared nurses into the clinical context. Nurses in clinical leadership and scholar positions may find, for example, that the research component of their

---

*As a teacher of a core master's level class that students often take early in their programmes, I have been fascinated over the years to note how prominent these rather negative attitudes are within the profession and how resistant they are to change. I do know that graduate students are increasingly recognising the "ambassador" role that they can play in helping their colleagues appreciate the value of the new learning they obtain from their graduate degree programmes, and to recognise that the confidence, critical thinking skills, and "big-picture" thinking that they begin to apply to their practise is not simply coincident with their going back to school. —Author

role is less valued than is the administrative aspect. As a result, although nursing has made great strides in cultivating a generation of accomplished researchers, this may have been at the expense of other critically important leadership roles. For example, many of the recent dean and director searches for Canadian nursing schools have been long and protracted, and it is generally understood that the available applicant pool has been diminished by other opportunities in research and scholarship as well as by an extended period of time in which nursing administrative scholarship was relatively unsupported. Thus, in contrast to the situation that faces the master's prepared nurse attempting to reenter the practise domain, doctorally prepared nurses graduate into a professional culture characterised by an inordinate valuing of specialised research training and acquiring protected time away from distractions to attain the highest level of research funding possible. In its own way, this attitudinal climate is as problematic and counterproductive as that of the academically resistant mainstream.

ISSUES AND CONTROVERSIES IN GRADUATE EDUCATION

In contrast to the career paths typical of many professions, nurses still perceive the option to take their graduate education in nursing or consider advanced study in other disciplines. Although the proliferation of programmes at the graduate level across the country and the increased availability of distance offerings have made higher degrees in nursing a viable option for all Canadian nurses, many decide to look elsewhere for their academic advancement. Certainly, the history of the nursing profession in Canada has been well served by many noted leaders who returned to the fold after completing their master's or doctoral degrees in such fields as education, psychology, business administration, public health, anthropology, medical sciences, or sociology. From those disciplines, we have derived benefits in theoretical diversity, methodology, and analytic processes. We also recognise that the world in which nursing is practised is inherently interdisciplinary and therefore that nurses have a natural affinity for the models, methods, and substantive knowledge of a range of disciplines.

At the same time, despite individual exceptions, leaders who lack an in-depth understanding of the complex theoretical, historical, and philosophical grounding of the nursing discipline can be considerably disadvantaged when they attempt to articulate a nursing perspective. Even more problematic may be that they do not even know they lack this understanding. Because nursing is and remains difficult to describe, delineate, and encapsulate in language, because of its ineffable nature and complexity, Canada needs a cadre of leaders who are adept at conceptualising the discipline and its contributions in a changing context. Because of this, although graduate preparation in nursing will remain a high priority for the discipline's development in this country, there are many opinions on how best to achieve it.

Theoretical Debates

An explicit concern for issues of a theoretical nature evolved in the second half of the 20th century in response to the explosion of new knowledge in the physical and social sciences and the availability of new theoretical challenges arising from the core projects of a variety of academic disciplines. Nursing theory emerged as a mechanism for organising and making sense of "this infinitely dynamic and complex body of information" so that nurses could use knowledge in a "professional, accountable, and defensible manner" (Beckstrand, 1978).

As the influence of physicians and the medical model on health care delivery systems expanded, new species of health care professionals and technicians proliferated, and nursing curricula evolved away from the more traditional medical science and apprenticeship structure, nurses began to recognise an urgent need to articulate the uniqueness and distinctiveness of their profession among others in the health care system (Chinn & Kramer, 1999; Engebretson, 1997). To do this, they began to create conceptual maps that would depict the manner in which nursing informational and decisional processes might relate to a theoretically infinite range of clinical situations (Ellis, 1968; Johnson, 1974; McKay, 1969; Wald & Leonard, 1964). In calling such conceptual frameworks "nursing theory," they located nursing thought within the rather rigid academic and scientific community of the era and thereby created a context within which nursing science could be legitimised and acknowledged (Cull-Wilby & Peppin, 1987; Jones, 1997).

The conceptual model-building era that lasted from the mid-1960s through the mid-1980s was remarkable in its optimism and enthusiasm for extending the boundaries of existing scientific and philosophical thinking. In a context in which theory development in science was understood to follow linear causation and reductionistic models, the nursing theorists were essentially attempting to capture complexity and infinite variation within a rigorous and systematic scientific matrix.

Lacking some of the philosophical and scientific innovations with which we can now reflect upon the project, some aspects of their efforts may seem naïve in retrospect. However, it can also be said that their efforts to develop a science accounting for both the generalities of substantive knowledge and theory as well as the particularities of an infinite range of new applications was impressive in its capacity to recognise the complexities inherent in excellent clinical nursing reasoning and to respect the diversities of expanding knowledge that nursing operates within (Barnum, 1994; Benner et al., 1996; Meleis, 1987; Raudonis & Acton, 1997; Thorne & Perry, 2001).

However, the model-building enterprise was not well understood within the dominant mainstream of nursing and, for the most part, remained a distinct enterprise from the research scholarship that developed through the latter decades of the century. As the theorists themselves became embroiled in debates about whose conceptual structure ought to dominate the discipline, much of academic nursing tired of the discourse and began to consider the theoretical debates a minor embarrassment in nursing's history. (Engebretson, 1997). Indeed, where comparative analysis of the theoretical models had been a prominent aspect of graduate education in nursing, many programmes eliminated the issue from their curricula in favour of a shift towards what Meleis (1987) termed the "substance" of nursing theory.

This distaste for the conceptual model debates left a theoretical vacuum into which a somewhat different version of theoretical contention emerged. Throughout the 1990s, one group of the theorists came to understand their ideas as entirely incommensurate with the dominant mainstream of nursing theorising and began to position their definitions of the role of the nurse as inherently distinct from those derived from dominant thinking. Using language such as "simultaneity" and "totality" to depict what they understood to be two mutually exclusive camps within nursing theory, these scholars attempted to effect a "paradigm shift" within nursing thought away from what they understood as reductionism, causality, and objectivity and towards holism, rhythmnicity, and subjectivity (e.g., Parse, 1987).

Because it is arguable that mainstream nursing theorising was evolving towards embracing aspects of those directions anyway, the "revolution" in nursing thinking became something of a turf war in which ideologic claims about the inherent intention-ality of theoretical positions took the form of abject generalisations about the beliefs and motives of those who did and did not sit on the same side of the paradigm fence (Thorne et al., 1999). Further, instead of welcoming debate, some proponents of simultaneity theory have elected to interpret challenges to the inherent value of simultaneity theories within the discipline as nothing more substantive than a "vicious diatribe" (Cody, 2000) and have even suggested that criticism from outside of that paradigm cannot be taken seriously because it is inherently misguided (Parse, 1998). Perhaps one advantage of this unfortunate turn of theorising is that it brought the relevance of theoretical thinking back into the forefront of academic nursing and stimulated many nurse scholars to pay attention to the debates. Because of this, critical analysis of the implications of theoretical positioning has come back into favor in graduate nursing education as a relevant and entirely necessary body of scholarship. Further, the explosion of misunderstanding and accusation among the discipline's theorists has forced academic nursing to recognise the imperative of understanding more fully its philosophical underpinnings.

Philosophical Challenges

Among the most overt and easily recognised philosophical challenges facing nursing scholarship from the 1980s to the present has been the qualitative–quantitative methodologic debate. Although research methodology has technical aspects, much of this debate underscores a number of much deeper and more complex philosophical schisms within the scientific and academic communities of which nursing is a member. Overt attention to the philosophy of science was at one time rare in nursing curricula at any level, but it is now well recognised as a hallmark of a credible graduate programme in the discipline and has crept downward into undergraduate curricula as well. Thus, an appreciation for the philosophical positioning of the ideas of the discipline has emerged as a critically important element in professional leadership.

As a result of the popularisation of Kuhn's (1962) treatise on scientific revolution, academic discourse is no longer characterised by indisputable facts and truths, but rather by claims and positions. In a climate in which postmodern thinking permeates society, knowledge previously considered immutable by virtue of its scientific grounding has become fodder for deconstruction and revisioning (Haack, 1998; Hacking, 1999). The evolution of scientific knowledge is no longer understood as linear and rational, but rather as an entirely human enterprise, subject to ideational and political pressures over time (Van Doren, 1991). What we knew to be true yesterday is entirely disputable today and may be considered reactionary tomorrow. For a discipline such as nursing, the dramatic shift from a realistic ontologic orientation, in which factual truths exist, towards consideration of knowledge as social construction, in which there may be different ways of understanding truth, has had tremendous appeal. For example, nurses know that every practise principle must have its legitimate variations and that every theoretical claim one might make about human health and illness experience will break down in the face of individual human uniqueness. To some degree, one might argue that theoretical relativism has always been philosophically consistent with the kind of flexibility and adaptability that is the hallmark of excellent nursing practise. Because of this, nursing scholarship has enthusiastically embraced qualitative methods, subjective knowledge, and critical-emancipatory inquiry as consistent with its general moral underpinnings.

In a climate in which theoretical truths are no longer as comfortable as they once were, however, many nurse scholars now find themselves struggling to find purchase on an increasingly slippery platform of disciplinary knowledge. For the profession to have a social mandate, certain basic philosophic truths or positions seem prerequisite. For example, although it might be interesting to philosophise about whether human pain and suffering exist apart from our ability to apprehend them subjectively, nursing is solidly morally bound to an assumption that they do and that nurses have an obligation to ameliorate them when possible, despite the individual variations they might manifest and the possibilities that they might simply be profound subjective constructions within the minds of those afflicted. Thus, in reaction to the notion that qualitative methods were more true to human subjective experience and therefore more relevant to the knowledge required for nursing practise, many scholars now recognise the inherent limits of any methodologic approach for generating knowledge suitable to a practise science. To develop useful knowledge in relation to a substantive field, for example, nursing might require population-based surveys, linear regression modelling, phenomenologic interpretation, and emancipatory action research. Thus, the members of the academy are scrambling to expand beyond their traditional methodologic expertise and develop the more rounded philosophical and methodologic buttressing that scholars of the future will require. For doctoral programmes in nursing, this means that skill within a range of inquiry methods, including qualitative research, quantitative research, and philosophical analysis, will be foundational to producing a new generation of excellent scholars.

Although traditional doctoral training has relied heavily on mentorship models, the scholarship of the future will inevitably require a shift in student and supervisor relationships. The postmodern challenge within academia has raised awareness that traditional science recreates itself, such that genuine innovation must inevitably resist and react against the dictates of older models and authorities. Of course, in the extreme version, the notion of expertise is rejected entirely (Thorne, 1999). However, although that extreme version clearly exists within the academic community in Canada (Good, 2001), nursing's professional practise mandates seem to have kept it somewhat more grounded in a perspective in which the ideas one holds have meaningful implications for the society we live in and the individuals who constitute it. However, it also seems quite common for Canadian nursing graduate students, especially those at the doctoral level, to view the scholarship forms of their mentors with a critical lens, to envision combinations of methodologic and philosophical approaches that extend beyond the specific expertise of their supervisors, and to chafe under academic regulations that create barriers to building their own programmes of scholarship in a less rigid and bounded science than did their predecessors.

Practical Challenges

Although many of these debates underscore the challenge of understanding the theoretical and philosophical nature of the discipline, there are also a number of somewhat technical and practical issues that relate centrally to the question of core disciplinary knowledge. Historically and currently, Canada has almost no dedicated source of funding for the development of nursing knowledge (the relatively minor amounts available from the CNF notwithstanding). The issue of a separate nursing fund was hotly debated during the developmental phase of transforming Canada's research infrastructure from the Medical Research Council and the National Health Research Development Program into the Canadian Institutes for Health Research. Although many nurses felt confident in their ability to compete for dollars with other disciplines in the context of the mandates of specific institutes, others recognised that an opportunity might be lost to sustain inquiry pertaining to the core of nursing. In other words, although new knowledge considered part of the national health agenda might be supported, that which would be considered specific to the discipline would be much more difficult to accomplish.

In many instances, this insight may have been elusive for those whose graduate preparation was outside the discipline, for whom the problems of core nursing knowledge seemed tangential to the larger enterprise. Given the contentious nature of the nursing theoretical debates, their reluctance to engage in these issues seems understandable. However, this tension between allegiance to "substantive" knowledge (such as children's health or family health) and "disciplinary" knowledge (such as the nature of nursing or the dynamics of clinical nursing reasoning) has played itself out in graduate nursing curriculum and programme development as well, with some nursing scholars advocating immersion in the substance and others pressing for the disciplinary competence within which to ground it. Ongoing debates with regard to the relative importance of such topics as the philosophy of nursing science in comparison to the interdisciplinary knowledge associated with distinct fields of nursing specialisation are likely to continue and to complicate curricular planning for the foreseeable future.

A related practical challenge derives from the applied and practical nature of the science of nursing. Although graduate education has not always been understood as an inherent adjunct to the practise of nursing, increasing numbers of master's and doctoral students seek advanced degrees for the explicit purpose of enhancing and strengthening their practise effectiveness. Although it has been natural for the discipline to consider the conduct and dissemination of research as a scholarly enterprise, the notion of practise scholarship has been much more difficult to articulate. Although many Canadian universities continue to support and encourage advancement of practise knowledge using a variety of strategies, the continuous pressure to evaluate the quality of academic units on the basis of the research dollars they attract and the publications they produce is unavoidable. Thus, particularly at the doctoral level, there has generally been less overt support for scholarship in the practise tradition than for more conventional health research scholarship, and students seeking to create practise scholar careers may find themselves seduced by the apparent credibility afforded the more usual career track strategies.

As graduate education continues to proliferate in this country, nursing will confront many permutations of the theoretical, philosophical, and practical challenges that have been mentioned. As graduate education becomes the norm rather than the exception, increasing pressure toward flexibility and access will inevitably occur, and smaller academic nursing units will start to feel left behind if they are not offering graduate degree programmes.

It will be interesting to observe whether the discipline will tackle such thorny issues as imposing limits on universities with insufficient resources to provide a full range of educational experiences to learners at the graduate level, or whether it will allow competitive market pressures to force the conditions in which programmes of questionable quality can proliferate.

CHALLENGES FOR GRADUATE-PREPARED NURSES

Nurses prepared at the graduate level are the current and future leaders of the profession in Canada. In that capacity, they are vulnerable to the effects of the current health care climate. Various health reforms since the 1990s in this country have reflected attempts to control health spending by shifting resources from the acute care to the community sector, mechanisms to rationalise resource allocation decision making, and efforts to bring health care system decision making closer to home within national regions (CNA, 2000). The strongly held principles articulated in the Canada Health Act, and traditionally embraced by nurses, have been challenged as never before in the context of this conflictual health reform climate (May & Ferguson-Pare, 1997). Nursing shortages and the "graying" of the profession (Bradley, 1999) occur in a climate in which nursing leadership is increasingly scarce (King, 2000).

The weight of navigating the discipline's journey through the health reform process over the next several decades will undoubtedly sit squarely upon the shoulders of practise leaders, many of them prepared at the master's level. Clearly, their capacity to make nimble adjustments in health human resource planning, economic accountability, health policy processes, and professional practise leadership will determine the shape of professional nursing for the next generation. Because these fields of inquiry have not been dominant within nursing's disciplinary scholarship over the most recent decades, there is a recognised shortage in scholarship related to nursing work, nursing service, and the delivery of nursing care. Because formal research scholarship has eclipsed academic and administrative leadership as a priority since the 1980s, it will take some time before graduate nursing programmes can take a sufficient shift in course to cultivate a new generation of professional leaders. In the meanwhile, collaborative partnerships will be essential between practise settings and universities to resolve the challenges inherent in the shortage of nursing personnel at all levels and in the conditions of nursing work. Thus, we can expect issues of the workplace to take an increasingly prominent position among the scholarship arenas of graduate education, such that issues traditionally considered the domain of the functional specialisation of nursing administration will become mainstream and foundational expectations of nursing in any leadership role.

Although the numbers of nurses entering graduate programmes continues to increase at all levels, the pressures on nurses to extend their academic commitment have also exponentially increased. First-rate graduates of master's programmes are quickly seduced into doctoral programmes, doctoral graduates are encouraged to shift immediately into postdoctoral training, and postdocs are expected to seek career award funding to protect their research investment. Although each of these progressions is laudable and necessary, it is also important for the profession to remain vigilant to the continuing need for nursing scholarship and leadership throughout the system. University (and college) programmes will increasingly be hungry for new faculty members to teach the next generation of nursing students, and clinical agencies will be desperate for nurses capable of combining practise knowledge with policy work, administrative strength, evidence-based practise development, and corporate leadership. As the current generation of faculty and administrators retires from the active roster, the demand for the next generation to fill the gaps will clearly exceed the current capacity of the profession to train and groom appropriate numbers. Thus, we can anticipate that the global effects of Canada's nursing shortage have only just begun.

In the current climate, the health care community will more urgently demand that the university play a strong role in resolving the critical human and material resource challenges that Canada will face in its development and delivery of health services to an increasingly diverse and complex population. Pressure to meet the emergent needs of the system will take the form of new professional practise roles, increasingly specialised training expectations, and greater numbers of excellently prepared graduates. Without dialogue and debate to create a national consensus on our shared beliefs, role definitions, and disciplinary core values, nursing may well experience discord and organisational disarray. And with the urgent demands on the system insinuating themselves on our education and practise contexts as well as on our research, it may be difficult in the next few decades to take the time we require to reflect on our past and direct our future.

STRATEGIES FOR ADVANCING GRADUATE EDUCATION

Canadian nurses have been strong advocates for the principles embedded in the Canada Health Act, and they have also been consistently proud of a national tradition of high-quality professional education and service delivery. As the pressures to increase the numbers of graduates inevitably lead to more programmes and more diverse programme delivery modes, it will be important for Canadian nursing to attend to the quality dimensions of the educational opportunities upon which its leaders build their professional careers.

At present, nursing has no quality monitoring mechanism at the graduate level. Programmes preparatory to professional licensure are all regulated by provincial statute and professional organisations, and there is a voluntary accreditation system by which the quality of baccalaureate nursing programmes is well supported. Although the CAUSN has created position statements on master's and doctoral education (Box 11.1), graduate programme approval is entirely within the authority of the individual university senate. The approval is typically based on the market demands of the specific institution as well as the degree to which it considers conventional academic quality criteria in its programme decisions.

Currently, at least four additional universities are in the process of preparing proposals to deliver doctoral programmes in nursing. Because doctoral students bring in fellowship dollars, increase the rate of faculty publication, and expand the research capacity of the organisational unit, many administrations may not be all that concerned that there is insufficient support within the department for core disciplinary knowledge, research training, or scholarly mentorship. Thus, as was predicted by Ada Sue Hinshaw at the doctoral forum in Toronto, we may find that doctoral degrees become possible under conditions in which the profession is not entirely well served.

Similarly, there is continuing pressure to expand the flexibility and accessibility of master's programmes. A review of the CNA's current programme listings suggests that most Canadian nursing master's programmes have some courses currently available by distance delivery mode or are working toward complete programme delivery online or using modern information technology. Although there is no doubt that these fulfill an identified need, the implications of responding to the pressure *en masse* ought to be an important agenda for national discussion and deliberation. Some of the less objective attributes of a high-quality master's programme, such as developing the skills of collegial networking, challenging one's own concepts and core values, and being mentored by knowledge brokers and generators within the discipline, all become experiences of a different nature when conducted in intellectual isolation. Thus, it seems more important than ever for Canadian nurses to remain vigilant to the question of quality monitoring of graduate education and to take ownership of the standards by which excellence (and mediocrity) can be judged.

Because the financial imperatives of universities will undoubtedly continue to create the conditions under which scholarship is evaluated in the external academic community, nursing academics and their leaders will have to find strategies by which a

BOX 11.1

CAUSN Position Statements (1998) on Graduate Education in Canada

ON MASTER'S EDUCATION

At the master's level, students analyse and critique research and theory in order to establish their utility for guiding nursing practice. Knowledge from their own investigations and those of others contributes to the development of the students' understanding of the relationships between research, theory, and practice. The focus of master's study is on the preparation of nurses with advanced skills in the practise of nursing. These skills are developed through testing of selected clinical interventions and the implementation of findings from the students' own investigations and those of other researchers. Students analyse and critique the theoretical positions of other nurses in order to establish relevance for practice and research.

More specifically, the master's curriculum should include a definitive practise component designed to enable students to view practice, research, and theory as a triad, each part of which strengthens the other. The program should also include a definitive research component. This is not only essential in relation to practise but also provides a base for those who wish to proceed to doctoral study. Provision should also be made for examination of current issues in health care and the ethical values that influence decision making. Individual programs may include both required and elective courses designed to prepare graduates to assume leadership positions in advanced practice, teaching or administration.

ON DOCTORAL EDUCATION

At the doctoral level, the emphasis is on the process of building theory and advancing nursing knowledge. Doctoral programs focus on advanced research training, for which a foundation has been laid at the master's level. The practise and research aspects of nursing are furthered within the intensive investigation of a particular nursing question. The knowledge gained through this process contributes to further theoretical development of nursing. The nature of doctoral preparation in nursing is based on the following assumptions:

- Nursing practise at present has a growing theoretical base which requires organization and systematization.
- Many nursing interventions are founded on rationales that have not been validated or critically examined.
- The theoretical base and scientific rationale for nursing practice can be further developed through nursing practice research.

(continued)

balance between lucrative and meaningful inquiry can be supported. At present in Canada, there is an influx of opportunity for funding research projects, programmes, and training centres within the national agenda of health system and health service demands. To the extent that nurses can align their scholarship with those national agendas as they unfold, they will be increasingly successful in attracting additional resources to their academic units. Unfettered adherence to these agendas, however, would have predictable and unacceptable effects on the culture and nature of nursing

BOX 11.1

CAUSN Position Statements (1998) on Graduate Education in Canada (Continued)

- Nursing needs to educate scholars with the analytical and research skills necessary for developing theories and methodologies appropriate to the study of questions unique to nursing and health promotion, health care delivery, and health care policy.

- As knowledge is gained through the research process and incorporated into practice, the effectiveness of health promotion and quality of nursing care will improve.

- Doctoral graduates are required for faculty positions in nursing education programs.

It is obvious from the preceding that the main emphasis at the doctoral level is the development of research and scholarly ability. The program should centre on the student's research questions, the vehicle for developing an understanding of research methodologies and techniques, and may include cognate courses closely related to the research problem. In addition, the program should include studies in the philosophical and ethical foundations of science and nursing theory as it is presently conceived.

The assumptions set forth above support the need for increasing numbers of nurses holding the doctoral degree in nursing.

Canadian Association of Schools of Nursing. Retrieved from www.causn.org/new/education/edpositionstatements.htm

academic departments. Within any department offering graduate degree programmes, it will remain important to have faculty who teach as well as do research, who engage in practise scholarship as well as traditional research, and who examine the philosophical and theoretical problems of the discipline as well as respond to the immediate expressed needs of the society around them.

Indeed, one of the most complex challenges for academic nursing will be to enact strategies and processes that reward a range of professional leadership and scholarship (Boyer, 1990; Glassick et al., 1997) and to create the kinds of learning environments that are grounded strongly within the discipline as well as active and credible in the larger arena. In support of this endeavour, it would be interesting to explore whether it might be timely to articulate and endorse national standards for graduate education in nursing.

Nurses in Canada have made great strides towards developing professional scholarship and academic credibility during an era in which the pressing problems of society have demanded unprecedented attention. They have attempted to stay true to a vision of professional integrity as they flow with the changing tides of acceptable inquiry methods and theoretical locations. In an increasingly interdisciplinary world in which truth is never static and credibility is always open for discussion, nurses have collectively assumed a rightful place in the academy, in the health care delivery and policy arenas, and in society. And, as Florence Nightingale might have reminded us, the worth of a society can be measured by the quality of its nursing.

SUMMARY

Graduate education has advanced rapidly from 1959—when the first master's degree was offered by the University of Western Ontario—to the turn of the century when 18 universities offered master's degrees and the first doctoral programme was offered at the University of Alberta. Current graduate nursing education in Canada appears to follow two tracks: advanced practise for those with master's degrees and research for those prepared at the doctoral and postdoctoral levels.

As the percentage of Canadian nurses with master's degrees rises, many programmes now focus on developing professional leadership and scholarship not only in academia but also in clinical practise. This phenomenon occurs in part because nursing's contribution to the Canadian health care system inherently depends on the application of knowledge in the practise arena.

A particular challenge for nurses pursuing master's level education is a reported lack of support from their colleagues in practise. Many do not recognize that greater education gives the profession an advantage—that "going back to school" is a way to prepare the profession for the future. Additional challenges for the profession include an insufficient number of adequately prepared nurse educators (with a significant percentage of educators nearing retirement age), controversy over what constitutes graduate education in nursing, how it ought to be funded and delivered, who should shape future development (academia or professional jurisdictions), and how to ensure quality programmes.

Canada needs a cadre of nursing leaders who are adept at conceptualising the discipline and its contributions in an ever-changing context of diverse theories and structures. Scholarship of the future will require increased and dedicated sources of funding and exploration and consensus with regard to issues, such as the philosophy of nursing science compared with the interdisciplinary knowledge associated with nursing specialisation; conduct and dissemination of research as a practise as well as scholarly enterprise; development of future nurse leaders; vulnerability of the profession to the health care/reform climate; and ownership of the standards by which excellence (and mediocrity) can be judged. New leaders and new programmes will also need to explore and implement collaborative partnerships between practise settings and universities with regard to personnel shortages, conditions of nurses' work, and challenges to increase administrative strength, implement evidence-based practise, and participate in corporate leadership.

Online RESOURCES

Add to your knowledge of this issue:

Association of Universities and Colleges of Canada	http://www.aucc.ca/en/index.html
Canadian Association of Nursing Research	http://www.canr.ca/
Canadian Association of Schools of Nursing	http://www.casn.org/new/index.htm
Canadian Health Services Research Foundation	http://www.chsrf.ca/
Canadian Institute for Health Information	http://www.cihi.ca
Canadian Nurses Association	http://www.cna-nurses.ca/default.htm

Reflections on the Chapter

1. What priorities and trends have most influenced the changes in Canadian master's and doctoral nursing degree curricula since the 1960s?

2. Attitudes towards graduate education within the mainstream practising nurse population may not have consistently supported nurses in their efforts to obtain master's or doctoral nursing education. Why do such attitudes exist? What social, political, and economic forces within nursing might contribute to their continuation?

3. It can be argued that many nurses with graduate degrees in the discipline are ambivalent about the value of studying "nursing theory," or the theoretical debates within the discipline. What characteristics of the theories or the understanding of them may have created this climate of misunderstanding?

4. As academic nursing evolves over the next 2 decades, how can it appropriately attend to a balance between core disciplinary knowledge and the substantive knowledge that will drive advances in clinical practise?

5. Should Canadian nursing leaders engage in formal dialogue about the future direction of graduate education in this country? If so, who ought to lead that discussion, and what should be its primary objective?

REFERENCES

Allen, M. (1986). The relationship between graduate teaching and research in nursing. In S. M. Stinson & J. C. Kerr (Eds.), *International issues in nursing research* (pp. 151–167). London: Croom Helm.

Association of Universities and Colleges of Canada (2001). Programs of Study Database [On-line]. Available: http://www3.aucc.ca:6666/dcu/docs/rootfolder/index.html (May 30, 2001).

Banning, J. A. (1990). Editorial: Nursing PhD comes to Canada. *The Canadian Nurse, 86*(11), 3.

Barnum, B. J. S. (1994). *Nursing theory: Analysis, application, evaluation* (4th ed). Philadelphia: JB Lippincott.

Beaton, J. (1990). Crises in graduate nursing education. *The Canadian Nurse, 86*(1), 29–32.

Beckstrand, J. (1978). The notion of a practice theory and the relationship of scientific and ethical knowledge to practice. *Research in Nursing & Health, 1,* 131–136.

Benner, P., Tanner, C. A., & Chesla, C. A. (1996). *Expertise in nursing practice: Caring, clinical judgement, and ethics.* New York: Springer.

Boyer, E. (1990). *Scholarship reconsidered: Priorities of the professoriate.* Princeton, NJ: The Carnegie Foundation for the Advancement of Teaching.

Bradley, C. (1999). Doing more with less in nursing work: A review of the literature. *Contemporary Nurse, 8*(3), 57–64.

Brink, P. J. (1991). Editorial: The first Canadian Ph.D. in nursing. *Western Journal of Nursing Research, 13*(4), 432–433.

Broughton, K., & Hoot, T. (1995). Commentary: Canada needs accessible masters' programs. *The Canadian Nurse, 91*(10), 55.

Canadian Association of Schools of Nursing (CASN) (1998). CASN position statements on education [On-line]. Available: http://www.causn.org/English/frame.htm (September 9, 2002).

Canadian Nurses Association (1977). Policy statement on doctoral and post-doctoral preparation in nursing [On-line]. Available: http://www.cna-nurses.ca/pages/education/educationframe.htm (May 20, 2001).

Canadian Nurses Association (2000). *Framework for Canada's health system.* Ottawa: Canadian Nurses Association.

Canadian Nurses Association (2001). Edufacts: Graduate distance education [On-line]. Available: http://www.cna-nurses.ca/pages/education/educationframe.htm (May 20, 2001).

Chinn, P. L., & Kramer, M. K. (1999). *Theory and nursing: Integrated knowledge development* (5th ed.). St. Louis: Mosby.

Cody, W. K. (2000). Paradigm shift or paradigm drift? A meditation on commitment and transcendence. *Nursing Science Quarterly, 13*(2), 93–102.

Cull-Wilby, B. L., & Peppin, J. C. (1987). Toward a coexistence of paradigms in nursing knowledge development. *Journal of Advanced Nursing, 12,* 515–521.

Ellis, R. (1968). Characteristics of significant theories. *Nursing Research, 17*(3), 217–222.

Engebretson, J. (1997). A multiparadigm approach to nursing. *Advances in Nursing Science, 20*(1), 21–33.

Ezer, H., MacDonald, J., & Gros, C. P. (1991). Follow-up of generic master's graduates: Viability of a model of nursing in practice. *Canadian Journal of Nursing Research, 23*(3), 9–20.

Field, P. A., Stinson, S. M., & Thibaudeau, M. F. (1992).

Graduate education in nursing in Canada. In A. J. Baumgart & J. Larsen, (Eds.), *Canadian nursing faces the future* (2nd ed.) (pp. 421–445). St. Louis: Mosby.

Ford, J. S., & Wertenberger, D. H. (1993). Nursing education content in master's in nursing programs. *Canadian Journal of Nursing Research, 25*(2), 53–61.

Gein, L. (1994). Defending the master's thesis in nursing graduate programs: The Canadian context. *Journal of Nursing Education, 33*(7), 330–332.

Glassick, C., Huber, M., & Maeroff, G. (1997). *Scholarship assessed: Evaluation on the professoriate.* San Francisco: Jossey-Bass.

Godkin, M. D., & Bottorff, J. L. (1991). Doctorate in nursing: Idea to reality. *The Canadian Nurse, 87*(11), 31–34.

Good, G. (2001). *Humanism betrayed: Theory, ideology, and culture in the contemporary university.* Montreal & Kingston: McGill & Queens University Press.

Griffiths, H. (2000). Nursing education at the crossroads. *Nursing BC, 32*(2), 21–23.

Haack, S. (1998). *Manifesto of a passionate moderate.* Chicago: University of Chicago Press.

Hacking, I. (1999). *The social construction of what?* Cambridge, MA: Harvard University Press.

Iwasiw, C. (1993). *Nursing faculty and doctorates: Doctoral preparation of nursing faculty in Canadian universities.* Unpublished doctoral dissertation, University of Toronto.

Jeans, M. E. (1990). Advancing doctoral preparation for nurses. *Canadian Journal of Nursing Research, 22*(2), 1–2.

Johnson, D. E. (1974). Development of theory: A requisite for nursing as a primary health profession. *Nursing Research, 23*(5), 372–377.

Jones, M. (1997). Thinking nursing. In S. E. Thorne & V. E. Hayes (Eds.), *Nursing praxis: Knowledge and action* (pp. 125–139). Thousand Oaks, CA: Sage.

Kerr, J. R. (1988). Nursing education at a distance: Using technology to advantage in undergraduate and graduate degree programs in Alberta, Canada. *International Journal of Nursing Studies, 25,* 301–306.

Kerr, J. R. (1995). The growth of graduate education in nursing in Canada. In J. R. Kerr & J. McPhail (Eds.), *Canadian nursing: Issues and perspectives* (3rd ed.) (pp. 407–424). St. Louis: Mosby.

Kerr, J. R., & McPhail, J. (1996). *Concepts in Canadian nursing.* St. Louis: Mosby.

King, T. (2000). Paradigms of Canadian nurse managers: Lenses for viewing leadership and management. *Canadian Journal of Nursing Leadership, 13*(1), 15–20.

Kuhn, T. S. (1962). *The structure of scientific revolutions.* Chicago: University of Chicago Press.

May, K. A. (2000). *Ensuring the future of Canadian nursing: A framework for a national nursing education strategy.* Ottawa: Canadian Association for University Schools of Nursing.

May, K. A., & Ferguson-Pare, M. (1997). Preparing nurse leaders for the future: Views from Canada. *Seminars for Nurse Managers, 5*(2), 97–105.

McBride, W. (1995). *State of the art and trends in graduate nursing programs in Canada.* Converging Educational Perspectives: An Anthology from the Pan American Conference on Graduate Nursing Education, Bogatá, Columbia, Oct 10–12, 1995 (pp. 255–257). NLN Pub. #19-6894.

McKay, R. (1969). Theories, models, and systems for nursing. *Nursing Research, 18*(5), 393–399.

Meleis, A. I. (1987). ReVisions in knowledge development: A passion for substance. *Scholarly Inquiry for Nursing Practice, 1*(1), 5–19.

Mussalem, H. K. (1965). *Nursing education in Canada.* Ottawa: Queens University Printer.

Nursing Education Council of British Columbia (2001). *Who will prepare the next generation of nurses?* Vancouver: Author.

Parse, R. R. (1987). *Nursing science: Major paradigms, theories, and critiques.* Philadelphia: W.B. Saunders.

Parse, R. R. (1998). The art of criticism. *Nursing Science Quarterly, 11*(2), 43.

Raudonis, B. M., & Acton, G. J. (1997). Theory-based nursing practice. *Journal of Advanced Nursing, 26*(2/1), 138–145.

Rodger, G. L. (1991). Canadian nurses succeed again! The launch of Canada's first doctoral degree in nursing. *Journal of Advanced Nursing, 16,* 1395–1396.

Thorne, S. (1999). Are egalitarian relationships a desirable ideal for nursing? *Western Journal of Nursing Research, 21*(1), 16–34.

Thorne, S. E., & Perry, J. A. (2001).Theoretical foundations of nursing. In P. A. Potter, A. J. Perry, J. C. Ross-Kerr, & M. J. Wood (Eds.), *Canadian fundamentals of nursing* (2nd ed.) (pp. 86–100). Toronto: Mosby.

Thorne, S. E., Reimer Kirkham, S., & Henderson, A. (1999). Ideological implications of paradigm discourse. *Nursing Inquiry, 6,* 123–131.

Trojan, L., Marck, P., Gray, C., & Rodger, G. L. (1996). A framework for planned change: Achieving a funded PhD program in nursing. *Canadian Journal of Nursing Administration, 9*(1), 71–86.

Van Doren, C. (1991). *A history of knowledge: Past, present, and future.* New York: Ballantine.

Wald, F. S., & Leonard, R. C. (1964). Toward development of nursing practice theory. *American Journal of Nursing, 13*(4), 309–313.

Wood, M. J. (1997). Canadian Ph.D. in nursing programs: A new age. *Clinical Nursing Research, 6,* 307–309.

Wright, L. M., Watson, W. L., & Duhamel, F. (1985). The family nursing unit: Clinical preparation at the master's level. *The Canadian Nurse, 81*(5), 26–29.

Zilm, G., Larose, O., & Stinson, S. (1979). *Ph.D (nursing).* Ottawa: Canadian Nurses Association.

12

Nursing Competence: Constructing Persons and a Form of Life

Mary Ellen Purkis ■ Sioban Nelson

Chapter Objectives

At the completion of this chapter, you will be able to:

1. Understand the historical and political evolution of nursing competencies.

2. Describe the mechanisms by which competencies become "facts" within nursing.

(continued)

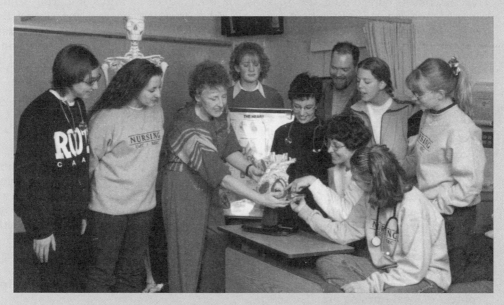

Used with permission of Faculty of Nursing, University of Calgary.

3. Articulate the relationships between competencies, accreditation, and auditing practices.

4. Trace the relationship between a competency framework and self-regulation.

5. Account for differences in competency development in Canada and elsewhere.

6. Discuss individual and organisational differences in responsibilities for nurse's competence.

Competencies are ubiquitous. Internationally, competency statements underpin curricula, define and maintain professional standards, delineate specialist practise, and perform a multitude of functions related to the accreditation and regulation of practise. A concise definition of competency according to the Alberta Association of Registered Nurses (AARN) states that "competence is the ability of the nurse to integrate and apply the knowledge, skills, judgement, and personal attributes required to practice safely and ethically in a designated role and setting" (AARN, 2000, p. 20).

A fairly recent occurrence in nursing's professional history, competency-based practise has transformed the Canadian nurse's manner of conceptualising and ordering practise. This chapter examines not only the success of the competency movement in Canada and abroad but also the possibility that the movement as conceived weakens nursing's influence in holding governments accountable for the resources that enable competence in practise.

This chapter explores the competency phenomenon by examining the genesis of competencies, considering the reasons for their success, and comparing Canadian competency models with others, such as those in Australia and the United States, where the competency movement in nursing has a slightly longer history. The range of competencies, the kind of nurse produced by competency-based formulations, and the applications of these competencies are discussed in relation to what they reveal about the nursing profession and its changing place in the health care system.

HISTORICAL UNDERSTANDINGS OF COMPETENCY STANDARDS

The Canadian competency movement is a fairly recent innovation adopted by nursing professional associations across the country to assist the process of determining whether educational programmes are preparing nursing students for entry into the profession of nursing. A national consensus process was engaged in by nurses across the country for a 2-year period (1995 to 1997) during which time the National Nursing Competencies Project (NNCP) was undertaken. At the culmination of this project, entry-level nursing competencies for licensed practical nurses, registered nurses, and registered psychiatric nurses were established. Each provincial association then went through a more local process of validating the relevance of the competencies within the context of local nursing practise settings.

This Canadian process was predated by processes in other countries that also culminated in the production of competency statements, and in each case, quite different processes developed. As an example, the next sections review processes for the development of practise competency statements in Australia and the United States.

Australian Approach

During the 1980s, the Australian federal government moved to reform and revitalise the economy and the workplace. Each profession was expected to develop competency-based standards. The goal was standardisation of education and portability of qualifications, which would thereby produce a more efficient workforce.

As part of this innovative and world-leading programme of initiatives, the National Training Reform Agenda and then the National Training Board (Gonzi et al., 1990) were established to review vocational education and training programmes across the country. The timing of these national initiatives was significant; the Australasian Nurse Registering Authorities Conference (ANRAC) had begun the process in 1986. Following a period of vigorous debate within the profession, Australian nurses took the lead in this movement and became the first profession or industry to develop national competency standards as part of the structural reform of the Australian workplace in its drive for market efficiency (Gonzi, 1993).

Nurses' enthusiasm for competencies has not been confined to Australia. From Benner's 1980s work in the United States that has had international impact (Borbasi, 1999; Gallaher, 1999; Hegedus & Pearson, 2000; Krugman et al., 2000; Sarvimaki & Stenbock-Hult, 1996; Thompson, 1999) to the formal requirements for continuing license to practise in Canada, competencies have been seized by nurses, employers, registration authorities, and educators as the scaffold upon which to design curricula, develop legislation, and assess continuing safety to practise.

American Approach

A major impetus for introducing competencies in the United States came from the Pew Health Professions Commission Taskforce on Health Care Workforce Regulation (Pew Commission) released in December 1995 (Sharp, 1998; Lassiter, 1997).

Aimed at reforming the health workforce regulation system, the Pew Commission disbursed grants totalling $300,000 to stimulate the health professions to restructure the health system in ways that focussed attention away from profit making and toward effective, competent practise.

In the manner of all successful innovations, competencies take the appearance of logical, even inevitable, developments (Lassiter, 1997). Their unproblematic and almost universal adoption by the profession internationally, however, merits reflection. How was it that competencies were so enthusiastically endorsed and adopted by nursing? How has the adoption of competencies as a framework for training, assessments, and professional development changed the way nursing understands itself? How have competencies changed the nurse? By what mechanisms have competencies become *facts* within nursing?

INVENTION OF COMPETENCIES

To explore these questions, one may follow an intellectual path developed by Osborne and Rose (1999) in their analysis of the creation of new phenomena. In examining the mechanisms by which competencies have become facts, the concern is in determining what facts have become *true* in our world (i.e., competencies) and how and with what consequences. It may be helpful to think along the following lines: that this is a matter of the emergence of certain descriptions *rather than others*; and that some descriptions will survive *if it is possible to do things with them* and use them *to produce effects*. So, the questions asked in this chapter are the following: How did competence emerge as a favoured way of making determinations about the ability of nurses to fulfill a particular role within society? What sorts of things become possible once a nursing association identifies particular competencies as being necessary attributes for nurses to demonstrate—and to demonstrate in particular ways? What are the effects produced in the world through these processes mandated by professional associations that demand competence from nurse members?

To the extent that these questions can be answered, one can say that the conditions underlying the creation of a phenomenon as set out by Osborne and Rose (1999, p. 373) are met. And, as a result, one may say that a particular knowledge practise has created a phenomenon. The significance of engaging in this analytic process is that it illustrates the socially constructed basis of the competency movement as it is currently being implemented within the Canadian context. As such, nurses are invited to examine for themselves a *range* of purposes the competency statements serve.

British sociologists Thomas Osborne and Nikolas Rose (1999) used the example of public opinion in their study of the way in which social sciences create phenomena. They argued that "new ways of describing and acting have been used to create all sorts of effects" (1999, p. 377). In the case of competency development, the manner in which this formulation of practise has "entered into the true" (Osborne & Rose, 1999, p. 367) can be productively analysed by considering the mechanisms that generate them and the conditions of their acceptance by the nursing profession worldwide.

For Osborne and Rose (1999), the target was the history and philosophy of science literature and what Osborne and Rose consider its failure to engage with the process through which the social sciences *actively create truths*. For us, as nurses, it is these processes, rather than the epistemologic concerns of Osborne and Rose, that are of primary concern. Namely, by what mechanisms have competencies become *facts* within nursing? Or, to paraphrase historian Peter Brown (1967, p. 393), what is the choice of problems that nursing regards as important? And why have these particular approaches been designed to particularise and solve those problems?

Evolution of the Canadian Competency Movement

The competency movement of the 1980s and 1990s has a particular genealogy. Fundamental to the successful application of a competency model are corresponding systems of accreditation and standardisation. Competencies can operate only within a framework that sets up standards for practise that arise from the quality assurance movement with its accreditation and auditing processes. After decades of refinement, the quality assurance movement achieved the extension of these accreditation and auditing technologies to the professions.

To implement the auditing of personnel within the total framework of industry accreditation, training and skill reviews became implicit components. It was the skill base of professionals, who ostensibly satisfied the training and educational preparation requirements for any audit procedures, that were targeted. Historically, the professions had been immune to ongoing review of their skill base (Angus, 1959). Therefore, it is significant that the competency movement breached the defenses of the professions and demanded they introduce processes to standardise curricula, implement skill audits for registration, and set in place processes to monitor life-long learning compliance (Fig. 12.1).

What is significant about these imperatives is that they have been facilitated, not by draconian measures, but by *self-regulation*. The success of the competency movement has been in its general acceptance as a framework that enables the more effective self-regulation at all levels: professional, organisational, and individual. These are not processes that individuals are forced to undertake but rather are engaged by individuals through self-review.

Early Frameworks of the Competency Movement

An example from Australia is a case in point. For Australian nurses, the competency movement had three main stages:

1. Development of standards for entry-level practise
2. Development of standards for advanced practise
3. Development of standards for specialty practise

Each stage involved different actors, served different objectives, and achieved distinct outcomes.

ENTRY-LEVEL COMPETENCIES

Entry-level competencies grew out of the 1984 in-principle decision of the Australian federal government that nursing education be moved from a hospital-based education system into the university sector, thereby setting a bachelor's degree as the entry-to-practise qualification for Australian nurses. Executing this momentous shift in the provision of nursing education involved a major reworking within the postsecondary education sector and the development of new curriculum standards. It also involved a period of intense collaboration among clinical leaders, registration authorities, professional and industrial associations, and the universities over curriculum, standards of practise, and registration (Australian Nursing Council, Inc. [ANCI], 1993).

The competency framework mandated by the federal government provided a timely mechanism for reconstituting nursing education and professional preparation. It was not uniformly welcomed by Australian nurses, however. Kim Walker, an Australian nurse-educator, assessed the competency movement as demonstrating rampant positivism that places nursing at the mercy of macro-political concerns (Walker, 1995, p. 97). Less sophisticated was the commonly held concern that nursing's professional aspirations may be damaged by the embrace of the competency movement. After all,

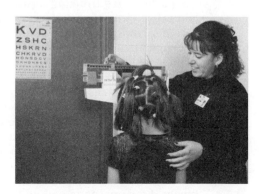

FIGURE 12.1. Used with permission, Faculty of Nursing, University of Calgary.

the Australian competency framework had emerged from the vocational education sector wherein skilled workers rather than professionals were prepared according to competency principles. For nurses who had finally achieved their goal of a university qualification for entry to practise, there was widespread concern that nursing curricula based on competencies reinforced the perception of nursing as a *skilled* rather than a *professional* pursuit (While, 1994; Pincombe, 1993). Despite these misgivings and strongly voiced opposition, government imperatives and the obvious benefits to industry prevailed. As sociologists Osborne and Rose (1999) argue, with the development of all phenomena constituted by the social sciences, "At a certain point, the controversy is settled. The phenomenon exists: now it is time for it to be investigated, explained. . . . It becomes a *usable* kind of thing" (p. 372, emphasis added).

In fact, it is this very *utility* of competencies that is so important. The process of developing competencies reveals this to be one of the most critical aspects of their success—*competencies are generated through consensus*. This has certainly been the case with nursing competency standards. "In fact the process actually reinforces consensus and the sense of objectivity of what has been discovered" (Osborne & Rose, 1999, p. 368).

In the case of undergraduate nursing, the universities, the profession, the unions, the regulators, and industry engaged in a process of structured consultations to agree on a set of competencies for entry-level practise. As Osborne and Rose (1999) noted: "One then observes a rather complex work of alliance between academic researchers and professionals and practitioners, in which the practitioners call upon the academics to boost their credentials, and the academics draw upon the pragmatic credit of their appeal to a professional audience to increase their likelihood of research funding and the like" (p. 390).

The process outlined here resonates with contemporary experiences of seeking research funding. Research grant-writers have developed strategies that capitalise on an "appeal to a professional audience"—at the same time, those same researchers experience the constraints such associations bring to the research endeavour.

ADVANCED-LEVEL COMPETENCIES

For the advanced-level practitioner, all the nursing organisations in the country engaged in a protracted series of consultations. An *action research project* was undertaken, leading to the development of consensus statements as to what constituted a generic set of competencies for advanced practise (Australian Nursing Federation [ANF], 1997). Action research was both a method to achieve the research aim of the production of advanced-level competencies and a process to develop participants' and the profession's thinking forward through the creation of such competencies. The collaborative philosophy of action research, where researchers and participants move together toward a shared change agenda, proved a useful approach to the development of competencies.

SPECIALIST COMPETENCIES

Finally, in the case of specialist nursing, such as that engendered by the Australian Confederation of Operating Room Nurses (ACORN), the creation of competencies served extremely useful functions. It, too, generated consensus among practitioners about the scope of specialty practise and engaged them in defining and delineating practise boundaries. Again, the favoured model was an action research design of multiple methods and a high level of participant engagement (ACORN, 1999). Action research provided the overall methodologic and theoretical framework for a project that involved a combination of qualitative and quantitative methods. Thus, at the end of the competency process, areas of specialty practise could be said to exist legitimately. A set of truths about that specialty were now written into the professional literature. The active constitution of the area was dynamically achieved through the enactment and reenactment of these competencies as the basis for recognition as a specialist practitioner. Through these processes, competencies can be said to exist as real things. And, by means of the creation of such realities, practises that may be as archaic as nursing itself can now be described in new and accountable ways.

These new realities are created in a systematic way that draws into play relations between state authorities, professional organisations, and individual nurses. Under *advanced liberalism*, which can be understood as a stance held in relation to questions of the governing of conduct of citizens, certain self-evaluative techniques related to competent practise (discussed later) provide the mechanism through which compliance with workplace reforms and improved efficiencies is achieved.

Compliance Initiatives

In the case of Australia, the federal government demanded compliance of all professional regulatory authorities. In the United States, nongovernmental but highly influential organisations (such as the Pew Commission) led the charge with funded programmes that set the agenda for workplace reforms through a competency framework.

In Canada, partnerships between the state (i.e., regionalised health authorities), professional associations, and other regulatory authorities and educators reframed both the expectations and the responsibilities of the profession and the individual practitioner. Regulatory authorities take responsibility to ask whether the practitioner remains competent to practise, but the practitioner is now expected to complete an official document and make an honest assessment of his or her competence. Self-declarations of competence need to be supported with a portfolio of evidence. The characteristics of this evidence are highly questionable when considered in relation to the stated goals of competency projects.

COMPETENCY MODELS AND IMPLICATIONS FOR NURSING

Since early in the year 2000, individual nurses across Canada have been receiving brightly colored print materials from their professional associations. These materials offer directions for nurses in each provincial jurisdiction on how to engage with a set of complex legal requirements in demonstrating their "continuing competence." The requirements for such demonstration have been established through provincial legislation and require that health care professionals forward documentary evidence of their alignment, as individual practitioners, with statements established by regulatory bodies to support their claims to competence in nursing practise. How are these textual materials being taken up by these regulatory bodies to become usable in ways anticipated by Osborne and Rose's argument about how phenomena are created?

"A key aspect of the creativity of phenomena in the social sciences pertains to the subjective attributes of the persons themselves: the kinds of persons they take themselves to be and the *forms of life they inhabit and construct*" (Osborne & Rose, 1999, p. 392, emphasis added). Of particular interest here is how the process of demonstrating competence has "produced a version of the world that [has] entered into the true" (Osborne & Rose, 1999, p. 367); that is, a process that is generally unquestioned by nurses who engage enthusiastically in the construction of themselves as particular sorts of competent practitioners—and significantly, nurses who will practise their competence within everyday circumstances that render invisible the responsibilities of the wider sociopolitical system for offering financial and material resources necessary to support competent practise.

A comparison of target audiences embedded in competency documents produced by professional organisations in Canada and Australia offers a starting point to question the emphasis on competence within these two particular jurisdictions. Evident in even an initial comparison of Canadian and Australian competencies is that the focus on the individual nurse in Canadian documents is largely missing from Australian documents.

Alberta Association of Registered Nurses Model

The AARN defines competence as "the ability of the nurse to integrate and apply the knowledge, skills, judgement and personal attributes required to practise safely and ethically in a designated role and setting" (AARN, 2000, p. 20). Other associations emphasise similar aspects of competence.

The AARN definition goes on to suggest to nurses that, "Just as nursing is more than a set of procedures or tasks, competence is *more than just a set of skills which must be performed safely and efficiently*. It is the integrating of knowledge with skills and applying it to the practice of nursing in a *safe, ethical* manner, based on the standards of the profession" (AARN, 2000, p. 20, emphasis added).

Safe practise is the central issue. The individuated nurse is the target of the message. That is, competence is defined against "the ability of the nurse" to enact specified knowledge functions, such as applying relevant knowledge to particular circumstances, practicing in a skilled manner, making relevant and appropriate judgements about the ever-changing condition of the patient, and so on. In this definition, there is no indication that the *context* within which opportunities to know particular things are embedded would have any influence on the nurse's ability to fulfill the required knowledge functions. The individuated focus is reinforced in additional ways: first in the reference to "personal attributes" and with this, the association of safety with ethics.

Safety is used in two different ways in this definition. *Initially*, nurses are informed that they are "required to practice safely and ethically in a designated role and setting." Next, they are advised that competence is "more than" safely and efficiently performed skills. An intellectual process of "integration and application" is signalled here, although the actual set of knowledges, skills, judgements, and personal attributes that constitute "safe and ethical" practise are left unspecified. (In a footnote, readers are advised that these attributes "include but are not limited to attitudes, values, and beliefs.")

Authors of the AARN definition of competency-based practise and the accompanying workbook containing explanatory notes provide some historical and political context for the focus on safe and ethical practise. Indeed, many regulatory bodies offer similar rationale for developing procedures to measure and monitor competence. That is, they establish a link between the requirements for demonstrating competence with legislative reviews of acts pertaining to health care professionals. Authors of the AARN document offer the following explanation for why AARN asks members to submit themselves to the competency review process (*note the primary reference to the impact of health service restructure):*

> Over the past ten years, the health care system has undergone massive changes, and the public has asked for reassurance that health professionals have maintained and upgraded their knowledge and skills for the role and setting in which they practise. The government has placed the responsibility for protection of the public on registering bod-

ies, such as the AARN, and has responded to this public request by requiring that the AARN and other regulatory bodies develop continuing competence programs for their members. In 1999, the Alberta government passed the *Health Professions Act* (HPA). It requires that all health professions develop a continuing competence program and that all health professionals demonstrate that they are maintaining their competence throughout their careers. This means that the AARN is required to develop a continuing competence program, and that, "regardless of the role or setting in which you work, you will need to fulfill the program requirements and demonstrate that you are continuing to be competent in your practice" (AARN, 2000, pp. 2–3).

Registered Nurses Association of British Columbia Focus

The Registered Nurses Association of British Columbia (RNABC) is quite explicit that specification of the *content* of safe and ethical practise is expressly *not* the point of the exercise of reporting on practise competencies by individual nurses. Instead, the exercise of competency review is designed to explicate a process that RNABC claims all nurses already engage in:

> RNABC's personal practice review requirements provide a framework for nurses to identify and address their learning needs. It offers a systematic approach for nurses to maintain their competence to practice and demonstrate accountability to the public. *The requirements are not designed to assess competence.* An underlying belief of the personal practice review requirements is that nurses are competent professionals. The additional continuing competence requirements provide an opportunity to formalize the process that registered nurses already use to maintain their competence to practice" (http://www.rnabc.bc.ca/contcomp/ explain.htm, emphasis added).

The RNABC offers the following rationale for establishing safe practise standards to its members:

> The Nurses (Registered) Act requires RNABC to establish and maintain a continuing competence program. This is a legislated mandate required of all health regulatory bodies in B.C. RNABC's personal practice review requirements provide a framework for nurses to identify and address their learning needs. It offers a systematic approach for nurses to maintain their competence to practice and demonstrate accountability to the public" (http://www.rnabc.bc.ca/contcomp/explain.htm).

As in the AARN statement, members of the RNABC are advised that the continuing competence programme is a "requirement" that the Association is mandated by provincial legislation to undertake. Also evident in this explanation are references to the fact that such programmes are not required only of nurses but that "all health regulatory bodies" in the province are required to address this mandate.

This might be interpreted as an attempt by RNABC to resist any breaching of its authority as a professional and autonomous body. But such an interpretation denies the extent to which such regulatory bodies are *networked* and, thus, discipline one another into forms of consensus and compliance. In claiming that the process merely formalises practises already engaged in by individual nurses, this statement too has an individuating effect. It pulls the individual nurse out of widely diverse practise settings and locates her or him in a space of accountability that is somehow supracontextual: individual accountability.

The authors of these definitions intend for the processes of integration and application to *move* nurses to engage in practises that are both *safe* and *ethical*. However, references to efficiency denote an organisational influence on nursing practise. In contrast to this, the reference to ethics denotes the centrality of the *individual, professional* nurse as holding primary responsibility for the conduct of safe and competent practise.

Manitoba Association of Registered Nurses' Position

Emphasising the point about "an increased awareness of health care issues [and] the changing roles of health care providers" in a way echoed in the AARN publication, the Manitoba Association of Registered Nurses (MARN) offers the following rationale for its introduction of competency procedures to its members:

> There is an increasing emphasis on and interest in the continuing competence of registered nurses and other health care professionals. This is due in part to an increased awareness of health care issues, the changing roles of health care providers, and the recognition that there is a link between quality care and the practitioner's competence to provide it (http://www.marn.mb.ca/continue.htm; Finochio et al., 1998).

The rationale for this explanation links it to the work of the Pew Commission. Mentioned earlier in the chapter, this commission's role was to develop *standard* competencies for a broad audience of health professionals. The report by Finochio, cited in the MARN rationale for the need to engage in a review of competence in practise (Finochio et al., 1998), refers to a report focussing on strengthening health care consumer protection within the United States. One of the major contributions of the commission was the development of "Twenty-One Competencies for the 21st Century." The list of 21 competencies appears in Box 12.1.

IMPACT OF CANADIAN COMPETENCY REQUIREMENTS ON NURSING

Two points stand out regarding the genesis of a rationale supporting the introduction of the continuing competence movement within the Canadian nursing professional body context:

- First, the competency requirement *is* directed at individual nurses—their knowledge, skills, and personal attributes. Nurses are targeted as responsible for the conduct of safe and ethical care—in the *absence* of any acknowledgement that the organisational context shapes possibilities and opportunities for engaging in ethical conduct (Latimer, 1998; Varcoe & Rodney, 2001).
- Second, the work of explicating nurses' competence in this highly individualised manner represents a significant departure from the way in which competencies were conceived of by those contributing to the Pew Commission's report, which is cited as a central, founding document supporting the development of nurse competencies in Canada.

As the list of 21 competencies indicates, those working within the context of the Pew Commission were setting forward an agenda designed to link consumers and providers. Such an agenda has a particular meaning within the largely for-profit health care industry of the United States. Consider the following data. The U.S. Census Bureau reports that for the year 1999, 15.5% of Americans were without health insurance for the entire year. Although criteria for *poverty* are not specified, this figure increases to 32.4% of poor people uninsured for the entire year of 1999. The Pew Commission's competency statements for the 21st century can be read as a national agenda for health care provision within the context of *inequitable* access to basic health care services.

In contrast to the situation in the United States, universal access to health care in Canada is mandated by federal statute in the form of the 1984 Canada Health Act (Gov-

BOX 12.1

Twenty-One Competencies for the 21st Century

1. Embrace a personal ethic of social responsibility and service.
2. Exhibit ethical behavior in all professional activities.
3. Provide evidence-based, clinically competent care.
4. Incorporate the multiple determinants of health in clinical care.
5. Apply knowledge of the new sciences.
6. Demonstrate critical thinking, reflection, and problem-solving skills.
7. Understand the role of primary care.
8. Rigorously practise preventive health care.
9. Integrate population-based care and services into practise.
10. Improve access to health care for those with unmet health needs.
11. Practise relationship-centred care with individuals and families.
12. Provide culturally sensitive care to a diverse society.
13. Partner with communities in health care decisions.
14. Use communication and information technology effectively and appropriately.
15. Work in interdisciplinary teams.
16. Ensure care that balances individual professional system and society needs.
17. Practise leadership.
18. Take responsibility for quality of care and health outcomes at all levels.
19. Contribute to continuous improvement of the health care system.
20. Advocate for public policy that promotes and protects the health of the public.
21. Continue to learn and help others learn.

From the Pew Commission (1998).

ernment of Canada, 2001). The Act mandates that health care be delivered through a funding structure whereby federal and provincial levels of government share costs through public, not-for-profit insurance providers. The key point here is that the relationship among governments, health care providers, and citizens seeking access to health care is vastly different between these neighbouring countries. The competencies set out by the Pew Commission reflect an interest in positioning health care delivery as a form of social responsibility. Ethical practise within this context reflects an interest in attending to the myriad ways in which people seeking health care might be discriminated against within the American context (Allen, 1996). That is, the competencies set out by the Pew Commission must be interpreted, in the American context, as politically motivated.

One may argue that the Pew agenda for social responsibility already underpins the Canadian system of publicly funded, universally accessible health care. And so the reference to this commission's work prompts many questions about how Canadian nursing regulatory bodies are defining ethical practise and how they intend that definition to be taken up by Canadian nurses. Before exploring this perplexing question, let's first examine the target of competencies in the Australian context. As suggested earlier, the competency agenda has developed quite differently within different national contexts. The Australian case illustrates this difference quite clearly.

Contrasts in Competencies

In stark contrast to the tone of the competencies developed in Canada are the competencies set out by the ANCI (2001) for beginning practise and the Advanced Nursing Competencies (ANF, 1997). In the ANCI's competency standards, one can see that organisations employing nurses and other health care workers are responsible for enabling competent practise.

Competency units (CUs) for registered nurses are established in four domains: professional and ethical practise, critical thinking and analysis, management of care, and enabling (Box 12.2). Even from these titles, it is possible to see some linkage to the competencies set out by Canadian professional bodies specifically in a stated interest in the domain of professional and ethical practise. However, the target for responsibility around the achievement of competent practise in this domain is rendered in quite different language within the detailed description offered. For instance, within this domain of professional and ethical practise, the first competency unit (CU 1) relates to "functions in accordance with legislation and common law affecting nursing practice." The specific competencies set out within this unit relate to a specific knowledge base: that of common law regulating safe practise. Nurses are responsible for knowing about this law, how it affects their actions, and what the reporting requirements are should they witness a breach of the law.

This statement is quite different from the lack of specificity related to knowledge requirements established for Canadian nurses. Similarly, CU 2 demands that nurses conduct nursing practise "in a way that can be ethically justified," again in relation to a specified document: the professions' code of ethics (Element 2.1).

The 14 ANCI competencies are targeted at entry- to practise-level nurses. Consequently, they focus on the responsibilities that the new nurse must be ready to shoulder as a registered professional. They incorporate expectations regarding the nurse's approach to nursing work by specifying the issues of research (CU 6), assessment (CU 7), planning (CU 8), and evaluation (CU 10). The competencies also place the nurse's role within the context of multidisciplinary teams and heterogenous service structures, emphasising the collaborative and collegial demands of nursing (CUs 8, 12, and 14).

Likewise, the competencies developed by the National Nursing Organisations (NNOs) with the ANF set the basis for advanced practise in the *work* of the nurse, as opposed to ethical or personal attributes of the nurse (Box 12.3).

As with the entry- to practise-level competencies, the function of ANF advanced nursing standards was consensus building. The advanced standards project set out to reflect current practise and to acknowledge the evolving national standards framework. Another goal was to meet the need to put in place standards that reflect the practise of nurses beyond the minimum level reflected in the ANCI competency standards. Additional objectives included informing ongoing professional education, contributing to ongoing development of specialty competency standards, and achieving endorsement by nurses across Australia (ANF, 1997, p. 6).

Thus, in the ANCI's minimum standards for practise, the ANF's advanced standards, and the separate specialty standards (such as those advanced by ACORN), the emphasis is on consensus building in a fractured educational and regulatory framework. Scope of practise, curriculum framework, and ethical and legal issues dominate, and the standards provide an ordered and coherent path around which these diverse practise and educational and regional interests can successfully cohere. As previously mentioned, the competencies also fill a void of public and professional confidence in consistency in the standard of nurse education since the abolition of state registering

BOX 12.2

Practice Domains and Units of Competency for Australian Nurses

DOMAIN: PROFESSIONAL AND ETHICAL PRACTICE

Competency Unit 1: Functions in accordance with legislation and common law affecting nursing practise.

Competency Unit 2: Conducts practise in a way that can be ethically justified (in relation to the professions' code of ethics [Element 2.1]).

Competency Unit 3: Protects the rights of individuals and groups in relation to health care.

Competency Unit 4: Accepts accountability and responsibility for own actions within nursing practice.

DOMAIN: CRITICAL THINKING AND ANALYSIS

Competency Unit 5: Acts to enhance the professional development of self and others.

Competency Unit 6: Values research in contributing to developments in nursing and improved standards of care.

DOMAIN: MANAGEMENT OF CARE

Competency Unit 7: Carries out a comprehensive and accurate nursing assessment of individuals and groups in a variety of settings.

Competency Unit 8: Formulates a plan of care in collaboration with individuals and groups.

Competency Unit 9: Implements planned nursing care to achieve identified outcomes within scope of competency.

Competency Unit 10: Evaluates progress towards expected outcomes and reviews and revises plans in accordance with evaluation data.

DOMAIN: ENABLING

Competency Unit 11: Contributes to the maintenance of an environment that promotes safety, security, and personal integrity of individuals and groups.

Competency Unit 12: Communicates effectively with individuals and groups.

Competency Unit 13: Manages effectively the nursing care of individuals and groups.

Competency Unit 14: Collaborates with other members of the health care team.

Source: (http://www.anci.org.au/competencystandards.htm).

examinations with the wholesale move of Australian nursing into the postsecondary education sector in the 1980s.

Australian Concerns: Corporate–Shared Responsibility

The focus of these standards appears to be on the scope of practise and the educational and professional preparation required of nurses rather than on the individual nurse's ability to meet the values set out in the formulated competencies. The *choice of*

BOX 12.3

Competency for Advanced Practise Nursing in Australia

The advanced practise competencies advanced by the Australian Nursing Federation (ANF) evince a pragmatic and contextualised view of nursing performance. These competencies set out 12 standards that provide a broad framework for advanced nursing practise. Essentially, they state that the advanced practise nurse:

- Uses multiple approaches to decision making
- Manages the care of individuals and groups
- Engages in collaborative practise to achieve patient outcomes
- Provides a supportive environment for colleagues
- Manages staff and physical resources
- Engages in ethically justifiable nursing practise
- Protects the rights of individuals and/or groups
- Engages in activities to improve nursing practise
- Develops therapeutic and caring relationships
- Fulfills the conduct requirement of the profession
- Acts to enhance the professional development of self
- Functions in accordance with the legislation and common law affecting nursing practise

From Australian Nursing Federation. (1997). *Competency Standards for the advanced nurse.* Melbourne: ANF Federal Office.

problem addressed by the Australian competencies was the development of national curricula and clinical experience requirements within the tertiary sector for new graduates and advanced practise in the clinical specialties.

Canadian Concerns: Individual Responsibility

These concerns appear largely absent from the Canadian competency material. One indication of the "choice of problem" Canadian competencies are trying to address can be found in Appendix 11 of the National Nursing Competency Project Final Report, which was published in 1997 (pp. 138–172). This section is entirely devoted to the complex task of discrimination between *shared* and *unique* competencies for the licensed practice and registered nurses. It even tabulates current (1996) and future (2001) competencies between the two levels of nurses. As such, the competencies attempt to clarify the muddy waters of multiple entry to professional practise.

By contrast, in Australia, the competency document is only directed at a specific level of professional nurse designation: the registered nurse. The problem of multiple levels of nursing practitioners, then, was not one requiring solution through the competency process in Australia. Instead, the competencies solved a problem of irregular educational standards across the country. In the shift of education for nurses from hospitals to universities, the process of national examination was lost. In this case, the competencies provided an informal framework for the evolution of a national curriculum, with recent calls for a national nursing curriculum based on competencies seeking to formalise this process (National Review of Nursing Education Committee, 2001).

The most radical example of departure from the pragmatic and context-based competency model of Australia comes from Alberta, where the focus is solely on the individual nurse and the nurse's capacity to determine continuing education needs and attend to them. The AARN triple component, "We Trust You, Tell Us, Show Us," asks reregistering nurses to assess their own practise according to the set standard (on a scale of 1 to 5), to collect feedback from colleagues and patients, and to develop an appropriate learning plan that is then to be evaluated. Set forth in writing, the AARN documents present a professional climate of not only self-surveillance but also co-surveillance, with substantiation of the individual nurse's claims to have achieved and maintained critical competencies required from those around her.

Written in the first person, the AARN continuing competence handbook leaves no doubt as to who is fully responsible for continuing competence in the nursing profession—the individual. Moreover, the confessional tone of the document is further heightened by requiring the nurse to identify limitations and define how to redress them. Given that the exercise is entirely subjective and that the document is unable to be verified, the document *radically fails* as a conventional audit of continuing competency.

But perhaps this is not the purpose. That these competencies institute mandatory reflective practise is illuminating, particularly because these reflective techniques are a means to reconstitute subjective attributes, performing a "specialized form of self-culture" (Nelson, 2000, p. 88). As the tool of choice by regulatory authorities, reflective practise provides the mechanism whereby nurses internalise the new professional ethos. Clearly, one can see that nurses are under surveillance by the registration authorities to make sure this reconstitution of the nurse is achieved.

FUTURE IMPLICATIONS: NURSING'S CHANGING PLACE

One thing that is clearly articulated and "enters the true" through the processes described in this chapter is a changing relationship between the public and those professionals who have undertaken advanced education to learn practises designated as effective in providing health care services. What the development of competencies signals is that an initial preparation as a nurse is no longer sufficient guarantee of the competence of that practitioner to deliver appropriate care. Instead, elaborate processes (which, as we have argued, fail on any conventional measure of competency audit) have been designed apparently to assuage the fears of the public that health care practitioners might somehow be "out of practise." Yet, no strong evidence exists that the public has expressed these fears. Instead, the competency movement seems to have emerged out of a much longer-term interest (of governments and, more locally and by implication, health service managers) in breaching the immunity held by professional groups to any sort of external review of the effectiveness of their skill base.

SUMMARY

The analysis of the competency movement in several jurisdictions establishes an argument that, particularly in the Canadian case, review processes fail to provide the very guarantee of effectiveness that the competency movement seeks. This does not mean, however, that the competency movement has failed. Instead, it has been spectacularly successful in producing a range of consensus statements that serve as powerful *narratives of consistency*.

Competencies fill a void of public and professional confidence in consistency in standards of nurse education. In Canada, registering examinations are devised at the national level. As such, diversity in the capacity to deliver on a range of health care services resulting from regional economic disparity can be masked by federal and provincial legislators through demands for professionals to create narratives of consistency. In contrast, the registration examination did not survive the shift from hospital schools to university-based education in Australia. In that context, competencies provided a surrogate framework for an evolving national curriculum.

Professional bodies such as ANF and AARN share an interest in demonstrating guarantees of competence to the public by responding to government demands. In so doing, however, they undermine their capacity to hold governments accountable for providing resources that make such competent practise much more likely.

The success of the competency movement within nursing deserves careful and cautious attention by the profession. Far from fulfilling the promise of detailing an evidential basis for professional practise, alignment with the competency movement alienates nurses as individuals and as members of a professional body from holding managers and governments accountable for the provision of resources, such as staff-to-patient ratios that enable nurses to work collaboratively with patients to deliver care that acknowledges and respects their goals for health. It is our belief that it is this sort of condition that underpins safe and effective care. Instead, by drawing on highly suspect strategies of self-surveillance and co-surveillance, the blame for poor practise outcomes can be placed on individual nurses who, it will be said, have proven themselves to be untrustworthy.

Online RESOURCES

Add to your knowledge of this issue:

The Canadian Nurses Association   www.cna-nurses.ca/
Provincial and Territorial Organisations

Registered Nurses Association of British Columbia	www.rnabc.bc.ca/
Alberta Association of Registered Nurses	www.nurses.ab.ca/
Saskatchewan Registered Nurses Association	www.srna.org/
College of Registered Nurses of Manitoba	www.crnm.mb.ca/
Registered Nurses Association of Ontario	www.rnao.org
College of Nurses of Ontario	www.cno.org/
Ordre des Infirmieres et Infirmiers du Quebec	www.oiig.org/
Nurses Association of New Brunswick	www.nanb.nb.ca/
Registered Nurses Association of Nova Scotia	www.rnans.ns.ca/about.html
Northwest Territories Registered Nurses Association	www.nwtrna.com

Other associations may be reached through e-mail addresses:

Association of Registered Nurses of Newfoundland	arnn@nf.sympatico.ca
Association of Nurses of Prince Edward Island	anpei@pei.sympatico.ca
Yukon Registered Nurses Association	yrna@yukon.net

Reflections on the Chapter

1. The authors of this chapter claim that despite the spectacular success of the competency movement in Canada, it undermines a nurse's capacity to hold governments accountable for providing resources that would make such competency possible. Do you agree with this argument? Support your position.

2. Go to your provincial web site (listed in references) and download the most recent document related to competencies for practise. Review this document and discuss how this fits or does not fit with the chapter.

3. Discuss with colleagues or classmates in practise what they see as the purpose of the competencies for practise documents. How does this fit with your view? How does your view fit with those of your colleagues in practise or the views expressed in this chapter?

4. Demonstrated evidence of competence is required by law in some provinces. What is the intended purpose of such legislation? What are the effects of such legislation for nurses? For health care organisations? For health care practises?

5. Discuss the implications of competencies for nursing curricula generally and for continuing education of nurses in particular.

6. What are your thoughts about the notion that nurses are targeted as responsible for provision of safe and ethical care in the absence of any acknowledgment that the organisational context shapes possibilities and opportunities of engaging in ethical conduct? Review existing documents on competencies for your province to see if and how this might be true. Take a stance that supports or challenges this claim.

7. In considering the chapter, the provincial documents, and your own thoughts on this matter, what issues can you identify for nurses, nursing practise, and the health of Canadians? What frameworks can you identify that help you to articulate these issues? What barriers can you identify to the resolution of these issues? What strategies can you suggest for the resolution of these issues?

REFERENCES

Alberta Association of registered Nurses (AARN). (2000). AARN Continuing Competence Handbook. Edmonton, AB: Author. Available at http://nurses.ab.ca/practice/Handbook.pdf

Allen, D. G. (1996). Knowledge, politics, culture, and gender: A discourse perspective. *Canadian Journal of Nursing Research, 28,* 95–102.

Angus, N.C. (Ed.) (1959). *The expert and administration in New Zealand.* London: Oxford University Press.

Australian Nursing Council, Inc. (1994). National validation of ANCI competencies for beginning level enrolled nurses across all areas of nursing practice: Report to ANCI Competencies Committee 1993. Canberra: Author.

Australian Confederation of Operating Room Nurses. (1999). Validation of ACORN Competency Research Project Report, Adelaide.

Australian Nursing Council, Inc. (2001). *ANCI national competency standards for the registered nurse and the enrolled nurse* [On-line]. Available: http://www. anci.org.au/competencystandards.htm (August 1, 2001).

Australian Nursing Federation. (1997). *Competency standards for the advanced nurse.* ANF Federal office, Melbourne.

Borbasi, S. A. (1999). Advanced practice/expert nurses: Hospitals can't live without them. *Australian Journal of Advanced Nursing, 16*(3), 21–29.

Brown, P. (1967). *Augustine of Hippo.* New York: Dorset.

Commonwealth of Australia. (1990). *The identification and assessment of competencies: The Nursing Project and its implications.* Department of Employment, Education and Training, Research paper No. 4, Canberra, AGPS.

Finocchio, L. J., Dower, C. M., Blick, N. T., Gragnola, C. M., & Taskforce on Health Care Workforce Regulation. (1998). *Strengthening consumer protection: Priorities for health care workforce regulation.* San Francisco: Pew Health Professions Commission.

Gallagher, L. (1999). Expert public health nursing practice: a complex tapestry. *Nursing Praxis in New Zealand, 14*(3), 16–27.

Gonzi, A. (1993). Competence and competencies: A global perspective. Paper presented at the First National Conference on Competencies in Nursing, Adelaide, 5–7 December, 1993.

Gonzi, A., Hager, P., & Oliver, L. (1990). *Establishing competency-based standards in the professions.* Department of Employment, Education and Training Research paper No. 1, Canberra, AGPS.

Government of Canada. (2001). *Canada Health Act overview* [On-line]. Available: http://www.hc-sc.gc.ca/main/hc/web/datapcb/datahins/chaover.htm (August 1, 2001).

Hegedus, K. S., & Pearson, G. S. (2000). Articulating professional nursing practice in Hungary: Ripples that extend to waves. *National Academies of Practice Forum: Issues in interdisciplinary care, 2,* 187–190.

Krugman, M., Smith, K., & Goode, C. J. (2000). A clinical advancement program: evaluating 10 years of progressive change. *Journal of Nursing Administration, 30,* 215–225.

Lassiter, F. (1997). Pew Commission's state initiatives program to Reform Health Care Work-force. Regulation grant activity update, [Health Policy Issues]. *AORN Journal, 6*(5), 923–926.

Latimer, J. (1998). Organizing context: Nurses' assessments of older people in an acute medical unit. *Nursing Inquiry, 5,* 43–57.

Masters, G. & McCurry, D. (1992). *Competency-based assessment in the professions.* Department of Employment, Education and Training Research paper No. 2. Canberra, AGPS.

National Review of Nursing Education Committee. (2001). *National review of nursing education.* Discussion paper, AusInfo, Canberra.

Nelson, S. (2000). *A genealogy of care of the sick: Nursing holism and pious practice.* Southsea, Hants: Nursing Praxis Press.

Osborne, T., & Rose, N. (1999). Do the social sciences create phenomena? The example of public opinion research. *British Journal of Sociology, 50*(3), 367–396.

Pincombe, J. (1993). *Competencies: do we need them?* Presented at the First National Conference on Competencies in Nursing, Adelaide, 5–7 December.

Sarvimaki, A., & Stenbock-Hult, B. (1996). Intuition: A problematic form of knowledge in nursing. *Scandinavian Journal of Caring Sciences, 10,* 234–241.

Sharp, N. (1998). October 1998 Pew Report: Supportive of NP goals. *Nurse Practitioner, 23*(12), 72.

Thompson, C. (1999). A conceptual treadmill: The need for "middle ground" in clinical decision making theory in nursing. *Journal of Advanced Nursing, 30,* 1222–1229.

Varcoe, C., & Rodney, P. (2001). Constrained agency: The social structure of nurses' work. In S. Bolaria & H. Dickinson (Eds.), *Health, illness and health care in Canada* (3rd ed.) (pp. 108–128). Toronto: Harcourt Brace.

Walker, K. (1995). Courting competency: Nursing and the politics of performance in practice. *Nursing Inquiry, 2,* 90-99.

While, A. E. (1994). Competence versus performance: Which is more important? *Journal of Advanced Nursing, 20,* 525–531.

13

Nursing, Technology, and Informatics: An Easy or Uneasy Alliance?

W. Dean Care ■ David Gregory ■ Christina Whittaker ■ Wanda Chernomas

Chapter Objectives

At the completion of this chapter, you will be able to:

1. Discuss the relationship between nursing and technology.
2. Describe the role of technology and informatics in nursing practice.
3. Explore the possibilities of the use of technology and informatics in nursing practice.

4. Discuss the issues related to applying technology and informatics in practice.
5. Identify the barriers to resolving these issues in practice.
6. Formulate strategies for resolving these issues in practice.

Teaching by videoconference to northern Manitoba. Used with permission of University of Manitoba, Faculty of Nursing.

It is the year 2005. Teresa Fraser, RN, BScN, has just completed a shift as triage coordinator at Health Care Inc. On this day, Teresa spent time interacting with post–cardiac surgery patients being cared for in their homes. She accessed and downloaded her patients' health care records from the local health care agency. She communicated with and visualised her clients through desktop videoconferencing hardware installed in their homes. She checked their vital signs and cardiac status through remote sensors, visualised skin color, and assessed mental health status through online testing. She filed a full report in the electronic health care record that is accessed and supplemented by other care providers. Teresa also spent 2 hours engaged in a chat room (virtual) discussion with a group of hypertensive patients. She then revised her web site on preoperative teaching for bypass surgery. This site is accessed by hundreds of current and prospective patients each month. Throughout the day, Teresa maintained ongoing communication with her patients by way of wireless electronic mail accessed through her palm-sized computer. A voice-activated documentation system permits her to maintain an instant record of her patients' health status through her palm pilot.

This brief vignette sets the stage for a discussion of the issues and trends arising from technology and informatics as they apply to nursing. Like this vignette, the chapter focusses on common uses and applications of technology in nursing practise and education. It also identifies issues arising from this technology and discusses the future of technology in nursing and health care. Relevant historical events are introduced within the chapter, particularly as they relate to the significant shift in Western society from an industrial focus to an information ethos. Both rely heavily on technology, but in vastly different ways.

The Industrial Age was characterised by an emphasis on productivity, efficiency, division of labour, and hierarchic organisations. In contrast, the Information Age is distinguished by a heavy dependence on telecommunications, knowledge and information explosion, global operations, decentralised organisations, and networked employees. The Information Age provides society with rapid access to information. In the area of health care, the Information Age fosters advances in health and telecommunications technology. These advances have had a profound effect on nurses and the organisations for which they work.

The relationship between technology and nursing has been marked by tension and unrest. Until recently, nursing and technology have been framed as a dichotomy—nursing at one end and technology at the other—polar opposites, in a sense. Technology has been viewed as masculine, scientific, mechanistic, and reductionistic. In contrast, nursing in this dichotomous thinking has been conceptualised as feminine, nurturing, a soft science, humanistic, and holistic. Thus, technology has been identified as innately negative and dehumanising to nursing—obstructing or impeding nursing care (Erlen, 1994; Gadow, 1988).

Understanding technology simply as "scientific care" and nursing as "sympathetic care" does great injustice to the science of nursing care (Sandelowski, 1999). Like technology, nursing care is based on science. Recently, technology and its relationship with nursing are considered in more sophisticated and complex terms. For example, nurses can use technology as an intentional way of expressing caring (Schoenhofer & Boykin, 1998). Expert nurses can and do use technologies as part of their holistic care (Sandelowski, 1998). In this way, nurses can potentially render technology as unobtrusive as possible while achieving maximum therapeutic benefit for the whole person (Purnell, 1998). With technology, nurses look beyond the technical to "touch" patients

(Ray, 1987, as cited in Sandelowski, 1998). Touch includes physical, psychological, emotional, and spiritual aspects of care.

Nurses serve as "cultural brokers" between technology and patients. In this broker role, nurses translate technology for patients and provide explanations about the technology. Bridging the worlds of technology and nursing care, however, is not without a host of challenges. Despite expert nurse clinicians and their brokering activities, these challenges have the potential to undermine the relationship between nursing and technology.

RELATIONSHIP BETWEEN NURSING AND TECHNOLOGY

What exactly is the relationship between nursing and technology? Nurses are rarely "at the table" in regard to developing technology. As a profession, nursing most often inherits or receives technology developed by other disciplines. Medical technology is not nursing technology, and yet this technology is imposed upon nursing (Purnell, 1998). This has, in great measure, contributed to the strained relationship between technology and nursing. Because of this *technologic inheritance*—an understanding of impact on the illness experience—how a disease or condition is experienced by a patient and integrated into her or his life remains mostly unknown with new technologies.

Additionally, the relationships among technology, patients, and nursing care are of great concern to nursing. Assessing the impact of technology entails considerations of efficacy, safety, cost, legal ramifications, and social and ethical impact on the lives of patients and their families (Purnell, 1998). This is supported by the Canadian Nurses Association (CNA) in the following statement:

> While technology has the potential to improve health care, science has advanced so quickly that some technologies have been put into use with little understanding of the possible impact on clients, families, health care professionals and the health delivery system. Nurses are often called upon to use technologies with limited training, and with little technical or administrative support. The introduction of new technologies can lead to higher overall costs, particularly if the technologies are not planned and managed properly (CNA, 1992).

The adoption of new technology also has an impact on the nature of nurses' work. Nurses incorporate technology into their work on a regular and ongoing basis. Nurses must learn how the new technology works, consider its demands for nursing time and knowledge, and decide how best to incorporate it into nursing care. One of the challenges of technology is that time previously dedicated to patient care may be short-shifted as a consequence of the technologic demands. Nurses use technology, and the data it produces, in clinical assessments, decision making, and nursing interventions. However, accompanying the technology are real time demands and an impact on independent nursing interventions. With the introduction of new technology comes a litany of tasks. For example, in combination chemotherapy, oncology nurses engage in the following activities: checking dosages, starting intravenous therapy, mixing and administering premedications, obtaining blood specimens, and giving antiemetic medications (Brown, 1992). These tasks draw upon the limited time available to oncology nurses as they provide patient care.

Nurses, as patient advocates, are concerned about the illness experience. It is nurses who attend to how new technologies impinge upon patients and their families. As Sandelowski (1998) observed, "nurses have a special 'angle of vision' by virtue of their distinctive epistemologic, social, and moral position on the front lines and at the point of impact of technologies on patient care" (p. 8). It is incumbent upon nurses to conduct research on the impact of technology on their work. This will provide valuable information to refine how and why technology is used in practise.

NURSING INFORMATICS

According to Simpson (1998), "part of the reason nursing informatics is so hard to define is because it's a moving target" (p. 22). An accurate definition of nursing informatics, however, is essential for understanding its role in practise. It will ensure that nurses are taught "not just how to use computers, but how to collect and use information to truly further care delivery" (Simpson, 1998, p. 24). Graves and Corcoran-Perry (1996) state that when applied to a discipline, informatics is "an application of computer science and information science to the management and processing of data, information and knowledge in the named discipline" (p. 15). Simpson (1999) further expands this idea to include in a definition, "all the activities involved in managing and processing nursing data for use in care delivery. It also includes conceptual frameworks and such theories as information processing and decision theory and language development and human-computer interfaces, among others" (p. 91).

Today's nurse is affected by an ever-changing health care system dominated by a focus on outcomes or evidence, performance measurement, and the use of technology to provide and support care delivery. Nurse educators generally lack the necessary knowledge and competence in information technology. As more patients become comfortable with information technology, expectations will be placed on nurses to have similar skills. "In fact, nurses may find that their patient education encounters will increasingly occur through distance technology" (Gassert, 1998, p. 266).

The rapid explosion of both computer technology and telecommunications makes it essential that faculty clearly articulate the need for information technology in nursing curricula. According to Gassert (1998), all nurses will need core informatics skills to practise effectively. These skills include word processing, electronic mail use, familiarity with a variety of spreadsheets and databases, bibliographic retrieval, and ability to develop graphic presentations and to access and critique web-based information.

APPLICATIONS OF NURSING INFORMATICS AND TECHNOLOGY IN PRACTICE

The application of nursing informatics as an umbrella concept takes various forms in practise. At this time, the most common form is telehealth, with the telephone, electronic mail, and web-based information as the vehicles for knowledge dissemination. Electronic health records are also discussed in this section.

Telehealth

The term *telehealth* encompasses a broad range of health care and service delivery systems provided through *distance* or *electronic* technology (Gassert, 2000). Telehealth can be defined as "the use of advanced telecommunications technologies to exchange health information and provide health care services across the geographic, time, social, and cultural barriers" (Reid, 1996).

The geographically dispersed population of Canada provides an ideal opportunity for the application of telehealth to reduce barriers related to health care access. Telehealth has the potential to provide borderless, seamless, and accessible health care in all reaches of the country, delivering fast, accurate diagnosis and treatment in situations where face-to-face visits may not be possible or feasible.

The proliferation of terms relating to care practises using distance technology has created confusion and difficulty when exploring related issues. Terms such as *telemedicine, nursing telepractise,* and *tele-education* are invoked in the literature. Collectively, they refer to different components of health care delivery through technology and, in certain instances, as subsets of telehealth. A national working group chaired by the CNA has defined *nursing telepractise* as patient-centred forms of nursing practise, which occur through, or are facilitated by, the use of telecommunications or electronic means. Nursing telepractise uses the nursing process, which encompasses patient assessment, planning and implementation through the provision of information, referral, education and support, evaluation, and documentation (CNA, 2000).

An example of nursing telepractise, Tele-HomeCare is the provision of a range of services to patients in their own homes through an integrated approach to service delivery by home and hospital care providers, a hospital-based monitoring centre, the use of videoconferencing equipment, and remote vital signs monitoring (Hospital for Sick Children, 2001). Through 24-hour interactive video systems, a patient can contact the nurse specialist any time for consultation on a wide range of issues that would previously require visits to emergency facilities either at great distance or considerable difficulty.

In real time, nurses can perform a wide variety of assessment, education, and intervention skills at varying frequencies. They can listen to heart and chest sounds, read and interpret electrocardiograms, assess wound status, review downloaded blood glucose information, and observe and educate the patient's self-care (Russo, 2001). The opportunities for nursing within this area may be limited only by the technologic resources available and the ability of nursing to advocate for our expanded role in implementation, care, and evaluation.

Within telehealth, the need remains for nurses to practise according to the established standards of practise, code of ethics, provincial legislation, and competencies of their regulatory bodies. Several related issues and challenges are apparent within the telehealth environment. There are standards of telephone practise in some jurisdictions. However, not all provinces have such policies for their practitioners. These telephone standards of practise do not address the range of practise now possible within a telehealth environment. Policies on the provision of telehealth across provincial registering bodies have yet to be developed through coordinated efforts. In addition, educational standards or credentials have not been established for this area of practise. Issues related to maintenance of privacy and confidentiality have not been addressed. Without the aforementioned issues being addressed, liability issues and employer responsibilities become unclear.

Some questions needing clarification are as follows:

1. What is the nurse's liability in regard to nursing care provided to patients who reside in a province where the nurse is not licenced to practise?
2. How do professional nursing organisations and regulatory bodies promote good practise, prevent poor nursing practise, and intervene or discipline as necessary when the nurse and patient may be thousands of miles apart and the interactions are electronic?
3. Are provincial associations ready to address these developing questions?

Care Delivery by Telephone

The earliest use of the telephone as a tool for providing public health or private duty nursing occurred in the early 1920s (Sandelowski, 2000). Only recently, however, has consultation with patients over the telephone become a distinct nursing intervention, with specialised protocols for practise.

Many of the current telephone health care delivery programmes evolved from the emergency room. However, telephone practise is no longer just an extension of emergency health service. Standards of practise have been developed for nursing care offered by telephone. Two examples of provincial standards from regulatory bodies include (1) the College of Nurses of Ontario: Telephone Nursing Practise Standards and (2) the College of Registered Nurses of Manitoba: Telephone Nursing Standards. A wide range of protocols also exists to guide nurses' decision making and judgment. Questions and issues remain regarding the frequency of review of protocols, the qualifications and training required of the practitioner, and nurses' involvement in developing the standards.

Manitoba's Health Links is an example of telephone technology that provides 24-hour province-wide nursing access for health information and advice. Experienced nurses with a broad range of expertise and constellation of skills usually provide this service. Another example is British Columbia's HealthGuide NurseLine, which makes 24-hour, toll-free province-wide nursing access available. Nurses use software to assist in guiding patients' health care decision making. NurseLine is part of an expanded programme endorsed by the Registered Nurses Association of British Columbia. The programme consists of a printed HealthGuide handbook and an online health database. Commercially available software can be customised, at a cost, to meet needs for evaluation and monitoring, including the number and type of calls and users, automated evaluation of disposition or outcome, patient satisfaction, and patient knowledge of services.

Whether the protocols are available online or on paper, telephone nursing can be contrasted to the more traditional triage. Telephone nursing uses nursing assessment to guide or coach the decision making of the patient concurrently with an empowerment approach rather than directed decisions. The inability for nurses to incorporate nonverbal patient behaviours can be viewed as a limitation, or as a challenge, to their assessment skills. However, the advent of visual images may address this limitation.

The Aboriginal Nurses Association of Canada (ANAC) supports the use of telehealth practises to improve the health of First Nations and Inuit communities. According to a recent discussion paper, "inequities exist in the health and the health care services of Aboriginal people compared to the general population of Canada" (ANAC, 2001, p. 9). The introduction of telehealth services into aboriginal communities has the potential to address these inequities. However, patients from these communities or others without a phone, computer, or computer skills are at a disadvantage. The introduction of advanced technology may create a two-tiered system: those people with financial and technical resources will have access to health services; those who do not will be disadvantaged.

Electronic Mail and the Internet

Electronic mail (e-mail) and the Internet are a means of providing telehealth services. As more patients become comfortable with and gain access to e-mail, this form of communication will be used increasingly as a means of contact and consultation with health care providers. Some patients may experience greater comfort using e-mail as a form of communicating at a distance, especially if their concerns are of a personal or sensitive nature. With e-mail, patients and nurses have some flexibility in regard to the timing of enquiries and responses. However, the issues of privacy and confidentiality remain unresolved. Additionally, it may not be possible to verify that the individual initiating communication is indeed the patient, nor that the question and the nurse's response will not be read by others. The e-mail response by the nurse could also be circulated to other care providers, with the nurse's response misinterpreted out of context to that particular patient or prior communication. The lack of live communication may belie the complexity of the patient's situation, leading to tendencies for both the patient and provider to simplify or exaggerate inadvertently their concerns, assessment, and response. *Liability for care practises and potential misdiagnoses or care provided through the medium of distance or electronic technology are issues warranting careful exploration.*

Health-Seeking Behaviours

Similarly, the Internet has provided the opportunity for health-seeking behaviour by patients, often before contact with a health professional. Potentially, the Internet offers privacy, immediacy, breadth of information, different perspectives, and infinite repetition of information (Bischoff & Kelley, 1999). Conversely, the potential for greater patient involvement in health choices can be overwhelming because of the variety and often-conflicting health information.

Patients and care providers may be unaware of how to evaluate the accuracy and credibility of web-based information. Provider resources for such evaluation are growing, as exemplified by the inclusion of guidelines and standards for web-based publishing on many web sites. The nurse may find her or his practise extending into patient education about how to evaluate Internet sites. Various local public and academic libraries are beginning to provide information on how to evaluate Internet sites. An example of such a service is the Consumer and Patient Health Information Service at the University of Manitoba.

Online Support Groups

In addition to its use for patient self-education, the Internet is used for support groups through online synchronous chat rooms (real-time discussion) and asynchronous interaction (any-time discussion), which provide patients with the opportunity to seek support and consult with others independently. The content of online health care and related discussions may vary according to the nature of the disorder and the composition of the group (White & Dorman, 2000). Topics may revolve around general themes, such as personal experience and opinion, encouragement and support, treatment, symptoms, alternative therapies, caregiver concerns, and coping strategies. As with electronic mail, using technology may ease communication by those who feel inhibited or who are geographically isolated. Future research will need to explore the role that nurses play in such online support groups, how effective groups are conducted, and the role of such groups in health promotion. Active participation or "listening" to online support groups also helps the nurse to understand better patients' concerns. Nurses need to be familiar with the opportunities that online support groups provide.

Despite the challenges of this technology, e-mail, the Internet, and telehealth prac-tises have the potential to decrease substantially the indirect and social costs of health care. Costs associated with travel to health care facilities and absenteeism from family, school, or work can be reduced. This is particularly relevant to patients and families isolated by geography or care needs.

Electronic Health Records

The definition that best summarises the intent of *electronic health records* (EHRs) is the health record of an individual that is accessible online from many separate, interoper-able automated systems within an electronic network (Office of Health and the Infor-mation Highway [OHIH], 2001). This definition infers the complexity of the issues involving EHRs, such as the additional resources, infrastructure, and economic chal-lenges related to access to an integrated electronic network, including the various regional, provincial, and federal approaches to health care delivery.

The move to EHRs has been stimulated by technologic development, increased social mobility, care by a wider range of health care professionals—all of whom will require information, and public and government demand for accountability (OHIH, 2001). Health care decision makers and policy analysts increasingly require access to data for the evaluation and support of appropriate health care programming. The availability of a patient's record electronically promotes accessibility of the information by a variety of health care providers who are involved in the patient's care and who are linked to the network. EHRs could eliminate duplication of services, improve efficiency of the system, and provide accurate documentation over time.

Patient access to health records also becomes a possibility with EHRs. Such access may support enhanced personal decision making in health behaviours. Poten-tially, patients can be more informed about their health status, which may facilitate discussions with health care providers. However, patient access may inhibit profes-sionals from freely recording data on sensitive issues, or offering controversial provi-sional assessments such as "patient is malingering." Patient access may also pose legal ramifications in certain circumstances, such as illicit drug use. Additionally, patients could misread or misinterpret findings in the health record, causing distress pending clarification.

As Nahm and Poston (2000) report, nurse and patient satisfaction with EHRs is mixed. Nurses identified a number of considerations in adjusting to EHRs, such as time required for charting; time for acquiring appropriate skills and knowledge; quality of documentation; change in care, charting, and privacy related to using bedside ter-minals; technologic difficulties, including "viruses" and "worms"; and potential changes in quality of patient care.

The benefit of wide and simultaneous availability of EHRs also raises concerns related to the potential threat to privacy of health records. Unanswered questions include the following:

- Who decides which health care providers have access to information about patients?
- Should the patient have a role in determining which health care providers are entitled to access?
- Should there be a mechanism to ensure informed consent around access?
- What mechanisms should be designed for the detection and sanction of access violations, and who should perform such monitoring?

Answers to these questions have ethical and legal implications and as such should be addressed before the health care system adopts EHRs as a primary means of record keeping.

ISSUES IN THE APPLICATION OF TECHNOLOGY IN NURSING PRACTICE

A study by Cooper and Powell (1998) revealed how technology created extreme uncertainty and profound physical, emotional, psychological, and spiritual vulnerability among patients undergoing bone marrow transplantation. It was, however, nurses who attended to these vulnerabilities. The researchers observed the following about how nurses incorporated technology as part of their nursing care.

> It is no exaggeration to suggest that these nurses created a sacred space in this highly technologic enterprise for patients to do the work of making meaning of the experience. . . . One extraordinary feature of this [nursing] care resides in the fact that it occurred in the context of a highly technical endeavour. Capturing the essence of this feat, one patient insightfully asked, "How can the nurses be at the end of technology [in a spectrum of technology and care] and thank goodness they are because I'm here today because of it—and then how can they be at this touch-feel end at the same time?" (p. 65).

Ethical Dilemmas

It is the nurse who experiences firsthand the ethical dilemmas associated with new technology. Ethical and moral knowledge moves nurses to action in relation to technology. Reproductive technologies, for example, are a special concern of women, their families, and practitioners. Within nursing, there is a substantial body of work related to the ethics of reproductive technology. Availability of genetic testing requires women to examine their personal situations and beliefs to determine whether they wish to access the technology. Nurses may need to provide counselling as a woman sorts through the best decision for her. Additionally, society at large varies in its perception of the right or the need of government, resource availability, funding, and community values to influence the utilisation and distribution of technologies.

Decision Making

Decision making regarding access to available technology has further ethical implications when technology is costly or in limited supply. Who should have access? What criteria should be used? Who should develop the criteria for access? These are some issues that emerge in the face of new technology. For example, at this time, not all people who need dialysis have access to this technology. One mechanism to address determination of access under high-demand, limited-availability situations is to refer decision making to review boards. Such boards establish criteria in reviewing candidates for access to the technology. Nurses may be members of such boards, or they may be called upon to assess a patient's suitability for access to the technology. Then, too, nurses are in positions to provide information, advocacy, and emotional support to patients and families denied access to these services.

Decision-making criteria to purchase technology or make it accessible to units are also limited (Purnell, 1998). In most instances, incorporation of technology onto nursing units occurs as a consequence of criteria established by medical and, increasingly, nonnursing administrators. As nurses are "left out" of technology development, they are similarly distanced from decision making related to technology application in their workplaces.

ISSUES IN THE ALLOCATION OF TECHNOLOGY IN EDUCATION

Timothy, a nursing student in 2005, is about to graduate. Timothy thinks he is well prepared to face a work world filled with technology. Computers were commonplace in his life as a student. Nursing Informatics was a required course that he took at the beginning of his programme. He used a word processing programme to construct and format papers. He found that electronic mail with Internet access was helpful to search web sites, stay in touch with classmates, keep informed about university and faculty information, and take courses offered by WebCT. He became adept at locating information through the worldwide web and skilled at critiquing the quality of the information. Timothy's programme offered him a number of options in course delivery. His favourite course offered by WebCT was Leadership in Nursing Practice. In this course, he had to apply course concepts in an assignment that had him plan how he would introduce practitioners, not knowledgeable about computers, to their use in patient education. He participated in courses that were videoconferenced to other sites. It was enlightening to hear the perspectives of students from the North because this was one of the places Timothy was considering for his senior practicum.

The computer is a significant tool for education and practise. Brown (1992) states, "to become appropriate role models for students regarding the use of computers, faculty must integrate computers into the curriculum and demonstrate comfort and lack of fear in using them" (p. 9). It is important to define what knowledge and skills in relation to computers will be required of students in nursing programmes. It is evident that if nurse educators want students to be able to use computers in their practise, they must become proficient and comfortable with computers in their own basic programmes. Saranto and Leino-Kilpi (1997) identified the following content areas for teaching information technology: introduction to computers, skills in software application, system security, data transfer, skills in computerised patient monitoring, how to teach about hospital information systems, how to teach nursing informatics, and the teacher's role.

Extent of Computer Literacy

Computers are available in most schools of nursing, but their use is neither systematically nor routinely included in programming, unlike the situation described in the above vignette. Until recently, no programme in Canada had a required nursing informatics course. Postsecondary institutions may believe that incoming students possess the necessary computer skills because of their experience with computers in primary and secondary schools. However, empirical evidence shows that although nursing students had access to computers in primary and secondary schools, they had limited opportunity to use them for tasks other than word processing (Gassert, 1998).

Many institutions of higher learning are increasing their use of computers and other technologic innovations. In some cases, technology is being used to address the issue of increasing student numbers, multiple-site campuses, declining numbers of faculty, and limited financial resources. The potential then exists that technology will become a means to address these complex administrative problems without due consideration for maintaining educational standards and quality programming. Educational facilities need to guard against the temptation of substituting quality of instruction for increased student access and financial gain.

Options for Distance Learning

Nursing education is experiencing unprecedented changes in student characteristics. The student of the 21st century is more likely to be older, in pursuit of a second degree or career, closely linked to a community, and working to balance career and home responsibilities (Bates, 2000). These demographics are fueling the need for educational facilities to consider distance-learning options. The same can be said for providing opportunities for practicing nurses who require enhanced job skills, such as physical assessment or leadership abilities.

Technology-based pedagogy enables us to conceive of education without the restrictions of the classroom; hence, the usual mechanisms and parameters around course delivery need to be rethought. For example, traditional lectures, which often are the foundation of content delivery in higher education, become nonexistent in a learner-centred, web-based environment. In this scenario, a faculty member and student may never see each other despite having lengthy "discussions" that have the potential to shape a student's thinking for life. At the same time, nursing education values strategies that facilitate the learning of a wide range of skills. Nursing education also values knowledge that includes assessment skills, promotion of health in families, adoption of the ethical values of the profession, and communications skills.

The use of technology in nursing education is not a recent phenomenon. Advances in technology have affected the way nurses have been educated since the late 19th century (Sandelowski, 1999). Instructional technology has evolved from the use of a chalkboard and overhead projector to innovations such as computer-assisted instruction, interactive television, presentation media, electronic mail, and virtual classrooms.

Learning Distribution Systems

Four general categories of distributed learning systems in use today support instructional delivery and communication. These include (1) print, (2) audioconferencing, (3) videoconferencing, and (4) computer technology (Billings & Bachmeier, 1994).

PRINT-BASED DELIVERY

Print-based and correspondence courses rely heavily on the print medium. This approach employs prepackaged courses and self-contained learning modules. Faculty–student interaction is limited to occasional telephone contact and written feedback on submitted assignments. In recent years, distance education providers have incorporated technologic advancements such as facsimile machines, electronic mail, and assignment submissions through the Internet to supplement print-based courses. This mode of course delivery requires maintaining an expensive and extensive infrastructure. A team of instructional designers, administrators, and support staff are needed to design, manage, plan, and implement the course beyond the work of the faculty member in teaching the course.

AUDIOCONFERENCE DELIVERY

Instructional delivery has been enhanced by advancements in digitalised audio capabilities. This medium includes two-way telephone interaction between the faculty member and groups of students gathered at remote sites. Courses can be offered anywhere in the world that has telephone lines. Audioconferencing provides for real-time delivery at a fairly reasonable cost. It is ideally suited to students who cannot attend courses offered on campus or who do not have easy access to computer technology. One drawback of this method is the lack of visual stimuli to enhance the teaching–learning experience. This is especially evident for students who have been exposed to video games, television, virtual learning experiences, and other hi-tech classes with slide presentations and graphic illustrations of course materials.

VIDEOCONFERENCE DELIVERY

Interactive video networks use compressed digital video technology to deliver two-way audio signals and visual images to distant sites. Although the initial investment in videoconferencing requires an expensive technologic infrastructure, ongoing costs are usually limited to long-distance telephone charges and technical support. Student participation is encouraged through the use of multimedia presentations and interactive capabilities. Recent innovations in technology include the development of desktop video applications and simulations.

This form of delivery best approximates a face-to-face learning experience. It also permits students in remote locations to have access to faculty expertise that they may not have available in their locale. However, the expectations of this technology are often exceeded by the realities of the technical difficulties that can occur. The more complex the technology, the more complex the problems. This is one reason that more technical support is needed before and during course delivery. Preparing for a videoconference course requires considerable preliminary planning, knowledge of the technology, and the ability to problem-solve and use the available technology to its fullest. Students on the receiving end tend to feel isolated from the faculty member, which may result in a perception of substandard and unequal treatment. Extensive faculty development is needed to assist educators to use this method of teaching.

WEB-BASED DELIVERY

To participate fully in a web-based course, students must have regular access to a computer with Internet capacity. Web-based delivery allows students to engage in online interaction with the teacher and other students in a virtual learning environment. The instructional medium is through such software programmes as WebCT and Blackboard. Interaction occurs through bulletin boards, chat rooms, and e-mail. Courses can be structured as synchronous (real-time) or asynchronous (anytime) offerings. This delivery method ensures that geographic and access barriers to education are virtually eliminated. As a result of this fairly recent movement to web-based instructional technology, the issues associated with this delivery system are emphasised in the following discussion.

ISSUES IN ADOPTING TECHNOLOGY IN NURSING EDUCATION

The adoption of advanced instructional technology, like web-based delivery, has become commonplace in higher education. It has been viewed as both an educational boon and a technologic "money pit." Using advanced instructional technology in higher education challenges educators to rethink the teaching and learning enterprise.

Changing Models

In the traditional paradigm of education, the faculty member is the "sage on the stage," with lectures being the dominant teaching practise. Students are expected to listen passively and absorb large quantities of content in a single serving. This "tell 'em and test 'em" approach sees the teacher as the expert and provider of information. In a learner-centred paradigm, the principles of constructivism, that is, "a learning philosophy that focuses on the ways in which individuals come to know or understand . . ." (Wambach et al. 1999, p. 268), can be applied in a web-based course. In this constructivist paradigm, teachers facilitate the learning process and, as such, become "guides on the side" for students.

Changing Roles

The adoption of technology in education requires a paradigm shift that has a dramatic impact on the faculty and student role. The role of facilitator has been commonly used to characterise how a faculty member functions in the technology-based pedagogy (Billings, 1997). In relation to web-based instruction, specific aspects of the faculty role have been defined as assisting with access and navigation, explaining expectations for students, clarifying the faculty role, stimulating critical thinking, sharing professional expertise, and providing encouragement to online students (VandeVusse & Hanson, 2000). This shift points to the large discrepancies between necessary computer skills for future nurses and the skills possessed by faculty (Austin, 1999; Carty & Rosenfeld, 1998). How will teachers be able to assist students to develop such skills without developing the computer knowledge and skills themselves?

Carryover to Curricula

Rapid advances in the use of technology in practise has put pressure on faculty to integrate the types of technology used in health care and nursing into already "packed" undergraduate curricula. Educational programmes need to make decisions about the extent of use of technology in the delivery of programmes. Will all teachers be expected to adapt their courses or teaching strategies to include advanced instructional technologies?

Demands on Time and Career Activities

The most troublesome area for faculty is time. The use of technology can increase the amount of time needed for teaching. This takes faculty away from other aspects of their academic roles and responsibilities, such as scholarly and research activities. VandeVusse and Hanson (2000) found online courses increased faculty workload, at least in the course development phase. Link and Scholtz (2000) support the premise of allocating preparation time to allow faculty to develop and deliver online courses.

One of the greatest barriers to implementing web-based instruction in higher education is the lack of recognition it affords faculty. University environments, in particular, place a higher value on the research and scholarly achievements of faculty than on teaching and community service. Faculty who persist in incorporating advanced instructional technologies in their courses serve the curriculum in significant ways, but they do so at the risk of jeopardising their academic careers. Faculties and schools of nursing need to make decisions about the value placed on using advanced technologies in their programmes.

Gains and Losses

One of the benefits of web-based, online instruction is increased access by students who live in remote locations. For example, education becomes a reality for underrepresented populations like the aboriginal community, although the concern with this instructional medium is the loss of face-to-face contact between teacher and students and among students themselves. What becomes of the high value placed on socialisation, role modeling, and development of the student–teacher relationship? Can a chat session replace the level of dialogue and discourse that exists in a traditional classroom? It is only after these issues are resolved that faculty will feel comfortable adopting this approach on a large scale.

Effect of Advanced Instructional Technology on Career Choices

There is a call for a critical examination of the use of and growing reliance on technology in education. Mallow and Gilje (1999) caution faculty about the rapidity of adopting technology in nursing education without careful thought about its impact. They note that research to date supports the effectiveness of technology in conveying factual information, and they report student satisfaction. However, little evidence exists regarding "student progress in affective domain criteria such as outcomes related to humanism, moral knowledge development, ethical development, interdisciplinary communication, or caring attributes." Mallow and Gilje recommend that educators consider the core values and social processes of the profession before using technology in the curriculum. Faculty often struggle to balance the use of technology with the need to develop valuable working relationships with students.

In Canada, it is becoming clear that certain areas within nursing practise are "passed over" by students in favour of more technologically challenging environments. Nursing students are drawn to the "power and prestige" of technology. This was substantiated in a longitudinal study by Australian researchers (Stevens & Crouch, 1998). Of note was how nurse educators and nurses in clinical settings championed high-technology areas of nursing practise (e.g., emergency room, intensive care nursing) and created favorable technologic bias in students. The 156 students who were studied responded accordingly and, upon graduation, gravitated towards these high-technology nursing practise domains. Because of this socialisation by educators and clinicians, students valued specialised training experiences (e.g., intensive care, spinal trauma, pediatric/neonatal intensive care) over basic nursing. Students and graduate nurses in the Australian study perceived that high-technology activities attracted power, prestige, and the nod from the elite of the profession, whereas basic nursing had low status and no power and was marginalised from the profession (Stevens & Crouch, 1998, p. 14). *At issue then, is how will the new generation of computer-literate, technologically savvy nurses be attracted to and retained in low-technology practise areas such as long-term care?*

Information and instructional technologies can enhance the quality of the educational experience if used for the right purpose. The adoption of advanced technology in education does not in and of itself guarantee a positive outcome. The question that must be asked is, how can this technology contribute to the overall effectiveness of the educational process in a way that maximises student learning? Until that question is adequately addressed, educators must be cautious of wading into the technologic sea.

FUTURE OF TECHNOLOGY IN EDUCATION AND PRACTISE

Although the future is unclear, one thing is certain: technology will continue to evolve and advance. The computer has become to the Information Age what the automobile was to the Industrial Age. The Internet is accessed by millions of people daily. The explosion of a digital society has brought about significant transformations in the way people interact, access and process information, and solve problems. Health care professionals are only beginning to appreciate the impact this revolution will have on the ability to deliver comprehensive and safe care. These challenging times call for health care professionals who can think critically and adapt to change quickly.

Impact of Nursing Science on Practise Technology

The development of nursing science, that is, knowledge relevant for nursing practise, will have an impact on the development and use of technology in nursing practise. Clinical nursing information systems, for data categorisation and storage, depend on the taxonomic structures developed to reflect the phenomena of the discipline (Graves & Corcoran-Perry, 1996). If nursing science continues to be reflected in numerous classification systems, those that are selected to frame data management programmes will have their presence more strongly embedded in the discipline.

Extent of Informatics in Curricula

At this point in nursing's history, it is not surprising that there is a need for more training, support, and research for optimal utilisation of computer technology and information systems for practicing nurses, educators, and undergraduate and graduate students (Link & Scholtz, 2000; Smith et al., 1998). As the next decades unfold, improved understanding and skills among all these groups are likely, as is concurrent acceptance of advanced information technology as part of nursing. The extent of inclusion of nursing informatics within nursing undergraduate curricula is now being discussed in faculties across the country. New curricula that emerge in the coming years will incorporate decisions about this vital question. Research into the effectiveness of advanced technology in nursing education will provide valuable information in refining how we incorporate technology into delivering nursing knowledge in undergraduate programmes.

Potential for Greater Learning Access

Technology has the potential to improve access to nursing education for those for whom geography or other barriers have prevented access of a university degree. This is a particularly significant issue in Canada for students who live great distances from major cities where higher education is more likely to be located. Today's public demands education that is convenient and flexible. Moreover, in the face of busy lives, the ability to access education from home is appealing. Developments in the kind of available distance education modalities have expanded the options available and increased the quality of communication that is now possible with students who prefer to obtain degrees from their living rooms.

Faculty and student roles will change as the means of communication between faculty and students takes different forms. This can also be said about nursing practise as technology is further incorporated into the health care system. Although computer skills and knowledge will be important in the 21st century, interpersonal relations that rely on basic language and communication skills will remain significant in the provision of nursing care. Being with patients and their families can be facilitated through technologic advances, for it is the way nurses enact their knowing with patients that defines the practise. Technology facilitates and alters this but does not replace nursing knowledge about the work with patients.

Whatever technologic innovations emerge in the future, nursing must remember that technology offers the profession tools to use in its mandate to provide care to individuals and their families in illness and in health promotion. Technology is a means towards the goal of health. Thoughtful development and use can serve nursing and recipients of care well.

SUMMARY

Nursing informatics—the application of computer and information science to managing, processing, and documenting nursing data—has a profound effect on nurses and the organisations where they work. The relationship between technology and nursing is marked by tension, with technology viewed as scientific, mechanistic, and reductionistic and nursing viewed as sympathetic, humanistic, and holistic.

The advent of nursing informatics presents challenges and opportunities. The Canadian Nurses Association recognises that technology can improve health care, but technology without training and support may also impact clients, families, health care professionals, and the health system in untoward ways.

Some applications of nursing informatics are telehealth (the use of advanced telecommunications technologies to exchange health information and provide health care from vast distances), video-conferencing, remote monitoring, and electronic health records.

Challenges associated with technology include "short shifting" as real time demands replace patient care with a litany of technical tasks and a focus on outcomes (evidence), performance measurement, and technical expertise that calls for acquiring related knowledge and competence in information technology.

Applied informatics will require nurses to adhere to standards of practise, a code of ethics, provincial legislation, and competencies established by regulatory bodies. To this end, nurses will need to develop or follow telephone standards of practise, policies on providing telehealth across provinces, educational standards and credentials, provisions for maintaining privacy and confidentiality, protocols to guide decision-making and judgment, and advice on professional liability issues and employer responsibilities.

Additional challenges to nursing practise are the geographic invisibility of the client and liability for care practises—potential malpractise or misdiagnoses—delivered by distance or electronic technology. On the other hand, changes influenced by informatics will be incorporated into the health care system, offering nurses tools to use in promoting health and caring for the sick.

Benefits to practise include greater client involvement in health-seeking behaviours and health choices, possibly because electronic communication is perceived to offer privacy, immediacy, breadth of information, and different perspectives.

Additional benefits apply particularly to education. One of the benefits of web-based, online instruction is increased access by students who live in remote locations. Information previously disseminated in classroom and in textbooks and other print media is now available to students and faculty in remote locations at nontraditional times. Examples include audio-conferencing, video-conferencing, and web-based information delivery. The benefits are obvious, as are the challenges prompted by change. Faculty must clearly articulate the need for information technology in nursing curricula to ensure that all nurses have the skills needed to practise effectively. Faculty must acquire technical skills and adjust to an altered role as collaborator, facilitator, and guide.

Online RESOURCES

Add to your knowledge of this issue:

BC Health Guide, BC Ministry of Health	www.bchealthguide.org
"The Role of the Nurse in the Use of Health Care Technology": Canadian Nurses Association	www.cnanurses.ca/ frames/ policies/policiesmainframe.htm
Canadian Society of Telehealth	www.cstsct.org/
COACH—Canada's Health Informatics Association	www.coachorg.com
Office of Health and the Information Highway, Health Canada	www.hc-sc.gc.ca/ohih-bsi/ menu e.html
e-Health: "From Vision to Action," a newsletter from Office of Health and the Information Highway, Health Canada	www.hcsc.gc.ca/ohihbisi/ available/newsbull/newsbull1 e. html#ehr
The Canadian Cochrane Network and Centre	www.hiru.mcmaster.ca/cochrane/ centres/canadian/links.htm
Healthwise Incorporated	www.healthwise.org/index2.html
"Nursing Now: Issues and Trends in Canadian Nursing," "Canadian Nurses Association Telehealth: Great Potential or Risky Terrain?" Consumer and Patient Health Information Service, University of Manitoba Health Sciences Libraries	www.cnanurses.ca/pages/ issuestrends/nrgnow/ telehealth great%20potential.htm www.umanitoba.ca/ academic support/ibraries/ units/health/reference/chis.html
TETRA (Telehealth and Educational Technology Resources Agency), Faculty of Medicine, Memorial University	www.med.mun.ca/telemed/
Telehealth Association of Ontario	www.rohcg.on.ca/tao/
The Hospital for Sick Children Telehealth programme	www.sickkids.on.ca/telehealth/ default.asp
British Columbia Health Industries Network	www.hinetbc.org/telehealth/ bcprojects.html
National Nursing Informatics Project	cnanurses.ca/pages/resources/nni/ national nursing informatics project.htm
International Council of Nurses (ICN) International Classification for Nursing Practice	www.icn.ch/icnp.htm

Reflections on the Chapter

1. From your experience, give examples of the application of technology and informatics in practise.
2. How would you describe the relationships between technology, informatics, and nursing practise in these examples?
3. Identify issues related to the use of technology in your practise or in practise situations you have observed.
4. What strategies have you used or observed being used to overcome barriers to the use of technology and informatics in practise?
5. What barriers have you experienced in using technology in your nursing studies?
6. What strategies have you used or could you use to overcome these barriers?

REFERENCES

Aboriginal Nurses Association of Canada (2001). *Impact of technology on Aboriginal nursing: A discussion paper.* Ottawa, Ontario: Author.

Austin, S. I. (1999). Baccalaureate nursing faculty performance of nursing computer literacy skills and curriculum integration of these skills through teaching practice. *Journal of Nursing Education, 38*(6), 260–266.

Bates, A. W. (2000). *Managing technological change: Strategies for college and university leaders.* San Francisco: Jossey-Bass.

Billings, D. M. (1997). Issues in teaching and learning at a distance: Changing roles and responsibilities of administrators, faculty and students. *Computers in Nursing, 15*(2), 69–70.

Billings, D. M., & Bachmeier, B. (1994). Teaching and learning at a distance: a review of the nursing literature. In L. R. Allen. (Ed.) *Review of research in nursing education* (Vol. 6) (pp. 1–32). Indianapolis: Indiana University School of Nursing.

Bischoff, W. R., & Kelley, S. J. (1999). 21st Century house call: The Internet and the world wide web. *Holistic Nursing Practice, 13*(4), 42–50.

Brown, J. (1992). Nurses or technicians? The impact of technology on oncology nursing. *Canadian Oncology Nursing Journal 2*(1),12–17.

Canadian Nurses Association (1992). *The role of the nurse in the use of health care technology.* Ottawa: Author. Available on-line: http://www.cna-nurses. ca/frames/policies/policiesmainframe.htm.

Canadian Nurses Association (2000). Telehealth: Great potential or risky terrain? *Nursing Now: Issues and Trends in Canadian Nursing, 9.*

Carty, B., & Rosenfeld, P. (1998). From computer technology to information technology: Findings from a national study of nursing education. *Computers in Nursing, 16*(5), 259–265.

Cooper, M. C., & Powell, E. (1998). Technology and care in a bone marrow transplant unit: Creating and assuaging vulnerability. *Holistic Nursing Practice, 12*(4), 57–68.

Erlen, J. (1994). Technology's seductive power. *Orthopedic Nursing 13,* 50–52, 56.

Gadow, S. (1988). Covenant without cure: Letting go and holding on in chronic illness. In J. Watson & M. Ray (Eds.), *The ethics of care and the ethics of cure.* New York: National League for Nursing.

Gassert, C. A. (1998). The challenge of meeting patients' needs with a national nursing informatics agenda. *Journal of American Medical Informatics Association, 5*(3), 263–268.

Gassert, C. A. (2000). Telehealth and nursing. In B. Carty (Ed.), *Nursing informatics: Education for practice.* New York: Springer.

Graves, J. R., & Corcoran-Perry, S. (1996). The study of nursing informatics. *Holistic Nursing Practice, 11*(1), 15–24.

Hospital for Sick Children (2001). *What is tele-home-Care?* [On-line]. Available: http://www.sickkids. on.ca/telehomecare/program.asp#whatis.

Link, D. G., & Scholtz, S. M. (2000). Educational technology and the faculty role: What you don't know can hurt you. *Nurse Educator, 25*(6), 274–276.

Mallow, G. E., & Gilje, F. (1999). Technology-based nursing education: Overview and call for further dialogue. *Journal of Nursing Education, 38*(6), 248–251.

Nahm, R., & Poston, I. (2000). Measurement of the effects of an integrated, point-of-care computer system on quality of nursing documentation and patient satisfaction. *Computers in Nursing, 18*(5), 220–229.

Office of Health and the Information Highway, Health Canada (2001). *Toward electronic health records* [On-line]. Available: http://www.hc-sc.gc.ca/ohih-bsi/ehr/ehr dse/ehr dse e.html#Overview.

Purnell, M. (1998). Who really makes the bed? Uncovering technologic dissonance in nursing. *Holistic Nursing Practice, 12*(4):12–22.

Ray, M. (1987). Technological caring: A new model in critical care. *Dimensions in Critical Care Nursing, 6,* 166–173.

Reid, J. (1996). *A telemedicine primer: Understanding the issues.* Billings, Montana: Art Craft Printers.

Russo, H. (2001). Window of opportunity for home care nurses: Telehealth technologies. *Online Journal of Issues in Nursing, 6*(3). Available: Http://www.nursingworld.org/ojin/topic16/ pc16toc.htm,

Sandelowski, M. (1998). Looking to care or caring to look? Technology and the rise of spectacular nursing. *Holistic Nursing Practice, 12*(4), 1–11.

Sandelowski, M. (1999). Troubling distinctions: A semiotics of the nursing/technology relationship. *Nursing Inquiry, 6*(3), 198–207.

Sandelowski, M. (2000). Thermometers and telephones: A century of nursing and technology. *American Journal of Nursing, 100*(10), 82–85.

Saranto, K., & Leino-Kilpi, H. (1997). Computer literacy in nursing: Developing the information technology syllabus in nursing education. *Journal of Advanced Nursing, 25*(2), 377–385.

Schoenhofer, S., & Boykin, A. (1998). Discovering the value of nursing in high-technology environments: Outcomes revisited. *Holistic Nursing Practice, 12*(4):31–39.

Simpson, R. L. (1998). A few points about point-of-care technology. *Nursing Management, 29*(11), 19–22.

Simpson, R. L. (1999). The state of nursing informatics. *Nursing Administration Quarterly, 23*(3), 90–92.

Smith, C.E., Young-Cureton, V., Hooper, C., & Dearner, P. (1998). A survey of computer technology utilization in school nursing. *Journal of School Nursing, 14*(2), 27–34.

Stevens, J., & Crouch, M. (1998). Frankenstein's nurse! What are schools of nursing creating? *Collegian 5*(1), 10–15.

VandeVusse, L., & Hanson, L. (2000). Evaluation of online course discussions: Faculty facilitation of active student learning. *Computers in Nursing, 18*(4), 181–188.

Wambach, K., Boyle, D., Hagemaster, J., Teel, C., Langner, B., Fazzone, P., Connors, H., Smith, C., & Forbes, S. (1999). Beyond correspondence, video conferencing, and voice mail: Internet-based master's degree courses in nursing. *Journal of Nursing Education, 38*(6), 267–271.

White, M. H., & Dorman, S. M. (2000). Online support for caregivers: Analysis of an Internet Alzheimer mailgroup. *Computers in Nursing, 18*(4), 168–179.

14

The Realities of Canadian Nursing Research

Dorothy Pringle

Chapter Objectives

At the completion of this chapter, you will be able to:

1. Appreciate the history of nursing research in Canada.

2. Identify significant milestones in the evolution of nursing research in Canada.

3. Describe obstacles nurses and nursing have had to overcome to develop research.

4. Describe how nurses can use research in their practise.

5. Identify challenges confronting the continued development of nursing research.

6. Discuss ways in which these challenges can be overcome.

Publications, professional conferences, poster sessions, and scholarship exchanges are key ways to disseminate the nursing research findings that are central to determining what constitutes "best practice." Photographer: Beverly Anderson. Used with permission.

Research has become an important force in Canadian nursing. This has not happened quickly, and whereas the ultimate impact of research is still not clear, it has the potential to revolutionise nursing. To illuminate the impact of research in nursing, this chapter traces the evolution of nursing research in Canada, examines the influence it currently has on nursing practise and education and how it exercises that influence, and speculates on the potential influence of nursing research. The chapter also explores the contribution nursing research has made to the health of Canadians. Finally, issues involved in getting nurses to become involved in the utilisation of research and the future of nursing research in Canadian health care are discussed.

THE EVOLUTION OF NURSING RESEARCH IN CANADA

This section could easily have been called the revolution in nursing research in Canada because the last four decades of the 20th century represent no less than a revolution. Revolutions are not one-battle affairs. They are fought over time and include many skirmishes as well as a few large-scale battles. Usually, only the battles make their way into the history books. Although there were no declarations of war and no lives lost, nurse–researchers in Canada struggled to establish nursing research firmly during the second half of the century and finally achieved that status in the 1990s.

The evolution of Canadian nursing research can best be appreciated against the landscape of its counterpart in the United States. Canada followed the American model of nursing education rather than the British model in that it identified nursing education as appropriately located in universities. This does not mean that all or even most nursing education occurred there, but in Canada, from 1919 onward when the University of British Columbia commenced a programme to prepare nurses for public health, nursing was associated with universities. This was very important in the evolution of nursing research because universities are where the vast majority of health-related research occurs. Furthermore, the usual academic progression of baccalaureate to master's to doctoral education was adopted in Canadian nursing (as it was in the United States), and this set the pattern for the preparation of nurse researchers in the same mould as other academic disciplines.

In Britain, the voyage has been more difficult than in North America because of early decisions that nursing education should occur in hospitals and that specialisation should be through hospital-based certification programmes rather than through the pursuit of master's degrees. Nursing education essentially did not move to universities until the 1990s. There were exceptions, such as the University of Edinburgh, which has had a nursing programme since the 1940s, but few nurses pursued their initial nursing education through university programmes.

Publishing Nursing Research

Nursing research began in Canada in the 1920s with a focus on nursing education. However, over the next half century, only occasional studies were conducted by the few people prepared to undertake research (Ritchie, 1992). This contrasts with the United States, where nursing research began developing momentum in the 1940s and 1950s. *Nursing Research*, the first research journal in nursing, was initially published in the

United States in 1952. The first nursing research text, *Better Patient Care through Nursing Research* (Abdellah & Levine), appeared in 1965. The impetus for much *early* nursing research came from McGill University and the leadership of Dr. Moyra Allen. Dr. Allen completed her Ph.D. at Stanford University and returned to Canada and to McGill. She saw the need for a nursing research journal to serve Canadian researchers, and *Nursing Papers* was launched in 1969 with just two editions per year. In 1975, *Nursing Papers* became bilingual, publishing both French and English articles and providing abstracts of the articles in the other language. The French language name, *Perspectives en Nursing* was added (Gottlieb, 1999) at that time. It was renamed the *Canadian Journal of Nursing Research/Revue Canadienne de Recherche en Sciences Infirmiéres* in 1988. Gottlieb traced the history of this journal in the editorial that introduced the 30-year anniversary edition published in 1999. Maintaining this journal represents one of the struggles in the development of nursing research in Canada. There was never enough money, manuscripts—particularly in the early days—were hard to come by, and circulation was low. However, it was crucial and remains so for Canadian nurse researchers to have a vehicle in which to publish their work, some of which addressed topics of particular interest to the Canadian scene; for example, the 2002 report by Butler and colleagues on a workshop held to develop a national strategy for integrating supportive care in research, practise, and policy. In addition, the editorials reflected issues in Canadian health care and nursing education and what research had to bring to these issues (Gagnon, 1999). The journal remains at McGill and issues four editions a year.

Many other journals have been established in Canada since 1969, including journals that support mainly specialty fields, for example, the *Canadian Journal of Cardiovascular Nursing and Perspectives* and the *Journal of the Gerontological Nurses Association.* Several of these journals began by publishing articles about clinical practise with very little research reflected in them. This has changed over the years. They all now publish reports of research on topics relevant to practitioners in their specialty area. Most have introduced peer review, which means that the reports submitted by the researchers are reviewed by people with research expertise in that field to determine whether the research is sufficiently sound to warrant publication. The reviewers are not informed who the authors are; hence, the peer review is called a "blind" review. This prevents the reviewers from bringing a positive or negative bias coloured by any relationship they might have with the authors of the research.

Canadian researchers publish well beyond journals based in Canada and well beyond nursing journals. However, many excellent nursing research journals are now available, including *Research in Nursing & Health,* the *Journal of Nursing Scholarship* (formerly *Image*), *Qualitative Nursing Research,* and the *Western Journal of Nursing Research.* Despite the excellence of many journals and the filter of the peer-review process, the caveat "reader beware" still holds true. The consumer of research must bring a critical perspective to reading all published research to determine whether the findings of the study can or should be generalised to their own practise.

Funding of Nursing Research

Until very recently, being a nurse researcher in Canada was very difficult. The conduct of research takes funds, and funds were scarce to support the kinds of research that nurses undertook. The Medical Research Council (MRC) of Canada was launched in 1960 with a mandate to "promote, assist and undertake basic, applied and clinical research in Canada in the health sciences" (MRC Act), but because of the meagre funding available, MRC decided to limit its support to biomedical research. This did not change in any fundamental way until the mid-1990s.

The alternative major national source of funding available to nurses (and other nonbiomedical researchers) was the National Health Research and Development Program (NHRDP) of Health Canada (previously Health and Welfare Canada). Unlike MRC, which operated in an arm's-length relationship with the government and could develop its own research priorities, NHRDP was a department of the government and was expected to support research that assisted the government to meet its objectives. The size of their budgets differed enormously: although MRC had a budget of about $150 million in 1990, the budget for the NHRDP was about one tenth of that and fluctuated every year depending on the government's largesse. Because NHRDP was the major general research fund available to nurses at the national level (i.e., not limited to a specialty area), the competition was fierce and the size of the available grants limited. Grants could be as large as $300,000 for a 2-year project, but most were less than $100,000 annually.

Despite the constraints of both a limited budget and government-directed focus, NHRDP proved to be a great benefactor of nurses. Many nurses who pursued doctoral education from 1975 until 2000 received fellowships from NHRDP that supported them during their studies. These fellowships were won in national interdisciplinary competitions that demonstrated nurses' ability to compete head-on with the best candidates from other health disciplines. The scientists who gained this training went on to become some of the best researchers in the country. Academically able, they were admitted to excellent research training programmes in nursing and other disciplines in Canada and elsewhere and worked with some of the best supervisors available.

NHRDP was also a source of funding for grants needed by nurses for the actual conduct of research. Charitable organisations with special interests in particular diseases, for example, the Heart and Stroke Foundation, the Diabetes Association, and the Cancer Society, raise money to support research into those diseases. Many tended to favour biomedical research because of its orientation to seek cures rather than research focussed on caring for individuals with the disease. However, some nurses were successful in receiving grants from competitions held by these organisations and built important research programmes based on this funding. Fortunately, the policies of many of these foundations evolved over the years, and nursing research is now part of the range of studies funded by them.

Because of the very limited funding available at the national level, the Canadian Nurses Foundation (CNF) was established by the Canadian Nurses Association (CNA) in 1962 initially to provide support for nurses studying at the master's and doctoral levels. (See Ritchie [1992] for a description of the development of the CNF.) In 1984, small grants for the conduct of research were added. As with many nursing-based endeavours, CNF has struggled since its inception to secure sufficient funds to keep itself in business. Much of its support has come from donations from nurse researchers themselves. In the days before NHRDP and MRC funding, CNF was frequently the sole resource nurses could turn to. Even today, CNF will fund studies that address uniquely nursing topics that would not likely be successful in interdisciplinary competitions. The investigation of nursing-specific themes, such as the nature of the nurse–patient relationship, are appreciated as vital to understanding nursing as a discipline in peer-review committees dominated by nurses. This is not necessarily true of interdisciplinary committees unless a strong nursing research advocate is a member of the committee. In 2002, CNF entered into a partnership with the Canadian Health Services Research Foundation (described later) to increase their resources substantially.

For the first time in its history, the funding future looks secure, and CNF will be able to support substantially more graduate fellowships at higher dollar levels and provide larger grants to support research projects.

The Social Sciences and Humanities Research Council of Canada (SSHRC) has been and continues to be an important source of funding for many nurse researchers. SSHRC is a national foundation, established in 1977 on the same basis as MRC, that is, arm's length from government. (The third national body in Canada that makes up the research funding triumvirate is the Natural Sciences and Engineering Research Council, or NSERC.) SSHRC also derives its funding from the federal government but always has had a substantially smaller budget than MRC. In 2001–02, its budget was $156.5 million. In contrast, the successor to MRC, the Canadian Institutes of Health Research (CIHR), has a budget of $560 million for this same year. As its name suggests, SSHRC funds research that examines questions relevant to the social, cultural, and economic dimensions of life. For many qualitative nurse researchers and those interested in ethical, historical, and psychosocial dimensions of nursing, SSHRC is a major source of funding. The peer-review committees understand and value qualitative methods to address questions and have expertise in content areas relevant to nursing. Nurses also have received doctoral fellowship support from SSHRC. However, the size of the overall budget dictates that most SSHRC grants are relatively modest in comparison to those available from MRC and CIHR.

Some provincial granting bodies have a tradition of providing funds to nursing research, for example, the Fonds de Researche Scientifique du Québec (FRSQ), the British Columbia Health Research Foundation, and the Ministry of Health of Ontario. The Ontario programme, which was an enormous contributor to nursing research in the 1980s and early 1990s (O'Connor & Bouchard, 1991), is no longer in operation, whereas the British Columbia Foundation was replaced by the Michael Smith Foundation for Health Research (MSFHR) in 2001 to honour British Columbia's first Nobel Prize winner.

In 1980, Alberta was enjoying a booming economy, and the government decided to invest some of the money not needed for current provincial needs into the Alberta Heritage Foundation for Medical Research (AHFMR). A $300 million endowment was created to fund basic biomedical and medical research. New research positions were created, and new competitions for doctoral and postdoctoral training were initiated. Nurses in the province objected, and after a major initiative led by Dr. Shirley Stinson of the University of Alberta, the Alberta Nursing Research Foundation (ANRF) was established in 1982 and provided with an expendable $1 million yearly budget. This contrasted with the large endowment provided for biomedical research but nevertheless was a breakthrough for nursing research in Canada.

The ANRF was certainly welcomed by nurse researchers in the province, but the fund was too limited to award large grants, for example, more than $100,000 per year for several years. Furthermore, it separated nursing from the more intense interdisciplinary competitions that one finds at the national level. Provincial competitions are good training grounds for learning to write strong, coherent grant applications that will survive and be successful at the national level. The Nursing Research Foundation was terminated in 1994. Again, Alberta nurses successfully mounted a campaign, and AHFMR expanded its mandate to include nursing research and nurse researchers among those eligible to compete for their funds. Since then, nurses have successfully competed for grants, doctoral and postdoctoral training awards, and research scholar awards to support young investigators. In fact, AHFMR has become a major source of support for nurse researchers in Alberta and a model of an innovative granting body for the rest of the country.

At the national level, a lot happened in the 1990s. The Canadian Health Services Research Foundation (CHSRF) was established in 1997 with an initial endowment of $66.5 million that was increased by an additional $60 million in 1999. Its mandate is to fund research on health services management and policy. In 1999, as a result of successful lobbying of Health Canada by the CNA, $25 million was allocated to CHSRF for the funding of nursing research over a 10-year period. CHSRF was the recipient of the funds because the CNA argued that workplace difficulties and workforce shortages were at crisis levels in Canada and required serious research attention. The agreement between Health Canada and CHSRF specified that $500,000 per year was to be spent on clinical research, whereas the rest was to go to health services and policy research relevant to nursing. CHSRF and CNF have developed the Nursing Care Partnership Fund for the administration of the clinical research dollars.

Almost simultaneously with the CHSRF developments, MRC—led by Dr. Henry Friesen—undertook a national study that resulted in a reinterpretation of its mandate to embrace all types of research. New peer-review committees were developed, and nurses and researchers from other disciplines, such as occupational and physical therapy, epidemiology, and family medicine, were able to compete. This was followed quickly by a redevelopment of the entire health research enterprise. The CIHR was approved by the government of Canada in June 2000. MRC and NHRDP, as such, ceased to exist, and CIHR became the depository for most health research funding.

Thirteen "virtual" interdisciplinary institutes were created to represent such diverse areas of science as genetics, aging, cancer, aboriginal health, and gender and health. Each institute reflects four pillars or types of research: basic biomedical, clinical, health services, and population health. A scientific director heads each institute and is assisted by an advisory board. CIHR started with a budget of $475 million, which increased to $560 million in the second year of operation. The target is to achieve $1 billion in funding annually by 2006.

Nurses are an integral part of CIHR. Dr. Denise Alcock, the Dean of Health Sciences at the University of Ottawa and the former Director of the School of Nursing, is a member of the Council, which is the policymaking body of CIHR. A nurse scientist, Dr. Miriam Stewart, is the scientific director of the Institute of Gender and Health, and another nurse, Earl Nowgesic, is the assistant director of the Institute of Aboriginal Health. There are nurses on most Institute Advisory Boards, and nurses sit on all the appropriate peer-review committees. They chair some committees and serve as scientific officers on others. Nurse researchers can now compete for much larger grants and take their place alongside scientists from all other disciplines.

The structure of CIHR was not what nursing had hoped for. Given the frustration created by MRC's exclusion of nursing research for so many years and the very tentative steps to include an applied research agenda in the 1990s, nursing had hoped that the new approach to research funding would include an institute for nursing research. However, very early in its development, CIHR embraced a strictly interdisciplinary agenda and declared that no institute would be disciplinary based. Despite this assertion, the Canadian Association of University Schools of Nursing (CAUSN) and the Canadian Association of Nurse Researchers (CANR) mounted a campaign for a nursing-specific institute. The two organisations successfully competed for funds from SSHRC and CHSRF to undertake a planning exercise for a new institute. Representatives met and debated the relative advantages of advocating for a nursing research institute versus a nursing and caregiving research institute. The latter was seen to accommodate an interdisciplinary thrust while acknowledging nursing as the lead discipline. The decision was made to go with the latter, and a proposal for such an institute was developed and submitted to the CIHR interim council, which acted as a planning committee. The application was not successful.

In the United States, nursing research has had a different history. After many years of concerted and well-coordinated lobbying by nurses, a National Center for Nursing Research was created in 1985 as part of the National Institutes of Health (NIH). The centre was elevated to the status of a National Institute of Nursing Research (NINR) in 1992. The American National Institutes of Health are organised very differently than their Canadian counterparts in that they have dedicated buildings, they conduct research within the institutes (intramural research), and they mount competitions for researchers to apply for funds (extramural research). They also have relatively large budgets, many in the billions of dollars, compared with Canada. NINR's autonomy and resources (a budget of $69,600 million in the U.S. in 1999) mean that American nurses are able to identify areas of particular interest to nursing or areas that require special attention and establish special competitions (in addition to their regular competitions) to drive research into them. For example, they have identified low-birth-weight infants, vulnerable populations, and people with HIV/AIDS as requiring specific nursing research attention.

Canadian nursing cannot do this under the CIHR structure and must seek other routes to gain attention for special needs areas. This battle for the recognition of nursing research is not over. Nurses are well positioned within the CIHR, and there is no reason to believe that individual nurse researchers will not do well in competitions for grant support. However, the discipline has yet to develop strategies for working with the various institutes so that nursing is heard when new initiatives are required to understand issues and problems that are either unique to nursing or in which nurses play a major role.

Preparation of Nurse Researchers

The conduct of nursing research depends on having well-prepared researchers. This requires programmes of study and funds for students while they study. Preparation at the doctoral level is seen as necessary for most people to undertake the role of principal investigator, the person who takes major responsibility for designing and managing research studies. Canada was late to develop doctoral programmes in nursing relative to other countries. Our first programmes occurred in the early 1990s, whereas the United States already had four doctoral programmes by 1975. By 1990, the United States had 45 programmes. Finland, Japan, Korea, and Thailand all had doctoral programmes in nursing by 1990.

In the mid-1980s, McGill University, followed closely by the University of Alberta, began to plan in earnest for doctoral programmes in nursing. In the case of McGill, the governing body of the faculty of medicine—of which the School of Nursing was a department—challenged the plan. The faculty of medicine did not think that nursing had demonstrated sufficient resources or a sufficient body of knowledge to justify a Ph.D. degree in the discipline. The faculty of nursing at the University of Alberta saw their programme approved at the university level, but the government was not prepared to provide funding for it. The faculty decided that it should not try to mount the programme in the absence of funds; essentially, they determined that if the doctoral programme could be mounted without additional government funding, even if it was difficult, the government would never provide the funds.

Both programmes went on hold while these internal and external political situations were resolved. However, both McGill and the University of Alberta had provisions within the universities that made it possible to admit individual students to studies in areas in which doctoral programmes were planned. Both nursing schools used these provisions to admit nurses to *ad hoc* studies, and several nurses were able to complete the requirements for a Ph.D. in nursing before formal programmes were established. This included Dr. Francine Ducharme, the first person to complete a Ph.D. in nursing in Canada. Dr. Ducharme completed her doctoral programme at McGill University.

After intensely lobbying the government, the University of Alberta received funding to begin a doctoral programme in nursing in 1991. The University of Toronto followed, as did the University of British Columbia in 1993. McMaster University and a joint bilingual McGill University–University of Montreal began programmes in 1994. These programmes started with small enrolments of between 3 and 5 students. By the year 2000, the programmes had grown, admitting 10 to 15 new students each year. Additional programmes have been added. The University of Calgary began a nursing Ph.D. programme, and a few universities either developed interdisciplinary programmes in which nursing participated, for example, the University of Victoria, or admitted individual students to study with specific supervisors, for example, the Universities of Saskatchewan and Manitoba. Dalhousie University, the University of Ottawa, and the University of Western Ontario are well advanced in their planning to offer doctoral programmes starting in 2003.

The graduates of these early programmes are becoming the major Canadian nurse researchers of the early 21st century. Dr. Ducharme holds the endowed Chair in Gerontological Nursing Research at the University of Montreal. Dr. Bonnie Stevens, another graduate of the *ad hoc* doctoral programme at McGill, holds the Signy Hildur Eaton Chair in Pediatric Nursing Research at the Hospital for Sick Children at the University of Toronto. Dr. Joan Bottorff, a graduate of the University of Alberta *ad hoc* programme, holds an NHRDP research scholar award, and Dr. Carole Estabrooks, another Alberta graduate, is a CIHR/MRC Health Scholar and an AHFMR Population Health Investigator, and she directs the Centre for Knowledge Transfer at the same university.

Like everything else in the establishment of the nursing research enterprise in Canada, the mounting of doctoral programmes did not come easily. Nursing had to prove itself once again as a legitimate academic field of study in several of the universities. Only a few faculties and schools actually received additional funding to support these programmes, and the rest stretched their budgets to include this new resource-intensive activity. Now this most important battle may be declared won.

These programmes provide the infrastructure for the continued production of researchers without which all the other elements of the conduct of research could not proceed. Furthermore, after 10 years of experience, a clearly Canadian model of the Ph.D. degree in nursing has emerged. Canadian programmes require only a few courses, four to five on average, including a course on the philosophic underpinning of science, in general, and nursing science, in particular, one or two research design and statistics courses and one or two courses on theories and content specific to the students' research. The dissertations are a very large component of the programmes and are begun immediately upon entering the programme. The dissertations are substantial in scope, and the supervisory committee is usually interdisciplinary in composition.

This model contrasts markedly with the design of doctoral programmes in the United States, which include a large number of courses, usually around 20, a smaller dissertation which the doctoral candidate does not begin until much of the course work is completed, and a supervisory committee composed largely of nurse scientists. In Britain, there is usually no required course work, and the entire focus of the Ph.D.

degree programme is on the conduct of the research, which is supervised by one individual.

All of these models are consistent with the approach to doctoral work in general in their host countries. One design is not superior to another, but they do tend to produce researchers with somewhat different strengths. Graduates of Canadian programmes have strong research design skills and an appreciation of what other disciplines bring to the conduct of research even when that research is focussed on answering questions relevant to nursing. This is an important orientation—given the strong interdisciplinary bent of the national funding agencies.

Funding to support nursing doctoral students has not proved as buoyant as the programmes themselves. The absence of a specific source of funds for nurses is felt every time CIHR releases the list of successful candidates for doctoral fellowships. There is an enormous demand for doctoral support, and CIHR funds fewer than 20% of the applications it receives. The limited access to funds means that many doctoral students work full- or part-time throughout their programmes. This tends to slow their progress and creates a great burden on the individual who may be raising a family at the same time. This is a continuing struggle and one that requires creative solutions by nursing agencies.

Although completion of a doctoral programme was sufficient to commence a research career until recently, it is increasingly common for graduates to undertake 2 to 3 years of postdoctoral studies before accepting an academic or research position. The graduates of Canadian nursing Ph.D. programmes have achieved a high level of success in national and provincial competitions for funding to support their postdoctoral work. Most Canadian funding sources require candidates to change their locations and their supervisors to get the maximum benefit from further studies. Postdoctoral work is intended to turn young researchers into independent researchers and render them competitive for grants, which Ph.D. studies alone sometimes cannot or do not do.

Research takes time: time to undertake the review of the current state of knowledge in the area of interest; time to assemble a research team and to meet with them; time to determine the most appropriate design, data gathering approach, and measurement instruments; time to figure out the data analysis strategies; and time to write the grant and get ethics approval. Because it is so time intensive, research frequently is relegated to second or third place behind other responsibilities. Nurses in academic settings find themselves with heavy teaching loads, which requires them to fit research into weekends and evenings. Similar dilemmas are faced by administrators and clinical nurse specialists, who have heavy demands on their time but are expected and encouraged to do research. One way of managing this is for the researcher to apply for a "personnel award." These awards have a number of different titles depending on the granting agency and the stage of the individual's career: research scholar, career scientist, scientist, and national scientist, among others. Personnel awards provide the researchers' employers with at least half of the researcher's salary, with an expectation that 75% of the person's time can be spent on research.

These awards are very important, particularly to young scientists who are just launching their independent research careers. As noted earlier, because MRC and most disease-related funding charities did not support nurses, they were dependent on NHRDP and a few provincial funding agencies for personnel awards. In the 1970s, Dr. Moyra Allen at McGill won an NHRDP National Health Scientist award to study the health-promoting activities nurses undertook at the nursing-run Health Station in Montreal. A few other nurses were awarded NHRDP research scholar funding. In the 1970s, awards were granted to Dr. Shirley Stinson of the University of Alberta and Dr.

Jacqueline Chapman at the University of Toronto; in the 1980s, awards went to Dr. Sharon Ogden Burke at Queen's University, Dr. Gina Browne at McMaster University, Dr. Joan Anderson at the University of British Columbia, and Dr. Janice Morse at the University of Alberta. These were important breakthroughs for nursing as a discipline, but they were too few to move the development of nursing science ahead at a pace that reflected the size of the profession. Much more was needed, particularly to assist young investigators to launch their research careers.

Dr. Ginette Rodger was executive director of the Canadian Nurses Association in the 1980s and in 1986 was appointed to the MRC Council. Only one nurse before her, Dr. Dorothy Kergin, then the director of the McMaster University School of Nursing had ever sat on the decision-making body of MRC. Dr. Rodger used this opportunity to encourage MRC to work with NHRDP to create a new set of research scholar awards for nurses only. After huge initial resistance, the agencies capitulated, and the Joint MRC/NHRDP Research Scholar awards were launched in 1988. Schools of nursing had to compete for these awards on behalf of their best young researchers. The programme got off to a rather slow start, but over the subsequent 7 years of its existence, 15 nurse researchers from eight universities received 5-year awards. (The 15 included Drs. Hilary Llewellyn-Thomas and Diane Irvine, University of Toronto; Annette O'Connor, University of Ottawa; Celeste Johnston, McGill University; Louise Levesque, Francine Ducharme, Lise Talbot, and Sylvie Robichaud; University of Montreal; Lesley Degner, and Linda Kristjanson, University of Manitoba; Sharon Ogden Burke and Carol Roberts, Queen's University; Marilyn Ford-Gilboe and Helene Berman, University of Western Ontario; and Janice Morse, University of Alberta.) Building on their earlier successes, some went on to compete for and receive NHRDP research scholar awards for another 5 years. These awardees, with few exceptions, have become leaders in nursing research in Canada.

Nurse researchers now compete for CIHR personnel awards along with all the best scientists from other health disciplines. They are enjoying a reasonable level of success. Is this another battle won in the road to research respectability and achievement or one that is still in progress? CIHR is still too new to be able to draw any definitive conclusions about whether nurses can continue to rely on it as a major source of support for funding that will allow them to devote a significant portion of their time to research. Although the absence of NHRDP as a consistent funding source is felt, several provincial governments offer competitions for these types of awards (Ontario, Alberta, Quebec), and nurse researchers have done well in them.

Research chairs are now a major resource on the national scene. There have been research chairs for many years, but the 1990s saw an avalanche of new chairs become available. The creation of named chairs became a popular fund-raising target for universities and hospitals. Dr. Ellen Hodnett assumed the first endowed research chair in nursing in Canada, the Heather M. Reisman Chair in Perinatal Nursing Research, a joint chair between Mt. Sinai Hospital and the University of Toronto. The Canadian Health Services Research Foundation (CHSRF) added five more nursing chairs in 2000. These chairs are not endowed but will support the incumbents for 10 years. Research chairs are filled by researchers who have international reputations for their work and who have made outstanding contributions to specific fields of knowledge. At the beginning of the 21st century, the number of newly endowed chairs is outstripping the number of senior nurse researchers available to fill them. The University of Toronto and its teaching hospitals alone have five endowed nursing research chairs they have been unable to fill. This is a new phenomenon for nursing (i.e., to have more resources than it is able to absorb), and it puts pressure on the discipline to continue to support young investigators, protect their time, and assist them to develop the reputations that will make them eligible to assume chairs in the future.

A final indicator of the maturing of nursing research in Canada is reflected in the amount of funding nurses are receiving to conduct their research. CAUSN compiled the research funding received by nurses as principal or co-investigators on grants throughout the 1980s, and O'Connor and Bouchard (1991) published the CAUSN results for the 1988–89 academic year. In total, nurses had received $4,491,000. Close to $3 million of these funds were received by universities in Ontario. Ten years later, in 1998, the total amount of grant money for research on which nurses were either principal or co-investigators essentially doubled to $8,584,611 (Table 14.1).

What followed over the next 3 years was an almost exponential growth in funding: $14,390,303 in 1999, $19,323,971 in 2000, reaching an all time high of $27,528,277 in 2001 (CAUSN, 2002). This escalating growth is attributable to both an increased number of nurses conducting research and an increase in the amount of funding available to do the work. By 1998, the first graduates of the Canadian doctoral programmes in nursing were applying for grants. The beginning productivity of this new stream of researchers bodes well for the future of research. Nurses are now successfully competing for funds provincially, nationally, and internationally. Several Canadian nurses (Dr. Janice Morse, University of Alberta, and Drs. Bonnie Stevens, Ellen Hodnett, and Souraya Sidani, University of Toronto) hold, or have held, NINR grants worth millions of dollars because they have been able to demonstrate that there is no one in the United States who can mount the same research as they are proposing.

INFLUENCE OF RESEARCH ON NURSING PRACTISE AND EDUCATION

After touring the status of historical and current nursing research in Canada, one is likely to ask what nursing research is and where it fits into the spectrum of human sciences research.

Research, and especially research in a profession like nursing, is a service to the people who require the assistance of nurses and to the health care providers, especially nurses, who provide that assistance. Some disciplines can investigate phenom-

Table 14.1 Summary of Research Funding by Region in Canada, 1998–2001

AMOUNT OF RESEARCH FUNDING ($)

REGION	1998	1999	2000	2001
Western Canada	2,041,378	4,127,076	5,585,288	11,433,161
Ontario	5,225,348	8,441,655	10,969,440	13,537,441
Quebec	203,454	172,245	467,328	721,818
Atlantic Canada	1,114,432	1,649,327	2,301,915	1,835,857
Total Canada	**8,584,612**	**14,390,303**	**19,323,971**	**27,528,277**

Source: Canadian Association of University Schools of Nursing, as of March 9, 2002.

ena simply to satisfy the curiosity of the investigators. Nurses do not enjoy that luxury. It should always be possible to explain the relevance of each research study that is undertaken.

Defining nursing research rather precisely occupied nurse researchers for several decades in the last century, but this question receives little attention now, and there is little angst about the answers. Bloch (1981) developed a model of nursing research and nursing science which nicely locates these within the larger landscape of science. She describes a communal pool of what she calls "fundamental research" to which researchers of all disciplines contribute. This pool includes knowledge about life, health, and disease. Before this knowledge can be applied directly in practise, it must first be translated into a series of interventions. Nursing develops its interventions based on this fundamental knowledge, as do all other applied disciplines, such as psychology and medicine. An important message in Bloch's perspective is that nursing must draw on knowledge developed by many other disciplines to develop interventions that are unique to its practise. These interventions are tested, and their results, taken together, form nursing science or the science of nursing practise. Nurse researchers have a responsibility to contribute to the pool of fundamental knowledge as well as to address questions that affect nursing practise. This perspective does not preclude researchers from other disciplines undertaking research on nursing practise problems.

The reality is that in addition to research that is of particular interest to nurses, nurse researchers work on many studies that do not directly impinge on nursing practise but to which they bring expertise that benefits the study. A good example of this is found in the work of Dr. Ellen Hodnett. The focus of her research is care of mothers and families during labour and delivery, particularly the benefits of one-to-one supportive care by nurses. However, Dr. Hodnett is part of a team of researchers that includes obstetricians, pediatricians, epidemiologists, and statisticians who study a whole range of issues related to perinatal care of women. Among many others, she was a co-investigator on a large international trial that investigated breech positions of babies and whether allowing breech deliveries or intervening with cesarean sections was more beneficial to the mothers and babies (Hannah et al., 2000). Clearly, nurses do not make decisions about cesarean sections, but they are parts of teams that make those decisions, and they need to understand the nature of the issues that drive decisions one way or the other. Furthermore, the care of women during the long difficult labour when a breech presentation is involved is of significant importance to nurses. Dr. Hodnett brought her deep understanding of perinatal care and her skill in designing multisite international randomised clinical trials to the team. The outcome of this particular study was interesting. The trial was terminated early because the evidence for both mothers and babies was overwhelmingly in favour of intervening and delivering the babies by cesarean section rather than letting the labour proceed to a vaginal delivery. This was not an outcome that the investigator team had predicted (Hannah et al., 2000).

Influence on Practise

Throughout the 1970s and part of the 1980s, much was made of nurses delivering theory-based practise. This referred most frequently to the grand theories that a number of nurses had developed to understand and explain patient behaviours and the relationships between what nurses did and the responses of patients to these interventions. Among these were King's Interacting Systems Framework, Rogers' Science of Unitary Human Beings, and Neuman's Systems Model (Fawcett, 1989). The term *the-*

ory-based practise is rarely heard now because the era of *evidence-based practise* has replaced it.

Evidence-based practise, which is sometimes referred to as *best practise*, means that the type of care delivered (or in health-promotion arenas, the health-promotion strategy used) is based on the best research evidence about that practise integrated with knowledge about the patient's preferences, culture, emotional status, information needs, and unique physiologic responses among other things.

Research is now regarded as central to the determination of what constitutes best practise. Basing care on research evidence was not possible until recently because there was simply not enough research available in most areas of nursing practise to influence the decision. This is still the case in some areas of nursing practise, such as the care of patients with dementia or chronic psychiatric disorders. Nevertheless, the evidence is mounting, and increasingly nurses can turn to research studies to help them determine what is best for individual patients or classes of patients; for example, patients being supported by mechanical ventilation or recovering from coronary artery bypass surgery. This represents a significant change in how nurses approach patient care and will change the view that nurses turn to each other rather than the research literature to answer questions about what is the most current thinking on the care of patients with specific problems.

One research study in an area tells us something about that area but is rarely sufficient in scope or size to support a change in practise. An exception might be a large, multisite, randomised control trial with thousands of patients enrolled, such as the study on breech births referred to earlier. Clinicians seek out a series of studies that focus on a specific type of practise, but this requires a method for integrating the findings from across the studies so that a determination can be made of what the true conclusion is. Two approaches are used: systematic reviews and metaanalysis. In *systematic reviews* (sometimes called *integrated reviews*), all the studies that bear on a topic are retrieved from published and unpublished sources, the individual studies are assessed for their methodologic quality, and then the findings from all the studies, taking into account the quality of the research, are examined to reach a decision on what is the state of knowledge on that topic (Mulrow & Cook, 1998). If possible, a recommendation is made to change practise. However, if the evidence is conflicted or the quality of the studies is poor, then a recommendation for further research is made specifying the questions it must address and the designs needed before a conclusion can be reached.

A *metaanalysis* takes the systematic review a step further and integrates the actual data from all the studies to reach a statistical decision about whether a particular intervention improves outcomes. This is reported in the form of an odds ratio or an effect size, depending on whether the data are continuous or dichotomous (Lau et al., 1998). This latter technique is applied mainly to analysis of findings from randomised controlled trials. Systematic reviews and metaanalyses are now commonly found in journals, and the Cochrane Library provides metaanalyses on a wide range of topics, including many that are relevant to nursing. These analyses are updated regularly as new research is published.

It is a common misconception that systematic reviews can be undertaken only on experimental research and that the randomised controlled analysis is the gold standard for all research (Jennings, 2000; Petticrew, 2001). Nursing research includes an increasing number of randomised controlled trials, but much of nursing practise does not lend itself to experimental treatment. Nursing relies heavily on qualitative research to help understand phenomena from the perspective of the patient; furthermore, interventions that include a strong interpersonal component are difficult to subject to the methodology of randomised controlled analysis. Nevertheless, nurses need to know what the state of knowledge is in the range of patient care issues that confront them. Systematic reviews provide a method for summarising the state of knowledge across the range of research methods used to address nursing research questions (Petticrew, 2001).

Conclusions from systematic reviews and metaanalyses frequently are integrated into clinical practise guidelines or care maps for patients who share a common diagnosis or clinical condition. Most of these guidelines are interdisciplinary in nature and provide the type and timing of tests, interventions, and medications across all the disciplines providing patient care.

The development of electronic databases has made the search for and location of research studies and systematic reviews immensely easier. Access to these databases in all hospital libraries and frequently through computers located on hospital patient care units or public health units has provided nurses with access to findings from research never before possible. As well, there are Internet websites that house clinical practise guidelines that teams of practitioners can access rather than having to start from scratch every time to develop their own. In practise, however, most teams find it difficult to incorporate other teams' guidelines without studying the issues, reading the original research or at least the systematic reviews, and finally adapting the guidelines to their own environments and patient populations.

As hard as it is to believe, doing the research and accessing the research reports, the systematic reviews, the metaanalyses, and clinical practise guidelines on patient care units are the easy parts of evidence-based practise. The difficult part is getting the individual practitioner—whether that person is a nurse, physician, or physical therapist—actually to change her or his practise to conform to the evidence. There is a huge gap between what is known as a result of research and its application in patient care. Research utilisation is a developing area of science, and Canadian nurse researchers, in particular Dr. Carole Estabrooks at the University of Alberta Faculty of Nursing, are taking a lead in explicating the factors that influence health professionals to use or ignore research findings in their practise. It seems that simply knowing what works best does not necessarily lead to practising on the basis of that knowledge. The issue is change and the difficulty in getting individual nurses and teams of nurses to become informed about research, give up their usual practise, and adopt new methods.

Several theories have been developed to try to guide research utilisation. The difficulty with many of them is their linearity (Kitson et al., 1998); that is, there are a series of steps that if followed in a simple straightforward manner will result in practise changes. The reality is quite different. Kitson and co-workers have proposed a conceptual framework that acknowledges how messy and complex the process is. Their framework for implementing research in practise explicates the formula: SI = f (E,C,F); that is, **S**uccessful **I**mplementation is a **F**unction of **E**vidence, **C**ontext, and **F**acilitation. Rather than treating this as a linear formula, the elements of evidence, the environment, and the presence of a facilitator whose role it is to make things easier for those being asked to change are considered simultaneously. Each of these components has several dimensions:

- Evidence includes research, clinical expertise, and patient choice.
- Environment incorporates an understanding of the culture, human relationships as explicated in leadership roles, and how the organisation measures its system and service performance.
- Facilitation involves determining how the facilitator uses interpersonal and group skills to influence change.

In this framework, each of the elements is assessed along a continuum (high to low). Depending on how the three elements are assessed, the facilitation approach changes (Kitson et al., 1998).

None of the research utilisation theories guarantees successful change to best practise; however, the theories represent the state of the art of our understanding about how to bring about practise changes early in our experience. Clearly, this is an area of great potential for future development, but the patients and the practitioners cannot wait until the "right" theory comes along that will guide change with more predictable results. The facilitators, nurse educators, and clinical leaders must use the theories and frameworks available now to approach research utilisation in as systematic a way as the theories allow.

A second force for research on the horizon is an increasingly better educated nursing workforce. Research will increasingly influence the way nurses practise as more nurses are educated to read research with authority, to conduct systematic reviews, and to seek out research as their first resource when trying to answer practise questions.

So far, this discussion on evidence-based practise has skirted the question on how much research actually influences current practise because the question cannot be answered definitively. In some settings, most frequently the highly specialised areas of practise like intensive care units, coronary care units, and transplantation units, clinical practise guidelines that incorporate best practises are widely used. Nurses in these units are challenging long-standing practises, such as the routine introduction of saline solution into artificial airways to facilitate suctioning of mucus. A number of well-designed studies demonstrate that saline solution does not necessarily improve suctioning and may harm the patient (Druding, 1997). In other units, the concept of best practise has not yet been discovered let alone incorporated into daily life. This will not continue for long. Nursing in Canada is in the very early days of research production and utilisation. Nursing practise will be influenced and changed as more nurses are educated to use research and as more nurses attend conferences in their specialty areas and hear presentations on research on common practises. Nursing practise will be influenced and changed as more nurses read their specialty journals and encounter not "let me tell you how we do it on our unit" articles but articles describing why questions were raised about a nursing practise and how research was conducted to answer those questions. Nursing practise will be influenced and changed as nurses change employment and move from units or organisations that operate on best-practise principles to ones that do not. It is possible to predict that by the end of the first decade of the 21st century, nursing practise will be greatly influenced by research. The term *best practise* may not be heard very commonly then because it will be so embedded in the daily life of nurses as not to require comment or attention.

Influence on Education

Nursing education has been profoundly affected by the development of research in terms of what is taught and who teaches it. Forty years ago, faculty members in university programmes were educated at the baccalaureate or master's levels, and teachers in diploma programmes themselves had only diplomas or baccalaureate degrees. Research had little presence in the programmes by virtue of the fact that little existed. Textbooks were the cornerstone of course work. In the 21st century, this has changed dramatically. Most university professors of nursing now hold a Ph.D., and the minimum preparation found throughout nursing education programmes is the master's degree. These are not just paper qualifications. They mean that the faculty in nursing programmes are both educators and researchers. This profoundly changes teaching.

The journal replaces the textbook as the source of knowledge. Students are guided to use the journal collection as their major resource. Increasingly, the assigned readings for courses are collections of research articles assembled and printed, in accord with Canadian copyright laws, and sold to students. Course content focusses on findings from research on the topic. Faculty members bring their own research into the classrooms to teach the content students are to acquire. If courses in the 21st century are taught the same way as they were even 10 years earlier, they are not reflecting the changes in knowledge nor the source of knowledge.

In larger research-intensive university programmes, opportunities are available to undergraduate students to work as research assistants on research projects throughout their education. This frequently serves as an incentive for these students to pursue graduate education immediately to acquire the research skills that will allow them to become principal investigators. They get bitten by the research bug, and they want to do it all.

Nursing is still struggling with how to make research an attractive and attainable career goal for an increased number of students entering the profession. Most students enter nursing to realise their desire to care for people who are ill. In the course of their studies, they find that many different career paths are available to them. If they are exposed to research and have the opportunity to participate actively in it, they come to see research as a possible future.

In schools of nursing with master's and doctoral programmes, undergraduate nursing students are exposed to graduate-level students in those programmes. The students interact in their roles as teaching assistants or in social encounters. This makes graduate education very real and attainable. If undergraduate students are not in a research-intensive environment, then faculty members have to use imaginative ways of making research live for the students. It may mean attending research days at other universities when faculty and graduate student research is presented or having researchers or doctoral students come and meet with students, present their work in interactive seminars, and discuss the realities of research careers. Students need encouragement to see graduate school as a logical step in their career plans. They also need tangible financial support to be able to pursue their education. Students who are excited by the possibilities of research, who in the course of their studies raise questions that have been investigated or can be investigated using research methods, and who challenge current practise are excellent candidates for future research careers in nursing.

CONTRIBUTION OF NURSING RESEARCH TO THE HEALTH AND HEALTH CARE OF CANADIANS

It would be very nice if the contributions of nursing research to Canadians' health could be numbered and neatly listed. It is not that simple. Nursing research has contributed in many different ways to Canadian's health and health care, but the nature of the research undertaken by nurses does not usually result in products like the identification of the gene for multiple dystrophy, the discovery of insulin, or the development of pablum—all the outcomes of medical research by Canadian scientists. Instead, nursing research has helped us to understand how parents manage multiple encounters with the health care system when they have a chronically ill child (Burke et al., 1991), how pain is experienced by premature infants in pediatric intensive care units (Stevens & Johnston, 1994; Stevens et al., 1994), how chronic illness is experienced and how people change their lives to cope with it (Paterson, 2001; Thorne & Paterson, 2001), how patients are comforted during painful treatments in the emergency rooms (Morse & Proctor, 1998), and how patients with cancer want to have control over the type and amount of their treatment (Degner, 1992). Much of what nursing research has done to date is inform clinicians (nurses and all health care professionals) of what patients are experiencing and what they prefer in the way of treatment, information, and approach. This positions the clinicians to work in more sensitive, helpful, and therapeutic ways with patients. Nurses increasingly are undertaking experimental research, whether it be randomised controlled trials or theory-based experimental studies advocated by Sidani as more appropriate for many of nursing's questions (Sidani & Braden, 1998). Randomised controlled trials have demonstrated how to control pain in babies undergoing such procedures as heel sticks (Stevens et al., 1999), how to help family caregivers of older people with dementia adjust to the institutionalisation of their relative (Ducharme et al., 2001), and how to use exercise to manage fatigue in patients with cancer (Graydon et al., 1998). These few examples all focus on what research by Canadian nurse researchers has contributed to our understanding of how to care for people having a variety of illnesses or undergoing medical treatment. Clearly there is much more; the journals are replete with reports of studies.

Nurses have also contributed research that has increased the health of Canadians. They have explored how to assist pregnant women and new mothers to stop smoking or to extend periods of nonsmoking (Johnson et al., 2000), and they have studied how to help mothers protect their infants from environmental smoke (Ratner et al., 2001). Much work has been done on how to reduce falls among individuals living in the community and in institutions because falls are a major contributor to morbidity, reduced quality of life, and premature death (Edwards et al., 1993; Gallagher & Scott, 1997; Morse, 2001). An inventory has been compiled of interventions carried out by public health nurses and other community health workers that are effective in improving health and preventing morbidity and mortality (Ciliska et al., 1996; Ploeg et al., 1996).

An area to which nurse researchers, and Canadian nurse researchers in particular, are making impressive contributions is in our understanding of how to staff and manage the health care system. Irvine Doran and McGillis Hall at the University of Toronto have undertaken a series of studies on the impact of staffing ratios and nursing skill mix on a variety of patient outcomes and several aspects of nurses' work (Doran et al., 2002; McGillis Hall et al., 2001). Tourangeau and colleagues at the University of Alberta have demonstrated that better nurse–patient ratios reduce the death rate among patients with cardiovascular disease and shorten their hospital stays (Tourangeau et al., 2002). An interdisciplinary team of researchers with nursing leadership (O'Brien-Pallas et al., 2002) found that nurses with baccalaureate degrees working in home care reduced the number of visits patients required to achieve the desired outcomes. O'Brien-Pallas (2002) has launched a programme of research to develop a model for explicating the complex phenomenon of determining the size and nature of the nursing workforce required to meet Canadian's health care needs in the future.

This type of research, which relies heavily on databases that house information about patient case mix, lengths of stay, and mortality, rather than on the collection of primary data, is increasingly important to our understanding of how to staff the health care system to achieve maximum efficiency and maximum patient outcomes. It is relatively new to nursing and requires that nurse researchers have the expertise to use, link, and extract data from these types of databases, which are a national resource. The Canadian health care system makes it possible to establish national databases drawn from the systems in each of the provinces that house information about patients, their diagnoses, treatments, lengths of stay, use of medications, and outcomes in terms of morbidity. Ontario is planning to establish databases that include patient outcomes reflective of nursing's input. These databases will allow questions to be answered regarding the relationship between nursing inputs such as skill mix (the proportion of registered nurses, licensed practical nurses, and nonprofessional workers), or the number of nursing hours per patient days, or the educational level and experience of nurses, and patient outcomes such as self-care ability and functional status (Pringle & White, 2002).

ISSUES FACING NURSING RESEARCH

A number of issues have been identified throughout this chapter, but the following three, in particular, deserve special attention:

- The need to produce sufficient researchers for the future
- The need to use the CIHR structure and resources to serve nursing research and the role of interdisciplinary research in nursing's future
- The need to increase research utilisation in practise

Shortage of Nurse Researchers

Canada entered the 21st century in the throes of a nursing shortage and with the probability that this shortage would intensify over the next decade. The shortage is distributed across all dimensions of the profession. There are insufficient staff nurses, too few nurse educators, and not enough senior researchers to fill the chairs available and not enough junior researchers to replace the cohort of researchers who will retire during the next 10 to 15 years.

Canada needs more nurse researchers, not fewer. Medical science is making enormous progress in addressing the treatment of disease. For every development in medical care, nursing must respond by determining patients' responses and needs and by developing interventions that complement the medical treatment. Furthermore, there is much catching up to do. Because the undertaking of nursing research is so recent, most of what nurses do and most of what patients experience and need to understand about their health situation has not been studied.

In an overall nursing shortage, every dimension of nursing competes with every other to attract nurses. When there are lots of well-paying positions, it can be very difficult to convince undergraduate students to forego immediate employment and stay in school to pursue research training or to leave well-remunerated positions and return to school. This difficulty is compounded in situations of insufficient funding to allow students to remain in school. The increasing cost of nursing education has resulted in more students graduating with debt. Most find it untenable to take on more debt in the course of acquiring graduate degrees.

Because nurse researchers compose the majority of nurse educators, unless incentives are put in place to make it possible for nurses to undertake graduate work, there will be not only insufficient researchers but also insufficient educators to prepare the nurses to staff the health system. In the United States in the 1960s, the federal government put in place "nurse traineeships" so that all students undertaking graduate degrees in accredited nursing programmes received a tuition waiver and a monthly stipend. The graduate programmes each received a negotiated number of traineeships; hence, it was not necessary for the students to compete for them because admission to the graduate programme guaranteed they would receive one.

There are alternative strategies that serve as incentives for nurses to seek advanced preparation:

- Academic debt forgiveness programmes if students pursue research training
- Tuition reimbursement programmes
- Special graduate scholarships
- Awards available to schools with graduate programmes.

With the exception of the small MRC/NHRDP research scholar programme of the early 1990s, Canadian nursing has not been the beneficiary of incentive programmes designed specifically to support nurses to achieve or accelerate research careers. And they are needed more now than ever before. However, they will not be successful unless young nurses see research or academic careers as attractive, achievable, and rewarding. Interested students need to be exposed to successful nurse researchers who are enthusiastic about their career choice and can serve as role models and mentors to less experienced nurses. Developing opportunities for young nurses or nursing students to work as research assistants to successful and positive researchers is an important recruitment device.

Creating incentive programmes to support nurses while they pursue graduate education and developing creative and stimulating opportunities to expose undergraduate and graduate students to see research as a viable and desirable career choice are desperately needed to ensure the future of nursing research.

Canadian Institutes of Health Research Structure

As noted earlier, Canadian nursing does not have its own institute within the CIHR structure and must seek other routes to attract attention for special needs areas. Furthermore, CIHR emphasises interdisciplinary research. Nurses are well positioned within the CIHR institutes, but the discipline has yet to develop strategies for working with the various institutes so that nursing is heard when new initiatives are required to better understand issues that are either unique to nursing or in which nurses play a major role.

The peer-review committees that review applications and make recommendations for grants to support research projects and personnel awards are separate from the CIHR institutes. Many of these peer-review committees include nurses but usually not more than one or two in a total membership of 12 to 15. When applications from nurses reach these committees, the nurse members may find themselves having to interpret the relevance of the project and to argue for its worth. Nursing must find a way to ensure that there are nurses on all peer-review committees to which nursing proposals might be assigned so that proposals are reviewed by knowledgeable researchers who respect the nature of the work.

Additionally, nursing needs to develop ways of connecting with CIHR institutes that have special relevance nursing, such as Cancer Research, Aging, Circulatory and Respiratory Health, Human Development, Child and Youth Health. These connections might be made through nursing's specialty organisations, such as the cancer nurses association, the cardiovascular nurses group, and the gerontologic nursing societies.

These specialty organisations could develop special relationships with their institute counterparts to design special initiatives that would serve nursing. Keeping in mind that the institutes must be interdisciplinary in their orientation, the initiatives would have to be of interest to other disciplines and incur their support. Interdisciplinarity in research has become the watchword of CIHR. As an organisation, CIHR is convinced that better research results from investigators from a variety of relevant disciplines working together and merging their expertise. This may be true. However, interdisciplinarity results from individuals well prepared in their own disciplines coming together. Interdisciplinarity depends first on disciplinarity. Preparing experts in their own disciplines in an environment that rewards interdisciplinary teams who write grants and conduct research is a real challenge and, in Canada, one that nursing must address.

Nurses will have to be creative to work with CIHR to ensure that nursing's unique needs and orientation are addressed. It will take imagination and relationship building different than the routes available to American nursing with their own NINR; however, it is not impossible, and nurses' presence in important positions throughout the institutes and on the CIHR Council is a good starting place.

Research Utilisation

A third critical issue facing nursing research is the need to accelerate the transfer of research into practise. As discussed earlier, the uptake of research into best practise is at an early stage of development in nursing and in all the health disciplines. The rate of research production in nursing, however, means that if the transfer process does not accelerate, research knowledge will languish in journals years before it is used in patient care. This is wasteful and unfair to the public that has funded the research in the first place. Nursing needs an understanding by and commitment from all practising nurses to attend to research findings and to seek opportunities to use the results of research in their practise. This means that nurses must be prepared in their initial education or through continuing education opportunities to read, comprehend, and critique research. It puts a special demand on nursing practise leaders, such as nurse managers, clinical nurse specialists, and nurse educators, to assist nurses to appreciate the value of research and to find creative ways of bringing research into practise. Organizations that employ nurses have a special responsibility to provide the resources and the infrastructure supports that make it possible for nurses to access research, to have time to read it, and to have individuals available to them to assist them in using it.

THE FUTURE OF NURSING RESEARCH

Notwithstanding the challenges confronting nursing and nurses in the creation of nursing research, the future has never been more encouraging, more robust, or more exciting. Nursing internationally, and particularly in Canada, has never before in its history had so many well-prepared and productive researchers. They are increasingly successful in funding competitions; they see their research published in the best nursing journals and highly regarded interdisciplinary and medical journals; they are sought out to participate in research studies examining a wide range of health issues; and they are well placed in the new structures that support Canadian health research.

The doctoral programmes that were created in the 1990s have proved to be solid and sustainable. Their products are credible and successful. The research conducted by the students is sound and relevant.

Canadians have every reason to be confident that the money they are investing in nursing research is paying off in better understanding of what matters to them about their health, how they can sustain their health, how their health care and nursing care can be better designed and delivered, and how they can achieve their objectives through the health care system. It is a good time to be a nurse researcher.

SUMMARY

Nursing research has been developing since the 1960s in Canada, and enormous strides were made in the 1990s. Doctoral programmes in nursing were launched, and more nurses than ever before achieved doctoral preparation. The funding environment changed, new sources of funds became available to support nursing research, and a number of opportunities developed to allow nurses to devote more of their time to the actual conduct of research. Nursing research achieved an increasing share of the research dollars that are distributed annually. These changes did not come easily. Opposition both inside and outside universities had to be overcome before the Ph.D. programmes became established, and nurses had to work very strategically to ensure that they gained access to the new sources of funding.

Research is now regarded as central to determining what constitutes best practise, that is, care delivered based on the best research evidence available combined with knowledge about the patient's unique circumstances. An understanding of how to bring about best practise and research utilisation more broadly is in its infancy, but new theories and robust programmes of research are slowly contributing to knowledge in this area.

Nursing education has been profoundly influenced by research. Nurse educators are better prepared and bring knowledge about research into their teaching. Increasingly, students are assigned journals rather than textbooks as their first source of information about patient care.

Despite its relative youth, nursing research has made major contributions to our understanding of what patients are experiencing and what they prefer in the way of treatment, information, or approach to their care; how to better care for patients experiencing a variety of health conditions; how to run the health care system more effectively and efficiently; and how to help people to live healthier lives. The potential for even more substantive contributions is immense, particularly because more research funding is available, and more nurse researchers are in positions to design, develop, and conduct programmes of studies.

Of the many issues facing nurses, three stand out: the challenge to prepare sufficient researchers to replace those who will retire over the next 10 to 15 years and to meet future demands; the challenge of using the structure and resources of the new CIHR to meet the needs of nursing research; and the challenge of dramatically increasing research utilisation in practise.

Future nursing research will help Canadians better understand how to sustain their health and how health care and nursing care can be better designed and delivered. Nurses have never before been as well prepared or had the amount of support available to them to meet these expectations.

Online RESOURCES

Add to your knowledge of this issue:

Alberta Heritage Foundation for Medical Research	**www.ahfmr.ab.ca**
Canada Association for Nursing Research (CANR)	**www.canr.ca**
Canadian Association of University Schools of Nursing (CAUSN)	**www.causn.com**
Canadian Health Services Research Foundation (CHSRF)	**www.chsrf.ca**
Canadian Institutes of Health Research (CIHR)	**www.cihr.ca**
Canadian Nurses Association (CNA)	**www.cna-nurses.ca**
Canadian Nurses Foundation (CNF)	**www.can-nurses.ca/cnf**
Fonds de Researche Scientifique du Québec (FRSQ)	**www.frsq.qc.ca**
Michael Smith Foundation for Health Research (MSFHR)	**www.msfhr.org**
Natural Sciences and Engineering Research Council of Canada (NSERC)	**www.nserc.ca**
Social Sciences and Humanities Research Council of Canada (SSHRC)	**www.sshrc.ca**

Reflections on the Chapter

1. Identify one or two nurse researchers whose work interests you. Trace their publications through the electronic databases such as CINAHL and MEDLINE. What journals are they publishing in? Are they working alone or with a consistent team of collaborators? How would you summarise their contributions?

2. Think about an area of practise that interests you, for example, managing the symptoms of children being treated for cancer or helping mothers maintain a sense of control during labour, and then develop a nursing practise question. Go to the electronic databases and search for research that addresses that question. Has research been done on it? If there is research, who has done it, and how much of it has been done by nurses? If there is no research, are there opinion pieces, editorials, or descriptions of how various places manage? Describe the state of knowledge at this time on the practise. Would you recommend research or more research on the question?

3. Think of one practise setting you have been in. What strategies are in place to apply research findings to practise? How successful are they? If there are no obvious strategies, describe what could be done to bring research to practise.

4. Go to the CIHR website, www.cihr.ca. Visit the web pages of the 13 institutes. Review their mission statements and the types of research they are interested in. How many are focussed on research that is relevant to nursing? Look at their staffing and members of their advisory boards. How many have nurses on their boards? Is there a relationship between their mission and research focus and the membership of their boards?

REFERENCES

Abdellah, F. G., & Levine, E. (1965). *Better patient care through nursing research.* New York: Macmillan.

Bloch, D. A. (1981). Conceptualization of nursing research and nursing science. In McCloskey, J. & Grace, H. (Eds.), *Current issues in nursing* (pp. 81–93). Oxford, UK: Blackwell.

Burke, S. O., Kauffmann, E., Costello, E., & Dillon, M. (1991). Hazardous secrets and reluctantly taking charge: Parenting a child with repeated hospitalizations. *Image: The Journal of Nursing Scholarship. 23,* 39–45.

Butler, L., Love, B., Reimer, M., Browne, G., Downe-Wamboldt, B., West, R., Banfield, V. (2002). Nurses begin a national plan for the integration of supportive care in health research, practice and policy. *Canadian Journal of Nursing Research, 33*(4), 155–170.

CASN (2002) Nursing Research Funding Database. Retrieved from www.casn.ca/new/research/CNRFD. htm.

Ciliska, D., Hayward, S., Thomas, H., Mitchell, A. Dobbins, M., Underwood, J., Rafael, A., Martin, E. (1996). A systematic overview of the effectiveness of home visiting as a delivery strategy for public health nursing interventions. *Canadian Journal of Public Health, 87*(3), 193–198.

Degner, L. (1992). Patient participation in treatment decision making. *AXON, 14,* 13–14.

Doran, D. I., Sidani, S., Keatings, M., & Doidge, D. (2002). An empirical test of the nursing role effectiveness model. *Journal of Advanced Nursing, 38*(1), 29–39.

Druding, M. C. (1997). Re-examining the practice of normal saline instillation prior to suctioning. *MED-SURG Nursing, 6,* 209–212.

Ducharme. F., Levesque, L., Gendron, M., & Legault, A. (2001). Development process and qualitative evaluation of a program to promote the mental health of family caregivers. *Clinical Nursing Research, 10*(2), 182–201.

Edwards, N., Cere, M., & Leblond, D. (1993). A community-based intervention to prevent falls among seniors. *Family & Community Health, 15*(4), 57–65.

Estabrooks, C. A. (1998). Will evidence-based nursing practice make practice perfect? *Canadian Journal of Nursing Research, 30*(1), 15–36.

Fawcett, J. (1989). *Analysis and evaluation of conceptual models of nursing* (2nd ed.). Philadelphia: F. A. Davis.

Gagnon, A. J. (1999). Do editors have anything to teach us? A review of 30 years of journal editorials. *Canadian Journal of Nursing Research, 30*(4), 23–26.

Gallagher, E. M., & Scott, V. J. (1997). The STEPS project: Participatory action research to reduce falls in public places among seniors and persons with disabilities. *Canadian Journal of Public Health, 88*(2), 129–133.

Gottlieb, L. N. (1999). From nursing papers to research journal: A 30-year odyssey [Editorial]. *Canadian Journal of Nursing Research, 30*(4), 9–14.

Graydon, J., Sidani, S., Irvine, D., Vincent, L., Bubela, N., & Harrison, D. (1998). Literature review of cancer-related fatigue. *Canadian Oncology Nursing Journal, 8*(Suppl 1), S5.

Hannah, M. E., Hannah, W. J., Hewson, S. A., Hodnett, E. D., Saigal, S., & Willan, A., for the Breech trial Collaborative Group. (2000). Planned caesarian section versus planned vaginal birth for breech presentation at term: A randomized multicentre trial. *Lancet, 356,* 1375–1383.

Jennings, B. M. (2000). Evidence-based practice: The road best traveled? [Editorial]. *Research in Nursing & Health, 23,* 343–345.

Johnson, J. L., Ratner, P. A., Bottoroff, J. L., Hall, W., & Dahinton, S. (2000). Preventing smoking relapse in postpartum women. *Nursing Research, 49,* 44–52.

Kitson, A., Harvey, G., & McCormack, B. (1998). Enabling the implementation of evidence-based practice: A conceptual framework. *Quality in Health Care, 7,* 149–158.

Lau, J., Ioannidis, J. P., & Schmid, C. H. (1998). Quantitative synthesis in systematic reviews. In C. Mulrow & D. Cook (Eds.), *Systematic reviews.* Philadelphia: American College of Physicians.

McGillis Hall, L., Doran, D. I., Baker, G. R., Pink, G. H., Sidani, S., O'Brien-Pallas, L. L. (2001). *The impact of nursing staff mix models and organizational strategies on patient, system and nurse outcomes. Final report.* University of Toronto.

Morse, J. M. (2001). Preventing falls in the elderly. *Reflections on Nursing Leadership, 27*(1), 26–27.

Morse, J. M., & Proctor, A. (1998). Maintaining patient endurance . . . the comfort work of trauma nurses. *Clinical Nursing Research, 7*(3), 250–274.

Mulrow, C., & Cook, D. (1998). *Systematic reviews.* Philadelphia: American College of Physicians.

O'Brien-Pallas, L. L., Doran, D. I., Murray, M., Cockerill, R., Sidani, S., Laurie-Shaw, B., Lochhaas-Gerlach, J. (2002). Evaluation of a client care delivery model, Part 2: Variability in client outcomes in community home nursing. *Nursing Economics, 20*(1), 13–21.

O'Brien-Pallas, L. (2002). Where to from here? *Canadian Journal of Nursing Research, 33*(4), 3–14.

O'Connor, A. M., & Bouchard, J. L. (1991). Research activities in Canadian University Schools and Faculties of Nursing for 1988-1989. *Canadian Journal of Nursing Research, 23*(1), 57–65.

Paterson, B. (2001). The shifting perspective model of chronic illness. *Journal of Nursing Scholarship, 33*(1), 21–26.

Petticrew, M. (2001). Systematic reviews from astronomy to zoology. *British Medical Journal, 322,* 98–101

Ploeg, J., Ciliska, D., Dobbins, M., Hayward, S., Thomas, H., & Underwood, J. (1996). A systematic review of adolescent suicide prevention programs. *Canadian Journal of Public Health, 87*(5), 319–324.

Pringle, D. M., & White, P. (2002). Nursing matters: The

Nursing and Health Outcomes Project of the Ontario Ministry of Health and Long Term Care. *Canadian Journal of Nursing Research, 33*(4), 115–121.

Ratner, P. A., Johnson, J. L., & Bottoroff, J. L. (2001). Mothers' efforts to protect their infants from environmental tobacco smoke. *Canadian Journal of Public health, 92,* 46–47.

Ritchie, J. A. (1992). Research issues. In A. J. Baumgart & J. Larsen (Eds.), *Canadian Nursing Faces the Future.* St. Louis: Mosby.

Sidani, S., & Braden, C. J. (1998). *Evaluating nursing interventions: A theory-driven approach.* Thousand Oaks, CA: Sage.

Stevens, B. J., & Johnston, C. C. (1994). Physiologic responses of premature infants to a painful stimulus. *Nursing Research, 43,* 226–231.

Stevens, B., Johnston, C., Franck, L., Petryshen, P., Jack, A., & Foster, G. (1999). The efficacy of developmentally sensitive interventions and sucrose for relieving procedural pain in very low birth weight neonates. *Nursing Research, 48,* 35–43.

Stevens, B. J., Johnston, C. C., & Horton, L. (1994). Factors that influence the behavioural pain responses of premature infants. *Pain, 59,* 101–109.

Thorne, S., & Paterson, B. (2001). Health care professional support for self care in chronic illness: Insights from diabetes research. *Patient Education and Counseling, 42,* 81–90.

Tourangeau, A. E., Giovannetti, P., Tu, J. V., & Wood, M. (2002). Nursing-related determinants of 30-day mortality for hospitalized patients. *Canadian Journal of Nursing Research, 33*(4), 71–88.

IV

Workplace Realities

15

Issues Arising From the Nature of Nurses' Work

Marjorie McIntyre ■ Carol McDonald

Chapter Objectives

At the completion of this chapter, you will be able to:

1. Understand the nature of nurses' work.
2. Discuss the significance of nurses' work issues.
3. Articulate selected issues arising from the nature of nurses' work.
4. Frame and analyse issues arising from the nature of nurses' work.

5. Identify barriers to resolving the issues arising in nurses' work.
6. Formulate strategies for resolving issues arising in nurses' work.
7. Trace the links between nurses' work, nurses' health, and the health of Canadians.

Nurses find more meaning and reward in their work when they can care for their patients as professionals and when the conditions of work support the scope of practice gained through education and experience. Photography by Larry Arbour. Used with permission of Faculty of Nursing, University of Calgary.

This chapter highlights relevant issues arising from the nature of nurses' work and the significance of these issues for the health of nurses and the health of Canadians who need nursing care. Issues arising from the nature of nurses' work are closely related to and sometimes overlap the issues arising within the environments in which nurses' work takes place. However, there is increasing Canadian and international research substantiating the importance of understanding the nature of nurses' work distinct from nurses' work environment. Therefore, this chapter focusses on the nature of nurses' work and the issues that arise from it.

THE NATURE OF NURSES' WORK

Themes throughout the literature on the changing nature of nurses' work include confusion about what constitutes nurses' work, the increasing demands of nurses' work, the lack of control that nurses have over the work they do, and the incongruity between what nurses are prepared as professionals to do and what they are expected to do in practise.

The lack of clarity in defining nurses' work is due in part to the lack of clear boundaries between nurses' work and nonnurses' work and the increasing expectation that nurses perform work other than nursing care. Changes in administrative structures and in the way auxiliary workers are utilised means nurses take on work that has been traditionally performed by others. In other situations, nursing practises have been relinquished to auxiliary workers. In addition to the increasing demand to do more work, nurses are also faced with the increasing demands of the work itself. Patients in care are more acutely ill, and the care nurses provide is increasingly complex. There are demands on nurses for increasing technical competence.

In practise, nurses are often faced with a lack of control over the work that they do. Decisions about what care will be provided, who will provide that care, and in what setting the care will be provided are made by someone other than the nurses expected to provide the care. Nurses' work often occurs in a climate of diminished resources without support to meet the demands of their work with competence and confidence. The increased demands of nurses' work and the lack of support provided to sustain the work may contribute to the disturbing reality that nurses are unable to nurse in the ways that they have come to expect they should. Nurses increasingly experience incongruities between the work that they are prepared to do, both educationally and philosophically, and the expectations that they encounter in practise.

THE SIGNIFICANCE OF NURSES' WORK ISSUES

Issues arising from the nature of nurses' work relate directly to the recruitment and retention of nurses, the health of the nursing workforce, and the quality of care that nurses are able to deliver. As discussed in earlier chapters, the belief that all we need to do to address the recurrent shortages of nurses is to produce more nurses overlooks the point that it is the issues arising from the nature of nurses' work that sustain and perpetuate nursing shortages. Unless the issues arising from the nature of nurses' work are addressed, it is unlikely that existing vacancies will be filled, that student enrollments will increase, or that nurses, given other opportunities, will stay in nursing. This chapter challenges the inevitability of health care systems doing more with less in the short term when downsizing and restructuring occurs at the expense of nurses' health and well-being (Tables 15.1 and 15.2).

ISSUES ARISING FROM THE NATURE OF NURSES' WORK

In the face of indisputable evidence that there are too few nurses to fill current positions and predictions that the shortage will worsen, there is only beginning recognition that issues related to the nature of nurses' work can and must change. In any discussion of nurses' work, one cannot overlook the nature of the work itself and the availability of nurses to do this work.

Lack of Clarity About What Constitutes Nurses' Work

Several situations contribute to the current confusion about what constitutes nurses' work. Increasingly, the boundaries are blurred between nurses' work and the work of others. Nurses are faced with a conundrum. On one hand, nurses are increasingly expected to be team players on interdisciplinary teams. On the other hand, management changes and the restructuring of work are eroding nurses' work.

In a discussion of the reengineering of hospitals and health care, White (1997) analyses the erosion of nurses' work in relation to the work of other professionals. Nurses work alongside other professionals, each with their own special training, licensing, and regulating bodies. Membership in professional organisations and collective bargaining groups protects professionals' jobs through legislated scope of practise and standards of care. The process that protects a job from erosion by others is called *sheltering.* It serves two purposes: the protection of quality care (to ensure safety to the public) and the protection of job "turf." Recent "restructuring" processes have undermined the sheltering of nurses' work and led to its being "unbundled" into a series of subtasks and delegated to a range of other occupational groups (White, 1997).

Concurrent with this unbundling of nursing practise, Baumann and colleagues (1998) urge nurses and other professionals that "care need not be the exclusive domain of one profession" and suggest that the "focus of decision making becomes the

Table 15.1. Employment Predictions for Nurses in 2011

BETWEEN 1993 AND 2011, NO. OF NURSES MUST INCREASE	LOW GROWTH: 23%	MEDIUM GROWTH: 34.5%	HIGH GROWTH: 46%
Number of RNs employed 1993	235,630	235,630	235,630
Number of RNs employed 1996	227,830	227,830	227,830
Projected number of RNs required 2011	290,000	317,000	344,000
Additional RNs required 2011	62,000	89,000	116,000
Projected number of RNs available 2011	231,000	231,000	231,000
Projected shortage of RNs	**59,000**	**86,000**	**113,000**

Source: Compiled from data collected by Canadian Nurses Association. Used with permission.

Table 15.2. Ratio of Practising Registered Nurses to Canadian Population

YEAR	NURSES: POPULATION
1978	1:115
1988	1:123
1998	1:133

Source: Compiled from data collected by Canadian Nurses Association (2000-2001). Used with permission.

patient, the family, and indeed the population, in partnership and collaboration with other professionals" (p. 1044). MacLeod (1994) supports this notion and suggests that in place of the narrowly defined scope of practise of today's health disciplines, new roles for health professionals will emerge. Despite the appeal of this team approach, one can not overlook the research showing "that hospitals that facilitate professional autonomy, control over practice, and comparatively good relations between nurses and physicians will be the ones in which nurses are able to exercise their professional judgment on a more routine basis, with positive outcomes of patient care" (Aiken et al., 1994, p. 772). Nursing studies show that nursing care delivery affects nurses, organisational outcomes, and patient outcomes. Higher ratios of registered to nonregistered nurses on a unit have been shown to produce lower incidence of adverse occurrences on inpatient care units (Blegen et al., 1998, p. 43). Research provides evidence that the lack of clarity of what constitutes nurses' work matters.

Increasing Demands of Nurses' Work

Although one can cite many examples of the increasing volume of nurses' work, it is important not to overlook the demands of increasing acuity and complexity of patient care. Baumann and coauthors (2001a) conclude that the discrepancy between the work demanded of nurses and what nurses can reasonably give because of increased patient acuity and complexity of care creates an imbalance that threatens the health of nurses and "puts patients throughout Canada at risk" (p. 4).

The care provided by nurses is thought to be more complex than ever before. O'Brien-Pallas and associates (2001) reported that the acuity of patients has increased steadily since 1994. Nurses have the added responsibility of providing care not only to individual patients but also to families and communities. This work suggests that nurses' work is increasingly physically, intellectually, and emotionally demanding (Baumann et al., 2001a). Studies also show that in addition to the increased demands brought on by patient acuity and complexity of care, the effects of hospital downsizing and restructuring have intensified nurses' work. The result is obvious: nurses work harder (Burke & Greenglass, 2000).

Other research highlights the "load" that nurses' work places on nurses (Gaudine, 2000). In a descriptive study in which 31 nurses were interviewed, Gaudine offers compelling narration of the experiences of workload and work overload from the accounts of these nurses. Although nurses' description of what constituted work overload varied significantly, a brief glimpse of the richness of these accounts is offered in the following examples. Simultaneous demands were apparent in situations in which study subjects talked about being expected to do more than one thing at a time and to be in more that one place at a time.

The following example illustrates one nurse's experience with simultaneous demands:

> A doctor is asking me questions. . . . Meanwhile a patient's relative is standing beside me and wants something, and the phone is ringing. I have to get a patient ready to go to X-ray. Then the doctor wants a dressing changed and I know the vitals need taking on my patient receiving blood. (Gaudine, 2000, p. 24)

In a second example of work overload, Gaudine (2000) describes "qualitative work overload" (p. 25) in which the nurses' experiences of work overload are attributed by the nurses to the unfamiliar nature of the work. The following example richly illuminates one nurse's experience with this:

> It was the night shift, and I had never done TPN before. I had eight charts to look over. The TPN lines hadn't been changed on days and had to be done for around 8 p.m. I spent a half hour with the procedure manual, which for me is useless. I want to see it, not just read it. The dressing set didn't have what the procedure book said it would. It was 9:30 p.m. by the time I finished it, and I hadn't even looked at the other patients' charts. (p. 25)

"Heavy load" is another dimension of the work that Gaudine describes. Heavy load involves situations in which there is just too much work to do, expressed by one nurse's response in the following example:

> I can't believe we have to be here for twelve hours and often have to miss our breaks. And I just get the expectations of nurses is really, like super nurse, to do an incredible amount, and I think it is just too much. To work twelve hours, and I can't even go out to lunch, like at any other job. (p. 25)

The final example of work overload is illustrated by a situation in which nurses are, by virtue of their competence and experience, responsible *directly* for the care of the patients assigned to them and also responsible *indirectly* for the patients assigned to other nurses on their unit. One of the nurses in Gaudine's (2000) study talks about this dilemma in a way that resonates with other accounts throughout the literature:

> Most (nurses) are more junior than me and may have trouble doing new things. . . . Just to be cautious, I stayed on the unit at break today, because there was a very sick child and so many new nurses. (p. 25)

Many researchers and practising nurses identify workload as the most significant issue for nurses directly and indirectly because of links between nurses' work, nurses' health, and the health of patients in their care (Baumann et al, 2001a; Burke & Greenglass, 2000; Cockerill & O'Brien-Pallas, 1990; O'Brien-Pallas et al., 1997; Schullenberger, 2000; and White, 1997.)

INCONGRUITIES BETWEEN NURSES' WORK AS TAUGHT AND PRACTISED

The lack of clarity about what constitutes nurses' work and the increasing demands of nurses' work life have hindered the development of a professional role for nurses. The professional role of nurses is further problematised by incongruities that exist between "nursing as taught and nursing as practiced, between nursing as experienced by nurses and nursing as perceived by others" (Ceci & McIntyre, 2001, p. 123). The incongruities that are raised "when nurses find themselves unable to nurse as they had envisioned, as they can or believe they should" (p. 123) undermines the meaning that nurses find in their work. Researchers who interviewed practising nurses claim "nurses find meaning in their work when they are able to care for patients performing in a way that conforms to the philosophy of care held by the nursing profession" (Baumann et al., 2001a, p. 8).

In considering the meaning that nurses find in their work, it is important to recognise that nurses have a different experience than other members of the health care system. And this difference, rather than being trivial or blatantly obvious, "holds ethical and political meanings and implications for nurses and for our practices" (Ceci & McIntyre, 2001, p. 127). The professional role for nurses, that is, their understanding of their scope of practise, develops through both education and practise experiences. For many nurses, this scope of practise makes central a holistic approach to the care of patients and their families. However, in contemporary practise, a "treatment-oriented medical model" often overrides the nurse's scope of practise (Baumann et al., 2001a, p. 9). When faced with demanding workloads and the dissonance of conflicting approaches to care, nurses' work becomes reconfigured as tasks. In addition, when nurses' interpretations of what is occurring in practise are excluded from policy discussions, "a sense of being incorrect, in some essential sense, in their understanding of themselves and their work comes into play" (Ceci & McIntyre, 2001, p. 123).

LACK OF CONTROL OVER THE WORK

The recently published *Commitment and Care: The Benefits of Healthy Workplaces for Nurses, Their Patients and the System* by Baumann and others (2001a), makes an important contribution to our understanding of issues arising from the nature of nurses' work in Canada. Drawing on the earlier work of Kristensen (1999), Baumann identified six principles that constitute an optimal work environment for nurses' social and psychological well-being. Baumann's work incorporates a review of current literature, including relevant policy documents on the topic and the findings of focus group discussions with nurses in practise across Canada.

This chapter draws on the findings of Baumann's work to support discussions of issues of control and support in nurses' work. *Control* as it is used here can be understood as both control over the work that nurses do and control over the ways in which that work is organised in practise. Baumann and colleagues introduce the finding that "establishing a professional role is a prerequisite for establishing control over practice" (2001a, p. 9). They further link control over practise to job satisfaction and greater latitude in decision making to decreased turnover of nurses in practise.

Baumann and others reported that focus group participants strongly supported the need for nurses to have input into the "patient-care decisions related to their practice" (2001a, p. 9). Nurses stressed the importance of having their say in "all aspects of care within their scope of practice, including serving as patient advocates" (p. 9). Nurses in this study experienced difficulty in playing "significant roles in policy-making" or in communicating "effectively with decision makers" because of being "under-represented in institutional hierarchies" (p. 10).

For nurses to experience control over their work, they must be central in the policy decisions that direct work-life issues, such as scheduling, full-time–to–part-time staff ratios, casual nurses, and auxiliary workers. Although nurses are often left with the responsibility of calling in relief staff and implementing mandatory overtime, there are still too few instances in which nurses have meaningful input into the policies that determine these arrangements. The failure to gain control over and have meaningful input into one's practise, generated by the demands of mandatory overtime and the high rates of relief staff, influence nurses' commitment to their practise and the decisions they make about remaining in practise. Nurses who are satisfied with their work and the organisation of their work schedules show a higher commitment to their practise. Research shows that the job satisfaction level of the nursing staff strongly determines the satisfaction level of the patients in their care (Baumann et al., 2001a).

Lack of Support for Nurses' Work

Central to the discussion of nurses' work is the decline of emotional and cognitive support available to nurses in their workplaces (Baumann et al., 2001a). In place of full-time positions, in which nurses knew the people they worked with and were familiar with their places of work, many working nurses have "moved away from the traditional workplace to a world where employers may offer part-time or casual work and employees have several jobs" (Baumann et al., 2001a, p. 7). In full-time long-term work situations, nurses' social support for dealing with professional and personal issues came from managers, supervisors, and colleagues. Cognitive support came from preceptors, mentors, and organisational policies that provided the needed in-service and continuing education for professional and career development.

In the absence of leaders to protect them from overwork, some nurses have turned to absenteeism as a way to deal with feelings of diminished competence, work overload, and mandatory overtime (White, 1997). Research shows a relationship between nurses' satisfaction with support in their work and absenteeism (Blythe et al., 2001). It is significant that nurses have lower rates of absenteeism in part-time than in full-time work, suggesting that absenteeism may be related to the strain of working longer hours (Burke & Greenglass, 2000).

During the restructuring of health care services, as nurses face increasing demands in their workload, the cognitive or educational support that could once be counted on has been withdrawn. The financial and professional support for ongoing education and in-servicing has diminished at a time when there is an increasing pressure for nurses to account for their continued competency. Despite the profession's commitment to advanced education among its members, employers provide little support or remuneration for the pursuit and attainment of advanced degrees (Table 15.3).

Table 15.3. Levels of Education Among Canadian Nurses

LEVEL	PERCENTAGE OF NURSES
Diploma	77.6
Baccalaureate	20.8
Master's	1.5
Doctorate	0.1

Source: Compiled from data collected by Canadian Nurses Association (2000-2001). Used with permission.

FRAMING AND ANALYSING ISSUES ARISING FROM THE NATURE OF NURSES' WORK

Issues arising from the nature of nurses' work and the conditions within and under which this work is performed are not new. Although the rationale for making nurses' work issues a priority has varied across time, overall, governments, employers, and even nurse leaders have failed to address adequately these issues in a way that has lasting effects.

Historical Understandings of Nurses' Work

In reviewing historical literature, one gets a sense that the nature of nurses' work has always been less than ideal (Gibbon & Mathewson, 1947). What we can learn from an historical analysis is how the issues have been sustained over time and the implications that this has for the current situation and for long-term planning of health care provision.

Despite the evidence of declining enrollments and an inadequate supply of nurses to fill current positions, many employers continue to assume that one can still "recruit women interested in self-denial, servitude and the expression of their natural qualities as women . . . the workplace still operates to some extent on that basis—expecting nurses to work harder than ever for less and less" (Stuart, 1993, p. 22). Although many nurses in the past expressed a deep dissatisfaction with nurses' work, what has changed is that today, nurses are more likely to view themselves as professional and their work as a career rather than understanding nursing as a calling to servitude. With this view of professional work, nurses who stay in the profession do so knowing they have choices. Nurses have many more opportunities to leave the profession and work elsewhere than in the past.

Social and Cultural Analysis

Priorities placed on nurses' work and the value attributed by society and by nurses themselves to this work have often been linked to economic rather than social realities (Donner et al., 1994). The issues arising from the nature of nurses' work would benefit from a social and cultural analysis that considers the social realities of nurses' lives, nurses' health, and the quality of patient care.

A social and cultural analysis reminds us that considering the realities of nurses' lives must include consideration of the realities of the lives of women in our society. Nurses facing issues of increasing demands and lack of support for their work simultaneously experience the demands of the multiple roles in their nonworking lives as women. Prevailing attitudes in society suggest that work and personal lives are separate domains. This attitude privileges particular members of society and fails to take into account the realities of the lives of women as mothers, care providers, community supporters, and volunteers juggled alongside their paid work as nurses. Issues that arise from mandatory callback, overtime, and the increased workload demands of nursing compromise the quality of nurses lives, their well-being, and their energy to participate fully in both their personal and professional lives.

The aging of the nursing work force is well documented in the literature (Table 15.4). Dominant views of society regarding the devaluing and dispensability of older workers threatens to undermine the contribution that nurses continue to make to the profession as they age. Operating on a framework that views all nurses as the same,

Table 15.4. Projected Number of Registered Nurses in 2011, by Age

AGE IN 2011 (YEARS)	RNS RETAINED FROM 1995	NEW RNS SINCE 1995	TOTAL	PERCENTAGE
≤24	-	3,438	3,438	1.5
25-29	-	18,112	18,112	7.9
30-34	-	21,996	21,996	9.5
35-39	2,824	24,715	27,539	11.9
40-44	18,642	14,133	32,775	14.2
45-49	30,314	7,856	38,170	16.6
50-54	32,242	4,759	37,001	16.0
55-59	30,855	2,253	33,108	14.4
60-64	14,475	940	15,415	6.7
65+	3,009	15	3,024	1.3
Total	**132,361**	**98,217**	**230,578**	**100.0**

Source: Compiled from data collected by Canadian Nurses Association (2000-2001). Used with permission.

with expectations that each nurse will perform the same work in a given setting, erases the realities of the differences among nurses, including the differences that may be associated with aging. A British Columbia setting provides a useful model that recognises both the realities of nurses' lives and the contribution that is fluid throughout nurses' careers. This programme enables senior nurses to be relieved of up to 30% of their patient assignment in return for mentoring new nurses (Baumann et al., 2001a).

Political Analysis

Typically, issues arising from the nature of nurses' work come to the foreground when recruitment and retention issues arise, but these issues tend to fade from public awareness and concern once the numbers (shortages) problem is averted. Significantly, once vacant positions are filled, concern about nurses' work tends to be put aside as a topic for serious debate for the nurses' themselves. The failure of governments, employers, professional organisations, and nurses themselves to address adequately the issues arising from the nature of nurses' work is linked to the failure to understand the implications of such conditions and their significance for the health of Canadians.

A political analysis asks who benefits from this issue being resolved and who benefits from things staying the same. Nurses and the patients they care for stand to benefit from the resolution of issues arising from the nature of nurses' work. Employers, however, may benefit from some of these issues remaining as they are. For example, the lack of clarity between nursing and nonnursing work allows employers to exploit nurses in assigning multiple roles to them. This exploitation serves managers well as nurses take on the work of other professionals and clerical staff when needed, but it undermines the control that nurses have over what constitutes nurses' work. When nurses are engaged in nonnursing work, in addition to their patient care, it is the patient care, the real work of nurses, that is compromised.

CRITICAL FEMINIST ANALYSIS

A critical feminist analysis directs us towards the consideration of power structures and ideologies and to the question of what it means to be a subject of one's own life. This analysis highlights how realities such as other people defining and controlling nurses' work influence how nurses see themselves. As a subject of one's own work life, nurses would retain control of their work and work arrangements, rather than being an object that is manipulated and controlled by structures of power.

Nurses are complicit in the maintenance of power structures when they fail to make central their own beliefs and ideas or the ideas of nurse leaders. *Complicity* as it is used here refers to the practise of nurses' participation in the perpetuation of power structures and unexamined ideologies that work against nurses.

ETHICAL ANALYSIS

Profession codes, such as the CNA *Code of Ethics* and the provincial and territorial scope of practise guidelines, direct nurses to advocate for patients in the provision of health care. Legislative acts, such as the Canada Health Act and the Health Professions Act, mandate nurses as professionals to provide competent, ethical care. Collective bargaining and labor laws are in place to protect nurses from the demands of overwork, to control the hours of work, and to ensure safe practise standards. Despite these multiple levels of regulation of nurses' work, governmental agencies and employers continue, uninterrupted, to demand work of nurses that erodes these guidelines.

Ethical questions are raised about the health of nurses and the subsequent health care provided to patients. These quandaries include the risks to patients when a nurse who has worked many shifts without a leave or entire shifts without a rest break becomes vulnerable to fatigue and a subsequent increased risk for making errors. Ethical questions may also evolve from the added responsibility felt by nurses when they are working with other nurses whose competence is compromised by unfamiliarity with the work demanded of them or with the fatigue of overwork.

BARRIERS TO RESOLVING ISSUES ARISING IN NURSES' WORK

One of the largest barriers to making decisions about the amount and nature of work one nurse can be expected to do is that there is little, if any, consensus on what nurses' work is and what it is not. For example, many systems designed to measure nurses' workload measure only a portion of the work done (O'Brien-Pallas et al., 1997). Typically, the focus of such systems are tasks performed without taking into account the complexity of the patient assignment, the nurses' knowledge and skill to provide the required care, and the context in which the care is to be provided. Incomplete assessment of what nurses know and do in their practise results in nursing effort and expertise being inadequately recognised or compensated (Baumann et al., 2001a, p. 5).

"Nurses' views of the world are both overshadowed and undermined" by the views of others who "define what nurses are and what nurses are for" (Ceci & McIntyre, 2001, p. 126). This places nurses in the "uncomfortable position of trying to render their perspectives believable or credible using terms of reference which are not necessarily their own" (p. 126). Many employers think of nurses as versatile. In addition to the care their education and experience have prepared them to give, they are known to be able to provide "services for which the hospital sometimes employ nurses' aides, secretarial and clerical personnel, lab technicians, pharmacists, physical therapists and social workers. They commonly assume hospital management roles after hours and (under certain circumstances) substitute for physicians in the community" (Stuart, 1993, p. 22).

A second major barrier to changing the issues arising from the nature of nurses' work is the failure of Canadians generally and governments and employers specifically to acknowledge the impact of the nature of nurses' work on nurses' health and on the health of patients. Nurses' work, in particular adequate staffing levels, has been linked through research to improved patient outcomes (Aitken et al., 1998) and to the health of nurses themselves (O'Brien-Pallas et al., 2001).

The reality that staffing decisions are based on funding rather than on the level of nurse preparation or the number of nurses needed to achieve the desired outcomes is the third barrier to resolving these issues. Despite the tools and systems available to help with making staffing decisions, the literature reviewed expresses skepticism about these tools and the need for senior nursing positions whereby those with the expertise would make these decisions. The staffing of patient care units must be based on the needs of the patients and the corresponding "staffing required to achieve desired outcomes" (Blegen et al., 1998, p. 49).

A fourth barrier that undermines the lack of control that nurses have over their work and that interfaces with the lack of clarity about what constitutes nurses' work is the balancing of the registered nurses–to–auxiliary worker ratio. It is not always easy or even possible to assess accurately how many registered nurses are needed to achieve desired outcomes of care. As discussed earlier, difficulty in assessing nurses' work is compounded by difficulties distinguishing nurses' work from other work that nurses do. Although existing tools for determining a good skill mix have been judged inadequate, there is support among nurses for refining these tools. In addition to the limitations of existing tools, however, the literature is very clear that much more important than the tools are the relationships among nurse managers, nurses, and other team members involved in and influenced by the staffing decisions made (Gaudine, 2000).

A fifth barrier to resolving issues of nurses' work conditions is a failure to see the link between job security and nurses' absenteeism from work, nurses' organisational commitment, and nurses satisfaction or dissatisfaction with work. Similar to other workers involved in research studies, nurses reported that job security, that is, being able to count on full-time work despite changes and restructuring, was associated with less absenteeism from work, more commitment to employers, and better physical and emotional health (Blythe et al., 2001).

A sixth barrier to resolving issues that arise within nurses' work is the failure of governments and others to account for the effects of restructuring on nurses' work. In a study conducted in three Ontario hospitals where restructuring had occurred, participants described that in every aspect of their work life, "relationships became less integrated, their work activities became less controllable, and the changes compromised their ability to deliver effective care" (Blythe et al., 2001, p. 61).

Baumann and associates (2001b) explored the implications of restructuring on the quality of nurses' work life. They reported that nurses who had been involved directly with the restructuring either through layoffs, moves to another unit, or moves to another workplace altogether reported being "more dissatisfied with their work environments" (p. 19). They expressed feeling "less confident in their practice" and were more "concerned about the impact of restructuring on patient welfare" (p. 19). Additionally, nurses experienced "less organisational commitment" than they experienced before restructuring (p. 19).

Another study makes a related but important addition to this work and cautions that research on nurses' experiences of downsizing and layoffs should focus not only on the effects of layoffs or transfers but also on those nurses who are not downsized or laid off. Nurses who remain in the same positions report high levels of stress and increased workload related to the staffing changes on the units (Maurier & Northcott, 2001).

STRATEGIES FOR RESOLVING ISSUES ARISING IN NURSES' WORK

Recent research studies provide compelling evidence that the issues arising from the nature of nurses' work can and must change (Baumann et al., 2001a). They challenge the notion that these issues are a problem for nurses to address. Instead, the studies assign responsibility for the current situation of nurses' work and the threat of a system-wide shortage of nurses with governments, employers, and professional organisations.

Strategies to overcome the existing barriers to resolving issues that arise from the nature of nurses' work are those that "enable nurses to practice in a way that optimises the use of their knowledge and expert judgment" in their practise (Laschinger et al., 2001, p. 240) "Work environments that provide opportunities to learn and grow" and "support creative strategies" in nurses' work are those that will be considered health promoting for nurses and those to whom they provide care (p. 240). Strategies increasing "decision-making latitude" (the extent to which a worker has control over the job and how it is done) will "moderate the effects of high levels of psychological demands" (p. 239) and enhance the quality of nurses' work life.

In her research on work overload, Gaudine (2000) stressed the importance of administrators listening carefully to the accounts of nurses' experiences of workload as part of verifying what a particular workload might be. Although one can make use of the tool available to get some indication of workload, one should not interpret the findings of such tools without considering the particularities of the nurse or nurses involved. An additional insight gained from Gaudine's study was that even in situations in which it is not possible to alter the workload or change the conditions at that particular time, taking the time to understand a particular nurse's experience of workload or work overload can make a contribution to the quality of a nurse's work life through validation and support.

In the United States and elsewhere, research on magnet hospitals, that is, hospitals that embody a set of organisational attributes that nurses find desirable and that are conducive to better patient care (Aitken et al., 1994), may provide valuable direction for strategies to mediate some of the issues arising from the nature of nurses' work. Kramer and Schmalenberg (1988) suggest "magnet hospitals may be dealing effectively with the nursing shortage by creating organizational conditions conducive to eliminating the shortage" (p. 13). They identified the following attributes of magnet hospitals:

- Innovative policies and practises
- Intelligent use of staff (nurses are not treated as replaceable parts in the bureaucratic machinery; rather, they are moved in teams)
- Informal communication lines and open-door policies
- Pervasive and deliberately promoted and promulgated quality care values, including (1) advocacy of education, drive for quality, and (2) autonomy valued (includes freedom to act and freedom to act and fail).

Aitken and colleagues (1994) extend the work on magnet hospitals which they identify as "like other hospitals except in the organization of nursing (p.784)." They produced evidence to show that the magnet hospitals in their study had lower mortality rates, suggesting that organisational factors such as the organisation of nursing care can be linked to better patient outcomes. Research is one of the most convincing strategies to support the link between nurses' work and positive patient outcomes.

In making reference to the many challenges and limited benefits that nursing offers today, the report of Baumann and associates (2001a) on the benefits of a healthy work experience for nurses predicts that if nursing is to "remain a viable profession, its status must be enhanced and the welfare of nurses promoted" (p. 13). In their policy synthesis on the benefits of a healthy work experience for nurses, and the patients they care for, Baumann and associates (2001a) stressed that governments, professional organisations, employers, educators, and researchers must act together to promote patient welfare by facilitating healthy work experiences for nurses. What follows are a selection of the key points identified by this research team.

Key points for governments include the following:

- Revise funding formulas to better support the many dimensions of nursing practise.
- Set rules for using the funds and monitor how they are spent.
- Support the welfare of nurses by providing funds to increase staff so that managers can assign workloads that consider the acuity and complexity of patient care.
- Ensure the supply of nurses in the future by investing in continuing education, including baccalaureate and postgraduate education.

Key points for professional associations and councils include the following:

- Continue to advocate for nurses and advise governments and employers to allow nurses to practise to their full scope.
- Share recruitment and retention strategies and promote nursing through advertising and marketing strategies.

Key points for employers include the following:

- Address staffing issues by hiring sufficient nurses to ensure a reasonable workload.
- Address issues of staff mix and full-time and part-time status.
- Work with unions to develop flexible scheduling that suits both nurses and employers.
- Engage nurses on units in the recruitment and hiring process.
- Adopt the most effective tools for measuring and allocating workload.
- Reward effort and achievement with economic remuneration and other rewards.
- Support nursing leadership and professional development.
- Monitor nurses' health.
- Promote recruitment and retention of graduates into the workforce.

Key points for educators include the following:

- In partnership with employers, governments, and nursing associations, integrate new nurses into the workplace through such strategies as clinical internships and cooperative programmes.

- Ensure a match between the curriculum and the skills required in the workplace.
- Teach leadership skills, health care policy, and work-life health issues for nurses.
- Work with nursing associations on scope-of-practise issues.

Key points for researchers include the following:

- Develop databases, workload-measurement instruments, and human resources forecasting tools.
- Conduct studies to evaluate the effectiveness of strategies to improve nurses' well-being.

The strategies suggested in this chapter are directed towards individuals and groups with the power to sustain or to revise the structures and ideologies that underlie the issues arising from the nature of nurses' work. Societal and cultural analysis, in particular, helps us to recognise that the burden for the resolution of these issues does not rest with individual nurses, but with governments, professional groups, employers, and labor groups.

What, then, is the role of the individual nurse in coping with and contributing to the establishment of a healthier work experience for nurses and subsequently improved patient care? Perhaps the most powerful action that individual nurses' can take is to disrupt or to interrupt the dominant discourse in health care and in society regarding the versatility and subservience of nurses. When given the opportunity, nurses' can make their voices heard with governments, professional associations, and labor groups by broadcasting the issues of justice and issues of health arising from the nature of nurses' work as it is currently experienced.

SUMMARY

Although historically the nature of nurses' work has been less than ideal, the changes in nurses' work and the issues that arise from this work in the past decade have seriously compromised nurses' ability to provide quality care in some circumstances and even adequate care in others. Nurses' work has undergone dramatic changes without corresponding support to moderate the effect of theses changes for nurses. Increased workloads and work overload, higher patient acuity and care complexity, and increased job insecurity in the workplace have had an overwhelming effect on how nurses experience their work. The impact of the issues that arise from the nature of nurses' work can be seen in the way nurses care for their patients and ultimately contributes to both the quality of nurses' work and the quality of care they are able to provide.

There is significant research evidence presented in this chapter to support the links between nurses' work, nurses' health, quality of nursing care, and patient outcomes. Studies support the link between the practise of nursing and hospital mortality and nurses' work satisfaction with better patient care (Aiken et al., 1994; Laschinger et al., 2001).

Barriers to resolving the issues arising from the nature of nurses' work are many, but the need to overcome these barriers and begin to address these issues has never been more urgent. Strategies for resolution involve the cooperation of governments, professional organisations, employers, educators, and researchers. The time to act is now.

Online RESOURCES

Add to your knowledge of this issue:

Canadian Health Services Research Foundations

Canadian Nurses Association   **www.cna-nurses.ca**

Provincial Organizations and Colleges

Registered Nurses Association of British Columbia   **www.rnabc.bc.ca**

Alberta Registered Nurses Association   **www.nurses.ab.ca**

Saskatchewan Registered Nurses Association   **www.srna.org**

Manitoba Association of Registered Nurses   **www.marn.mb.ca**

Registered Nurses Association of Ontario   **www.rnao.org**

College of Nurses of Ontario   **www.cno.org**

Ordre des Infirmiéres et Infirmiers du Québec   **www.oiiq.org**

Nurses Association of New Brunswick   **www.nanb.nb.ca**

Registered Nurses Association of Nova Scotia   **www.rnans.ns.ca**

Reflections on the Chapter

1. From your own experience in practise, describe situations that support or challenge what you have read about the nature of nurses' work.

2. How do you account for the current issues arising from the nature of nurses' work in your practise or practicum areas? Who might you ask or where might you look to gain an understanding of these current issues?

3. Researchers have located the responsibility for the issues arising from the nature of nurses' work with governments, employers, and professional organisations. Support or challenge this view.

4. Can you identify other barriers than those listed in this chapter to resolving the issues related to the nature of nurses' work?

5. What other strategies might you suggest for resolving issues related to the nature of nurses' work?

REFERENCES

Aiken, L. H., Smith, H. L., & Lake, E. T. (1994). Lower Medicare mortality among a set of hospitals known for good nursing care. *Medical Care, 32*(8), 771–787.

Aitken, L., Sloane, D., & Sochalski, J. (1998). Hospital organization and outcomes. *Quality of Health Care 7*(4), 222–226.

Baumann, A., Deber, R. B., Silverman, B. E., & Mallette, C. M. (1998). Who cares? Who cures? The ongoing debate in the provision of health care. *Journal of Advanced Nursing, 28*(5), 1040–1045.

Baumann, A., Giovanetti, P., O'Brien-Pallas, L., Mallette, C. M., Deber, R., Blythe, J., Hibberd, J., & DiCenso, A. (2001b). Healthcare restructuring: The impact of job change. *Canadian Journal of Nursing Leadership, 14*(1), 14–20.

Baumann, A., O'Brien-Pallas, L., Deber, R., Donner, G., Semogas, D., & Silverman, B. (1996). Downsizing in the hospital system: A restructuring process. *Healthcare Management Forum, 9*(4), 5–13.

Baumann, A., O'Brien-Pallas, L., Armstrong-Strassen, Blythe, J., Bourbonnais, R, Cameron, S., Doran,

D., Kerr, M., Gillis-Hall, L., Vzina, M., Butt, M., & Ryan, L. (2001a). *Commitment and care: The benefits of health workplaces for nurses, their patients and the system. A policy synthesis.* Canadian Health Research Foundation. Ottawa: Government of Canada.

Blegen, M. A., Goode, C. J., & Reed, L. (1998). Nurse staffing and patient outcomes. *Nursing Research,* 47(1), 43–50.

Blythe, J., Baumann, A., & Giovqanetti, P. (2001). Nurses' experiences of restructuring in three Ontario hospitals. *Journal of Nursing Scholarship,* 33(1), 61–68.

Burke, R. J., & Greenglass, E. R. (2000). Effects of hospital restructuring on full time and part time nursing staff in Ontario. *International Journal of Nursing Studies,* 37(2), 163–171.

Ceci, C., & McIntyre, M. (2001). A 'quiet' crisis in health care: Developing our capacity to hear. *Nursing Philosophy* 2(2), 122–130.

Cockerill, L., & O'Brien-Pallas, L. (1990). Satisfaction with nursing workload systems: Report of a survey of Canadian hospitals. Part A. *Canadian Journal of Nursing Administration,* 3(2), 17–22.

Donner, G., Semogas, D., & Blythe, J. (1994). *Towards an understanding of nurses' lives: Gender, power and control.* Toronto: Quality of Nursing Worklife Research Unit.

Gaudine, A. P. (2000). What do nurses mean by workload and work overload? *Canadian Journal of Nursing Leadership,* 13(2), 22–27.

Gibbon, M., & Mathewson, M. (1947). *Three centuries of Canadian Nursing.* Toronto: MacMillan.

Kramer, M., & Schamalenberg, C. (1988). Magnet hospitals: Part 1, Institutions of excellence. *Journal of Nursing Administration,* 18(1), 13–24.

Kristensen, T. S. (1999). Challenges for research and prevention in relation to work and cardiovascular diseases. *Scandinavian Journal of Work, Environment and Health,* 25(6), 550–557.

Laschinger, H. K. S., Finegan, J., Shamian, J., & Almost, J. (2001). Testing Karasek's demands-control model in restructured health care settings: Effects of job strain of staff nurses' quality of work-life. *Journal of Nursing Administration,* 31(5), 233–243.

MacLeod, S. (1994). A new breed of health care professionals. *Odyssey,* 1(1), 45-51.

O'Brien-Pallas L., & Baumann, A. (1992). Quality of nursing work life issues: A unifying framework. *Canadian Journal of Nursing Administration,* 5(2), 12–16.

O'Brien-Pallas L., Irvine, D., Peereboom, E., & Murray, M. (1997). Measuring nursing workload: Understanding the variability. *Nursing Economics,* 15(4), 171–182.

O'Brien-Pallas L., Thomson, D., Alksinis, C., & Bruce, S. (May, 2001). The economic impact of nurse staffing decisions: Time to turn down another road? *Hospital Quarterly,* 4(3), 42–50.

Shamian, J., & Villeneuve, M. (2000). Building a national nursing agenda. *Hospital Quarterly,* 4(1), 16–18.

Stuart, M. (1993). Nursing: The endangered profession. *The Canadian Nurse,* April, 19–22.

Shullenberger, G. (2000). Nurse staffing decisions: An integrative review of the literature. *Nursing Economics,* 18(3), 124–132, 146–148.

White, J. P. (1997). Health care, hospitals, and reengineering: The nightingales sign the blues. In A. Duffy, D. Glenday, & N. Pupo (Eds.), *Good jobs, bad jobs, no jobs: The transformation of work in the 21st century.* Toronto: Harcourt & Brace.

CHAPTER **16**

The Workplace Environment

Marjorie McIntyre

Chapter Objectives

At the completion of this chapter, you will be able to:

1. Identify issues that are relevant to providing quality practise environments in nurses' workplaces.

2. Articulate and analyse issues that arise in nurses' workplaces.

3. State past and current barriers to providing quality practise environments.

4. Formulate strategies to resolve nurses' workplace issues.

5. Recognise the conflicting loyalties between the goals of the organisation and nurses' professional goals.

Nurses work in many environments and adapt to many conditions. The setting for these nurses is the inner city. Photography by Chuck Russell. Used with permission of *Canadian Nurse*.

This chapter articulates and critically analyses issues arising within nurses' workplaces, particularly those issues that obstruct the development and maintenance of quality practise environments by nurses. The chapter also proposes some strategies for resolving these issues. For the most part, nurses' work environments are and always have been complex, and barriers to providing quality professional practise environments are considerable. However, given the authority, adequate resources, and support of colleagues, it is assumed at the outset of writing this chapter that nurses can provide such quality practise environments as those envisioned by the Canadian Nurses Association (CNA).

According to the recent position statement on nurses' work environments prepared by the CNA in 2001, nurses have an obligation to their patients to demand practise environments that have the "organizational and human support allocations necessary for safe, competent and ethical nursing care" (p. 1). The CNA position states that a quality nursing practise environment for professional nurses is one in which "the needs and goals of the individual nurse are met at the same time the patient or client is assisted to reach his or her individual health goals, within the costs and quality framework mandated by the organization where the care is provided" (p. 1). CNA holds that the development and support of quality practise environments for professional nurses is a responsibility shared by practitioners, employers, regulatory bodies, professional associations, educational institutions, unions, and the public.

Provincial professional organisations and unions unanimously support the CNA position statement that nurses have an *obligation* to their patients to demand practise environments that allow for the provision of safe, competent, and ethical nursing care. However, coupled with their support, the Canadian Federation of Nursing Unions (CFNU, 2002) and several provincial professional organisations (Alberta Association of Registered Nurses [AARN], 2002; Registered Nurses Association of Nova Scotia [RNANS], 1996) also claim that a safe and secure work environment is an undeniable right of every nurse and is an essential element of providing quality care.

THE NATURE OF NURSES' WORKPLACES

Although it is impossible to make broad statements about the provision of quality practise environments by Canadian nurses, several very important themes are evident in the literature. The most central theme is that when nurses have little control over their work and few resources to support their work, nurses' satisfaction with their work is eroded, and patient care is eventually compromised (Aiken et al., 1994, 1998; Akyeampong & Ulsacas, 1998; Baumann et al., 2001; Lachinger et al., 2001; Leveck & Jones, 1996). The issues arising from the nature of nurses' work and from the workplace itself are interrelated; both contribute to nurses' experience of job satisfaction, recruitment and retention, and well-being. However, this chapter focusses on the issues directly related to workplaces and, in doing so, highlights important differences that lead to specific strategies for change.

Many writers and researchers have linked Canada's current nursing shortage to inadequate and inferior work environments (Ceci & McIntyre, 2001). Baumann and others claim, "Canada's nursing shortage is at least in part due to a work environment that burns out the experienced and discourages new recruits. But that environment can be changed" (2001, p. iii). Despite the seriousness of the real and potential short-comings of nurses' work environments, there is evidence that governments, employers, and nurses' themselves are taking action to improve the situation. Further, there is an acknowledgment on the part of these groups that they must work together to create and maintain healthy nurse workplaces. Research suggests that recruitment and retention strategies will only be successful if this action is implemented on a large scale (Sochalski, 2001).

What does this mean for new nursing graduates? Understanding what constitutes a healthy work environment and selecting those environments in which to work will positively affect not only the individual's work-life experience but also the quality of care that that individual is able to deliver. As more desirable work environments are created, nurses already in practise will undoubtedly be attracted to those employment situations, promoting the continued production of healthy work environments. Many employers are beginning to offer onsite services to nurses and other employees that have been identified as indicative of a quality work environment. These services include but are not limited to the following:

- Provision for onsite child care
- Safe, accessible, and affordable parking
- Nutritious and hot food services 24 hours a day
- Onsite fitness centres and classes
- Wellness programmes, such as smoking cessation, back care, and stress management
- Counseling for mental health issues and substance use and misuse
- Programmes for workplace safety
- Programmes to reduce workplace violence

In addition to these services, research (Baumann et al., 2001) shows that the workplace for professional practicing nurses would be improved through the integration of these initiatives:

- Support for new nurses through mentoring programmes
- Support for continuing and advanced education
- Nurses' participation in policy and governance
- Clear distinction between nurses and nonnurses' work
- Provision of adequate resources, including human and material resources

WORKPLACE ISSUES

Despite the positive initiatives of select groups of employers, for many Canadian nurses, the realities of the workplace continue to be reflected in themes of professional and social isolation; issues of workplace safety and workplace violence; and disrupted workplaces, resulting in alienation from nurse leaders, peers, and other professionals; inadequate educational, mentorship, and orientation programmes; decreased levels of support for professional development; and the failure of governments and the public to recognise and support the need for change in nurses' workplaces. Despite the well-documented lack of control over their work and work environments, nurses continue to be held accountable for, and in some cases hold themselves accountable for, providing quality practise environments and safe, competent, ethical care. The following sections contain an expanded discussion of each of these issues.

Workplace Isolation

A review of recent literature on social support in the workplace and an examination of current employer practises suggest that nurses' commitment to their employing organisations has decreased (Baumann et al., 2001). This diminished commitment is due, at least in part, to a belief that employers no longer support them. The dismissal of chief nursing officers, head nurses, and middle managers during restructuring has meant that nurses received less professional support on the job. Unit nurses do not have the opportunity to build relationships with their managers, an important source of professional and social support in the past. The nurse working in the practise environment has no one to turn to for professional support, such as advice on patient- or unit-related problems.

Nursing teams that take time and commitment to build have been decimated by the redeployment of nurses from their accustomed practise environments. This redeployment of nursing teams has also reduced the collaboration in patient care and relationships with other health care professionals because of the uncertainty of professional practise environments. One example of organisational initiatives to create healthy workplaces is the Victoria Order of Nurses in the Ottawa region. In this setting, nursing teams have been established to support nurses working with specialised groups of patients. In these teams where nurses are able to develop and utilise their expertise, nurses not only nurse better but also derive more satisfaction from their work (Baumann et al., 2001).

Although many, if not all, nurses experience some degree of professional and social isolation in their workplaces, rural nurses, community health nurses, and new graduates are nurses whose sense of isolation can be linked clearly to the workplace. The following sections discuss this select group of nurses to serve as exemplars of experiences of workplace isolation.

THE EXPERIENCES OF RURAL NURSES

Whereas nurses working in rural locations have more independence in their practise than other nurses have, they have other workplace issues to contend with. Rural nursing environments often include both inpatient and outpatient practise areas, and rural nurses attend to medical, surgical, obstetric, paediatric, and emergency room patients possibly on the "same shift and frequently alone" (Winters & Mayers, 2002, p. 79). Scharff (1998) describes experienced rural nurses as "expert generalists" in that they must know a great deal about a "variety of practise areas," possess a "high level of flexibility, work independently, transition smoothly from one task to another and one patient to another" in constantly changing environments (p. 20). However, not all nurses working in the rural setting have the experience and education needed to provide care in such varied situations. Nurses working in isolated communities seldom have the opportunities to update their knowledge and skills that nurses working in major centres have. Rural nurses face professional isolation in that there are not always other nurses to draw on.

These nurses may find themselves alone with professional care and decision making while paradoxically being highly visible to the community. "Nurses working in sparsely populated areas lack anonymity, which means they are visible and identifiable within their communities and experience diminished personal and professional boundaries" (Winters & Mayer, 2002, p. 79). An example of the conflict that can arise from high visibility or lack of anonymity for a nurse in a small community is demonstrated by a nurses' privileged access to confidential information about community members. Unlike nurses in larger centres, rural nurses cannot avoid social interaction with patients and their families. In instances in which a patient's circumstance has social consequences, such as alcohol or substance abuse, the nurse can be placed in an uncomfortable or conflictual situation.

COMMUNITY AS WORKPLACE

Although much of the distance nurses experience from leaders, peers, and other professionals can be attributed to restructuring and deployment of nurses, in some cases, the particular workplace undermines the relationship of nurses and the leaders who work there. Home care nurses practise in isolation and frequently provide home nursing care that remains invisible to administrators of home care services and to the decision makers who fund these programmes. Nurses who work in home care settings may be asked to exclude patients they have been providing nursing care to from their caseload. These excluding practises are based on criteria set by administrators rather than on what the home care nurses know from providing nursing care. Purkis (2001) describes how home care nurses find themselves caught in the tension between what they know particular patients need and what administrators and government agencies expect nurses to provide.

Nurse administrators who supervise home care nurses are also caught in a tension, but their conflicts are different. Nurse administrators are situated between the home care nurses' desire to base their decisions for excluding patients from services on their professional assessment and the pressure they face as administrators "to reduce the deficits in the face of major cuts in federal health and social spending" (Purkis, 2000, p. 142).

MENTORSHIP AND ORIENTATION PROGRAMMES FOR NEW GRADUATES

Another group of nurses for whom the professional practise environment is an issue are the new graduates whose precarious job situation as an occasional "on-call" nurse has become a way of life (Viens, 1996). To understand better what it means for new graduates to fit into current practise environments and to understand the rate at which new graduates leave the profession, Viens explored the experiences of 31 new graduates over 18 months from five different Quebec hospitals. New graduates, in this study, discovered very early on that "they have entered a brave new world where the work situation proves to be very different from what they have been taught" (p. 44). In the absence of the stability that a consistent environment might bring, new graduates struggle for "professional survival." Adapting to a constantly changing environment produces what Viens (1996) in her study has dubbed the "functional nurse"—the nurse who learns to be "available at all times, to provide care with no continuity and without any hope of ever belonging to a unit" (p. 44). Is it any wonder these new graduates question the quality of care they give or their future as nurses? How is it that new graduates are expected to take their place in this constantly changing practise environment?

In an initiative to support new graduates, the Calgary Health Region has hired nursing instructors to orientate and mentor new staff. Numerous innovative programmes across the country support new graduates and their mentors through the provision of release time and reduced responsibilities for both participants. Examples of these programmes are in St. Michael's Hospital in Toronto, in the Winnipeg Health Authority, and through British Columbia's Health Action Plan (Baumann et al., 2001).

Workplace Safety

Of the many risks nurses are exposed to in the workplace, the risk of injuring themselves when providing nursing care is a primary concern. A fact sheet released by the Workers' Compensation Board (WCB) of British Columbia (2000a) reported that from 1994 to 1998, about 36,000 injury claims were made in the health care industry. The average injury rate for health care workers in British Columbia was 7.4, compared with an average rate of 4.8 for other workers in British Columbia—54% higher than other workers. Of the injuries reported, overexertions caused by "patient/resident" and "material" handlings were the most common. About two thirds of injuries reported were classified as strains, and one third of these were classified as back strain. Registered nurses figure prominently in 25% of these claims. Although this report is limited to reports of injury in British Columbia, similar findings are available from other provincial WCB reports.

According to Statistics Canada, nurses' job-related injuries are more costly than those of so-called high-risk occupations, such as firefighter or police officer. Poor workplace maintenance, inadequate equipment, and supply shortages increase nurses' risk for injury (Baumann et al., 2001, p. 4)

Workplace Violence

Research findings show that nurses experience high rates of verbal and emotional abuse, physical violence, and sexual harassment in their work. As levels of frustration and violence in society generally increase, so does the likelihood that nurses will be assaulted or abused in the workplace (CNA, 1996c).

A background paper also prepared by WCB of British Columbia (2000b) reported that health care workers experience acts of violence more often than any other group of workers in British Columbia. They also have more compensable claims and lose more days of work as a result of acts of violence than any other group. Findings of a survey of selected hospitals in Alberta indicate that a significant number of nurses (169 of 1,000) reported experiencing at least one form of violence in the previous *five* shifts (Duncan et al., 2000, 2001). These nurses also reported that although patients were the most frequent source of all types of violence, the sources of 35% of incidents of emotional and verbal abuse were physicians, co-workers, families, and visitors. In a Nova Scotia study, 80% of respondents to a survey reported experiencing some form of violence in their nursing careers (Cruickshank, 1995), and many reported that they had been victims of more than one type of violence: 63% of respondents reported having experienced harsh or insulting language; 25% had been verbally threatened with physical harm; 35% had attempts of physical harm made against them; 24% were sexually harassed in the workplace; and 21% were victims of a physical attack. According to the findings in this study, violence in the workplace is widespread, occurring in all practise settings: acute care settings, emergency departments, critical care units, psychiatric inpatient units, community health agencies, and homes for special care.

Less visible and perhaps less recognised are the experiences of violence that nurses face based on personal attributes, such as age, race, ethnicity, or sexual orientation. Gay and lesbian people, for example have "historically been treated with insensitivity, antagonism, and discrimination in their health care encounters" (Misner et al., 1997, p. 179). This knowledge of the prevailing attitudes of health care providers towards minority groups promotes the invisibility of health care providers who are themselves members of minority groups. In considering the attributes of a safe practise environment for nurses, one should consider institution policies and the unit milieus that accommodate and support differences among nurses.

Employers are demonstrating an increased awareness of and decreased tolerance for violence in the workplace through public education programmes (Boxes 16.1 and 16.2). Although many organisations are offering programmes to assist nurses in dealing with potentially violent situations and to provide support in dealing with the aftermath of violent events, current research suggests that there is continued underreporting of violent incidents by nurses (Whitehorn, 1997). See Box 16.3 for more information. Ongoing intervention and awareness of the factors contributing to workplace violence is essential in attaining a safe workplace for nurses (Box 16.4).]

Disrupted Workplaces

During restructuring, health care organisations decreased their level of support for professional development. The shift to programme management meant that mentoring and evaluation of junior nurses became less common and resources for continuing

---

BOX 16.1

Canadian Federation of Nursing Unions Workplace Violence Program

- No nurse should work alone at any time.
- Individual nurses must report acts and refuse to tolerate violence and harassment.
- Issues around prevention must be examined to create a physical environment which discourages aggressive behavior. Environment includes the layout and the climate of the workplace. It is the responsibility of employers to provide a safe workplace and put in place a zero-tolerance policy.
- Education must be an integral part of prevention. All student nurses and nurses must be prepared to assess signs of potential violent behaviour and have the skills to defuse or cope with escalating situations. It must be clear that violence or threats of such are unacceptable. There must be an awareness of the consequences of such actions.
- Employers must be accountable to provide administrative structure and support procedures to manage violent situations, including security, equipment, and personnel. An emergency response team must be prepared to deal effectively and safely with aggression.
- Employers must be accountable to provide a follow-up program which includes a clear method of documentation; nurses being advised of their rights if charges are to be laid; follow-up and support mechanisms by the employer when charges are laid; and employee assistance programs with critical incident stress debriefing available for nurses who are victims of violence in the workplace.
- Levels of governments must provide the legislative mechanisms and adequate resources to ensure safe workplaces.
- Nursing organisations must provide advocacy and information.

Source: Canadian Federation of Nursing Unions.

BOX 16.2

Factors Contributing to Workplace Violence

- Environmental factors, such as inflexible institutional rules and policies; restrictions on activities, noise, or inappropriate lighting levels; busy or high-activity times; and invasion of personal space, units, or areas housing patients (e.g., emergency department settings).
- Staff dynamics (conflict among staff members) and staff attitudes (anxiety or ambivalence towards the prevention and management of aggression). Staff behaviour (tone of voice, body language, overt aggression) may also influence the risk for violence.
- Organisational policies and educational programs which lack the policies or programmes aimed at preventing and reducing the incidence and impact of violence in the workplace.

Source: Nova Scotia Nurses Union, 1995.

education were often eliminated. Today, staff shortages make attendance at educational courses difficult even when they are available. In 1988, the CNA developed a position statement on nurse administrators that emphasised the role of the nurse administrator in providing an environment conducive to quality patient care and nurses' well-being. In 1993, the CNA developed a position statement on the role of chief nursing officers, and in 1996, it developed a position paper on nursing leadership. These statements have been repeatedly updated and offer clear direction for change.

Recent hospital downsizing and restructuring have undermined existing leadership structures and the vision the CNA documents provide for nursing. Significantly, positions such as the chief nursing officer are being eroded. In some instances, they have disappeared altogether. Changes in the role of nurse managers have led to these roles becoming more diffuse with "a broader scope of services to administer and more managerial tasks to accomplish" (McGirr & Bakker, 2000, p. 7). These changes tend to distance managers from practise and give added professional practise and coordination responsibilities to staff nurses at a time when fewer nurses are available.

BOX 16.3

Factors Influencing Underreporting of Violent Incidents

- Violence is often perceived to be part of the job.
- Potential reporters perceive no benefit from reporting (assumption that nothing will be done).
- Specific incidents are not perceived as violent by the nurse involved.
- Nurses fear employers will blame them for provoking the incident.
- Nurses fear they will be perceived as unable to manage aggressive incidents.

Source: Whitehorn, 1995.

BOX 16.4

Employer Responsibility in Providing a Safe Work Environment

Employers are responsible to provide administrative support and structures to promote the safety of all employees, including nurses. Policies and procedures are the first step in ensuring a safe workplace. Security equipment and personnel should be provided as well as education in preventing and responding to violence. Facilities should be planned or modified to discourage aggressive behavior. Clear documentation processes and follow-up mechanisms that support the nurse should be in place. This follow-up should provide critical incident stress debriefing and, if necessary, support for the nurse through the process of laying charges.

FRAMING AND ANALYSING WORK ENVIRONMENT ISSUES

The following section draws on selected frameworks to analyse issues that arise for nurses in providing quality practise environments. The organising theme of the discussion is the contradiction inherent in nurses' obligation to demand quality practise environments when they have neither the authority nor the resources to fulfill such an obligation. Making this focus explicit is not intended to undermine the importance of the work of past and current political activists in nursing but rather to highlight the need for change.

Several discourses influence the frameworks used to analyse the issues that arise for nurses in providing quality practise environments. *Discourse* as it is used here pertains to the "social practices, values and cultural beliefs that prevail in a given culture or subculture at a specified historical moment, and shape the collective sense of what is right, proper, worthwhile or valuable" (Thorne et al., 1996, p. 2). When engaging in these discussions, it is important to remember that discourses that promote an understanding of nursing are more than mere ways of thinking; they are also ways of constituting the knowledge, practises, subjectivities, and relationships of power which together make up the meanings of nursing (Weedon, 1999).

Historical Analysis

Historically, nurses account for nearly two thirds of the health sector labor force. Today, they form the single largest health profession in Canada. The origin of the main issue for nurses—the tension between obligations and rights related to nurses' workplaces—dates back to the origin of nursing itself. Given society's views on women in general and nurses in particular, one of the ways nurse leaders have been able to gain support for nurses' work was by agreeing to conform to existing power structures. This conformity meant complying with existing patriarchal expectations of women's work and unquestioning acceptance of the subservience assigned to such work. This is not to say that nurses have not contributed significantly through their work, but rather, others have both administrative and financial control of the environments in which nurses have worked. Nurses historically have held and continue to hold key leadership positions, and in that capacity, they have been able to influence change. However, the past is littered with toppled leaders, the fragmentation of our workforce, and fluctuating control over our resources.

Given the necessity of placing nurse leaders outside collective bargaining units, nurse leaders are vulnerable to changes controlled by others. To date, nurses have not been the developers and shapers of policy and legislation. Nurses' "views on policy matters have rarely been heard and found plausible, much less accepted" (Baumgart, 1998, p. 131). Participation in policy at all levels would promote nurse leaders' input on decisions and protect established and worthwhile programmes. Nurses' consistent participation in these decisions could counteract the short-term planning and shifting priorities of government bodies with a 4-year mandate.

SIGNIFICANT CHANGES IN THE WORKPLACE

Shaped by cultural influences, profiles of the nursing workforce and nursing workplaces have changed over time. Nurses have always worked in a wide variety of settings in providing care to individuals and families who are experiencing stress. Anger and aggressive behaviors have always been and continue to be responses to anxiety experienced in illness situations. What seems to have changed over time, however, is that illness may be exacerbated by other stresses, such as family disintegration, inadequate social services, underemployment, unemployment, or poverty. Combined with the increasing unpredictability of professional practise environments, these societal stresses increase nurses' risk for workplace violence, burnout, and emotional exhaustion.

EFFECTS OF CHANGE

Historically, nurses have worked in institutions, communities, and patients' homes. Although the places where nurses work have not changed that dramatically, the delivery of care has been significantly influenced by societal and cultural changes. For nurses, the concentration of health care services in large centres, coupled with the closure of smaller hospitals, means that nurses spend more time commuting between patients' homes and community centres. In addition to the nursing care provided in the traditional settings, new practise settings have opened up. Nurses work with the homeless on the streets, in isolated nursing stations in the north, onsite in occupational health positions, and in remote international communities. Whether the setting is traditional or not, the setting itself may put the nurse who works there at risk. What is of equal concern is that nurses, who are fully aware of the risks, usually lack both the authority and resources to change these professional practise environments (Table 16.1).

Table 16.1 Where Do Nurses Work?

PLACES OF EMPLOYMENT	NO. OF NURSES	PERCENTAGE OF NURSES
Hospitals	148,647	65.20
Nursing homes	28,178	12.40
Community and home care	23,661	10.40
Family practice and physicians	5,763	2.50
Educational institutions	5,611	2.50
Other	15,970	7.00
Total	**227,830**	**100.00**

Source: Registered Nurses Management Data, Statistics Canada, 1996.

Social and Cultural Analysis

Although there are many ways to provide a social and cultural analysis of the issues arising in nurses' workplaces, this discussion focusses on prevailing attitudes in society about the issues; values and priorities of the dominant culture as they influence the issues; and the ways in which these values and priorities confer privilege on the dominant culture over other members of society. That nurses need to have control and the reasons they need control over their workplaces is well documented in the nursing literature. Yet, a prevailing attitude in society is that things are fine as they are. Although the public for the most part seems aware that nurses' work environments are less than ideal, there is little evidence that employers and decision makers at all levels of government imagine that things could be otherwise. Why is this?

Professional organisations and individual nurses have lobbied, and continue to lobby, government representatives for changes that would empower nurses to control their workplaces and that would provide the resources needed for safe, competent, and ethical nursing care. Yet as our history unfolds, it is the values and priorities of the dominant culture rather than those that are representative of nursing or the recipients of nursing care that continue to influence this issue.

Despite a growing awareness of how professions whose members are predominantly women are disadvantaged, decisions about nurses' work and their workplaces continue to be made by nonnurses. Decisions about nurses' work and nurses' work environments are increasingly based on criteria derived from business models, management models, and economic models rather than related to the needs of the populations nurses serve (White, 1997; Taft & Steward, 2000).

Nurses and their managers continue to hear explanations of budget cuts that have forced them to reconceptualise services without the opportunity for nurses or their leaders to provide input about what patients need in terms of care. Moreover, nurses themselves have insufficiently understood and critiqued the ways in which these values and priorities put the needs of the dominant culture over other members of society (Davies, 1995).

According to Davies (1995), in her work *Gender and the Professional Predicament of Nursing*, an understanding of the nursing world must be found in the "gendering of social institutions, in the dynamics of the devaluation of nursing work that this produces and the discourses of diminishment that accompany this" (p. 180). Together, according to Davies, the gendering, the devaluation, and the diminishment of nurses "trivialize the work of nursing, belittle the people who carry it out putting them in a position of impossible choices" which in turn leads them "to doubt the caliber of their leaders and of themselves" (p. 180). Thankfully, Davies concludes her work on a much more positive note. Through her work, she has come to see how these existing models of organising institutions are socially and historically constructed and therefore the place where new constructions, new history can be created. It is Davies' view that nurses could take the lead in addressing these changes, to be a part of new constructions. One of the ways of deconstructing particular views and reconstructing new ones is through a critical feminist analysis.

Critical Feminist Analysis

A feminist analysis looks beyond the experiences of a particular nurse—woman or man—to the structures and ideologies that influence these experiences. Past and existing government and employment structures have shaped policymaking so that nurses are bypassed as decision makers and controllers of the resources needed for safe and competent nursing practise. A feminist analysis is intended to promote understanding of the views and the effects of the views held by others about nurses' abilities and realities. It is not that others view nurses as unable to take responsibility for shaping quality workplaces; rather, the prevalence of patriarchal views is such that empowering nurses as responsible policymakers has not been seriously considered.

A feminist analysis is also useful in that it insists that nurses explore their own participation in the realities of nursing, which makes nurses—mostly women—more aware of how they participate in perpetuating patriarchal views. Put another way, feminist analysis helps us to understand our own complicity in sustaining structures and ideologies that foster misinterpretation of women's and nurses' experiences.

Nurses have not always supported leaders or nurses who worked to bring about changes in workplace environments. A feminist analysis of a nursing issue is useful also because it increases knowledge and awareness of relevant power structures, thereby positioning nurses to participate more effectively in changing them. Although various approaches may guide feminist analysis, support for issues related to nurses' workplace comes from challenging the following:

- Structures and ideologies that contribute to errors or myths about a nurse's abilities or realities
- Power inequities (and the hierarchic and patriarchal structures of institutions) over patients
- Power and authority of structures that interfere with one's right to have control of one's life

A feminist analysis is often done concurrently with a political analysis in which one takes the following into account: Who benefits from this issue being resolved? Who benefits from the status quo? What is the relationship between knowledge and power in this situation? How do ageist, sexist, racist, and ablest ideologies influence our understanding of this issue? How do dominant ideologies keep nurses from accepting their own ideas or those of their leaders over those imposed by other authorities?

Political Analysis

In situations in which nurses face the challenge of providing quality workplaces for their practise, they commonly struggle in less-than-ideal situations to provide adequate care. Nurses and the recipients of nurses' care could certainly benefit from the resolution of issues related to quality in the workplace. One may argue that the continued exploitation of nurses is unacceptable. One may also argue that nurses who continue to function in less-than-ideal situations are unlikely to go on doing so given that many more desirable opportunities are available. It is difficult to formulate an argument that someone benefits from nurses working in inferior work environments, and yet it is not that difficult to point out that others do benefit from the exploitation of nurses.

One may argue that funding to address these issues is not available or that short-term savings are at the expense of nurses' health and the health of all Canadians in the long term. It is not that the health of Canadians is at risk because nurses work in inferior environments; it is that nurses are unlikely to continue working in high-risk situations. As such, the staff needed to provide care that promotes and sustains the health of Canadians will be unavailable (Ceci & McIntyre, 2001).

Economic Analysis

An economic analysis highlights how the forces of supply and demand work in a particular issue. For issues related to nurses' workplaces, one may explore the influence nurse leaders have in challenging purely cost-containment strategies when the health of Canadians is thought to be at risk. A purely economic analysis of these issues could lead and has led to nurses being asked to do more with less. Sochalski (2001) reminds us that "economics provides the framework for the allocation of resources," and the economics question facing nursing is not what the value of nursing care is but rather "how to allocate this valuable resource to best meet the health care needs of our patients and our population" (p. 15).

The difficulty talking about health care and nursing care in purely economic terms is that it overlooks other costs. What needs to be made more transparent to the public is the high cost and incredible waste of resources resulting from the short-term slashing of funds, closure of needed health facilities, and withdrawal of life-sustaining services. An ironic point to consider here is that the position statement obligating nurses to demand quality practise environments includes a phrase suggesting that this be done "within the costs and quality framework mandated by the organisation where the care is provided" (p. 1). The concern is that such wording supports the claim that governments would provide differently if they could, a point that in many cases has been accepted without question.

BARRIERS TO RESOLUTION

One of the most important strategies for moving an issue towards resolution is identifying barriers that may impede the resolution process. Identifying barriers increases opportunities for resolution through such means as mediation, collaboration, or negotiation.

As stated earlier, the major barrier to resolving issues arising in nurses' professional practise environments is nurses' lack of authority and resources to influence the quality of their workplace environments. Despite this lack of authority and control, nurses and others continue to hold nurses accountable for providing safe and ethical practise environments. Until policies are enacted that authorise nurse leaders to control decisions and manage resources in the workplace, the current situation is unlikely to change. Until nurses see themselves and their leaders as agents of change, it is hard to imagine such change occurring.

A second barrier is the complexity of nurses' workplaces. It is not always well understood what needs to change, and what constitutes a risk for nurses needs to be better defined and understood. For example, a number of contributing factors have been known to exacerbate the risk for violence or trigger potentially violent situations in the workplace (see Box 16.1 for more information). Despite some excellent programmes on quality workplaces in all provinces and the territories, the high incidence of violent events and workplace injuries suggests that nurses are not accessing these programmes or that programmes are not what are needed to address these issues.

A third barrier is that nurses and employers have come to accept what on closer scrutiny is unacceptable. For example, the failure of nurses to report violent events and employers' failure to address these are also barriers (see Box 16.2 for more information).

A fourth barrier is the lack of understanding of what constitutes quality workplaces in the first place. Although a great deal of research has been done (Bourbonnais et al., 1998; Laschinger et al., 2001; O'Brien-Pallas et al., 1997), and reports synthesising this research and making recommendations for change have been carried out (Baumann et al., 2001; Corey-Lisle et al., 1999; Greenglass & Burke, 2001; McGirr & Bakker, 2000; Sochalski, 2001), the resources to carry out these recommendations are not in place. The issues surrounding nurses' work, the conditions of nurses' work, and the quality of nurses' workplaces are often talked about and researched together. Considering issues of the workplace apart from issues of nurses' work could account for how these issues and the strategies for resolving these issues are different.

The final barrier is the lack of resources to make the changes that need to be made. Nurses and others involve themselves in explanations suggesting that everything that can be done is being done, or that the resources to improve nurses' workplaces are simply unavailable. These explanations act as a barrier to change because they overlook the high cost of failing to create and sustain healthful workplaces for nurses.

STRATEGIES FOR RESOLUTION

The first step in formulating strategies for resolving workplace issues is addressing the most central theme in the literature and across all practise environments: control over the workplace and resources to support nurses' work and quality environments. The following strategies are designed to give agency to nurses; the intention of these strategies is not to imply that the responsibility for resolution of these issues lies only with nurses or nurse leaders.

Strategies to address these issues include the following:

- Nurse leaders, practitioners, educators, researchers, leaders in professional organisations, and heads of collective bargaining groups need to continue negotiating for the involvement of nurses at all levels in decisions affecting practise, patient care, and the work environment. Nurses need to be in a position to authorise and provide the resources to delegate both nursing work and non-nursing work to unregulated workers. Nurses need flexibility in the scheduling of work hours to balance personal needs with organisational needs and the right to decide on their availability for overtime. Nurses have the right to control their professional and social lives.
- New graduates support the imperative for quality work environments when they understand what constitutes a good environment and select employers who demonstrate evidence of interest and resources that produce such workplaces.
- Nurses need to take the lead in and insist on being full participants in development and implementation of policy to support the health, safety, and well-being of nurses. To be implemented, these policies require administrative and government support through the provision of human and material resources for them.
- To address issues related to the risk for work-related safety and violence, nurses need to support the call of professional and collective bargaining units for zero tolerance of workplace violence. In addition, employers need to be held accountable to governmental agencies for providing up-to-date and well-maintained space and equipment in nurses' workplaces to avoid workplace injury.
- Nurses must continue to lobby for the development of policy and research to support evidence-based decision making as an important element of quality nursing practise.

- Nurses also need to be involved in decisions and policies related to health care technology. Nurses need opportunities to learn about communication and information technology tools to take responsibility and be held accountable for providing quality practise environments.
- To implement and sustain change, nurses need to enlist the support of governments in obtaining needed resources. Nurses also need to collaborate with employers in restructuring workplaces so that nurses have the authority to control their work. Nurse educators, researchers, policy developers, and leaders must present a unified argument focussed on the need for change and how changes can be implemented. Professional organisations and collective bargaining units need to continue their efforts to keep governments, employers, nurses, and the public informed of the risks involved for nurses and health care if these changes are not addressed.

SUMMARY

This chapter identifies several important issues for nurses on the topic of nurses' work environments. A central issue identified is the incongruity between nurses being obligated to demand quality workplaces for the provision of safe, competent patient care and the reality of nurse leaders, practitioners, educators, and researchers having neither the authority nor resources to act on such an obligation.

Related workplace issues explored are professional and social isolation; risks for workplace violence; alienation from nurse leaders, workplace peers, and other professionals; inadequate education, mentorship, and orientation programmes; decreased levels of support for professional development; and the failure of governments and the public to understand and support the needed changes in nurses' work environments.

New graduates and more experienced nurses provide nursing care in a wide variety of workplaces, among them acute and long-term care institutions, rural areas with limited facilities and professional staff, patients' homes, and community settings. Several frameworks, including historical, sociocultural, political, economic, and critical feminist, are used to analyse nurses' workplace issues. Such analyses help nurses to identify barriers to fulfilling the obligation to demand quality work environments.

Strategies for overcoming barriers to fulfilling their obligations and demands include negotiating politically and professionally for inclusion in health care and workplace policy decisions as well as the material resources to support policy. Given the authority, adequate resources, and support of colleagues, nurses can provide quality practise environments as those envisioned by the CNA.

Online RESOURCES

Add to your knowledge of this issue:

International Council of Nurses	*www.icn.ch*
Canadian Nurses Association	*www.cna-nurses.ca*
Canadian Federation of Nursing Unions	*www.nursesunions.ca*

Provincial and Territorial Organisations

Registered Nurses Association of British Columbia	www.rnabc.bc.ca
Alberta Association of Registered Nurses	www.nurses.ab.ca
Saskatchewan Registered Nurses Association	www.srna.org
College of Registered Nurses of Manitoba	www.marn.mb.ca
Registered Nurses Association of Ontario	www.rnao.org
College of Nurses of Ontario	www.cno.org
Ordre des Infirmiéres et Infirmiers du Québec	www.oiiq.org
Nurses Association of New Brunswick	www.nanb.nb.ca
College of Registered Nurses of Nova Scotia	www.rnans.ns.ca
Association of Registered Nurses of Newfoundland and Labrador	www.arnn.nf.ca
Association of Nurses of Prince Edward Island	www.iwpei.com/nurses
Northwest Territories Registered Nurses Association	www.nwtrna.com
Yukon Registered Nurses Association	e-mail: yrna@yknet.ca

Reflections on the Chapter

1. Which of the workplace issues described in the chapter have you observed in your own practicum experience? What other examples can you add?
2. Identify the appropriate documents that provide direction for nurses and their employers in the provision of professional practise environments.
3. What are the barriers in your practise environment to nurses providing safe, ethical care? How would you resolve these?
4. Of the strategies offered for resolving the issue, which have you seen implemented in practise?
5. What are your views on the strengths and limitations of the strategies presented in this chapter or that you have seen utilised in the practise setting?
6. Identify at least one issue for nurses in the provision of a safe professional practise environment for their work.
7. What other strategies can you suggest for the resolution of this issue?
8. How would you describe the stand of your provincial professional organisation on this issue? How would you account for this stand?

REFERENCES

Aiken, L., Sloane, D., & Sochalski, J. (1998). Hospital organizations and outcomes. *Quality in Health Care, 7*(4), 222–226.

Aiken, L., Smith, H., & Lake, E. (1994). Lower medicare mortality among a set of hospitals known for good nursing care. *Medical Care 32*(8), 771–787.

Akyeampong, E., & Usalcas, J. (1998). Work absence rates, 1980–1997. *Statistics Canada,* Cat No. 71-535-MPB, no. 9.

Alberta Association of Registered Nurses (2002, Sept). Supports for safe practice environments. Retrieved from: http://nurses.ab.ca/issues/safer.html

Baumann, A., O'Brien-Pallas, L., Armstrong-Strassen, Blythe, J., Bourbonnais, R, Cameron, S., Doran, D., Kerr, M., Gillis-Hall, L., Vzina, M., Butt, M., & Ryan, L. (2001*). Commitment and care: The benefits of health workplaces for nurses, their patients and the system. A policy synthesis.* Canadian Health Research Foundation. Ottawa: Government of Canada.

Baumgart, A. (1998). Nurses and political action: The legacy of sexism. *Canadian Journal of Nursing Research, 30*(4), 131–142.

Billay, E. (2002). Safety and risks for RN's on home visits. *Alberta RN, 58*(2), 14–15.

Bourbonnais, R., Comeau, M., Vezina, M., & Dion, G. (1998). Job strain, psychological stress and burnout in nurses. *American Journal of Industrial Medicine, 34,* 20–28.

Canadian Nurses Association. (1996a). *Chief executive officer.* Ottawa: Author.

Canadian Nurses Association. (1996b*). Nursing leadership.* Ottawa: Author.

Canadian Nurses Association. (1996c*). Violence in the workplace/nurse abuse.* Ottawa: Author.

Canadian Nurses Association. (1996d). *Resources, research and education initiatives on nurse abuse/violence in the workplace.* Ottawa: Author.

Canadian Federation of Nurses Unions (2002, Sept). Violence in the workplace. www.nursesunions.ca/ps/violenceworkplace.shtml.

Ceci, C., & McIntyre, M. (2001). A quiet crisis in health care: Developing our capacity to hear. *Nursing Philosophy 2*(2), 122–130.

Corey-Lisle, P., Tarzian, A., Cohen, M., & Trinkoff, A. (1999). Healthcare reform: It's effect on nurses. *Journal of Nursing Administration, 29*(3), 30–37.

Croker, K., & Cummings, A. L. (1995). Nurses' reactions to physical assault by their patients. *Canadian Journal of Nursing Research, 27*(2), 81–93.

Cruickshank, C. J. M. (1995). Nurse abuse: A study of workplace violence in Nova Scotia. *Nurse to Nurse, 6*(2), 12.

Davies, C. (1995). *Gender and the professional predicament in nursing.* Philadelphia: Open University Press.

Duncan, S., Estabrooks, C. A., & Reimer, M. (2000). Violence against nurses. *Alberta RN, 56*(2), 13–14.

Duncan, S. M., Hyndman, K., Estabrooks, C. A., Hesketh, K., Humphrey, C. K., Wong, J. S., Acorn, S., & Giovannetti, P. (2001). Nurses' experience of violence in Alberta and British Columbia hospitals. *Canadian Journal of Nursing Research, 32*(4), 57–78.

Forbes, S. (1996). *Critical incident stress: Signs, symptoms, and interventions.* Halifax: Author.

Greenglass, E., & Burke, J. (2001). Stress and effects of hospital re-structuring in nurses. *Canadian Journal of Nursing Research, 33*(2), 93–108.

Laschinger, H., Finegan, J., Shamian, J., & Almost, J. (2001). Testing Karasek's demands control model in restructured health care settings: Effects of job strain on staff nurses, *Nursing Administration, 31*(5), 233–243.

Levek, M., & Jones, C (1996). The nursing practice environment, staff retention, and quality of care. *Research in Nursing and Health, 19*(4), 331–343.

Mayer, D. (2002). Special feature: An approach to cardiac care in rural settings. *Critical care Nursing Quarterly 24*(4), 75–82.

Marck, P. (1993). Abuse in the workplace: A symptom that signs alone won't cure. *AARN Newsletter, 49*(7), 31–33.

McCaskill, L. (1990). Dealing with nurse abuse. *Canadian Nursing Management, 27,* 25–33.

McGirr, M., & Bakker, D. (2000). Shaping positive work environments for nurses. *Canadian Journal of Nursing Research, 13*(1), 7–14.

McGuinness, S. (1992). Nurse abuse: Inhumanity tolerated. *AARN Newsletter, 48*(4), 17–18.

Misner, T., Sowell, R., Phillips, K., & Harris, C. (1997). Sexual orientation: A cultural diversity issue for nursing. *Nursing Outlook, 45*(4), 178–181.

National Federation of Nurses' Unions (1991). *Position statement on violence in the workplace.* Ottawa: Author.

O'Brien-Pallas, L., Irvine, D., Peereboom, E., & Murray, M. (1997). Measuring nursing workload: Understanding the variability. *Nursing Economics, 15*(4), 171–182.

Purkis, M. (2001). Managing home nursing care: Visibility, accountability and exclusion. *Nursing Inquiry, 8*(3), 141–150.

Registered Nurses' Association of British Columbia. (1990*). Information for nurses: Dealing with abusive behavior.* Vancouver: Author.

Registered Nurses' Association of Nova Scotia. (1996). *Violence in the workplace.* Dartmouth: Author.

Registered Nurses' Association of Ontario (1994). *Nurse abuse.* Toronto: Author.

Scharff, J. (1998). The distinctive nature and scope of rural practice: Philosophical bases. In H. J. Lee (Ed.), *Conceptual basis for rural nursing* (pp. 19–38). New York: Springer.

Sochalski, J. (2001). Nursing's valued resources: Critical issues in economics and nursing care. *Canadian Journal of Nursing Research, 33*(1), 11–18.

Taft, K. & Steward, G. (2000). Clear answers: The economics and politics of for-profit medicine. Edmonton: Duval Gaske.

Thorne, S., McCormick, J., & Carty, E. (1996). Deconstructing the gender neutrality of illness and disability. *Health Care for Women International 18*, 1–16.

Viens, C. (1996). The future shock of nursing graduates. *Canadian Nurse 92*(2), 40–44.

Whitehorn, D., & Nowlan, M. (1997). Towards an aggression-free health care environment. *Canadian Nurse, 93*(3), 24–26.

Weedon, C. (1999). Feminism, theory and the politics of difference. London: Blackwell.

White, J. P. (1997). Health care, hospitals, and reengineering: The nightingales sign the blues. In A. Duffy, D. Glenday, & N. Pupo (Eds.), *Good jobs, bad jobs, no jobs: The transformation of work in the 21st century.* Toronto: Harcourt & Brace.

Whitehorn, D. & Nowlan, M. (1997). Towards an aggression-free health care environment. *Canadian Nurse, 93*(3),24–26.

Winters, C. and Mayer, D. (2002). Special feature: An approach to cardiac care in rural settings. *Critical Care Nursing Quarterly, 24*(4), 75–82.

Workers' Compensation Board of British Columbia. (2000a). *WCB fact sheet. Health care industry: Health care sector* [On-line; news release]. Available: www. worksafebc.comcorporate.

Workers' Compensation Board of British Columbia. (2000b). *Preventing violence in health care: Five steps to an effective program.* Vancouver, BC: Author.

17

Unionisation: Collective Bargaining in Nursing

Marjorie McIntyre ■ Carol McDonald

Chapter Objectives

At the completion of this chapter, you will be able to:

1. Understand the significance of issues related to collective bargaining for nurses.

2. Describe the breadth and scope of collective bargaining groups and the issues they address for nurses.

(continued)

In many cases, collective action leads to collective bargaining. Here, the Saskatchewan Union of Nurses (SUN) shines a bright light on nurses' working conditions.

3. Explore personal, professional, and societal assumptions about unionism.

4. Discuss the events that led to the separation of professional organisations and collective bargaining groups.

5. Identify legislation that has shaped nurses' collective action.

6. Discuss the influence of public support on nurses' collective bargaining.

This chapter highlights issues that arise from nurses' unionisation and collective bargaining activities. It introduces collective bargaining and the issues that arise from nurses' relationships with unions and unionisation. Next, it presents a selection of issues that arise for nurses within the context of unions and collective bargaining, along with their significance. It then uses a framework by which to analyse issues, drawing on historical, social-cultural, political, ethical-legal, critical feminist, and economic perspectives. Lastly, the chapter addresses barriers to nurses' participation in the collective bargaining process, along with strategies to increase nurses' understanding of the issues that surround unions and collective bargaining.

The intent of this chapter is to make visible the current situation for nurses in collective bargaining in Canada and to provide nurses with a framework by which to analyse these issues. Although nurses' collective bargaining procedures affect many people, the principal participants in collective bargaining include two groups: "nurses and their unions" and "employers and their organizations" (Hibberd, 1999, p. 506). Governments also are involved; they "fund hospitals and community health-care agencies," create labour laws, and also are responsible for protecting the public interest (p. 506).

In Canada the direction for union certification comes from provincial labour legislation. The labour relations system is decentralised much like that of the health care system, leaving responsibility for collective bargaining mostly with the provinces. Because each province and territory has its own labour legislation, the formation of unions and collective bargaining procedures tend to vary from province to province, which is "why nurses are entitled to strike in some provinces and not in others" (Hibberd, 1999, p. 506) (Box 17.1).

COLLECTIVE BARGAINING

Collective bargaining refers to the activities that nurses and their unions are involved in to negotiate working conditions and remuneration. A collective agreement, the product of collective bargaining, is a "contract of employment" (Hibberd, 1999, p. 506).

In most situations, unions now act as the bargaining agents for many nurses in Canada. Prior to the establishment of independent unions for nurses, collective bargaining took place through nurses' provincial or territorial professional associations. Before the establishment of professional organisations, nurses were self-employed and singularly negotiated salary and work conditions with their employers. Independent

---

BOX 17.1

Glossary: Terms of Labour

Collective agreement-a contract of employment.

Collective bargaining-the procedures and processes that all nurses are involved in to negotiate working conditions and remuneration.

Grievance-a claim that one or more of the provisions of a collective agreement have been violated, accompanied by a request for compensation.

Negotiation-give-and-take process in which multiple parties meet to discuss issues, present requests, and settle demands.

Mediation-process by which all parties involved in conflict agree to reach a decision that all parties can accept.

Arbitration-process by which a final decision is made by a third party.

Lockout-the employer locks employees out of the work setting.

Ratified agreement-contractual process in which the provisions in a contract are agreed upon by both parties and by which both parties are duty-bound to honor until such time as a new contract is negotiated.

Work-to-rule-job action taken to challenge contract provisions, such as refusal to work overtime, restriction of activities to the practice of nursing, and refusal to do nonnursing work.

Strike-withdrawal of services; a *legal strike* involves action permitted by existing labour laws; an *illegal strike* involves action in defiance of existing labour laws.

Source: Hibberd, J. Working with unions. In J. Hibberd & L. Smith (Eds.), *Nursing management in Canada* (2nd ed., pp. 505-524). City: Publisher, with permission.

---

unions certified by provincial labour relation systems have now been in place for nurses in each of the provinces and territories in Canada for more than 3 decades.

The board of Canadian Federation of Nurses Union (CFNU) includes elected representatives from each of the provincial member unions except Quebec. The CFNU represents 122,000 nurses, including registered nurses, registered psychiatric nurses, and licensed practical nurses, and is the largest organisation of nurses in Canada. Founded in 1981, the CFNU provides a national voice for the concerns of Canadian nurses as well as resources to support provincial union activities (Connors, 2002) (Table 17.1).

Issues Arising from the Unionisation of Nurses

The impetus for this chapter is the assumption that many nurses experience ambivalence regarding participation in, and support of, collective bargaining. Nurses' ambivalence is assumed to link to complex unresolved issues within the collective bargaining process. What follows is the identification and discussion of selected issues.

1. Nurses experience tension between unionism and professionalism.
2. Conflict exists over participating in job action that involves the withdrawal of services.
3. Nurses face alienation from co-workers whose views differ from theirs.
4. Conflict-of-interest legislation divides nurses and their leaders.

Table 17.1   Differences Between Unions and Professional Associations

	PROFESSIONAL ASSOCIATION	UNION
Membership	All registered nurses in the province	Excludes management and administration
Legislative authority	Health Professions Act	Provincial Labour Relations Boards
Mandate	To promote the profession of nursing and to protect the public interest	To advance social, economic, and general welfare of nurses
Roles	Registration of members	The regulation of relations between nurses and their employers
	Regulation and discipline of members	The negotiation of written contracts with employers
	Scope of practise; standards of care and competency	The promotion of the knowledge of nurses through education and research
	Represents the concerns of its members to government, the public, and allied health professions	The promotion of the highest standards of health care
	Provision of educational loans and scholarships	The promotion of unity within the labour movement, the nursing profession, and other allied fields
		The promotion of occupational health and safety

Information modified from data provided by United Nurses of Alberta at *www.una.ab.ca.*

5. Ambiguity exists as to what constitutes "essential services."
6. Pay equity (equal pay for work of equal value) is an issue.
7. Knowledge of collective bargaining, its history, and its legislated authority is inadequate.
8. The nature of relationships among nurses' unions, governments, and employers is adversarial.

TENSION BETWEEN UNIONISM AND PROFESSIONALISM

Nurses' ambivalence also can be understood as a tension between "unionism" and "professionalism." Conflict is created for individual nurses who hold membership in union and professional organisations. These organisations hold differing mandates that occasionally could be seen as at cross-purposes. The central focus of nursing unions is its members' remuneration and working conditions, whereas the central focus of professional associations is the maintenance of standards of care and the protection of the public. The history of nursing reflects nurses' unresolved tensions between the interests of quality care for patients and the interests of a quality work life for nurses who provide that care.

In a study exploring nurses' perceptions of the coping of colleagues during the fall-out from a strike, Hibberd and Norris (1991) reported that nurses' strikes and other forms of job action "place nurses in the dilemma of having to chose between loyalty to patients in providing uninterrupted services, and loyalty to peers in collectively pursuing improvements to working conditions and socio-economic status" (p. 52). In a practice discipline in which interpersonal relationships between colleagues can affect the delivery of quality of care, it is important to consider the effects of conflicting feelings both within the individual nurse and in relationships with peers.

CONFLICT OVER PARTICIPATING IN JOB ACTION THAT INVOLVES THE WITHDRAWAL OF SERVICES

Despite the increasing unity of nurses regarding the need for collective bargaining, nurses remain divided when it comes to making decisions about job action. Nurses' dissonance on this issue can be linked to the adversarial nature of this discourse in media coverage, in collective bargaining legislation, and in the message heard in day-to-day life (Hibberd, 1992b). Some of this dissonance can be traced to 1944, when the Canadian Nurses Association (CNA) approved collective bargaining for practicing nurses but rejected the idea that nurses would even consider the withdrawal of services (Jensen, 1992). Since that time, provinces have taken different fragmenting stands based on the differing provisions of provincial legislation. As a result, nursing organisations have been fragmented, and the possibility for solidarity for Canadian nurses as a group has been disrupted. Despite the increasingly unified stand of nurses regarding the need for collective bargaining, there remains less solidarity over what constitutes acceptable job action (Kerr, 1996b).

NURSES FACE ALIENATION FROM CO-WORKERS WITH DIFFERING VIEWS

Nurses identified the importance of aligning their views with colleagues, co-workers, and nurse leaders for "fear of alienation" from them. In Hibberd and Norris (1991) study, nurses identified the most powerful reason for joining a strike was "fear of peer pressure and possible retribution" (p.50) if they chose to cross their own picket lines. Nurses in this study also feared that not aligning with a majority decision could result in adverse personal consequences. One nurse expressed her concern in this way: "If you ever cross the picket line, they [co-workers] never let you forget it. The people you work with will never, ever forget that you crossed" (p.50). Given the centrality of interpersonal relationships for nurses' work, these tensions are extremely important to nurses and their workplace environments.

CONFLICT OF INTEREST LEGISLATION

Conflict-of-interest legislation has divided staff nurses from administrative nurses, leaving the staff nurses without managerial support and managers without the security of a collective agreement. In 1973, a controversy erupted over who would be certified as the official bargaining unit for a group of Saskatchewan nurses. Prior to this time, the professional organisations, which included nurse managers, had carried out collective bargaining. A question was raised of whether the staff nurses' association, part of the professional association, should continue as the bargaining agent or if independent unions should be formed. The controversy was resolved in favor of a union. The 1973 Supreme Court ruling "ultimately required that a separate and completely independent nursing union or unions be formed to assume the collective bargaining function for general staff nurses" (Ross-Kerr, 1998, p. 274). By 1981, the "transition from responsibility vested in professional associations to responsibility vested in independent nursing unions had taken place in every province in Canada" (p. 274). The tension for nurses created by this change from professional organisations to unions as their collective bargaining agent remains.

On one hand, the conflict-of-interest concern of nurse managers evaluating staff nurses is defensible. Nurses need to be able to bargain independently of administrators. On the other hand, this legislation has the potential to create a rift between staff nurses and their leaders (McPherson, 1996). Nurse leaders in their capacity as representing employers and acting on their behalf were cut off from the larger group of nurses. One could even argue that unionization divided the group that the professional association had contained. A further concern that can be linked to much of the current ambivalence to this 1973 legislation is the vulnerability of nurse leaders to lose their positions in cost-containment strategies and the fragmenting effects of these cuts in staffing on nurses as group. Important highlights of this issue are the effects of the legislation on nurses and nursing. This is not a comment for or against nurse unions but rather a reminder for nurses to be cognizant of the effects of this legislation.

AMBIGUITY ABOUT WHAT CONSTITUTES ESSENTIAL SERVICES

From the inception of collective bargaining in nursing, the understanding that essential services would be in place and would not be compromised by any job action has been a given. What complicates this tenet of collective bargaining agreements is that it is "not inherently obvious" (Ross-Kerr, 1998, p. 280) which services are essential. Even in those provinces where there is some agreement as to what constitutes such services and guidelines are in place to identify "how essential services should be put in place in the event of a strike" conflicts can and still do occur (p. 280). Ambiguity as to what constitutes "essential services" complicates nurses' decision-making about supporting strikes and about how to act during a strike.

PAY EQUITY: EQUAL PAY FOR WORK OF EQUAL VALUE

The issue of pay equity, equal pay for work of equal value, both complicates and is complicated by negotiations involving the gendered nature of nurses' work (Day, 1993). Despite general agreement by most members of society that women generally and nurses particularly have the right to equal pay for work of equal value, salary inequities remain the reality for many Canadian nurses. The major challenge of pay equity is and always has been the lack of clarity about what constitutes nurses' work. Once the nature and scope of nurses' work is agreed on, there is the added difficulty of finding a comparable group in which the dominant gender is male to assess equity (Schriber, 1992). As long as the values associated with nursing and nurses' work are not made explicit, both nurses and their employers go on accepting the way things are. However, with pay equity legislation forcing "nurses to articulate the value of nurses' work" (p. 19) and administrators to make explicit "how much (or how little) they value nursing work"(p. 19), the status quo can never be the same.

NURSES' INADEQUATE KNOWLEDGE OF COLLECTIVE BARGAINING, ITS HISTORY, AND ITS LEGISLATED AUTHORITY

Interviews conducted with nurses during strikes suggest that an important issue for the nursing unions is lack of sophistication about understanding collective bargaining, its history, and its legislated authority (Day, 1993; McPherson, 1999). Nursing curricula have been slow to provide the knowledge needed for nurses to understand collective bargaining, its history, and its place in the nurse's work life (Day, 1993).

Despite significant public relations work by unions and professional associations, practicing nurses do not always well understand the need to belong to both a professional organisation and a union. Such misunderstanding can be traced to nurses' lack of familiarity with the legislation that mandated the need for independent unions and professional associations and the scarcity of political and historical collective bargaining in nursing curriculum. Even today, nurse educators are ambivalent about the place of collective bargaining in nursing and the role of unions in the profession. This, of course, can result in differences in the way this knowledge is presented, or not, to students. Also, until very recently, many textbooks for nursing programmes were American and were therefore more reflective of the American labour situation.

Even when nurses understand the diverse purposes of unions and professional organisations, the resistance to accepting the need for two organisations may arise from the burden of paying dues to both organisations. Another possible reason for some nurses' ambivalence is that nurses may not comprehend the breadth and scope of what unions have to offer. Typically, many nurses and the public equate unionism with strike action and financial remuneration.

A review of national and provincial web sites reveals that, currently, nursing unions across Canada are taking action to raise awareness of recruitment and retention issues, increase nursing seats in educational institutions, and to increase nurses' autonomy, power, and control in the workplace. Union leaders are speaking out on issues of access to quality basic care, Medicare, and the universality of the health care system (Table 17.2). Union organisations are developing strategies to partner with professional organisations, employers, and governments to address issues of nurses' work life and to improve nurses' relationships with employers.

ADVERSARIAL NATURE OF RELATIONSHIPS BETWEEN NURSES' UNIONS, GOVERNMENTS, AND EMPLOYERS

Talk of cost containment and rollback of nurses' salaries are common at collective bargaining tables across the country. It is hard for nurses and their unions to get ahead when they need so much energy just to maintain the collective agreement provisions they already have achieved. Despite gains for many Canadian nurses at bargaining tables from 1998 to 2001, constant governmental talk of cost containment and restructuring strategies is and always has been accompanied by the possibility of the loss of significant gains for nurses.

Nurses and their unions, particularly in provinces that have removed the right to strike, put themselves, their union, and their certification to collective bargain as a group at risk when they engage in illegal strikes. However, when nurses see themselves as losing what they have gained through 3 decades of past collective bargaining, it is not that difficult to understand their willingness to take such risks.

In the United Nurses of Alberta's (UNA) illegal strike of 1988, the employer was poised to roll back a significant percentage of the salary increases and contract provisions gained in previous collective bargaining. Although faced with heavy fines for an illegal strike, on January 25, 1988, some 11,000 nurses from 96 hospitals left their work and picketed for 19 days in −30°C weather (Ross-Kerr, 1998). The union paid the fines but stopped the rollbacks and other provisions that employers were negotiating to take away. Nurses made other gains on this illegal strike: the public strongly supported the nurses' collective bargaining despite the disruption it created, and nurses who had previously not participated in strike actions (because they were illegal in their places of employment) joined the nurses on the picket lines. Strategically planned on the eve of the Calgary Winter Olympic games, the strike by the UNA nurses showed that they would not tolerate unjust treatment. Although it is true that "illegal strikes by unions are becoming more common, that nurses have been willing to engage in them has been shocking to many" (p. 283).

Although the issues overlap and are not representative of all issues that arise for nurses in the collective bargaining process, they are issues that have been present in nurses' collective bargaining since its inception (McPherson, 1996). The multiple tensions that exist for nurses are further complicated by society's expectations of nurses and the media's questionable accounting of these expectations (Day, 1993). In many cases nurses' ambivalence toward collective bargaining can be traced to their reluctance to be involved in strikes or other forms of job action involving withdrawal of services. In other cases, however, particularly in the past, the ambivalence can be linked to the somewhat naïve belief still held by some nurses that employers will treat nurses fairly without such action (Jensen, 1992).

Significance of Addressing Collective Bargaining Issues

The restructuring of the health care system throughout the 1990s has shifted the priorities for nurses and significantly affected the conditions in which nurses work. Although nurses have made notable gains in their salaries in many provinces, shifting priorities within provincial health care systems in recent decades have influenced working conditions in ways that are reminiscent of working conditions of nurses in much earlier times. Canadian nurses continue to struggle with their work being recognised and valued in society, establishment of safe and healthy work environments, and reasonable work-life demands.

In the past, nurses were more able to rely on the leadership and mentorship of senior nurses. In many instances, these long-established relationships were eroded in the restructuring of health care workplaces. Although one could argue that leadership within unions is a constant support for practicing nurses, the need remains for every nurse to understand the contribution that she or he can make to the resolution of the issues that are addressed through collective bargaining. Further, there is need for some form of connection between the collective bargaining engaged in by nurses, their provincial professional associations, and the national professional association.

FRAMEWORK FOR ANALYSING COLLECTIVE BARGAINING ISSUES

A framework for analysis highlights how the issues surrounding nurses' ambivalence are constituted for nurses in relation to the collective bargaining process. In some instances nurses' ambivalence can be linked to the history of nursing and of collective bargaining itself. Nurses' ambivalence reflects prevailing societal attitudes about women's work, nurses' work, and the gendered nature of workplace realities (Stuart, 1993). This framework for analysis draws on historical, sociocultural, political, ethical-legal, critical feminist, and economic discourses. These discourses are more than ways of thinking; they reflect the practices and social values that contribute to our understandings of the nurses' experience of collective bargaining (Thorne et al., 1996).

Historical Analysis

An historical analysis helps to identify the events and conditions that have led to the development of the issue. Nurses' living and working conditions, in the early 20th century, can best be described as deplorable. Hospitals were almost completely staffed by student nurses. In situations in which graduate nurses were hired, they were treated as students: salaries, holidays, sick time, and benefits were almost nonexistent, as were standards of practise and regulation of working conditions. Nurses often worked in private homes and relied on their employer's goodwill for their well-being; some nurses working for only room and board. Nurses were vulnerable to workplace discrimination rooted in "age, physical attraction and ethnicity" (Jensen, 1992, p. 558).

Faced with abysmal working conditions and unsympathetic employers, nurses had little choice but to organise collectively. Although practicing nurses at the time recognised the need for a collective voice, the consideration of collective organisation generated ambivalence in many nurses from the outset. As a group of women, nurses found an uncomfortable fit with both the idea of lobbying government for the legislation needed to form a professional organisation and the thought of aligning themselves with labour unions. Nurses first organised themselves collectively in the late 1920s into professional organisations. Although these professional organisations were able to influence schools of nursing and the regulation of nurses, they had little influence on issues of nurses' remuneration and working conditions. (Jensen, 1992). In 1944, a full 2 decades after the formation of professional organisations, the CNA approved the involvement of professional associations in collective bargaining. Despite this approval for collective bargaining, the national organisation strongly opposed strike action or any form of job action that involved withdrawal of services by nurses. The professional association of British Columbia was the first to be certified as a bargaining agent in 1946 (Jensen, 1992). Throughout the middle decades of the 1900s, professional associations represented nurses in the collective bargaining process.

EMERGENCE OF UNIONS

Although collective bargaining units within professional organisations made considerable gains, the success of professional associations in the collective bargaining process was compromised by the competing interests of bedside nurses and nurses in management and administrative positions, all of whom were legitimate members of the professional associations. This inherent bias came to prominence with a 1973 Supreme Court challenge mandating the separation of bargaining units from organisations in which administrators were members. This challenge was intended to address the many situations in which managers were in conflict of interest with the requests of staff nurses. This separation of nurses from their nursing leaders also has contributed to their ambiguous support for unionisation. The separation process divided the membership. Nurse leaders were excluded; today, they still remain unprotected by collective bargaining.

Historically, the relationship between nurses and their leaders was one of solidarity. Conflict between nurses and their managers, according to McPherson (1996), was mitigated by shared experiences of education and practice. Divisions among nurses "were reflected but also resolved within the organizational structures they sup ported" (p. 261). Professional nursing associations, which combined trade union activity with professional organisational duties (Table 17.3), created solidarity amongst its members– "a solidarity built in part on the gender of its members" (p. 262).

Social and Cultural Analysis

According to Jensen (1992), nursing is steeped in a tradition of nurturing and care for others, with less attention given to meeting assertively nurses' own needs. Some nurses continue to associate unionisation with labour unrest, when, in actuality, it is unions that have worked to address and improve working conditions for nurses for more than 3 decades. This history of nurses as selfless caregivers has, however, made it difficult for nurses to conceive of themselves as adversarial participants in unionism. "Paradoxically, under labor law, the process of coming to agreement is structured as adversarial and promotes conflict rather than resolution. By law, unions must take the initiative in the process and, as a result, tend to be blamed when two parties fail to come to agreement" (Jensen, 1992, p. 558). This adversarial stance continues to fuel the flames of conflict between nurses and their unions, between unions and nurses' professional organisations, and between both of these groups and provincial governments. It is important not to locate this adversarial stance with unions but to look to the legislative authorities behind such a stance.

Labour legislation also plays a role in nurses' pay equity issues. Some segments of society have made progress regarding work equity and the rights of workers, but the gendered nature of nurses' work continues to confound nurses' collective bargaining efforts. Although one could argue that nurses have made tremendous gains, particularly in the area of wages, nurses continue to be frustrated with only minimal gains for improved conditions of their work and workplaces. The progress that has been made has not been without personal angst for nurses, originating in prevailing attitudes of society. This tension pits nurses against other nurses, their leaders, and the public and, more importantly, creates an inner turmoil for nurses. The ultimate struggle for nurses is being caught between knowing that improving their own working conditions will positively affect patient care and the concern that society will see their efforts as self-serving.

Political Analysis

A political analysis is useful to highlight the ways in which nurses influence others, particularly those with the power to make changes. Nurses are well positioned with their privileged access to patients' experiences within the health care system to know what needs to change within this system. In this capacity, nurses have been able to make many significant contributions. However, nurses have been less successful in convincing governments that the conditions of nurses' work and the quality of work environments significantly influence the quality of care that patients receive. If nurses' salaries are not competitive with other choices nurses can make, the recruitment and retention of qualified experienced nurses will be impossible.

It is these issues that nurses and their unions have brought to the bargaining table time and time again. It is these issues that influence nurses to participate in illegal strikes. Nurses, more than other members of society, can see that, unless salaries and working conditions are comparable with other work of equal value, there will not be nurses. Although nurses have used many ways to communicate this message, to influence decision makers to make changes, some would argue that it has been through strikes–legal and illegal–that nurses have been most able to inform Canadians of these issues and exercise influence in these changes.

Ethical-Legal Analysis

An ethical-legal analysis highlights the laws, legislative acts, and professional codes that inform, constrain, or otherwise influence an issue. The issue of nurses' ambiguous relationship with unionisation is fueled by the tension between and among legislative acts, codes, and laws. For example, unions have traditionally drawn on the Charter of Human Rights to support job action as an essential right in collective bargaining,

Table 17.2 Formation of Canadian Nurses' Unions		
PROVINCE	**UNION**	**DATE OF INDEPENDENCE**
British Columbia	BCNU	1981
Alberta	UNA	1977
Saskatchewan	SUN	1974
Manitoba	MNU	1975
Ontario	ONA	1973
Quebec	FIIQ	1987
Newfoundland and Labrador	NLNU	1974
New Brunswick	NBNU	1978
Nova Scotia	NSNU	1976
Prince Edward Island	PEINU	1988

Source: Jensen, P. (1992). The changing role of nurses' unions. In J. Larsen & A. Baumgart (Eds.), *Canadian nursing faces the future* (pp. 557-572). City: Publisher, with permission. *Canadian nursing faces the future.*

which for nurses and others deemed to be providing essential services was countered by a Supreme Court of Canada ruling in 1987. The CNA's Code of Ethics (1997), has recognised nurses' right to collective bargaining action on the condition that steps are taken to ensure the reasonable safety of clients. Despite the amazing efforts of nurses to provide essential services and participate in strikes, nurses have lost the right to strike in many provinces.

When nurses face conflicting directions from their professional organisations, unions, and the legal system regarding the ethicality of collective bargaining and job action, the situation is confounded. Nurses cannot resolve their positions based on consistent and clear external leadership. What further contributes to nurses' ambiguity is the knowledge that some of the most successful collective bargaining, enjoying resounding public support, has taken place as "illegal" action. One could argue that existing legislation not only confounds this situation but also is at the heart of the difficulty. Do existing laws make fulfilling nurses' ethical obligations to provide competent care impossible?

Critical Feminist Analysis

A feminist analysis helps us to understand the structures and ideologies that foster misrepresentation of women's and nurses' (women and men) experiences. Nurses' reluctance to become involved in union activity can be tied to the patriarchal nature of their relationships with their employers, the gendered nature of nurses' work as feminine, and the gendered nature of labour unions as masculine. Nurses have had difficulty in "identifying with the male-dominated, working-class labour union movement" (Jensen, 1992, p. 559). In its place nurses have relied on the benevolence of their employers believing that if they worked hard as loyal employees, they would be rewarded justly.

According to Day (1993), women face a work-life dilemma: they are trained to be responsible on the one hand and made to feel guilty on the other. Despite the propensity of health care facilities to layoff workers and eliminate jobs regularly, despite the consequent overcrowding of hospital emergency rooms and growing surgical waiting lists, the nurses (mostly women) who protest such conditions by leaving their jobs are censored for abandoning services considered to be "essential." What's more, the "media blame the women for lack of care" (p. 93). This is the hallmark of patriarchal thinking. This is where a critical feminist analysis is most needed in nursing.

Economic Analysis

Nurses' salaries have been and continue to be the pivotal point both for nurses' unions and employers' organisations in negotiating a collective agreement. For the nurses, equitable salaries indicate the value attributed to their work; to employers, salaries are the largest item on their budgets. The political and economic environment is also likely to have a significant influence on how nurses and employers approach collective bargaining. In an economic recession, nurses and their unions are likely to make job security a priority rather than demands for salary increases. Employers involved in collective bargaining in a recession are more likely to be looking for wage concessions or rollbacks.

In many instances, economic considerations dominate collective bargaining processes and agreements. When significant salary increases are gained, concerns are raised about how existing budgets can accommodate this and how increased salaries for nurses could mean fewer available positions. In these cases, the decision to cut positions rather than reassess budget allocations suggests that decisions are based on what governments have budgeted versus what is needed to provide safe and competent nursing care to Canadians. In some instances, Alberta is a good example: budgets have been called into question for creating the impression that there is a shortfall when in reality no shortfall existed (Taft & Steward, 2001).

BARRIERS TO RESOLUTION

One of the greatest barriers to resolving the issue of nurses' ambivalence in participating in the collective bargaining process is the failure of nurses to comprehend fully the scope and role of unions. Although one can make a strong argument for the increasing participation and support by nurses of union work when collective bargaining agreements are being renegotiated, one cannot overlook the importance of the work that needs to be done by unions going forward. Nurses' involvement ensures that issues addressed in collective bargaining are the issues that nurses see as relevant. Nurses need access to such knowledge and to ways of conceptualising issues for their own practise. To increase their interest and participation in union activity, they can also benefit from knowledge of the history of collective bargaining in nursing, the legislation that authorises nurses' unions to engage in collective bargaining, and the societal structures and ideologies that shape nurses' views of collective bargaining.

A second barrier concerns the many different realities of nurses' collective bargaining. Nurses' collective bargaining is a provincial matter; hence, the provisions of the collective agreement vary significantly across provinces and territories. The solidarity that could be achieved through the national organisation, the Canadian Federation of Nurses Unions, by such a large group is compromised by the differences in provincial provisions in collective bargaining. Even provincial unions do not represent all nurses in the provinces. Federal union groups represent nurses who work for federal institutions. Federal labour codes direct these unions, contributing to further fragmentation of Canadian nurses.

As discussed earlier, nurses' collective bargaining excludes nurse leaders. Nurse leaders, often the most highly educated nurses in Canada, work across the bargaining table from staff nurses. The best of nursing expertise is in an adversarial position to the nurses who perform the day-to-day work of nurses. Nurse leaders speak with a knowledge grounded in practise, but they do not speak for practicing nurses. Nurse leaders have been co-opted to speak for employers who have different goals and purposes in the collective bargaining process. Sometimes, they speak for practise, but no one hears them. If they are heard, their own jobs are in peril. Our leaders are positioned as the adversaries of nurses and their unions. They are expendable. They are vulnerable. In our current system, nurse leaders and their positions are unprotected by collective bargaining. Nurses and nursing are divided by this system. Nurse leaders are lost to practicing nurses and to the patients who entrust practicing nurses to care for them.

A third barrier for nurses and their unions is isolation. The interests of unions by virtue of legislative mandates are in conflict with the interests of nurses' professional organisation because professional associations include nurses involved in evaluation of staff nurses. The interests of nurse unions are in conflict with the interests of government agencies that are positioned in opposition to nurses as they carry out their role of protecting the public interest. Although one can convince a government representative that nurses' working conditions are connected to and inseparable from nurses' work with patients, elected representatives are vested to spend public funds wisely. Put another way, elected officials are influenced by structures of power, where nurses' working conditions and the quality of patient care are important but not central to decision making.

A final barrier for nurses is a certain naïveté about unionisation and the collective bargaining process itself. Despite abundant evidence to the contrary, a considerable number of nurses have operated and continue to operate under the assumption that dedicated and loyal employees will be adequately recognised and rewarded. There are many examples of nurses' unconscious complicity in ideologies that sustain nurses' work as service, that support prevailing societal attitudes about nurses' work as women's work and labour unions as working-class male organisations (McPherson, 1996). The literature holds countless examples that call nurses to join in solidarity, that invite the 250,000 Canadian nurses to speak with one voice, to listen to one another, to empower themselves and each other, to collaborate with others, and to think about alternatives to strike action (Ritchie, 1990). Regardless of how well intentioned such messages are, this professional rhetoric create barriers to our understanding of what has to change. Collective bargaining has become part of what many nurses do to improve the quality of care they provide and the places in which they work. Although many barriers exist for nurses in resolving issues in and related to the collective bargaining process, the major barrier is nurses' ambivalence about collective bargaining itself.

STRATEGIES FOR RESOLUTION

One of the first and more important strategies to resolve issues surrounding nurses' involvement in collective bargaining is education. In the case of nursing students, nursing curricula need to include the various viewpoints of those involved in nurses' collective bargaining: nurses' views, nurses' unions views, the professional association views, employer organisation views, government agency views, and the views of consumers. Students need opportunities to understand and learn to critique the structures and ideologies that dominate their lives as men and women.

In the case of graduate nurses, the same materials need to be made available through continuing education workshops, conferences, and in-service speakers. Scholarship in the field of unionisation needs to be further developed to include feminist approaches to the conceptualisation of nurses' work to highlight the value attributed to nurses. Work and the gendered nature of nurses' work must be understood as located within relationships of power; and nurses need opportunities to explore collective bargaining as well as other strategies to engage in such relationships.

A second strategy that would move this very complex issue towards resolution involves efforts to make collective bargaining activities by all participants more transparent. That is, decisions and the reasons behind particular decisions need to be made explicit. Nurses and their unions can make public the accomplishments of unions. They can also publicise the need to maintain the tension with bargaining units to accomplish and then to maintain the provisions of collective agreements.

A third strategy is to foster partnerships between unions, government, and professional associations with a goal of understanding the different perspectives that each brings to the bargaining table. The differences between nurses' professional organisations and nurses' unions are often oversimplified. Professional organisations do focus on the safety of the public, and unions and organisations do focus on remuneration and work life of nurses. In these ways, these organisations are differently focused. What is even more important to highlight but more difficult to articulate are the ways in which these two organisations work and have the potential to work even smarter on common areas of interest. Governments also stand to benefit from partnering with nurses' professional organisation and their unions. Although much of the rhetoric from the media would suggest that these three groups are always and already positioned in adversarial positions, an argument could be made that the health of Canadians might be better served through the partnering of these groups. Given that the media has become a powerful influence on public awareness, the ability of such partnerships to bring the media onside to support the outcomes of this partnering is pivotal.

SUMMARY

This chapter explores the realities of today's nurses and their unions in an overview of nurses' experiences with collective bargaining. Significant dates, events, and legislation are discussed. Central to these discussions are the issues that collective bargaining and unionisation present for nursing. Although nine issues thought to arise in collective bargaining and unionisation for nurses are presented, these issues cohere and overlap around one central theme, nurses dilemma of ambivalence on the one hand and a growing awareness of the need for solidarity to influence change on the other.

A framework for analysing these issues uses historical, social-cultural, political, ethical-legal, and critical feminist approaches. Questions are raised about the barriers to resolving these issues and strategies are presented to begin to move these issues toward resolution.

A review of the excellent scholarship on unionisation in the Canadian nursing literature suggests that more research and more writings of a critical interpretive nature are needed. Despite this, what has been written points the way to an exciting future for nurses.

Nurses are reclaiming their connection with their feminist past and forging the way to a future where nurse unions and nurses' professional organisations will create the collective needed to improve the quality of the care nurses provide and of the workplaces where this care is provided.

Nurses can and must speak in one voice to challenge those structures and ideologies that impede our progress. Success depends on nursing's ability as a profession to create a rightful space for nurses and their unions.

Online RESOURCES

Add to your knowledge of this issue:

British Columbia Nurses' Union	www.bcnu.org
United Nurses of Alberta	www.una.ab.ca
Saskatchewan Union of Nurses	www.sun-nurses.sk.ca
Manitoba Nurses Union	www.nursesunion.mb.ca
Ontario Nurses Association	www.ona.org
Federation des infirmiers du Quebec	www.fiig.gc.ca
Newfoundland Labrador Nurses Union	www.nlnu.nf.ca
New Brunswick Nurses Union	www.nbnu-siinb.ca
Nova Scotia	www.nsnu.ns.ca

Reflections on the Chapter

1. In 1944, the CNA approved the principle of collective bargaining for nurses. What legislation that was passed just before this influenced this approval?

2. How might you account for the slow response of the provinces to act on this approval of collective bargaining by the national body?

3. What prompted Alberta nurses finally to move to have the Registered Nurses Act amended in 1966 to allow for collective bargaining between staff nurses' associations and their employers?

4. Two Supreme Court of Canada rulings (in 1973 and 1987) have significantly influenced the nature of nurses' collective bargaining. State the rulings and discuss their effects on nurses' collective bargaining.

5. In nurses' collective bargaining pay equity, the right to equal pay for work of equal value has been an issue. What is the nature of this issue?

6. How do nurses describe the dilemma that the issue of strikes and withdrawal of services presents for them?

7. Nurses' salaries are and continue to be central in collective bargaining between nurses' unions and their employers. Discuss the different viewpoints held by nurses and their employers on nurses' salaries.

8. Despite the significant increases in wages gained through the collective bargaining of nurses' unions, there has continued to be a proliferation of strikes by nurses. How might you account for that?

9. Why is it that nurses can strike in some provinces and not in others?

REFERENCES

Canadian Nurses Association. (1997). Code of Ethics for Registered Nurses.

Coburn, D. (1999). Professional autonomy and the problematic nature of self-regulation: medicine, nursing and the state. *Health & Canadian Society, 5*(1), 25–53.

Connors, K. (2002). Values guided care: evidence based decision. Presentation to the Future of Health Care in Canada May 28, 2002. Retrieved June 19, 2002 from http://www.nurseunions.ca/cb/index/shtml.

Day, E. (1993). The unionization of nurses. In P. Armstrong, J. Choinere, and E. Day (Eds.), *Vital signs: nursing in transition (pp. 242–265)*. Toronto: Garamond Press.

Grand, N. (1971). Nightingalism, employeeism and professional collectivism. *Nursing Forum, 10*(3), 289–299.

Hibberd, J. (1999). Working with unions. In J. Hibberd & L. Smith (Eds.), *Nursing Management in Canada* (2nd ed., pp. 505–524). Toronto: W.B. Saunders.

Hibberd, J., & Norris, J. (1991). Strikes by nurses: perceptions of colleagues coping with the fallout. *Canadian Journal of Nursing Research, 23*(4), 43–54.

Hibberd, J. (1992). Strikes by nurses: Incidence, issues and trends. *Canadian Nurse, 88*(3), 26–31.

Hibberd, J. (1992). Strikes by nurses. In J. Larsen & A. Baumgart (Eds.), *Canadian Nursing Faces the Future (pp. 574-595)*. Toronto: Mosby.

Jensen, P. (1992). The changing role of nurses' unions. In J. Larsen & A. Baumgart (Eds.), *Canadian Nursing Faces the Future (pp. 557-572)*. Toronto: Mosby.

McPherson, K. (1996). The price of generations: Canadian nursing under Medicare (1968-1990). In *Bedside matters: the transformation of Canadian nursing (pp. 248-349)*. Toronto: Oxford University Press.

Ritchie, J. (1990). Feeling empowered. *The Canadian Nurse, 86*(1), p. 3.

Ross-Kerr, J. (1998). The rise of unions in Alberta. In J. Ross-Kerr (Ed.), *Prepared to care: nurses and nursing in Alberta 1859-1996*. Edmonton: University of Alberta Press.

Ross-Kerr, J. (1998). The rise of unions in Alberta. In J. Ross-Kerr (Ed.), *Prepared to care: nurses and nursing in Alberta 1859-1996*. Edmonton: University of Alberta Press.

Schriber, R., & Nemetz, E. (1992). Pay equity for Ontario nurses. *Canadian Nurse, 88*(9), 17–19.

Stuart, M. (1993). Nursing: the endangered profession. *Canadian Nurse, 89*(4), 19–22.

Taft, K., & Steward, G. (2000). Clear answers: the economics and politics of for-profit medicine. Edmonton: Duval Publishing House.

Thorne, S., McCormick, J., & Carty E. (1996). Deconstructing the gender neutrality of chronic illness and disability. *Health Care International for Women 18*, 1–16.

18

Ethical and Legal Issues in Nursing

Laurie Hardingham

Chapter Objectives

At the completion of this chapter, you will be able to:

1. Defend the importance of ethical and legal issues for nursing practise.

2. Describe the difference between ethical and legal issues.

3. Articulate relevant ethical and legal issues.

4. Understand the implications for individual nurses and for the nursing profession when ethical and legal issues are not resolved.

5. Identify some of the barriers to, and strategies for, resolving ethical and legal issues.

6. Identify some of the ethical and legal resources available to nurses.

Laurie Hardingham, nurse and senior Fellow in Clinical Ethics, with members of the Clinical Ethics Group, the Toronto Rehabilitation Institute/University of Toronto Joint Centre for Bioethics. Used with permission.

This chapter introduces readers to some ethical and legal issues in nursing and provides an overview of their significance to nursing practise. Specifically, readers are given a case, and some of the legal and ethical issues in the case will be identified. Examining the case will help readers to explore, articulate, analyse, and generate resolutions to the issues.

STORY: THE WINNIPEG NURSES

Chapter 1 of the *Report of the Manitoba Pediatric Cardiac Surgery Inquest* (Sinclair, 2000) begins:

> Pediatric cardiac surgery is one of the most professionally difficult and personally satisfying medical disciplines in which to work. It demands precision and accuracy from the surgeon, as well as a high degree of efficiency and teamwork from other doctors, nurses, and technicians who form its operating-room teams (p. 3).

Sometimes called the Sinclair Report, the inquest report tells the story of 12 children who died and the health care providers who worked with them during 1994 in the Pediatric Cardiac Surgery Program at the Winnipeg Health Sciences Centre.

The programme was suspended in February 1995, following an external review. When many parents of the children who died demanded a public inquiry into their children's deaths, the Chief Medical Examiner for the Province of Manitoba ordered an inquest, which commenced hearings in December 1995. The hearings lasted until the fall of 1998; the Report was released in the fall of 2000.

The 900-plus page report found that the programme had a mortality rate more than twice as high as similar programmes. The most heart-wrenching part of the report is the narrative of the children and their parents and the treatment of nurses—these were two of the four central themes recorded at the inquest.

History of the Programme and Nursing Concerns

Since the 1994 restart of the cardiac surgery programme, the operating room and intensive care nurses had concerns. They worried about the lack of preparation, about the problems in surgery, and about the many complications. As the deaths continued, the nurses voiced their concerns to their supervisor, to physicians and surgeons, and to the director of nursing.

The nurses "were never treated as full and equal members of the surgical team" (Sinclair, 2000, p. viii). Their concerns were ignored, and the programme continued. The nurses continued to keep notes and speak out to their supervisors. Finally, after the 12th child died, the programme was suspended.

Inquest Findings

The Report found that the nurses did nothing wrong; in fact, they did many things that were right. However, the nurses continue to wonder if events might have been different had they acted differently.

After several children had died, one of the nurses, Carol Youngson, decided to attempt to limit her contact with parents. She could no longer take the children from their parent's arms into the operating room. She told the officials at the inquest that she had considered telling parents to "take your baby and run" (Sinclair, 2000, p. 355).

When asked why she did not warn the parents, she stated that had she done so, "all hell would have broken loose." She felt that she would have been perceived as overly emotional and that, although she could have perhaps saved one child, there would have been more children coming in, and nothing would have changed. She would have lost her job. Less experienced nurses would be hired, and the programme would continue; it would not have been stopped (Sinclair, 2000, p. 355).

Using this story as a background for analysis, nurses can examine relevant ethical and legal issues and try to uncover what it means to practise ethically and legally in the difficult environment that is health care today. Although the story of the nurses in the Winnipeg Pediatric Cardiology Program is a particularly dramatic one, it raises many issues that concern nurses across the country on a daily basis.

WHAT IS ETHICS?

Ethics is the philosophical study of morality, the study of what is right and wrong behaviour. Studying ethics enables us to examine the things that influence our moral decisions, our obligations and duties to others, our character, the nature of "good," and the underpinnings of what makes a good society.

A subset of ethics is applied ethics, in which ethical theory is applied to real-life situations. This can be divided into various categories, such as bioethics (the study of ethics in the life sciences), business ethics (the study of ethics in the business world), or environmental ethics (ethics related to the natural world and our relationship to it).

Bioethics can be broken into several subspecialties, for example, biomedical ethics (the study of ethics in the medical profession), health care ethics (ethics in the health care setting), or nursing ethics (applied ethical theory in nursing). This chapter focusses on bioethical issues, with a particular emphasis on those that arise for nurses and in the nursing profession.

RECOGNISING ETHICAL ISSUES

Because ethics is the study of right and wrong behaviour, it involves the analysis of what we "ought" to do, what our duties and obligations are to other people, and what kinds of behaviour we should expect from others.

What guides this analysis? How do we determine what is the right (and the wrong) action in specific situations? When other people think differently about what actions are morally right, how do we defend our beliefs, and question others about theirs?

Moral philosophers and ethicists are not moral experts claiming to have the answers to these questions. They can, however, offer rational grounds or bases for our moral beliefs and help us sort out difficult problems. Although they cannot be the "moral conscience" of society, ethicists have knowledge of moral theory, which is the systematic, critical study of the basic underlying principles, values, and concepts utilised in thinking about moral life (Boetzkes & Waluchow, 2000).

IDENTIFYING AND ARTICULATING ETHICAL ISSUES

The identification of an ethical issue is not always a straightforward activity. For example, when consent for surgery was obtained, but the problems in the Pediatric Cardiology Surgery Program were not divulged, the surgeon might have justified the situation by claiming that he was maintaining public confidence in the programme. And perhaps the administrators viewed the issue as one of risk management. The nurses, on the other hand, saw the problem as an ethical issue. They believed that the parents were not given all the information they needed to give informed consent that was consistent with their values and beliefs. The issue of informed consent was identified both by the nurses and later by the Sinclair Report as an important ethical issue in the Winnipeg situation. This issue can be examined in greater detail to see how ethical analysis can help in identifying difficult problems.

Informed Consent: Example of an Ethical Issue

One of the major issues explored in the Report was whether the families of the deceased children were fully informed of risks and benefits of surgery before giving their consent to the surgical procedures involving their children. The following story is told in the Report:

Mary Jane Wasney's nephew was scheduled for cardiac surgery in June 1994 at the Health Sciences Centre (HSC). Mary Jane, a surgical nurse at HSC, had heard about the deaths of a number of children undergoing cardiac surgery, and she knew that operations were taking longer than expected. Concerned, she spoke with Carol Youngson, the senior nurse in charge in cardiac surgery. Carol advised her to speak with Joan Borton, a nurse clinician at HSC. Mary Jane went to Joan in tears, worried that her nephew was going to die. Joan suggested that Mary Jane could get her nephew "referred out of the province" and advised her to talk to the acting section head of pediatric cardiology. The cardiologist acknowledged that there was a "learning curve in any new program," but stated that he was confident that Dr. Odim could do the nephew's surgery.

Still concerned, Mary Jane asked several of the anesthetists in the programme for advice. In her testimony at the inquest, she recalled that all three anesthetists she spoke with recommended against having the operation done in Winnipeg. In the end, the nephew was operated on in Saskatoon. (Sinclair, 2000).

Many people do not have access to the information that Mary Jane had. If you were the parents or a close relative of this child, would you have wanted to be informed about the problems in the surgical programme? The inquest judge thinks that you would, and the inquest judge went on to make several recommendations regarding informed consent that, if adopted, would change our idea of what is sufficient information to give informed consent.

THE RIGHT TO BE INFORMED

It is now widely recognised that a patient has the right to be informed about proposed treatment and to decide whether to consent to that treatment. For consent to be valid, it must have the following attributes:

- It must be provided by a competent person.
- It must be informed (i.e., appropriate and sufficient information must be given in a way that the patient understands, and the informer must be satisfied that the patient understands).
- It must be voluntary (i.e., without undue coercion or pressure).

How much information must a physician provide? Until recently, the courts recognised a Professional Standard: Physicians must provide the amount of information that the average, prudent, reasonable physician would provide in a similar situation.

Physicians would have fulfilled their legal obligations if they provided information to a patient in accordance with the practise among their colleagues. However, the law of medical consent has changed recently. The current standard appears to be patient centred. The information provided is sufficient if it meets the standard that a reasonable, average patient in that patient's situation would expect (Baylis et al., 1995).

The Sinclair Report (2000) reviews recent case law that suggests it is not only the patient (rather than the physician) who should decide whether medical treatment will be performed (and where and by whom it will be performed), but it is also a doctor's duty to inform the patient of all material risks. What is material is determined by asking the question, "What would a reasonable patient want to know?" Material risks are also those risks that pose a real threat to the patient's life, health, or comfort.

Merely having a signed consent form in which it is acknowledged that the nature of the operation has been explained to the patient does not necessarily prove that the duty to inform has been observed. For example, in an Ontario case in which a surgeon had failed to disclose to his patient that he had little experience with the technique being used, the trial judge held that the surgeon failed in his duty to his patient by not disclosing his inexperience and by failing to give his patient the opportunity to have the procedure performed by another, more experienced surgeon.

In light of such cases, the Report states that when a person has been deprived of the opportunity to make a proper decision regarding treatment and when there is a significant risk that would affect the judgement of a reasonable patient, then in the normal course, it is the responsibility of the physician to inform the patient of that significant risk—if the information is needed by the patient to determine for himself or herself what course he or she should follow (Sinclair, 2000).

The Report concludes that the evidence suggests that the parents of the children involved in the Winnipeg cases were not as fully informed as they were entitled to be. The Report made several recommendations to both the Manitoba Department of Health and the hospital aimed at improving the process of consent and communication with families. These recommendations suggest that the information required is much more than is commonly given. It is the kind of information that the Winnipeg nurses wanted to give to the parents.

Increasing the standard for informed consent certainly involves not only physicians but also others in the health care environment. Those who recognise problems with consent in specific cases have a moral obligation, if not a legal obligation, to ensure that fully informed consent is obtained.

ETHICS INFORMS LAW

The last chapter in the Manitoba Pediatric Cardiac Surgery Inquest Report concludes:

> The thrust of the recommendations in this chapter is not punitive. The need is to improve the health-care system so as to prevent the recurrence of events that occurred in 1994. It is necessary to accept that the health-care system will not improve if people act solely on the basis of a fear of consequences for themselves or their careers. Instead, the recommendations are intended to establish a structure within which highly skilled and talented people can establish a health-care team that continually works together to provide a high standard of care. All of the comments and recommendations in this chapter are intended to fulfill this objective. (Sinclair, 2000, p. 466)

As the Report clearly points out, often nurses are the first people on the health care team to perceive a problem in the informed consent process. This is because nurses have access to information about health care professionals, programmes, and institutional problems that most patients do not. Because they usually are more familiar with patient and family values, nurses can appreciate when these patients and families need to know more to make an informed and reasoned decision about medical care.

The standards of informed consent imposed by recent court decisions and recommended by the Winnipeg inquest report have implications for nurses. Nurses need to be aware of the requirements for informed consent and the kinds of disclosure that are seen as relevant by the courts (Hardingham, 2001a, 2001b).

LEGAL RESPONSIBILITIES OF NURSES

What legal responsibilities do nurses have regarding informed consent? To answer this question, it is important, first of all, to distinguish between two kinds of situations:

- Getting patient consent for what nurses do
- Participating in the consent process for what other health care professionals do

For the first kind of situation, the Canadian Nurses Protective Society (CNPS) cautions: "A nurse carrying out an invasive nursing procedure should provide an explanation and document that the explanation was given and consent obtained" (CNPS, 1994, p.13). Further, the CNPS states: "Any touching of a client requires verbal, and in some cases, written consent. Legal experts suggest that the person carrying out the treatment should provide the relevant information to the client. So, nurses should be aware of disclosure and consent requirements, and they should be sure to chart that these requirements were met. Failure to obtain consent can result in professional sanctions, civil liability and/or criminal charges."

For the second type of situation (e.g., when nurses witness the signing of a consent form for a surgical or medical procedure to be performed by a physician), nurses are not responsible for providing information. The physician, as the caregiver performing the treatment, must provide this. Nurses do, however, have an ethical responsibility to inform the physician when there is evidence that the patient does not have enough information to make an informed decision or that the decision is otherwise not fully informed. If the physician does not remedy the situation, nurses have a role to play as patient advocates in such situations. Under both the *Code of Ethics* and the nursing practise standards, each nurse as an individual practitioner has responsibilities to the patients in his or her care. For example, under the value of "choice," the *Code* states:

> Nurses provide the information and support required so that clients, to the best of their ability, are able to act on their own behalf in meeting the health and health care needs. Information given is complete, accurate, truthful, and understandable. When they are unable to provide the required information, nurses assist clients in obtaining it from other appropriate sources. (CNA, 2002)

These ethical responsibilities may become legal responsibilities if the provincial nursing practise standards or *Code of Ethics* (CNA, 2002) are recognised by a court of law as guidelines for what a reasonable nurse would do in a specific situation.

ETHICAL OR LEGAL ISSUE? ALIKE BUT DIFFERENT

As the preceding analysis points out, ethical and legal issues are closely linked. A legal action and an ethical action one might consider taking may be the same action—but not necessarily. For example, a nurse working in an emergency setting might be reluctant to report suspected child abuse to the authorities, which is required by law, because by doing so, she might lose the trust of the family and in turn discourage them from seeking needed medical help for their child or children in the future. The nurse's values suggest that the ethical thing to do would be to work with the family as long as possible to determine whether there is actual abuse or to refer the family to appropriate resources to help them resolve significant problems.

Like all professionals, however, nurses operate within a framework of legal as well as ethical rules and guidelines. (See Box 18.1 for a review of informative resources.) The legal rules that nurses must follow include those that apply to all members of society. In addition to these, nurses as professionals have legal and ethical duties that flow from their obligation to serve the public interest and the common good (Keatings & Smith, 2000). Having a unique body of knowledge, skills, and expertise, nurses have been granted certain rights and privileges by society. In return for this, society holds nurses to high standards of professional, moral, and ethical competence. To balance these responsibilities, nurses must be familiar with the legislation that governs nursing practise and the relevant policies, codes, and standards of practise, as well as with their rights and privileges as professionals.

BOX 18.1

Book Review

The following resources are suggested for increasing knowledge and skills for legal and ethical practice.

- Keatings, M. & Smith, O. B. (2000). *Ethical and legal issues in Canadian nursing* (2nd ed.), Toronto: W.B. Saunders Canada.

This book explores the ethical and legal challenges that nurses meet in everyday practise. It is a good resource for nurses on the Canadian legal system, how nursing is regulated in this country, and professional conduct, misconduct, and malpractice.

- Yeo, M. & Moorhouse, A. (Eds.) (1996). *Concepts and cases in nursing ethics* (2nd ed.). Peterborough: Broadview Press.

Focusing on the ethical dilemmas faced by nurses who work in the "front lines" of the health care system, this book has many excellent case studies that illustrate how ethical theory can be applied in nursing practise.

- Boetzkes, E. & Waluchow, W. (2000). *Readings in health care ethics.* Peterborough: Broadview Press.

This recent anthology contains an excellent introductory chapter on ethical justification and theory, "Ethical Resources for Decision Making," as well as a well-chosen selection of readings, both well-known and newly written, in the main areas of health care ethics.

- Thomas, J. & Waluchow, W. (1998). *Well and good: A case study approach to biomedical ethics* (3rd ed.). Peterborough: Broadview Press.

This text uses a case study approach to health care ethics, with brief but good discussion on ethical theory. Included are some well-known Canadian cases, such as the "mercy killing" by Robert Latimer, the assisted suicide of Sue Rodriguiez, and the pregnancy solvent-abuse case of Mrs. G., as well as little-known real-life cases.

- Canadian Nurses Association. (1998). *Everyday ethics: Putting the Code into practice.* Ottawa, ON: Author.

This workbook is designed to help Canadian nurses reflect on the *Code of Ethics* and incorporate ethics into their practises. It provides three different ethical decision-making models, with examples of each, and resources for group discussion.

The Need to Understand Legal Requirements

There are four reasons why nurses should be familiar with the law and have a basic understanding of Canada's legal system. First, the CNA *Code of Ethics* and each provincial regulatory body impose certain requirements with respect to nurses' level of professional knowledge and skill. If nurses do not meet these requirements, they are open to disciplinary action from their professional governing body and, if the conduct is serious enough, the courts.

Second, nurses have access to drugs that are regulated both by legislation and hospital procedures governing their use, dispensation, and handling. They need to know the relevant laws and policies that apply to drugs.

Third, nurses need to be familiar with legal requirements because everyday actions and decisions made by nurses affect the basic rights of their patients. Nurses need to know what those rights are and how to respect and protect those rights.

Finally, nurses have access to confidential information about individual patients, and they are both legally and ethically obligated to keep such information confidential and not divulge it without patient consent; although in some cases, nurses are required to divulge such information in court—in the form of testimony—or to report information, such as that related to child abuse (Keatings & Smith, 2000).

The legal system is founded on rules and regulations that guide society in a formal and binding manner. Although constructed by individuals and capable of being changed by the judiciary or legislative enactments, the legal system is a general foundation that gives continuing guidance to health care professionals regardless of their personal views and values system. For example, the law recognises the competent patient's right to refuse treatment. A patient has this right whether or not the health care providers agree with the patient's choice. This right, however, is not absolute. If there are overriding state interests, treatment may be mandated against a patient's or parent's wishes. Some examples of this are a court order to fluoridate the water supply or to perform a blood transfusion for a child whose parents refuse such treatment because of religious beliefs. One may have difficulty reconciling law and ethics in areas that transect both, such as issues of death and dying, abuse of others, or futility of health care. Legal and ethical issues are often entwined.

One way of differentiating between legal and ethical issues is that laws may be seen as external to oneself, being imposed from the outside. Ethics, on the other hand, can be viewed as something internal to oneself. Although this is often true, there are exceptions. Professional codes of ethics may be seen by some as imposed externally, although the aim might be to have nurses internalise their professional ethics during their education. And if people agree with the laws of society, they may have internalised them. Someone might believe that it is always ethical to obey the laws of the society in which they live. Another distinction might be that one might obey the law because it is prudent to do so, that actions that disobey the law might result in some harm. Ethical actions, on the other hand, are done because they are the right things to do, not because of fear of being punished.

The Need to Incorporate Law and Ethics Into Practise

In the story at the beginning of this chapter, the Winnipeg nurses advocated repeatedly for their patients but seemed to get nowhere. We might here ask the following question: If nurses are unable to fulfill the requirements in the *Code of Ethics* and their nursing practise standards, are these requirements then empty ones? If they are not empty, then nurses must be able to incorporate them into their nursing practise.

However, a nurse who chooses to be a patient advocate by disclosing directly to a patient that there are problems with a specific health care professional or programme may be legally open to a charge of defamation. If following the requirements means that nurses must perform heroic acts, such as putting their jobs at risk by repeatedly taking their concerns to upper management or by blowing the whistle (informing) on wrongdoers, then for most nurses, the requirements may seem to be empty. Is this an unsolvable problem for nurses?

ISSUES OF MORAL INTEGRITY

A major issue that arises for nurses facing difficult situations is how they can maintain moral integrity, or a sense of moral wholeness, when their values go unheeded and they see themselves as powerless to influence change. As Redman and Fry (2000) point out:

> It is no surprise that nurses experience ethical conflicts while providing care. They are individuals with personal and professional values; they ply their skills in institutions in conjunction with other professionals—all of whom have different values. They provide nursing care to patients who may have religious, cultural, and moral values quite different from their own. (p. 360)

This kind of values conflict often leads to problems within the health care setting. In an analysis of five studies on nurses' ethical conflicts, Redman and Fry (2000) found two underlying themes:

1. Evidence of widespread conflict between professional, corporate, and societal definitions of aadequacy of care.
2. Evidence of differences in the philosophical orientations of the various health professions. For example, nurses believe that they value patient autonomy more than physicians value patient autonomy.

Redman and Fry ask two questions: Will the differences and the concerns of nurses be seen as worthy of attention? In practise settings, what kind of moral agency of nurses will be supported? These are important questions because nurses make daily decisions in their work with patients. Some of these are moral decisions, and when nurses act deliberately on moral decisions, they are moral agents. As moral agents, nurses are required to examine, or reflect on, their actions.

Familiar to anyone who has taken a philosophy course, Socrates' assertion that "the unexamined life is not worth living" indicates how important thinking, self-analysis, and reflection are to understanding the world and our part in it. When feelings of distress arise, almost everyone examines the choices they have made and wonders if things would have turned out differently if different decisions had been made and different actions had been taken.

Health care professionals do this a lot and, in fact, are encouraged to do so. For example, the Alberta Association of Registered Nurses (AARN) requires, in their Continuing Competence Program, that nurses conduct a "review of one's own nursing practise to determine learning needs and incorporate learning to improve one's own practise." The key to this process is "reflection on your practice against the Nursing Practice Standards" (AARN, 2000, p. 8). In other words, nurses are asked to reflect on the extent to which their practise meets the standards.

Reflection is serious thinking about something, thinking that "reflects" back to us what we believe or value, so that we can understand better why we think that way. If we can find no good reasons for our beliefs, then we may need to think about whether we should change them.

Thomas and Waluchow (1998) use the idea of "reflecting" in their description of three levels of response to a moral question or problem:

1. The expressive level
2. The pre-reflective level
3. The reflective level

At the expressive level, responses are unanalysed expressions or feelings which, in themselves, do not constitute any kind of justification or reason for the response. The emotional response that "this is just not right!" when a nurse is upset is an example of the expressive level.

At the pre-reflective level of response, justification is given by reference to values, rules, and principles that are accepted uncritically. Most often, justification is made by reference to a "conventional" or commonly agreed-on standard or rule. We do not stop to think why we should act or base our judgements on these rules or whether they are good standards to adopt.

At the reflective level of response, moral judgements are based not entirely on blindly accepted conventional norms but rather on principles, rules, and values to which we ourselves consciously subscribe. A rational moral agent operating at the reflective level should be prepared to offer a reason for a moral judgement. Thus, moral reflection serves to concentrate one's thoughts back on a problem or an idea. This is not a new activity; it is something most of us have been doing all our lives. However, as moral agents, we need to think reflectively about constructing and evaluating the reasons for our rules and beliefs and to set out standards we can use to judge these reasons as good or poor ones. We need to direct our attention explicitly towards things that we normally take for granted, to examine carefully our beliefs and opinions and the evidence we have for them.

Reflection and Integrity

May (1996) includes critical thinking as an important aspect of moral integrity. Integrity means completeness or wholeness, and when we refer to our moral integrity as a person and as a professional, we think about the relationship of our actions to our beliefs. This relationship is very important to our self-concept.

According to May, the development of a critical point of view means that we need to view moral integrity not as holding steadfastly to a code of conduct or rules that others have provided—even if we approve of the code or rules—but rather "as a form of maturation in which reflection on a plurality of values provides a critical coherence to one's experiences" (May, 1996, p. 16). Achieving integrity means developing a critical perspective, a standpoint from which one can examine and then endorse or reject new social influences.

Implicit in this view is the requirement that our choices must be our own. We mature not merely by being socialised to accept certain values and beliefs but also by becoming committed to certain values and beliefs as a result of critical reflection. When our actions are in harmony with those values and beliefs, we have personal integrity. Acting at the pre-reflective level is a type of externally directed behaviour, the blind following of standards or norms set by someone else. Although not necessarily bad (sometimes conventional norms are capable of reasoned defense and can be fully justified morally), our conventional standards and rules must always be subject to scrutiny. Perhaps there are much better rules that we should try to persuade others to adopt. Or, perhaps existing conventions are morally objectionable.

What happens when moral integrity is compromised? Webster and Baylis (2000) distinguish among three kinds of experiences. *Moral dilemmas* arise when there are obligations to pursue two or more conflicting courses of action and no obvious reason to prefer one course of action over the other. Moral dilemmas also arise when some evidence suggests that a particular course of action is morally right, other evidence suggests that it is morally wrong, and in each case the evidence is inconclusive.

Moral uncertainty occurs when one is unsure what moral principles or values apply, or even what the moral problem is. Sometimes all that is required is more information to resolve the uncertainty, but at other times, the uncertainty can persist.

Moral distress is experienced when there is an inconsistency between one's beliefs and the actions that one actually takes. This inconsistency is usually because the person knows what is the right thing to do, but fails to do it (or fails to do it to his or her satisfaction) for such reasons as an error of judgement, a personal failing (e.g., a weakness or crimp in one's character, such as a pattern of "systemic avoidance"), or other circumstances beyond one's control, such as when one lacks the authority to act.

Redman and Fry (2000) found that studies of nurses and ethical conflicts show that moral uncertainty is rare. Most nurses believe that they understand the nature of the conflict; however, about one third of the nurses studied experienced moral distress. Nurses also perceived an organisational disinclination to deal with physicians when the ethical conflicts involved physicians, making nurses believe that these kinds of conflicts were unresolvable.

When situations that contribute to moral distress are not resolved, the result can lead to *moral residue*, "that which each of us carries with us from those times in our lives when in the face of moral distress we have seriously compromised ourselves or allowed ourselves to be compromised" (Webster & Baylis, 2000, p. 218). Moral residue results from the lingering distress that accompanies times when people compromise their basic values and principles. Moral residue can be profound and lasting, concentrated in our thoughts, and usually very painful because it threatens and sometimes betrays deeply held and cherished beliefs and values.

Carol Youngson, the Winnipeg nurse who could no longer take the children from their parents' arms into surgery, experienced profound moral distress which remains with her as moral residue (Armstrong, 2001). Youngson and the other nurses involved in the Pediatric Cardiac Surgery programme found that their personal moral integrity was compromised because a combination of fear, uncertainty, and doubt led them to question their values and their actions. They set aside actions that they might have performed, for example, to warn the parents or to go to the press, because these actions did not appear to be options open to them at the time.

Unfortunately in today's health care system, each professional may not have the time and the environment for the kind of critical reflection on values that might be required. And it is not clear that a distinction can be drawn between personal and professional integrity. In the same way, it is difficult to distinguish between errors caused by individual actions and errors resulting from systemic causes. However, in both situations, the individual is harmed when she or he experiences serious moral compromise. As May (1996) and Webster and Baylis (2000) point out, compromised integrity irreversibly alters the self. "One does not experience serious moral compromise and survive as the person one was" (Webster & Baylis, 2000, p. 224). When such change prompts the person to know with greater clarity what she will or will not tolerate or cooperate with in the future, then it can be change for the better. The change can be harmful, however, if the person adapts by constantly shifting his or her values. As time passes, the person's values become so changeable that it is nearly impossible to articulate what she or he sincerely believes. The person then becomes desensitised to wrongdoing and willing to tolerate morally questionable or morally impermissible actions.

Webster and Baylis (2000) also suggest that moral residue may actually lead to error; commonly, the error will take one of three forms:

1. Denial of the incoherence between beliefs and actions
2. Trivialisation of the incoherence between beliefs and actions
3. Unreflective acceptance of the incoherence between beliefs and actions

Very often, the structure and culture of the clinical setting are factors that contribute to such errors. For example, ethical issues can be camouflaged in the ordinariness of things, when familiar nonmoral language and categories are used to describe normative issues. The culture can appear to be willing to dismiss or trivialise certain ethical concerns and overlook or sidestep others. Therefore, we need to ask not only about the quality and clarity of thinking in terms of knowledge and analytical skills but also about whom we are in situations that arise and about the relationships we have, or expect to have, with colleagues and the wider health care community.

Moral Dilemmas

Bruce Jennings (1996) makes a useful distinction between two types of moral dilemmas. There are, first, those moral dilemmas inherent in the human condition, and second, those moral dilemmas created by institutional structures. The first type of dilemma, Jennings says, is unavoidable. The second type can often be avoided by altering institutional structures. Jennings claims that an important part of professional ethics is to be open to the possibility of avoiding moral dilemmas by modifying the institutions within which they work. In other words, we need to identify whether the moral dilemmas that we face are somehow inherent in our moral agency itself or whether the dilemmas are artifacts of specific institutional structures.

Those types of moral dilemmas that are artifacts of specific institutional structures require change in those structures. Both the *Code of Ethics* and the many nursing practise standards recognise this, calling attention to the value of practise environments conducive to safe, competent, and ethical care and the organisational supports needed in the practise setting. What is implicit in both the *Code of Ethics* and standards of practise documents is that professional nurses working in institutional settings cannot practise ethically without the required support.

Does this let nurses off the hook? Not exactly. First of all, even if nurses recognise that without change in the institutional structure they cannot practise ethically, they are still in a difficult situation, often facing severe moral distress. The Winnipeg nurses agonised over the deaths of the children. They continued to press for change, despite sarcasm and criticism from other members of the health care team (Sibbald, 1997). Second, the *Code of Ethics* explicitly states that nurses must work both individually and in partnership with others to improve practise environments and to address unsafe practise issues (CNA, 2002).

Nurses and Professional Integrity

Many bioethicists make a strong argument that such moral concepts as integrity and responsibility need to be understood as embedded in social structures (May, 1996; Webster & Baylis, 2000; Sherwin, 2000). For a professional, this means that professional ethics not only are embedded in individual conscience but also result from interactions between persons. Thus, to have moral integrity as professionals, individuals must do more than simply adhere to what their conscience tells them. They need to evaluate critically the standards that they as professionals are required to follow, both as individuals and collectively with others in their profession.

As we saw earlier, acting at the pre-reflective level is a type of "externally directed behaviour," whereby standards or norms set by someone else are followed blindly (Thomas & Waluchow, 1998). This is not necessarily bad. Sometimes, conventional norms are capable of reasoned defense and can be fully justified morally and therefore would be good standards to adopt. However, our conventional standards and rules must always be subject to scrutiny. Perhaps there are much better rules, and we should try to persuade others to adopt them. Or, perhaps existing conventions are morally objectionable. For example, the convention—followed until fairly recently—whereby nurses always deferred to physicians and obediently complied with their orders is now seen as unacceptable.

To have moral integrity, nurses need to assess the standards, codes, and rules that they are asked to follow in their practise. They must have good reasons for accepting them. This requires not only reflection on whether their practise follows codes of ethics and nursing practise standards but also reflection on the codes and standards themselves. Nurses ought to determine whether they are genuinely in accord with them and why. Reflective practise means thinking about standards, codes, and practises from a critical point of view and sharing this responsibility with other nurses.

Does reflective practise take time? Yes! It takes time to become familiar with the standards and practises nurses are asked to follow in their professional lives as well as to subject these standards and practises to a critical point of view. Do nurses have time for reflective practise? Perhaps not always, but they need to find space for reflection because nurses are morally and legally required to do so. Reflective practise might be time-consuming and frustrating, yet it offers the best hope for nurses' work to be responsive to the needs of their patients and society.

BARRIERS TO RESOLVING ETHICAL AND LEGAL ISSUES

Nurses are accountable to individual patients, their families, health care team members, employers, the profession, and society as a whole. As well, they also have rights as professionals. These multiple obligations can present difficulties and complicate the identification of barriers to the resolution of problems.

Lack of Workplace Supports

Kelly (1998) carried out a study that describes, explains, and interprets how new graduate nurses perceived their adaptation to the "real world" of hospital nursing. This study examines the major influences on the new graduates' moral values and ethical roles in the 2 years following their graduation. Kelly found that the nurses went through a complex psychosocial process to preserve moral integrity and maintain a valued professional identity. This process resulted in a struggle that led to moral distress. Kelly concluded that the self-doubt and confusion from intense stress resulted in greater reliance on others as references for self-evaluation. She found also that individual ethical standards are influenced by group norms and that the environment in which nurses work and the practise and support of their more experienced colleagues is very important in the maintenance of professional values and a professional identity. With the results of Kelly's work in mind, it is very important to have the kinds of practise setting which some authors have described as a "moral community" (Storch, 1999).

Conflict: Ambivalent Views and Approaches to Issues

Another barrier exists in the ways that society views health care hierarchies and concepts. For example, the notion of respect for patient autonomy, broadly recognised as the principle that patients have the authority to make their own decisions about their health care, occupies a prominent place in bioethics. However, Sherwin (2000) points out that feminists and others feel deeply ambivalent about the ideal of autonomy. Although it is woven throughout many feminist approaches, Sherwin points out that the ideal of autonomy is in need of a specifically feminist analysis.

Although there are many good reasons why respect for personal autonomy is important, there are also many problems with the autonomy ideal. Its main problem for many feminists is the focus on the individual that it usually takes. For many people, and especially for women, life is not lived in a vacuum, in which the decision maker acts in isolation. Decisions are made taking into consideration the relationships to other human beings, whether they are close relationships, such as those with parents, children, partners, or less intimate relationships, such as those in communities or professional–client relationships.

Sherwin proposes an alternative conception of autonomy, which she calls "relational autonomy." Although not denying that autonomy ultimately resides in individuals, Sherwin's concept takes into account the impact of social and political structures, especially sexism and other forms of oppression, on the lives and opportunities of individuals. "It realizes that the presence or absence of a degree of autonomy is not just a matter of being offered a choice. It also requires that the person have the opportunity to develop the skills necessary for making the type of choice in question, the experience of being respected in her decisions, and encouragement to reflect on her own values" (Sherwin, 2000, p. 79).

Applying the term relational autonomy to the full range of human relations, both personal and public, allows a political dimension to come in. It "makes visible the importance of considering how . . . social factors affect women's decision making" (Sherwin, 2000, p. 82) and how the place of nurses within the institutional context influences their ability to provide good nursing care.

Looking again at the Winnipeg nurses' story, the notion of relational autonomy is an excellent one. The nurses were concerned about their relationships with the children who were their patients, with the parents and families, with other members of the health care team, and with the wider community. In their decision making, they considered all of these groups, as well as the kinds of authority and influence that nurses had within the team, and decided that such actions as quitting or going public with their concerns would not be helpful. They continued to press for change through the proper channels but remained distressed about taking the children into the operating room. Their worry that the parents didn't know enough about the programme to make good decisions for their children's treatment was a constant source of pressure for them. On the other hand, the nurses realised the complexity of the relationships in health care and that the relationships depended on trust and cooperative action. Warning the parents or going to the press could do irreparable damage to trust and cooperation. The nurses felt that their own autonomy was diminished when their concerns went unheeded, leading some of the nurses to "silence themselves" (Sinclair, 2000, p. 478).

Sherwin (2000) also agrees that the moral community in which health care professionals work is important. Relational autonomy demands that appropriate structural conditions be met.

Limited Resources

Relational theory reminds us that material restrictions, including very restricted economic resources, "constitute real limitations on the options available to the agent. Moreover, it helps us to see how socially constructed stereotypes can reduce both society's and the agent's sense of that person's ability to act autonomously. Relational theory allows us to recognise how such diminished expectations readily become translated into diminished capacities" (Sherwin, 2000, p. 79).

The diminished capacities of the Winnipeg nurses resulted from, among other things, the lack of vehicles through which nurses could report incidents and concerns without risk for professional reprisal, the subservient position that nursing occupied within the organisation, and the failure to involve nurses in the planning process of the Pediatric Cardiac Surgery Program (Sinclair, 2000).

STRATEGIES FOR RESOLUTION OF ETHICAL AND LEGAL ISSUES

Once an ethical or legal issue for nurses is identified and analysed, many strategies can be implemented to address and resolve it. Strategies include, but are not limited to, the following:

- Review the *Code of Ethics*. The *Code* is reviewed every 5 years, and nurses' input is invited for this process. If you identify an issue that does not seem to be addressed in the *Code*, you could volunteer to contribute to the *Code's* review.
- Become familiar with the legislation, standards, and policies that apply to nursing practise. When you cannot conform to them, document the problems. Incident report forms, professional responsibility forms, and other ways of reporting concerns should be utilised.
- Ask for advice and support. Nurses' stories are of immediate interest in the political sphere, especially those that deal with ethical issues. Respect confidentiality, but try to find ways to broaden the approach to your issues. For example, contact your professional association or union for advice, support, and assistance to resolve concerns.
- Work to establish a moral community in your workplace. Participate actively on ethics committees, ethics rounds, and the like, in hospitals and health care organisations. Most hospitals have an ethics committee, an ethics consultation service, or other ways of dealing with ethical issues for accreditation purposes. Bringing instances or concerns forward can often bring them to the attention of

people who can take action to resolve them. Suggest a nursing ethics interest group or brown-bag lunch in your workplace to learn more about ethics and discuss problems.

- Identify what you can do both as an individual and as part of a group to build a supportive moral community in your workplace. Research shows that the culture, the amount of support from colleagues, and the kind of environment in which nurses work are important components to ethical practise (Kelly, 1998).
- Call the risk management committee's attention to a legal problem or a potential legal problem in a hospital or other health care facility where you work. This alone may be enough to have action taken. Also, for legal issues, there is expertise and assistance available from professional nursing organisations.

SUMMARY

Consider again the distress of the Winnipeg nurses in the Pediatric Cardiac Surgery Program. They were not facing moral uncertainty. They did not have a moral dilemma: they knew what the right thing to do was, and they did it. However, their concerns and attempts to use proper process did not help. They could have said, "We followed the policies, we took our concerns to the people we were supposed to report to, and so our responsibility is ended." But they did not: they continued to reflect on their concerns and continued to speak up for their patients. They decided that whistle blowing or warning the parents might cause more problems. They thought it better for the children if they remained on the job and continued to try to work for institutional change. Carol Youngson and the other nurses suffered moral distress, and the resulting moral residue remains with them, possibly forever (Armstrong, 2001).

The issues around informed consent are not the only legal and ethical issues arising out of the Winnipeg story. Other issues include those of truth telling, whistle blowing (going outside of the organisation with information about harms or wrongdoing), nurse–patient relationships, conflicts between members of the health care team, and gender issues. However, the analysis presented around informed consent may act as a prototype that gives the reader a sense of what approaches to take to other issues.

This chapter addresses the significance of legal and ethical issues to nurses. It points out reasons that nurses should be familiar with laws, codes, standards, and policies that apply to nursing practise.

The chapter also emphasises the importance to nurses of being able to identify, articulate, and understand ethical and legal issues, and the problems that result when this does not happen. Identifying barriers to ethical and legal nursing practise is an important step for nurses to take.

The task of overcoming those barriers to ethical and legal nursing is one that cannot be undertaken only by individuals. Nurses are vulnerable when faced with legal and ethical issues. They require knowledge about the law and about ethics and the realisation that they need to work individually and collectively to move identified issues towards resolution.

Online RESOURCES

Add to your knowledge of this issue:

Canadian Nurses Association   **www.can-nurses.ca**

CNA has various documents available, including several *Ethics in Practice* documents, *Nursing Now* documents, and the *Code of Ethics for Registered Nurses*, all available on their website.

Canadian Nurses Protective Society (CNPS)   **www.cnps.ca**

CNPS is a nonprofit society owned and operated by nurses for nurses. CNPS offers legal liability protection related to nursing practice to eligible registered nurses by providing information, education, and financial and legal assistance. Available on the website are 13 *InfoLaw* bulletins, a case study section, frequently asked questions, articles on legal issues, and protection from CNPS of interest to nurses.

Bioethics for Clinicians   **www.cma.ca/cmaj/series/ bioethic.htm**

Originally published in the *Canadian Medical Association Journal* (CMAJ), there are currently 27 articles in this series available on the CMAJ website. Aimed at clinicians and primarily physicians, these brief, easy-to-read articles use case examples as a basis for discussion and examination of ethical issues commonly encountered by clinicians in their work life. Seventeen of these are also available in a book.

Centre for Applied Ethics, University of British Columbia **www.ethics.ubc.ca**

Click on Starting Points in Applied Ethics to find resources for health care ethics.

Reflections on the Chapter

1. From your practise experience, can you identify examples of ethical and legal issues? How do you know that they were either ethical or legal issues? Were the two categories intertwined? If so, how were they intertwined?

2. Have you experienced moral uncertainty? A moral dilemma? Moral distress? What steps, if any, did you take? Looking back, what, if anything, would you do differently?

3. Think of the resources that are available to you to help you with ethical and legal issues. How would you go about accessing them?

4. Identify at least one ethical issue that seems to be prevalent in nursing practise. Is this issue one that is discussed publicly? What are the barriers to effective resolution to this issue? How are nurses approaching this issue and the problems it presents?

REFERENCES

Alberta Association of Registered Nurses. (1999). *Nursing practice standards*. Edmonton: AARN.

Armstrong, S. (2001). The crying shame. *Chatelaine, March,* 86–94.

Baylis, F., Downie, J., Freedman, B., Hoffmaster, B., & Sherwin, S. (1995). *Health care ethics in Canada.* Toronto: Harcourt Brace Canada.

Boetzkes, E., & Waluchow, W. *Readings in health care ethics.* Peterborough: Broadview Press, 2000.

Canadian Nurses Association. (2002). *Code of ethics for registered nurses.* Ottawa: CNA.

Hardingham, L. B. (2001a). Ethics in the workplace: Raising the standards of informed consent. The Winnipeg Inquest. *Alberta RN, 57*(1), 22–23.

Hardingham, L. B. (2001b). Ethics in the workplace: Nurses and Informed consent: Lessons from the Winnipeg Inquest. *Alberta RN, 57*(2), 22–23.

Jennings, B. (1996). The regulation of virtue: Crosscurrents in professional ethics. In R. A. Larmer (Ed.), *Ethics in the workplace: Selected readings in business ethics* (pp. 397–404). Minneapolis/St.Paul: West Publishing.

Keatings, M., & Smith, O. B. (2000). *Ethical and legal issues in Canadian nursing* (2nd ed.). Toronto: W. B. Saunders Canada.

Kelly, B. (1998). Preserving moral integrity: A follow-up study with new graduate nurses. *Journal of Advanced Nursing, 28*(5), 1134–1145.

May, L. (1996). *The socially responsive self: Social theory and professional ethics.* Chicago: The University of Chicago Press.

Redman, B. K., & Fry, S. T. (2000). Nurses' ethical conflicts: What is really known about them? *Nursing Ethics 2000, 7*(4), 360–366.

Sherwin, S. (2000). A relational approach to autonomy in health care. In Boetzkes, E., & Waluchow, W. (Eds.), *Readings in health care ethics.* Peterborough: Canadian Nurses Protective Society. Broadview Press.

Sibbald, B. (1997). A right to be heard. *Canadian Nurse, 93*(10): 22-98.

Sinclair, C.M. (2000). *Report of the Manitoba pediatric cardiac surgery inquest* [On-line]. Winnipeg: Manitoba Provincial Court. Available: http://www.pediatriccardiacinquest.mb.ca.

Storch, J. (1999). Ethical dimensions of leadership. In J. M.Hibberd & D. L. Smith (Eds.), *Nursing management in Canada* (2nd Ed., pp. 351–367). Toronto, ON: W. B. Saunders Canada.

Thomas, J., & Waluchow, W. (1998) *Well and good: A Case study approach to biomedical ethics* (3rd ed.). Peterborough, ON: Broadview Press.

Webster, G. C., & Baylis, F. (2000). Moral residue. In S. B. Rubin & L. Zoloth (Eds.), *Margin of error: The ethics of mistakes in the practice of medicine.* Hagerstown, MD: University Publishing Group.

19

Issues of Gender and Power: The Significance Attributed to Nurses' Work

Carol McDonald

Chapter Objectives

At the completion of this chapter, you will be able to:

1. Identify ways of thinking about power structures, including ideologies, social discourses, and the discursive process.
2. Understand the conceptualisation of gender as socially constructed, the process of naturalising knowledge, the location of gender as residing both within and beyond the individual, and the ways in which

gender knowledge is bound by cultural, temporal, and social realities.
3. Recognise gender as one of a number of intersecting identities, including race, class, age, ethnicity, and sexual orientation, through which we are uniquely constituted as persons.

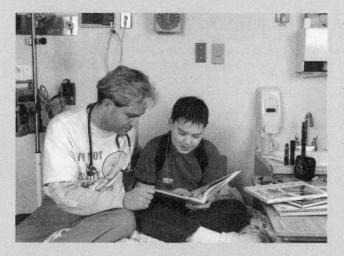

The identification of nursing as a gendered occupation is nothing new. A man who chooses nursing as a profession is inevitably identified as a "male nurse," whereas a woman is rarely referred to as a "female nurse." In nursing practice today, the concept of a profession as gender specific is rarely validated. Rather, the attributes of knowledge, skill, effectiveness, and care empower all nurses. Photograph by Larry Arbour. Used with permission of Faculty of Nursing, University of Calgary.

4. Articulate the nature of nurses' work, nurses' knowledge, and nurses' public representation as gendered and discuss the historical social discourses of women's work and nurses' work that have contributed to this understanding.

5. Discuss the barriers that interfere with the resolution of issues that arise from relations of power and gender and the significance attributed to nurses' work.

6. Identify strategies that will serve to interrupt the taken-for-granted notions of gendered work that underlie the devaluing of nurses' work.

This chapter presents opportunities to consider the idea that societally derived concepts about gender are inherent in claims about the value of nurses' work and the importance of nursing knowledge. The chapter challenges readers to look beneath the taken-for-granted assumptions about what is called women's work in general and nurses' work in particular. In reconsidering what we think we know, we come to see the web of social discourses through which work, knowledge, and nursing itself are inscribed with meanings of gender.

Ideas about women and ideas about women's work and whether this work requires significant knowledge, responsibility, and skill contribute to the devaluing of nurses' work by society. This chapter examines historical changes in the valuing of work that is ordinarily performed by women. It suggests that the devaluing of nurses' work and knowledge stems from cultural power arrangements. The impact of *discourses of care,* or ideas about care as central to nursing practise, on the value attributed to nurses' work are examined as well.

GENDER AND POWER: ARTICULATING THE ISSUE FOR NURSING

How do concepts of gender and power arise in a discussion of the issues currently affecting Canadian nurses in education and in practise? Gender is a concept in our society that is simultaneously taken for granted and poorly understood. In this chapter, gender refers to the ways in which a person lives her or his life that demonstrates or reflects masculinity and femininity. As the chapter explores, gender can be thought of as constructed through social influences outside of a particular individual. And although there is undoubtedly some interrelationship between biologic sex and gender, this chapter addresses gender as distinct from the categories of biologic sex.

As nurses, we seldom think about the preponderance of practicing nurses who are women. When we do reflect on the gender division in nursing, we may think no further than "the numbers," that is, the distribution of genders in the profession. However, the issues of gender and power, as they relate to nursing, are more complicated than the biologic sex of those who practise nursing. Moreover, gender itself is not an "issue" in nursing. The fact most practising nurses are women is not in itself problematic. What is problematic for the profession is that gender is inextricably linked to relations of

BOX 19.1

Glossary of Terms and Definitions

This list describes the way some terms have been used in the content of this chapter. They should not be taken as absolute definitions of the words.

Complicity—our own participation in, for example, supporting or reinforcing societal norms that undermine the value of women's work.

Essentialising—seeing something as representative of all members of a particular group or category. For example, essentialising nurses' work in a woman's domain implies that there is something about nursing that could only be performed by women.

Discourses—"social practices, values and cultural beliefs that prevail in a given culture or subculture at a specific historical moment and shape a collective sense of what is right, proper, worthwhile or valuable" (Thorne et al., 1995, p. 2).

Discourses of care—the ways in which ideas about care have been represented in nursing, particularly the values and beliefs that have placed care central to nursing practice.

Discursive process—how we learn to be and to behave in particular ways through the messages received in social discourses.

Gender—the ways in which femininity and masculinity are reflected in the lived life. Gender is distinct from the biological sex of a person. Culturally, there is value attached to particular genders and the way in which that gender is performed.

Ideologies—not merely ideas, but a powerful and authoritative voice in society that tells us who we are and how we are to behave.

Location of gender—gender is constructed through the interaction of the person with the social realities, values, and beliefs of a culture at a particular time in history. In this sense, gender resides both within and beyond the individual.

Naturalised—when some quality is taken to be innately, or obviously "the way it is," without questioning the beliefs on which that assumption is formed. For example, the symbol of a "woman" (wearing a dress) and a "man" (wearing pants) have become naturalised in our culture to represent the washrooms in public places to be used by women or men. Although there is nothing innately natural about these signs being men or women, we have come to interpret them unquestioningly this way.

Reinscribing—reinforcing or reproducing a concept or belief, at times without the thoughtful intention of doing so.

Social construction—ideas, concepts, and roles that are understood to be formed or built up through the agreed-on ideologies of a society.

Transparency—the ways in which we can see something clearly, or obviously (high transparency), or in which something is obscured from our view. For example, increasing our awareness of material and social realities that contribute to gendering of nurses' work will improve our ability to see, to make transparent to us, the manner in which nursing is undervalued because it is "women's work."

power. And it is this connection of gender and power that underlies and fuels issues related to the devaluing of nurses' work and the subordination of nurses' knowledge.

The discussion of power, and particularly relations of power as they affect nursing, may rouse a certain discomfort within nurse-readers, in view of the societally ingrained reluctance to examine our own power (Falk Rafael, 1996). However, because nursing as a profession has been largely composed of women, who are socialised to avoid discussions of power, we must venture into this deliberation.

This chapter explores and raises questions about *value and worth*, particularly the value and worth attached to the gendered nature of work, of knowledge, of nursing. These concepts of value and worth are the commodities of power. *When we talk about the value of nurses' knowledge or the ways in which work that is called women's work is devalued, we are talking about power.*

In exploring the significance of gender in relation to nursing practise, nursing knowledge, and nurses themselves, we may begin by acknowledging the complexity of gender *per se*. Then, we need to explore ways of thinking about gender beyond distribution, beyond the numbers of nurses who are female or male. These ways of thinking about gender will anchor us in the world of social realities where nursing is practised and where concepts of gender and gender practises are formed.

The first section of this chapter explores the theories that support an understanding of the gendered nature of work, knowledge, and the individual nurse. Grounded in feminist thought, this way of conceptualising gender and its effects in the social world is useful in understanding the significance of nurses' work.

Understanding Gender

As concepts, gender, women's work, and nursing itself derive their meaning in society through *social construction*. Social construction means that ideas, concepts, and roles are understood to be formed or built up through the agreed-on ideologies of a society. Ideologies, in this sense, are not merely ideas, they are imbued with power. They become the authoritative voice in society through which we come to understand ourselves. Ideologies tell us who we are, what we are to think, and how we are to behave (Althusser, 1971).

The power of ideologies lies in the authority that has us view much of our world as "natural" (obvious). *Nurse*, for example, is not a naturally occurring phenomenon, but the concept of *nurse* may become naturalised through ideologies about what constitutes or makes up the role of nurse. Although we may acknowledge intellectually that there is no natural role or personality attributable to *nurse*, we often, unthinkingly, act as if the opposite is so. The opportunity and the challenge in considering the social construction of nursing, gender, and "women's work" is twofold:

- To disrupt the thinking that supports taken-for-granted notions.
- To question the source of ideologies on which the "natural facts" are based.

Thinking in a way that interrupts that which is taken for granted helps us to recognise our own participation and complicity in supporting (reinscribing) ideologies that contribute to the undervaluing of nurses' work and nursing knowledge (Fig. 19.1).

Gender as Social Construction

What does it mean to think of gender as socially constructed? How does this way of understanding gender benefit one's thinking about issues of gender and power in nursing as a profession and in nursing practise?

FIGURE 19.1. The symbols of a "woman" (wearing a dress) and a "man" (wearing pants) have become naturalised in our culture to represent the washrooms in public places to be used by women or men. Although there is nothing innately natural about these symbols being men or women, we have come to interpret them unquestioningly in this way.

That people are gendered is taken for granted in everyday life and, although central to our experience of the world, is seldom thought about beyond the surface level. The lack of clarity between concepts of gender and biologic sex supports the tendency to keep our understandings of gender superficial. From the moment of birth, the biologic sex of the newborn is announced in a public way. This proclamation, biologically driven, determines much of the future of the child's life. Or does it?

In the text, *Revisioning Gender*, Nakano Glenn notes that "feminist scholars adopted the term *gender* precisely to free our thinking from the constrictions of naturalness and biological inevitability attached to the concept of sex" (1999, p. 4). In this sense, gender moves us to a broader understanding of what it is to live one's life in ways that reflect masculinity and femininity. Butler (1990), a prominent feminist thinker, discusses gender not as the expression of an internal identity but rather as a performance in which the person acts a script that is written in and through social discourses. In this context, *discourses* are "social practices", values and cultural beliefs that prevail in a given culture or subculture at a specific historical moment and shape a collective sense of what is right, proper, worthwhile or valuable" (Thorne et al., 1995, p. 2).

It is through these social discourses that we are inscripted with the knowledge of what it is to live a particularly gendered life. Although Butler maintains "that there is nothing about a binary gendered system that is given" (1990, p. 282), the scripts that are currently provided and normalised through social discourses offer little alternative to the categories of male and female. A concept of gender that surpasses biologic determinism provides the possibility, at least, of recognising and valuing the masculine and the feminine that resides within each of us.

Crucial to this understanding is what may be called the *location of gender*. Although the biologic anatomy of an individual resides with that person, gender as a social construction is located in a more complex way, both within and beyond the individual. The *construction of gender*, meaning the ways in which gender identities are acted out and the value attached to gender, originates outside of the individual person, in society. Notions of gender are constructed through the ideologies of the culture; they become known to us through social discourse. Gender knowledge is situated in particular temporal and social realities that are largely taken for granted by members of the culture. This taken-for-grantedness reflects our participation in the ideologies of the society in which we reside. In other words, we are complicit in reinforcing the ideas that define and structure what are accepted as normal, gender-appropriate behaviours and beliefs in our immediate culture and time.

The often-unexamined evidence of the ways in which gender knowledge is bound by cultural, temporal, and social realities surrounds us. When a child is born, how others respond to the news "It's a girl!" or "It's a boy!" is heavily influenced by the gender knowledge of the particular culture in a particular time in history. The proclamation communicates not only the sex of the child but also the meaning and value that is held for this young gendered life. Through the powerful ideologies of the culture, parents, family members, and strangers take up the life of the child as gendered, in effect, teaching the child to be in the world in gender-appropriate ways. As adults, we come to perform our gender roles, in large part, as they are prescribed through these social discourses.

Gender as Part of Identity

In recognising how dominant social discourses influence who we are to be, the production of identity becomes a discursive process (Scott, 1992). The term *discursive process* refers to how we learn to be, in particular ways, through the messages we receive in social discourses. Our concept of ourselves as gendered is one way in which we become subjects with particular identities. As we move on to consider some of the implications of what it means to be gendered subjects, we need to bear in mind that gender is but one component of our identity that is formed through discursive processes.

The gendered self is one of a number of the selves or identities through which we are uniquely formed as people. The gendered self intersects with other identities, such as race, class, age, ethnicity, and sexual orientation, in the constitution of each individual. The experience of living one's life as a black, young, middleclass, heterosexual, male, nursing student may be quite different from the experience of living as a white, middle-aged, poor, lesbian, single mother, nursing student. The difference of experience, although influenced by gender and what it means to be gendered in particular ways, is constructed through the material realities, such as economics and availability of social resources, as well as the influence of dominant social discourses.

The idea of the intersecting identities of nurses is addressed in Reverby's (1987) historical critique of American nursing. In her exploration of some of the historical unrest in the discipline, Reverby suggests that class differences among individual nurses and between groups of nurses with diverse training contributed to an internal hierarchy within nursing. Although the oppression of women was a reality for these nurses, they were also bound by their own participation in classist assumptions and ideologies. In this case, the "commonalities of the gendered experience could not become the basis for unity as long as hierarchical filial relations, not equal sisterhood, underlay nurses lives" (Reverby, 1987, p. 201). Reverby describes a situation in which the class identities of these nurses held more influence than their shared gender identity.

In essence, ideologies that become imbued with power carry societal authority to tell us who we are. Allen, writing of the postmodern critique in nursing, calls us to notice and to question "the ways in which discourses function as regimes of power, where knowledge and power interact to normalise or legitimate specific interests" (1992, p. xiv). The power attributed to particular social positions and particular identities, including gender, is neither random nor benign. Collins, a black feminist scholar, reminds us that "race, gender, social class, ethnicity, age and sexuality are not descriptive categories applied to individuals. Instead these elements of social structure emerge as fundamental devises that foster inequity in resulting groups" (1997, p. 376). This reminder challenges us to question the centrality of power in gendered identities as they are formed through the discursive process.

THE EFFECTS OF GENDER IN NURSES' LIVES

Once we think of people as gendered through a discursive process influenced by the social and material realities of a culture at a particular time, we can see that the gendering process extends beyond individuals—to institutions, organisations, and bodies of knowledge. Although it may be obvious that gender does not explicitly reside in these locations, it is also true that gender attributes are assigned to, or play themselves out in, various institutions. In this way, particular work becomes gendered in our minds. The implications of gendered institutions and gendered knowledge are profound. Gender in our society is not value neutral; thus, the gendered nature of knowledge, work, and institutions impacts the value given to that knowledge or work in our society.

The Gendered Nature of Work

"The gendered division of labor in the home and in the work place is part of a negotiated order that is accomplished within the social context of a prevailing set of normative conceptions or ideologies, about what activities are appropriate for men and women" (Angus, 1994, p. 24).

In exploring the working lives of Canadian women, Angus notes that the "labour force is characterised by marked horizontal (occupational) and vertical (hierarchical) gender divisions" (1994, p. 32). What this means is that women in preponderate numbers enter a limited subdivision of the workforce: a subdivision understood to be gender-typed as "women's work." Among these occupations resides that of nursing, composing part of about 80% of women workers who are "employed in labor-intensive occupations . . . concentrated in the public sector . . . where cost containment has produced additional burdens and frustration" (Angus, 1994, pp. 32, 38).

Angus's (1994) work also comments on the vertical division of labour by gender in certain occupations. This refers to the socially created reality that occupations dominated by men are better rewarded than those dominated by women. According to Angus (1994), this is attributable to the dominant discourses in our society that support the valuing of technical skill over interpersonal skill. It is also evident that within many occupational groups, women are less likely to be promoted to administrative positions or to be financially rewarded as generously as their male counterparts.

Although this argument within the nursing profession is open to contestation, the challenges that women often negotiate as the primary caregiver in their personal or familial situation with the demands of professional nursing practise are rigorous. The requirements of personal responsibilities may be experienced as incompatible with the additional demands of administrative work or participation in professional or union organisations, thus limiting the participation of nurses—in particular, women nurses—

from positions of power and politics (Angus, 1994). This is not to suggest that men in nursing may rise to particular positions by virtue of being men, but it does open questions about the social landscape on which the realities of the demands of labour reside. Other questions may be raised as well. How do these social arrangements contribute to what some have called an "over-representation (of men) in top positions compared with their minority status in the profession" (Davies, 1995, p. 9)?

A feminist critique would suggest that we resist the temptation to assign responsibility for the work-life choices that women are forced to make to the individual nurse. Instead, we might examine the social conditions of nurses' lives, such as primary caregiving responsibility and a lack of child-care resources, and the incompatibility of these social realities with the career demands of nursing.

Nursing practise has long been equated with "female virtues"—the virtues of care, nurturance, and altruism. In an exploration of classism, genderism, and racism in nursing, Turkoski notes that, historically, nursing has been "described in purely genderised terms as: 'women's mission, ministry, humanitarian service,' a 'service of womanly duty and conscience' and 'the noblest and most womanly of professions'" and reminds us that these descriptions "reinforced the assumption that nursing is essentially related to one's biological makeup" (1992, p. 162). "Gentleness and quietness were required of Nightingale's nurses, and many nurses in today's work force that 'trained' in the 1960s and earlier can attest to the importance attached to those virtues" (Falk Rafael, 1996, p. 9). Some of those nurses, who are still in practise, were expected to demonstrate as their "professional" behaviour, unquestioning deference to physicians, for example, standing when physicians entered the room, vacating chairs and opening doors for them, as well as obediently, even unthinkingly, carrying out physicians orders. Abbott and Wallace argue that although "nurses no longer see themselves as handmaidens to doctors, they have remained trapped in their status as subordinate to doctors" (1990, p. 22). In support of this argument, Abbott and Wallace remind us of nurses being accountable for administering medication which they are not authorized to prescribe.

In an article discussing the tensions between power and caring in the nursing profession, Falk Rafael itemises the characteristics traditionally associated with femininity and masculinity as follows (1996, p. 5):

FEMININITY	*MASCULINITY*
Submissiveness	Strength
Helplessness	Aggression
Dependency	Mastery
Tenderness	Independence
Nurturance	Logic
Altruism	Being unemotional
	Competitiveness
	Ambition

Falk Rafael (1996) notes that these traditional notions of femininity and masculinity have been *constructed* in a way that associates the masculine with power and the feminine with care. She reminds us that knowledge is developed and propagated in particular ways to maintain power. The "scientification" of knowledge over the past several hundred years demonstrates the systematic devaluing of the feminine. The "denigration of women and that which is feminine has been entrenched in all of civilisation's major institutions" (Falk Rafael, 1996, p. 6). In this conceptualisation, *care* is constructed as a female virtue and one that holds little esteem in Western society. How do we reconcile this devaluing of *care* with the centrality of *care* to the nursing profession?

Fisher, in exploring gender and power in nursing, locates a discourse of care as having "played a central role in the constitution of nursing as a gendered profession" (1993, p. 117). The association of nursing with care is complicated by the social belief in care as an *innately* female quality. When viewed as natural or essential—meaning innately residing in all women—the idea of care may contribute to undermining the value of nurses' work. When care is undervalued, as a feminine virtue, the devaluation extends beyond the individual nurse, be that nurse a woman or a man, to the work itself.

How is it that the value of care has been so compromised by society? A feminist historical analysis connects the value attached to work ordinarily performed by women in the public sphere to the changing value attached to work performed by women in the private sphere (Bunting, 1992). In preindustrial times, before the advent of large-scale productivity and commercialisation, the work ordinarily performed by women was associated with the maintenance and care of home and family and was more closely aligned, in worth, to the work ordinarily performed by men. The refocussing of modern society on a production- and wage-oriented economy resulted in a devaluation of the care-work ordinarily performed by women in the private sphere. Women were placed in the "position of performing services and producing products for the family that have no recognised market value" (Bunting, 1992, p. 58). Along with Bunting, we might wonder about the "connections between the devaluing of women's care in the home and the difficulty of gaining recognition for *nurses'* contributions of care" (1992, p. 60). Bunting (1992) finds a relationship between the invisibility and taken-for-grantedness of caregiving in the private sphere, based on the absence of financial remuneration, and the low status of nursing as a profession. Are there, then, in the social discourses of care, blurred boundaries between work that is "recognised, valued, and paid for . . . [and] work [that] is treated as a labor of love or duty" (Bunting, 1992, p. 61)?

Condon suggests we consider the feminist understanding of Fisher and Tronto that appreciates caring as a "positive dimension of our lives that has been socially devalued by a patriarchal and capitalistic order" (Condon, 1992, p. 73). In this way, the concept of care continues to be valued, and the effort is directed towards interrupting the social discourses that contribute to the devaluing of care. In contrast to duty and calling, which she calls "old masculine metaphors," Condon maintains that care provides an "infinitely more authentic metaphor grounded in the experience of women and capable of being practiced by anyone who chooses it as a social, as well as a professional, ethic" (1992, p. 81).

The Gendered Nature of Knowledge

"Ideas about women, about women's work and how it does or does not require significant knowledge, responsibility, and skill are embedded in nursing and become part of nursing's taken-for-granted reality" (Ceci & McIntyre, 2001, p. 121).

In considering the gendered nature of knowledge, and particularly the impact of gendered knowledge on nursing practise, we may ask, What counts as knowledge? Who decides what counts as knowledge? How might we understand the significance of knowledge gendered in particular ways? McIntyre suggests that "nursing knowledge is inextricable from the assumptions and values underlying its generation. Explicating the assumptions underlying different approaches to knowledge generation in nursing. . . helps nurses avoid unquestioning conformity to existing knowledge" (1999, p. 46).

Through time, nurses have been influenced by the discourses around several bodies of knowledge. Before the industrialisation of nursing, women healers and caregivers were privileged to gynocentric (feminine-centred) knowledge, for example, midwifery and herbal pharmacology, as well as the knowledge necessary for the care of home and family (Ginzberg, 1999). These areas of knowledge have lost value in the foreground of Western science and scientific knowledge, which was produced with an androcentric (masculine-centred) focus. Critiques of science, in the 20th century, suggest that "knowledge produced by the sciences is part of the social and political tradition within which it is produced" (Welch, 1999, p. 423). Such critiques support the notion that particular "women's activities haven't been called 'science' for *political* reasons, even when those activities have been model examples of inquiry leading to knowledge of the natural world" (Ginzberg, 1999, p. 441).

In her work, *Gender and Science*, Fox Keller, a scientist and feminist, explores the "historically pervasive association between masculine and objective, more specifically between masculine and scientific" (1999, p. 427). She addresses this notion as having reached near mythical status as "it has simultaneously the air of being 'self-evident' and 'nonsensical'—the former by virtue of existing in the realm of common knowledge and the later by virtue of . . . conflicting with our image of science as emotionally and sexually neutral" (Fox Keller, 1999, p. 427). She cautions, however, of the potential for unexamined myths to affect subversively our thinking. How, for example, might the masculinity associated with the knowledge we call science influence what counts as nursing knowledge?

The kinds of knowledge that are valued and prioritised in nursing education are clearly reflective of the gendered nature of the profession. The association of early nursing education with "womanly virtues," as discussed earlier, continues to be relevant in what Rafferty calls the "intellectual and social subordination of nurses" (1996, p. 1) and in the "deep anti-intellectual prejudice attached to woman's work in general" (1996, p. 1). The concept of the mandate of nurses' education towards producing graduates of a particular moral character remains covertly present in social discourses and reinforces the location of nursing within the "natural" domain of womanhood.

In discussions of Project 2000, regarding nursing education in Britain, Davies found among healthcare professionals the "distinct echoes . . . of the historical equation of nursing with the female sex, of the view that a good nurse is born, not made, that a good woman is a good nurse" (1995, p. 114). Davies (1995) reports, in her gender analysis of the profession, on the belief held by nurses and other health care professionals that the work of nursing is a practical skill that does not require advanced education in the sciences or in theory, but is best developed through an apprenticeship model of learning. Mackay also argues that there is a "tension between a vocational and a professional view of the nurse" (1998, p. 62) in Britain. She notes that although this may not be directly acknowledged by nurses, the "concept of vocation is embedded in many of the accepted practices and attitudes within nursing, such as being of service to others and putting others first" (Mackay, 1998, p. 63).

Is this discussion relevant to Canadian nurses and to the education of nursing students in Canada? Although some may argue that the Canadian Association of Nurses has advocated the baccalaureate entry to practise since 1993, the view of nursing as a vocation may be held by numbers of nurses in practise. In discussing the situation in Canada, Armstrong (1993) presents student nurses as apprentices and points out the financial inequities between these students and apprentices in male-dominated occupations. Despite the endorsement of baccalaureate entry to practise and the increasing academic preparation of nurses, the gender issues of nurses remain.

These conflicted ideals regarding the meaning and methods of nurse education raise resounding questions. Whose purpose is being served through the deintellectualisation of nurses' education? How does the apprenticeship model serve the economic and labour needs of hospitals and the health care systems? What is the meaning for nurses of an education that prepares them to develop "character" and practical skills while undervaluing the development of intellectual pursuit in independent thinking, analysis, and problem solving, to say nothing of the theoretical knowledge underlying the practise of manual or technical skills? How does the intellectual devaluing of nurses' knowledge, reinscribed by particular health care professionals, contribute to the marginality of the nurse's position in the health care system?

The Gendered Nature of the Nurse

"Nursing has always been a much conflicted metaphor in our culture, reflecting all the ambivalences we give to the meaning of womanhood" (Reverby, 1987, p. 207).

At any given point in time, there may be multiple discourses participating in the construction of the nurse as subject. Put another way, social discourses present an image of what it is to be and to practise as nurse. "Just as the cosmetic and fashion industries created the 'ideal woman,' so nursing texts, be they in popular press, television, or textbook form, create images of the ideal nurse" (Cheek & Rudge, 1994, p. 589). These idealised images of nurse are by no means unified. Part of the complexity of attaining the ideal is that it comprises mixed and conflicting messages and changes over time.

Regardless of the variables that form this ideal—including race, ethnicity, age, and sexuality—"both the nurse and the work of nursing are firmly associated in the public mind with the female sex" (Davies, 1995, p. 2). The naturalness of a woman performing as a nurse is reflected in the fact that "a man in the same job will be described not just as a nurse but as 'male nurse' " (Davies, 1995, p. 2). As suggested by Davies in the introduction to her text, *Gender and the Professional Predicament in Nursing*, "a closer acquaintance with nursing, however, shatters any cozy image of women doing work that is somehow *natural* to them and hence being entirely comfortable in and satisfied with the role they have chosen" (1995, p. 2, emphasis added).

A current American television portrayal of an emergency room nurse as an autonomous, independent, respected, and compassionate professional conveys a particular appeal to nurses entering the profession. The actual social and material realities of this nurse's professional world may, in fact, be as much of a fabrication as the professionally submissive representation of the fictional Dr. Welby's nurse, several decades ago. Both of these media portrayals of the nurse reflect an idealised image of "woman" formed through the prominent social discourses of the day. Although these images differ vastly from one another, they both present an idealised image of nurse-woman.

Is it possible that the public propagation of these ideals serves to undermine a more accurate representation of the nurse's lived experience, both in the eyes of the public and in the eyes of nurses themselves? Kalisch and Kalisch (1987) would concur that through the 19th and 20th centuries, media representations of the nurse have contributed to a narrow and undervalued image of nursing, drawing strongly on a received view of the nature of woman. We are challenged by nursing scholars to "raise questions about those discourses and ways of thinking, in the world or in us, which diminish nursing" (Ceci & McIntyre, 2001, p. 121). Among the discourses that require our ongoing interrogation are those that present a gender-idealised image of the nurse.

BARRIERS TO AND STRATEGIES FOR ISSUE RESOLUTION

Several barriers to resolving the issue of gender-related devaluing of nursing practise and profession need to be identified before strategies for change can be devised.

Identifying Barriers: Furthering Our Understandings

"The dilemma of nursing is too tied into the broader problems of gender and class in our society to be solved solely by the political efforts of one occupational group" (Reverby, 1987, p. 207). The barriers to the resolution of issues of gender and power in nursing are embedded in societal ideology. As nurses, we require both the knowledge and the willingness to critique and to challenge these social discourses. In particular, we can consider the following barriers that impair movement towards understanding the issues:

1. The gendered nature of work in general, and nurses' work in particular, is concealed—or implicitly present—in nursing practise. Although the effects of gendering on nursing practise are part of our experience, there is a lack of discussion that identifies these experiences as the problematic effects of gender and power.
2. The effects of power and gender in nurses' work and nursing knowledge are taken for granted in nurses' practise and education. The lack of transparency regarding the gendered nature of nurses' work (see barrier 1) contributes to our inability to question the embedded assumptions regarding gender and nurses' work.
3. Historically, nurses have lacked a critical feminist analysis that provides a framework to critique and question the taken-for-granted social discourses of gender, nurses' work, and the valuing of care in society.
4. Although the gendered divisions of labour have long been ingrained in society, only recently has the gendered nature of work been called into question in academic discourses that are accessible to nursing.
5. Understandings of the gendered nature of nurses' work are impaired by the larger lack of clarity and articulation of the nature of nurses' work in general. The inaccurate and limited public representations of the nurse and nurses' work contribute to the limited understanding and devaluing of nurses' work and nursing knowledge.
6. Individual efforts to disrupt the taken-for-granted ideas of gender require one to challenge social discourses and dominant views. This necessary strategy produces a barrier for the individual by placing her or him in a tension with commonly held societal views.

Devising Strategies: Voice and Action

1. Several of the barriers to resolving issues of gender and power, and their impact on the significance attributed to nurses' work, could be broken down by providing knowledge regarding the gendered nature of nurses' work, both historically and as it is currently embedded in nursing practise. The knowledge necessary for a thorough understanding of gender and power issues is complex and requires familiarity with a structure that can be used to critique and challenge the taken-for-granted assumptions embedded in these

issues. Knowledge of the gendered nature of nurses' work may be supported by feminist analysis, which focusses on the idea of power embedded in ideologies and the formation of gendered subjects through social discourses. This knowledge and the means to illuminate and question assumed truths belongs in nursing curricula, beginning early in undergraduate nursing education. Much of the complexity of this knowledge lies in our lack of familiarity with concepts of gendering and social construction. As nurses become fluent in knowledge and language, the transparency regarding the gendered nature of nurses' work will be improved.

2. As identified in the barriers (see earlier), there is a tension generated between the origin of social discourses of gender and the value of particular types of work in society, and the disruption of these discourses must begin at an individual level. Important strategies to interrupt discourses that undermine the significance attributed to nurses' work begin with increasing our own awareness of these taken-for-granted discourses in our daily lives. Influencing these discourses in ways that call into question "the way things have always been, or have always been done" requires confidence and courage for the individual nurse.

3. The "action" required to change or disrupt large social ideologies can begin with wondering about the following:

   - What it is we think we "know"
   - The effects of taken-for-granted "truths" on the valuing of nurses' knowledge and practise
   - The ways in which we reinscribe social discourses of gender in our own practise

4. As members of society, nurses and women have been socialised to suppress difference. To challenge effectively what is taken for granted about the role of gender and its powerful influence on nurses' work, we must be willing to notice difference and to acknowledge the way that differences, such as gender, class, race, ethnicity, and sexual orientation, matter in the ways our identities are lived and viewed by the world.

5. Social discourses of gender are more than ideas.

They are intimately connected to the social and material realities of our lives. Exerting influence that will change or disrupt discourses of gender necessitates action that will improve, in particular, the material realities of women's lives. This means, for example, advocating for changes in the workplace that support the lives of women as they negotiate family and work responsibilities and demands. Adequate resources for child care and family responsibilities are gendered workplace issues. Attending to these needs influences the value and respect attributed to women's multiple roles, including the significance attributed to nurses' paid work.

SUMMARY

This chapter explores multiple issues associated with the gendered nature of nurses' work, of nursing knowledge, and of the public representation of the nurse. Central to the issue are the social discourses about gender that are inherent in the value attributed to nurses' work and the importance attached to nurses' knowledge.

One question examined is this: Is the value accorded to nurses' work representative of the societal devaluing of work that is ordinarily performed by women? The exploration extends our understanding of gender and power in nursing beyond the idea of the "distribution of gender" in the profession. The significance of nurses' work and the value accorded this work are steeped in societal structures and ideologies that surpass the particular gender of the nurse who is performing the work.

The gendered nature of nurses' work and education has been with us since the inception of nursing. The gendered division of labour has historically placed nursing in the realm of women's work, a division that was supported through the early educational programme for nurses that focussed on "womanly virtues" and "moral character." The legacy of this account of nursing has been the conceptualisation of care as both an innately feminine virtue residing in all women and a discourse central to nursing practise. The significance of nurses' work parallels the devaluing of care in a society that has increasingly valued science and a production-focussed economy.

Given the early image of nursing as a natural extension of feminine virtues, we may be tempted to assign responsibility for "gendering" to the pioneering women of nursing practise and education. This chapter argues that the gendering of work occurs, not with particular individuals, but through society's discourses, embedded with ideologies.

The current, and perhaps more difficult challenge, is to recognise the less overt but no less present discourses of gender that structure current nursing practises. These discourses of gender—the nature of the work called women's work, and the value that is afforded to caregiving in our society—underlie the significance of nurses' work.

In locating the discourses of gender in society, we need not look beyond ourselves. Our complicity is evident as we participate in the reinstatement of gendered discourses birthed in the societal ideologies from which we cannot extricate ourselves. The challenge, then, is to look for opportunities to recognise and to disrupt the taken-for-granted notions that define and constrain the possibilities for gendered people who are practising and being nurses.

Reflections on the Chapter

1. How do you understand gender as socially constructed? What are the implications of your understandings for nurses, for nurses' work, for nursing as a profession?

2. What does a feminist analysis of gender add to our understanding of the value and conditions of nurses' work?

3. What are the benefits and limitations of placing gender in a central place in our analysis of nurses' work? How does gender intersect with other realities and conditions of nurses' lives?

4. Provide an example of your own participation in a taken-for-granted, socially sanctioned norm regarding gender, from your own nursing experience. In retrospect, how might you have acted to interrupt this particular social discourse around gender?

REFERENCES

Abbott, P., & Meerabeau, L. (Eds.). (1998). *The sociology of the caring professions* (2nd ed.). London: University College of London Press.

Abbott, P., & Wallace, C. (Eds.). (1990). *The sociology of the caring professions.* London: The Falmer Press.

Allen, D. (1992). Introduction. In J. Thompson, D. Allen, & L. Rodrigues-Fisher (Eds.), *Critique, resistance and action: Working papers in the politics of nursing* (pp. xi–xvi). New York: National League for Nursing Press.

Althusser, L. (1971). Ideology and ideological apparatuses. In B. Brewster (Trans.). L. Althussey (Ed.) *Lenin and philosophy and other essays* (pp. 123–172). London: New Left Books.

Angus, J. (1994). Women's paid/unpaid work and health: Exploring the social context of everyday life. *Canadian Journal of Nursing Research 26*(4), 23–42.

Armstron, P. (1993). Women's health care work: Nursing in context. In P. Armstrong, J. Choiniere, & E. Day (Eds.). *Vital Signs: Nursing in Transition.* Toronto: Garamond Press.

Bunting, S. (1992). Eve's legacy: An analysis of family caregiving from a feminist perspective. In J. Thompson, D. Allen, & L. Rodrigues-Fisher (Eds.), *Critique, resistance and action: Working papers in the politics of nursing* (pp. 53–68). New York: National League for Nursing Press.

Butler, J. (1990). Performative acts and gender constitution: An essay in phenomenology and feminist theory. In S. Case (Ed.), *Performing feminisms: Feminist critical theory and theatre* (pp. 270–282). Baltimore, MD: The John Hopkins University Press.

Ceci, C., & McIntyre, M. (2001). A "quiet" crisis in health care: Developing our capacity to hear. *Nursing Philosophy 2*(2), 121–127.

Cheek, J., & Rudge, T. (1994). The panopticon revisited? An exploration of the social and political dimensions of contemporary health care and nursing practice. *International Journal of Nursing Studies, 31*(6), 583–591.

Chinn, P. (1999). Gender and nursing science. In E. C. Polifroni & M. Welch (Eds.), *Perspectives on philosophy of science in nursing: An historical and contemporary anthology* (pp. 462–466). Philadelphia: Lippincott Williams & Wilkins.

Collins, P. H. (1997). Comment on Hekman's "Truth and method: Feminist standpoint theory revisited": Where's the power? *Signs: Journal of Women in Culture and Society, 22*(2), 375–381.

Condon, E. (1992). Nursing and the caring metaphor: Gender and political influences on an ethics of care. In J. Thompson, D. Allen, & L. Rodrigues-Fisher (Eds.), *Critique, resistance and action: Working papers in the politics of nursing* (pp. 69–84). New York: National League for Nursing Press.

Davies, C. (1995). *Gender and the professional predicament in nursing.* Philadelphia: Open University Press.

Falk Rafael, A. (1996). Power and caring: A dialectic in nursing. *Advances in Nursing Science 19*(1):3–17.

Ferree, M.M., Lorber, J., & Hess, B. (Eds.). (2000). *Revisioning gender.* New York: AltaMira Press.

Fisher, S. (1993). Gender, power, resistance: Is care the remedy? In S. Fisher & K. Davis (Eds.), *Negotiating at the margins: The gendered discourses of power and resistance* (pp. 87–121). New Brunswick, NJ: Rutgers University Press.

Fox Keller, E. (1999). Gender and science. In E. C. Polifroni & M. Welch (Eds.), *Perspectives on philosophy of science in nursing: An historical and contemporary anthology* (pp. 427–439). Philadelphia: Lippincott Williams & Wilkins.

Ginzberg, R. (1999). Uncovering gynocentric science. In E. C. Polifroni & M. Welch (Eds.), *Perspectives on philosophy of science in nursing: An historical and contemporary anthology* (pp. 440–450). Philadelphia: Lippincott Williams & Wilkins.

Kalisch, P., & Kalisch, B. (1987). *The changing image of the nurse.* Menlo Park, CA: Addison-Wesley.

Mackay, L. (1998). In: Abbott, P., & Meerabeau, L. (Eds.). (1998). *The sociology of the caring professions* (2nd ed.). London: University College of London Press.

McDowell, L. (1999). *Gender, identity and place: Understanding feminist geographies.* Minneapolis: University of Minnesota Press.

McIntyre, M. (1999). The focus of the discipline of nursing: A critique and extension. In E. C. Polifroni & M. Welch (Eds.), *Perspectives on philosophy of science in nursing: An historical and contemporary anthology* (pp. 46–54). Philadelphia: Lippincott Williams & Wilkins.

Nakano Glenn E. (2000). The social construction and institutionalization of gender and race: An integrative framework. In M. M. Ferree, J. Lorber, & B. Hess (Eds.), *Revisioning gender* (pp. 3—43). New York: AltaMira Press.

Neil, R., & Watts, R. (Eds.). (1991). *Caring and nursing: Explorations in feminist perspectives.* New York: National League for Nursing.

Rafferty, R. (1996). *The politics of nursing knowledge.* London: Routledge.

Reverby, S. (1987). *Ordered to care: The dilemma of American nursing, 1850–1945.* Cambridge, UK: Cambridge University Press.

Scott, J. (1992). Experience. In J. Butler & J. Scott (Eds.), *Feminists theorize the political* (pp. 22–40). London: Routledge.

Thorne, S., McCormick, J., & Carty, E. (1996). Deconstructing the gender neutrality of chronic illness and disability. *Health Care for Women International, 18*(1), 1–16.

Turkoski, B. (1992). A critical analysis of professionalism in nursing. In J. Thompson, D. Allen, & L. Rodrigues-Fisher (Eds.), *Critique, resistance and action: Working papers in the politics of nursing* (pp. 149–166). New York: National League for Nursing Press.

Welch, M. (1999). Science and gender. In E. C. Polifroni & M. Welch (Eds.), *Perspectives on philosophy of science in nursing: An historical and contemporary anthology* (pp. 423–426). Philadelphia: Lippincott Williams & Wilkins.

PART V

Societal Issues: Challenges for Nursing Practice

20

The Consumer Movement

Isobel Boyle

Chapter Objectives

At the completion of this chapter, you will be able to:

1. Understand the evolution of the consumer movement in health care.

2. Explore societal influences on the consumer movement in health care.

3. Discuss the patients' rights for informed consent.

4. Analyse the trends, issues, and barriers to public participation.

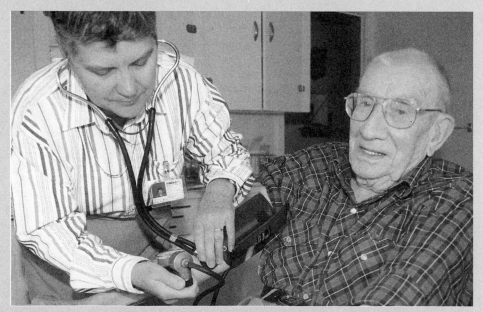

Photograph by Larry Arbour. Used with permission of University of Calgary.

5. Articulate the role of nurses as advocates.
6. Examine the effects of the consumer movement on nursing.

7. Identify future trends in the consumer movement in health care.

A *consumer* may be defined as a person who purchases or uses goods (such as food and clothing) or services (such as health services) to satisfy various needs. A consumer has both rights and responsibilities. With respect to rights, a consumer is entitled to receive the full goods and services that he or she has purchased or been promised. With respect to responsibilities, a consumer is responsible for being well informed before buying or using goods and services, for making sure that those goods and services are delivered and are what the consumer contracted for, and for initiating action so that problems related to consumed goods or services are resolved quickly and satisfactorily. Consumer rights and demands are important forces for any change.

The demand for health care is affected by the illnesses consumers experience, their tastes and preferences, their income, and their knowledge about health care (Milburn & Griffith, 1991). Consumerism in health care occurs at both the individual and collective level. At an individual level, treatment decisions may be made, whereas collectively, consumerism may influence health services and policy. It has been argued that "consumerism" is one of the main influences on health policy (Calnan & Gabe, 2001, p. 119). Groups, such as those composing the women's health movement, wellness advocates, and self-help movements, have heightened awareness of the rights of consumers and the desire for greater public accountability in health care decision making.

HISTORY OF THE CONSUMER MOVEMENT

The Consumers' Association of Canada (CAC) was formed in 1947 and continues today. CAC focusses on a broad range of topics, including food safety, health, trade, financial services, communications industries, and other marketplace issues as they emerge. The CAC brings consumers together to establish standards to ensure that safe, high-quality goods and services are available in Canada at affordable prices (CAC, 2001).

Consumers' Rights and Responsibilities

The CAC, along with professional associations such as the Canadian Medical Association and the Canadian Nurses Association, lobbied successfully for the passage of Canada's Health Act (1962) and universal medicare (1966). Consumer rights in health care were defined as early as the 1970s. These rights included:

> . . . the right to be informed, the right to be respected as the individual with the major responsibility for his own health care, the right to participate in decision-making affecting his health, and the right to equal access to health regardless of the individual's economic status, sex, age, creed, ethnic origin and location. (Storch, 1982, p. 186)

The establishment of these rights in health care has been viewed as the beginning of the health care consumer movement in Canada. The balance between benefits and costs determines health care preference, and, although benefits include collective goals, personal costs are notably the dominant factor (Singer, 1995). To achieve these consumers' rights, it became incumbent on governments, health administrators, health professionals, and consumers to work collaboratively in establishing legislation and policy.

Consumers are more than mere recipients of goods and services, particularly in health care. They want and need to be partners in seeking and obtaining appropriate health care services directed towards helping themselves. There is a need for an interdependent relationship, in which consumers of health care are advised and consulted, rather than the historical relationship wherein consumers depended on the decisions of health care professionals.

Today, CAC defines the needs of consumers in the areas of protection, safety, information, education, choice, participation, compensation, and environment. The CAC has many national issues committees, networks, and task forces that have consumer representation to establish policies within a set of general, consumer-oriented principles. Foremost among these principles are the rights to choose and to be heard as consumers. Examples of these committees include the Environmental Network, the National Health Council, Policy Advisory Group, Standards Task Force, Food Labelling, and Health Care Services.

Many individual health care institutions have developed or adopted a Patients' Bill of Rights. In the United States, the American Hospital Association has developed a Patients' Bill of Rights which is used nationally. In this document, consumers' rights are similar to those articulated by the CAC. The Patients' Bill of Rights strives to ensure that all patients know what their medical choices are, are aware of any risks from procedures and treatments, and understand how they may be involved in research and how this may affect them. Respectful communication between consumers and health professionals is expected. Obtaining complete information in understandable terms is emphasised.

Factors Influencing Rights and Responsibilities

On a societal level, demographic factors, such as affluence, education, and the age of the population, influence demand for health care. Increased coverage of medical topics in the popular media, as well as the availability of medical information on the Internet, has created a more knowledgeable public. Across Canada, telephone lines staffed by health professionals offer free health information 24 hours a day, 7 days a week. The objectives of these lines include increasing health education of the public and improving consumer satisfaction. Statistical analysis of the use of these lines demonstrates continually increasing demand indicating that individuals want to be empowered and to take charge of their health care (Fig. 20.1). Blomqvist (1979) noted that the "the market mechanism provides an effective signalling device through which consumers' relative valuation of different goods and services is transmitted to producers, and the allocation of productive resources is indirectly guided by individual preferences of the consumers" (p. 10).

Consumers are demanding quality care, courteous service, and personal concern from health care providers. Increasingly, institutions and facilities are attempting to measure quality of care provided to meet health care consumers' demands. Consumers also want to know their health care options. They want to have access to knowledge-

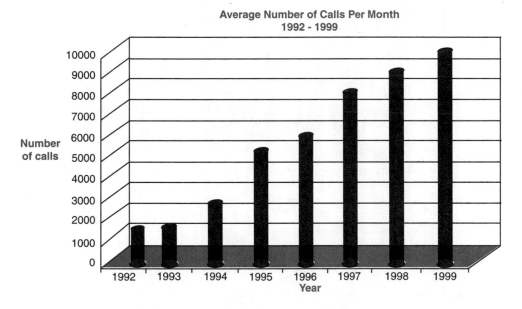

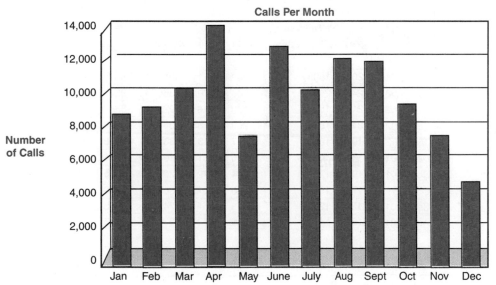

FIGURE 20.1. The average number of calls to Health Line increased more than tenfold from 1992 to 1999. More recent statistics show a continuing and increasing trend of usage (Source: Health Line, www.thehealthline.consumer. Provided by Kevin Wilson Health Line, University of Alberta.

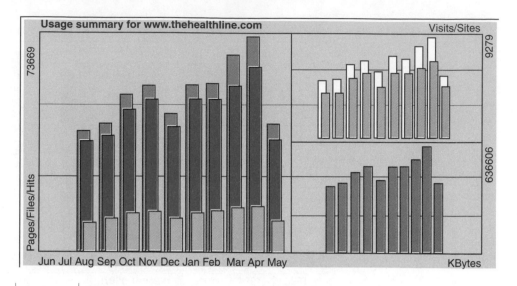

Summary by Month									
Month	**Daily Avg**				**Monthly Totals**				
	Hits	**Files**	**Pages**	**Visits**	**Sites**	**KBytes**	**Visits**	**Pages**	**Files**	**Hits**
May 2002	2047	1805	427	262	4611	398866	5522	8976	37905	42997
Apr 2002	2455	2131	512	309	7376	636606	9279	15382	63940	73669
Mar 2002	2161	1887	474	270	6716	592238	8382	14703	58505	66999
Feb 2002	2139	1867	490	263	5976	536176	7366	13730	52293	59902
Jan 2002	1917	1687	431	247	6043	533253	7678	13377	52323	59442
Dec 2001	1474	1289	354	196	4751	410467	6096	10983	39988	45723
Nov 2001	1937	1730	434	244	5872	522552	7345	13025	51907	58124
Oct 2001	1721	1540	391	220	5351	486703	6840	12147	47746	53351
Sep 2001	1391	1231	337	173	4154	374395	5203	10124	36956	41759
Aug 2001	1689	1495	360	216	4072	353121	4973	8281	34392	38862
Totals						4844377	68684	120728	475955	540828

FIGURE 20.1. (Continued)

able professionals and to accurate and current health information. They want to have choices to ensure that the drive for excellence in health care continues.

Consumerism Worldwide

The World Health Organization's (WHO's) vision, as articulated in the 1986 Ottawa Charter, was an attempt to emphasise health promotion and disease prevention. The report, *Achieving Health for All by the Year 2000*, focussed on the need for greater individual involvement in developing a healthy lifestyle, satisfactory relationships, and interdependency with professionals. "The WHO 1986 conference changed the model of health service delivery from the biomedical to a social model of care, recognising that community members have been excluded not only from consultation about individual health issues, but from health service policy making in general" (Crichton, 1997, p. 66). This model of health and the ensuing activity is referred to as the *wellness movement.*

However, the largest health expenditures continue to be focussed on acute care and the treatment of illness. Although there is some movement towards healthy lifestyle changes, consumers with chronic illnesses still demand the majority of treatment and care, leaving little money for prevention strategies. Attempts throughout the 1990s to restructure the health care system with a greater emphasis on health promotion have been restricted; restructuring has been financially driven to save money. As a result, services and the number of beds for acute care have been reduced. At the same time, the demand for services and beds has increased as more sophisticated diagnostic measures have been developed and implemented and as more people live longer. Krueger Wilson and Porter-O'Grady, in their 1999 book entitled *Leading the Revolution in Health Care, Advancing Systems, Igniting Performance,* state that to change the health care system, we must have a greater emphasis on life management processes instead of just illness treatment. This shift will demand a more dynamic relationship between consumers and health care providers.

INFLUENCES ON THE CONSUMER MOVEMENT

A number of sociologic factors have influenced the consumer movement in health care. These include the women's movement, an aging population, and the emergence of self-help groups and patient representatives. Traditional assumptions have been challenged as greater demands have been placed on the health care system.

The Women's Movement

In an edited collection of papers related to health care and women, Gallant and coauthors (1997) describe how the women's movement has broadened the definition of women's health beyond women's health care and has educated women to become informed consumers when making health care decisions. The focus on women's health has intensified since the 1980s. Women who previously accepted any medical recommendation at face value began to ask health care professionals about the availability of alternate treatments. For example, radical mastectomies were frequently the norm for women in the 1960s and early 1970s, but as more information about breast cancer became available, women began questioning their physicians and advocating for less deforming surgeries. Maharaj (1999) describes the role of women's advocacy groups in shaping the Canadian health care system. She describes these groups as agents for change and system "watchdogs" (p. 260).

The concern about issues in woman's health continues to grow. To meet the goal of improving and advancing women's health, Women's Health Council groups have been established in most Canadian provinces. Largely because of partnerships and collaboration with consumers, health care groups, governments, and other public and private groups, advancement in women's health has been stimulated, and changes are occurring.

Although the changes in health services for women are positive, evidence of inequities in the conduct of research for women's health issues continues to exist. The formation of the Centres of Excellence in Women's Health (2001), funded by Health Canada, attempted to strengthen policy-focussed research on women's health in Canada. These centres were directed to making the Canadian health system more responsive to the needs of women. Opportunities for collaboration among community-based women's health groups, service providers, and academic researchers continue to be encouraged in the interest of the promotion of women's health. Centres are located in British Columbia, the Prairies, Montreal, and Atlantic Canada.

An Aging Population

In the consumer movement, the influence of the "baby boomers" has been significant, particularly in health care. Baby boomers represent the population born in the 20 years from 1947 to 1966 (Foot & Stoffman, 2000, p. 15). This largest cohort of the population makes decisions not only for themselves but also for their parents and children. Maloney and Paul (1991) in their essay, "The Consumer Movement Takes Hold in Medical Care," state that baby boomers want more information, involvement, control, and choice regarding the services they buy (including medical care) than did previous generations. This influence was evidenced by increased family participation in obstetric and pediatric units in the late 1970s and early 1980s. Participation by fathers or significant others in the delivery room became a norm. Parents demanded to be with their children in hospitals and to be part of the decision-making process in the treatment of their children. Consumer advisory groups have become an expected component within hospital and community health organisations. Consumer input is now standard within many institutions. Community involvement has been incorporated into the Canadian Council of Health Services Accreditation Standards (2002).

"An older population is more demanding and more knowledgeable about the products and services it needs and is less willing to tolerate poor service" (Foot & Stoffman, 2000, p. 223). Advances in medical science have improved the life expectancy of Canadians. Despite these advances and public health initiatives, as the baby boomers grow old, the burden of chronic illness grows as well, and the demand for a more responsive health care system increases. Then, as the demand for health services grows, so grows the fear that the health care system will be unable to meet the demands. It will be incumbent on this group of consumers to participate in the system at all levels.

More than half of the nurses in the workforce today are members of the baby-boomer generation. These nurses are beginning to retire and will continue to do so for the next 20 years. Meanwhile, proportionately fewer nurses are entering the workforce. Nurses are involved as professionals in the health care system, but on a personal level, they are among the consumers demanding services for their children, their parents, and themselves. Meeting these demands is the challenge for governments, nursing associations, and administrators.

Self-Help Groups

Self-help groups exemplify increased consumerism in health care. Peer self-help groups offer guidance, information, and support to individuals experiencing a variety of medical, societal, or behavioural conditions. Frequently, they have formed as groups seeking support and are typified by their absence of professional leadership. Professionals are consulted but do not take the leadership role. In addition to providing information and support to others, these groups discuss issues and develop strategies for action and interaction with health professionals and the health care system. Some groups lobby the health care system and governments in the interest of advocating for members of the group represented. These groups identify their own issues rather than rely on the agendas of the health care community (Leigh, 1994).

Self-help groups are available for most diseases, particularly those of a chronic nature. They are becoming more prevalent with increased numbers of patients using the worldwide web for information and communications. The American Self-Help Group Clearinghouse provides a database of more than 900 national and international self-help support groups for various health problems. These groups range from those advocating and supporting people with disabilities to those providing support and information on such diseases as rare blood disorders. The medical community has raised some concern regarding the value of these groups. Criticisms by some physicians and others include the potential for providing misinformation, promoting a strong emphasis on illness and potentially encouraging unconventional therapies. However, others value self-help groups for the experience and the support that individuals in the group provide to members within the group.

Among the most prevalent self-help groups are those associated with cancer. People with cancer are demanding that nonmedical support services become an integral part of cancer care (Leigh, 1994). The increased information available on early detection and treatment options has increased long-term survival rates for people with cancer. While supporting each other, these survivors and other groups identified with other chronic conditions advocate for appropriate information and care. They are active participants in identifying issues related to their diseases. They also seek help from health professionals, politicians, or whoever may be in the best position to assist them. They support each other in the demand for effective communication with health care providers. Moreover, they demand accountability not only from professionals but also from the health care system.

Patient Representatives

During the 1970s, a new group of hospital workers emerged. Known as *patient representatives*, these hospital workers help patients and their families to address special needs that may arise in the course of treatment. Patient representatives are not only involved in advocacy; they also pinpoint potential problem areas and get involved in conflict management and dispute resolution (Beardwood et al., 1999, p. 371).

Responsibilities of patient representatives will vary from hospital to hospital but generally include the following:

- Providing information on patients' rights
- Acting as an intermediary between the hospital or department and the patient to bring about the most effective health care treatment
- Investigating and directing inquiries and complaints to appropriate staff
- Advocating for patients and their families
- Acting as an intermediary to administration on behalf of patients and their families

Patient representative positions were first evident in children's hospitals throughout Canada and the United States but are now established in most hospital and medical care centres. There are no official, specific requirements for this field. Hospitals and other employers establish their own educational and work experience requirements to meet specific needs of the settings in which the representatives will work. Many of these workers have backgrounds in health care, education, human resource services, or communications. Patient representatives have been effective in participating in the change of hospital policies, procedures, and services to health care consumers.

ISSUES FOR HEALTH CARE CONSUMERS

Health Care Reform

Health care reform in Canada has generally been viewed as a cost-saving measure rather than a real reform or change to the way health care is delivered. Each province has attempted to incorporate different ways of accommodating the increasing demand for health care spending and the reduced federal budgeting for health care. District or regional authorities were formed, inpatient beds were eliminated, and every health care sector was restructured. Reform included the corporatisation of many hospitals and other health care units. Rewards to authorities and districts were based on meeting budgets rather than on the quality of health care delivery. Reports of emergency room backups, waiting lists for surgery, and other concerns related to effective and safe delivery of health care were reported in the media daily. Consumers voice concerns that health care is not just a social right but also a consumer right—a right for the individual (Beardwood et al., 1999).

Health care reform has created mixed meanings and diverse intentions. Consumers are no longer passive recipients of health care. They demand information and quality in health care delivery. At the same time, there is a movement to involve consumers in decision making that will have system-wide repercussions. Members of the public, as well as officials who govern professional associations, are being elected to regional health boards.

Informed Consent

An inherent health consumer's right is that of informed consent. Giving informed consent to a health procedure or treatment means that a patient or a responsible caregiver (if the patient is incapacitated) is able to make a decision that is achieved by receiving and understanding all the information that he or she needs to make a decision regarding treatment or nontreatment. Informed consent implies both a legal and moral obligation on the part of patients and health professionals. The patient's signature on a form denotes the legal responsibility he or she accepts. In turn, health professionals have a legal and moral obligation to give adequate health information. True informed consent allows patients to make an autonomous decision about treatment based on the information they receive. This process involves more than the giving and receiving of information. Many patients want to be a partner in the decision-making process. Key issues of informed consent include the following:

- Understanding treatment options, including the associated risks and benefits
- Appropriate communication
- Respect for the decisions that patients make

O'Connor (1997), in her analysis of decision support for patients, notes that "the rise of consumerism and patient empowerment has shifted the emphasis from the more passive informed consent to informed choice" (p. 8).

Switanskowsky (1998) describes informed consent as being at a "crossroads between the traditional, paternalistic, harm-avoidance model and the autonomy enhancing, patient-focused model" (p. 119). The harm-avoidance model may be viewed as paternalistic and one in which the patient consents to treatment by passively accepting the treatment prescribed by physicians or other health care providers. In the autonomy-enhancing model, both the patient and the physician or other health care provider must be viewed as contributing to the process. There is growing recognition that patients' values, preferences, and lifestyle must be incorporated into the process of informed consent. This process involves a partnership in which both parties have something essential to contribute to the process of being informed. The provider has expertise in a particular area of treatment, whereas the patient possesses self. This knowledge may be about the medical condition, family values, or other personal idiosyncrasies affecting the patient's ability to make an informed decision. Inherent in the concept of patient rights is the right to be informed.

Consumers of health care increasingly seek knowledge to inform their consent—or dissent. The sources for information include family, friends, the popular media, available literature, and the Internet (Box 20.1). The completeness and accuracy of this information vary and challenge health care providers to ensure that patients obtain the best possible information. Adequate information is required before patients can be meaningful participants in their own care.

Privacy and Confidentiality

As more patient information becomes available electronically, there is concern about access to personal information. Concerns about preserving a patient's right to privacy and limiting access to patient data have given rise to both federal and provincial legislation, such as the Manitoba Provincial Health Information Act (PHIA) and the Ontario Municipal Freedom of Information and Protection of Privacy Act (MFIPPA). Patients have advocated for and must be able to expect that access to their information will have appropriate, reliable, and consistent standards. With increased technology, such as electronic records used to communicate patient information, the issues of privacy and confidentiality present new challenges.

Consumer Participation

The National Forum on Health (1997) noted the concern Canadians have regarding the erosion of the health care system. Consumers are not mere recipients of health serv-

BOX 20.1

Questions To Ask Your Doctor Before You Have Surgery

- Why do I need this surgery?
- What alternatives to surgery are available?
- What is the surgeon's experience?
- What kind of anaesthesia is available?

Adapted from the American Agency for Health Care Policy and Research. (2001). [On-line]. Available: http://www.ahrq.gov/qual/kffhigh.htm.

ices. A consumer-based approach to health care implies that consumers become active participants in decisions related to health care. "The concepts of community empowerment and participation reflect a commitment to such precepts as the common good and shared responsibility for health" (Minkler, 1994, p. 406). Consumers act as partners in both the definition of issues and the development of solutions to address these issues.

The concept of community participation has been endorsed at many levels within the health care system. Community representation is seen on hospital boards, community health organisations, and boards of professional organisations. Higgins (1999) notes that many sources support public participation in both health promotion and community development. Consumer representation on health-related boards and committees provides a unique perspective. Many boards are now required by law to include public representation. These members are chosen by governments to represent constituents, socioeconomic groups, regions or the public at large, or they may be chosen by a general assembly. This is exemplified across Canada by the appointment of consumers to the provincial professional nursing boards.

Consumers are now viewed as major stakeholders in health care. The increasing need for broad involvement comes at a time when Canadians, as a population, are adopting a broader definition of health and acknowledging the wide range of factors that contribute to the health of the population. Studies have demonstrated that consumers can be influential both in improving their own health outcome as well as influencing policies issues. "Consumers reap the benefits, but also bear the financial and clinical burdens, of research and medical practice" (Hiller et al., 1997, p. 1280).

However, what public participation really means remains ambiguous. Who are the public representatives? Who do they represent? What information do these representatives need to give meaningful input into decision making? What is the level of participation by these individuals? Individuals chosen as public representatives are often characterised by "their skill in public speaking, ability to understand policy and technical language, familiarity with meeting etiquette and professional status that motivates and enables them to become involved" (Higgins, 1999, p. 30). The question remains as to their ability to understand and represent the issues of the public they represent.

Controlling health care costs is now a top priority for both the federal and provincial governments. The federal government has increased the shift of fiscal and moral responsibilities to the provinces. In turn, the provincial governments are attempting to shift responsibility for making difficult decisions regarding resource allocation to communities and consumers. There is a desire to increase public accountability for decisions on the allocation of health care resources. This trend has the potential to make providers more accountable to the communities that they serve. What is the consumer's role in this process?

Charles and DeMaio (1993) note that roles and the context in which public participation exists must be defined in order for meaningful decision making to occur. Additionally, the level of participation of these representatives is important to note. Public or lay representatives may have a role as individual consumers of health services, or they may have a broader public or community perspective. Clarification of the roles that representatives have influences their level of participation. Frequently, lay representatives are intimidated by the expertise of the various health professionals. Lay representatives do not always have the necessary knowledge to participate fully. Sometimes, the perspectives that they bring to the table are not valued. Consultation, participation, and opinions may be sought from public representatives for information gathering but may or may not be used when policy decisions are made. There is no guarantee that individual views will be taken into account. Representatives and professionals must understand the role of public representation. Public representatives may advocate for a specific group, but they need also to take responsibility for obtaining the knowledge necessary to be active participants in the decision-making process.

To be effective, public participants must be viewed as equal partners with the health policymakers. They need to be acknowledged and respected for the contributions that they bring to the discussion. They need to be involved in the development, management, and operation of services as well as the assessment of need. "Control is no longer found in unilateral ownership or decision making. Instead, control is a function of the character and kind of risk sharing that service partners agree to bear together and therefore is negotiated between partners" (Krueger Wilson, 1999). In Canada, public participation on many district authorities is beginning to move towards a partnership with the professionals that will see greater public involvement in health care planning and decision-making responsibilities.

An example of the shift from consultant to active participant in decision making can be seen in the evolution of Family Advisory Committees in children's hospitals. The primary mandate of these committees is to support and enhance the highest quality of family-centred care. An example of this mandate can be seen in the Winnipeg Children's Hospital position statement on family centred care (1999). Initially, these committees developed in the 1980s and early 1990s. Family input was explored through consultation, focus groups, and surveys. This information may or may not have been used in decision making with regard to hospital planning and policy. Over time with clarification of roles and the sharing of knowledge and expertise to make decisions, strong professional and family partnerships have evolved.

IMPLICATIONS AND ISSUES FOR NURSES

As health care professionals and consumers of health, nurses play a pivotal role in health care delivery. They are influential by their sheer volume as well as the professional role that they play. Public opinion polls continue to show that nurses are held in high regard. The public trusts nurses. Nurses are involved in all aspects of the health care continuum. Nurses are educated to act as patient advocates and to engage actively in health care education regardless of their practise sites. The consumer movement has placed greater demands on nurses to fulfill these roles.

Patient Advocacy

Advocacy is identified as a prominent role for nurses. Shellian, former President of the Alberta Nurses Association, describes advocacy as happening in the things nurses do to make a critical difference for people, "Advocacy in nursing is a quality we all recognize" (1997, p. 34). The Canadian Nurses Association *Code of Ethics* (2002) states, "Nurses put forward, and advocate, the interests of all persons in their care. This includes helping individuals and groups gain access to appropriate health care that is of their choosing" (p. 15).

This advocacy role involves giving information to patients, speaking out for patients, and helping patients speak out for themselves. Consumers need health information about particular conditions as well as information on how to navigate the health care system. They also need opportunities to discuss issues of concern. However, nurses may not feel comfortable or believe they have the knowledge and skills to address patient concerns. Additionally, many nurses do not believe they have the time to address the questions.

Informed consent exemplifies the role of the nurse as advocate. Nurses obtain consent for nursing care and give information about procedures. Although informed consent for surgery and many other procedures is generally viewed as the responsibility of the physician, the nurse is frequently in the position to ensure that the patient has been given all the necessary information to make appropriate decisions. The *Code of Ethics for Registered Nurses* (CNA, 2002) further states: "nurses respect and promote the autonomy of persons and help them to express their health needs and values, and to obtain appropriate information and services" (p. 11).

Informed consent is a complex issue, and careful assessment of the patient's level of understanding is required. Different professionals may be involved. Nurses may view the responsibility of obtaining informed consent as solely that of the physicians. Lack of knowledge about a specific treatment or perceived lack of time may inhibit the nurse's involvement. However, nurses can assist patients in making informed choices by assessing their level of understanding and helping them question the benefits and risks of the proposed treatment.

What happens when the nurse feels that the patient does not have the needed information to make an informed decision? This leads to ethical and moral dilemmas for nurses as they are torn between their role of patient advocate and their loyalty to their employer and to the other professionals with whom they work. The events leading to the *Report of the Manitoba Pediatric Cardiac Surgery Inquest* (Sinclair, 2001) exemplify this dilemma. Nurses questioned the information that had been given to parents as well as the skill of the physician performing the procedures. They were torn between their role of advocacy for their patients and their loyalty to other professionals. At some point in their careers, most nurses face situations in which they question the safety of practises they witness, and this dilemma arises.

Nurses have a right and a responsibility to provide information to their patients even if information is in conflict with physicians or other professionals. Ultimately, loyalty to other professionals must be limited by doing what is good for the patient (Hinam, 1999). In addition to information regarding procedures, consumers are now demanding information about the competencies of health team members. Consumer groups such as the Coalition for Improved Access to Physician Profiles are demanding information about a surgeon's experience (Winnipeg Free Press, January 2001). In some jurisdictions, this demand has been acknowledged, and access to information about a physician's professional experience and expertise is available.

Patient Education

Health education has always been a primary role for nurses. As consumers of health care become more informed, there is a greater demand for the education that nurses provide. As patient advocates, nurses have a responsibility to give their public the information needed to make intelligent decisions regarding their health care plan, including choices regarding treatment. Providing consumers relevant, current, and accurate information is an important role for nurses.

Consumers obtain their health information from many sources, family, friends, books, popular media, health information telephone centres, the world wide web, and health professionals (Table 20.1). The accuracy and quality of this information will vary. It is difficult for nurses to assess the reliability of the multiple sources of information

Table 20.1. Statistical Breakdown: Consumer Use of The Health Line

YEAR	TOTAL NO. OF CALLS RECEIVED	AVERAGE NO. OF CALLS PER MONTH
1992	10,584	882
1993	12,888	1,074
1994	27,876	2,323
1995	67,061	5,588
1996	90,707	7,559
1997	101,801	8,483
1998	102,551	8,546
1999	115,132	9,594

Source: http://www.thehealthline.com/consumer.htm.

and make recommendations. The challenge for nurses is to help patients to sort the available information so that they can make informed choices. It is important that consumers understand their role as primary providers of their own care, and health care professionals need to view themselves as partners providing professional expertise.

The many available choices influence consumers, and several strategies may be used to assist patients in obtaining health information. Nurses must use their assessment skills in deciding what information is needed, evaluating the patient's level of understanding, and identifying the supports needed to assist the patient in decision making. Information can be given to the patient, but ultimately it is up to the patient to use or not use this information. Nurses cannot be expected to be experts in all areas of health care, but fortunately, specialisation in nursing has created individuals with rich knowledge in their defined field. For nurses, the challenge remains to teach consumers how to access information and resources appropriate to their individual needs and values so that they feel confident in making health care decisions and managing their own care.

Complaints

As consumers learn more about their own health and the health care system, their expectations and demands increase. When the expectations and demands are not satisfied, complaints are inevitable—particularly when a system is faced with the financial, technologic, and human stressors that affect the current Canadian health care system. For the most part, institutions are rewarded more for fiscal responsibility than for improving the health of citizens. In Ontario, for example, an increase in complaints to the College of Nurses was reported (Beardwood et al., 1999). Originally, the primary source of complaints was employers, mainly hospitals; but the source has now shifted to the public. Beardwood and colleagues note that "ideological changes that have recognised the supremacy of individual rights and the importance of satisfying consumer expectations give much greater validity to patients' expectations" (1999, p. 365). This report exemplifies the increase in numbers of complaints made to most health professional regulatory bodies across the country.

The effects of workplace stresses have changed working environments for nurses, often making it difficult for them to meet their professional standards. When nurses do meet their professional standards, it may be at personal cost. Media accounts abound with stories of unsafe working conditions, delayed services, stress, and burnout for nurses. Nurses report workplace concerns to their employers and to their professional organisations. This has prompted some professional organisations to publish position papers and guidelines to deal with stress and workplace environments (Manitoba Association of Registered Nurses, 2000). Governments and regulatory and union bodies have undertaken numerous workplace studies. Changes in workplace environments will be slow given human and fiscal restraints, within the current economic climate.

Nursing regulatory boards exist to protect the public, not the nursing profession. Public participation on regulatory boards serves to expand the regulatory bodies' awareness of changing health needs of the public and their preferred ways of meeting these needs to ensure that the regulatory body is responsive and accountable to the public that it serves. With the increased participation of the public on nursing regulatory boards, the general public's awareness of the role of these regulatory bodies has grown, and these public representatives are aware of, and involved in, the complaint process. Criticisms of the complaints and discipline procedures of regulatory organisations have resulted in even greater public input into the discipline process.

Although complaints to regulatory bodies are increasing, they are still relatively few in comparison to the number of registered nurses. However, complaints regarding incompetent care may be underreported to regulatory bodies for a number of reasons. Although patient representatives in many institutions deal with complaints from the public, there remains a reluctance to register complaints with the regulatory bodies because this may necessitate a prolonged involvement in a complaint or disciplinary procedure or there may be fear of a wrongful dismissal.

Then, too, consumers may complain about deficient care to seek personal rectification or to advocate changes in the system. The complaint process is time consuming and dissatisfying to both the nurse and the complainant. "The process individualizes the problem and deflects attention from the problems of system change" (Beardwood et al., 1999, p. 370). It is likely that complaints and consumer involvement in the complaint process will continue to increase. The challenge is for nurse leaders within workplaces to examine systems to support nurses in their work environments. Those within regulatory bodies are also challenged to make the complaint and discipline process less cumbersome and dissatisfying to both nurses and the public.

SUMMARY

This chapter addresses the significance of the consumer movement on health care and particularly on the role of nurses. As consumers have influenced policy within the system and the accountability of governments and health care professionals, the consumer movement has led to many positive outcomes for individuals, groups, and the health care system.

Consumerism occurs at both the individual and the collective levels. Consumers have voiced their rights and expect that health professionals will honour those rights. These expectations have been influenced by the shift from illness care to health promotion, the women's movement, and the aging population.

Consumers, however, must become partners in the process and not just recipients of service if they are to help themselves. Control of health and the health care system is not found in unilateral ownership or decision making; rather, it can be found in a partnership between consumer and provider that will ultimately determine the direction for the health care system.

Nurses continue to play important roles as advocates and educators. Both roles are paramount in the informed consent process. It is not merely knowledge that is needed for consent but also a partnership in which the patients bring values and preferences into an autonomy-enhancing model of informed consent.

Increased public participation in all levels of the health care system will challenge the concept of partnership. As consumers become more involved, they will take a more active role in the management of changes to the health care system. Leaders must critically work through the changes that are required to embrace the consumer-provided partnership.

Online RESOURCES

Add to your knowledge of this issue:

American Agency for Health Care Policy and Evaluation — www.ahrq.gov/qual/kffhigh.htm

Centre of Excellence for Women's Health — www.cewh-cesf.ca/indexingeng.html

Consumers Association of Canada — www.consumer.ca

Consumer Support Groups — www.wwdmoz.org/Health/ Consumer Support Groups

Family Advisory Committee — www.sickkids.on.ca

Reflections on the Chapter

1. Identify ways for the public to have more meaningful participation in health boards.
2. What does it mean to be a board member?
3. Identify and discuss some barriers to public participation.
4. What influence has the consumer movement had on the concept of informed consent?
5. Do you think the discipline process is the same across all professions? Should it be? Support your position.

REFERENCES

Alberta Centre for Well-Being. (2002). [On-line]. Website retrieved from www.thehealthline.com, now Alberta Centre for Active Living, www.centre4activeliving.ca.

American Agency for Health Care Policy and Evaluation. (2001). [On-line]. Available: http://www.ahrq.gov/qual/kffhigh.htm.

Anderson, J. M. (1996). Empowering patients: issues and strategies. *Social Science & Medicine, 43,* 697–705.

Beardwood, B., Walters, V., Eyles, J., & French, S. (1999). Complaints against nurses: A reflection of 'the new managerialism' and consumerism in health care? *Social Science and Medicine, 48,* 363–374.

Blomqvist, A. (1979). *The health care business: International evidence on private versus public health care systems.* Vancouver, BC: The Fraser Institute.

Calnan, M., & Gabe, J. (2001). From comsumerism to partnership? Britain's national health service at the turn of the century. *International Journal of Health Services, 31*(1), 119–131.

Canadian Nurses Association (2002). *Code of Ethics for Registered Nurses.* Ottawa: Author.

Centre of Excellence for Women's Health. (2001). [On-line]. Available: http://www.cewh-cesf.ca/indexingeng.html.

Charles, C., & DeMaio, S. (1993). Lay participation in health care decision making: A conceptual framework. *Journal of Health, Politics and the Law, 18*(4), 881–904.

Consumers Association of Canada. (2001). About us. [On-line]. Available: www.consumer.ca/aboutus/aboutus/cfm.

Crichton, A. (1997). Community participation in health service policy making in Canada. *Bibliotheca Medica Canadiana, 19*(2), 66–69.

Foot, D. K., & Stoffman D. (2000). *Boom, bust and echo profiting from the demographic shift in the 21ˢᵗ century.* Toronto: Stoddart.

Gallant, S. J., Puryear, K., & Royal-Schaler, R. (1997). *Health care for women: Psychological, social and behavioural influences.* Washington, DC: American Psychological Association.

Griffiths, H. (1993). Supporting the advocacy role. *Nursing BC, Nov.–Dec.,* 25–26.

Kerr, J., & MacPhail, J. (1991). *Canadian nursing: issues and perspectives* (3rd ed.). St. Louis: Mosby–Year Book.

Higgins, J. (1999). Closer to home: The case for experiential participation in health reform. *Canadian Journal of Public Health, 90*(1), 30–33.

Hiller, E., Landenburger, G., & Natowicz, M. (1997). Public participation in medical policy-making and the status of consumer autonomy: The example of newborn screening programs in the United States. *American Journal of Public Health, 87*(8), 1280–1287.

Hinam, I. (1999). Winnipeg's pediatric cardiac inquest: The ethical issues. *Canadian Operating Room Nursing Journal, December,* 13–16.

Krueger Wilson C., & Porter-O'Grady, T. (1999). *Leading the Revolution in Health Care Advancing Sys-*

tems, *Igniting Performance* (2nd Ed). Gaithersburg, Maryland: Asper Publications.

Care, *Advancing Systems, Igniting Performance* (2ⁿᵈed). Gaitherburg, MD: Aspen Publications.

Leigh, S. (1994). Cancer survivorship: A consumer movement. *Seminars in Oncology, 21*(6), 783–786.

Maharaj, R. (1999). The role of women's advocacy groups in shaping Canadian health care policy. *Women's Health Issues, 9*(5), 259–263.

Maloney, T., & Paul, B. (1991). The consumer movement takes hold in medical care. *Health Affairs, 10*(4), 268–279.

Manitoba Association of Registered Nurses (2000). *Supportive practice environments: A discussion paper.* Winnipeg: Author.

Milburn, L., & Griffith, H. (1991). Economic issues in health care in nursing. In J. Creasea & B. Parker (Eds.), *Conceptual foundations of professional nursing practice* (pp. 107–128). St. Louis: Mosby–Year Book.

Minkler, M. (1994). Worksite health, practitioners' forum. *American Journal of Health Promotion, 8*(6), 403–412.

National Forum on Health (1997). *Canada health action: Building on the legacy.* Ottawa: Author.

O'Connor, A. M. (1997). Consumer/patient decision support in the new millennium: Where should our research take us? *Canadian Journal of Nursing research, 29*(3), 7–12.

Redden, C. (1999). Rationing care in the community: Engaging citizens in health care decision making. *Journal of Health, Politics, Policy and Law, 24*(6), 1363–1687.

Shellian, B. (1997). Registered nurses and advocacy: Helping others speak up. *Alberta RN, 53*(3), 33–34.

Sinclair, M. (2001). *The report of the Manitoba Pediatric Cardiac Surgery Inquest.* Provincial Court of Manitoba. Winnipeg: Government of Manitoba.

Singer, M. A. (1995). Community participation in health care decision making: Is it feasible? *Canadian Medical Association Journal, 153*(4), 421–423.

Storch, J. (1982). *Patients' rights, ethical and legal issues in health care and nursing.* Toronto: McGraw-Hill, Ryerson.

Switankowsky, I. (1998). *A new paradigm for informed consent.* Lanham, MD: University Press of America.

Winnipeg Children's Hospital (2001). Mission Statement. Available: http://www.hsc.mb.ca/childrens/information.htm

21

Violence and Abuse: Ending the Silence

Elizabeth Thomlinson

Chapter Objectives

At the completion of this chapter, you will be able to:

1. Identify many forms of violence and abuse.
2. Analyse political, legal, and ethical factors related to violence and abuse.
3. Relate the effect of violence and abuse to the health of individuals.
4. Evaluate the impact of violence and abuse on the health care system.
5. Examine factors that contribute to the continued silencing of victims of violence and abuse.
6. Differentiate facilitators and barriers to resolution of various issues and generate strategies to address violence and abuse.

Poem reproduced with permission of Mabel Cook, a member of Mosakahiken Cree Nation, who has spent many years working to prevent abuse and violence within aboriginal communities. Her primary focus has been the youth of the communities. She has been a magistrate and currently is a community mediator in northern Manitoba.

Waiting to Be Seen and Heard

 There are so many of us that cry out in agony
To no-one in particular because nobody cares to hear
People pass us by and never look beyond our exterior
Our bodies grow simply because it's the cycle of life.

When you look at us with contempt and mistrust
We feel that all you see is potential problems
Of young people not knowing how to be responsible
For you think we solve life's problems with violence.

Has it ever occurred to you to ask me how I feel?
We cry in vain in hopes that you will actually see
See the chaotic mess we strive to untangle
Trying to understand why you chose to hurt us.

Why don't you look deep within our very being
To find small defenseless children cowering in fear
Our growth was stunted because of a violent episode
One we did not ask for but received anyway.

You talk about us so negatively because we react in anger
Anger because we cannot tell anyone of our secret
Anyone who can take us on a journey of healing
Anyone who wishes to make us understand this cruelty.

You shattered what faith we had in humanity
For now we have built a wall around us where we cower
Cowering in fear wondering when you will come for us
To shatter our already battered and imprisoned spirit.

You have done much work on compiling information about us
Information that makes for good reading but does very little
We need you to take it to people who want to fight for us
Even the government sends men to war to kill others
    for freedom.

What about us? We are being killed Spiritually, Emotionally
Physically, Mentally, Sexually, and it is a slow death
We feel every fiber of our soul quivering in pain wanting
    freedom
Wondering who will see and hear to finally end this abuse.

— *Mabel V. Cook*

Since the late 1970s, there has been a growing recognition that violence and abuse in their many forms have a significant impact on the health of individuals specifically and on the Canadian health care system in general. According to the Canadian Nurses Association (CNA), "violence is now recognized as a social act involving a serious abuse of power" (CNA, 1996, p. 1).

Violence consists of exerting power over another person to control, disempower, or injure the other. As a social act, violence crosses legal, ethical, and health care boundaries with serious moral, sociocultural, political, and personal ramifications for society (Hoff, 1994). Violence is perpetrated against people of all ages, in every socioeconomic sector of society, and in all societies around the globe. Young people, elderly people, and people with disabilities are among the most vulnerable. The long-term negative effects of violence have enormous implications for the victims as well as for all facets of society.

Discussion of violence is an everyday occurrence in the media. Although Canadian culture officially condemns violence, it is often glorified in film, television, books, and music. The long-held myth that the family is a safe haven for all of its members has been dispelled through frequent accounts highlighting the magnitude of the violence and abuse within that setting. In the workplace, there are ever-increasing numbers of stories of violent occurrences leading to injury and even death.

It is not possible in one chapter to present an in-depth coverage of this complex topic. Rather, this chapter highlights some of the multiple forms of violence, the association with the health of individuals, and the role nurses and the nursing profession can and should take to address issues of violence and abuse. There is a vast array of multidisciplinary sources of information, including print based, film, and audio, on the topic of violence. The chapter is meant to stimulate a rudimentary recognition of the topic, and readers are encouraged to expand their knowledge and understanding through the numerous other sources that are available. To begin, definitions of the multiple forms of violence and abuse are presented in Box 21.1.

THE MANY FORMS OF VIOLENCE

Most people agree that *violence* is an act of physical force aimed at hurting, harming, or injuring another person, group, or object. The word *violence* is derived from the Latin infinitive *violare*, to violate, rape, or injure. Violation of another person not only may result in visible physical harm but also may result in emotional trauma that is as equally harmful as physical battering. Within this chapter, the terms *violence* and *abuse* are used interchangeably, although abuse may not entail physical trauma. The CNA focusses the discussion of violence on two major points:

- *Interpersonal violence* includes violence that occurs within relationships as well as that experienced from strangers and acquaintances. All types of violence are encompassed by the term, including violence against children, women, and elders; abuse of spouses or partners; violence within the context of dating; violence witnessed by children; and abuse and neglect of frail and vulnerable persons. Abuse may also be perpetrated by professionals.
- *Violence in relationships* of kinship, intimacy, dependency, or trust can take the form of physical assault, emotional abuse, intimidation, sexual assault, neglect, deprivation, and financial exploitation. Although these forms of violence occur most often in families or within intimate relationships, they can also occur within the health care system (CNA, 1996, p. 1).

BOX 21.1

Forms of Violence and Abuse

PHYSICAL

Slapping, kicking, hitting with a fist, beating, choking, shoving

Using a weapon against another

Forcibly restraining, confining, or kidnapping another

SEXUAL

Forcing another to perform sexual acts, e.g., fellatio

Forcing another to have sexual intercourse

PSYCHOLOGICAL

Name calling, humiliating another, verbally degrading another

Harming property or pets

Creating an atmosphere of fear and terror

Using threats and coercion

Witnessing assault or abuse of another (parent, grandparent, sibling, friend, etc.)

Infantilization

FINANCIAL

Taking or withholding money

Extorting funds or property

Taking control of all expenditures

Forcing another to stop working and become dependent

Selling the home or possessions of elderly people without their consent

SOCIAL

Imposing (forced) isolation from friends and other family

Monitoring all phone calls and connection with others

PHYSICAL NEGLECT

Failing to provide food, clothing, shelter, or medical care

Failing to supervise children or elders appropriately

The multiple definitions of violence and abuse influence how we view violence and where we place emphases. Terms such as *family violence, domestic abuse, interpersonal violence*, and *violence in relationships* tend to downplay the gender relationships in violence and phrase the behaviour in gender-neutral language. Although some authorities suggest that women are equally violent in their actions, the reality remains that most perpetrators of violence in families are heterosexual males, and the victims of the most violent crimes are women and children (Canadian Public Health Association, 1994; Bunge & Locke, 2000; Hoff, 1994). Terms such as family violence locate abuse within the family, diluting society's influence and effects. Nurses must be aware of how the terminology that is used affects the perceptions of professionals and society at large. The use of language that downplays gender relationships and societal influences is one of many issues that arise within the topic of violence and abuse.

HISTORICAL PERSPECTIVES ON VIOLENCE AND ABUSE

The abuse of children and of female partners has deep historical roots. Even today, abuse is condoned within many societies in the world. Throughout history, children have been sacrificed to appease the gods, killed if they suffer handicapping conditions, and beaten and tortured to rid them of demons or to educate them (Humphreys & Ramsey, 1993). It was only in 1962 that Dr. Henry Kempe coined the term "battered child syndrome" (Helfer & Kempe, 1968), which was the impetus for educational campaigns and increased efforts within the American states and Canadian provinces to protect children from violence and abuse.

Humphreys and Ramsey (1993) noted that it was the interaction of several factors that focussed societal attention and helped raise public concern regarding child abuse. They suggested that the public was affected by the violence in Southeast Asia, namely the Vietnamese conflict, and the rising homicide rates in United States society. Other factors that heightened public awareness of violence were the women's movement and the interest demonstrated by social scientists studying the phenomenon. The combination of these variables led to multiple studies on violence and abuse, with resultant books and articles on the topic. Social agencies were formed, the Society for the Prevention of Child Abuse and Neglect was developed, and laws mandating the prevention of the abuse and neglect of children were updated. In Canada, child welfare falls within the mandate of individual provinces. Applicable legislation can be obtained from each provincial government's web site.

Equally, the abuse of female partners has deep historical roots, with the Bible providing "the earliest prescription for physical punishment of wives" (Campbell & Fishwick, 1993, p. 73). According to these authors, documentation of wife beating can be found throughout European literature—women accused of adultery could be killed with impunity, and instructions for "correcting" wives by beating were available.

In other countries throughout the world, husbands may be punished only if their abusive behaviour is "excessive" (Duffy & Momirov, 2000). Despite the efforts of the Indian government to suppress "dowry deaths," women continue to be murdered or harassed to commit suicide when the husband and his family are not satisfied with the money and valuables brought to the marriage. Media reports of the flogging of a Nigerian girl who had a child out of wedlock caused outrage around the world; however, the beating proceeded shortly after her infant's birth (Imam, 2001). Similarly, the violence by stoning and beating committed against women in Afghanistan for infractions, such as having an ankle exposed, highlight violence against women that is ongoing worldwide.

The prevalence of elder abuse only began to be recognised in the 1970s with initial efforts to "identify the kind and extent of abuse and neglect of seniors" (MacLean & Williams, 1995, p. xi). The Manitoba Association on Gerontology was the first provincial association to begin addressing this subject by developing guidelines to identify elder abuse and protocols for practise (Interdepartmental Working Group on Elder Abuse and Manitoba Seniors Directorate, 1993). In Canada, a nurse, Elizabeth Podnieks, is a leader in the study of elder abuse (Podnieks, 1985; Podnieks et al., 1990; Podnieks & Baillie, 1995). The national prevalence study that she undertook emphasised the scope of elder abuse in Canada and laid the groundwork for further research and intervention efforts.

There has been a tendency to treat violence from a generic perspective (Duffy & Momirov, 2000) without addressing the effects of class, race, sexual orientation, and ethnicity on the extent and impact of violence for aboriginal women, immigrant and refugee women, black women, people with disabilities, gay men, and lesbian women. The historical and cultural context adds a complex dimension to the analysis of violence and abuse.

STATISTICS IN THE CANADIAN CONTEXT

There is general acknowledgment that multiple factors are at play in the underreporting of violence and abuse. A personal need to keep any incidents of violence secret, shame on the part of the victim and the perpetrator, dependency of the victim on the perpetrator, ignorance of resources, fear of repercussions, and an inability to seek help because of forced restraint all contribute to a code of silence. For women living in rural and remote regions of the country, distance and a lack of resources hinder attempts to escape an abusive relationship. This helps keep the true number of incidents of violence concealed. These factors compound the difficulties for young people, elderly people, people with disabilities, and immigrants and other women who do not know where to seek help and do not have the physical means to do so.

A leading study that attempted to ascertain the violence women experienced, especially by their intimate partners, was the 1993 Canadian Violence Against Women Survey (CVAWS) (Bunge & Locke, 2000; Duffy & Momirov, 2000). Findings from this study indicated that 29% of women had experienced at least one episode of violence and that two thirds of these women reported that it had happened more than once. A second major survey undertaken to examine violence and abuse was the 1999 General Social Survey on Victimization (GSS) (Bunge & Locke, 2000). About 26,000 people were selected through random-digit dialing and interviewed from February to December 1999. The findings from this survey, from the Uniform Crime Reporting Survey (UCR2), and from the Homicide Survey form the basis for the report, "Family Violence in Canada: A Statistical Profile 2000" (Bunge & Locke, 2000). The UCR2 collected information of criminal offences reported to police. Victims only report these offences after a lengthy process that includes multiple decisions concerning the implications of reporting. Equally lengthy and complex are the decisions the criminal justice system then makes about whether to lay charges. This is a complicated process, and many cases are never reported.

Methodologic variations between surveys on violence and abuse result in differences in the data that have been compiled. Caution must be taken when comparing the results between studies because of these differences. There are often differences in time frames, definitions, and terminology between studies that may result in findings that require careful examination before any similarities and differences can be discussed.

Violence Against Women

Criticisms regarding the use of the terms *spousal abuse, conjugal violence, partner violence*, and *domestic abuse* centre on the implication that the abuse that women direct against male partners is equal, in nature and degree, to that committed by men against female partners (Campbell & Fishwick, 1993). There remains a consensus in the statistics on violence and abuse that women continue to suffer the most severe, repetitive, protracted forms of abuse, often resulting in injury and requiring medical attention (Bunge & Locke, 2000; Dobash & Dobash, 1979). There is also concurrence in the research that female to male violence results from acts of self-defense (DeKerseredy & Kelly, 1993). This is consistent with the fact that men reported far greater incidents of hitting, kicking, biting, and having objects thrown at them than did women (Bunge & Locke, 2000). The concerns regarding the impact of terminology in focussing attention away from the reality of who constitutes the majority of abusers must be kept at the forefront while reading the following statistics.

Findings of the 1999 GSS suggest that within the previous 5 years, 7% of people who were married or in common-law relationships experienced some form of violence from their intimate partner, with the rates for women and men being similar (Bunge & Locke, 2000). However, the report "Family Violence in Canada: A Statistical Profile 2000" emphasises that the most severe and consistent forms of violence were reported by women. Women were three times as likely as men to report having been beaten (13% versus 4%). Women were also far more likely than men to be choked and sexually assaulted or to be threatened with a weapon. Men reported a higher incidence of being slapped, having something thrown at them, or being kicked, hit, and bit. During the same 5-year period, the police were involved in 37% of cases with female victims and 15% of cases with male victims.

There was a slightly greater proportion of women younger than 34 years of age who reported being abused, as did more women in common-law relationships than those who were married (Bunge & Locke, 2000). Periodic bouts of heavy drinking, more than the frequency of the abuser's drinking, were related to episodes of violent behaviour. A question that could be asked is whether the abuser became equally violent with people outside the home or confined the violent actions to those within the home.

Although this section focusses on violence and abuse within families, it must be noted that 23% of women are sexually assaulted by strangers (Matas, 2001). In 1997, there were 89 reported sexual assaults per 100,000 people in the population (Statistics Canada, 1997). The province of Saskatchewan reported the highest number of assaults, whereas Quebec reported the fewest. From the findings of anonymous surveys, it has been estimated that as many as 90% of sexual assaults, however, are never reported.

Comparisons with national studies in the United States and Britain produced findings that were similar to the Canadian statistics (Bunge & Locke, 2000, p. 26). Women reported being beaten or choked more often than men and were more likely to suffer injury when they were abused. Tham and colleagues (1995) noted that 40% of people presenting to psychiatric services reported a history of some abuse, whereas 24% reported being victims of domestic violence, the ratio of women to men in this group being 2.75:1.

Violence in Gay and Lesbian Relationships

Until recent decades, there have been relatively few studies of violence in gay and lesbian relationships. Ristock (2001) conducted a multisite qualitative study of violence experienced in lesbian relationships. Service providers (counselors, shelter workers, and social workers) who participated in focus groups noted that basing their efforts on heterosexual dynamics limited their practise. Ristock highlighted that some concerns were raised—chief among them that drawing attention to violence in lesbian relationships will detract from feminist efforts to raise awareness that violence perpetrated by men continues to be a significant social issue.

Although the focus on gender-based violence is challenged by the reporting of same-sex violence, these reports emphasise the need for the further examination of power and control as key factors in violence and abuse. Key questions that may be asked are, Where is power held within a society? and What is the relationship between gender and power? Of importance in this discussion is the relationship to the social context in which this violence occurs. Victims of same-sex violence may fear being stigmatised as gay or lesbian and may expect their complaints will be trivialised (Duffy & Momirov, 2000). In a society that remains largely homophobic, the dynamics of violence within same-sex relationships are even more complex than those of opposite-sex relationships. This complexity will continue to contribute to the silencing of the issues in violent and abusive same-sex relationships.

Abuse and Neglect of Older Canadians

One of the leading studies on the abuse and neglect of older Canadians found that 4% of respondents reported financial, material, and verbal abuse by family members and other people (Podnieks et al., 1990). Ten years later, 7% of older adults in the GSS reported experiencing emotional abuse in the form of name calling, being put down, being isolated from friends and family, or financial abuse by a spouse, caregiver, or child (Bunge & Locke, 2000). One must keep in mind that older people may be reluctant or afraid to report abuse by family members for various reasons, among them dependency, feelings of shame, or fear of retaliation.

Little research has been undertaken on violence and abuse of elderly people living in institutions. Anecdotal and case study reports have been the source of information on abuse within residential care settings. Overt acts of physical abuse included extensive use of restraints, hitting, pinching, and shoving (Wiehe, 1998). Limiting freedom and choice, providing inadequate nutrition, and isolating people were among the more covert acts of abuse. In these cases, it was people who had responsibility for the care of the residents who often were the abusers—the people who were in power.

In police-reported statistics of elder abuse, most offenders are strangers and people outside the family. According to statistics from the Incident-based Uniform Crime Reporting Survey, older Canadians were 67% more likely to be abused by strangers than by family members (Bunge & Locke, 2000). Although the numbers are relatively small, people who deliberately target elderly people in home invasions and fraud are prominently figured in the media.

Violence Against Children and Youth

Child maltreatment is an all-encompassing term that includes physical, sexual, and emotional abuse and neglect of children. Although child maltreatment is recognised as a significant problem in Canada, there is no data set that consolidates all of the provincial statistics to present a comprehensive national picture. Data on cases of child maltreatment are based on child welfare caseloads, police files on assault and homicide, and hospitalisations for violence-related injuries (Bunge & Locke, 2000). Child welfare is a provincial responsibility, and although each province has legislation defining child abuse and neglect, a lack of common definitions across jurisdictions precludes the formation of a single national data set.

Although there are mandatory reporting laws for child abuse, it is accepted that official accounts of child maltreatment underestimate the prevalence because of the failure to report by perpetrators and victims, by community members who observe abuse, and by professionals who fail to recognise the maltreatment (MacMillan et al., 1997). According to the findings from the *Ontario Health Supplement* that focussed on child physical and sexual abuse, males reported being physically abused more often than did females, whereas females reported more cases of sexual abuse. Girls also reported experiencing higher rates of physical and sexual abuse conjointly. A previous retrospective study of child sexual abuse in Canada (Badgley et al., 1984) provided similar statistics for child sexual abuse: 6% for males and 13% for females. It is thought that despite the existence of mandatory child abuse reporting laws, as many as 90% of cases are not reported to child welfare authorities (MacMillan et al., 1997). At issue is why, with mandatory reporting laws for child abuse and neglect, underreporting persists. A question for professionals and for society is why and how this silence regarding a significant social and health problem continues.

Children and youth represented 60% of sexual assaults reported in Canada in 1999 and 20% of physical assaults (Bunge & Locke, 2000). Acquaintances were the primary abusers (52%), with the remaining perpetrators being family members (24%) and strangers (19%). Girls were victimised more often than boys in 80% of sexual assault cases and 53% of physical assault cases.

Violence in First Nations Communities

The Aboriginal Justice Inquiry in Manitoba noted that "violence and abuse in aboriginal communities has reached epidemic proportions" (Hamilton & Sinclair, 1991, p. 481). Among the health concerns of aboriginal community members were family violence and physical and sexual abuse, which they believed were prevalent in their communities (Smylie, 2001).

In one survey of community members, 63% of respondents reported they had experienced violence and abuse, whereas 76% were aware that family members had been abused (Thomlinson et al., 2000). However, only 37% disclosed their violence to people in authority. Fear of repercussions and a lack of trust that reporting would introduce a change contributed to this lack of reporting. According to the Report of the Royal Commission on Aboriginal Peoples, although it is impossible to ascertain the full extent of violence in aboriginal communities, the topic is distinctive from other communities in that "it [violence] has invaded whole communities and cannot be considered a problem of a particular couple or an individual household" (1996, p. 56). The interrelationship of poverty and social and economic marginalisation of many aboriginal communities is believed to contribute to an increase in violence and abuse (Hamby, 2000). Without efforts that will substantially change conditions in the community, attempts to address violence will continue to experience only minor success.

Dating Violence

As they do in other forms of violence, women suffer more severe, pervasive, and systematic victimisation in dating relationships (Canadian Public Health Association, 1994) than do men. According to a survey of college and university students, 45% of women reported being sexually assaulted while in a dating relationship, 79% had been psychologically abused, and 35% had been physically abused (DeKerseredy & Kelly, 1993). DeKerseredy & Kelly caution that although this survey pointed to high percentages of dating violence, these statistics should be regarded as underestimates for similar reasons to other forms of violence and abuse.

Violence in the Workplace

Studies on the violence nurses face in the workplace suggest that up to 70% of nurses have been abused or threatened on the job, including being hit, kicked, verbally abused, and sexually harassed (Canadian Public Health Association, 1994). According to Mireille Kingma, nurse consultant with the International Council of Nurses (ICN), "72% of nurses do not feel safe from assault in their workplace," while "97% of nurse respondents in a British survey knew a nurse who had been physically assaulted in the past year and up to 95% reported having been bullied at work" (ICN, 1999b). This topic has been extensively covered in Chapter 6 and is only mentioned here to remind readers that workplace violence and abuse represent an equally significant concern with their own specific issues.

One of the issues that is relevant to the safety of nurses and which ultimately affects the recruitment and retention of nurses in the workplace is the continued lack of reporting and tolerance of abuse against nurses. Of the 5,000 nurses who responded to a survey by the Manitoba Association of Registered Nurses (1989), between one fourth and one third noted that they chose to ignore abusive behaviour directed towards them in the workplace. Factors affecting the decision to ignore the abuse are relevant to the analysis of this issue.

TRYING TO UNDERSTAND: THEORETICAL PERSPECTIVES

Since the 1970s, a number of theoretical approaches have been proposed in the attempt to understand factors related to the violence and abuse of people, mainly women and children (Campbell & Fishwick, 1993; Duffy & Momirov, 2000; Gelles, 1980). Gelles classified three different types of models: the psychiatric or intraindividual model, the social-psychological model, and the sociologic model. The focus of assessments and interventions varies depending on the type of model to which one subscribes: individuals, individuals in context, or society at large. Beliefs and myths regarding violence and abuse that arise from the underlying theoretical framework will affect how one chooses to interact with individuals who are experiencing abusive situations.

From Inside the Individual

Intraindividual explanations focus on abusive men as psychopaths and the women victims as masochists. Innes and associates (1991) noted that studies focussing on the mental health of men and women in abusive relationships demonstrated a bias against women by blaming the victims. Campbell and Fishwick (1993) contend that vestiges of the masochism myth remain today when authors suggest that a woman provoked a man to batter her. As early as 1979, Walker (1979) stated that by blaming the victim, men are ultimately excused of their abusive behaviours. Innes and associates (1991) further noted that men rarely demonstrate the same violent actions outside the home but confine their abuse to where they will avoid castigation.

Environment and Interaction

The *social-psychological* model focusses on the interaction of the environment and the individual and the family. In child abuse cases, Helfer and Kempe hypothesised that an interaction occurs between the child, the caretaker, and the circumstance that predisposes toward violence (Helfer, 1973). Social learning theory (Bandura, 1969) is the basis for the suggestion that growing up in violent homes predisposes children towards violent behaviour (Duffy & Momirov, 2000). This model has been used to explain the intergenerational transmission of violence wherein each generation of a family continues the violent and abusive behaviours that were perpetrated against them or that they observed against others in the family.

Tolerance of Violence

Sociologic models contend that violence and abuse occur in environments that tolerate, and even foster, violent actions. Garbarino's ecologic model of child abuse stresses the effect of the continued support of force in the care of children and multiple factors that affect the family (Garbarino, 1977; Garbarino, 1995; Garbarino & Kostelny, 1992; Garbarino & Sherman, 1980). A key component of this model is the incorporation of societal beliefs and values along with other factors that affect the family, such as housing, poverty, social supports, and reactions of others in the family and community.

Feminist Perspective

Feminist analysis emphasises the role of patriarchal culture in legitimising male violence against both women and children (Duffy & Momirov, 2000). The power and control that men in society hold in the corporate world, in government, in religious institutions, and in society as a whole facilitate male use of power and control in the home (Wiehe, 1998). Violence and abuse ensure continued control over women and children. Feminist analysis has contributed to the exploration of violence through examination of how race, culture, disability, social class, age, and sexual orientation affect experiences women of all ages have in society. Duffy and Momirov (2000) suggest that inclusion of violence in lesbian relationships in this dialogue has forced feminists to focus more attention on the issues of power and control rather than remaining concentrated on gender-based relationships.

Larger societal variables, including historical and cultural perspectives, are relevant to the analysis of violence within First Nations communities, among immigrant women, and among those living with disabilities. Prejudice, economic marginalisation, and social powerlessness are key factors in the lives of both the abused and the abusers.

IMPACT ON HEALTH AND THE HEALTH CARE SYSTEM

Violence and abuse present formidable costs to society and to the health of individuals and families. These costs translate into expenditures to the Canadian health care system when victims seek medical care. Estimates have been made that more than 100,000 inpatient hospital days can be attributed to violence (Canadian Public Health Association, 1994). With hospital bed costs ranging from $400 to $800 a day in current dollars, this would result in expenditures between $40 and $80 million annually in this country as a result of violence. There are no estimates of how many emergency room visits are related to violence, but at an estimated $150 per visit (hospital and physician costs), these visits would be a substantial drain on health care budgets. It is also not possible to estimate the amount of money spent on prescription drug use by battered women and other victims of violence and abuse.

Various sources estimate that abused women suffer losses of up to $7 million annually in wages and productivity (Duffy & Momirov, 2000). Financial costs to police, child welfare and victim counseling services, the court system, social services, shelters, and foster home care, as well as costs incurred for imprisoning offenders, for second-stage housing, and the incalculable costs in human suffering, contribute to the impact of violence and abuse on individuals and society.

Depression, feelings of powerlessness, alcoholism and drug use, ongoing difficulties to trust and develop relationships, and suicidal ideation and death are the individual costs to the victims of abuse and to children who witness violence and abuse (Sleutel, 1998; Wiehe, 1998). Battered women are at substantial risk for posttraumatic stress disorder (PTSD) (Wiehe, 1998), with rates ranging between 40% and 50% of serious depression and PTSD in samples of women who have been battered (Campbell, 1999).

The Canadian Public Health Association (1994) cites a significant relationship between attempted suicide and the experience of abuse and violence. One third of the respondents in one survey noted that they had attempted suicide as a result of their abuse (Thomlinson et al., 2000). Equally disturbing were the numbers of respondents in that study who continued to think about committing suicide.

One of the more frightening aspects of violence and abuse is the number of women who are murdered by intimate partners. One study of homicide revealed that 58% of female victims had been either married to or sexually intimate with their murderers (Dobash & Dobash, 1979). Other studies found that up to 71% of homicide victims were previously abused by their killers (Campbell & Fishwick, 1993; Wiehe, 1998). Battered women are extremely aware that the most dangerous time for them is when they decide to leave an abusive relationship (Langford, 1996). Over a 20-year period from 1979 to 1998, three times as many wives as husbands were killed by their spouses (Bunge & Locke, 2000). For every 1 million couples, 10 wives and 3 husbands were murdered by their partners.

Physical and sexual abuse of children leads to severe, long-term emotional and academic problems. Abused children have difficulty concentrating, have little anger control, may suffer from eating disorders, and are at high risk for dropping out of school (Wiehe, 1998). Koniak-Griffin and Lesser (1996) found that child maltreatment was a significant predictor of self-injurious behaviour and attempted suicide. In Canada in 1997 to 1998, childhood admissions for acknowledged cases of assault and other maltreatment such as battering, rape, fighting, strangulation, firearms, and stabbings were 2,359 per 100,000 population (Bunge & Locke, 2000). A total of 38 in every 100,000 children under the age of 1 year were admitted to a hospital as a result of child abuse. Considering that many more cases of abuse are never reported or go unrecognised, these are significant numbers. The costs to the health care system and in lost human potential and suffering because of the maltreatment of children and youth is incalculable.

There is a growing awareness that even if they themselves are not abused, children who live in a home where mothers are battered and where violence between parents occurs experience PTSD (Humphreys, 1993). Behavioural responses of these children include truancy, disturbed sleep patterns, decreased school performance, lack of positive peer relations, increased worry for their mothers, and fear. Children who are exposed to violence and abuse learn that violence is the way to settle problems and achieve their own ends (Beauchesne et al., 1997). Pynoos and Nader (1990) examined four main types of symptoms experienced by children who have observed violent and abusive incidents: PTSD, grief reactions, separation anxiety symptoms, and exacerbation or renewal of previous symptoms. They found that exposure to violence may have long-term detrimental effects on a child's cognitive development.

ISSUES FOR NURSES AND THE NURSING PROFESSION

Nursing associations at all levels, provincially, nationally, and internationally, advocate that nurses take an active role in addressing problems of violence by increasing their knowledge of issues associated with violence and abuse (American Nurses Association, 1994; CNA, 1996; Alberta Association of Registered Nurses et al., 1999). The associations advocate zero tolerance for interpersonal violence and violence in the workplace. What issues, then, should nurses be informed of and what information should they incorporate into their nursing practise?

Language

The use of gender-neutral language in discussing all types of interpersonal violence has diluted the issue so that there is a perception that violence and abuse are committed equally by men and women in society. A careful examination of the statistics on the types and circumstances surrounding any violence and abuse provides a more comprehensive picture of what actually is occurring. Nurses, as professionals and as members of society, have a role to play in recognising that the use of a particular language can obscure and slant perceptions of what really is happening in violent and abusive relationships.

Lack of Understanding

A second issue arises from a lack of understanding about the pervasiveness of violent behaviours. Multiple myths about violence and abuse affect how health care professionals respond to, and treat, people involved in violent situations. One myth that continues to pervade society is that it is mainly people living in poverty who act violently towards others. Health care providers, then, do not consider that professionals and people from upper socioeconomic brackets could be victims or perpetrators of violence within their families. The effect of holding this perception is that poor people may be stereotyped as violent and the effects minimised as being part of the culture, whereas others receive little intervention because "it [violence] cannot possibly be happening in that home."

Other Issues

Other issues that require analysis include the following:

- The persistent underreporting of child abuse cases
- The question of whether there should be compulsory reporting of violence between adult partners who are treated within the health care system
- The need for a reporting mechanism for cases of abuse of elders who live outside of institutions in their own homes or the homes of family members
- The continuing belief that intervention in violence and abuse is not a health care issue but a social service issue
- The ongoing lack of reporting of violence against nurses in the workplace

BARRIERS TO RESOLUTION

The pervasiveness of abuse and violence through all ages, classes, cultures, races, across genders, and across political boundaries nationally and internationally underlies and hampers efforts to address the issues surrounding the topic. This pervasiveness means that victims of violence, as well as the perpetrators, are in all sectors of society, including the health care professions. The strong need to deny abuse, to keep silent, pervades society. This social and political reality counters efforts for change. The silence that has permitted and even encouraged violence and abuse is complex, not easily understood, and universal.

A key factor that reinforces the silencing of abuse is a societal belief in the sanctity of the family: what occurs within the walls of the home is private. A belief that parents and spouses are permitted to control what goes on in the family and to discipline family members is another component. Gender-based power that underlies society, as was noted previously in the chapter, affects relationships at all levels. The perpetrators of abuse may be in positions of power in government, justice, and throughout the rest of society. Secrecy permits them to continue to abuse. Power in relationships such as nurse–patient interactions contributes to the opportunity for abuse to occur. There is sometimes little recognition given to the type and amount of power that health professionals hold over their patients.

Another element may be the helplessness that professionals feel regarding their inability to understand and to intervene in abuse between adults. It is easier not to ask questions about violence than to ask questions that might reveal an abusive relationship and not know how to interact and intervene. Professionals may subvert their assessment by the manner in which they ask questions regarding violence. Those who choose to speak out may be silenced by co-workers and others who wish to have the abuse and violence remain secret. The complex interactions that yield this ongoing silencing suggest there may be no easy solutions.

STRATEGIES FOR RESOLUTION

No one profession can successfully work toward ending the silence about abuse and violence in isolation from others. Developing partnerships with victims of violence will require a concerted effort by professionals to gain the confidence and trust that victims must achieve before alliances can be established. Although this is a time-consuming process, effective intervention programmes can develop out of these alliances. To aid in developing understanding interdisciplinary courses in the education setting is a beginning.

Interdisciplinary Education and Intervention

A key issue *more than a decade* after the federal government convened interdisciplinary consultations across the country to address violence and abuse is the persistent lack of interdisciplinary education programmes and intervention protocols for health and social service professionals. This issue is particularly relevant to nurses because they are in key positions to advocate for patients, to educate others, to promote healthy relationships, to identify abuse and violence, and to intervene. To act, nurses must be knowledgeable about the topic, they must comprehend the education that the professionals with whom they work have, and they must understand the roles that each has in addressing violence and abuse.

A curriculum guide for nurses was developed by Hoff and Ross (1993) and then followed by an interdisciplinary curriculum guide for health care professionals (Hoff, 1994). Although some education on violence and abuse has been incorporated into curricula of health care professionals, the need for interdisciplinary courses to aid in developing a comprehensive prevention and intervention programme remains.

Victims of violence continue to report that health care professionals focus on the injuries that have been sustained yet ignore any other aspects of the situation (Sleutel, 1998). Additionally, nurses and doctors acknowledged that they defer asking questions that may lead to disclosure of violence and abuse (Campbell et al., 1993). Moreover, victims have accused them of being judgemental, uncaring, and the least helpful category of professionals to whom they have gone for assistance (American Academy of Nurses Expert Panel on Violence, 1993, p. 87).

The CNA's *Code of Ethics* (1997), the practise standards and expectations for nurses across the country (Alberta Association of Registered Nurses et al., 1999), and the ICN (1999a) have set guidelines for zero tolerance of violence and abuse. This unanimity across all levels of nursing highlights the importance given to the problem presented by the diverse types of violence. Other associations and organisations have also recommended the need for the education of health care professionals (MacLean & Williams, 1995; MacLeod, 1991; McCullough, 1994). Despite this convergence of opinion and the consensus that everyone has the right to a life free of violence and abuse, the development of interdisciplinary curricula has been slow.

Political Action

The societal and cultural issues underlying the reticence to deal with issues involving violence and abuse are key factors affecting the procrastination in developing joint curricula.

In a circular fashion, the approach of health care professionals to focus on the short-term treatment of the signs and symptoms of violence places the onus on the individual to correct the problem and does not demand change within society. Compartmentalisation and a focus on the physical effects of violence and abuse also, then, do not require that professionals accept responsibility to address the broader implications of abuse and violence.

Continued joint efforts of the professional associations, at the national and provincial levels, are needed for developing interdisciplinary curricula on abuse and violence. As with all other issues, there must be individuals within the various organisations who will advocate for these education programmes. The efforts to lobby faculties of nursing, medicine, dentistry, physiotherapy, and occupational therapy must be undertaken by those who recognise and believe in the need to address this issue. An example of an organisation that could be utilised in this lobby in Western Canada is RESOLVE (Research and Education for Solutions to Violence and Abuse), an interdisciplinary community and academic organisation working towards ending abuse and violence (RESOLVE, 1999). Joint research and education organisations exist in other regions of the country (see Online Resources at the end of the chapter for several addresses and links), and the involvement of professionals from multiple disciplines, working with community members, strengthens the efforts and potentiates success. The commitment of time and energy to establish working relationships with members of other disciplines can facilitate efforts to address this issue.

SUMMARY

The enormity and pervasiveness of violence and abuse across society are emphasised and validated by the thousands of books and articles on the topic. The financial and human costs of violence are incalculable but extensive, affecting intimate relationships and all segments of society, particularly the vulnerable: elderly people, disabled people, First Nations members, immigrants and minorities, and children. Violence in the workplace affects nurses and other health professionals.

Nurses are in strategic positions to address issues of violence and abuse because they are among the most trusted professionals, are accessible to the public, and are often the first professionals met by those seeking health care.

Nurses, therefore, must become knowledgeable about violence and abuse, develop the skills to assess and intervene in cases of violence and abuse, and work in interdisciplinary teams to provide comprehensive care. To do any less is a disservice to patients and the profession.

Online RESOURCES

Add to your knowledge of this issue:

British Columbia Institute Against Family Violence	www.bcifv.org
Family and Intimate Partner Violence Prevention Team	www.cdc.gov/ncipc/dvp/ fivpt/fivpt.htm
Family Violence in Canada	www.statcan.ca/english/ freepub/85-224-XIE/free.htm
Hot Peach Pages	www.hotpeachpages.org
Muriel McQueen Fergusson Centre for Family Violence Research	www.unbf.ca/arts/c/fvr
National Clearinghouse on Family Violence	www.hc-sc.gc.ca/hppb/ familyviolence
National Council on Child Abuse and Family Violence	www.nccafv.org
National Council Against Domestic Violence	www.ncadv.org
Research and Education for Solutions to Violence and Abuse	www.umanitoba.ca/resolve

Reflections on the Chapter

1. What images do you have when you hear the terms *family violence, woman abuse, abuse of the elderly*? Who are the main characters in your images and what are they doing?

2. Compile a list of accounts from newspapers, television, and radio in the past week that dealt with violence and abuse. What impact would these incidents have on the health of the population? Were health issues addressed in these accounts?

3. If you have had a patient divulge that she or he has been abused, what steps were taken to assist this person? What steps might you take having read this chapter? What resources could you draw on to guide your actions?

4. What attitudes have you heard expressed that would provide a caring atmosphere for any person (patient or nurse) who divulges abuse? What attitudes would hinder or suppress disclosing this type of information?

5. On which of the many facets of violence and abuse would you choose to focus your attention if you were asked to undertake a project of prevention? Where would you begin your efforts?

6. What resources are available in your work environment that would help you care for and deal with the emotional impact of working with victims of violence?

REFERENCES

Adler, C. (1996). Unheard and unseen: Rural women and domestic violence. *Journal of Nurse-Midwifery, 41*(6), 463–466.

Alberta Association of Registered Nurses, College of Licensed Practical Nurses, & Registered Psychiatric Nurses of Alberta. (1999). *Joint statement on family violence* [On-line]. Available: http://www.nurses.ab.ca/ARNDocs/Family_violence.htm. Edmonton, AB: Authors.

American Academy of Nurses Expert Panel on Violence. (1993). Violence as a nursing priority: Policy implications. *Nursing Outlook, 41*(2), 83–92.

American Nurses Association. (1994). *Workplace violences:* Can you close the door on it? (WP-5): Author. Retrieved April 18, 2001 from http://www.nursingworld.org/dlwa/osh/wp5.htm

Badgley, R. F., Allard, H. A., & McCormick, N. (1984). *Sexual offences against children* (Catalogue No. J2-50/1984E). Ottawa, ON: Department of Supply and Services.

Bandura, A. (1969). Social-learning theory of identificatory processes. In D. A. Goslin (Ed.), *Handbook of socialization theory and research* (pp. 213–262). Chicago: Rand McNally.

Beauchesne, M., Kelley, B. R., Lawrence, P. R., & Farquharson, P. E. (1997). Violence prevention: A community approach. *Journal of Pediatric Health Care, 11*, 179–188.

Bunge, V. P., & Locke, D. (2000). *Family violence in Canada: A statistical profile 2000* [On-line]. Available: http://www.statcan.ca (Catalogue 85-224-XIE Canadian Centre for Justice Statistics). Ottawa, ON: Minister of Industry.

Campbell, J., & Fishwick, N. (1993). Abuse of female partners. In J. Campbell & J. Humphreys (Eds.), *Nursing care of survivors of family violence* (pp. 68–106). St. Louis: Mosby.

Campbell, J., McKenna, L., Torres, S., Sheridan, D., & Landeburger, K. (1993). Nursing care of abused women. In J. Campbell & J. Humphries (Eds.), *Nursing care of survivors of family violence* (pp. 248–289). St. Louis: Mosby.

Campbell, J. C. (1999). *Safety planning based on lethality assessment for partners of batterers in treatment.* Paper presented at the Partnerships to Enhance Victim Safety Conference: Criminal Justice & Advocacy Responses to Domestic Violence, Troy, NY [On-line]. Available: http://www.opdv.state.ny.us/criminal_justice/ojpconf.lethality.htm.

Canadian Nurses Association. (1996). *Interpersonal violence* [On-line]. Available: http://www.cna-nurses.ca/pages/policies/interpersonal%5Fviolence.html). Ottawa, ON: Author.

Canadian Nurses Association. (1997). *Code of ethics.* Ottawa, ON: Author.

Canadian Public Health Association. (1994). *Violence in society: A public health perspective* (Issue Paper). Ottawa: Author.

DeKerseredy, W. S., & Kelly, K. (1993). The incidence and prevalence of woman abuse in Canadian university and college dating relationships. *Canadian Journal of Sociology, 18*(2), 137–159.

Dobash, R. E., & Dobash, R. P. (1979). *Violence against wives.* New York: Free Press.

Duffy, A., & Momirov, J. (2000). Family violence: Issues and advances at the end of the twentieth century. In N. Mandell & A. Duffy (Eds.), *Canadian families: Diversity, conflict, and change* (pp. 290–322). Toronto, ON: Harcourt Canada.

Garbarino, J. (1977). The human ecology of child maltreatment: A conceptual model for research. *Journal of Marriage and the Family, 39*, 721–735.

Garbarino, J. (1995). Growing up in a socially toxic environment: Life for children and families in the 1990s. In G. B. Melton (Ed.), *The individual, the family, and social good: Personal fulfillment in times of change* (Vol. 42, pp. 1–20). Lincoln: University of Nebraska Press.

Garbarino, J., & Kostelny, K. (1992). Child maltreatment as a community problem. *Child Abuse and Neglect, 16*, 455–464.

Garbarino, J., & Sherman, D. (1980). High-risk neighborhoods and high-risk families: The human ecology of child maltreatment. *Child Development, 51*, 188–198.

Gelles, R. J. (1980). Violence in the family: A review of research in the seventies. *Journal of Marriage and the Family, 42*, 873–885.

Hamby, S. L. (2000). The importance of community in a feminist analysis of domestic violence among American Indians. *American Journal of Community Psychology, 28*(5), 649–669.

Hamilton, A. C., & Sinclair, C. M. (1991). *The justice system and aboriginal people.* Winnipeg, MB: Queen's Printer.

Helfer, R. (1973). The etiology of child abuse. *Pediatrics, 51,* 777–779.

Helfer, R., & Kempe, C. H. (1968). *The battered child.* Chicago: University of Chicago Press.

Hoff, L. A. (1994). *Violence issues: An interdisciplinary curriculum guide for health professionals* (H72-21/129-1995E). Ottawa, ON: Mental Health Division Health Canada.

Hoff, L. A., & Ross, M. M. (1993). *Curriculum guide for nursing: Violence against women and children.* Ottawa, ON: University of Ottawa.

Humphreys, J. (1993). Children of battered women. In J. Campbell & J. Humphreys (Eds.), *Nursing care of survivors of family violence* (pp. 107–131). St. Louis: Mosby.

Humphreys, J., & Ramsey, A. M. (1993). Child abuse. In J. Campbell & J. Humphreys (Eds.), *Nursing care of the survivors of family violence* (pp. 36–67). St. Louis: Mosby.

Imam, A. (2001, April). Nigerian women's group condemns whipping [On-line]. Available: http://www.web.net/~matchint/en/apr01/nlapr01_3.htm.

Innes, J. E., Ratner, P. A., Finlayson, P. F., Bray, D., & Giovannetti, P. B. (1991). *Models and strategies of delivering community health services related to woman abuse.* Edmonton, AB: University of Alberta.

Interdepartmental Working Group on Elder Abuse and Manitoba Seniors Directorate. (1993). *Abuse of the elderly: A guide for the development of protocols.* Winnipeg, MB: Government of Manitoba.

International Council of Nurses. (1999a). *Abuse and violence against nursing personnel* [On-line]. Available: http://www.icn.ch/psviolence00.htm. Geneva: Author.

International Council of Nurses. (1999b). Increasing violence in the workplace is a threat to nursing and the delivery of health care (March 8, 1999) [On-line]. Available: www.icn.ch/prviolence_99.htm.

Koniak-Griffin, D., & Lesser, J. (1996). The impact of childhood maltreatment on young mothers' violent behavior toward themselves and others. *Journal of Pediatric Nursing, 11*(5), 300–308.

Langford, D. R. (1996). Predicting unpredictability: A model of women's processes of predicting battering men's violence. *Scholarly Inquiry for Nursing Practice: An International Journal, 10*(4), 371–385.

MacLean, M. J., & Williams, R. M. (1995). Introduction. In M. J. MacLean (Ed.), *Abuse & neglect of older Canadians: Strategies for change* (pp. ix–xii). Toronto, ON: Canadian Association on Gerontology and Thompson Educational Publishing, Inc.

MacLeod, L. (1991). *Freedom from fear: A woman's right, a community concern, a national priority* (C91-099010-7E). Ottawa, ON: Secretary of State Canada Multiculturalism and Citizenship Canada.

MacMillan, H. L., Fleming, J. E., Trocme, N., Boyle, M. H., Wong, M., Racine, Y. A., Beardslee, W. R., & Offord, D. R. (1997). Prevalence of child physical and sexual abuse in the community. *Journal of the American Medical Association, 278*(2), 131–135.

Manitoba Association of Registered Nurses. (1989). *Nurse abuse report.* Winnipeg, MB: Author.

Matas, R. (2001, March 24, 2001). "He said if I ever told anyone, he will kill me when he gets out." *Globe and Mail,* pp. A9–10.

McCullough, I. (1994). *A challenge for health: Making connections within the family violence context* (Discussion papers on health/family violence issues H39-292/1-1994E). Ottawa, ON: Health Canada.

Podnieks, E. (1985). Elder abuse: It's time we did something about it. *Canadian Nurse, 81*(11), 36–39.

Podnieks, E., & Baillie, E. (1995). Education as the key to the prevention of elder abuse and neglect. In M. J. MacLean (Ed.), *Abuse and neglect of older Canadians: Strategies for change* (pp. 81–93). Toronto, ON: Canadian Association on Gerontology and Thompson Educational Publishing, Inc.

Podnieks, E., Pillemer, K., Nicholson, J. P., Shillington, T., & Frizzell, A. F. (1990). *National survey on abuse of the elderly in Canada.* Toronto, ON: Ryerson Polytechnic Institute.

Pynoos, R. S., & Nader, K. (1990). Children's exposure to violence and traumatic death. *Psychiatric Annals, 20*(6), 334–344.

Report of the Royal Commission on Aboriginal Peoples. (1996). *For Seven Generations* (Vol. 3). Ottawa, ON: Libraxus Inc.

RESOLVE. (1999). Winnipeg Foundation Funds RESOLVE Newsletter. In B. Comaskey (Ed.), (Vol. 1, pp. 1). Winnipeg, MB: Author.

Ristock, J. L. (2001). Decentering heterosexuality: Responses of feminist counselors to abuse in lesbian relationships. *Women & Therapy, 23*(3), 59–72.

Sleutel, M. R. (1998). Women's experiences of abuse: A review of qualitative research. *Issues in Mental Health Nursing, 19,* 525–539.

Smylie, J. (2001). A guide for health professionals working with aboriginal peoples: Health issues affecting aboriginal peoples. *Journal of the Society of Obstetricians and Gynecologists of Canada, 100,* 54–68.

Statistics Canada (1997). *Graphical overview of crime and the administration of criminal justice in Canada, 1997* (Catalogue No. 85F0018XIE). Ottawa, ON: Minister of Industry.

Tham, S. W., Ford, T. J., & Wilkinson, D. G. (1995). A survey of domestic violence and other forms of abuse. *Journal of Mental Health, 4,* 317–321.

Thomlinson, E. B., Erickson, N., & Cook, M. (2000). Could this be your community? In J. Proulx & S. Perrault (Eds.), *No place for violence: Canadian aboriginal alternatives* (Vol. 1, pp. 22–38). Halifax, NS: Fernwood Publishing and RESOLVE (Research and Education for Solutions to Violence and Abuse).

Walker, L. E. (1979). *The battered woman.* New York: Harper & Row.

Wiehe, V. R. (1998). *Understanding family violence: Treating and preventing partner, child, sibling, and elder abuse.* Thousand Oaks, CA: Sage Publications.

22

Environmental Health and Nursing

Elizabeth Thomlinson

Chapter Objectives

At the completion of this chapter, you will be able to:

1. Identify some common environmental health hazards in your geographic region.

2. Examine the nursing profession's impact in addressing environmental issues.

3. Generate ideas about how individual nurses can affect issues of environmental health.

4. Evaluate how your nursing curriculum integrates health and the environment.

Across Canada, the relationship of the environment to the health of individuals and families is a serious concern. Emissions from gas plants or other environmental pollutants are just a few of the potential hazards to health. Individual nurses and the nursing profession can promote greater societal health through the tradtional routes of nursing practice, education, and research.

This we know . . . the earth does not belong to man, man belongs to the earth.

All things are connected, like blood which connects one family. Whatever befalls the earth befalls the children of the earth. Man did not weave the web of life; he is merely a strand in it.

Whatever he does to the web, he does to himself.

—*Chief Seattle, 1854 Suqwamish and Duwamish*

In a world that is increasingly affected by globalisation, swift transportation, almost instant communication, global warming, the extinction of multiple species of plants, animals, and birds, and the rapid transfer of diseases around the globe, humans are as closely linked to the health of their environments as they were at the dawn of human history. Environmental hazards, the health of the earth, and the health of the earth's inhabitants are inseparable. The interdependence of all species on the earth and the physical environment cannot be overemphasised. The concepts of person, environment, health, and nursing, which form the metaparadigm of the nursing profession, underscores this interdependence, but a perusal of issues texts for nurses uncovered little discussion of environmental health.

Although this chapter does not focus on the conservation of natural resources, it does underscore how environmental hazards contribute to adverse health outcomes for humans. It is hoped that readers will examine the regions and communities where they live and work to gain awareness of the connection between their own environments and the health of the residents. The need to be aware of how environmental hazards impact human health is important for nurses regardless of their practise setting—be it community, long-term or acute institutional care, or occupational health. All too often when concerns regarding environmental health issues surface, they are so far removed from the daily lives of most people that little attention is paid to the issues raised. Only when the media highlights major problems, such as the deaths from *Escherichia coli* bacteria resulting from contaminated water sources in Walkerton, Ontario (Ahluwalia, 2000), do citizens become concerned about the possibility of similar events in their own neighbourhoods.

There is no doubt that human health is affected when the environment or ecosystem is damaged (McMullan, 1997). The term *environmental health,* as used in this chapter, refers to freedom from illness related to the exposure to environmental contamination, hazards, or toxins that are detrimental to health. In the discussions that follow, the term *environment* includes the physical, social, political, legal, psychological, and cognitive environments of individuals, their families, and their communities. As scientific knowledge increases and social and political values change, the definitions of, and factors related to, environmental health will also change.

Reference resources for this chapter include government agency web sites, national and international nursing association web sites, newspapers, and a variety of professional literature in addition to what is available in the Canadian nursing literature. A limited number of the many Canadian and American web sites that are available for research and information are listed at the end of the chapter (see Online Resources). Readers are encouraged to examine the vast body of literature on the topic of environmental health, ranging from extensive research reports found in journals such as *Environmental Health Perspectives, Environmental Health,* and *The Ecologist* to general literature that alerts the public to issues of concern in the environment. The impact of Rachel Carson's books, including *The Silent Spring* and *The Sea Around Us,* and the efforts of David Suzuki, among others, in raising awareness of the destruction of our physical world have been incalculable.

HISTORICAL LINKS BETWEEN ENVIRONMENT AND HEALTH

The effect that a healthy, or conversely an unhealthy, environment has on human health is not a recent discovery. Early civilizations were aware of the impact of the environment on health. The Minoans (3000 to 1430 B.C.), Mycenaeans (1430 to 1150 B.C.), and Romans (509 B.C. to 476 A.D.) all built extensive drainage and water systems as well as baths and toilets (McGuire & Eigsti-Gerber, 1999) in response to related environmental health hazards of pestilence and disease. Early Hebrew writings included a code on hygiene, whereas the ancient Egyptians (3100 B.C. to 600 A.D.) developed safe water and sewer systems. As civilizations rose and fell, this knowledge and the systems that had been developed were often forgotten or destroyed.

Plagues resulting from contamination of water sources and the spread of disease through animal vectors have been documented throughout history. Through the introduction of public health measures such as providing a clean source of drinking water and the safe disposal of sewage and other wastes, great improvements were made in the health of populations; these are key elements that remain as important as ever (Clark, 1999; McDevitt & Wilbur, 2002). A major turning point in history however, was the Industrial Revolution that began in Great Britain in the early 1700s and spread to Europe and North America. Industrialisation resulted in a shift from what had been a rural, agricultural economy to one that was urban and factory-based with concomitant problems of pollution from large steel foundries and the burning of fossil fuels. The impact of the Industrial Revolution extended far beyond the production of goods and material to changes in governments, the use of resources in the world, material benefits for some of the world's population, and wars and exploitation of many populations. Modern transportation and communication, the globalisation of markets, and the even more rapid destruction of habitats are evident today. Nurses have been integral participants in examining and changing some of the harmful environmental conditions to improve public health.

In *Notes on Nursing*, Florence Nightingale (1860) observed that environmental factors had a key impact on health and disease:

> In watching diseases, both in private homes and in public hospitals, the thing which strikes the experienced observer most forcibly is this, that the symptoms or the sufferings generally considered to be inevitable and incident to the disease are very often not symptoms of the disease at all, but of something quite different—of the want of fresh air, or of cleanliness, or of punctuality and care in the administration of diet, of each or of all of these. (p. 5)

Further, Nightingale noted that there were "five essential points in securing the health of houses" and by extrapolation the health of the population: "pure air, pure water, efficient drainage, cleanliness and light" (1860, p. 14).

Other nurses who actively advocated for safe water, sewage, and sanitation systems, which they incorporated into their health promotion and education practises, included Lillian Wald (1915) and Mary Breckenridge (1952) (Eigsti-Gerber & McGuire, 1999). Wald was the founder of modern public health nursing, working in New York to improve the health of children in particular. Breckenridge incorporated principles of environmental health in her community health practise in rural Kentucky that resulted in lowered infant mortality. Before the establishment of large hospitals and the focus on care in hospitals, most early nursing practise was carried out in the community. Nurses were cognizant of the environmental conditions in which their patients lived and worked. The shift to the majority of nursing practise being concentrated within institutions separated nurses from the environmental effects that had been more readily apparent.

Current environmental debates centre on global warming as a result of the burning of fossil fuels (Foley, 2001; Last et al., 1998), destruction of habitat around the world (Malcolm et al., 2002), and the potential for unrestrained population growth to outstrip the ability to produce enough food to feed the world's citizens (Brown et al., 2001). Multiple charters, agreements, summits, and conventions have been held to examine the health of the world's citizens; globalisation and global issues related to the environment; access to safe water and food; and global warming as well as the sociopolitical causes and impact of poverty and the economic disparity that exists among nations within the context of a "sustainable global ecosystem" (Hilfinger Messias, 2001, p. 10). A proliferation of treaties and accords since the 1970s has resulted in more than 240 international agreements (Brown et al., 2001).

Brown and colleagues noted that the 1987 Montreal Protocol on Substances that Deplete the Ozone Layer led to the gradual phasing out of the use of chlorofluorocarbons that damage the stratosphere. The 1997 Kyoto Protocol to the 1992 United Nations (U.N.) Framework Convention on Climate Change has been much more contentious, with the United States refusing to ratify the treaty that requires industrialised nations to cut carbon dioxide emissions by 6% to 8% by 2008 to 2012. A major concern remains regarding the ability to police these agreements and end environmental crime that is fueled by greed and the self-interests of individuals, corporations, and governments.

While recognising positive global effects linked to health, sanitation, and urban reclamation, Berlinguer (1999) raised concerns regarding pollution, depletion of natural resources, global warming, and the declining quality of life—particularly in urban centres and in developing nations. He noted that people in the lowest socioeconomic classes suffer the greatest damage because they lack the resources and facilities to preserve their health.

In all nations, the poorest residents tend to live in substandard housing in densely populated communities in close proximity to industrial areas where the potential for contamination and hazardous waste leakage are the highest (Chaudhuri, 1998). Within Canadian society, members of First Nations communities are especially at risk for health problems related to unsafe drinking water, lack of adequate sanitation, and substandard housing (Health Canada, 1999b). Environmental contaminants such as polychlorinated biphenyls (PCBs) used in electrical and hydraulic equipment, dioxins from bleaching wood pulp with chlorine, and mercury from old industrial practises and long-range transport have been found in fish and marine mammals throughout the country. This has resulted in a contaminated food supply, particularly for aboriginal people in the north and those who follow a traditional diet.

ENVIRONMENTAL HEALTH HAZARDS

Around the world, life expectancy has increased and morbidity and mortality have decreased as a result of significant improvement and availability of safe water and sewage systems and better nutrition and housing. Individuals, communities, and governments need to be conscious that these gains do not overshadow current and developing environmental problems. The World Health Organization (WHO) notes that about 2 million children younger than 5 years of age die annually because of unsafe drinking water and lack of sanitation. Air pollution is responsible for up to 20% of childhood mortality (WHO, 2001). A WHO taskforce has been established to promote the identification, assessment, mitigation, and prevention of environmental hazards specifically "to prevent disease and disability in children associated with chemical and physical threats" (WHO, 2001).

Various U.N. agencies participated in a global environmental assessment by providing data and information on environmental issues within their particular mandates (U.N. Environmental Programme, 1999). This assessment was undertaken in response to the need to build a consensus on priorities regarding the environment. According to this report, increased industrialisation around the world has contributed to environmental deterioration resulting from air and water pollution, waste dumping, and increasing ill health, especially among the poor. Environmental contaminants include biologic agents, inorganic and organic chemicals, radiation, and particulate matter (Box 22.1).

Contaminants follow pathways from the time they are released into the environment until people, animals, or plants come in contact with them. These *exposure pathways* consist of five components that need to be examined when tracing sources of contamination (Health Canada, 1998). The components include the following:

- Source of contamination; for example, emissions, waste water and disposal sites, volcanoes, fires, household products
- Medium through which the contaminant travels; for example, water, soil, air, food products
- Point at which people come into contact with the contaminant
- Person, animal, or plant that is the receptor of the contaminant
- Route of exposure; for example, inhalation (gases, vapours, or particulate matter), dermal contact (working in contaminated soil or swimming in contaminated water), or ingestion (contaminated food or water)

Many symptoms exhibited by people exposed to environmental contaminants can be attributed to other causes, making it difficult to establish an exact cause and effect. It is therefore important when assessing exposure to environmental contaminants to take as broad a perspective as possible to include all potential environmental factors.

Water Safety and Pollution

Water is fundamental to all life on the planet. Uneven distribution of this resource around the globe means that some regions, such as Canada, have an abundance of fresh water, whereas other regions, such as the Middle East and northern Africa, suffer from a shortage. It is estimated that 500 million people in the world live in countries that are short of water and that by 2025, this number will dramatically rise to 3 billion (Mitchell, 2001). Water use worldwide has risen sixfold between 1900 and 1995, more than double the population increase.

In countries such as Canada, the abundance of water has led to waste and increased pollution of this resource. Although water is the ultimate renewable resource, major problems now exist in that water sources are polluted with chemicals, fertilizers, heavy metals, hydrocarbons, and raw sewage (Robson & Schneider, 2001;

BOX 22.1

Selected Environmental Contaminants

BIOLOGICAL AGENTS

Bacteria such as *Escherichia coli*

Protozoa

Viruses

Fungi

Algae

House dust mites

Pollen grains

Moulds

CHEMICAL CONTAMINANTS

Organic substances, such as: fluorine, chlorine, bromine, iodine, nitrogen, sulfur, phosphorus, carbon, polychlorinated biphenyls (PCBs), DDT, dioxins, benzene, malathion, toluene, dioxane

Inorganic substances, such as: ozone, nitrogen oxides, sulfur dioxide, lead, mercury, cadmium, arsenic, uranium, beryllium, chromium

RADIATION

Microwaves

Ultraviolet light

Low-frequency electromagnetic fields

Sound

PARTICULATE MATTER

Fine dust

Smoke from forest fires and burning stubble

Asbestos

Cigarette smoke

U.N. Environmental Programme, 1999; Wanke & Saunders, 1996). Industrial waste, runoff from large-scale farming operations, and the dumping of garbage in uncontrolled waste sites leads to continued pollution. In the report "Health and the Environment," Health Canada (1997) noted that in a 1993 study, 40% of 1,300 rural wells in Ontario had undesirable levels of chemical or microbiologic contaminants. This report also stated that many Canadian residents have detectable traces of contaminants in their blood, hair, and body tissues.

Underground aquifers are being drained more quickly than they are being replenished. Global warming has led the atmosphere to retain more water in the form of water vapour, which decreases the volume of water returned in the form of rain. An example of the overuse of subterranean water is the High Plains Aquifer that extends underground from South Dakota to Texas in the United States. The level of water has dropped by more than 40 metres as the population uses the water for irrigating land that was once barren. Political solutions suggested by American politicians and entrepreneurs to this water depletion are the bulk sale of water from Canada and the desalination of ocean water for human use. The short- and long-term effects on the environment of either of these proposals are not known.

The need to provide a safe drinking water supply has been highlighted by recent outbreaks of *E. coli* in the water supply at Walkerton, Ontario, and *Cryptosporidium* species found in the water in North Battleford, Saskatchewan. The *E. coli* outbreak led to multiple gastrointestinal illnesses and ultimately to the deaths of nine people (Ahluwalia, 2000). Contamination of the water sources from manure from cattle farms in the area and the inadequate treatment of the water is a suspected cause of this outbreak. The impact of these outbreaks has heightened public awareness and increased the need to examine and question water safety in the communities.

Cryptosporidium, although not a new organism, is becoming more prevalent. Animals and humans shed this protozoan parasite in their feces. The consumption of contaminated water or food, ingestion of recreational water, or contact with infected people can lead to infection. There are potentially life-threatening consequences for immunosuppressed people who become infected (Physicians for Social Responsibility, 2001b). Proper filtration, distillation, or reverse osmosis processes must be used to ensure that the organism has been removed from the water supply. *Giardia lamblia* is another parasite endemic to the ecosystem. *G. lamblia* causes gastrointestinal infections and can also produce life-threatening effects in an immunocompromised individual. Contamination of water supplies with various microbial contaminants leads to multiple boil-water alerts annually in all provinces.

In 2001, a government roundtable found that although water quality is a serious problem throughout the country, there is particular concern regarding water supply to First Nations communities. A Health Canada report in 1995 signalled that 171 communities (one in five) had water systems that could negatively affect the health of the citizens (MacKinnon, 2001). Minimal improvements have occurred during the intervening years. As of 2001, there were no national regulations in Canada regarding water protection and safety, an indication that future disasters can and will continue to occur.

Air Pollution

Many regions of the world suffer from air pollution that leads to illness and death. In South America, about 4,000 premature deaths are estimated to occur annually in Sao Paulo and Rio de Janeiro as a result of severe air pollution (U.N. Environmental Programme, 1999). The very young and the very old suffer a greater burden from air pollution than do people in the interim age ranges. The risk from air pollution for children increases because they breathe more rapidly and inhale more pollutants per pound of body weight than do adults. A wide range of negative effects from air pollution include impaired pulmonary function; reduced physical performance; multiple visits to physicians, emergency rooms, and hospitals; and premature death (Health Canada, 1998).

Air pollutants are generated from burning fossil fuels, such as oil, coal, gasoline, and diesel fuel in vehicles and power generators. Industries, such as pulp and paper mills, oil refineries, and ore smelters, contribute to air pollution. Oil, natural gas, and coal production has resulted in Alberta emitting 30% of the carbon dioxide, 26% of the nitrogen oxide, and 23% of the sulfur oxide emissions generated in Canada (Environment Canada, 2000a). Asthma is a respiratory disease that can be triggered by airborne contaminants. Air pollutants, such as ground-level ozone, sulfur dioxide, and particulate matter, are believed to be key factors in increased asthma rates (Last et al., 1998). Pope and colleagues (2002) analysed the correlation of the mortality statistics of participants in the Cancer Prevention Study II who resided in American metropolitan areas where pollution data were available. They demonstrated that fine particulate air contamination is associated with cardiopulmonary and lung cancer mortality (p. 1137) and presents a significant risk factor to population health.

An exponential incidence of asthma in children in Canada has occurred in the 1990s. Rates of hospitalisation for boys increased by 27% and for girls by 18% (Health Canada, 1997). This raised annual hospital admissions to more than 60,000. According to Last and associates (1998), hospital admissions in Ontario for acute bronchitis, bronchiolitis, and pneumonia in children younger than 1 year of age "can be attributed to the summer pollutants, ozone and sulphates" (p. 21). In the United States, asthma is now the most prevalent childhood illness (Physicians for Social Responsibility, 1997). As well, since the 1970s, there has been a significant increase in the death rates from asthma of people 70 years of age and older.

Some authorities suggest that it would cost $6 billion to implement a programme to decrease air pollution by developing cleaner vehicles and fuels in Canada (Health Canada, 1998, p. 121). On the other hand, savings to the health care system are estimated to be $24 billion as a result of eliminating many of the negative health effects of air pollution. Improving ambient air quality in Canada alone could amount to $8 billion in health care savings over the next 20 years (Last et al., 1998). Last and associates suggest that the reduction of motor vehicle emissions would result in savings to the forest and agricultural sectors of the Canadian economy of between $11 and $30 billion.

Although chemically the same, ground-level ozone (found within 11 kilometres of the earth's surface) and the "ozone layer" (found between 11 and 47 kilometres above the earth in the stratosphere) need to be differentiated from each other. The ozone layer acts as a barrier against ultraviolet (UV) radiation (particularly UVB rays) from the sun (Health Canada, 1998). As this layer is damaged or destroyed by chlorofluorocarbons, more radiation penetrates to earth. The result is an increase in skin cancer, particularly melanomas. There is also evidence that UVB exposure increases the risk for cataracts (Institute of Medicine, 1995).

Ground-level ozone, or smog, forms when nitrogen oxides and volatile organic compounds react in the presence of sunlight (Health Canada, 1998). This occurs on hot, still, summer days, and the resultant air pollution can lead to adverse cardiac and respiratory effects. Again, those most affected are elderly and very young people. As the earth's average temperature rises, it is expected that more hot summer days with smog advisories or warnings will occur.

PCBs, dioxins, and other organic compounds can travel long distances through the air before being deposited on the land or in bodies of water. These toxins accumulate in the food chain, where they become a hazard to people who consume fish and wildlife as food, particularly when they are ingested faster than they can be excreted (Health Canada, 1998). There is grave concern that seals and other Artic animals are contaminated and pose a risk to Inuit communities that rely on these animals as a source of food.

Chemical Pollution

Humans are slowly coming to realise the effects of the huge quantities of manmade chemicals that have been discharged into the environment since the 1940s (Physicians for Social Responsibility, 1994). Excessive use of fertilizers, pesticides, and heavy metals such as arsenic, cadmium, lead, and mercury has polluted the land (U.N. Environmental Programme, 1999). Local sources of contamination such as sewage and waste disposal and industrial discharge can be more readily identified. More diffuse contamination occurs through runoff from fields and lawns, motor vehicle emissions, and the long-distance contamination of acid rain (which develops from sulfur dioxide and nitrogen oxides from coal-fired power plants, smelters, and vehicular emissions). *The Health and Environment Handbook for Health Professionals* prepared by Health Canada and the Ontario Ministry of the Environment (1998) notes that there are "300 industrial sites" in Ontario "that discharge directly into rivers and lakes" and "another 12,000 that dump their waste into municipal sewage systems that cannot adequately treat toxic chemicals" (p. 38).

Many of these chemical pollutants remain in the environment for long periods. They can be ingested and then accumulate in the tissues of humans if their excretion does not occur as quickly as their intake. Dioxins, furans, and PCBs build up in fatty tissue, whereas metals such as lead, mercury, and cadmium are stored in the liver, kidney, and bone. Mercury can be found in many lakes and rivers, where it converts to a toxic substance methyl mercury that can affect the nervous systems of humans and animals (Environment Canada, 2000b). An additional concern is long-term arsenic ingestion (through drinking water), which increases the risk for skin, bladder, lung, kidney, and other cancers (Physicians for Social Responsibility, 2001a). The impact on human health of long-term low-level exposure to many chemical pollutants is unknown. Concerns focus on immune system suppression, neurologic and behavioural changes, and the role that chemical toxins play in initiating cancer.

The term *pesticide* refers to a variety of chemicals that control weeds (herbicides), bacteria (disinfectants), fungi (fungicides), insects (insecticides), and rodents (rodenticides). Pesticides are widely used in agriculture and forestry to protect crops and forests. Large amounts of fertilizer and herbicides are used annually in urban and suburban environments in the care of lawns and golf courses. In Canada, more than 500 active ingredients have been registered for use as pesticides (Health Canada, 1998). There is a growing movement within some towns and cities across Canada to ban the use of herbicides because of the risk to human health (Box 22.2).

Of grave concern are the implications for the health of residents who live in the immediate vicinity of toxic waste sites or who now live in what was once a contaminated industrial site (Carruth et al., 1997). There are no biologic markers by which the level of exposure can be determined for many of the chemicals that are discharged into the environment. Further, the long-term impact of long-term exposure to some contaminants, such as malathion, is not known. Key concerns related to long-term exposure include the following:

- Those in lower socioeconomic conditions are often the people who live in areas closest to polluted sites.
- As knowledge of chemical pollutants grows, standards may change; that is, norms that were once considered safe may be upgraded to levels considered a health risk.
- Exposure to toxins may occur and may be undetected over extended periods of time.
- Exposure to contaminants may occur through multiple pathways (air, water, soil) and enter the food chain in numerous ways, making detection more difficult.

BOX 22.2

Selected Environmental Health Concerns

CONCERNS RELATED TO GENERAL ENVIRONMENTAL HAZARDS

Cancer

Genetic mutation

Birth defects

Neurologic effects, such as cerebral ataxia, neuropathies, and encephalitis

Heat prostration, injuries, and death from weather and climate extremes

Joint and muscle pain or weakness

Organ damage

Reproductive damage

Developmental and behavioural abnormalities

Respiratory disorders: asthma, bronchitis, emphysema

Gastrointestinal diseases, such as cholera and other infections, caused by *Escherichia coli, Giardia lambia,* or *Cryptosporidium species*

Death

CONCERNS RELATED TO NURSING WORKPLACE HAZARDS

Infectious diseases

   Hepatitis A, B, and C

   Tuberculosis, measles, rubella, influenza

   Human immunodeficiency virus (HIV)

Exposure to toxins

   Cytotoxic drugs

   Anesthetic gas waste

   Ethylene oxide, gluteraldehyde, and formaldehyde

Radiation

Stress

Violence

- Action to curb exposure to contaminants has not kept pace with society's abilities to detect contamination (Canadian Nurses Association, 2000).
- Canada is without longitudinal research regarding the effects of individual contaminants as well as the combined effects from multiple sources of contamination (Canadian Nurses Association, 2000).

Inside Environments

The Ottawa Charter for Health Promotion credits adequate shelter as having a major effect on health. According to the report from the federal, provincial, and territorial governments, *Toward a Healthy Future: Second Report on the Health of Canadians,* one in five Canadians who rent accommodations are living in substandard housing (Health Canada, 1999b). The people who most often live in these conditions are single-parent families, particularly ones in which parents are younger than 30 years old; individuals with mental health problems, and senior citizens living alone. Of grave concern are the inadequate housing and crowded living conditions under which aboriginal people live. This may be a major contributor to the fact that aboriginal children suffer from much higher rates of respiratory and other infectious diseases than do nonaboriginal children (Health Canada, 1999b).

Health Canada estimates that Canadians spend up to 90% of their time indoors in their homes, work sites, and other buildings. In addition to outdoor contaminants, which can also be found indoors, the inside air may contain tobacco smoke, formaldehyde, vapours from household products, carbon dioxide, and biologic agents such as bacteria, fungi, moulds, viruses, and mite byproducts (Health Canada, 1998). The health of the residents may be adversely affected if the concentrations of any of these contaminants rise too high. The growing trend toward weatherising homes and buildings in the interest of conservation may result in a lack of adequate air exchange because the ventilation systems were not designed for these well-insulated and sealed buildings. Therefore, the potential for contaminant buildup increases.

A principal contaminant in indoor environments is tobacco smoke, including sidestream smoke emitted from cigarettes, pipes, and cigars between puffs and mainstream smoke that is exhaled by smokers. It is estimated that there are 300 deaths from lung cancer in nonsmokers annually in Canada as a result of environmental tobacco smoke (ETS) (Health Canada, 1998, 1999b). In addition, ETS is considered a significant cause of cardiovascular disease and death in nonsmokers.

Canadian children are at an increased risk for health effects from ETS because they spend more time indoors than do children in many other countries. As mentioned previously, children have smaller airways and breathe more rapidly than do adults, thus inhaling more pollutants per kilogram of body weight. In the United States, authorities estimate that 11% of asthma cases, about 350,000 cases of bronchitis, and 152,000 cases of pneumonia are a consequence of ETS (Health Canada, 1998). More than one third of households with children younger than 15 years of age also have a smoker in the family. Authorities suspect that exposure to ETS during childhood may be associated with increased pulmonary disease and cancer.

There is a wide variation among provinces in the control and restriction of smoking in public areas. Restrictions against smoking range from being limited to designated smoking areas to a total ban on smoking on public premises. As the public becomes more aware and concerned with the health risks attributed to ETS, smoking bans may become more stringent.

Contaminated Social Environments

If consideration of environmental health risks is confined to the effects of pollution and hazards within the natural environment, a key component of the settings in which individuals and families live will be ignored. Impoverished neighbourhoods with substandard housing, abject poverty, homelessness, visible signs of people who are substance abusing and drug dealing, and violence and crime within the community are examples of contaminated social environments. The impact on the physical, psychological, and emotional health of individuals living in such environments can be severe.

The national crime rate in Canada, including homicides, attempted murder, robbery, break-ins, motor vehicle theft, and impaired driving, has doubled since the 1960s (Health Canada, 1999b). Of significant concern is the fact that the rate of young people charged with violent crimes is more than double the rate of a decade ago. As well, the effects of violence in the schools and the impact of bullying, leading to the suicide deaths of teenagers, has been frequently in the news (Cox, 2002). There has, however, been a drop in the national crime rate since it peaked in 1991. An actual decrease of 19 homicides in which firearms were used (193 versus 212) occurred between the years 1996 and 1997. This is in contrast to the United States, where a proliferation of handguns contributes to an increased homicide rate. In that country, 17% of deaths in the workplace were homicides, with gunshots accounting for 82% of that total (Institute of Medicine, 1995). Almost 1,000 workers are murdered on the job annually in the United States, with homicide being the number one cause of women's deaths in the workplace (International Council of Nurses, 2001).

If the social environments in which people live are violent, degrading, and impoverished, there is a significant negative impact on the health of the residents. These negative effects are further compounded by the toxic waste sites and heavy industry that are often physically juxtaposed to these communities. Health care professionals need to take into account the entire environmental context of the people and communities with which they are working.

NURSING AND ENVIRONMENTAL HEALTH

A press release by the ICN noted that "over 1 billion persons in developing countries live without adequate shelter or [un]acceptable housing, 1.4 billion lack access to safe water, and 2.9 billion people have no access to adequate sanitation" (International Council of Nurses, 2000). All of these environmental conditions continue a cycle of ill health that has negative consequences for the general welfare of individuals, families, communities, and nations.

The CNA position statement entitled *The Environment is a Determinant of Health* states that "the CNA will work with others in the health and social sectors to influence decisions that impact the environment and thus human health" (Canadian Nurses Association, 2000). Of particular concern are the long-term health effects of contaminants on children. In a joint statement, the CNA and the Canadian Medical Association (CMA) indicate that "a healthy environment is fundamental to life, and attention to the effect of the environment on human health is imperative if we are to attain the goal of health for all" (CNA/CMA, 1996).

Multiple sources note, however, that nurses consider themselves unprepared to address environmental health issues, nurses are not aware of regulations and policies that affect the environment and health, and nurses believed they were not competent to recognise the health effects of environmental contaminants (Bellack et al., 1996; Green, 2000; Institute of Medicine, 1995). It is important to question why, with the plethora of scientific and popular literature available on environmental health issues, nurses do not consider they have the knowledge and skills required to address these issues.

First and foremost, nurses require knowledge about the particular environmental issues that affect their own health and practise of nursing. Nurses themselves face particular health risks from infectious diseases, chemicals, radiation, air pollution (such as moulds) within their work sites, physical injuries, and even violence in the community and the workplace. To address these concerns, it is important to examine the roles nurses have involving environmental health, the competencies that are required, and the methods to achieve these competencies regardless of their work setting.

Practise Roles and Competencies

Nurses are frequently the only health care professionals who enter the homes, workplaces, and communities of the individuals and populations they serve (Institute of Medicine, 1995). Practising nurses require the skills to identify environmental hazards that may be related to the health concerns faced by an individual or a population. According to Eigsti-Gerber and McGuire (1999), nurses require the education to act as investigators, educators, and advocates in environmental health issues for individuals, families, and communities. To do this, they must be aware of the environmental hazards that cause or exacerbate particular diseases in the population. To assist in assessment, diagnosis, intervention, planning, and evaluation, nurses also need basic knowledge of the following:

- Potential hazards in a geographic region
- Routes by which people may become infected (the exposure pathways)
- Prevention and control strategies
- Adult learning principles
- Referral agencies and resources (Institute of Medicine, 1995)

It is important to understand provincial and federal government legislation, policies, and regulations related to environment and health. As noted before, many Canadians are surprised to find that uniform standards for water safety do not exist in this country, a fact that was highlighted in the light of the Walkerton *E. coli* illnesses and deaths. Knowledge of who should, and how to, advocate for safety standards and regulations is essential if change is to occur. (Note: The use of the strategies of letter writing, presenting resolutions, lobbying politicians and others in power, outlined in Chapter 1, can be used to address issues that have been analysed and clearly articulated.) See Box 22.3 for an example of a resolution presented to the International Council of Nurses by Canadian nurses.

It is also essential to recognise the ethical implications of actions undertaken by individuals, corporations, and governments that affect the environment and health. The enhancement of education on environmental health for nurses who compose the largest group of health professionals has the potential to affect significantly the health of individuals, families, and populations.

Education and Professional Development

Requests from the public for information on health concerns related to the environment are growing (Health Canada, 1998). Many sources recommend that all nurses require a basic knowledge of environmental health hazards, risks, prevention strategies, and health promotion (Bellack et al., 1996; Green, 2000; Institute of Medicine, 1995; McGuire & Eigsti-Gerber, 1999). To suggest simply that environmental health be added into the already full curricula of nursing programmes has the potential for failure before it is even considered. There must be an examination of how the content and skills required for practise could be integrated within various courses throughout undergraduate and graduate educational programmes as well as continuing education programmes for practising nurses.

However, adding into every health history the question, "Is there something in the environment that causes or exacerbates this condition?" would raise awareness of the impact of the environment both for nurses and patients. Continuing education pro-

BOX 22.3

Example of a Canadian Nurses Association Resolution On Chemicals, Pesticides, and Contaminants

Whereas, People the world over are increasingly concerned about threats to the environment and are demanding that these be addressed by their government;

Whereas, There is increasing evidence that the extensive use of chemicals and pesticides has a negative effect on our environment and our health;

Whereas, There is evidence that certain substances such as polychlorinated biphenyls (PCBs) are concentrated in mothers' milk, and that some chemicals and pesticides are chronic carcinogens;

Whereas, One hundred (100) nations committed to ratify the World Declaration on the Survival, Protection and Development of Children and the Plan of Action following the United Nations World Summit for Children (September 1990);

Whereas, The Plan of Action addressed the need to preserve and create healthy environments for children;

Whereas, Findings of research into the effects of chemicals and pesticides on immune system competence would give guidance regarding necessary actions to protect children from the effects of these substances;

Therefore be it

Resolved, That the International Council of Nurses and its member associations call on all governments to support research on the role of chemical contaminants in altering immune system competence; and epidemiological studies on mothers and children to determine the effects of present contaminant loads on children.

Accepted by the International Council of Nurses Council of National Representatives, Madrid, Spain, June 1993 (CNA/CMA, 1996 #22).

grammes could be developed on emerging concerns in environmental health, risk communication, and referral to resources and agencies. Some suggestions for incorporating environmental health information into a nursing curriculum are proposed in Table 22.1.

Research

Relatively little research with a nurse as the principal investigator or connected to a nursing organisation has been conducted on environmental health (Institute of Medicine, 1995). Because of the complexity of health and environmental concerns, interdisciplinary research that included professionals from a wide range of disciplines could prove to be the most effective method to examine environmental health-related issues. Research on which to base best-practise standards and educational programming is desperately needed. The development of nurse researchers interested in conducting studies with nurses and other practising professionals is of paramount importance. Primary to the conduct of research are the availability of and access to funding support for the conduct of this research. Of equal value is the dissemination of the results

Table 22.1. Integrating Environmental Health Issues Into Nursing Curricula

COURSE	COMPETENCY	TYPE OF CONTENT
Health assessment	Assessment and critical reflection	History taking; educating regarding risk
Introduction to nursing	Basic knowledge	Concepts relating environment and health
Medicine, pediatrics, maternal/child, family	Assessment and critical reflection	Relationship of environmental factors, such as water safety and air pollution, to health
Research	Basic knowledge; issues related to implementation of studies on the environment	Current research on nursing, health, and the environment
Issues and trends	Assessment; advocacy; team relationships	Policies, issues, and trends
Leadership	Advocacy; ethics; ability to initiate projects	Policies, procedures, legislation, roles of professional associations
Community	Working in multidisciplinary teams; advocacy; basic knowledge regarding population health risks; community development; empowerment of patients	Hazards; exposure pathways; prevention; program planning

of research to nurses, other professionals, government officials, and the public. Nurses are to be encouraged to publish and present in both professional and public arenas to achieve as broad a distribution as possible.

SUMMARY

Multiple environmental concerns, including water safety, air purity or pollution, chemical spills and spread, the growing contamination of inside environments, and violent surroundings are a serious concern across Canada, as is the relationship of the environment to the health of individuals, families, and populations whether in the home, community, or workplace. The information in this chapter represents a snippet of the volumes of literature available on the topic.

Individual nurses and the nursing profession can play a role in improving societal health through the traditional routes of nursing practise, education, and research. Examination of issues that arise within the topic of health and the environment is a complex process. Using a consistent process (such as the one presented in Box 22.4) is an effective method to examine critically the issues that arise. Questions that help clarify each stage of the analysis are included. See Chapter 1 for additional interpretation of the process.

BOX 22.4

Steps for Resolving Issues

Using a format that outlines the process in a stepwise fashion is a helpful strategy for resolving an issue. The example below addresses the effects of the environment on health.

Topic identification: Environment and health

Societal values: Greater concern if local? Less concern if more distant? Are there economic factors that will preclude resolution? What other points?

Nurses assumptions: What perspectives are important here?

Conceptualisation of the issue: What is the definition of the issue? An example of an issue related to the topic is that nurses continue to identify their lack of education and skills regarding the environment and health.

Significance of the issue: How important is the issue and to whom?

Analysis: What is the background? Who in society is affected? Who benefits by change in the issue? Who benefits by the situation staying the same? What are the politics that surround the issue? Who is involved? Are there ethical ramifications?

Strategies for resolution: What can be done? What will be most effective? Who will and should act on these strategies? What barriers will hamper resolution?

Online RESOURCES

Add to your knowledge of this issue:

Canadian Nurses Association	http://www.cna-nurses.ca
David Suzuki Foundation	http://www.davidsuzuki.org
Environment Canada	http://www.ec.gc.ca/
Environmental Protection Agency (U.S.)	http//www.epa.gov/
International Council of Nurses	http://www.icn.ch/
International Development Research Centre	http://www.idrc.ca/ecohealth/indicators
National Academy Press	http://nap.edu
National Center for Environmental Health	http://www.cdc.gov/ncehhom/htm
Physicians for Social Responsibility	http://www.psr.org
Toxnet	http://toxnet.nlm.nih.gov/
World Health	http://www.who/int/peh
Worldwatch Institute	http://worldwatch.org

Reflections on the Chapter

1. Cite specific examples from courses in your nursing program that link health and environmental conditions.
2. Name three health issues related to environmental factors that have been in the news recently in your local region and in your province/territory. Were nurses evident in the discussions?
3. What evidence is there that global climate change will affect the health of individuals and communities across the globe?
4. What legislation has your provincial/territorial government or the federal government passed in the last year regarding pollution/contamination in the environment?
5. What types of medical waste might have an impact on the environment? What is the potential for contamination or pollution to occur from medical waste? Where and how might this contamination or pollution happen?
6. What impact will the spread of diseases such as the West Nile virus have on health and environmental issues for Canadians? What implications does the increasing call for the control of pesticides have for the spread of disease?

REFERENCES

Ahluwalia, R. (2000, Posted May, 2000). Ontario's rural heartland in shock. *CBC TV News.*

Bellack, J. P., Musham, C., Hainer, A., Graber, D. R., & Holmes, D. (1996). Environmental health competencies: A survey of U.S. nurse practitioner programs. *Journal of Nursing Education, 35*(2), 74–81.

Berlinguer, G. (1999). Globalization and global health. *International Journal of Health Services, 29*(3), 579–595.

Brown, L., Flavin, C., French, H., Abramovitz, J., Dunn, S., Gardner, G., Mastny, L., Matoon, A., Roodman, D., Sampat, P., Sheehan, M., & Starke, L. (2001). *State of the world 2001.* New York: W.W. Norton & Company Ltd.

Canadian Nurses Association. (2000). *The environment is a determinant of health: Position statement* [Online]. Available: www.cna-nurses.ca, pp. 1-2). Ottawa, ON: Author.

Canadian Nurses Association/Canadian Medical Association. (1996). *Joint CNA/CMA position statement on environmentally responsible activity in the health sector.* (pp. 1–6). Ottawa, ON: Author.

Carruth, A. K., Gilbert, K., & Lewis, B. (1997). Environmental health hazards: The impact on a Southern community. *Public Health Nursing, 14*(5), 259–267.

Chaudhuri, N. (1998). Child health, poverty and the environment: The Canadian context. *Canadian Journal of Public Health, 89*(Suppl. 1), S26–S30.

Clark, M. J. (1999). *Nursing in the community: Dimensions of community health nursing* (3rd ed.). Stamford, CT: Appleton & Lange.

Cox, K. (2002, April 13). Teen gang demanded money, father says. *The Globe and Mail,* p. A9.

Environment Canada. (2000a). *Canada's clean air picture: Prairies and the North* [On-line]. Available: www.ec.gc.ca/air/pnr_e.htm.

Environment Canada. (2000b). *Clean air* [On-line]. Available: www.ec.gc.ca/air/menu_e.shtml.

Eigsti-Gerber, D., & McGuire, S. L. (1999). Teaching students about nursing and the environment. Part 1: Nursing role and basic curricula. *Journal of Community Health Nursing, 16*(2), 69–79.

Foley, D. (May 2001). *Fuelling the climate crisis: The continental energy plan.* Vancouver: David Suzuki Foundation.

Green, P. M. (2000). Taking environmental health education seriously. *Nursing and health care perspectives, 21*(5), 234–239.

Health Canada. (1997). *Health and environment: Partners for life* (Cat. H49-112-1/1997E). Minister of Public Works and Government Services Canada.

Health Canada. (1998). *The health and environment handbook for health professionals* (Cat. No. H46-2/98-211-2E). Minister of Public Works and Government Services Canada.

Health Canada. (1999a). *A second diagnostic on the health of First Nations and Inuit people in Canada* [On-line]. Available: http://www.hc-gc.ca/english/archives/releases/2000_20ebk2.htm.

Health Canada. (1999b). *Toward a healthy future: Second report on the health of Canadians* (Cat H39-468/1999E). Minister of Public Works and Government Services Canada.

Hilfinger Messias, D. K. (2001). Globalization, nursing, and health for all. *Journal of Nursing Scholarship, 33*(1), 8–11.

Institute of Medicine Committee on Enhancing Environmental Health Content in Nursing Practice.

(1995). *Nursing, health, & the environment.* Washington, DC: National Academy Press.

International Council of Nurses. (2000). *Poverty impacts on health: Nurses remind G8 leaders* (pp. 1–2) [On-line]. Geneva: Author. Available: www.icn.ch/pr13a_00.htm.

International Council of Nurses. (2001). *ICN on occupational stress and the threat to worker health* (pp. 1–6). Geneva: Author. Available: www.icn.ch/matters_stress.htm.

Last, J., Trouton, K., & Pengally, D. (1998). Taking our breath away: The health effects of air polution and climate change. Vancouver: David Suzuki Foundation. Available at www.davidsuzuki.org.

MacKinnon, M. (2001, July 18). Vital to improve water quality on reserves, group says. *The Globe and Mail,* p. A5.

Malcolm, J., Liu, C., Miller, L., Allnutt, T., & Hansen, L. (2002). *Habitats at risk: Global warming and species loss in globally significant terrestrial ecosystems.* Gland, Switzerland: World Wide Fund for Nature.

McDevitt, J., & Wilbur, J. (2002). Locating sources of data. In N. Ervin (Ed.), *Advanced community health nursing practice* (pp. 109–148). Upper Saddle River, NJ: Prentice Hall.

McGuire, S. L., & Eigsti-Gerber, D. (1999). Teaching students about nursing and the environment. Part 2: Legislation and resources. *Journal of Community Health Nursing, 16*(2), 81–94.

McMullan, C. (1997). *Indicators of urban ecosystem health* [On-line]. Available: http://idrc.ca/ecohealth/indicators_e.html. International Development Research Centre.

Mitchell, A. (2001, June 4, 2001). The world's `single biggest threat.' *The Globe and Mail.*

Nightingale, F. (1860). *Notes on nursing: What it is and what it is not.* (Reprinted London: J.B. Lippincott Company, date unknown.). New York: D. Appleton and Co.

Physicians for Social Responsibility. (1994). *Environmental pollutants & reproductive health: What primary care physicians should know* [On-line]. Available: http://www.psr.org.

Physicians for Social Responsibility. (1997). *Asthma and the role of air pollution: What the primary care physician should know* [On-line]. Available: http://www.psr.org.

Physicians for Social Responsibility. (2001a). *Arsenic: What health care providers should know* [On-line]. Available: http://www.psr.org.

Physicians for Social Responsibility. (2001b). *Cryptosporidium: What health care providers should know* [On-line]. Available: http://www.psr.org.

Pope, C. A., Burnett, R., Thun, M., Calle, E., Krewski, D., Ito, K., & Thurston, G. (2002). Lung cancer, cardiopulmonary mortality, and long-term exposure to fine particulate air pollution. *Journal of the American Medical Association, 287*(9), 1132–1141.

Robson, M., & Schneider, D. (2001). Environmental health issues in rural communities. *Environmental Health, 63*(10), 16–20.

United Nations Environment Programme (1999). *Global Environment Outlook GEO-2000* [On-line]. Available: http://www.unep.org.

Wanke, M. I., & Saunders, D. (1996). Survey of local environmental health programs in Alberta. *Canadian Journal of Public Health, 87*(5), 345–350.

World Health Organization. (2001). *The gateway to children's environmental health* [On-line]. Available: http://www.who.int/peh/CEH/index.htm.

23

When Difference Matters: The Politics of Privilege and Marginality

Christine Ceci

Chapter Objectives

At the completion of this chapter, you will be able to:

1. Discuss multiple interpretations of difference.

2. Discuss social, political, and historical influences on our understanding of difference.

3. Explore the concept of difference as a relationship.

4. Critique the concept of difference as deviance.

5. Identify assumptions underlying ideas of normality.

In what ways do differences matter and to whom? Whle these boys appear to be friends of the same age, they may come from different cultures, economic levels, and belief systems. Photography by Larry Arbour. Used with permission of the Faculty of Nursing, University of Calgary.

This is a chapter about difference, or more specifically, about the challenges and resistances we encounter, both from others and from within ourselves, when we try to move beyond the superficial and the obvious in our efforts to understand difference. The obvious approach calls on us to define differences, to list them, to create categories, to suppose that the significance of any particular difference is clear or uncontested. The obvious approach often assumes that the meaning of various "basic differences," reflected in categories such as sex, race, or class, is given to us; that trusting the evidence of our senses, we can read off the surface the difference of another. This is the kind of thinking we want to let go of in this chapter. That is, the thinking that says to us that difference is simply a characteristic, a trait or a description easily assigned to another whose difference is obvious to us.

This is not to say, however, that activities of defining or categorising are not sometimes useful but rather to suggest they almost always stop too soon. Though we often may need to begin by organising our observations, in themselves, definitions, categories, labels, and lists are inadequate for understanding difference. In fact, in this chapter, the tendency these activities express of locating difference outside of ourselves and the processes of our own understanding is conceptualised as a problem. Further, this is posed as a particular problem for nurses in part because of the privileged access we have to other lives. As nurses, we encounter people in their most vulnerable moments and so have opportunity to cause harm by unthinking adherence to the false and damaging beliefs and assumptions often contained in categories and labels. A willingness to question our own thinking, then, seems an obviously necessary task for nurses.

A PHILOSOPHICAL APPROACH TO UNDERSTANDING DIFFERENCE

Raising questions about the meanings of difference requires that we examine the various ways difference has been constructed in historical and contemporary situations. By reflecting on the examples explored in this chapter, we can ask who has defined difference in different situations and for what purposes have particular boundaries between groups been inscribed. On what basis are claims to difference made? How have the meanings of particular differences been contested? In what ways do differences matter and to whom? The historical examples allow us the distance to reflect on how particular ideas of difference have played themselves out but also, when considered alongside contemporary situations, enable us to trace similarities and extend our analyses from one context to another. For the same reason, that is, so that we may observe the similarity in processes of differentiation, a variety of what are commonly viewed as differences are explored. In each case, however, the difference discussed, for example, race or sex, is not understood as a thing in itself but rather as an outcome of social processes of differentiation. Difference, then, is understood in this chapter as a relational concept, whereby the meaning of any particular difference depends on relationship and context.

Admittedly, this is a more philosophical approach to difference than some readers may be expecting, but if we wish to understand the complexity of ideas of difference, we must be willing to raise questions of meaning, a project which requires from us a certain amount of thoughtfulness. As used here, thoughtfulness refers to a conscious and critical engagement with our current understandings of difference, an engagement that encourages us to question what we think we already know. This, then, is the purpose of this chapter: *to problematise difference.* We will proceed by exploring the discourses and ways of thinking that define difference and consider the social contexts and conditions through which differences come to matter.

HISTORICAL AND CONTEMPORARY CONSIDERATIONS

Accounting for difference among people, in situation and status, in privilege and power, has long been a preoccupation of Western societies. From at least as early as Plato's argument for the naturalness of unequal social status for men, women, and slaves, the purpose of these narratives has been, with few exceptions, to explain and justify the prevailing social order. Throughout Western history, dominant belief systems suggested that people were positioned in particular ways in society because of inborn differences in capacities and worth. These differences were often understood as determined by what were considered unalterable laws of nature. The differences in situation between men and women, rich and poor, races and cultures were all informed by ways of thinking that assumed the properness and inevitability of existing social roles and hierarchies. These ways of thinking, which interpreted selected anatomic, biologic, and phenotypic differences as signs of inherent worth, were typically generated by people who occupied positions of privilege in the same social order they sought to justify. For example, even as late as 1919, the American psychologist H. H. Goddard could publicly argue that "the people who are doing the drudgery are, as a rule, in their proper places" (cited in Gould, 1996, p. 191).

The Significance of Marginalised Perspectives

Understanding and explaining difference, and arguing the grounds upon which differences are seen to lie, continues to be a major concern in Western societies but with one significant change. Many of those theorising difference today have a stake in transforming rather than justifying existing social arrangements. For some, challenging what are considered inadequate interpretations of difference is related to awareness of the growing complexity of our societies, to increasing racial and ethnic diversity, and to the persistence of social inequities. In some respects, it is the presence of oppositional social movements—that is, groups organised around a shared commitment to eradicate social, political, and economic inequities—that has placed the need to rethink difference on the public agenda. Oppositional social movements question the validity of social norms and challenge ideas and practises viewed as contributing to the oppression, exclusion, and exploitation of marginalised groups. Marginalised groups—those that have been excluded from the social mainstream, including groups representing the interests of women, people of colour, people living with poverty, gays and lesbians, or people with disabilities—pose alternative explanations for their experience and position in the social world. In doing so, they challenge the seeming naturalness of existing social roles and arrangements.

The challenges these movements offer are practical and material, having to do with access to resources and opportunities. They are also philosophical, having to do with how we perceive and interpret our worlds. That is to say, part of the challenge of oppositional social movements is the challenge they present to our commonsense understandings of society. For example, a challenge people living with poverty may pose to members of dominant groups is whether, in doing the "drudgery," they are in fact in their proper places or whether larger social and economic processes limit their opportunities. To understand this situation adequately, we need to ask who is doing what jobs in society. Are some groups disproportionately responsible for the dull, menial, and fatiguing work? How do we explain this? Similarly, some women have argued that it is not a law of nature that they be primarily responsible for the care of children and have instead raised questions about how the caring work of society is allocated and rewarded.

When given voice, members of marginalised groups point out the inaccurate and limited nature of many dominant social narratives, those common, familiar stories we draw on almost unthinkingly to understand our world. For example, there are dominant social narratives which explain the presence of poverty in our society. Chief among these are those that suggest that poor people are responsible for their poverty by virtue of their own inadequacies—this is the "flawed character" view of poverty (Banyard & Graham-Bermann, 1995). This explanation of poverty is partial and inadequate because it locates the "problem" of poverty inside the person and obscures the social, political, and economic arrangements which create and sustain poverty.

Marginalised groups also question the ability of those in positions of privilege to know or understand the experience of less powerful groups. By contesting the adequacy of dominant perspectives and hence their reasonableness as the justification for existing social relations, and by offering alternative perspectives, marginalised groups challenge the authority of those in positions of privilege to speak for, or represent the interests of, all of society. Developing more inclusive interpretations of society and more just practises involves taking these concerns of marginalised people seriously. It also involves recognising that the experiences of many members of society are ignored or distorted by dominant social narratives. Although these narratives are commonly held to explain or describe all of reality, they more often depict only the experiences or situation of a particular social group.

The Insufficiency of Dominant Perspectives: False Universals

History holds many examples of these ostensibly universal discourses revealed instead to refer only to the experience of particular dominant groups. For example, understanding "man" as equivalent to "human" has, in many cases, been demonstrated to be a false universal. The falseness becomes apparent when excluded groups claim the benefits of these discourses or positions for themselves, but because they are not members of dominant groups, their claims are disallowed or unacknowledged.

In 1929, to cite a well-known example from Canadian history, a particular group of Canadian women demanded to be considered persons under the law. They argued that, in practise, the apparently inclusive and gender-neutral legal concept "person" excluded women. Their argument demonstrated that their female bodies were, in this case, a difference from a male standard that mattered in terms of their rights and privileges in society. Yet many of those who successfully argued that this gender difference should not matter, and who advocated for the legal personhood of Canadian white women, did not similarly champion the legal rights of, for example, aboriginal women. In this case, "gender" for aboriginal women was inflected by race in a way that mattered for the status of First Nations women, whose right even to vote was not achieved until many decades after other Canadian women.

Similarly, in the late 19th century when American white women organised to gain the right to vote, their failure to include women of colour provoked ex-slave Sojourner Truth to ask, "Ain't I a woman?" Though she was, of course, biologically female, the dominant social ideology concerning women merged the term "woman" with particular and culturally specific ideals of femininity. "Real" women were gentle, passive, physically frail, in need of male protection, and white. "Real" women did not work the fields, never "plowed and planted, and gathered into barns" (Truth, 1851 cited in Trinh, 1989, p. 100). Truth's words challenged the then dominant conceptualisation of woman because an affirmative answer to her challenge would have required a rethinking of what being a woman, in that time and place, meant. Her black body and her experiences as a black woman were differences that mattered in terms of *her* rights and privileges in society.

These two examples from "women's" history demonstrate how a supposedly neutral and inclusive category such as "woman" often disregards the experience of entire groups of women who do not fit the tacit conceptualisation on which it is based. These examples also suggest that practises of exclusion have adverse consequences for the status of those excluded.

Nursing and Exclusionary Practises

Organised nursing in Canada, particularly through the early 20th century, was not immune from this kind of exclusionary practise. In their efforts to elevate the status of nursing, the nursing profession and health care administrators promoted nursing as a bastion of feminine respectability. They defined nursing according to a particular paradigm of appropriate femininity that drew on racist and classist stereotypes to exclude certain women from education and employment. Canadian historian of nursing Kathryn McPherson (1996) writes, "Because nursing relied on an image of feminine respectability to legitimate nurses' presence in the health care system and their knowledge of the body, respectability was constructed in a racial and national context" (p. 17). She also claims, based on the evidence of historical records, that "nurses' respectability and definition of gentility were European in origin. White, native-born Canadian women were expected to bring their superior sense of sexual and social behaviour to the bedside" (McPherson, 1996, p. 17). Though some women of colour and immigrant women were able to obtain nursing training, they were expected to provide service only to their "own" communities. "In the eyes of hospital administrators and nursing leaders, Canadian women of non-European heritage could not be relied on to reflect the morality of health at the bedside" (McPherson, 1996, p. 17). And in fact, until after the Second World War, "administrators remained convinced that the very presence of non-White attendants might exacerbate the health problems of White patients" (McPherson, 1996, p. 17). As McPherson argues, these kinds of beliefs suggest that nursing's exclusivity was "not merely the innocent by-product of objective standards" (1996, p. 17).

As a result, nursing in Canada was "the preserve of white and Canadian-born women" (McPherson, 1996, p. 17) for most of the 20th century. Even though nursing shortages since World War II have necessitated an opening of occupational boundaries, issues of racism and workplace discrimination persist in nursing. In 1992, for example, a group of African Canadian nurses successfully argued in front of the Ontario Human Rights Commission that they experienced racial discrimination and harassment in their workplace (McPherson, 1996). This suggests that, although the face of nursing has changed significantly in recent decades, nursing is also a product of a society in which whiteness is systematically privileged (Dyer, 1997). Having a body, a particular and specific body which is not only sexed but always simultaneously raced and classed, is almost always a difference that matters. The meanings and implications of these differences and others are considered in this chapter.

THE CHALLENGE OF DIFFERENCE

Part of the challenge that difference offers us is that our knowledge of the world is always limited by our positioning within it. This means that where and how we are located in the social world influences our experiences, our ways of thinking, and the discourses available to us to shape and express our understanding. Discourses consist of beliefs, assumptions, and statements that, though rarely conscious, form our possibilities for knowledge. A discourse of nursing, for example, includes the ways we speak of nursing as well as the ideas, rituals, practises, and social power relations that make nursing a recognisable entity. However, at any point in time, nursing is intersected and influenced by many, sometimes competing, discourses. For example, there are discourses that define nursing as caring, as vocation, or as skilled women's work and others that emphasise the instrumentality or technical nature of nursing work.

To add to this complexity, our positioning in the world is often ambiguous, characterised by multiplicity rather than singularity. For example, a particular woman's understanding of what it means to be a woman is determined not only by her gendered difference from men but also by the many facets of her difference from other women. The meaning of being a woman will always be coloured by the things a woman is and does, whether she is poor or a mother, a refugee, or a lesbian or whether she works as a nurse, an engineer, or a prostitute or receives social assistance. All of the features of her life texture what being a woman means, just as being a woman changes the meaning of all else that she is and does. What is significant here are the ways in which our circumstances and situations affect the nature of our experiences, what we take as fact, what we consider to be normal or natural, and the ways this changes over time and across society (Ceci, 2000).

The Canadian population is stratified by many relations of difference, and encountering difference is part of everyday life. But not all differences matter in the same way. Rather, it is our interpretations of difference—not specific differences in themselves—that influence whether and how they will matter. That our perspectives are limited and partial is not a problem, particularly not one that we can overcome. Limitedness is accepted simply as the character of our situation. However, in light of the limitedness of our perspectives, how do we proceed in a world with other people in it? To respond to this question, we can explore various interpretations of difference and hope to develop new understandings of what difference means in our lives and in our practises. Though difference as an issue is not resolvable, we can explore what it means to name difference. We can consider what it means to practise nursing with respect for difference. Our concern here is with both the meanings attributed to difference and the implications of these meanings in people's lives.

THEORISING DIFFERENCE

We begin with two related questions. First, what does the term *difference* mean? And second, what does it mean to theorise difference? A *difference*, to our commonsense at least, *is that which distinguishes one thing from another*. Though this seems a fairly straightforward definition, it does not tell us whether difference is a feature of the thing itself or if distinguishing difference is a function of our habits of perception. That is, do we assign difference because something *is* different or because we are accustomed to perceiving it *as* different? Is it even possible to discriminate between these two activities? This is where theorising enters the picture. Theories shape our seeing and our possibilities for interpretation. They "provide us with a way of ordering, understanding and capturing aspects of reality" (Cheek & Purkis, 1997, p. 160). Though theories can guide us in picking out features of the world which we then treat as significant, they can also blind us to other, equally important aspects of reality.

Theories organise the way in which a phenomenon such as difference will be perceived and represented (Cheek & Purkis, 1997). Described in these terms, theory is not just something located in books or classrooms; rather, all of our seeing and understanding should be thought of as theoretical. That is, our interactions with reality should be understood as informed beforehand by our beliefs, assumptions, and expectations. Like scientists, researchers, and others who consciously use theory, we too are guided in our lives, in our practises, "by a certain conception of the way things are," (Caputo, 1987, p. 215), by theories. For example, emphasising the primacy of race in social classifications systems can be understood not simply as a reflection of a reality that contains people who have skin of various hues but as a testament to theories which say this must be important. Or, as Ahmed (1998) writes, "bodies are never simply bodies: they are always inscribed within a system of value differentiation" (p. 27), a system which asserts which features of the body, which of its diverse aspects are worth paying attention to.

The Influence of Theories on Perception: Race as a Category

A good example of how particular theories influence our perceptions of the world is found in theories that suggest that racial differences are important units of analysis. Those who hold these views, consciously or unconsciously, will assume that just knowing a person's race can tell us important things about them. Race becomes a category that is "internalized into ways we think about other people . . . and ourselves" (Allen, 1996, p. 99), and stressing its significance leads us to perceive people initially and sometimes chiefly in terms of skin colour and phenotype. Race, understood as visible difference, becomes one of the first things we see and interpret as meaningful when we look at a person. But is race, aside from the meanings we attribute to it, an important difference? And how do we know this? And then, how do we incorporate into our analysis the contemporary scientific evidence that demonstrates that race, as a meaningful biologic category, is not real (Alcoff, 1999)?

In societies that continue to categorise, classify, and rank people according to a conception of race that suggests innate, immutable differences among groups, how do we account for the fact that the "overall genetic differences among human races is astonishingly small" (Gould, 1996, p. 353)? How do we account for the fact that there are no such things as "race genes" or genes that are present in certain races but lacking in all others? Does knowing of this "remarkable lack of genetic differentiation among human groups" (Gould, 1996, p. 352) alter our understanding of what we have become accustomed to perceive as intrinsically and biologically distinct groups?

These are important questions because they ask us to reconsider our common-sense belief that race constitutes an obvious and important biologic difference among people. One would expect that these questions would direct us to seek other explanations, other than the biologic that is, for the tenacity of racial categorisation and ranking in our societies. Yet despite significant efforts in this direction, "scientific" research seeking to establish innate difference among groups continues unabated (Brah, 1996).

THE CLASSIFICATION OF BODIES IN HISTORY

A useful location from which to begin to rethink race and racial classification systems is history. Here we can see that race has not always been understood as especially relevant, even though in Western societies, skin colour and phenotype are currently considered important signifiers of difference (Weedon, 1999). Rather than disclosing fixed and stable natural categories, the salience of race as a significant social difference has changed over time. And because it has a history, we can see how human beings have made it. Specifically, its history reflects the development of the natural sciences in the 18th and 19th centuries. Racial categories were constructed by biologists and anthropologists as part of a project to order and classify the entire natural world (Alcoff, 1999; Gould, 1996; Weedon, 1999).

In addition, early scientists did not simply describe the realities they observed but rather interpreted difference in light of their preexisting values, beliefs, and judgements. That is, they ranked perceived differences in body type and appearance according to preconceived notions of character and worth. "The meanings attributed to nineteenth-century racial categories included value judgements about beauty, intellect, morality, emotionality, sexuality and other physical capacities" (Weedon, 1999, p. 153). These judgements, which always assumed the inherent superiority of the white races, came in handy because they "justified colonialism, the slavery of Africans, and the appropriation of African, Asian, and American land and human resources by whites" (Essed, 1996, p. 7). These practises came to be seen as the natural outcome of inborn inequalities between the "races."

In addition to interpretations of the meaning of skin colour, 18th-, 19th-, and 20th-century scientists theorised links between particular physical features and what were believed to be inborn characteristics, such as intelligence or criminality. High foreheads, low brows, small heads, large jaws, big arms, as well as skin colour were all interpreted as direct and uncomplicated reflections of character and capacity. Yet there are literally thousands of ways to measure the human body, and any investigator convinced beforehand by a theory, such as the hierarchic ordering of races, could easily choose the measurements, inadvertently or not, which would subsequently prove his* theory true (Gould, 1996). These theories of the meanings of racial difference, which can be grouped under the general heading of biologic determinism or sociobiology, take bodies as "their referent and guarantee," and view bodies as the definitive and transparent source of differences among groups (Weedon, 1999, p. 13). Classifying people according to visible difference is a process which "seeks to systematize differences and to relate them to differences of character and worth" (Dyer, 1997, p. 20).

A CONTINUING PRACTISE

Though one might expect this kind of thinking to have disappeared by now, in some ways, it has simply become more sophisticated. As outmoded and offensive as these views are, recent publications, such as Herrnstein and Murray's (1994) *The Bell Curve: The Reshaping of American Life by Difference in Intelligence* and Rushton's (1995)

---

*Scientists in this time and place were almost exclusively male.

Race, Evolution and Behaviour, suggest that no matter how often these concepts are exposed as vacuous by reputable thinkers, there will be someone—charlatan, fraud, or disingenuous scientist, politician, or social commentator—who is convinced that race and other physical features are important explanations and guarantees of social difference.

The Significance of Theorising Difference

Recognising that our understanding is theoretical, and therefore that our interpretations of difference are informed beforehand by theory, is important for at least three reasons. First, this allows us to appreciate that certain features of the world, particularly those we tend to take for granted as naturally occurring, are in reality shaped by our preexisting theoretical commitments and assumptions, commitments and assumptions we have simply by virtue of being born into a culture. For example, we may assume that race is an important biologically based difference among groups not only because of the "evidence" of our senses but also because our cultural and social experience supports this theory. It is, at some level, obvious to us.

Second, awareness of what we take for granted allows us to attempt to make the beliefs and assumptions that inform our theoretical views explicit rather than implicit. The theoretical perspective informing our assumption about the significance of racial categories is often called *biologic determinism*. This theory supports several propositions, including that of H. H. Goddard: "the people who are doing the drudgery are, as a rule, in their proper places" (cited in Gould, 1996, p. 191). People are believed to be located where they are in the social world essentially for biologic reasons.

Third, consciousness of the specific ways of thinking which influence our understanding allows us to consider the reasons we might choose to hold one theoretical position rather than another. We might ask: What are the views of the people doing the drudgery concerning their proper place? Are their views even available to us? Why might people in positions of privilege hold their views? In what ways do social arrangements, the allocation of privileges and resources, work to justify a particular social order and the ways of thinking which support it? If race is not an important biologically based category, what kind of category is it? Social? Political? What purpose does it serve?

DIFFERENCE AS DEVIANCE:
A CASE OF BIOLOGIC DETERMINISM IN PRACTISE

Different theories—meaning different ways of ordering and interpreting the world—are more than just words. Theories have tangible effects in the world because of the ways in which they shape institutions and practises. That is, the way something is understood, including the *kind* of problem it is seen to be, has implications for how we think it should be addressed. By focussing in some detail on a particular episode in Canadian history—the pre- and post–World War II preoccupation with the discourses and practises of social hygiene and eugenics—it is hoped that we can achieve some insight into how this happens. We can then take our understanding of this situation and use it to create new understandings of how issues of difference are theorised in our current contexts.

Part of the usefulness of knowing our own history lies in the ways it can help us to understand how others have attempted to respond to complicated issues, and perhaps even to locate the origins of our own ways of thinking. If we can do this, we can begin to recognise our beliefs as a particular way of thinking rather than the truth, and reflect on how ideas we may hold have played themselves out in other times and places. Understanding how and why particular ideas may resonate for us or seem so obviously true offers us the opportunity either to take these ideas up more consciously and deliberately or to develop alternative points of view.

Eugenics and Social Hygiene in Canadian History

Eugenic discourses advocating the necessity of intervening in the course of human reproduction flourished openly in many Western countries for the first half of the 20th century fueled by the fears and uncertainties of a rapidly changing world and "consuming concern about the health and welfare of the race" (Dowbiggin, 1997, p. 165). In Canada, the social problems and public health challenges associated with increased immigration and urbanisation led many prominent political figures and public health advocates, respected physicians, and psychiatrists to preach a gospel of social hygiene and racial purity rooted in the widespread fear that "traditional Canadian ideals, values and attitudes . . . were disappearing" (Dowbiggin, 1997, p. 134). Erroneously claiming that science could correct the hereditary "deficiencies" believed to cause poverty, crime, and vice, many influential public figures across the country advocated sterilisation, segregation, and eugenic immigration restrictions as essential strategies for both public health and social reform (Dowbiggin, 1997). Swept up in the limitless possibilities for advancement that science seemed to offer, and by the expanding authority of medical and scientific discourses to pronounce on all areas of human life, claims that these measures would improve public health were claims that almost no one doubted (Paul, 1998). Faith in science, in its neutrality and objectivity, convinced many proponents that their positions were purely objective, inevitable, and rational responses to the "facts" of scientific knowledge. Such certainty did more than merely mask the cultural values latent in eugenic discourses, it made dissent seem both irrational and irresponsible.

As a pseudoscientific theorising of difference, eugenic thinking was and is an argument for the biologic innateness of particular defining traits, most notably a belief in the hereditary determination of intelligence and character. Thriving particularly during the economically troubled 1930s, eugenic discourses explained social problems in terms of individual inadequacies, inadequacies defined in terms of, and relying for meaning on, preexisting social structural relations of class, gender, and race (Valverde, 1991). The physically and mentally subnormal, the different, the deviant, the feeble-minded, the unfit, the defective were categories encompassing those with actual physical and mental illness as well as children who merely performed poorly on standardised tests, unmarried mothers, labour activists, aboriginal people, immigrants of colour, and other nonwhites. These groups were assigned the blame for many social problems and were viewed as posing a threat to the smooth functioning of society through their supposedly inborn propensity for violence, crime, and aberrant sexual behaviour. So widespread was this way of thinking that even labour unrest was understood by some not as the product of problematic social arrangements but as the result of defective brains (Dowbiggin, 1997).

During these years, it was clear to many influential Canadians that if a particular class of human life was to be preserved and enhanced, then preventive measures to control and contain those who threatened the existing social order, both through their dangerous behaviours and the economic burden their care represented, must be undertaken. This, a social argument, attained greater legitimacy and authority when it was rendered in scientific terms, terms which transformed complex social problems into mere matters of health and disease inviting medical intervention.

Although eugenic thinking could be found everywhere in Canada, only 2 of 10 Canadian provinces enacted sterilisation acts—Alberta in 1928 and British Columbia in 1933. Other provinces debated these issues but chose not to create legislation, which is not to say that involuntary sterilisation procedures were not performed across Canada without benefit of a law (McLaren, 1990). Eugenic policies, often framed in the language of social hygiene or cleanliness, were directed towards creating stronger, healthier societies through weeding out those deemed unfit in the dominant discourses of the day (Pernick, 1997). Across Canada there was a general consensus, among dominant groups at least, that controlling the reproduction of some groups, segregating those deemed defective, and restricting immigration on eugenic grounds were warranted public health measures.

Yet it is clear that the problems that eugenic policies were meant to address were very much problems of difference. As Canadian society was becoming more and more obviously heterogeneous, the fear that Canadian values and ideals were being lost was prevalent among more established groups. Eugenic policies were articulated from this centre, that is, by members of dominant groups, and had their greatest effects on society's weakest or most marginalised members. Differences that mattered were clearly framed by categories of class, race, and gender.

For example, in the case of eugenic sterilisations, the supposedly scientific and rational decisions made by eugenic boards clearly revealed the decided influence of social criteria of normality and value (Dowbiggin, 1997; McLaren, 1990; Paul, 1998; Pernick; 1997). Those sterilised tended to be female, young and inexperienced, poor, rural, a member of a racial or ethnic minority group, and unmarried. In other words, those referred for sterilisation procedures were rarely members of the dominant group; rather, as Pernick (1997) observed, "race, class, ethnic, religious and sexual prejudices determined who was defined as unfit" (p. 1770).

Difference as Deviance: Assumptions of Normality

As noted previously, eugenic discourses explained social problems in terms of individual inadequacies, inadequacies that were thought to be reflected in and confirm one's proper position in society. These arguments typically focussed on individual deviance from a supposed norm and gained legitimacy when they were communicated in scientific and medical terms that diagnosed those outside the dominant social order as diseased. Thus, complex social problems were transformed into matters of health and illness.

Yet, even though it is common to treat concepts of health and illness as matters of fact (Caplan et al., 1981), ideas of both health and illness are only meaningful in relation to some prior conception about what is normal (Susser, 1981). And normal itself is not a neutral term with clear and self-evident meaning; rather, ideas of normality are constructed within particular sociohistorical contexts and always contain an evaluative element concerning what is understood to be usual, acceptable, and valued.

Concepts of normality require value judgements to be made, and their use implies the presence of a regulative structure which produces both the normal and the not normal. Because ideas of normality are most often produced and employed by those in positions of social dominance, the experience and values of dominant groups tend to represent that which is then thought to be normal for everyone. For example, many school-aged children were labeled feeble minded or subnormal in the early decades of the 20th century after failing to pass standardised intelligence tests. These tests contained what we now recognise as "arbitrary norms of intellectual achievement" (McLaren, 1990, p. 38). Rather than providing objective, scientific measures of intelligence as it was then believed, these tests reflected the experiences and values of the dominant group who produced them. Children who were not members of this group were less likely to perform well. In some instances, then, what is conceived of as deviance from normality might be more usefully and accurately understood as a distant or marginal relation to a powerful centre. This was certainly the experience of many Canadians labeled different or deviant during the years when eugenic policies and practises were prevalent.

Eugenic Practises and Public Health: Nursing Roles

In considering the role of nursing in the implementation of eugenic practises and policies, it is important to recognise that there were links between eugenic discourses and public health goals, beliefs, and values, what has been called "the convergence between genes and germs" (Pernick, 1997, p. 1769). With very little tolerance for difference, the supposedly defective, unfit, and subnormal were constructed in dominant discourses as deviant and diseased. And because public health nurses were concerned with protecting the health of society in general from any number of sources of disease, their goals were apparently congruent with those of the eugenicists whose interpretations of health and illness dominated public discussions.

Segregation, institutionalisation, and restrictive immigration were all conceptualised as necessary social and mental hygiene measures intended to stop the spread of an unseen contagion, and to sterilise meant, in eugenics as in bacteriology, "to eliminate agents that cause disease" (Pernick, p. 1769). Thus, in some ways, nurses' actions in implementing these policies and practises, actions which included assessing children in homes and schools, identifying candidates for sterilisation, making referrals to eugenics boards, providing operating room assistance, and assisting in the "Canadianising" of new immigrants (Mansell & Hibberd, 1998), were simply extensions of the nursing role to care for the health and welfare of the population, at least as that task was then defined.

NURSING PRACTISE AND DOMINANT THINKING

This last point, however, is where difficulties for nurses may arise. Nursing and nurses are constituted within the dominant society and within the possibilities and constraints of particular sociohistorical contexts. The conduct of nurses, in this time and place, should be understood in relation to the lesser status of women in society, the subordination of nurses in the health care hierarchy, the rewards nurses received for compliance, as well as the absence of an alternative discourse or way of thinking about difference. Nurses consented to what was dominant in medical and societal thinking, to a particular understanding of difference influenced by the tenets of biologic determinism, a theory that we now clearly understand as informed by false beliefs and assumptions and as having caused significant harm to vulnerable people. This consent was not particular to nurses but rather a reflection of prevailing attitudes and beliefs or, as Mansell and Hibberd (1998) have written, "nurses handled, managed, and controlled individuals in order to maintain a society that adhered to the wishes of the dominant group, of which they were part" (p. 9).

Significance for Contemporary Nursing

The purpose here, however, is not to suggest that nurses were right or wrong in terms of their participation but rather to consider the implications for ourselves, as nurses, of the possibility that we also may become the means through which social and moral harms are perpetrated. Nurses must consider these issues simply because nurses are often in the position of implementing policies not necessarily of their own making, of supporting and sustaining particular social and political arrangements of health care. It is a dilemma for nursing that although much of our work, particularly in the area of public health, involves the care of socially, economically, and politically marginalised or disadvantaged people, the dominant voices in defining health and health care policies rarely come from these groups. Thus, in their roles as "conduits into the lives and social spaces of groups otherwise beyond the reach of social agents of authority" (Rafferty et al., 1997, p. 3), nurses may have a special responsibility to be attuned to the differences of marginalised perspectives.

DIFFERENCE AS RELATIONSHIP

The meanings given to difference, whether that difference is named in terms of gender, race, class, intellectual ability, or sexual orientation, assume immediate significance for people because these meanings are used to circumscribe and explain experience, to influence both the lived meanings and material realities of a life. The meanings given to femaleness, for example, have been important to women "because they were used to determine and limit the social and economic spheres to which women had access" (Weedon, 1999, p. 10). Consider these words of the late 19th-century founder of social psychology, Gustave Le Bon: "All psychologists who have studied the intelligence of women, as well as poets and novelists, recognise that they represent the most inferior form of human evolution and that they are closer to children and savages than an adult, civilized man" (Le Bon, 1879, cited in Gould, 1996, p. 137). Le Bon goes on to describe women, who with the rare exception he suggests may be ignored as being "as exceptional as the birth of any monstrosity," as typically and naturally illogical, irrational, childish, capricious, and unreliable. Given that this is, in Le Bon's view, the nature or essence of woman's being, education for women, as well as any role for women outside the home, was seen not only as a wasteful indulgence but also as against nature and therefore dangerously aberrant.

As ludicrous as this now sounds, the importance for women lies not only in the aspersions cast on their character and capacities, though these are not insignificant, but also in the ways in which these types of views have limited and constrained women's access to resources and opportunities for so many years. Women, in all their various social locations, have learned "who [they] are and how to think and behave through discursive practices" (Weedon, 1999, p. 104). As these social and political practises of thinking and theorising have become entrenched through institutions such as psychology (medicine, religion, philosophy, and law), the difference of being a woman has come to matter in ways that have had and *still* have real material consequences for women. The meanings attributed to sex differences have justified the social, political, and economic inequality of women. These kinds of practise have had similar consequences in the lives of others who are marginalised and diminished on the grounds of their difference from a dominant group.

The difference of women, which is clearly meant to be understood as the difference between men and women, and most probably the difference between men and women of a particular race and class, is articulated by Le Bon as naturally occurring inferiority and lack. This is clearly not a neutral difference, for example, one which would mean simply not the same. Rather, difference is organised in terms of a relationship in which one side is understood as being or setting the standard the other fails to achieve, a process still quite common in Western thinking.

Dualism and Difference

Western societies have tended to arrange many important features of the world into oppositional and exclusive dualities, necessary hierarchies whose meaning both reflects and sustains clear and pervasive differences in social power and status. Male/female, white/black, rich/poor, straight/gay are examples of dualisms which organise difference in crude, yet highly effective, structures in which one side of the duality is clearly meant to be understood as superior to the other. The other in each case is named and defined in relation to the dominant group, whose power in some respects resides in the very capacity to create the kind of relationship which establishes "us here and them over there" (Trinh, 1990, p. 371), to name and to define those not themselves as "other." In the case of Le Bon described previously, the claim is made that *us here men* are plainly the natural social masters of *them there women*—a crude but unquestionably effective process of differentiation and social categorisation.

LIMITATIONS OF DUALIST THINKING

In dualistic thinking, difference is organised into simplistic, oppositional, and exclusive categories. This occurs despite the limited explanatory power such frameworks for understanding hold. As well as reducing our understanding of men and women, for example, to terms of difference and suggesting that women and men should only be understood in opposition to one another, dualistic thinking tends to erase differences among women and suggests that women should be understood only in terms of sameness—both clearly inadequate proposals. Strictly dualistic conceptualisations of difference limit our understanding of the multiple and shifting ways we are positioned in relation to others. A white middle-class or affluent woman may find herself and her opportunities limited in relation to the men in her life, but she may exercise power in her relation to other, less advantageously positioned men and women. Sometimes, the difference of gender may be in the foreground; at other times, race, class, and sexual orientation may be the differences that matter—sometimes singly, sometimes all at once.

Difference as a Relation Between Margin and Centre

It is important to recognise that when we are perceiving difference, a relationship of some sort or another is being inferred, although the fact of relationship is often assumed rather than plainly stipulated. That is to say, there is a norm or a standard to which we refer, consciously or unconsciously, implicitly or explicitly, when we identify someone or something as different. The identification and production of difference, then, is bound up with assumptions concerning the socially, culturally, and politically relevant features of persons, which in Western societies have generally corresponded to the ways in which we are categorised according to gender, race, sexual orientation, and class. These differences mark people *as* different in relation to a dominant and presumably unmarked group, a group which in Western societies has tended to be composed of white, propertied, able-bodied, heterosexual males.

In this way, our identification of difference can be understood as the recognition of a particular relation between margin and centre, between dominant and subordinate groups, with the differences that matter most arising in the context of relations of power. Relations of power are intrinsic to all social relations, but of particular concern are those that establish access to such things as resources, opportunities, and knowledge: "power takes many forms, affecting access to material resources as well as questions of language, culture and the right to define who one is" (Weedon, 1999, p. 5).

Thus, besides trying to understand the processes through which difference is produced, understanding who defines whom *as* different is also always of significance. These relations of difference attain their significance for us when they result in structures of inequality or patterns of disadvantage: "Differences between individuals and groups—between sexes, classes, races, ethnic groups, religions and nations—become important political issues when they involve relations of power" (Weedon, 1999, p. 5).

Processes of Differentiation

Difference is produced through social processes of categorisation. Some feature of a person is selected as significant and defined against a backdrop of dominant assumptions, beliefs, and values and in relation to that which is believed to be usual or traditional, normal, or natural. These activities of selection and interpretation, however, cannot be thought of as politically neutral: "Both the construction of commonality among subjects and the assertion of difference between subjects are rhetorical and political acts, gestures of affiliation and disaffiliation that emphasizes [sic] some properties and obscures others" (Felski, 1997, p. 17). For example, designating income level as a person's most significant characteristic brings to the fore a single aspect of a person's identity while rendering invisible much else that the person is and does. Income level stands in for a more particularised explanation of life and circumstances and allows people living with poverty, for example, to appear as an undifferentiated mass. Conceptualising difference as a relation rather than a thing in itself, and instead of a feature of persons which exists independently of our theorising about it, encourages us to inquire into the social relations through which differences that matter are produced.

For nurses, coming to understand the ways in which marginalised populations are related to the dominant social centre means theorising how apparently neutral differences are the result of structures of inequality or patterns of disadvantage affecting particular groups in particular ways. The prevalence of poverty among women provides a good example because women's poverty is both disproportionate and relatively intransigent. Women as a group are more likely than men as a group to live in poverty, and even though women have made gains in many areas of life, this situation has remained relatively unchanged. In 1997 in Canada, for example, 2.8 million women, or 19% of the total female population, were living in low-income situations (Statistics Canada, 2000). Although improved access to education, increased participation in the labour force, smaller family sizes, and changes in the structure of family living have improved the lives of many women, women in all age categories and family types are still much more likely to be poor than are men.

Single mothers and elderly women continue to be those with the greatest likelihood of living in poverty, and there is an especially high incidence of poverty among women of colour, immigrant women, First Nations women, and women with disabilities. Each of these groups, in addition to being female, departs in some way from a dominant societal norm circumscribed by a white, middle-class, male, heterosexual, youth-oriented, able-bodied perspective. Not only is the other defined and named in relation to this dominant group, but also relations of power and privilege are structured or shaped by this relationship.

For both women as a group and women with particular differences, distance from this centre can be seen as having the power to shape both social relations and individual experience. Poverty, given this situation, could be theorised as being neither inherent nor accidental but rather as centrally about power, and society's economic organisation could be one way in which relations of power are enacted in many women's lives, determining their success in obtaining both material and social resources. This type of thinking would stand in opposition to views which suggest that women are disproportionately poor because they are flawed in some way. Being female in our society is clearly a difference that matters, a difference from a male norm, a difference whose consequence may be read in the likelihood of living in poverty.

Differences and Relations of Power

The social relations which work to construct the lived meanings, as well as the material realities of differences, such as gender, race, sexual orientation, and class, can also be understood as relations of power. In fact, to raise the question of difference in the context of social relationships requires that we recognise that our interpretations of difference are always and in every case the "effects of many types of power relations" (Weedon, 1999, p. vii).

Attending to power means understanding that activities of labeling, defining, and categorising are power moves and often result in some members of society being subjected to and by the power of others: "those who claim a dominant position can presume the right to determine which aspects of identities are core, and by which aspect others will be known" (Kaplan, 1997, p. 34). The power exercised by dominant groups to name the differences that matter includes the capacity also to determine the kind of difference something is understood to be. That is, is a particular named difference cultural, political, natural, or biologic? Is it normal or pathologic? Acceptable or perverse? Power is what makes differences matter—the power to impose definitions, to determine meanings, to shape reality.

For example, in a context in which heterosexuality is assumed dominant and is believed to be "normal," sexuality for gay men and lesbians, whether they wish it to or not, may become their significant defining feature, the aspect by which they will be known. To say of someone that "she is lesbian" has a different meaning and effect than to say "she is heterosexual" because, in our society at least, heterosexuality is assumed; it is not to be different at all. In naming a woman lesbian (which must be understood as different than naming oneself), a particular difference is called into being, a difference which matters in part because of its relation to a dominant centre and to ideas of normality. In addition, a different kind of knowledge of the person is assumed, a knowledge which seems to be saying that the most important thing about this woman is her sexuality, and it is important not because of the meanings it holds for her but because it differs from a supposed norm. For those who are marginalised in relation to a dominant centre, the consequences of being categorised in this way can be quite serious and range from having reduced access to resources and opportunities to the failure to have one's understanding or interpretation of one's own experience matter. A peculiar silencing occurs when what becomes most important about a person is how they are defined by others, by their perceived relation to the dominant group, to a supposed norm or centre.

THE DISTINCT REALITIES OF OTHERS

It has become a cliché to suggest that, as a society, we must learn to live with difference. This can mean anything from halfheartedly agreeing to merely tolerating difference to the desire to embrace and celebrate diversity among people. Where we locate ourselves in this situation will depend, to some extent at least, on how we have chosen to interpret difference.

In the case of racial differences, for example, we have seen that even though many continue to believe that the meaning of race is located in biology, actual genetic differences between races are insignificant—the meaning of racial difference is not self-evident in the sense of being directly attributable to nature. Yet even though race is a constructed rather than natural category, race, whether we are privileged or marginalised because of it, remains a compelling force in all of our lives, shaping our understandings of ourselves, our relationships with others, our possibilities and constraints.

Race in our social worlds is important because we attribute particular meanings to it. We should probably be willing to ask ourselves, what is it, exactly, that we think race means? As we notice a person's skin colour, their appearance, what do we think we already know about that person? Is reading off the surface in this way anything more than a reflection, not of the person, but of ourselves, of our own and our society's beliefs, assumptions, and biases?

Similarly, the meanings of gender, sexuality, and economic status, to name only a few of the differences which constitute our social worlds, can also be understood in this way, as constructed within social relationships and as deserving of the same kind of questioning. These are categories which, like race, have the effect of seeming natural but which, in order to be realised, virtually always require value judgements backed up by the authorising practises of various institutionalised discourses, such as those of medicine or law or religion. And these are only some of the most obvious differences, those that are enforced and reinforced by relations of power.

For nurses, in our privileged and intimate relationships with others, we must not only resist racist, sexist, classist, and heterosexist definitions of people, we must also be willing to reconcile the innumerable significant and insignificant ways we may differ from one another. Naming difference is not simply a descriptive act but one that creates a relationship that is often, though not always, a relation between margin and centre, dominant and subordinate groups. In part because of the power we hold to influence events and experience, we must take the distinct realities of others seriously. Nursing and nurses are embedded in a larger social world and because of this, we are not free of the constraints and prejudices that shape all of society. Yet, "consequences are enacted by nurses, not as individuals, but because they are part of a larger system" (Liaschenko, 1998, p. 76). We have, perhaps, a greater responsibility than others for a critical consciousness of the beliefs, values, and assumptions which shape our thinking and inform our actions.

But what does this mean, this challenge that nurses practise with respect for the distinct realities of others? In the first place, it means that it is necessary for nurses to understand that there exist many competing discourses which make truth claims about people, that these truth claims do not exist equally, and that some versions of the world and some voices are privileged over others (Weedon, 1999). If as Sherwin (1992) has suggested, people's health needs "vary inversely with their power and privilege in society" (p. 222), then nurses need to recognise that quite often the people who are the focus of their attentions are also the ones whose voices are silent or silenced in determining the practises and processes of health care. Respect for difference, for the distinct realities of others, requires, at the very least, a willingness to reevaluate what will count for us as important sources of knowledge and meaning. We must develop a capacity to hear the voices of the least powerful.

Second, nurses need to understand that they themselves are socially, culturally, economically, and politically situated. That is, we are "located at particular positions, each of which enables and constrains the possibilities of experience" (Grossberg, 1996, p. 99). Our "situatedness" means that we are not necessarily going to be able to understand the experience of others, and this knowledge of our limitations is simply the unavoidable character of our situations. But knowing of the partiality and limitedness of our own perspective is also what can compel us to seek other views, to acknowledge that our own understanding is rarely adequate or sufficient (Strickland, 1994). Practicing with respect for the distinct realities of others means recognising that the singular significant characteristic of nursing practise is that someone else is there, someone who must be allowed to speak to us, to really tell us something.

Difference for nurses can mean diversity, a recognition of plurality and multiple points of view. This is important, but there is another meaning of difference that may be even more meaningful for nursing, a meaning of difference which has its roots in the essential alterity of others—the inescapable otherness of others. This is what Caputo (1993) calls the "difference that makes a difference" (p. 56) wherein "everything turns on a respect for difference, for the other one" (p. 60). This is difference that is singular, focussed on this person, this particular other who is before me, here and now. The ethic of a nursing relationship is such that the presence of this particular other is fundamental rather than incidental to how we will proceed, an ethic that is compromised whenever we assume we already know the meaning of another person's life.

SUMMARY

In this chapter, difference has not been presented as an issue to be resolved but rather as a feature of the world that we must consciously consider. Difference is conceptualised as a relationship, the meaning of which is determined in part by how we choose to interpret our worlds. Familiar frames of reference, such as definitions or categories, have been presented as inadequate for truly understanding difference. These have been critiqued for the ways they mask complex and changing social relationships and conceal social processes of differentiation.

What has been raised for consideration in this chapter is how particular differences are constructed and how the meanings attributed to them come to matter in economic, social, and political domains. We are asked to think about how various categories of difference become invested with particular meanings rather than take the meanings of what are named as important differences to be self-evident.

Online RESOURCES

Add to your knowledge of this issue:

Canadian Nurses Association

www.cna-nurses.ca

Differences (a journal of feminist cultural studies mainly, but not exclusively, about gender)

www.press.uchicago.edu/
cgi-bin/hfs.cgi/66/
indiana/diff.ctl

Dialogues in Diversity at the University of Michigan

www.dialogues.umich.edu

Interactive small-group exploration of emerging issues, case studies, and current research

www.ilr.cornell.edu/depts/WDN

Focus on women's issues, oppression, and race

www.worldtrust.org

Reflections on the Chapter

1. From your practise experience, identify differences that seem to matter. Who has named and identified these differences as significant? In what ways do they matter and to whom?

2. Using the questions and analysis highlighted in this chapter, explore how difference is a concern or feature of your practise. What difference does it make to conceptualise difference as a relationship rather than a characteristic or trait?

3. Because difference is not an issue to be resolved, how would you proceed in your practise, given that the world is full of difference? Identify the assumptions and beliefs that influence your understanding and interpretation of difference.

REFERENCES

Ahmed, S. (1998). *Differences that matter: Feminist theory and postmodernism.* Cambridge: University Press.

Alcoff, L. (1999). The phenomenology of racial embodiment. *Radical Philosophy 95,* 15–26.

Allen, D. (1996). Knowledge, politics, culture and gender: A discourse perspective. *Canadian Journal of Nursing Research, 28*(1), 95–102.

Banyard, V., & Graham-Bermann, S. (1995). Building an empowerment policy paradigm: Self-reported strengths of homeless mothers. *American Journal of Orthopsychiatry, 65*(4), 479–491.

Brah, A. (1996). *Cartographies of Diaspora: Contesting identities.* London: Routledge.

Caplan, A., Engelhardt Jr., H., & McCartney, J. (Eds.). (1981). *Concepts of health and disease: Interdisciplinary perspectives.* Reading, MA: Addison-Wesley.

Caputo, J. (1993). *Against ethics: Contributions to a poetics of obligation with constant reference to deconstruction.* Bloomington: Indiana University Press.

Caputo, J. (1987). *Radical hermeneutics: Repetition, deconstruction and the hermeneutic project.* Bloomington: Indiana University Press.

Ceci, C. (2000). Not innocent: Relationships between knowers and knowledge. *Canadian Journal of Nursing Research, 32*(2), 57–73.

Cheek, J., & Purkis, M. (1997). "Capturing" nursing? Theories concealed in writings about nursing practice. *Social Science in Health, 3*(3), 157–163.

Dowbiggin, I. (1997). *Keeping America sane: Psychiatry and eugenics in the United States and Canada, 1880–1940.* Ithaca, NY: Cornell University Press.

Dyer, R. (1997). *White.* London: Routledge.

Essed, P. (1996). *Diversity: Gender, color and culture.* (R. Gircour, Transl.). Amherst: University of Massachusetts Press.

Felski, R. (1997). The doxa of difference. *Signs, 23*(1), 1–21.

Gould, S. (1996). *The mismeasure of man* (Rev. ed.). New York: W. W. Norton.

Grossberg, L. (1996). Identity and cultural studies: Is

that all there is? In S. Hall & P. Du Gay (Eds.), *Questions of cultural identity* (pp. 87–107). London: Sage.

Herrnstein, R., & Murray, C. (1994). *The Bell curve: The reshaping of American life by difference in intelligence.* New York: Free Press.

Kaplan, A. (1997). How can a group of white, heterosexual, privileged women claim to speak of "women's" experience? In J. Jordon (Ed.), *Women's growth in diversity: More writings from the Stone Centre* (pp. 32–37). New York: Guilford Press.

Liaschenko, J. (1998). Moral evaluation and concepts of health and health promotion. *Advanced Practice Nursing Quarterly, 4*(2), 71–77.

Mansell, D., & Hibberd, J. (1998). "We picked the wrong one to sterilize": The role of nursing in the eugenics movement in Alberta, 1920–1940. *International History of Nursing Journal, 3*(4), 4–11.

McLaren, A. (1990). *Our own master race: Eugenics in Canada, 1885–1945.* Don Mills, ON: Oxford University Press.

McPherson, K. (1996). *Bedside matters: The transformation of Canadian nursing, 1900–1990.* Toronto: Oxford University Press.

Paul, D. (1998). *The politics of heredity: Essays on eugenics, biomedicine and the nature–nurture debate.* Albany, NY: University of New York Press.

Pernick, M. (1997). Eugenics and public health in American history. *American Journal of Public Health, 87*(11), 1767–1772.

Rafferty, A., Robinson, J., & Elkan, R. (Eds.). (1997).

Nursing history and the politics of welfare. London: Routledge.

Rushton, P. (1995). *Race, evolution and behaviour.* New Brunswick, NJ: Transaction.

Sherwin, S. (1992). *No longer patient: Feminist ethics and health care.* Philadelphia: Temple University Press.

Statistics Canada (2000). *Women in Canada, 2000: A gender-based statistical report.* Ottawa: Author.

Strickland, S. (1994). Feminism, postmodernism and difference. In K. Lennon & M. Whitford (Eds.), *Knowing the difference: Feminist perspectives in epistemology* (pp. 265–274). New York: Routledge.

Susser, M. (1981). Ethical components in the definition of health. In A. Caplan, T. Engelhardt, & J. McCartney (Eds.), *Concepts of health and disease: Interdisciplinary perspectives* (pp. 93–106). Reading, MA: Addison-Wesley.

Trinh Minh-ha, T. (1990). Not you/like you: Post-colonial women and the interlocking questions of identity and difference. In G. Anzaldua (Ed.), *Making face, making soul: Creative and critical perspectives by feminists of colour* (pp. 371–375). San Francisco: Aunt Lute Books.

Trinh Minh-ha, T. (1989). *Woman, native, other: Writing postcoloniality and feminism.* Bloomington: Indiana University Press.

Valverde, M. (1991). *The age of light, soap, and water: Moral reform in English Canada, 1885–1925.* Toronto: McClelland & Stewart.

Weedon, C. (1999). *Feminism, theory and the politics of difference.* Oxford: Blackwell.

24

Challenges for the New Millennium: Nursing in First Nations Communities

Fjola Hart Wasekeesikaw

Chapter Objectives

At the completion of this chapter, you will be able to:

1. Describe the relationship between the colonisation of First Nations people and health-related issues.

2. Analyse the significance of concepts of population health in addressing issues of inequity.

Nursing students from the University of Manitoba Baccalaureate Nursing Program, Norway House, are dedicated to advancing health care among the First Nations. Front row (l-r): Cheryl McKay, Georgina Henry, Tena Flett, Harriet Hart, and Barb Queskekapow; back row (l-r) Tracy Fosseneuve, Allison Saunders, Kim Cooper, Glenda Muskego, and Stacy Dixon. Photograph by Lorraine Robertson. Used with permission of University of Manitoba.

3. Examine the diversity of views of health held by the First Peoples in Canada, the First Nations.

4. Interpret the significance of cultural resurgence, community development, and the expressed need to widen the scope of health and transfer of health care services to First Nations communities.

5. Evaluate the role of nurses and nursing in the delivery of health care services to First Nations communities in Canada.

6. Examine the following issues confronting nurses in the provision of health care services to First Nations people:
   - Population demographics and the relationship to the health care needs
   - Transfer of health care services in relation to nursing issues
   - Need for cultural competence
   - Educational needs of nurses working in First Nations communities

This chapter introduces the reader to issues related to health, health care, and nursing with First Nations people in Canada and presents basic information to facilitate greater understanding of First Nations people. Key to understanding is recognition of the great diversity among First Nations communities and the views of health held by First Nations members. Also discussed are the relationship between the historical attempts for enfranchisement of First Nations people and health-related issues and the significance of cultural resurgence among First Nations in community development. How these factors influence the practise of nursing in Canada and how, in turn, nurses can potentially influence the health care of First Nations people will be explored. Current issues related to the nursing and delivery of health care to First Nations people will be identified.

DIVERSITY OF THE FIRST PEOPLES

The 560 First Nations in Canada constitute a diverse population of descendants of the First Peoples of North America. Many of these nations are further grouped into tribal councils, which provides unity and greater political power as well as combined resources among nations. Each First Nation has its own reserve land base, traditional territories, culture, and language.

First Nations are part of a larger group of aboriginal people and are descendants of the First Peoples of North America. As defined in the Canadian Constitution Act, the term *aboriginal* refers to First Nations, Inuit, and Metis. All aboriginal people originate from 11 different language families (Smylie, 2000, p. 1072). These language families are Algonkian, Athapaskan, Haidan, Iroquoian, Kutenaian, Salishan, Siouan, Tlingit, Tsimshaian, Wakashan, and Inuit. Each language family inhabited traditional territory in Canada. Out of these families spring 50 distinct languages.

According to the Indian Act, an act of the Canadian Parliament, First Nations members are legally defined as "Indians." The Indian Act, first passed in 1876, was designed to administer programmes to Indians for the purpose of assimilating them into Canadian society; the Act also determined who was legally defined as an Indian. There have been many revisions to the Indian Act since its inception, but the purpose remains the same. Each person who is deemed to be legally Indian has a registration number to reflect her or his population number within her or his band or First Nations community.

Some First Nations members are also referred to as having "treaty" status. This term applies to those First Nations that signed treaties with the British or Canadian governments. Between 1817 and 1929, the First Nations conducted negotiations with the British government or with Canada in the right of the Crown, resulting in the signing of more than 20 international treaties. Through this treaty process, the Treaty Nations agreed to cede certain lands for use and settlement in return for specific guarantees. These guarantees are the treaty rights of First Nations. The treaties reserved lands and resources for continued use and existence as Nations. The treaties also guaranteed specific social and economic rights to ensure continued strong First Nations governments. For example, the Natural Resources Transfer Agreements of 1930 guarantee that First Nations people residing in Manitoba, Saskatchewan, and Alberta have the right to hunt, trap, and fish except for commercial purposes (Indian and Northern Affairs Canada, www.ainc-inac.gc.ca/pr/pub/ywtk/ index e.html). Ultimately, the First Nations leadership guaranteed the right to be born and live as a First Nations person.

The term *Indian* originates from early explorers to North America who thought they had discovered India. First Nations members assert that the roots of the term Indian are deemed inappropriate and serve to reflect a history of colonialism. To reflect more appropriately that they are descendants of the First Peoples on this continent, the First Nations have determined that they would be identified accordingly.

EUROPEAN RELATIONSHIP WITH FIRST NATIONS

What is the significance of the impact of colonisation on the lives and ways of living of First Nations families and communities in Canada? *Colonialism* (a result of colonisation) is considered to be control by one power over a dependent area or people. The term also refers to policy based on such control. Before contact with European colonisers, the First Peoples had their own systems of government, trade, and health care. After confederation, Canada began to displace the First Nations from their traditional territories to make room for the ever-increasing influx of European settlers. Government policies were developed to protect, civilise, and assimilate the First Peoples into Canadian society. The final outcome of these measures was cultural genocide. The process undertaken to achieve this end would greatly affect the mental, physical, and spiritual health of First Nations. The inherent oppressive and suppressive nature of these policies has had, and continues to have, far-reaching negative effects on First Nation governance and cultural identity.

Because of the extensiveness and length of the time during which colonisation took place, this chapter presents no more than a brief overview. The risk in attempting to discuss the historical highlights is the potential to oversimplify the European relationship with the First Nations and the long-lasting negative effects on the population. With this in mind, the history will briefly cover the following key phases:

- Cooperation, nation to nation
- Colonisation and its effects on the health of First Nations members and their communities
- First Nations' cultural resurgence

Cooperation Among Nations

Colonisation did not begin at the point of original contact between the Europeans and First Nations. Unlike the history between the First Peoples and European settlers in the United States, where wars established the dominance of European culture, the initial relationship between the First Peoples and first the French and then the British in Canada was one of mutual tolerance and respect. The social, cultural, and political differences between these societies were maintained. This reflected how First Nations related to each other. The newcomers came to a continent that was already inhabited by diverse nations of indigenous people who formed alliances and good relations with each other to access and distribute their tribal resources (Dickason, 1994, p. 76).

The First Peoples had their own economic, health, political, and social systems that were developed within their communities according to their traditions and the need imposed by their environments. When the first Europeans came into contact with the First Nations, each thought of the other as distinct and autonomous. Each nation continued to govern its internal affairs. Nations cooperated in areas of mutual interest and were connected in various trading relationships and other forms of nation-to-nation alliances.

The Royal Proclamation of 1763 demonstrates that the partnership between First Nations and the British Crown was one of cooperation and protection. In exchange for cooperation in the partnership that characterised the relationship between them at that time, the King of England extended royal protection to the First Peoples lands and political autonomy. When Canada was formed in 1867, a legislative basis for dealing with the Indian people as nations had already been established.

Colonisation and the Effect on First Nations

The written word reflects an author's attitude and beliefs, and so it was that the plans of action or policies to carry out the government laws reflected the attitudes of the people who wrote these policies. The Indian Act was the legislative vehicle for implementing policies to civilise, protect, and assimilate the Indian people (Tobias, 1991). There is no one single event that marked the beginning of these colonial practises. Rather, they began with the attitudes of the time and laid the foundation for a series of actions that deemed the Indian people as inferior beings. Government laws still reflect these attitudes today; in doing so, these laws continue to perpetuate a colonialistic attitude.

A series of actions led to the proclaiming of the Indian Act. This was one act of many that laid the foundation for the civilisation programme that was developed in 1828 and gave rise to the reserve system that became a social laboratory designed to enable Indian communities to adopt European values (Tobias, 1991). This programme established Indians in isolated, fixed locations where they could be educated, converted to Christianity, and transformed into farmers. The goal was to eradicate the First Peoples' values through education, religion, new economic and political systems, and a new concept of property. Not only was the distinct cultural group to disappear but so, too, was the laboratory where these changes were brought about. It was assumed that each Indian person who became enfranchised would also take his share of the land from the reserve.

The Assembly of the United Canadas of the Gradual Civilization Act of 1857 provided the criteria for determining whether an Indian person qualified to become enfranchised. A special board of examiners determined each applicant's merit based on whether the person was educated, free from debt, and of good moral character. If so, the person was awarded 20 hectacres of land within the colony and "the accompanying rights" as a citizen of the Dominion (Milloy, 1991, p. 147). One of the accompanying rights was the opportunity to vote in the country's elections. And so, it was assumed that Indian people would sever ties with their communities and embrace colonial living and values.

The British North America Act of 1867, establishing the Canadian nation, also contained the forerunner of the Indian Act and placed First Nations, and lands reserved for them, under the legislative authority of the Canadian federal government. The Indian Act was amended almost every year to address unanticipated problems in carrying out the government policies. The need for policy revision also reflected resistance by First Nations people to change their values and cultural ways (Milloy, 1991). The amendments persisted on a course to erode the land base of First Nations, wipe out traditional political governance, and smother traditional ways of expression and living. Some effects of the amended Indian Act include the following:

- *The erosion of the protected status of reserve lands.* In 1894, the government leased reserve land held by physically disabled Indian people, widows, orphans, or others who could not cultivate their lands (Royal Commission on Aboriginal People, 1996a). These tracts of land were not surrendered, nor was approval required by the First Nations communities for the government simply to take over the land and lease it to European settlers. Later in 1918, the leasing of reserve lands without being surrendered was broadened to include any uncultivated lands if the purpose of the lease was cultivation or grazing. Only Indian people who were able to cultivate their land were allowed to keep tracts of reserve land. This was in violation of treaty obligations connecting Canada to the Royal Proclamation of 1763, wherein Indian title to land and the need to obtain proper surrender of Indian lands was identified.
- *The undermining of traditional political processes used by First Nations communities.* The federal government determined how First Nations community leadership was to be elected and interfered with the decision-making processes of the communities' affairs. The superintendent of Indian affairs determined the time, place, and manner in which the elections took place (Milloy, 1991). In addition, the governor could remove a chief or councilor from office if he thought the leader was dishonest, intemperate, or immoral. The interpretation of these terms and how they were applied to each case was left to the governor's advisors and departmental agents. The extent to which community members participated in the elections was limited to all males over the age of 21 years who could vote for their officials. The chief and council were forced to function within a foreign-designed and foreign-controlled system.

Federal authority also set a bureaucratic system of controlling the communities' affairs. The nature of the concerns in which the chief and council could make decisions was preset; in addition, each decision was subject to confirmation by the Governor (Cassidy & Bish, 1989). The chief and council functioned within a narrow federally controlled context such as making bylaws for a variety of purposes. Some of these bylaws include the control of band membership; provision of public health; regulation of commerce, traffic, construction, and buildings; assurance of the observance of law and order; prevention of disorderly conduct and nuisances; construction and maintenance of water supplies, roads, bridges, and other public works; regulation of animal populations; and removal of trespassers from reserve land. By interfering with the governing processes of First Nations communities, the federal government undercut the authority of the First Nations communities' leadership.

- *The suppression of the traditions and values of First Nations.* In a concerted effort to extinguish any traditional beliefs and practises in the First Nation community, laws were enacted to ban all practise of traditional ceremonies and to control Indian movement from one reserve to another (Milloy, 1991). It was thought that intertribal gatherings, celebrations, and ceremonial practises were the primary obstacles to Indian people becoming Christians. In 1884, the potlatch and the Tamanawas dance were prohibited, with a jail term of 2 to 6 months for conviction of any Indian who engaged or assisted in these dances. In later years, further amendments banned the practise of other traditional dances such as the Blackfoot sun dance. In part, the system was an attempt to control discussion between political and spiritual leaders living on various reserves. In 1885, Indian people were prohibited from travelling off their reserves without written authorisation of the Indian agent on the reserve. These laws were designed to suppress historical, social, and political organisation of First Nations societies and governments.

Government laws and policies have systematically assaulted First Nations in their spiritual practises and in their social organisation, governance, and economic activities. For many First Nations, the residential school system in which the state and church attempted to capture and socialise First Nations children was the sharpest cut of all (Royal Commission of Aboriginal Peoples, 1996b). The residential school experience left in its wake dislocation and a strong sense of loss for individual students and their families, with rippling, cumulative intergenerational effects on First Nations communities. Dislocation from one's community effected many losses, including culture, language, spirituality, identity, pride, self-respect, and ability to parent. This left many communities trapped between what remains of traditional ways of doing things and the fear of importing too much more of mainstream Canadian cultural values into reserve life. The residential school system insult to the spirit of the First Nations people has had, and continues to have, destructive effects on families and communities. It is important to recognise however, that colonisation processes have not been successful in eliminating First Nations. Rather, they have propelled First Nations to embark on reviving traditions and proclaiming their identity.

Attitudes and policies reflecting the colonial system continue today because the present health care and government systems exist on a foundation of protection, civilisation, and assimilation (Smylie, 2000). This has repercussions for the relationships between the First Nations people and their health care providers.

CULTURAL RESURGENCE OF FIRST NATIONS AND COMMUNITY DEVELOPMENT

The First Nations cultural resurgence and community development share similar roots and are closely intertwined (Elias, 1991). In the 1960s, First Nations people demanded the right to set their own cultural course. They spoke out about indigenous perspectives on development (Elias, 1991). Their voices were significant in creating a pathway upon which community development could be used to bring about economic and social changes in First Nations communities.

Until 1951 when the Indian Act was revised, laws banned First Nations members from attempting to organise themselves. With the revisions to the Indian Act, First Nations members (McFarlane, 2000) began the enormous task of developing political organisations to strengthen and improve the situations of First Nations people. Members began travelling from community to community, discussing issues and potential actions to change the conditions within the communities. Over the ensuing decade, tension between First Nations and the government of Canada developed. The early 1960s was a time when government control was so deeply entrenched that policy controlled almost every aspect of First Nations people's lives, interests, and concerns. For example, the Indian Act affected the family unit in that it provided for arbitrary enfranchisement of an Indian woman who married a person who was not registered as an Indian. Within a family unit, women's status as band members could cease depending on whom the female siblings married. Concomitant with this example, the Wildlife Act prohibits any Indian person from giving meat to a non-Indian. The non-Indian person in this case could be a sister who is enfranchised.

First Nations people set out to challenge policies reflecting a belief that Canadian institutions alone could prescribe solutions to the problems faced by First Nations people. They had different ideas about dealing with their own issues. Provincial organisations were developed to deal with concerns facing the status of Indian people. Nationally, the first status Indian organisation, the National Indian Brotherhood, was started in December 1968. (Note: The term status Indian is applied to an Indian person who is registered under the Indian Act.) The National Indian Brotherhood gave a single voice to all status Indian people in Canada (McFarlane, 2000). Of particular significance was the First Nations response to the White Paper, a Canadian government policy statement in 1969 that aimed to abolish all First Nations rights, including rights to reserve lands. The First Nations response shifted the nature of the relationship the First Nations would have with the government of Canada; the response would be key in moving away from a relationship whereby Indian people were the wards of the state. First Nations governing their own affairs would provide a basis for developing community-specific health and healing systems.

MIYUPIMAATISSIIUM: BEING ALIVE WELL

Miyupimaatissiium, or "being alive well," is seen as an interdependent relationship people have with the natural world and with keeping one's spirit strong (Adelson, 1991; Hamilton & Sinclair, 1991; Malloch, 1989). Culture, language, and traditions used to express concepts similar to that of *being alive well* vary from one First Nations community to another. To the members of a First Nations Eastern Ininiwuk (known as "human beings" and also known as the Cree people) community in the province of Quebec, Ininiwuk food is essential to miyupimaatissiium. Game and fish are a requirement for miyupimaatissiium and symbolise essential aspects of Ininiwuk life.

In the natural world, "eating well" means to the people in this community that one has been eating *bush food* (from the land), and from this, it can be assumed that there has been a good hunting season. In turn, a good hunting season signifies that one has the physical strength required to work in the bush. Miyupimaatissiium is evidence of an experienced hunter and of a woman who has the skills and ability required for preparing the meat and hides. The spiritual aspect of eating well is at the moment when the animal chooses to give itself to the hunter. The relationship between an Ininiwuk hunter and the animals hunted for food is based upon mutual respect. A cyclical affinity between the Ininiwuk (human being), hunting, the land, and food incorporates all aspects of life and so too, being alive well. Miyupimaatissiium is a holistic concept encompassing people in relation to their environment and all that is within the universe. The Royal Commission of Aboriginal Peoples (1996c) identified that holism is an integral part of aboriginal health and healing systems.

Health Status of First Nations People in Canada

The First Peoples enjoyed good health in the Americas; then, as result of European contact, the decimation and extinction of many First Peoples followed. The effects of infectious diseases, such as smallpox, were devastating to the health and cultures of the First Peoples (Podolsky, 2000). They suffered many losses, ranging from decreased size of the community to a strong sense of personal and collective loss. The epidemics resulted in declining fertility rates because infected women were unable to conceive or carry their pregnancy to term and also in decreased chances of conceiving as result of population loss and subsequent lack of partners. Loss of relatives and large numbers of community members resulted in loneliness, grief, and depression. Loss of leadership, warriors, and hunters and reduced size of communities made it difficult to protect territorial boundaries (Ray, 1974). This further resulted in migratory shifts in the tribal territories and the modification of economic roles from trappers to middleman traders. Canadian historian Olive Dickason presented to the members of the Royal Commission of Aboriginal Peoples reasons for the impressive state of good health of the First Peoples and then related the impact of infectious diseases on their health and well-being:

> Some analysts argue that disease agents themselves were rare in pre-contact America until the tall ships began to arrive with their invisible cargo of bacteria and viruses. What is more likely is that Aboriginal people had adapted well to their environment; they had developed effective resistance to the micro-organisms living along side them and had knowledge of herbs and other therapies for treating injury and disease . . . some . . . died prematurely. But more stayed well. Or recovered from illness, and thus lived to raise their children and continue the clans and the nations. Aboriginal populations fluctuated largely in relation to food supply.

> Hundreds of thousands . . . died as a result of their encounters with the Europeans . . . infectious diseases were the greatest killer. Influenza, measles, polio, diphtheria, smallpox, and other diseases were transported from the slums of Europe to the unprotected villages of the Americas. . . . Aboriginal people were well aware of the link between the newcomers and the epidemics that raced though their camps and villages. During the eighteenth and nineteenth centuries, their leaders sought agreements or treaties with representatives of the British crown aimed at ensuring their survival in the face of spreading disease and impoverishment. In the expectation of fair compensation for the use of their lands and resources and in mounting fear of the social and health effects of Euro-Canadian settlement, many Aboriginal nations, clans and families agreed to relocate to camps, farms, villages or reserves distant from sites of colonial settlement. Many did so in the belief that the Crown would guarantee their wellbeing for all time. Given the gulf that separated Aboriginal and non-Aboriginal cultures, it is not surprising that the meaning of those oral and written agreements has been a matter of conflicting interpretation ever since (Royal Commission of Aboriginal Peoples, 1996c, p. 112).

Epidemics occur when the complex relationship between human populations and their social and physical environments are altered, disrupted or conducive to the flourishing of microorganisms (Waldram et al., 1995, p. 43).

Use of a Population Health Approach to Address Inequity

Population health includes a study of the determinants of health and disease, health status, and the degree to which health care affects the health of the community (Shah,

1998). An examination of the determinants of health helps to identify and then address inequities within the health care system (Evans et al., 1994). Many First Nations have identified the significance of clean drinking water; safe, uncontaminated food; reliable sanitation; comfortable housing and workplaces; and adequate employment as essential to the health of the population (Royal Commission on Aboriginal Peoples, 1996c; Evans, 1999). The health of a community is largely determined by the behaviour, the food available, and the nature of the environment of its residents.

Human poverty is any fundamental need that is not adequately satisfied (Neef et al., 1989). Some First Nations communities have come to know many faces of poverty related to low socioeconomic status. Poverty is also related to marginalisation and the imposition of alien values on local and regional culture (Aboriginal Nurses Association of Canada [ANAC], 2001b). Health involves more than physical integrity of the body; it includes social and political concerns and the relationship of individuals to the environment in which they live. Community development is an avenue for facilitating active participation of each member in a community. Resources to improve the health and social conditions of people may be hidden. They are both personal and social in nature. For example, one of these resources is First Nations' determination in obtaining community control and adequate resources to design health, social, and political systems that are of their choosing and reflective of their community's culture.

The Royal Commission on Aboriginal Peoples articulated in *Gathering Strength* (1999c) that aboriginal people want to access health and healing services and achieve health status equal to those of the general Canadian population.

Access to Health Care: A Fiduciary Responsibility

The federal government has a fiduciary responsibility for ensuring the delivery of health care to the members of First Nations communities (Venne, 1997). However, the government of Canada has not acknowledged this responsibility. The relationship between the government of Canada and its fiduciary responsibility for delivering health services to First Nations is based on the medicine chest clause of Treaty Six (1876). Treaty Six specifically mentions medical care in two clauses. The first refers to measures to be taken by the Indian agent when Indian people in their charge were subjected to pestilence or famine. The second clause refers to the medicine chest that was kept at the house of the Indian agents.

> Clause 1 of Treaty #6—That in the event hereafter of the Indians comprised within this treaty being overtaken by any pestilence or by a general famine, the Queen on being satisfied and certified thereof by her Indian Agent or Agents will grant to the Indians assistance of such character and to such extent as her chief Superintendent of Indian Affairs shall deem necessary and sufficient to relieve the Indians from the calamity that shall have befallen them.
>
> Clause 2 of Treaty #6—That a medicine chest shall be kept at the house of each Indian Agent for the use and benefit of the Indians at the discretion of such Agent.

Treaty six process reflected the cultures of the participants: the representatives of the Crown and the leadership of the First Nations people. However, the significance of these cultural contexts, such as the oral tradition, is not reflected in the final agreement.

HEALTH CARE IN NORTHERN AND ISOLATED COMMUNITIES

From the end of the 19th century, semi-trained government agents, members of the Royal Canadian Mounted Police, and missionaries provided health care services. Graham-Cumming wrote in 1967 that the first Department of Indian Affairs, established in 1880, was not originally concerned with First Nations health problems (as cited in Waldram et al., 1995). Then, after decades of ignoring the health of First Nations people, the government of Canada began to develop a system of primary care clinics, a public health programme, and regional hospitals. This was done primarily to stave off the threat of tuberculosis epidemics spreading to the general Canadian population. Indigenous healing ways were absent from this health care system. Medical personnel devalued the practise of indigenous medicine by determining it to be nothing more than witchcraft and sorcery. As a result of this and government policy, the people who practised traditional medicine feared persecution and went underground with their skills and knowledge.

Nurses and doctors, employees of the federal government of Canada, were integral to delivering health care to First Nations. Nurses have served as entry to this Western model of health care in First Nations and Inuit communities since the beginning of the 20th century (Young, 1984). In response to the health care needs of the First Peoples, the Department of National Health and Welfare established the nursing station model as the centre for providing medical services in northern communities (Waldram et al., 1995). In 1922, a mobile nurse-visitor programme was implemented to provide both medical and nursing care services in communities. The first nursing station was opened in 1930 on the Fisher River reserve in Manitoba. By 1935, the Medical Branch of the Department of Indian Affairs employed 11 field nurses who joined a team of medical officers and Indian agents with medical training to provide services to First Nations and Inuit communities. Nurses in these stations provided all primary care with only radio contact with physicians, and patients were evacuated to southern urban hospitals for more comprehensive treatment. By the mid-1950s and into the 1960s, a total of 37 nursing stations in northern Canada had become integral to accessing health care in First Nations, Inuit, and Metis communities.

Nurses in northern First Nations settings have provided care and continue to practise within the sphere of advanced practise (Lemphers, 1998). In addition, many function collaboratively within a community-based health and social team comprising community health representatives and social service workers.

Widening the Scope of Health: A First Nations Perspective

On a path leading towards control of their own communities' affairs, First Nations people expressed dissatisfaction about the state of the health care services available to the people in their communities. These concerns were based on the health status of their communities' membership and the development of programmes by the government without consultation with First Nations people. This would prove to be the beginnings of First Nations health care delivery systems. In 1971, the First Nations of Manitoba prepared a declaration aimed to achieve a just and mutually satisfactory relationship with the people of Canada (The Indian Tribes of Manitoba, 1971). In doing so, they identified social inequities as a factor that contributed to the negative health status of First Nations people. They outlined a number of strategies to help address these concerns. The following strategies pertain to the provision of nursing services in First Nations communities:

- Shift nursing services from a focus on acute care to health promotion and disease prevention.
- Educate public health providers so that they are better able to work effectively with people with low income.
- Educate all health professionals so that they are prepared to assume positions of shared responsibility for health care with community members. It was recommended that First Nations people be involved in the planning and decision-making processes relating to health.

In *Gathering Strength,* the Report of the Royal Commission of Aboriginal Peoples (1996c), First Nations protested when the government attempted to reduce noninsured health benefits, such as prescription drugs and eyeglasses, dental work, and transportation costs for medical services. They argued that treaty rights were being violated because changes were being made without negotiation with First Nations. Then, in 1979, the federal government acknowledged the following:

1. Community development as a key strategy for improving First Nations health
2. The continuing responsibility of the federal government for the health and well-being of First Nations people and Inuits
3. The essential elements of the Canadian health care system, including the federal and provincial jurisdictions. In response to the First Nations and Inuit dissatisfaction with the health care system, the government launched an inquiry.

Justice Thomas Berger (1980), in his Report of the Advisory Commission on Indian and Inuit Health Consultation, proposed mechanisms that included First Nations consultation in the development of community-controlled health and healing systems. His report was described as "radical" by the Royal Commission on Aboriginal Peoples (Cited in Royal Commission on Aboriginal Peoples; 1996c). Despite the proposed changes, First Nations were cautious of the proposed federal government initiatives on transfer. They expressed their unease at the federally initiated Community Health Demonstration Program that began in 1981. Why should First Nations have to prove to the federal government that they could manage their own community affairs? The community health projects were implemented to provide information about costs for First Nations control of health services (Health Canada, 1999). When the demonstration projects were completed in 1987, First Nations communities participated in the federal initiatives for transfer process to administer the control of federally sponsored health care programmes. The transfer of health care services to First Nations communities continued to be fraught with controversy. Culhane Speck (1989) identified gaps in the transfer process. First, the Canadian government refused to accept legal responsibility for Indian health. The evidence for this was the exclusion of noninsured health benefits. Second, in contrast to the understanding that control by First Nations would develop community-based and culturally designed health programmes and services, the government's interpretation was that administrative control would be transferred to the First Nations only for certain existing health programmes. The education component that would be required to develop culturally appropriate systems would not be funded. Specifically, there would be no upgrading and clinical training for nurses and other community programme personnel. This would have far-reaching ramifications for nursing services in First Nations communities.

Transfer of Health Care Services to First Nations

In all, 276 First Nations communities have taken on the administrative responsibility for health care services—either individually or collectively—through multicommunity agencies or tribal associations (Health Canada, 2001). In addition, 75 First Nations communities are involved in the pretransfer process. Communities that have completed the transfer process are employers for nurses and other health care personnel in their communities.

Every community is unique in the manner in which it establishes its own health and healing system. The extent and manner in which traditional views about health are used in developing the system or in influencing existing health care services will lie with each community. The Royal Commission on Aboriginal Peoples (1996c) proposed that new aboriginal health and healing systems embody the following four essential characteristics:

1. Pursuit of equity in access to health and healing services and in health status outcomes
2. Holism in approaches to problems and their treatment and prevention
3. Aboriginal authority over health systems and, where feasible, community control over services
4. Diversity in the design of systems and services to accommodate differences in culture and community realities

The key to restoring well-being among aboriginal people originates from within aboriginal cultures (Royal Commission on Aboriginal Peoples, 1996c). There will likely be as many variations of health care delivery systems as there are First Nations communities in Canada. Self-determination in the development of community health care systems is essential.

CLIMATE FOR CHANGE: NURSING IN FIRST NATIONS COMMUNITIES

Nurses have played a vital role in the delivery of health services in First Nations communities over the past century. Nursing is at a critical crossroads in addressing the health care needs of people living in First Nations communities. Improving the overall health status of First Nations people is the impetus for creating more effective ways of delivering nursing care services that reflect the health and healing systems determined by each community or tribal council. Aboriginal nursing services are an integral part of a First Nation community's health and healing system. A community's processes for economic development and participation in transfer of health care services can serve as vehicles for making these changes. This would require nurses to learn how the First Nations community or tribal council in which they work views health and healing, whether community development is being used, what is being planned, and what changes have been made. Having this information will provide the nurse with context and an understanding of the health care priorities selected by the community. These are important elements of a population health approach and the use of community development principles in providing nursing care in First Nations communities.

First Nations communities face many challenges, and some of these are barriers to the delivery of effective health care services (O'Neil et al., 1999, p. 147). Some of the barriers include the following:

1. *Scarce resources.* Beginning in 1995, the federal government capped increases in spending directed to First Nations and Inuit health services.
2. *No real autonomy for First Nations communities who have assumed administrative responsibility for health services.* Coupled with limited resources, a lack of planning for the increasing need for trained personnel to fill positions in a community's health and healing system, and a lack of resources to train personnel, communities have inadequate resources to develop new models of health programming. Unless nurses collaborate with community members and communities at large to overcome this major barrier, health programmes to address the need will not be realised.
3. *Emphasis on curative services.* The Canadian health system's focus on curative services and the poor health of many First Nations means that the limited health resources are focussed on treatment services.
4. *Emphasis on physical health.* The Canadian health system ignores holistic health and culturally based health programming.
5. *Lack of attention to health promotion and disease prevention.* With the emphasis on curative programming, there are few resources for innovative health promotion and prevention.
6. *Lack of health service integration.* There is no single, concerted approach to improve health through addressing the determinants of health, including economic development, employment, housing, and education. This void is mainly because of the lack of integrated health services between the federal, provincial, and community jurisdictions.
7. *Diminished traditional role of women.* Reflective of Western models of governance that have replaced the traditional hereditary system, the role of indigenous women as central in sustaining the health of communities has been weakened.
8. *The legacy of enforced dependency.* Communities have had to rely on the Canadian government-directed approaches to health services; thus, members have not had opportunities to develop integrated, effective First Nations health strategies.

Many First Nations face obstacles in delivering health care services to their community members. Subsequently, each of these barriers produces challenges for nurses and nursing. Current issues in the provision of nursing care to First Nations in Canada include the following:

- The significance of population demographics in relation to the health care needs of First Nations.
- The effect of transfer of health care services and community development as a climate for change in providing nursing care to First Nations, including issues faced by nurses in relation to transfer of health care services.
- The need to develop cultural competence in providing meaningful nursing care to First Nations through education, research, and practise.
- Barriers to accessing services in the health care system.
- The scarcity of First Nations people in all of the health professions.

Population Demographics

First Nations people are demographically distinctive from the Canadian population. They are similar, however, to the aboriginal population in that they are younger and experience higher fertility and mortality than the general population (Norris, 2000). Fertility and mortality affect the current and projected First Nations age-sex structure. The contrast between First Nations and the general population within the scope of cur-

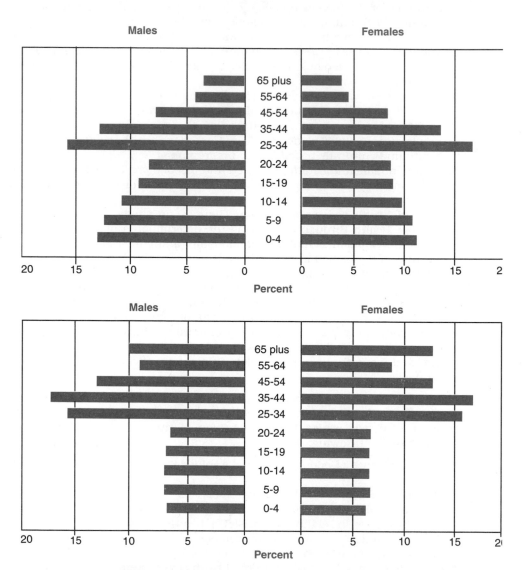

FIGURE 24.1. (Above) Percentage distribution by age group and sex of aboriginal population; (Below) Percentage distribution by age group and sex of total Canadian Population, aboriginal and nonaboriginal people (Source 1996 Census data, *Statistics Canada*).

rent and projected age and sex configurations provides a basis for developing an understanding about the health care needs of First Nations people (Fig. 24.1). Knowledge of the migration patterns of young First Nations women to and from reserves can also affect the nature of health care services provided both on and off the reserve. Demographic profiling serves as a valuable frame of reference within which to determine appropriate health care programming now and in the future.

In 1996, the median age of First Nations people was 25 years compared with the median age of the general population falling in the 35–44 year range; and 35% of children under the age of 15 years are First Nations, but this group makes up only 21% of the general population. In contrast, only 7% of the First Nations adults are 55 years of age or older, compared with 20% of the general population. However, analysis of census data and influencing factors suggests a shift to an aging First Nations population in the future. Although both the First Nations and general Canadian populations will be aging because of declining mortality and fertility levels, they will age differently. Norris (2000) projects that between 1996 and 2021, the proportion of young people 18 years of age and younger in the First Nations population will decline from about 40% to 28% (p. 209). The labour force and the elderly groups will significantly change from between 4% and 9% to between 55% and 63% of the First Nations population during the same time period. The First Nations population will be shifting from youth into the older labour force age groups, while the general population will be aging from the workforce age group into the retirement age group. The age configurations between First Nations and the general community will continue to differ in future decades. For example, the median age for First Nations people in 2021 is projected to be 32 years; whereas in the general population, it is expected to be 40 years. Infant, child, and teenage health programmes are essential to prevent chronic diseases such as type II diabetes and heart disease from developing during the middle years in First Nations adults.

Fertility and mortality affect the age and sex configuration among First Nations people. Although higher than in the general population, First Nations fertility has been declining since the 1960s. This is attributed to the use of contraceptives. Consequently, the size of aboriginal families is decreasing numerically, and aboriginal women are having children later in life and spacing them farther apart (Romaniuc, 1987).

Mortality rates for First Nations have declined since the turn of the 20th century. However, the life expectancy of First Nations members continues to be shorter than that of the general population. In 1995, the life expectancy in the general Canadian population was 75.4 years for men and 81.2 years for women. Life expectancy at birth increased from an estimated 33 years of age around the 1900s to about 69.1 years for men and 76.2 years for women in 1995. The leading causes of death among the First Nations are accidents, poisonings, and violence.

The increase of First Nations life expectancy is due to the decrease in infant (a child who is less than 1 year of age) mortality and the influx of Bill C-31 registrants who tended to be relatively young. In the early 1900s, about 25% of First Nations infants died within 1 year of their birth. The infant mortality rate continues to be high among First Nations: 3.5 times higher than the national rate (Statistics Canada, 1996). Particularly alarming is the fact that First Nations babies between the age of 28 days and 1 year died at a rate that was up to 5 times greater than the national average in 1995. The major causes of postneonatal death among "registered Indian" infants in 1994 were sudden infant death syndrome, congenital anomalies, respiratory infections, and injury.

Bill C-31 is the prelegislation name of the 1985 Act to Amend the Indian Act. This amended act eliminated certain discriminatory provisions of the Indian Act, including the section that resulted in Indian women losing their Indian status when they married non-Indian men. Bill C-31 enabled people affected by the discriminatory provisions of the old Indian Act to apply to have their status restored. Since 1985, about 105,000 people have successfully regained their Indian status (Department of Indian Affairs and Northern Development, 1997).

Most First Nations members who migrate do so between cities and reserves (Norris, 2000). Specifically, of those who migrated between 1991 and 1996, about 60% moved from reserves to urban areas, and about 70% moved from the cities to the reserves. More First Nations people are moving to the reserves, and as a result, reserves are serving more people. However, this gain is relatively small in relation to the reserve population. Norris (2000) surmises after the examination of the Department of Indian Affairs and Northern Development's 1996 Indian Register and adjusted census data that about 60% of registered First Nations people live on reserve. The initial percentage was adjusted for undercoverage and incomplete enumeration of reserves. The extent to which First Nations people migrate to and from reserves affects the health needs of First Nations, both on and off reserve.

Young First Nations women are similar to the general population and other aboriginal groups in that they tend to be the most mobile in a population (Norris, 2000, p. 184). In 1996, First Nations women, especially those between the ages of 15 and 24 years, migrate from the reserve to urban areas significantly more so than men of the same age range. Women who attend postsecondary education influence this pattern. It is also noted that undercoverage in census among young adult males may attribute to these findings. Within the urban setting, First Nations people and, in particular, young First Nations women, change their principal place of residence more than any other aboriginal group (nonstatus, Inuit, and Metis). This is with the understanding that aboriginal people tend to move at a higher rate than the general Canadian population (Norris, 2000). Between 1991 and 1996, among registered First Nations adults 20 to 24 years of age, 840 in every 1,000 registered First Nations women living off reserve had moved.

Nursing Issues Related to Transfer of Health Care Services

Many nurses who are employed by First Nations communities that are administering their own health care services state the professional administrative structure and standards could no longer be guaranteed in their practise (ANAC, 1995, 2001a). When the administration of health care services is transferred from Health Canada to a First Nations community, nursing service delivery also becomes the responsibility of that community. However, many communities were inadequately prepared through the transfer process to organise an effective system of nursing services (ANAC, 2000). Subsequently, nursing service structure and processes for supporting nurses at the community level were developed on an individual community or tribal council basis (ANAC, 2001a). The ANAC held nursing roundtables across Canada from 1986 to 1995 in which band-employed nurses clearly identified key issues surrounding health transfer, the delivery of nursing services, and the health of First Nations people in communities. Over the years as communities completed the transfer process, these concerns became reality to the nurses and their employees.

In *Issues Verification: Current Nursing Workplace Issues and Best Practices in Aboriginal Communities: A Literature Review and Analysis,* ANAC (2002) the main workplace issues in the contemporary context were compiled by examining literature, surveys, and reports and other information ranging from the time of band nurse workshops to the present. One conclusion, in particular, was clear: Issues that were articulated more than 10 years ago at the ANAC Band Nurse Workshops continue to be pertinent. Indeed, they have now been identified as requiring strategic planning and research in the area of best practises. Issues related to transfer are identified in the following reports of the ANAC:

- *Community Workshops Report, 2001–2002. ANAC Community Awareness Campaign.*
- *Developing Best Practice Environments. Best Practice Model Development in Aboriginal Communities. Final Report. January 2002.*
- *Supervision of Nurses in First Nation Communities: What are the Gaps? A Literature Review and Analysis. January 2002. Final Report.*
- *Community Orientation for Newly Employed Nurses. Components of a First Nations Community Orientation Template. March 2002. Final Report.*

Since the Indian Health Transfer policy was initiated in 1986, more than 40% of communities that were eligible have signed agreements for the health transfer initiatives. Although Health Canada has the structure and organisation for delivering nursing services, First Nations communities did not have the experience and expertise to develop them, nor the financial resources to implement them.

Some key components for nursing services are nursing management and supervision, orientation, ongoing education, professional development, and a system of performance appraisal and evaluation. Substantive liability coverage and standards to practise nursing in the advanced role are also required to be available to nursing personnel. Standards of practise are established and regulated by professional nursing organisations. Only a few provincial professional nursing organisations have developed guidelines for use by employers and nurses to address advanced nursing practise.

A lack of understanding regarding the infrastructure required for nursing services may have been partly due to a shift in understanding about jurisdiction, self-government, and the role of the Medical Services Branch (MSB) of Health Canada. It was apparent that the nursing services department that was in place before transfer initiatives did not meet the nursing service needs of a transferred community. Communities gained through trial and error; others may have had the resources to redesign nursing services for their communities. Many communities engaged in the transfer process in isolation and so struggled to create effective community-based nursing services.

In the *Survey of Nurses in Isolated First Nations Communities: Recruitment and Retention Issues* (ANAC, 2000), several leaders from First Nations, who were considering transfer or were in pretransfer stages, and First Nations authorities who had taken over management of nursing services provided their suggestions and recommendations to address conditions successfully. One of these was to create mechanisms for First Nations authorities to exchange information and facilitate mutual learning and collaboration as they go through the transfer process. The development of best practise models is one way of sharing solutions between communities and nurses.

ANAC has identified a number of key issues directly related to the transfer of health care to First Nations communities:

1. Nurses, their employers, and professional nursing associations lack understanding about liability coverage as it pertains to scope of practise. Nursing legislation differs from province to province on the degree of protection provided to

nurses who are functioning in advanced nursing practise. What are the implications of this legislation for the nurse and the employer?

2. Nurses are uncertain about how to support the community in which they are employed in the design of new programme initiatives. Many transferred communities choose to take on this type of initiative by reallocating community funds. However, many First Nations communities consider the incorporation of cultural and traditional knowledge into these new health and healing systems as being desirable but unattainable. This is largely because of the cost of such initiatives and lack of personnel who have the skills to help the community create these kinds of systems.

3. Nurses who are newly employed in a First Nations community are unclear about the manner in which they can become involved with the community. This can be a challenge for the nurse because community members may view nurses as being part of the Western health care system. Or they may see that nurses parachute into a community to work only for a short time, and then they are gone. The legacy of colonisation and illness prevail in some communities, and in others, only remnants are evident.

4. Nurses are not clear about the jurisdictions within which First Nations authorities are operating when considering the delivery of various community programmes. In some cases, the jurisdiction rests with the First Nations government, whereas in other cases, it may be the federal government. How does a nurse determine where the accountability for a programme lies?

5. In some First Nations communities, the nurse reports to a nonnursing supervisor such as the Director of Health. The nurse, supervisor, and community leadership may not be aware of the ramifications of this. There is potential that the supervisor may lack understanding about the role and function of nurses and may lead to overruling nursing decisions and potentially eroding quality care.

6. Nurses may not be aware that nurse managers are key to creating effective community-based nursing services. Their role is pivotal in working with community leadership, health service directors, community members, and nursing staff to create mechanisms for effective quality nursing care.

Other issues that have been identified include the following:

7. Some band-employed nurses do not feel that they have the respect of the community in which they are employed. This is evident when there is interference with the nurses' decisions.

8. The retention of nurses in First Nations communities depends on the quality of the practise environment. What are the key elements that need to be in place to ensure this quality is retained in the community workplace?

9. The employers of nurses may not be aware of the need for professional performance appraisal and evaluation.

Cultural Competence and Effective Health Care Programming

For many nurses, working with First Nations presents an opportunity to provide nursing care in a culture different from one's own. This also creates opportunities to positively affect nurse–patient relationships. Community development principles can affect the development of relationships with a community's leadership and its members (Shuster et al., 2001). Nurses who see themselves as partners with a community recognise that the strengths of the community will form a basis for organising and improving the health of that community. The development of this kind of relationship could be profound for nurses as well as empowering and liberating for community members. The opportunity for a deeper understanding and in many instances the need for patience will help to convey an attitude that will foster the kind of relationship that First Nations patients would find helpful as they manage their health care needs.

Cultural competence includes an understanding of the perspectives and behaviours patients have about health and illness, family health care decisions, treatment expectations, and compliance with health care treatment plans (Lester, 1998). Cultural competence moves away from viewing how patients can fit into the nurses' world and way of doing things to examining how nurses may understand and fit into the patient's world (St. Clair & McKenry, 1999). Nursing research reinforces these elements of culturally competent approaches in the prevention and treatment of chronic disease among aboriginal people. For example, programming and services must take into account the historical, social, and cultural factors surrounding chronic disease (Gregory et al., 1999). Having this understanding influences how one will approach each patient within a community.

Nurse–patient relationships are affected by the perceptions that community members have about nurses and the nursing profession. First Nations people consider nurses and other health care providers to be a part of a health care system rooted in colonisation. Indeed, elements of colonisation continue today and affect nurse–patient relationships, in turn positively or negatively affecting access to health care services by First Nations members.

Access to Services

First Nations people experience a sense of isolation and marginalisation when using general Canadian health care services (Dion Stout et al., 2001; Saunders, 1999). These experiences prompt many First Nations people to use health care services unwillingly or to avoid using them at all. A sense of isolation begins with having to leave one's home and community and, in many cases, travel great distances to access health services for specialised treatment. These distances tend to be geographic, but there are other kinds of distances, too. A key issue identified in the literature on aboriginal health is that aboriginal people face racism, prejudice, or insensitivity from the health care professionals from whom they are seeking services (Royal Commission on Health of Aboriginal People, 1996c; ANAC, 2000).

One method to ensure that comprehensive care is available to First Nations people is to assess their experiences with mainstream health care services. After the barriers and supports for patients have been identified, health policies and practises can be instituted to provide equitable services to all patients. The effectiveness of the nurse–patient communication can impose or remove barriers for persons seeking care. Dion Stout and colleagues (2001) compiled findings from the National Workshop on Aboriginal Women's Health Research held in Ottawa, in March 2001, and from results of research affiliated with the Centres of Excellence of Women's Health and Women's Health Bureau of Canada. Some of the most important findings include the following:

1. In an exploration of barriers and supports encountered by pregnant and parenting women entering addictions programme in Vancouver and Prince George, British Columbia, Poole and Isaac (2001) made a series of recommendations to redress the stigma, shame, and prejudice experienced by substance-abusing

mothers and pregnant women. A number of supports were identified, ranging from those provided by families to those provided by health care professionals.

2. An assessment of the positive and negative aspects of aboriginal women's experiences with mainstream health care services was completed in the Carrier First Nation reserve community (Browne et al., 2000). Health professionals were respectful of this community's cultural heritage and shared knowledge and decision making with patients about their health care. However, health professionals also learned that they dismissed or trivialised the women's concerns, judged in stereotypical negative ways, or demonstrated no regard for the patients' personal circumstances. The adoption of health policies and practises that incorporated the concept of cultural safety were among the recommendations made to address these concerns. Evaluation of other health service programmes identified the following items as areas to address:
   - The importance of asking the aboriginal clientele themselves about their needs and priorities in accessing health care services
   - The need to provide support in tandem with services
   - The need for culturally appropriate services
   - The use of patient health outcomes as indicators for effective services
   - The necessity of being familiar with the socioeconomic issues relevant to patients
   - The development of awareness of the daily living contexts of patients
   - Knowledge of the history of community social supports

3. An assessment of the degree to which the service needs of aboriginal women were met by the Vancouver Native Health Society located in Downtown Eastside of Vancouver British Columbia was carried out by Benoit and Carroll (2001). Interviews with service providers and a series of focus groups with aboriginal women helped researchers to identify a number of access barriers, including the following:
   - A lack of sufficient security and anonymity while accessing clinic services
   - The use of Western approaches to counseling and the exclusion of more traditional aboriginal forms of healing
   - The general lack of female health care providers on staff

Guidelines and policy statements originating with health professional organisations can provide insight and significant information about developing culturally appropriate relationships with aboriginal people. Statements (Smylie, 2001) that have been developed in collaboration with aboriginal people and endorsed by the national aboriginal organisations add credibility to the content of the documents. Ethically, nurses are bound to respect culturally diverse clients (Canadian Nurses Association, 2002).

According to the College of Nurses of Ontario, patient-centred care requires that nurses recognise the patient's culture, the nurse's culture, and how both impact the nurse–patient relationship. Consequently, culturally sensitive care is the recognition of the similarities and differences between the patient's culture and that of the nurse. Nurses enhance their ability to provide patient-centred care by reflecting on how their own values and beliefs impact the relationship (College of Nurses of Ontario, 1999).

SUMMARY

Nursing in First Nations communities presents many challenges. At the forefront is the need to understand indigenous history, starting from the time when only First Peoples inhabited North America. The relationship of First Nations with the Crown of England and later the government of Canada beginning with the treaties and then the Indian Act, the goal of colonisation to obliterate First Nations peoples' cultures and assimilate them into mainstream society, and First Nations' cultural resurgence and determination to obtain self-government are important parts of this history.

Both community development and transfer of health care services are integral to the development of culturally specific community health and healing systems. Population health is a way of identifying determinants of health to address inequities in

Online RESOURCES

Add to your knowledge of this issue:

Assembly of First Nations	http://www.afn.ca
Aboriginal Nurses of Canada	http://anac.on.ca
Indian and Northern Affairs Canada	www.ainc-inac.gc.ca/pr/pub/ ywtk/index_e.html
National Aboriginal Health Organization	http://naho.ca
Report of the Royal Commission on Aboriginal Peoples	http://www.libraxus.com.rcap

health care. Nurses are also challenged to understand the relationship between population demographics and the development of relevant health programmes. Nursing issues related to the transfer of health care services to First Nations communities will require critical analysis and collaborative efforts to effect optimal resolutions.

Reflections on the Chapter

1. How have teachings regarding First Nations health care been included in your nursing programme? Where are you able to obtain further information?
2. Using the determinants of health, examine the impact on the health of First Nations members and their communities.
3. Name four health care needs in First Nations communities. What are some strategies for dealing with them?
4. Using First Nations demographic data, determine two health issues that could become priorities by the year 2020.
5. Identify four approaches that will enhance nurse–patient communication with a First Nations person.

REFERENCES

Aboriginal Nurses Association of Canada (1995). *Band nurse workshops, Halifax, Montreal, Saskatoon, Vancouver: Summary report, March 1995*. Ottawa: Author.

Aboriginal Nurses Association of Canada (2000). *Survey of nurses in isolated First Nations communities:*

Recruitment and retention issues. Final report, September 8, 2000. Ottawa: Author.

Aboriginal Nurses Association of Canada (2001a). *Recruitment and retention workshop. Final Report, May 2001*. Ottawa: Author.

Aboriginal Nurses Association of Canada (2001b). *Sub-*

mission to the commission on the future of health care in Canada. Commissioner: Roy J. Romanow, Q. C. (November 1, 2001). Ottawa: Author.

Aboriginal Nurses Association of Canada (2001c). *The Aboriginal Nurses Association of Canada Submission to the Canadian Advisory Committee, November 19, 2001*. Ottawa: Author.

Adelson, N. (1991). "Being alive well": The praxis of Cree health. *Arctic Medical Research, 50 (Supplements)*, 230–232.

Benoit, C., & Carroll, D. (2001). *Marginalized voices from the downtown eastside: Aboriginal women speak about their health experiences*. Toronto: National Network on Environments and Health.

Browne, A., Fiske, J., & Thomas, G. (2000). *First Nations women's encounters with mainstream health care services and systems*. Vancouver: British Columbia Centre of Excellence for Women's Health.

College of Nurses of Ontario (1999). *A guide to nurses for providing culturally sensitive care for registered nurses and registered practical nurses in Ontario*. Author.

Culhane Speck, D. (1989). The Indian health transfer policy: A step in the right direction, or revenge of the hidden agenda? *Native Studies Review, 5*(1): 187–213.

Department of Indian Affairs and Northern Development (1997). Definitions [On-line]. Available: http://www.inac.gc.ca/pubs/information/info101.html.

Dickason, O. P. (1994). *Canada's First Nations: A history of founding Peoples from earliest times*. Toronto: McClelland & Stewart.

Dion Stout, M., Kipling, G. D., & Stout, R. (2001). *Aboriginal women's health research, synthesis project*. Final report. Centres of Excellence for Women's health program, Women's Health Bureau, Health Canada.

Evans, R. (1999).

Evans, R. G., Barer, M. L., & Marmor, R. (Eds.) (1994). *Why are some people healthy and others not? The determinants of health of populations*. New York: Aldine de Gruyter.

Garret, J. T. (1991). Where the medicine wheel meets medical services. In S. McFadden (Eds.), *Profiles in wisdom: Native elders speak about the earth*. Santa Fe, NM: Bear & Company.

Gregory, D. (1986). *Nurses and human resources in Indian communities: Nurse perceptions of factors affecting collaboration with elders and contact with traditional healers on Indian reserves and in health centres in Manitoba*. Unpublished master's thesis, University of Manitoba, Winnipeg, Manitoba.

Gregory, D. Whalley, W., Olson, J., Bain, M., Harper, G., Roberts, L., & Russell, C. (1999). Exploring the experience of type 2 diabetes in urban Aboriginal people. *Canadian Journal of Nursing Research, 31*(1), 101–115.

Hamilton, A. C., & Sinclair, C. M. (1991). *Report of the aboriginal justice inquiry of Manitoba: Vol. 1. The justice system and aboriginal people*. Winnipeg: Queen's Printer.

Hart-Wasekeesikaw, F. (1996). *First Nations People's perspectives and experiences with cancer*. Unpublished master's thesis, University of Manitoba, Winnipeg, Manitoba.

Health Canada (1999a). *Ten years of health transfer. First Nation and Inuit control. April 1989-March 1999*. Ottawa: Minister of Public Works and Government Services Canada.

Health Canada (1999b). *A second diagnostic on the health of First Nations and Inuit People in Canada* [On-line]. Indian and Northern Affairs Canada. Available: www.ainc-inac.gc.ca/pr/pub/ywtk/index_e.html.

Lemphers, C. (1998). Perspective. Northern nursing: A type of advanced nursing practice. *AARN Newsletter, 54*(1), 11, 23.

Little Bear, L. M., Boldt, M., & Long, J. A. (Eds.). (1989). *Pathways to self-determination: Canadian Indians and the Canadian state*. Toronto: University of Toronto Press.

Malloch, L. (1989). Indian medicine, Indian health. Study between red and white medicine. *Canadian Woman Studies, 10*(2 & 3), 105–112.

Martin, D., & Gregory, D. (1996). An ethnographic study exploring quality of worklife issues of outpost nurses in northern Manitoba. In J. Oakes & R. Riewe (Eds.), *Issues in the north: Vol. 1* (pp. 7–15). Edmonton: Canadian Circumpolar Institute.

McFarlane, P. (2000) Aboriginal peoples in Canada: Demographic and linguistic perspectives. In D. Long & O. P. Dickason (Eds.), *Visions of the heart, Canadian aboriginal issues* (2nd ed. pp.). Toronto: Harcourt Canada.

Milloy, J. S. (1991). The early Indian Acts. In J. R. Miller (Ed.), *Sweet promises: A reader on Indian–white relations in Canada* (pp. 145-154). Toronto: University of Toronto Press.

Neef, M. (1989)

Norris, M. J. (2000). Aboriginal peoples in Canada: Demographic and linguistic perspectives. In D. Long & O. P. Dickason (Eds.), *Visions of the heart, Canadian aboriginal issues* (2nd ed., pp. 167–236). Toronto: Harcourt Canada.

O'Neil, J., Lemchuk-Favel, L., Allard, Y., & Postl, B. (1999). Community healing and Aboriginal self-government. In J. H. Hylton (Ed), *Aboriginal self-government in Canada* (pp. 130–156). Saskatoon, Saskatchewan: Purich.

Podolsky, (2000).

Poole, N., & Issac, B. (2001). *Apprehensions: Barriers to treatment for substance-using mothers*. Vancouver: British Columbia Centre of Excellence for Women's Health.

Ray (1974)

Romaniuc (1987).

Royal Commission on Aboriginal Peoples (1996a). *Report on the royal commission on aboriginal peoples. Vol. 1, Chap. 9.1: Protection of the reserve land base* [On-line]. Ottawa: Government of Canada. Available: http://www.indigenous.bc.ca/v1/vol1ch9s9tos9.14.

Royal Commission on Aboriginal Peoples (1996b). *Report on the royal commission on aboriginal peoples. Vol. 2: Restructuring the relationship* [On-line]. Ottawa: Government of Canada. Available: http://www.indigenous.bc.ca/v2/vol2ch1

Royal Commission on Aboriginal Peoples (1996c). *Report on the royal commission on aboriginal peoples. Vol. 3: Gathering strength.* Ottawa: Government of Canada.

Saunders, Whalen (1999). Cultural sensitivity, a matter of respect. *Canadian Nurse, 95*(9), 43–44.

Shah, C. (1998). *Public health and preventive medicine* (4th ed.) Toronto: University of Toronto.

Smylie, J. (2001). Society of Obstetricians and Gynaecologists policy statement. A guide for health professionals working with aboriginal peoples: Cross cultural understanding. *Journal for Society of Obstetricians and Gynaecologists, 100*, 157–167.

Smylie, J. (2000). Society of Obstetricians and Gynaecologists policy statement. A guide for health professional working with Aboriginal Peoples: The sociocultural context of aboriginal peoples in Canada. *Journal for Society of Obstetricians and Gynaecologists, 100*, 1070–1081.

Tobias, J. L. (1991). Protection, civilization, assimilation: An outline history of Canada's Indian policy. In J. R. Miller (Ed.), *Sweet promises: A reader on Indian-white relations in Canada* (pp. 127–144). Toronto: University of Toronto Press.

Venne, S. (1997). Understanding Treaty 6: An indigenous perspective. In M. Asch (Ed.), *Aboriginal and treaty rights in Canada. Essays on law, equality, and respect for difference* (pp. 172–207). Vancouver: UBC Press.

Wabung (1971).

Waldram, J., Herring, D. A., & Young, T. K. (1995). *Aboriginal health in Canada: Historical, cultural, and epidemiological perspectives.* Toronto: University of Toronto Press.

Young, K. (1984). Indian health services in Canada: A sociohistorical perspective. *Social Science and Medicine 18*(3): 257–264.

25

The Spirit of Nursing: Ghost of Our Past or Force for Our Future?

Tracey Carr

Chapter Objectives

At the completion of this chapter, you will be able to:

1. Appreciate the historical and theoretical roots of spirituality in nursing practise.

2. Identify contemporary barriers to the provision of spiritual nursing care.

3. Explore the structure of health care's current hegemony (power structure).

4. Understand how this power structure contrasts with notions of caring, holism, and spirituality.

Used with permission: Faculty of Nursing, University of Calgary.

5. Discuss how health care's current structure affects the lifeworlds of nurses and patients.
6. Explore the growing resistance toward current thinking and the call toward a revaluing of spirituality in nursing practise and health care, in general.

This chapter addresses a fundamental contradiction that prevails in nursing practise in today's health care environment. It is this: Although spirituality is at the core of nursing practise and the essence of nursing in theory, spirituality dwells in the periphery in practise and education. To begin understanding the underpinnings of this riddle, consider the historical relevance of spirituality to nursing practise. Then consider some contemporary issues that contribute to the suppression of spiritual aspects of nursing care not only in practise but also in educational environments. Specifically, consider the argument that these environments are dominated by forms of thought, such as formal means–end rationale, corporatism, the biomedical model, and professionalisation, that collide with the forms of thought required to understand and engage in spiritual nursing care.

Next, explore the growing disillusionment and resistance to these dominant forms of thought and consider whether the resistance hints at future change and provides hope for restored humanity in health care and the return of spirituality to the core of nursing practise.

NURSING'S THEORETICAL AND HISTORICAL COMMITMENT TO SPIRITUAL CARE

A survey of contemporary nursing textbooks and periodicals finds them infused with the notion that nursing is not merely a job but also a moral ideal. It is a profession committed to the protection, preservation, and enhancement of human health and dignity. Its primary mandates are to give care and compassion and to protect, preserve, and promote health and well-being. In addition, nurses are expected to assume a significant role in assessing patients' spiritual needs and in providing spiritual care (O'Brien, 1999, p. 119).

Contemporary textbooks devote entire chapters to this aspect of care, with titles such as "Spiritual Health," "Spirituality and Religion," and "Spirituality," (Kozier et al., 2001; Potter & Perry, 2001; Taylor et al., 2001). These chapters include such topics as spiritual health, spiritual problems, assessment of patients' spiritual needs, religious practises, spirituality and family needs, spirituality and the nursing process, and nursing diagnosis of spiritual distress (O'Brien, 1999, p. 119).

The notion of spiritual care as reflected in these contemporary nursing texts has a long tradition. When any one thinks of the historical roots of the nursing profession, one of the first names that comes to mind is Florence Nightingale. Nightingale was at once a mystic, a scientist, a visionary, and the founder of modern nursing as we know it today in the Western world. "She forever changed human consciousness, the role of women, and nursing and public health systems in the middle of the 19th Century" (Dossey, 1998, para. 10). Although the nursing schools she established were secular, Nightingale taught, practised, and wrote about nursing with spiritual and religious inspiration. Nightingale viewed spirituality as intrinsic to human nature and the deepest and most potent resource for healing (Macrae, 1995, p. 8). In *Notes on Nursing*, Nightingale (1860/1969) writes that "Nature [i.e., the manifestations of God] alone cures. . . . And what nursing has to do . . . is to put the patient in the best condition for nature to act upon him" (p. 133). In line with this thinking, Nightingale viewed nursing science and science in general as intimately intertwined with human spirituality (Macrae, 1995).

Nightingale, however, was far from being the first to link nursing and healing to spirituality. Since the early Christian era, nursing practise in the Western world has been viewed as a religious vocation or calling (Donahue, 1985). According to O'Brien (1999), deacons and deaconesses and Roman matrons are considered the earliest forerunners of professional nursing. However, she points out that it was with the advent and rise of monasticism that the work of nursing began to become institutionalised. For example, Hildegard of Bingen (1098–1179), German abbess, visionary, musician, writer, and nurse, was one of the most outstanding mediaeval monastic women. Hildegard's extensive contribution to medicine, nursing, and theology are widely recognised. She, like Florence Nightingale, is described as a mystic who had an early awareness of the body–mind–spirit connection. She wrote "that the body can be afflicted with sickness and torments only the spirit can heal" (Lachman, 1993, p. 10, as cited in O'Brien, 1999).

Spiritual Basis of Nursing

In Canadian history, nursing practise itself and its link with religion and spirituality began on the first day of August 1639, when three Augustinian nuns arrived on the shores of Quebec following a voyage from France. Their mission was to provide care to the native peoples of New France. This caring and healing work was central to their Christian beliefs. The influence of the French nuns was profound. In fact, it has been said that if it were the English rather than the French who colonised along the St. Lawrence River in the 17th century, the history of nursing in Canada would have been very different (Gibbon & Mathewson, 1947, as cited in Ross-Kerr & MacPhail, 1996). This is because Henry VIII had expelled all of the nursing orders of nuns from London's hospitals, and nursing in England was facing demise. However, the Protestant Reformation did not take hold in France, and that resulted in no interruption to their system of nursing either at home or abroad. So, while nurses in England "were replaced by those of the Sairey Gamp type satirized by Dickens," French settlements in Quebec continued to be run under the French system of nursing by nuns "who were highly committed to their work and under whom the quality of care was excellent" (Ross-Kerr & MacPhail, 1996, p. 2). The influence of these religious orders on the history of nursing in Canada lasted for centuries. Not until June 10, 1874 was the first secular nursing school founded upon the Nightingale model established. Even within Nightingale's secular model, however, a strong link continued to be forged between healing and spirituality.

Religious Basis of Nursing

A religious basis of nursing care persists today. A recent study of 66 American nurses from various religious affiliations (39 Roman Catholics, 25 Protestants, 1 Jew, and 1 without a religious affiliation) found that most of these nurses continued to describe nursing as a vocation or calling (O'Brien, 1999). Additionally, many contemporary authors writing about spirituality and nursing practise explicitly refer to nursing as a calling (Bradshaw, 1994, 1996; O'Brien, 1999; Shelly & Miller, 1999). The notion of a calling has direct roots in religiosity, as Max Weber articulated so clearly (Weber, 1904–1905/1958). As a concept, it was born out of the Protestant Reformation during the 1600s and is grounded upon the Calvinist idea of predestination. Predestination holds that every soul is predestined for heaven or hell, and one can do nothing during life to affect one's ultimate fate. There are, however, signs that one may be among the elect. One of these signs is success in one's work, or calling. It is worthwhile, therefore, to work hard in one's calling because it not only shows that one is graced by a favourable fate but also contributes to the glory of God and God's plan for the individual (Bierstedt, 1974).

From the original concept of calling as put forth by the Calvinists grew the more general Protestant orientation towards attaching religious significance to one's work. The concept of calling imparted a religious significance to everyday worldly affairs, and every legitimate calling has exactly the same worth in the sight of God (Weber, 1904–1905/1958). Therefore, today, when we speak of nursing as a calling, when we talk about being "called to care," we are linking our practise either consciously or unconsciously to its spiritual and religious roots.

CONCEPTUALISATION OF THE ISSUE: THE RIDDLE OF SPIRITUALITY IN CONTEMPORARY NURSING PRACTISE

Despite the strong historical link between spirituality and nursing practise, and despite the fact that nurses have always viewed spiritual care as an essential aspect of practise, a perplexing riddle has emerged. Spirituality, which is central in nursing theory and history, is peripheral in nursing practise and education.

Several recent studies show that a significant number of nurses do not view themselves as skilled spiritual caregivers and that they rarely attend to this dimension of practise. For example, a survey of 176 registered nurses conducted by Piles (1990) found that only 11% of the nurses surveyed included spiritual interventions in care planning. A total of 65% believed that they were inadequately prepared to perform spiritual care. Similarly, Highfield and Cason (1983) conducted a descriptive study of 100 oncology nurses and found the nurses surveyed had limited ability to recognise signs of spiritual health and believed that spiritual needs occurred infrequently.

In their descriptive study of 750 registered oncology, hospice, and parish nurses, Sellers and Haag (1998) found referral to clergy as the most frequently identified spiritual nursing intervention. This finding suggests reluctance on the part of nurses to provide spiritual care themselves. Adding to these findings are studies revealing that nurses receive little or no theoretical grounding in the spiritual dimension. In fact, the spiritual dimension is not formally integrated within most programmes of nursing education (Harrison, 1993; McSherry and Draper, 1997; Narayanasamy, 1993; Ross, 1994). As McSherry (1998) points out, "if nurses are to provide spiritual care, there is a need to address this omission within existing curricula" (para. 6).

It should be reiterated that modern nursing theory takes for granted the holistic care of patients. Nursing code emphasises care of the whole person, including spiritual aspects, and the nursing process includes spiritual well-being in its evaluation of patient's needs (Mayer, 1992, p. 28). Why, then, is nursing care of the spiritual dimension commonly neglected or delegated to other professionals, such as clergy? And why is this aspect of care not addressed by nurse educators? More research is needed to better understand these questions.

Some nurses think that the holistic philosophies behind nursing theory may be pushed into the periphery in practise settings, at least in part, because they collide with the essence of the current power structure that dominates Western health care. This is characterised by health care's current orientation toward formal means–end rationality (a form of thought that guides human action). What exactly is the meaning and impact of this formal rationality? How does it influence our everyday experiences and the meanings we attribute to them?

IMPACT OF THE ISSUE ON NURSING: THE CHALLENGE OF HEALING AMIDST HEALTH CARE'S HEGEMONY

Hegemony refers to cultural or ideologic domination by the ruling class, which produces spontaneous or voluntary subordination of the masses. This subordination occurs not just in the political and economic spheres but also in every aspect of social life and thought. Hegemony thus entails a system of ideologic domination and subordination (Gramsci, 1971). Some nurses contend that the hegemony in health care hinges on formal rationality. Rationality refers to the particular form of thought used to guide human action (Albercrombie et al., 1994, p. 346). There are four types of rationality: theoretical, practical, formal, and substantive, summarised in Box 25.1.

- *Theoretical rationality* refers to "a conscious mastery of reality through the construction of increasingly precise abstract concepts rather than through action" (Kalberg, 1980, p. 1152). In the nursing profession, theoretical rationality is exemplified in the ongoing development of nursing theory.
- *Practical rationality,* on the other hand, refers to every way of life that views and judges worldly activity in relation to the individual's purely pragmatic and egotistic interests. This type of rationality leads to means–end rational action at the level of individual interests. People who practise practical rationality merely calculate the most expedient way of dealing with the difficulties presented in everyday life. In nursing practise, this type of rationality is reflected in the daily care routines developed by nurses to create a predictable, efficient, and controlled work environment.
- Whereas practical rationality indicates a means–end approach to solving problems at the individual level, *formal rationality* employs a similar means–end rational calculation but does so through reference to universally applied rules, laws, or regulations. "To the degree that sheer calculations in terms of abstract rules reigns, decisions are arrived at 'without regard to persons'" (Kalberg, 1980, p. 1158). This is the "spirit" of bureaucracy (Weber, 1968, p. 979 [565], as cited in Kalberg, 1980, p. 1158). Institutions guided by formally rational principles make decisions on the basis of means–end calculations "regardless of either their effect on individual persons or the degree to which they may violate ethical substantive rationalities" (Weber, 1968, p. 85 [44–45], as cited in Kalberg, 1980, p. 1159). Decisions made by health care administrators often exemplify formal means–end rationality. For example, decisions to layoff nurses, close hospital beds, and so forth are often made on the basis of means–end

BOX 25.1

Forms of Rationality

Theoretical—Concept of reality based on precise abstract concepts

Practical—Concept of reality related to the individual's purely pragmatic and egotistic interests; involves a means–end approach to solving problems at the individual level

Formal—Concept of reality involving means–end approach to solving problems based on universally applied rules, laws, or regulations (bureaucracy)

Substantive—Concept of reality based on clusters of values (also called *value postulate*), such as human dignity, spiritual well-being, and other principles inherent in holistic nursing

financial calculations alone and without the input of patients, nurses, or physicians (i.e., the experts).

- *Substantive rationality* directs humans not purely in means–end calculation of solutions but also in relation to a value postulate. Value postulates are not just single values, such as valuing of human dignity, but also are entire clusters of values, such as those values (including the value of human dignity) found under the value postulate of holistic nursing practise. "Formal rationalities have stood in the most direct antagonism to many substantive rationalities. The recurrent conflict of these types of rationality has played a particularly fateful role in the unfolding of rationalization processes in the West" (Kalberg, 1980, p. 1157).

Ultimately, the issue of spirituality's place in nursing practise reflects this conflict: the conflict between the predominantly formal rationality of health care bureaucracy and science and the predominantly substantive rationality of spiritual care.

Why do we as citizens and as health care providers and consumers accept the rule of our formally rational health care system? One can argue that the predictability, calculability, and routine of modern institutions, such as health care institutions, "provide individuals with a reasonable sense of security in the context of modern complexities" (Giddens, 1990, as cited in Besecke, 2000). However, one could also argue that this order and predictability could create the problem of meaninglessness, whereby the routines of everyday life make it difficult to raise existential questions or find meaning in one's experience (Giddens, 1990, as cited in Besecke, 2000).

What, then, is left of our existential lifeworld experience? What happens to meanings that transcend general and universally applied formulas, rules, laws, and regulations? *Lifeworld* "refers to the everyday world as it is experienced by ordinary men and women" (Albercrombie et al., 1994, p. 238). Experiences and meanings in the lifeworld are immensely complex and varied. However, there are four "fundamental existential themes that probably pervade the lifeworld of all human beings regardless of their historical, cultural, or social situatedness" (van Maanen, 1997, p. 101). These themes include lived space, lived body, lived time, and lived other. They can be differentiated but not separated. Together, they form the intricate unity we call our lifeworld, "but in research we can temporarily study the existential in their different aspects, while realizing that one existential always calls for the other" (van Maanen, 1997, p. 105).

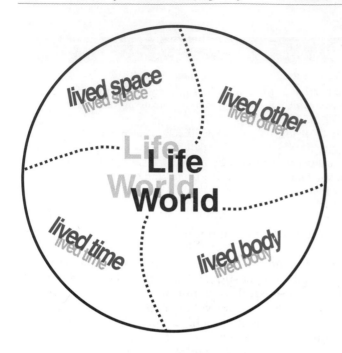

FIGURE 25.1. Lifeworld: The Lifeworld encompasses four fundamental existential themes: lived space (how you feel in the space you're in), lived body (your experience of self), lived time (perception of time as long or brief—rather than measure of time), and lived other (experiences and relationships).

Living in Health Care's Corporate Space and Time

Lived space is not mathematic dimensions of length, height, and width. Lived space is *felt space*. We do not normally reflect on felt space, and it is difficult to put into words. Yet we know that the various spaces we find ourselves in affect how we feel. Large crowded spaces can make us feel small and insignificant, the shelter of our homes can make us feel loved and secure, and the expansive view of the ocean can make us feel free. "In general, we may say that we become the space we are in" (van Maanen, 1997, p. 102).

What does the space of the health care system, particularly hospital space, do to us as nurses and patients? It can inflict fear or comfort; it can be liberating or oppressive, it can instill hope or dread; it can be nurturing or damaging. With restructuring in health care that began in the early 1990s, we are hearing more and more that the lived experience of hospital space is fearful, oppressive, and damaging both to nurses and patients. Nurses are finding, indeed, that they "are becoming the space they are in" because in it, it is impossible to be anything else. This space does not provide sufficient room for nurses to be comforters and nurturers. Various practicing nurses describe how they have had to forego their ideals of providing holistic care and have surrendered to the task and efficiency orientation of the structure they are in. Perhaps this surrender is best captured in this sad phrase heard in a variety of settings: "Nursing? . . . it's just a job for me now." Clearly, this statement does not suggest that a nurse's work is infused with spirituality or that the nurse is providing deep, meaningful holistic care.

Although lack of money is often blamed for the inability of nurses and patients to provide adequate, let alone spiritual or holistic, care, it can be argued that insufficient funds are not the central problem. Instead, it is proposed by some that the current health care crisis is rooted in the growing domination of formal rationality over substantive rationality. Ralston Saul (1999, p. 9) argues that major public policies, such as universal health care, work if they are driven by ideas—or substantive rationality. Such ideas have the power to drive even the most impossible-to-imagine projects. After all, the idea of universal health care was born out of and first realised at the height of the Great Depression in the most severely depressed province—Saskatchewan. At that time, the premier was Tommy Douglas, who was committed to equal access to health care. This commitment, which he and the majority of Canadians shared, represented a value postulate; it represented substantive rationality. This substantive rationality actually worked with formal rationality until a nationwide universal health care system was born under the Medical Care Insurance Act of 1966.

Unfortunately, since its enactment, this idea-driven policy gradually became administration driven, which is to say that form superseded content (Saul, 1999, p. 10). The "form" of health care administration is shaped as a corporate or classic bureaucratic structure. In a *classic bureaucratic structure,* each official has a specific job description and knows precisely his or her area of responsibility, whom he or she controls, and whom he or she must report to and be accountable to. This system is rational and efficient because each official knows his or her duties, and actions are not arbitrary but are governed by formal rules. Thus, any qualified person can take over any specific post and know what to do (Weber, 1968/1921, as cited in Chapman, 1982, pp. 51–52). However, although such a system may be efficient, in many cases it is too rigid. "The rules (often described as red tape) do not allow for personal discretion and do not adapt easily to change" (Chapman, 1982, p. 52).

One can argue that such a corporate, form-driven system does not work "no matter how hard you try to apply all of the administrative solutions being proposed" (Saul, 1999, p. 10). Moreover, "the more efficient you make a Medicare system, the less well— the less effective—it will work" (p. 10). Why? Because efficiency is driving the machine, leaving "the ideas to follow hobbling behind" (p. 10). When this happens, the system loses its direction, and people start claiming that this direction can be regained by implementing greater efficiency. Of course, direction cannot be gained by efficiency because efficiency has no content (Saul, 1999).

Another important aspect of health care bureaucracy is the trend to eliminate expertise from managerial positions. Nurses and doctors are accepting (or being forced to accept) corporatism, whereby policies that directly affect their work are being developed and implemented by administrators who know nothing about the work of nurses and doctors. The only thing these administrators know about is administration. Saul (1999) warns that such abdication of the expert role in policy development is "a dangerous flaw in the Western democratic system" (p. 12). When experts in the content of the system, such as nurses and doctors, disappear into their specialisations, they experience greater and greater difficulty talking to each other. Without communication, nothing is left to hold the Medicare system together "except policy, or purpose, which is very hard to pursue without the participation of the experts" (Saul, 1999, p. 11).

How can a bureaucratic health care system understand the notions of spirituality and holistic care? How can it justify the need patients have for more time with their nurses when these needs cannot be codified, keyed into the machine, and analysed fully in terms of cost–benefit ratios? This is where bureaucracies fall short.

A result of the administrative machine driving the health care system is restructuring. What does restructuring mean and how is it affecting nurses and patients? Restructuring, a process that has been underway in Canadian and American health care systems since the early 1990s (Heitlinger, 2000; O'Connell, 2000), has been linked to bureaucratic decision making. The aim of restructuring is increased efficiencies. The means to meet this end involve reducing both government funding and the size of the health care workforce; closing, merging, or otherwise "rationalising" hospitals; off-loading more work to community-based (largely unpaid) care; privatising through contracting out; transforming full-time nursing positions into part-time ones (the so-called casualisation of the nursing profession); fragmenting, deskilling, and intensifying nurses' work, and pressing for greater productivity and efficiency (Heitlinger, 2000, p. 1–2). What is often left out of restructuring is the effect this process has on patients and on nurses.

This process has left nurses feeling demoralised and devalued. Many who were eager graduates in the early 1990s spent the subsequent 10 years as casual nurses waiting by the phone to be called in to work. Many await calls not only from different hospital wards but also from different hospitals. Under these unpredictable, sporadic, and multisetting work conditions, nurses find the ideal of establishing deep, meaningful, and spiritually inspired relationships with their patients a nearly impossible vision. Continuity of care is violated, and the casual nurse seldom feels like a legitimate member of a patient's health care team.

Restructuring has further stifled spiritual or holistic patient care by *deskilling* nursing, that is, "by dividing nursing work into discrete tasks and progressively allocating many of these tasks to less well-trained and lower-paid workers" (Heitlinger, 2000, p. 2). In such a system, oral medications are administered by one worker, intravenous medications by another. Likewise, bathing, ambulation, dressings, diagnostic tests, physical assessments, and so forth are increasingly performed by separate workers on the same patients. This is not just antithetical to any concept of holism, it is dangerous. No one person oversees the patient as a whole. The patient's self and body are divided into discrete jobs performed by separate individuals. Nurses can and should be responsible for most of the tasks just described for each of their patients—everything from the bed bath to central line care or cardiac monitoring. Carrying the responsibility not only ensures that somebody is responsible for and sees the whole patient but also ensures that the nurse has fewer patients and spends more time being present for and with each. These important aspects of healing, unfortunately, remain unrecognised by the health care bureaucracy.

Restructuring as a product of corporatism has been planned and executed without the input of experts and without the input of front-line workers, such as nurses. As mentioned, decisions are made on the basis of rational means–end calculation—no ideas, values, or emotions enter in. What happens when nurses do not have a say in what happens to their patients? Although this situation makes nurses feel stripped of their professional status and autonomous practise, it has more serious consequences for the patient. Consider the following scenario related recently by a nurse:

> For the past 3 months on our floor [Geriatric Rehabilitation], we had an elderly woman who was awaiting placement. Out of the blue, for no reason other than efficient use of hospital bed space, "they" decided to transfer her to the Geriatric Family Practice ward. She cried and refused to go but was transferred anyway. The nurse's protests also went unheard. Once on her new ward she became confused, refused to eat, required a 1:1 sitter, and then soon expired.

This nurse attributes the patient's death directly to the transfer and indirectly to the lack of nursing and patient input in the decision as well as to the lack of value for holism and human caring by hospital administration.

An account from another nurse follows:

> We are told that the hospital's restructuring is aimed at increasing efficiencies. . . . We tell Mr. Smith that we are sorry he has waited 30 minutes for pain relief, but due to management efficiencies, his duty nurse, who called in sick, was not replaced. We are embarrassed when we explain to Mrs. Jones that although she has been coming to our unit for a few years, and she knows all the staff and feels comfortable with our care, hospital restructuring means that her next admission could be in one of four different wards. And we are sorry we do not know which nurses will be looking after her (O'Connell, 2000, p. 28).

These scenarios leaves one wondering how nurses can ensure that the needs of their patients are met holistically when they have little to no control over where their patients will be placed and who will be caring for them.

As mentioned, the experience of each existential theme or circumstance is influenced by the other. In the case of health care, the theme of lived space has a particularly strong impact on lived time. *Lived time* refers to "subjective time as opposed to clock time or objective time" (van Maanen, 1997, p. 104). Lived time speeds up when we are busy or enjoying ourselves and slows down when we are bored or anxiously awaiting something.

In health care, the ethic of efficiency compresses lived time for nurses. They rarely have enough time to do their assigned work comfortably in the fashion they were taught. Instead, they must rush through everything from medication administration to bereavement care. There is never enough time. The ethic of efficiency often creates quite the opposite effect for patients. As they wait for their call bells to be answered, their treatments to be given, their doctors to visit, time drags at a painfully slow rate. "Minutes may seem like hours, hours like days" (Toombs, 1992, p. 15). This slow experience of time is often compounded with physical pain and discomfort, fear, and uncertainty. As a consequence, the gap between nurses' and patients' experience of lived time can lead to stress, frustration, and misunderstandings between them. Furthermore, the nurse who manages to uphold the ethic of efficiency and completes her tasks at "supernurse" speed can be perceived as commendable by the hospital but uncaring and harried by patients and families (Chapman, 1982, p. 61). Hence, the nurse finds it difficult, if not impossible, to uphold the institutional ethic of efficiency and also to uphold the professional ethics of holism and caring.

Corporation, restructuring, and the value of efficiency are the ideologic strongholds of the health care institution. They form the basis of its current structure. They create a lived space and a lived time that is oppressive, fear-filled, demoralising, and antithetical to any concept of holism or spiritually informed care. Nurses and patients wishing to change this lived space and time face a formidable opponent, who, because of its formally rational orientation, tends to subordinate individuals to given realities and concomitantly to oppose all orientation based on transcendence of daily routine. "Such persons [or agents, institutions] often mistrust not only striving after impractical values of 'the beyond,' whether religious or secular Utopia, but also the abstract theoretical rationality of all intellectual strata" (Kalberg, 1980, p. 1152).

Formal rationality is also evident in the science of health care and medicine. Such science has been dominated by the positivist tradition. Like formal rationality, positivism relies on universal and generally applied principles, rules, and regulations. For example, "positivism accepts the idea that a single scientific method is applicable to all fields of study. It takes the physical sciences as the standard of certainty and exactness for all disciplines. Positivists believe that all knowledge is inherently neutral. They feel that they can keep human values out of their work" (Ritzer, 1996, p. 284). When this kind of science is applied and used to direct care, it influences patients' existential experience of lived body and lived other.

Lived Body as a Biomedical Machine

Lived body refers to the fact that "we are always bodily in the world. When we meet another person . . . we meet that person first of all through his or her body" (van Maanen, 1997, p. 103). Indeed, it is because of our bodies that we exist. In this view, the body is more than a biologic organism; it is the means to our experience of self. However, like the administrative "body" of the health care system, the human body, as cared for within it, is also viewed by many as a "machine." Indeed, it has been proposed that a vast majority of people in industrialised nations, when in medically defined situations, implicitly view the body as a biologic machine, functioning as an integrated whole and having highly specific parts and organs located and described with considerable accuracy. It is assumed by definition to be a biologistic entity, to be "experienced" in a similar fashion, and to be capable, within limits, of more or less comparable levels of performance and function for members of the same age and sex (Manning & Fabrega, 1973, pp. 254–255).

The similarities of this biologic or biomedical view to formal rationality are implicitly evident in its basic tenets. These tenets hold that the body is partitioned internally; that it is experienced comparably from person to person, situation to situation, culture to culture; that senses are universal; that disease is a universal and cross-culturally invariant phenomenon; that boundaries between the mind, body, and spirit are present and not problematic; that birth and death are biologic processes; and that the body should be seen by people as natural, objective, and value neutral (Manning & Fabrega, 1973, p. 255).

This biomedical view of the body has produced and continues to produce extraordinary discoveries that have saved or greatly improved the health and quality of life for countless individuals. Most nurses would never want to minimise this contribution, which they depend upon in their own practises. Modern biomedicine has much to offer to humankind. It is possible, however, to have too much of a good thing, to be thrown off balance by adhering to only one practise or paradigm, and this is a concern. In the zealous endorsement of the biomedical model, we have left behind other paradigms and perspectives of the body and illness experience that would ensure a balanced and holistic view. Most of us, for example, would agree that the body is more than a complicated machine. This acknowledgement, however, is not reflected in current health care delivery practises. Instead, modern medical care maintains a focus on the body as a machine in need of repair, neatly separated from the mind and soul of the person to which it is attached. This separation of body and mind is known and commonly referred to as the *Cartesian split* or *Cartesian dualism*. (Anderson & Kirkham, 1999, p. 53).

The Cartesian split not only separates the body from the self but also omits the self or person to whom the body belongs, "the person whose body it is" (Toombs, 1988, p. 201). With a focus on the body as a broken machine in need of repair, disease becomes the central concern. Disease in the biomedical view is conceptualised in terms of abstract quantitative data, and the subjective experience of the patient is discounted as irrelevant or unreliable. For example, in an article published in *Lancet*, a physician explains that he and other physicians alike generally regard social matters, such as socioeconomic status, marital status, and religion or spiritual factors, "as private and personal, not the business of medicine, *even if they have health implications*"

(Sloan et al., 2000, p. 666). This statement by a contemporary physician supports the claim that "the medical language and clinical vernacular reflect the message that disease counts: the human experience of illness does not" (Toombs, 1988, p. 202). Indeed, "medicine is humanist only to the extent that it takes into account the full humanness of patients" (Toombs, 1988, p. 202).

When nurses and doctors view the body as an object separate from the person, there is a possibility that the patient will feel reduced to being an object and sense a loss of personhood. "This feeling is intensified when, nurses, physicians, and other health care professionals . . . probe body openings and parts in order to examine or reveal body functioning. Instrumentation assists in these activities, separating even human touch from the process. Body parts, fluids, and emanations (sputum, feces, urine, sperm) are seen as discrete, detached, physical, independent units having no moral, sacred, personal, or unique meanings. They may in consequence be used to diagnose and treat impersonally defined illnesses" (Toombs, 1988, p. 276).

This Western biomedical model is a distinct culture. Like most cultures, it has much to offer. However, it must not be viewed from within or without as "embodying the absolute truth . . . to which all other cultures must unquestioningly submit" (Coward & Ratanakul, 1999, p. 3). Its strength and its weakness should be identified. Knowledge from other cultural perspectives should be respected and incorporated where possible. For example, we can learn from folk cultures that view the mind and body as a continuum, not a dichotomy, and that see illness not as experienced by a single person but as experienced by the relevant social unit in which it occurs. In such cultures, caring ceremonies are directed at mobilising these interpersonal networks, "and they cannot, as in modern societies, be seen as directed solely toward rectifying either a disordered mind or a dysfunctional body" (Manning & Fabrega, 1973, p. 280). If body, mind, and spirit continue to be viewed as separate spheres, and if the objective detached body continues to be our focus in the practise environment, the spirituality inherent in nursing will remain central in theory but peripheral in practise.

Lived Other: Caring for or Controlling

"*Lived other is the lived relation we maintain with others in the interpersonal space we share with them*" (van Maanen, 1997, p. 104). One may argue, then, in nursing and health care in general, that our existential experience of lived other has come to be as detached and objectified as our experience of lived body. How has the objectification of *lived other* come to pass, especially in nursing, a profession theoretically and historically founded on the practise of human-to-human caring?

To begin to understand the felt need to adopt and adjust to the dominant power structure (hegemony) and the steps nurses take to fit in and feel legitimate within the structure, we need to examine the history of nursing as a profession and the tensions inherent within the caring professions. Maternal feminism was the underlying ideology spurring the movement of women into the public sphere during the first wave of feminism. Although narrow, biologically deterministic, and conservative, this ideology gave middle- and upper-middle-class women of the late 19th century a cause around which to unite, foster a feminine consciousness, enter the public sphere, and contribute to the caring and betterment of society. This need to care for society was spurred by the adverse social conditions created by urbanisation and industrialisation. It was also fuelled by the Christian reform movements of the late 19th century. The Christian reform movement was motivated by the need to make the church socially relevant, to base it on more than faith alone. Such a church, it was hoped, would be able to withstand the threatening tides of biblical criticisms, Darwin's theory of evolution, and the ascent of science in general (Baines, 1993).

It was in this context that the roots of the modern-day caring professions of nursing, teaching, and social work were planted. Each profession was based on the maternal ethic of care and duty. Nursing education, for example, was founded on the Florence Nightingale model, which was not simply preparation for an occupation; it was character training for life. This training emphasised moral development, loyalty, proper behavior and comportment, order, discipline, and respect for hierarchic control.

Although maternal feminism created these new roles and occupations for women in the public sphere, it also reinforced the traditional role of women as subordinate caregivers. For instance, although Nightingale envisioned nurses as independent and confident women who would define a clear role for themselves in the hospital hierarchy, she also emphasised efficiency and the standardisation of procedures which limited initiative and independence and reinforced the male-dominated hierarchy (Baines, 1993, p. 49).

As these tensions and contradictions grew in nursing and other female-based caring professions, leaders began to advocate professionalisation as a means to achieve both status and autonomy (Baumgart & Larsen, 1988). *Professionalisation*, as it materialised in the late 19th century, was a process in which white, middle-class men carved out new roles and ultimately obtained monopoly for their services. Critiques of professionalisation suggest that although special knowledge and expertise are characteristics attributed to professions, the key element is social power (Baines, 1993). The movement in the caring professions towards professionalisation, thus, served only to compound existing tensions, tensions which continue to plague succeeding generations of nurses, teachers, and social workers.

Why the tensions? Because women's caring—that is, the mental, emotional, and physical work involved in looking after, responding to, and supporting others—contrasts sharply with the emphasis on objectivity, technique, and efficiency held within male-dominated professions. Indeed, within the "professional" milieu, caring is rarely recognised as work at all (Pascall, 1986, p. 70). Instead, caring is presumed to be something women do "naturally," thus rendering the labour involved invisible (Baines et al., 1993, p. 14). However, this presumption "fails to consider the significance of socially patterned roles and the process of socialization through which sex is translated into gender as women and men learn to incorporate into their behavior and attitudes, assumptions related to masculine and feminine roles" (Baines et al., 1993, p. 18). In other words, caring is natural for women, because they have learned and practised the skills required to be caring.

When these caring skills are transferred into the public sphere by way of the caring professions, the status of women in these roles is only marginally enhanced (Baines et al., 1993, p. 30). This devaluing of caring may explain in part why for the first time since the late 1980s through to the millennium, the professions of nursing, teaching, and social work are facing competition as women flock to the more prestigious "male" professions of law, medicine, and engineering. Although this exodus from female-dominated professions is, of course, related to improved equality of women, it is no doubt also related to the undervaluing and underrewarding of these same professions. "The reality may be that women have begun to believe that the work they do in these fields has little value" (Baines, 1993, p. 37).

As mentioned, many leaders in the caring professions have attempted to rectify their devalued position in the public sphere by adopting the values and behaviors associated with professionalisation. Adoption of the professional posture and values, however, sets up many paradoxes. For instance, how can one be at once emotionally involved, loving, present for, equal to, and also objective, detached, efficient, and expert?

To resolve these tensions and to improve status, many nurses have moved closer to professionalism and further from their roots in women's caring. This movement has been unfolding for more than 50 years. Some believe that nursing, as a result, has forgotten its origins. "Nursing is [now] nervous about identifying with anything relating to caring or feminine energy" (Watson, 1999, p. 14).

FUTURE IMPLICATIONS: COUNTER-HEGEMONY AND VOICES OF CHANGE

The hegemony in health care mirrors the general hegemony characteristic of Western civilisation because Western civilisation, too, is dominated by formally rational thought (Kalberg, 1980; Watson, 1999). However, a unique and important characteristic of Western thought is its liberal nature. Liberalism permits and even encourages critique of itself. Such a critique of the forms of thought dominating contemporary Western health care exists and is growing. For instance, authors writing about health care from both inside and outside perspectives remark that despite the magnificent accomplishments of modern medicine, something vital has been left out. This vital omission does not concern our physical bodies but our very being, our personhood, our souls (Saul, 1999; Watson, 1999). This is the aspect of our experiences in health and illness that transcends our physical bodies and that must be addressed by health care practitioners. "For almost the entire span of human history, healers accepted this idea; it is only in the latest heart beat of history that we have abandoned this idea as unscientific" (Watson, 1999; p. viii). Such abandonment has resulted in the existential state we find health care in today; a state that has been referred to as health care's "dark night of the soul" (Watson, 1999, p. vii).

Yet, even in the midst of this crisis and disillusionment, many nurses continue to find ways to provide spiritual care or attribute spiritual meaning to the care they give. This care comes in many forms and is viewed differently from nurse to nurse. However, broadly shared themes of what it is and how it is delivered emerge. Examples of such themes are found in recent interviews conducted with current nursing leaders. For example, Professor Dianne McCormack from the Department of Nursing at the University of New Brunswick in Saint John describes spiritual care as *being connected and fully present with a person or persons*. She adds:

> The notion is also about journeying. I think when I enter into the journey, I have then entered into spiritual care, and I cannot walk out of the journey at my own will. Once I enter into it, I want to go to the end of the journey with the person, and I find it very hard to step back.

Leticia Adair, former nursing educator and current Refugee Support Coordinator with the Red Cross in Saint John, New Brunswick, explains spiritual aspects of her care strengthen her as much as her patients:

> That emotional and spiritual side of a person is what holds them together many times, and I think that is what makes people really come through so many challenges when they arrive. . . . It is really incredible what people can endure. One of the things that is really important to keep in mind is how much hope plays a part in everything in our lives—the hope to have a better life, the hope to have freedom, the hope to be safe—it really drives a

person to look for a better life and maintains them. So, really, you can witness the spirit that a person has prevailing in them. It keeps them going. I think more than what I give is what I learn from people, and I think it really reenergises me. You are really seeing the spirit come through in these people who really endure and can still be happy.

Betty Hitchcock, former nursing educator, current Regional Director of Big Brothers/Big Sisters of Saint John, and breast cancer survivor, says that spiritual nursing care is about "focussing on the person, and leaving what is going on outside the patient's room behind you when you go in." According to Betty, spiritual nursing care is also about being open and being in a constant attitude of caring: "I think it's an openness, it's an attitude, it's a way of being. It's about letting the patient know you are receptive to them and their questions. I think a patient can tell very quickly whether you are receptive or not." For more from these interviews, see Box 25.2.

The voices and stories of these nursing leaders join in a growing call to acknowledge and reaffirm the importance of holism, spirituality, and transcendent meaning in health and healing. The call is also a call for change. Indeed, some predict that the most exciting breakthroughs of our time "will occur, not because of technology, but because of an expanding concept of what it means to be human" (Aberdene & Naisbitt, 1992, p. 16). For nursing practise, this means releasing and valuing the "repressed healing capacity of feminine energy, symbolized across time by women in general and nurses in particular—male and female alike" (Watson, 1999, p. xiii). It also means honouring the sacred by attending to the nonphysical, spiritual dimensions of existence; honouring the connectedness of all; honouring the unity of "mindbodyspirit"; and creating a healing (not corporate) space (Watson, 1999).

Although these ideas may seem marginal, idealistic, or even unrealistic, there is evidence that they are being incorporated into the mainstream.

For example, the American Holistic Nurses Association and the International Association for Human Caring are singularly committed to ushering holistic healing back into nursing. They call for a metaphorical relighting of the lamp and light of nursing's past calling (Bradshaw, 1996; O'Brien, 1999; Shelly & Miller 1999; Watson, 1999). Nursing's past calling is tied to the ethic of care, which characterises women's unique pattern of moral development. The pinnacle of this form of moral development is establishing growth-fostering connections in relationships, rather than the widely accepted masculine model of growth of an inner separation, autonomous reasoning, and individuality (Gilligan, 1997; Miller, 1986; Miller and Stiver, 1997).

This ethic of care can be further tied to the concept of *yin* in Chinese Taoism. In Chinese Taoism, *yin* is feminine energy, and *yang* is masculine energy. Taoists believe all life consists of the constant interplay of these vital energies. In this cosmology, the passive yin (everything female) and the active yang (everything male) give rise to everything in the world (Shepherd, 1993, p. 8). In the yin–yang system, no part has a life of its own but exists in complementary interaction with the other. Yin and yang work together to constitute equilibrium and harmony. Though opposites, they are not necessarily antagonists. "This can be nursing and medicine, instead of both competing for the same yang energy. This does not deny that nursing, as yin energy, contains a spot of masculine energy. Likewise, within yang medicine, there is a dot of nursing, the yin energy" (Watson, 1999, p. 75). If this balance is not achieved, if nursing continues to compete for the same yang energy, and if nursing fails to mature into its own sacred healing practise, some argue that it will remain in a technical and dependent position within the patriarchal system of medicine (Watson, 1999).

Text continues on page 488

BOX 25.2

Interviews on the Spirit

Providing spiritual care and attributing spiritual meaning to the care they give is characteristic of nurses. Although the perception of spirituality is usually very personal and different for the individual nurse, broad concepts of spirituality are common among the profession. Some excerpts from interviews about spirituality are shared here as an illustration.

- Professor Dianne McCormack from the Department of Nursing at the University of New Brunswick in Saint John describes spiritual care as *being connected and fully present with a person or persons.*
- Leticia Adair, former nursing educator and current Refugee Support Coordinator with the Red Cross in Saint John, New Brunswick, finds that *spiritual aspects of care strengthen her* as much as her patients.
- Betty Hitchcock, former nursing educator, current Regional Director of Big Brothers/Big Sisters of Saint John INC., and breast cancer survivor, says that spiritual nursing care incorporates *focus on the person, an openness, a receptive attitude, and a way of being.*

INTERVIEW WITH PROFESSOR DIANNE MCCORMACK

Interviewer: *I just want to start by talking generally about what spirituality and spiritual care mean to you....*

Dianne: ...you can't separate it—spirituality and spiritual care. Spirituality is more than the religious connotation. It is more related to connectedness and the notion of being fully present with the person or persons....It also includes the environmental context the person is in. If I am not really connected with the environment, I cannot have a full connection with the person....I guess the notion is journeying, and until I get connected with that environment, I really don't go on the journey....when I enter into the journey, I then enter into spiritual care, and I cannot walk out of the journey at my own will. I want to go to the end of the journey with the person. I think it is both that personal connection and an environmental connection....

Interviewer: *What do you mean by environmental connection?*

Dianne: Well, the work environment can enhance spiritual care or it can hinder it. But in spiritual care the person's environment becomes part of my environment and I enter into this experience [the connection] with them....it might only be their physical environment, but it usually includes their family context, their community context, and beyond that....I was visiting an elderly woman to follow-up with her diabetes....Family well known in the community, good church-going family, well respected, and an elderly mom in her eighties whom I visited. She recognized my willingness, I think, to go on this journey with her. Her issue was how could she prepare for death, when she was so terrified. I spent many hours with her talking....She was more my teacher, than I was her teacher....but we were totally connected. We had a mission and a purpose together. It got to the point where both of us felt a little overwhelmed. There was one particular clergy in the community who was very good at helping people pass from one life into the next, but he wasn't of her denomination. This is a small town (soft chuckle). You have to get this picture, because you went to your one and only faithful church. So, we had to figure out a way for her to meet him [the minister] without the family or her minister knowing...she didn't

(continued)

BOX 25.2

Interviews on the Spirit (Continued)

want to offend her own minister. It was quite a plot we had to develop (soft chuckle). He [the other minister] agreed to meet with us, and we met in a safe place eventually, and he helped us both....it wasn't a whole lot of time between that experience and her death. It was just so pleasant, because she was so ready and so prepared. She had dealt with her fear of dying, and she was able to let go of that fear. I felt privileged just to be a part of that experience.

Interviewer: *And you said he [the cleric] helped you too.*

Dianne: Yes. He helped me to celebrate life....from that experience I learned to ask people if there was anything they wanted to talk about, and to be there. But if you ask the question, you've got to be there to go on the journey. You can't just say it as you are walking out the door, and you can't just say it and not listen to the answer. And if you hear the answer, you may have to act on it. Usually if you talk enough through conversation—great intervention—if you talk it out, you are able to help people sort out some of the struggles they are facing.

INTERVIEW WITH LETICIA ADAIR

Interviewer: *Leticia, could you tell me about what spirituality and spiritual care mean to you?*

Leticia: The emotional and spiritual side of a person is what holds them together...and what makes people come through so many challenges....One of the things that is important to keep in mind is how much hope plays a part in everything in our lives—the hope to have a better life, the hope to have freedom...drives a person...and maintains them....so, you can witness the spirit that a person has prevailing in them. I think more than what I give is what I learn from people, and I think it really reenergises me....

Interviewer: *How do you see spirituality influencing your practice?*

Leticia: I think if you don't have that component, you burnout. Like seeing the person as a whole, you have to see your practice as a whole. There are times when you say this is really, really bad. I can't cope with this, but yesterday or the day before this turned out just right, and this person was able to provide me with this insight. So it helps. When you see a person...cope with so many things and still be able to survive, to laugh, or to have hopes, it is really incredible. It makes you grow....For me I see the religious part of spirituality as being really crucial. I think the only way to translate or practise your religion is for people to see it and to make it visible.

Interviewer: *You suggested that your personal commitment can be contagious. You can inspire other people....*

Leticia: Yes, because when you really believe in somebody, it is not something intellectual, it is not something visible, it is not something you can do by being very brilliant. It is a spiritual thing that shows. It is not something you can pretend. You can't do anything about it unless you have it. When you really believe in what you are doing, I think that reflects in a lot of things that you do, because you are always open to that situation.

Interviewer: *Do you think that nursing students can be taught this kind of thing?*

Leticia: I think it is a very personal thing. Nursing is one of the professions that draws people who want to do it, because they have that vocation....You cannot teach it, but you can foster it. We cannot be too idealistic, you also need good salaries and working conditions, but to continue the kind of work that nurses

BOX 25.2

Interviews on the Spirit (Continued)

do, such an incredible component of it is the spiritual element. If you don't have it, then you break down.

INTERVIEW WITH BETTY HITCHCOCK

Interviewer: I am interested to know what spirituality and spiritual nursing care means to you. Could you please share with me some of your thoughts and insights regarding this aspect of nursing care?

Betty: Well, to begin, I don't think you can do anything on a higher level, unless you've done a really good job with the basics. You can't really go on and do anything else, if the patient is uncomfortable. Also, I've heard a lot of people say that because of financial restraints and because of cutbacks and all of this, they don't have time for this and they don't have time for that. My philosophy is, I guess, whatever they do have time for can be done in a method that is spiritual. It doesn't matter to me whether it's making the bed, doing a dressing, or passing medications; you can do it in a way that is a spiritual way, that upholds the patient's spirituality.

Interviewer: Can you tell me a little more about how nurses can still provide spiritually meaningful care in the midst of cutbacks and time constraints?

Betty: I think the fact that we don't have time is sometimes an excuse. You've got to prioritize....I think you can be in an attitude of caring, an attitude of listening, an attitude of receptivity to what the patient has to say to you and what his or her needs are, no matter what you are doing.

Interviewer: How do you describe a nurse who displays an attitude of caring and receptivity?

Betty: I guess somebody that really focuses on the patient. I always used to tell nursing students..."When you go into the room you focus on the patient and leave the rest of the baggage out there, because this patient has got something very important going on." I think the person that is in tune with spiritual needs will do that—will automatically focus on the patient—and I think patients know whether you are focused on them or whether your mind is down the hall.

Interviewer: How would you approach spiritual matters with patients?

Betty: Patients who have things around them sometimes will indicate...if they have some scriptures or a book that is of a spiritual nature, I would comment on that or just let them know that I was open. Sometimes when you are a patient, you are unable to do the kinds of things you would do ordinarily for your spiritual health, such as read the scripture. It's nice during those times to have someone to do it for you. Sometimes just offering something like, "I've noticed you've got your scriptures here. Do you have a favorite passage? Would you like me to read it?" Maybe five minutes spent reading to that patient would be more important than all the other care that they could have. When I was in the hospital a couple of years ago, when I was very, very sick with cancer, there was a man in the next room—I never saw him, but I could hear him—and he would call almost every five minutes for the nurse. He had his bell or he would holler. He wanted this, he wanted that, or he wanted the other thing. It always amazed me how patient the nurses were with him. They would come in and every time, "Now Mr. So-and-So, what can I do for you now?" He really didn't want anything. He wanted to know they were there, and they were so good with him.

How can we prevent this situation? How can we value and realise women's unique ethic of caring, yin energy, and healing potential? The answers to this problem are not simple. There is no easy way for women to realise their ethic of care and yin energy while simultaneously seeking autonomy and equality within the caring professions. Consistent with the principles of balance in Taoism, "the answer does not lie in either a glorification of caring or a repudiation of professionalism" (Baines, 1993, p. 66). Either route would throw off the balance required to run a system as complex as health care. What is implied here is the need in modern society to somehow blend and balance caring and professionalism, to embrace transcendent meaning without sacrificing a commitment to modern rationality, and to expand our definitions of knowledge and science to fill the "emotionally hollow, aesthetically meaningless, and spiritually empty" (Pirsig, 1974, p. 102) nature of modern-day reason.

Currently, tensions exist between these dyads. These tensions rest fundamentally on the antagonism between substantive rationality and formal rationality and between transcendent meaning and modern reason. To overcome these tensions, a new language is needed—one that questions the systematic routines of modernity and refocusses social attention on existential questions and women's ethic of caring, all of which are currently repressed by contemporary institutions (Giddens, 1990; Gilligan, 1982).

Work by social theorists suggests that development of such a language could enable people to relate to, value, and realise transcendent meaning, substantive rationalities, and women's ethic of caring within a rationalistic context (Habermas, 1984, 1987; Giddens 1990, 1991; Gilligan, 1982). Work in the sociology of religion provides an example of such a language. This is known as the language of *reflexive spirituality*, which is a cultural language people use to talk with each other about transcendent meaning. The language incorporates simultaneous commitments both to modern rationality and to the value of transcendent meaning. Reflexive spirituality should be considered a cultural resource that modern North Americans are using to create the guiding transcendent meanings for a rationalised society (Besecke, 2000).

This phenomenon, although increasingly present in modernity, is not new. Indeed, it can be argued that the spirituality that guided Florence Nightingale through her life's work as a mystic and founder of modern-day nursing was reflexive in nature. Like modern reflexive spiritualists, Nightingale mentally "stood back" from her own perspective and recognised its situation in an array of possible perspectives. She maintained an awareness of the wide variety of religious meanings available and engaged in a critical and intentional assimilation of those meanings into her own spiritual outlook (Calabria, 1997; Dossey, 1998; Macrae, 1995). In further keeping with reflexive spirituality, Nightingale embraced transcendent meanings without sacrificing her commitment to rational thought. She saw no conflict between spirituality and science. "Indeed, Nightingale referred to the laws or organising principles of the universe as the 'Thoughts of God'" (Macrae, 1995, p. 9)

Furthermore, Florence Nightingale's mysticism itself may be linked to modern rationality. Early sociologists, such as Max Weber, expounded that mysticism as an idea system inhibits the development of rationality (Ritzer, 1996). However, there has since been a long tradition of both theoretical and empiric work that actually linked mysticism with modern rationality (Troeltsch, 1931; Campbell, 1978; Swatos, 1983; Paul, 1993; Roof 1993a, 1993b, 1998, 1999, as cited in Besecke, 2000). The argument underlying this association is that mystics are individuals who believe they are privileged to direct knowledge of God or ultimate reality. This knowledge is gained by direct experience through one or more of the five senses. Hence, "mysticism makes sense to many . . . because it seems to share with scientific rationality a value for empirical observation" (Besecke, 2000, p. 9). Thus, even through her mysticism, it can be argued that Florence Nightingale blended transcendent meaning without sacrificing her commitment to rationality.

Perhaps Nightingale's spiritual and scientific orientation provides us, as modern-day nurses, with clues that will help us strike a balance in our practise between caring and professionalism, between formal rationality and substantive rationality, and between transcendent meaning and modern reason. Blending wisdom gained across time in this way may result in a new form of nursing, nursing that realises its potential, nursing that may be called *neo-Nightingalism*.

SUMMARY

Research and experience indicate that spirituality, although at the core of nursing theory and history, is peripheral in practise and education. In terms of the lived experience of nursing practise, this situation creates a dissonance between what we are called upon to be and do and what our work environment permits us to realise.

The forces behind this dissonance, that is, factors in the social context of nursing practise that render spirituality and holistic care marginal, result from the collision of substantive rationality of spirituality and spiritual care and the formal means–end rationality of the current structure of the Western health care system. This oppressively authoritarian structure has a negative impact on nurses' and patients' experience and existence—their existential experiences—lived space, lived time, lived body, and lived other. It has pushed aside the initial, holistic, and traditional role of nurses as providers of physical and spiritual health care, healers of body and spirit.

Briefly, for today's nurse, lived space is experienced as corporate space rather than as nurturant space; lived time is experienced as efficient and compressed time rather than as shared time; lived body is experienced as a mechanised self rather than as an embodied self; and, finally, lived other is experienced largely through power rather than caring relations.

Fundamentally, these experiences are rooted in formal rationality and related forms of thought, including corporatism, the received view, the biomedical model, and the phenomenon of professionalisation. These thought forms serve as the ideologic basis of the current hegemonic structure.

The future, however, holds promise. More and more people are disillusioned with current medical practises and structures. They call for change, for the reestablishment of balance within the system. They call for health care bureaucracy, science, and practise to be guided by humanity, not just rationality. These voices of change constitute counter-hegemony—a counter movement. They beckon the spirit back into nursing, not as a ghost of the past but as a force for the future.

Online RESOURCES

Add to your knowledge of this issue:

American Holistic Nurses' Association

http://www.ahna.org/home/home.html

Alternative Medicine

http://www.pitt.ed/.cbw/altm.html

Canadian Association for Pastoral Practice and Education

http://www.cappe.org/

CareNurse

http://www.care-nurse.com

Catholic Health Association of Canada

http://www.chac.ca

International Association of Human Caring

http://www.humancaring.org/

Nurses Christian Fellowship International

http://welcome.to/NCFI

Dying With Dignity: A Canadian Society Concerned With the Quality of Dying

http://www.Web.apc.org/dwd/

Hospital Chaplains' Ministry of America, Inc.

http://www.hcmachaplains.org/

Whole Nurse

http://www.wholenurse.com/

Reflections on the Chapter

1. Reflect on and write down what spirituality and spiritual care mean to you.
2. During one of your clinical shifts, observe for spiritual care and spiritual care opportunities. Was spiritual care given? Why or Why not?
3. Ask your patients about the role their spirituality plays in their health and illness experiences. Compare their responses.
4. Identify barriers to the provision of spiritual nursing care.
5. Formulate strategies that address the barriers to the provision of spiritual nursing care for nursing practise and those responsible for providing health care resources.
6. Explore the implications for nursing education of the following statement "Spirituality, which is central in nursing theory and history, is peripheral in nursing practise and education."

REFERENCES

Albercrombie, N., Hill, S., & Turner, B. S. (1994). *The Penguin dictionary of sociology.* London: Penguin Books.

Aberdene, P., & Naisbitt, J. (1992*). Megatrends for women.* New York: Villard Books.

Anderson, J., & Kirkham, S. R. (1999). Discourse on health: A critical perspective. In H. Coward & P. Ratanakul (Eds.), *A cross-cultural dialogue on healthcare ethics* (pp. 47–67). Waterloo, ON: Wilfrid Laurier University Press.

Baines, C. (1993). The profession and an ethic of care. In C. Baines, P. Evans, & S. Neysmith (Eds.), *Women's caring: Feminist perspectives on social welfare* (pp. 36–72). Toronto: McClelland & Stewart Inc.

Baines, C., Evans, P., & Neysmith, S. (1993). Caring:

Its impact on the lives of women. In C. Baines, P. Evans, & S. Neysmith (Eds.), *Women's caring: Feminist perspectives on social welfare* (pp. 11–35). Toronto: McClelland & Stewart Inc.

Baumgart, A. & Larsen, J. (1992). *Canadian nurses facing the future* (2nd Ed.). St. Louis: Mosby Year Book.

Besecke, K. (2000, August). Speaking of meaning in modernity: *Reflexive spirituality as a cultural resource.* Paper presented at the annual meeting of the Association for the Sociology of Religion, Washington, D.C.

Bierstedt, R. (1974). *The social order* (4th ed.). New York: McGraw-Hill Book Company.

Bradshaw, A. (1994). *Lighting the lamp: The spiritual dimension of nursing care.* Harrow, Middlesex, England: Scutari Press.

Bradshaw, A. (1996). The spiritual dimension of hospice: The secularization of an ideal. *Social Science and Medicine, 43*(3), 409–419.

Calabria, M. D. (1997). *Florence Nightingale in Egypt and Greece: Her diary and "visions."* New York: State University of New York Press.

Campbell, C. (1978). The secret religion of the educated classes. *Sociological Analysis, 39,* 146–156.

Coward, H., & Ratanakul, P. (1999). *A cross-cultural dialogue on healthcare ethics.* Waterloo, ON: Wilfrid Laurier University Press.

Chapman, C. M. (1982). *Sociology for nurses* (2nd ed.). London: Bailliere Tindall.

Donahue, M. P. (1985). *Nursing the finest art: An illustrated history.* St. Louis: C. V. Mosby.

Dossey, B. (1998). Florence Nightingale. *Journal of Holistic Nursing, 16*(2), 111(54 pp.) [On-line]. Available: EBSCOhost/Academic Search FullTEXT Elite86190.

Gibbon, J. M., & Mathewson, M. S. (1947). *Three centuries of Canadian nursing.* Toronto: Macmillan.

Giddens, A. (1990). *The consequences of modernity.* Stanford: Stanford University Press.

Giddens, A. (1991). *Modernity and self-identity: Self and society in the late modern age.* Stanford, CA: Stanford University Press.

Gilligan, C. (1982). *In a different voice: Psychological theory and women's development.* Cambridge, MA: Harvard University Press.

Gilligan, C. (1997). In a different voice: Women's conceptions of self and morality. In D. Tietjens Meyers (Ed.), *Feminist social thought: A reader* (pp. 549–582). New York: Routledge.

Gramsci, A. (1971). *Selections from the prison notebooks* (Q. Hoare & G. Nowell-Smill, Eds. & Trans). New York: International Publishers.

Habermas, J. (1984). *The theory of communicative action. Vol. 1: Reason and the rationalization of society.* Boston: Beacon Press.

Habermas, J. (1987). *The philosophical discourse of humanity: Twelve lectures.* Jurgen Habermas: translated by Frederick Lawrence. Cambridge, MA: MIT Press.

Harrison, J. (1993). Spirituality and nursing practice. *Journal of Clinical Nursing, 2,* 211–217.

Heitlinger, A. (2000). *The impact of healthcare restructuring in Canada on the nursing profession.* Paper presented at the 12th Annual Meeting of the Society for the Advancement of Socio-Economics, London School of Economics, London, UK, July 7–10, 2000.

Highfield, M., & Cason, C. (1983). Spiritual needs of patients: Are they recognized? *Cancer Nursing, 6*(3), 187–192.

Kalberg, S. (1980). Max Weber's types of rationality: Cornerstones for analysis of rationalization processes in history. *American Journal of Sociology, 85*(5), 1145–1179.

Kozier, B., Erb, G., Berman, A. J., & Burke, K. M. (2001). *Fundamentals of nursing: Concepts, process, and practice* (6th ed.). Englewood Cliffs, NJ: Prentice Hall.Lachman, B. (1993). *The journal of Hildegard of Bingen.* New York: Bell Tower.

Macrae, J. (1995). Nightingale's spiritual philosophy and its significance for modern nursing. *Image—The Journal of Nursing Scholarship, 27*(1), 8–10.

Manning, P. K., & Fabrega, H. (1973). The experience of self and body: Health and illness in the Chiapas Highlands. In G. Psathas (Ed.), *Phenomenological sociology: Issues and applications* (pp. 251–304). New York: John Wiley & Sons.

Mayer, J. (1992). Wholly responsible for a part, or partly responsible for a whole? The concept of spiritual care in nursing. *Second Opinion, 17*(3), 26–55.

McSherry, W. (1998). Nurses' perception of spirituality and spiritual care. *Nursing Standard* [On-Line], *13*(4), 36-40. Available: Elsevier, Data Base: Elsevier Journals (licenced access only) [1999, July 12].

McSherry, W., & Draper, P. (1997). The spiritual dimension: Why the absence within nursing curricula?. *Nurse Education Today, 17,* 413–417.

McSherry, W., & Draper, P. (1998). The debates emerging from the literature surrounding the concept of spirituality as applied to nursing. *Journal of Advanced Nursing, 27,* 683–691.

Miller, J. B. (1986). *Toward a new psychology of women* (2nd ed.). Boston: Beacon press.

Miller, J. B., & Stiver, I. P. (1997). *The healing connection: How women form relationships in therapy and in life.* Boston: Beacon Press.

Narayanasamy, A. (1993). Nurse awareness and educational preparation in meeting their patient's spiritual needs. *Nurse Education Today, 13*(3), 196–201.

Nightingale, F. (1969). *Notes on nursing.* New York: Dover Publications (Original work published in 1860).

O'Brien, M. E. (1999). *Spirituality in nursing: Standing on holy ground.* Toronto: Jones and Bartlett Publishers.

O'Connell, B. (2000). Research shows erosion to advocacy role. *Reflections on Nursing Leadership, Second Quarter,* 26–28.

Pascall, G. (1986). *Social policy: A feminist analysis.* London: Tavistock.

Paul, G. E. (1993). Why Troeltsch? Why today? Theology for the 21st century. *Christian Century, 110,* 676–681.

Piles, C. (1990). Providing spiritual care. *Nurse Educator, 15*(1), 36–41.

Pirsig, R. M. (1974). *Zen and the art of motorcycle maintenance: An inquiry into values.* New York: Morrow.

Potter, P. A., & Perry, A. G. (2001). *Fundamentals of nursing: Concepts, process, and practice* (4th ed.). St. Louis: C. V. Mosby.

Ritzer, G. (1996). *Sociological theory* (4th ed.). New York: McGraw-Hill.

Roof, W. C. (1993a). Toward the year 2000: Reconstructions of religious space. *Annals of the American Academy of Political and Social Science, 527,* 155–170.

Roof, W. C. (1993b). *A generation of seekers: The spiritual journeys of the baby boom generation.* San Francisco: HarperCollins.

Roof, W. C. (1998). Modernity, the religious and the spiritual. *Annals of the American Academy of Political and Social Science, 558,* 211–224.

Roof, W. C. (1999). *Spiritual marketplace: Baby boomers and the remaking of American religion.* Princeton, NJ: Princeton University Press.

Ross, L. (1994). Spiritual aspects of nursing. *Journal of Advanced Nursing, 19,* 439–447.

Ross-Kerr, J. (1997). A heritage of healing: Reflections on nursing in Canada. *Reflections, Third/fourth Quarter,* 52–54.

Ross-Kerr, J., & MacPhail, J. (Eds.). (1996). *Concepts in Canadian nursing.* Toronto: Mosby.

Saul, J. R. (1999). Healthcare at the end of the Twentieth Century: Confusing symptoms for systems. In M. A. Sommerville (Ed.), *Do we care? Renewing Canada's commitment to health* (pp. 3–20). Kingston: McGill-Queen's University Press.

Sellers, S. C., & Haag, B. A. (1998). Spiritual nursing interventions. *Journal of Holistic Nursing* [On-line] *16*(3), p. 338, 18p. Available: EBSCOhost, Data Base: Academic Search Elite (licenced access only) [1999, June 20].

Shelly, J. A., & Miller, A. B. (1999). *Called to care: A Christian theology of nursing.* Downers Grove, IL: InterVarsity Press.

Shepherd, L. J. (1993). *Lifting the veil: The feminine face of science.* Boston: Shambhala Publications.

Sloan, R. P., Bagiella, E., & Powell, T. (2000). Religion, spirituality, and medicine. *Lancet, 353,* 664–667.

Swatos, W. H. (1983). Enchantment and disenchantment in modernity: The significance of "religion" as a sociocultural category. *Sociological Analysis, 44*(4), 321–338.

Taylor, C., Lillis, C., & LeMone, P. (2001). *Fundamentals of nursing: The art and science of nursing care* (4th ed.). Philadelphia: Lippincott Williams & Wilkins.

Toombs, S. K. (1988). Illness and the paradigm of lived body. *Theoretical Medicine, 9,* 201–226.

Toombs, S. K. (1992). *The meaning of illness: A phenomenological account of the different perspectives of physician and patient.* Boston: Kluwer Academic.

Troeltsch, E. (1931). *The social teachings of the Christian churches.* London: George Allen & Unwin.

van Maanen, M. (1997). Hermeneutic phenomenological reflection. In M. van Maanen (Ed.). *Researching lived experience* (2nd ed.) (pp. 77–109). London, ON: The Althouse Press.

Watson, J. (1999). *Postmodern nursing and beyond.* Toronto: Churchill Livingstone.

Weber, M. (1958). *The protestant ethic and the spirit of capitalism.* (T. Parsons, Transl.). New York: Charles Scribner's Sons. (Original work published 1904–05.)

Weber, M. (1968). *Economy and society* (edited by Guenther Roth and Clause Wittich). New York: Bedminister. (Original work published 1921.)

PART VI

Leadership and Change

26

Innovation and Contemporary Nursing Leadership

Deborah Tamlyn ■ Sandra Reilly

Chapter Objectives

At the completion of this chapter, you will be able to:

1. Analyse proposed changes pertaining to the role of nurses in the delivery of health care.

2. Describe the implications for nursing leadership associated with the transformation of the health system.

3. Suggest alternatives to the current health care delivery system.

4. Formulate questions related to the leadership role of nurses in the Canadian health system.

5. Discuss the importance of innovation as it relates to leadership in the health care delivery system.

6. Discuss the competencies now required of nursing leaders.

Ginette Lemire Rodger, President of Canadian Nurses Association.

The premise of this chapter is that Canadian nurses will need to adopt a new style of leadership (Chow et al., 1999) to participate in reshaping the delivery of health care. Certainly, most will agree that rapid changes in the 1990s produced considerable confusion and anxiety among health care professionals. As this transition continues, so too will the demands on nurses to assume significantly different leadership competencies. How well they meet these challenges will determine the quality of health care now and in the future.

Many words and phrases describe what has happened to nursing in regard to the Canadian health system. Alternatively, generic terms, such as *reshape* or *reform* or *restructure*, are used to describe the changes taking place. Useful in drawing attention to what has happened, these terms provide little, if any, information about what nursing leaders need to know if they are to make their contribution to the process of health care change. This chapter begins with a brief description of the new processes that have become so confused, that health care systems now have to readjust to rectify past decisions.

For their part, nursing leaders need to reset their perspectives to prepare for their new role as knowledge workers (Drucker, 1999). In 1959, Drucker (1994) coined the term "knowledge-worker" to describe the emerging class of new workers in postindustrial America. Unlike the earlier industrial worker, this new worker requires significant "formal education and the ability to acquire and to apply theoretical and analytical knowledge" (p. 62). For the knowledge-worker, the operative words are acquire and apply. That is, because knowledge, especially in the sciences, doubles every 18 to 24 months, a knowledge-worker has to learn continuously throughout his or her career. Similarly, citing the neurosurgeon as an example, Drucker also believes that abstract ideas primarily become meaningful in a knowledge society when they are applied to a problem. Consequently, the knowledge-worker typically displays his or her knowledge by applying it to concrete problems, which often require manual handling.

The demand for more applied education to solve complex problems leads to more specialisation among workers. Typically, as a worker learns more and more about less and less, he or she increasingly depends on others for those skills outside his or her scope of knowledge. As such, you most often find the knowledge-worker on a team within a knowledge-intense organisation.

Certainly, they can succeed only if they recognise that the operative word for nursing practise has become *innovation* (a concept, thing, procedure, or practise that individuals or groups see as new). In this regard, nursing leaders, both formal and informal, can take a page from management, which teaches that change produces opportunity that gives rise to innovation. Accordingly, nursing leaders, who typically work in knowledge-intense organisations, have to become expert in diffusing innovation in order to make changes.

HISTORICAL CONTEXT OF CONTEMPORARY NURSING LEADERSHIP

Like their colleagues in medicine, psychology, pharmacy, and social work, to name a few, nurses at the turn of this century find themselves without their traditional sense of purpose and autonomy (Storch & Stinson, 1988). Nurses now come under the direct authority of managers who are largely driven by financial considerations. They find themselves measured against outcomes that bear little resemblance to the profession's ideologic values and must respond to management—without input from nurses—designs of specific nursing activities. *This loss of purpose and autonomy* comes about because nurses remain lax in demonstrating how patients benefit from their interventions or in proving that nurses represent an efficient means of increasing productivity.

We are not the first to recognise that the current situation in nursing cries for a remedy (Nunn, 2001). Nevertheless, unless these problems are addressed, patient care suffers as nurses become demoralised by a pervasive sense of mistrust in the system. This mistrust likely accounts "for decreased commitment and job performance" (Corey-Lisle et al., 1999, p. 36). Regrettably but understandably, the consequence is that fewer nurses seem willing to assume leadership roles. In other words, at the same time nursing faces significant challenges, it lacks a cadre of leaders ready to provide direction to the largest group of well-educated professionals in the entire health care system.

Changing Health Care Landscape

Changes to the Canadian health care system became commonplace by the 1990s. Many practicing nurses remember how as students they received their training in a hospital system with expressed religious and para-militaristic overtones. Supported by the scientific management principles of Frederick Taylor (1947), training emphasised the command-control practise model that employed a strict hierarchical approach and invested all authority in physicians. By the 1990s, memories of these practises were increasingly distant. Although such practises should no longer have currency, the paradigm shift from such linear, top-down, deterministic thinking has only just begun.

A few words about this paradigm shift seem in order. Sometime after World War II, North America began changing from an industrial to a service economy. This change, with its emphasis on meeting human needs, began a transformation that questioned the century-old conviction in measuring human success solely by scientific, industrial, and material progress. Instead of extolling reason and order, society began to place increasing importance on the rights and needs of individuals.

Social commentator Alvin Toffler (1980) believes that the self-help and wellness movements represent tangible evidence of how these changes will eventually affect the practise of health care. Instead of behaving strictly as passive consumers of health care, individuals eventually became active "prosumers," which Toffler describes as a combination of producer and consumer. According to his logic, as patients more and more *actively participate* in *managing* their own care, we can expect a decrease in paternalistic, authoritative physician-centred thinking (Bulger, 1999).

Certainly, as patients gain a greater role in decisions about their care, nurses can expect greater accountability in their nursing practises. Because many patients see nurses as social and economic equals, nurses enjoy special access in helping patients to become informed consumers and to manage their chronic health problems. Nurses will also play a role in helping communities to become more responsible for their own health as health promotion gains wider acceptance. The emergence of nurse practitioners certainly testifies to a public willingness for nurses to expand their scope of practise.

Nurses can reasonably expect that the transformation of society and the health care sector will undoubtedly present increased opportunities and challenges for nurses to provide more comprehensive care for patients. Certainly, with society's ability to transfer large amounts of information electronically by the Internet, knowledge has become even more critical to any interaction between health professionals and their patients (Spitzer, 1998). With their newly found knowledge, patients can demand the best possible care. In such an environment, nurses can expect their traditional job titles, with their well-defined scopes of responsibilities, to disappear as health care systems devise new multiskilled teams.

The changes currently facing nursing reflect those occurring in the wider society, which appears ready to change the essence of health care delivery. The accompanying challenge appears nothing less than stupefying. How can the Canadian health care system operate efficiently and effectively, especially when an aging population, with heightened expectations of health care, demands increasingly expensive and complex treatments to increase its quality of life?

Nursing Leadership and Reform of the Health Care System

In many ways, the situation for nurses is emblematic of the aforementioned issues. Better educated and frequently expected to exercise initiative, nurses nevertheless remain limited by traditional and legal restrictions that go back decades. Without strong leadership models for alternative kinds of practise, nurses likely face the ongoing dilemma of how to actualise the self-care and wellness movements. For example, consider the challenge that nurses face of educating policymakers and the public that a comprehensive health care system equally considers health protection and health promotion when designing its activities. Heavily invested in a hospital system, organised around body parts and diseases, society appears reluctant to challenge the traditional medical approach. In short, nursing leaders have to divest society of the belief that health care represents only sickness care.

Extraordinarily complex, health care requires that providers pay attention to the person, the environment, and the system. Yet, like other professions, nursing currently lacks the tools for assessing and providing comprehensive care outside the hospital setting. Unless leaders address this failure, nursing faces an uncertain future (Spitzer, 1998). Indeed, according to Spitzer (1998), any profession that fails to redefine itself during this transformation "can be consumed, reduced, transformed or expelled out of the system as it reorganises and adapts" (p. 168).

To repeat the obvious, the current health care system in North America begs for nursing leadership. Nevertheless, according to Porter-O'Grady and Krueger-Wilson (1995), nursing, like other health professions, lacks a "ready and able group of leaders waiting in the wings . . . [and] institutions of higher education are just barely changing their curriculums to fit the new reality" (p. 298).

To correct this oversight, doctoral students, enrolled in the Faculty of Nursing at the University of Calgary, examine leadership as *the critical element* in health care reform. They understand that leadership roles are important not only in administrative matters but also in clinical and research areas. One particular course, "Contemporary Issues in Health Care," required of all doctoral students, who participate by videoconferencing and audioconferencing from across Canada, invites national leaders to discuss health care reform issues from multidisciplinary perspectives. The syllabus for this course reminds students that

> [t]he last decade of the twentieth century witnessed a revolution in health care. Largely driven by fiscal constraints, policymakers . . . downsized the health care system. In time, consumers accepted shorter hospital stays, postponements for specialized diagnoses and treatments, and more technologically elaborate home care programmes. Noticeably, the system provided few opportunities for consumers to engage with practitioners in revamping the system.

As eventually became evident, the imposition of budgetary constraints alone has limited usefulness. It too easily focuses on achieving efficiencies at the expense of ensuring and improving outcomes. And because health care ultimately concerns matters of life and death, such oversights affect more than quality of life issues. Downsizing, without adequate strategic thinking, raises questions about standards of care. In the face of these "realities," health care practitioners have to reexamine how they can collaborate with consumers to redesign the delivery of care. If they do any less, they effectively deny their expertise to consumers and fail to provide "leadership" to their colleagues.

In addition to fiscal constraints, other changes, more social than economic, require reexamination of the health care system. Delegated and narrowly defined roles, with carefully proscribed responsibilities, dominated by strict hierarchical relationships characterized the modern era. Today, as part of an ongoing paradigm shift from the modern to the postmodern era, rationality and centrality no longer dictate organizational behavior. In the postmodern era, roles have become interdependent and flexible. Consumers, policymakers, and practitioners expect to share responsibility in setting the agenda for new multidisciplinary health teams, sometimes organised on an *ad hoc* basis (Reilly & Tamlyn, 2001, pp. 2–3).

Nursing leaders who have participated as guest lecturers in this course include Geertje Boschma (AB), Bob Calnan (BC), Barbara Downe-Wamboldt (NS), Dana Edge (AB), Francine Girard (AB), Helen Glass (MAN), Wendy Harper (AB), Kathryn King (AB), Diana Mansell (AB), Helen Mussallem (BC), Ginette Lemire Rodger (ON), Sheila Robinson (AB), James Rankin (AB), Judith Shamian (ON), and Shirley Stinson (AB).

A recognised nursing leader and past president of the Canadian Nurses Association (CNA), Ginette Lemire Rodger looks at these unprecedented changes already underway as vindication for all the reforms asked for by nurses over the past 20 years. Although still unrealised, these reforms include, among others, the following:

- Concentrating on "health, not just health care"
- Arranging for more "health services in the community, not just in hospital"
- Developing "multidisciplinary networks of practitioners, educators, researchers, and managers, not just solo players" with something to offer patients
- Welcoming "public participation in shaping the system, not just public consultation"
- Focussing on "intersectoral health, not just health care"
- Using "appropriate technology, not just 'high tech' "
- Directing attention to "ecology, not just environment" (Hibberd & Rodger, 1999, p. 261)

Ultimately, in Rodger's opinion, the implementation of these reforms promises to value and utilise the skills of nurses for the betterment of the health care system.

NEW RELATIONSHIP BETWEEN WORKERS AND THE SYSTEM

Whatever transformations result from health care reform, the movement toward more people-centred health care is certain to proceed. Along with it, other innovations are likely to occur. According to Porter-O'Grady (1995), we will see the transformation of health delivery services proceed along several lines. Services will become more integrated, with the development of more structures that provide a continuum of care. Nurses, like other professionals, will recognise the social reality of the self-help and wellness movements and enter new partnerships with the community.

There is evidence that some organisations appear ready to accept such innovative thinking by abandoning the hierarchical, expert-driven way of thinking. For example, consider the seemingly innocuous decision by the Calgary Regional Health Authority (CRHA), after only 7 years since its inception, to rename itself. In June 2001, it became known as the Calgary Health Region (CHR).

According to a press release, members of the staff helped prompt the decision, when they requested a more collaborative nomenclature. By omitting "Authority," with its emphasis on hierarchical thinking, from its title, the CHR now permits "individual sites, portfolios, and programs" to identify themselves in all their correspondence (http://www.crha-health.ab.ca/frontlines/issue41_1.htm, 2001). Accordingly, "The [revised] name Calgary Health Region . . . is a much better reflection of the collaboration between hospitals, community care providers, physicians, nurses and a wide range of other care providers and partners in the community" (p. 2).

This thinking extends to the organisation's new logo. Whereas the previous one symbolised a linear system that promoted a power relationship between the organisation and the community, the new logo expresses a "caring, accessible and integrated" delivery system that recognises how all human activity integrates "people, growth and the cycle of life" (p. 2).

The obvious differences between the logos emphasises the transformations associated with health reform (Fig. 26.1). The previous logo and its use of the word Authority presumed a hierarchical relationship between provider and the community. It implied the organisation functioned in a stable environment with predictable problems and routine responses. Power rested in the vertical relationship between professionals and patients. In this system, professionals had strictly defined roles, supported by intractable relationships among different specialties or disciplines. The new logo opens the organisation to change and possibly innovation. Highly suggestive of an organisation ready to adapt and even introduce new systems, the new logo has a dynamic quality. It suggests fluidity, participatory decision making, and openness to innovation. With a more horizontal arrangement of power, the new logo implies a nonlinear decision-making process more in keeping with complex, multifaceted, systemic health problems in the 21st century.

Note that although the focus of this chapter is not on integrated delivery systems, they do have relevance to nursing leadership because some believe that integrated delivery systems compromise any leadership role for nursing (Pinkerton, 2000). For those interested in the subject, the first issue of *Healthcare Papers* (2000) examines the arguments for and against the adoption of integrated delivery systems in Canada.

FIGURE 26.1. Obvious differences between logos emphasise the transformations associated with health reform. The current logo (above) suggests a dynamic organization that is adaptable and open to change; the earlier logo (below) with the word *Authority* suggests a hierarchical relationship between provider and the community.

The name change of the Calgary Health Region makes a point about contemporary health organisations. They typically represent the ultimate learning environment. Sorrells-Jones (1999) states that any organisation in which 40% or more of the workers use information to solve problems, as well as generate ideas and services, ranks as a knowledge-intense environment. In such a place, knowledge work takes precedence. The organisation expects its workers to do "nonroutine, unpredictable, nonlinear, multidisciplinary, nonrepetitive activities in a long time frame with evolving goals" (Beyerlein et al., 1995, p. x).

In such an organisation, workers represent more of a resource than an expense because human capital has as much, if not more, importance to the organisation's mission as its property or equipment. To succeed, the organisation has to attract the right kind of people and provide them with "flat, agile structures, open information, power that moves to expertise, and systems that create knowledgeable employees" (Lawler, 2001, p. 17), who want nothing less than to devise innovative solutions to practical problems.

Obviously, knowledge workers have a substantive, if still undefined, role in formulating policies and practises. The organisations, if they seek credibility with their workers, want to include their workers' input and innovative ideas. In the end, the job falls on leaders inside and outside the organisation to emphasise the critical role of innovation to this process.

CALL FOR A NEW KIND OF NURSING LEADERSHIP

By now, everyone understands that successful organisations, like their workers, embrace change. Yet, as world-renowned authority on corporate management Peter Drucker (1999) tells us, "one cannot manage change. One can only be ahead of it" (p. 73). If one accepts this reasoning, it then follows that organisations or professions require leaders who can remain in front of change. Or in Hibberd & Rodger's (1999) words, "nursing requires visionaries, who see the future in terms of its possibilities."

The call for nursing visionaries seems a daunting quest, but it is attainable. Drucker (1999), for one, has some specific advice. A leader, who embraces change, examines, among other things, every "product," "service," and "process" for its usefulness. If it fails this test, the "change leader" abandons it. As importantly, abandonment does not necessarily mean obsolescence. It often means reorganisation to make the proper use of the product, service, or process. Certainly, the changing role of professional nurses demonstrates that nursing continually abandons some services or processes only to replace them with more useful evidence-based endeavors. Such change, to use Drucker's expression, represents a kind of "organised improvement" because it purposefully increases efficiency and effectiveness by staying ahead of change.

Nursing history also serves to teach us that challenges, albeit daunting, are not insurmountable. About 40 years ago, nursing leaders, who long ago recognised the dangers of routinising nursing practise, envisioned nursing practise as more collaborative. They advocated abandoning the 100-year-old hospital-based training system, with its adherence to the militaristic principle of obedience to authority. In its place, they proposed that a baccalaureate education become the entry point for nursing. These leaders faced serious opposition. The struggle continues as demonstrated by recent efforts of some provincial legislators to reopen hospital diploma nursing programmes. Nursing requires visionaries, who understand the importance of advanced education in preparing nurses for expanded responsibilities in reshaping the health care system.

Challenge to Leaders of Nursing Change

There is no debate about the challenge that awaits the leaders of nursing change. By their own account, Canadian nurses believe that they are underutilised and undervalued by the health care system. They state as much in two Canadian reports.

Health Canada (The Office of Nursing Policy, 2001) acknowledges a sense of appreciation and recognition as among the most important qualities nurses want in their workplace. Indeed, nurses report "lower levels of autonomy, poorer relationships with physicians and less job satisfaction" (p. 5), leading to more job-related stress than any other group of health care workers.

In another report, the Registered Nurses Association of Ontario (March, 2000) attribute inappropriate "workloads and the lack of professional development opportunities" to "fragmented patient care and the disillusionment of nurses with their profession" (p. 8). The report goes on to make 89 recommendations to improve nursing. Generally divided into two categories, the recommendations focus on providing more educational opportunities for nurses or ensuring that nurses enjoy more responsibilities in keeping with their abilities.

If a sense of undervaluation and underutilisation lies at the centre of nurses' dissatisfaction, it also represents the major challenge facing nursing leaders: how to reestablish nurses' trust so that they once again have confidence in the Canadian health care system (Shamian, 2000).

Attributes of Contemporary Nursing Leaders

Whether nurses have a role in supporting health reforms largely depends on the availability of nursing leaders in clinical, research, and administrative areas. These special individuals, according to Hibberd and Rodger (1999), possess four primary attributes. Nursing leaders have an ability to translate a *vision* into reality, the *knowledge* and the *confidence* to deal with uncertainty, and at the same time a commitment to maintain their *visibility* as nurses. These attributes are more like personal characteristics of someone who demonstrates leadership ability. Their usefulness largely corresponds to what management refers to as human resource skills. Goleman (1997) refers to this as "emotional intelligence." Highly pragmatic and relational, these attributes describe what a professional brings to his or her work.

VISION

Nursing leaders demonstrate vision when their ideas successfully bond the mission of the organisation with the larger purposes of society and the ideals of the profession. That is, nurses expect a high order of satisfaction from their work. Too frequently, they feel their special skills are undervalued and underutilised. Successful nursing leaders take their insights and create a vision that compels the participation of others. In so doing, nursing leaders actually stimulate innovation because they envision what will happen.

KNOWLEDGE

For the transformation of the health care sector to occur with minimal disruption, nursing leaders also have to possess comprehensive knowledge about the nature of change in the larger society as well as in specific areas of the health care sector. That is to say, nursing leaders see themselves and their organisations within the new paradigms and help others to do the same. They have the skills to organise activities without polarising other team members along professional, departmental, or specialty lines. Such knowledge obviously goes beyond mere understanding because it includes the appreciation of what constitutes the essence of the new paradigm inherent in the information age.

CONFIDENCE

Confidence represents the most personal and least tangible of the attributes associated with successful leadership. According to Hibberd and Rodger (1999), "nursing needs confident leaders who have self-esteem and are able to live with insecurity" (p. 264). Not only do they think outside the box, they also possess the fortitude to express ideas that run counter to the prevailing wisdom. For example, although public participation represents a fundamental tenet of the "new public health," consultation between communities and providers largely represents an unrealised goal. A successful nursing leader challenges traditional practises and helps the system make the necessary adjustments as to how the system interacts with the community.

VISIBILITY

An equally important attribute of successful nursing leadership is visibility. Here we have one of those paradoxes so typical of this period of transformation. At the same time that health care reforms have downgraded the role of professionals (Storch & Stinson, 1988), the complexity of health care tells us that professionals still play an essential part and that health care organisations have to support them. Hibberd and Rodger (1999) lament recent decisions to eliminate "nursing positions at the policy and senior-management levels of health-care agencies" (p. 265). Although nurses still hold management portfolios, now they more often function as health care leaders, not necessarily as nursing professionals. This omission of professional credentials from the administrative work of nurses has serious consequences. For certain, nursing runs the risk of becoming "invisible and disposable." And this diminished profile of nursing can lead to unnecessary fatalities because of lower standards of care.

The above situation raises a substantive problem. By "making assumptions about the nature of the [clinical] task, [hospital] reformers make assumptions about the nature and role of professionalism" (Southon & Braithwaite, 1998, p. 26). They assume that clinical protocols can predict clinical problems and that individual needs are reducible to classification. Whether one agrees that such changes devalue professionals, it seems obvious that professional assessments—at least for individual patients—count for less. This conundrum raises an important question for nursing leaders. How does the system deliver health services efficiently without compromising the effectiveness of these services?

CIRCUMSTANCES AND SOURCES THAT PROMOTE INNOVATION

Innovation is one of those familiar words that seemingly has limited application. Certainly, most human behaviour appears more repetitive than imaginative. Health professionals, no less than other workers, usually take comfort in the security of repeating what they know from experience, works. Consequently, people usually come up with fresh ideas only when circumstances compel them.

Drucker (1998) appreciates how events initiate and promote the innovative process and how they refer indirectly to leadership. In "The Discipline of Innovation" (1998), Drucker assigns a critical, if largely unspecified, role to the vision and knowledge required of change leaders. In several places, he makes clear that innovation occurs only when a change leader takes a highly visible position on changes that are taking place. Without trivialising the process whereby innovation occurs, Drucker implies that innovation occurs because the right *person* is in the right *place* at the right *time.*

Drucker believes that innovation represents a critical function of any organisation, whether a multinational corporation, a public service institution, or family business. Indeed, only through innovation can an organisation develop practical solutions in an environment of rapidly changing markets and technologies.

Drucker organises all innovation around various kinds of opportunities, divided into two classes or sources. One, *internal sources*, refers to opportunities that arise within the organisation. The other, *external sources*, considers opportunities that turn up outside the organisation.

Internal Sources of Innovation

Internal sources of innovation arise within the organisation, and workers are likely to know about them first. Unlike external sources of innovation, internal sources are more symptomatic than causal. They are likely to have already occurred. As such, they require little effort to make them functional.

UNEXPECTED SOURCES OF INNOVATION (NOT TO SERENDIPITY)

Sometimes success is fickle. Many times, it arrives unannounced, and it occurs in the most unlikely places. When success occurs serendipitously, organisations sometimes see it as anomalous and even label it as "unsound, unhealthy, and obviously abnormal" (Drucker, 1998, p. 38). Why do people mistrust this kind of success? Some people have an inherent suspicion of anything unfamiliar. Or they believe that change suggests incompetence. Or they wonder if change in one area will prompt other organisational changes that risk offending special interests or dominant groups.

Drucker (1998) tells the story of the inventor of procaine (Novocain), who refused to market it to dentists. Throughout his life, he remained committed to his original idea that procaine belonged exclusively to surgeons, who, he stubbornly believed, needed a new form of anaesthesia. For years, he travelled to dental schools criticising dentists' use of his invention. He was unable to evaluate his invention for what it offered humankind.

Similarly, organisations often lack the tools with which to appreciate success, especially qualitative success. To redress any lack of "vision, knowledge, and understanding" (Drucker, 1998, p. 41), organisations continuously have to ask themselves the question, "What basic changes are now appropriate for this organisation in the way it defines its business?" (p. 42). To answer the question, change leaders systematically have to investigate and analyse events for concealed successes.

INCONGRUITIES

Drucker defines an incongruity as "a discrepancy, a dissonance, between what is and what 'ought' to be, or between what is and what everybody assumes it to be" (Drucker, 1998, p. 57). Like the other sources of innovation, incongruities invite change. Unlike other sources, however, incongruities are solely qualitative and clearly definable within specific industries, markets, or processes. They are divided into four kinds:

- *Incongruity between economic realities.* An example drawn from the health care sector points out that innovative responses to incongruities exhibit a simple and obvious quality. For many families, a hospital emergency room (ER) became a primary care provider. Whatever the complaint, the ER was the first choice whenever a health problem arose. The resultant expense forced some ERs to close or some patients to wait unconscionably long times at others. Staff knew this but, mired in traditional practises, did nothing about it. Eventually, financial considerations prevailed. A combination of expediency and new management practises gave rise to emergent care centres outside of hospitals, where nonemergency cases receive attention around the clock.

- *Incongruity between assumptions and reality.* If people make assumptions that fail to agree with reality, their efforts to initiate change will also fail. After a decade of success in reducing HIV/AIDS transmission among homosexuals, health promotion efforts stalled because policymakers assumed that the homosexual population knew everything about the prevalence and transmission of the disease. Only after incidence of disease began to increase did community action teams devise a simple and focussed campaign directed at this population. Although the jury is still out, early results look promising.

- *Incongruity between perceived and actual values and expectations.* Of all incongruities, those between organisations and their clients occur most frequently. That is, it is not unusual that organisations wrongly or mistakenly perceive what their clients actually want. The very nature of the relationship *fosters* these misperceptions. Consider health care, especially obstetrics, palliative care, geriatrics, and pain management. Physicians and nurses typically presume that they know the meaning of health care for patients in these specialties. They usually define it in absolute terms and apply it equally to every patient. Yet, as the increasing popularity of doulas makes evident, expectant mothers want something more than the traditional obstetric experience.

- *Incongruity within the rhythm or logic of a process.* People within an industry or market often know that something is "out of sync" in a process or the way things are done. They come to this understanding by way of their experiences. In this regard, because of the continuity of care they provide patients, nurses have the benefit of knowing more about the operations of an organisation than other groups. In a regular column, "Nurse(s) to Know," which first appeared in 1998, *The Canadian Nurse* profiles each month one nurse who has acted in an innovative manner. One story illustrates how one nurse became an agent for an internal source of innovation. The article tells how she, working in an overcrowded maximum-security jail, realised that bureaucratic bungling and malfeasance interfered with the delivery of nursing care. She consulted with other professionals and prepared a report that led to the complete review of the situation. Ultimately, her innovative action led to improved services to a highly marginalised population.

NEED

A major source of innovative opportunity, "process need" begins with a job that needs doing. The innovator focusses on a task and "perfects a process that already exists, replaces a link that is weak, redesigns an existing old process around newly available knowledge" (Drucker, 1985, p. 69). This highly successful kind of innovation comes in response to a problem everyone in the organisation knows about but has never paid much attention to correcting. The innovation, once designed, is immediately accepted because it is obviously called for.

INDUSTRY AND MARKET CHANGES

Although their size appears to indicate otherwise, markets or industries are fragile. They disintegrate and reinvent themselves more quickly than most people imagine.

The Canadian Nurse provides another good example of how a nurse became a source of innovation in her practise. The graduate of a diploma programme, who returned to school for her baccalaureate and master's degrees, she created a role for advanced practise nursing in cardiology, when it had yet to exist in her province. To establish her credentials as a practitioner, she took it upon herself to complete a medical school course in physical assessment. In the same innovative manner, she went on to establish a preadmission programme for assessing cardiac patients about to undergo catheterisation. In effect, at a time when the system had only begun to make adjustments to increase the effectiveness and efficiency of its operations, she had already exhibited leadership ability.

Similar changes occurred in the health care system. When wounded veterans returned home after World War II, Canada built more hospitals. This growth demanded more workers, which then saw the introduction of new occupations, including technicians, therapists, and auxiliary personnel. As a system becomes more complex, it also demands innovation. For example, once almost all physicians had their own practises. Today, most work along with partners in group practises or have salaried positions in health care organisations. This happened because the complexity of health care services requires a more elaborate management system, which individual practitioners find unaffordable.

External Sources of Innovation

External sources of innovation arise from outside the organisation. Although less reliable and predictable than the internal sources of innovation, these three external sources do have certain advantages. Inasmuch as they arise from within the environment, they appear highly visible and of much greater consequence.

DEMOGRAPHICS

Described as predictable, unambiguous, and clear, demographics commonly refer to population characteristics such as gender, race, occupation, income, distribution, and other statistical characteristics. The term applies equally to the psychosocial events that influence how populations behave. For example, the development of birth control, the decision by women of child-bearing age to postpone marriage or pregnancy, and the rise of the two-income family are as critical to any explanation of recent population trends as is the number of people of child-bearing age. When analysed, demographics provide helpful information to guide preemptive action or change organisational strategies. Besides the obvious effects of an aging population, what other demographic events will influence nursing services? Consider the recruitment and retention of nurses. Within a decade, a worldwide shortage of nurses will decrease by more than half. Besides increasing the number of graduates, what other measures are available?

PERCEPTUAL CHANGES

A highly qualitative matter, perception concerns how individuals interpret facts. In other words, do they see a glass 50% filled with water as half full or half empty? Many North Americans, despite the remarkable advances in medical technology seem obsessed with aging or the disabilities ordinarily associated with growing old. Pharmaceutical companies realise this and focus on products that reduce or eliminate incontinence, maintain sexual potency, or reduce hair loss. What demands will an aging population, with heightened expectations of the health care system, make upon society and their families? Perception will also influence what innovations change leaders in nursing will devise.

KNOWLEDGE-BASED CHANGES

Innovation also occurs as the result of scientific or intellectual accomplishments. These accomplishments differ from all other sources of innovation primarily because of the lead time, failure rate, predictability, and challenges inherent in such work. For example, even when pharmaceutical companies receive permission for fast tracking "miracle drugs," the time between development and large-scale production can be a decade or more. The diffusion of intellectual innovation may take even longer. Although the Internet promises faster dissemination of ideas, especially with the emergence of English as a second global language, societies reluctantly change how they think. For this reason, change leaders of knowledge-based innovation have to possess a clear focus, comprehend the scope of the changes, know how to sell their ideas, and understand the expected outcomes.

DIFFUSION OF INNOVATION

How innovation is shared or diffused in a knowledge-intense organisation has critical importance. Not surprisingly, the subject has received considerable study.

Over 80 years in development with about 4,000 publications on the topic (Rogers, 1995), diffusion of innovation theory provides the most comprehensive framework for understanding the communication process whereby participants "create and share information with one another to reach a mutual understanding" (p. xvi). In other words, diffusion of innovation theory offers one explanation for the dissemination of innovative ideas among individuals in a social system.

Innovation provides individuals or organisations with alternatives with which to solve problems. In this lengthy process, individuals and organisations, not knowing for certain whether a solution works, vigilantly have to collect information to cope with the uncertainty inherent in the process.

As Everett Rogers (1995) points out, the diffusion of innovation follows an S-shaped curve over time. Figure 26.2 presents an amalgamation of Roger's S-shaped curve with Drucker's seven sources of innovation. This representation agrees with what management and communication science teaches us. First, according to Drucker, innovation occurs in response to various internal and external environmental sources. Second, as Rogers points out, once introduced, innovation takes a diffused path as it makes its way from one person to another. The conceptualisation in Figure 26-2 represents how Drucker's sources of innovation hypothetically interrelate with Rogers' diffusion theory.

Remembering what Drucker tells us about the sources of innovation, we can now concentrate on how change leaders win over others to their innovative products, services, and processes. According to Rogers, diffusion of innovation consists of four elements: innovation, communication channels, social systems, and time.

Innovation

An innovation is completely circumscribed by its newness. That is, to qualify as an innovation, the idea, practise, or object has to seem new to the individual. The individ-

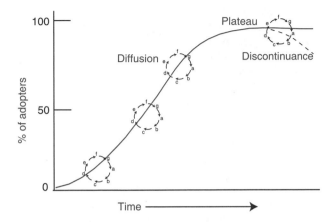

FIGURE 26-2. The relationship between the sources of innovation (Drucker, 1985) and the diffusion of innovations (Rogers, 1995). Key: (a) Unexpected outcomes; (b) incongruities; (c) process needs; (d) industry and market changes; (e) demographics; (f) changes in perception; (g) new knowledge.

ual can know about the idea or practise or object beforehand, but it remains innovative if he or she never formed any judgements or was asked to adopt it previously. In effect, innovations are not necessarily original. They are only relatively new. Individuals judge innovations in terms of other ideas, practises, and objects, which they have accepted or adopted in their lives. If anything, the decision of whether to adopt an innovation depends on its usefulness.

Communication

The diffusion of or communication about an innovation is "a process in which participants create and share information with one another in order to reach a mutual understanding" (Rogers, 1995, p. 35). Diffusion is a social process whereby individuals channel or share their evaluations about an innovation to one another. Because this process is highly subjective, *homophily* plays an important part in the effectiveness of any communication. Defined as the degree to which individuals share the same attributes, homophily includes factors such as social status, education, and the like. Rogers believes that an increase in homophily likely results in an increase in communication.

Social Systems

Defined "as a set of interrelated units that are engaged in joint problem-solving to accomplish a common goal," a social system includes "individuals, informal groups, organisations, and/or subsystems" (Rogers, 1995, p. 23). Within the social system, the diffusion of information largely depends on the social relationships or communication networks among members. Some members, labelled "opinion leaders," have leadership positions because they regularly succeed in influencing the attitudes and behaviours of others. These opinion leaders earn and maintain their positions by reason of "technical competence, social accessibility, and conformity to the system's norms" (Rogers, 1995, p. 27). Because they exemplify the best in the system, these opinion leaders usually occupy a privileged position within the communication network. Linked to other individuals within the social system, they appear more knowing and innovative, if the system is so inclined.

Time

The fourth element in the diffusion process, time plays an essential part in diffusion. That is, insofar as the diffusion of innovation represents an information-gathering and processing activity, time becomes critical to diffusion.

Rogers (1995) reduces time in the diffusion process into five steps. *Knowledge* comes about when an individual or any decision-making (organisational) unit begins to evaluate an innovation. *Persuasion* occurs when an individual or unit forms an opinion about the innovation. *Decision* happens when an individual or unit undertakes activities in support or rejection of an innovation. *Implementation* happens when the individual or unit applies the innovation. Finally, *confirmation* occurs when the individual or organisational unit looks for others to reinforce the earlier decision to implement the innovation.

The period of time required to complete a successful diffusive process describes the slope of the S curve in Figure 26.2. That is, if the quantity (distribution) of individuals or units that adopt an innovation is plotted against the vertical line and the required time is plotted against the horizontal line, then the rate of a successful diffusive process typically appears as an S curve. In other words, as more individuals or units adopt an innovation, the diffusion curve climbs to a point where the trajectory of adoption levels off on a plateau, when fewer and fewer individuals or units, who have not adopted the innovation, remain.

As Figure 26.2 makes clear, the discontinuance of an innovation can also occur. Certainly, given the vibrant and dynamic character of the various internal and external sources of innovation, elaborated on by Drucker, discontinuance likely occurs more frequently than not. That is, individuals can always discontinue a previously accepted innovation. They may want to replace it with another, more applicable innovation. Then again, other innovations are rejected because of disenchantment. That is, individuals or units become dissatisfied with the outcomes associated with the innovation. Whether this results because of a failure to consider all the consequences of adopting a particular innovation or because long-term outcomes differ markedly with short- or intermediate-term outcomes matters little. Remember that pragmatism drives the diffusion of innovation and that any innovation deserves discontinuance if it no longer has a perceived advantage.

RELATIONSHIP OF INNOVATION TO NURSING LEADERSHIP

Apropos to any discussion of how innovation relates to the reform of health care, the innovative accomplishments of Canadian nursing leaders deserve mention. This task presents more than the usual difficulties because nurses typically do not share their innovations with the wider community. Nurses who closely work with small groups of colleagues seldom receive the recognition that they deserve (Beason, 2000).

Fortunately, for nearly the past 35 years, the Government of Canada, through the Office of the Governor General, has recognised the outstanding achievements and lifetime contributions of those Canadians, including 37 nurses, who have made significant contributions to our society (http://www.gg.ca/honours/ordersrch e.html). Created in 1967, the Order of Canada lies at the centre of Canada's system of honors. Divided into three levels, the Order of Canada includes, in ascending order: Members, Officers, and Companions. Of the nurses who received the Order, 25 are Members, 11 are Officers, and 1 is a Companion (Table 26.1).

The only recipient of the highest level of the Order of Canada is Dr. Helen K. Mussallem. Her accomplishments make her emblematic of the innovative contributions of all the nurses who have received the Order. Highlighting only some of those instances in which Dr. Mussallem had the distinction of being first or truly innovative makes the point that nurses have made sizeable and innovative contributions to health care.

Dr. Mussallem stands as the first Canadian nurse to earn a doctoral degree in nursing. Her published dissertation, from Teachers College, Columbia University, pro-

Table 26.1 Nurse Leader Recipients of the Order of Canada (1969–2002)

NAME	DATE INVESTED	NAME	DATE INVESTED
Moyra Allen, **O.C.**	1987	Kathleen Mary Jo Lutley, **C.M.**	1987
Myra M. Bennett, **C.M.**	1974	Dorothy A. Macham, **C.M.**	1981
Rae Chittick, **C.M.**	1975	Louise Y. Maheu, **C.M.**	1992
Christina Cole, **C.M.**	1992	Edith E. Manuel, **C.M.**	1990
M. Dorothy Corrigan, **C.M.**	1978	Helen McArthur, **O.C.**	1972
Lyle Creelman, **O.C.**	1971	Maura McGuire, **O.C.**	1967
Josephine Gibbons, **C.M.**	1992	Cécile J. G. Montpetit, **C.M.**	1990
Alice Girard, **O.C.**	1968	Helen K. Mussallem, **C.C.**	1992
Helen Preston Glass, **O.C.**	1989	Edith B. Pinet, **C.M.**	1979
Jean Goodwill, **O.C.**	1992	Edith May Radley, **C.M.**	1981
E. Prudence Hockin, **C.M.**	1980	Helena F. Reimer, **C.M.**	1974
Margaret M. Hunter, **C.M.**	1985	Vera Roberts, **C.M.**	1987
Jane L. Hutchings, **C.M.**	1973	Margaret Sinn, **C.M.**	1977
Audrey Jakeman, **O.C.**	1969	Shirley Stinson, **O.C.**	2002
Jean Cecilian Leask, **O.C.**	1973	Margaret M. Street, **C.M.**	1982
Denise Lefebvre, **O.C.**	1983	Juliette A. St. Pierre, **C.M.**	1976
Marie Lemire, **O.C.**	1969	Constance Alexa Swinton, **C.M.**	1987
Clara Yee Lim, **C.M.**	1979	F. Elva Taylor, **C.M.**	1991
Millicent Loder, **C.M.**	1983	D. Ethel Williams, **C.M.**	1985

C.M., **Members of the Order of Canada** are recognized for distinguished service in or to a particular group, locally or field of endeavour; O.C., **Officers of the Order of Canada** are recognized for national achievement and merit of a high degree; C.C., **Companions of the Order of Canada** are recognized for outstanding achievement and merit of the highest degree, especially service to Canada or humanity at large.

vided the impetus to subsequent significant innovations in Canadian nursing education. In addition, she holds the distinction of being the first nurse to address the Annual Assembly of the Canadian Medical Association. She also conducted a survey for the Royal Commission on Health Services (Hall Commission) and a national survey of Canadian Schools of Nursing. She served as Chair (and the only Canadian) on the World Health Organization Scientific Group on Research in Nursing, and the Economic Council of Canada. She worked on the formation of the Commonwealth Nurses Foundation and received a Commonwealth Lectureship. She has also completed international assignments in 37 developing countries under the auspices of the World Health Organization, Pan American Health Association, Commonwealth Foundation, and CIDA (Communication Services, CNA, July 23, 2001).

Undeniably, today's nurses have a plethora of opportunities to introduce innovation into the health care environment. Porter-O'Grady (2000) classifies these innovative opportunities into three categories of change: knowledge-based, perceptual, and unexpected.

Other leaders who have been recognised nationally included recipients of the prestigious Jeanne-Mance Award (Table 26.3) given by the CNA, and the Ethel Johns Award (Table 26.2), given by the Canadian Association of University Schools of Nursing (CAUSN).

Knowledge-Based Changes

The first source of innovative opportunity arises from outside the organisation. Like Drucker, who also classified such opportunities as "knowledge-based changes," Porter-O'Grady (2000) thinks of technologic innovations as limitless opportunities that will significantly increase the independence of patients, who will function more as prosumers. With increased home care, outpatient services, day surgery, and effective health promotion programmes, there will be a decrease in the number and size of hospitals. Future nursing leaders need to abandon thinking that forces dependencies on patient services that warehouse the chronically challenged or economically marginalised. Nursing leaders already recognise that the task is not to fill beds but to reframe the notion of long-term care so that individuals can devise more ingenious solutions to life's challenges. In this way, patients become more responsible, and nurses become more resourceful in improving the effectiveness and efficiency of health care services.

Table 26.2 Nurse Leaders Who Received the Ethel Johns Award (1988–2002)

DATE	NAME	DATE	NAME
1988	Dr. Dorothy Kergin	1996	Dr. Alice Baumgart
1990	Professor Joan Gilchrist	1997	Dr. Denise Alcock
1992	Sister Jeanne Forest	1998	Dr. Susan E. French
1993	Professor Marie France Thibaudeau	1999	Dr. Helen Glass
1994	Dr. Moyra Allen		Dr. Marilyn Wood
		2000	Dr. Shirley Stinson

Table 26.3 Nurse Leaders Who Received the Canadian Nurses Association Jeanne-Mance Award (1971–2002)

DATE	NAME	DATE	NAME
1971	Dr. Helen McArthur	1986	Dr. Dorothy Kergin
1974	Dr. Lyle Creelman	1988	Dr. Maria Rovers (posthumous)
	Dr. Alice Girard	1990	Dr. Shirley Stinson
	E. A. Electa MacLennan	1992	Dr. Helen Glass
1977	Dr. Rae Chittick	1994	E. Louise Miner
1979	Moyra Allen	1996	Margaret Neylan
	Dr. Huguette Labelle	1998	Peggy Anne Field
1980	Dr. Helen K. Mussallem	2000	Dr. Dorothy Pringle
1982	Dr. Verna Huffman Splane		
1984	Dr. Florence Emory		
	Sister Denise Lefebvre		

Perceptual Changes

Whatever nurses think about the newfound importance of economic outcomes in health care, managerialism now drives health care services. Nurses and other professionals have to grow accustomed to this perceptual change (Reilly & Tamlyn, 2001). Targets and outcomes have come to replace goals and plans as costs and resource allocations have come to enjoy new prominence in health care jargon. The challenge that awaits the next generation of nurses is how to devise strategies whereby nurses exercise "responsible autonomy." Not the kind of traditional professionalism to which nurses are accustomed, this new way of doing things nevertheless holds out considerable promise, if nursing leaders will devise more innovative approaches to health care. Only then will nurses become more like knowledge workers, which will allow them to function outside the strict hierarchical system now undergoing transformation.

Unexpected Changes

Porter-O'Grady (2000) speaks of a new foundation for health care when he describes the diminution of an overbuilt hospital system. In this new era in which human capital counts for as much as buildings, equipment, and real estate, nursing leaders have to recognise this event as yet another unrealised opportunity to restructure health care delivery. They have to devise innovative responses to enable nurses to expand their scope of responsibilities beyond the hospital structure. If nurses are to fulfill society's expectations of them, they must welcome public collaboration in moving health services out of the hospital into the community. They must share their vision that health promotion is as important as health protection. They must embrace educational opportunities to increase their competencies so they can become more accountable.

NEW BLEND OF NURSING LEADERSHIP COMPETENCIES

Earlier in this chapter, the discussion of Rogers' (1995) diffusion of innovation emphasised that opinion leaders exhibit "technical competence, social accessibility and conformity to the system's norm" (p. 27). To elaborate on these behaviours and thereby gain a fuller understanding of the theoretical basis, examining the relationship between diffusion theory and social learning theory may be helpful.

Rogers comments that social learning theory (Bandura, 1995) applies directly to diffusion theory. That is, each relies on modelling to explain how individuals learn from one another. According to both theories, individuals learn by observing the verbal and nonverbal behaviour of others. And both stress that the exchange of information is critical and that such communication exchanges help explain changes in behaviour.

A thorough discussion of Bandura's social learning theory goes beyond the scope of this chapter. Fortunately, the interested reader has numerous sources with which to explore the subject, including *Self-Efficacy in Changing Societies* (Bandura, 1995). Therein, Bandura offers his explanations for how people think, feel, and act.

Briefly, according to Bandura (1995), people strive individually and collectively, which Bandura labels as self-efficacy and collective-efficacy respectively, to control their lives. He defines self-efficacy as the belief "in one's capabilities to organise and execute courses of action required to manage prospective situations" (p. 2). Although self-efficacy accentuates self-direction, Bandura makes clear that self-efficacy also lies at the centre of collective-efficacy, or a group's belief in its ability to act on its own behalf. Such thinking finds support in the fact that individuals make up the group and therefore affect and are affected by the groups to which they belong.

Bandura (1995) recognises that in a period of "drastic technological and social change," individuals face "unique opportunities, challenges and constraints." How well they meet these challenges depends on their own sense of self-efficacy because it plays "a paramount role in how well . . . [individuals] organise, create, and manage the circumstances that affect their life course" (p. 35). In other words, how individuals feel about themselves affects their lives at home and at work.

Bandura and Rogers believe that all of life is a learning experience. Informed by systems and human ecological thinking, they theorise that individuals are influenced by their inner ideas and feelings as well as by exterior events. Because individuals learn on their own and from each other, they cannot help but influence others within their social network. When such influences extend to new ideas, we describe them as *innovative*. And the individuals who sponsor the diffusion of innovation are known as *leaders*.

This chapter began by discussing the changeover, or reform, from an expert-driven to a more people-centred health care system. Assuming that health care reform in a knowledge-intense society requires innovation and that the innovative process requires leadership, nurses need "change leaders," if you adopt Drucker's expression, or "opinion leaders," if you prefer Rogers' term, in order to participate in transforming the health care system. These change or opinion leaders, like their colleagues whom they hope to influence, must recognise that their success ultimately depends on their ability to promote innovative applications to the challenges of health care reform.

The fact that hospitals and similar institutions are knowledge-intense organisations means that today's nursing leaders primarily act as facilitators and integrators rather than as administrators. Cooperative rather than paternalistic, this new relationship accepts the notion that knowledge workers become more capable when they share their intellectual resources. As such, these leaders accentuate the development of competencies and capabilities and emphasise the acquisition of self-sustaining, adaptive behaviours among nurses. By emphasising the acquisition of new knowledge and skills, these nursing leaders strengthen and support new strategies with which to implement the external and internal demands for innovation. By focussing on team development, today's nursing leaders strengthen the work of the profession and increase the likelihood of implementing its collective vision.

SUMMARY

This chapter examines nursing leadership as an important factor in health care reform or the diffusion of innovation. Consideration is first given to the changing health care environment and to the leadership role played by nurses in health care reform. Regrettably, nursing, like other knowledge-intense occupations, currently lacks a sufficient cadre of visible and vocal leaders required to develop innovative strategies to address these challenges.

Described as visionary, knowledgeable, confident, and highly visible, these leaders must possess the special ability to promote innovation. They must also know how to diffuse innovative ideas within an organisation. In so doing, they influence others on the health care team to implement new strategies that increase the effectiveness and efficiencies of the system.

Online RESOURCES

Add to your knowledge of this issue:

Health Canada—The Office of Nursing Policy—Health Policy & Communications	**onp-bpsi@hc-sc.gc.ca**
Registered Nurses Association of Ontario	**www.rnao.org**
Canadian Association of Schools of Nursing	**www.casn.org**
The Peter F. Drucker Foundation for Nonprofit Management	**http://drucker.org** and **http://pfdf.org/innovation/index.html**

Reflections on the Chapter

1. Select from among your student experiences an example of how nurses introduced an innovation. Identify the sources of the innovation and critical steps in the innovation process.

2. From your most current clinical practicum, suggest some innovative ways to increase effectiveness or efficiency. Describe the leadership attributes or competencies called for in the innovation process.

3. This chapter discusses the changing health care environment in terms of nursing leadership. How can a new graduate prepare for such a role?

4. Hibberd and Rodger's four attributes of leadership are meant to apply to one individual. Can you provide examples of how different nurses, whom you have observed, displayed one of these attributes?

REFERENCES

Bandura, A. (1995). Exercise of personal and collective efficacy in changing societies. In A. Bandura (Ed.), *Self-efficacy in changing societies* (pp. 1–45). New York: Cambridge University Press.

Barker, A. M. (1990). *Transformational nursing leadership*. Baltimore: Williams & Wilkins.

Beason, C. F. (2000). Advancing innovative nursing practice. *Nursing Clinics of North America, 35*(2), 569–577.

Beyerlein, M. M., Johnson, D. A., & Beyerlein, S. T. (1995). (Eds.) *Advances in interdisciplinary studies of work teams. Vol. 2: Knowledge work in teams.* Greenwich, CT: Jai Press.

Bradham, D. D., Mangan, M., Warrick, A., Geiger-Brown, J., Reiner, J. I., & Saunders, H. J. (2000). Linking innovative nursing practice to health services research. *Nursing Clinics of North America, 35*(2), 557–568.

Bulger, R. J. (1999). What will health care look like in the future? In E. J. Sullivan (Ed.), *Creating nursing's future issues, opportunities and challenges.* St. Louis: Mosby, pp. 14–31.

Burns, N., & Grove, S. K. (2001). Utilization of research to promote evidence-based nursing practice. In *The practice of nursing research* (4th ed., pp. 683–714). Philadelphia: W. B. Saunders.

Calgary Health Region (2001). A (slightly) new name and a new look for the region. [On-line]. Available: http://www.crha-health.ab.ca/frontlines/issue41_1.htm.

Chow, M. P., Coffman, J. M., & Morjikian, R. L. (1999). Transforming nursing leadership. In R.W. Gilkey (Ed.), *The 21st Century Health Care Leader* (pp. 290–298). San Francisco: Jossey-Bass.

Coyle, L. A., & Sokop, A. G. (1990). Innovation adoption behavior among nurses. *Nursing Research, 39*(3), 176–180.

Corey-Lisle, P., Tarzian, A. J., Cohen, M. Z., & Trinkoff, A. M. (1999). Healthcare reform: Its effects on nurses. *Journal of Nursing Administration, 29*(3), 30–37.

Drucker, P. (1994, November). The age of social transformation. *The Atlantic Monthly,* pp. 53–56, 59, 62, 64, 66–68, 71-72, 74–78, 80.

Drucker, P. F. (1999). *Management challenges for the 21st century.* New York: Harper Business.

Drucker, P. F. (1998). The discipline of innovation. *Harvard Business Review 76*(6), 149–157.

Drucker, P. F., Dyson, E., Handy, C., Saffo, P., & Senge, P. M. (1997). *Harvard Business Review, 75*(5), 18–32.

Drucker, P. (1985). *Innovation and entrepreneurship: Practice and principles.* New York: Harper & Row.

Ferrence, R. (1996). Using diffusion theory in health promotion: The case of tobacco. *Canadian Journal of Public Health, 87*(Suppl. 2), 24–27.

Frankel, B. G., Speechley, M., & Wade, T. J. (1996). *The sociology of health and health care: A Canadian perspective.* Toronto: Copp Clark Ltd.

Goleman, D. (1997). *Emotional intelligence.* NY: Bantam Books.

Halverson, P. K. (1999). Leadership skills and strategies for the integrated community health system. In R. W. Gilkey (Ed.), *The 21st century health care leader* (pp. 142–148). San Francisco: Jossey-Bass.

Hein, E. C. (Ed.) (2001). *Nursing issues in the 21st century.* Philadelphia: Lippincott Williams & Wilkins.

Hibberd, J. M., & Rodger, G. L. (1999). Contemporary perspectives on leadership. In J. M. Hibberd & D. L. Smith (Eds.), *Nursing management in Canada* (pp. 259–277). Toronto: W. B. Saunders.

Kirkwood, R., & Bouchard, J. (1992). *Take counsel with one another: A beginning history of the Canadian Association of University Schools of Nursing 1942–1992.* Ottawa: Canadian Association of University Schools of Nursing.

Kizer, K. W. (2000). Promoting innovative nursing practice during radical health system change. *Nursing Clinics of North America, 35*(2), 429–441.

Laschinger, H. K., Finegan, J., Shamian, J., & Casier, S. (2000). Organizational trust and empowerment in restructured healthcare settings. *Journal of Nursing Administration, 30*(9): 413–425.

Lawler, E. E. (2001). The era of human capital has finally arrived. In W. Bennis, C. M. Spreitzer, & T. G. Cummings (Eds.), *The future of leadership* (pp. 14–25). San Francisco: Jossey-Bass.

Longwoods Publishing Corporation. (2000). New models for the new healthcare. *Healthcare Papers, 1*(2).

Marriner-Torney, A. (1996). *Guide to nursing management and leadership.* St. Louis: Mosby.

Nunn, K. (2001, February). *What about nursing leadership? A discussion paper for the nursing leadership conference.* Paper presented at the Nursing Leadership Conference, Ottawa.

The Office of Nursing Policy, Health Canada (2001). Healthy nurses, healthy workplaces. *Proceedings of the National Stakeholder Consultation Meeting.* Ottawa: The Office of Nursing Policy, Health Policy & Communications Branch.

O'Neil, E. (1999). Core competencies for physicians. In R. W. Gilkey (Ed.), *The 21st century health care leader* (pp. 269-277). San Francisco: Jossey-Bass.

Pinkerton, S. (2000). Organizing nursing in an integrated delivery system (IDS). In N. Chaska (Ed.), *The nursing profession: Tomorrow and beyond* (pp. 681–690). Thousand Oaks, CA: Sage.

Porter-O'Grady, T. (2000). Visions for the 21st century: New horizons, new health care. *Nursing Administration Quarterly, 25*(1), 30–38.

Porter-O'Grady, T., & Krueger-Wilson, C. (1995). *The leadership revolution in health care: Altering systems, changing behaviours.* Gaithersburg, MD: Aspen.

Registered Nurses Association of Ontario (2000). *Ensuring the care will be there: Report on nursing recruitment and retention in Ontario.* Toronto: Registered Nurses Association of Ontario.

Reilly, S. M., & Tamlyn, D. (2001). The function of

health knowledge teams in building a learning environment. *Proceedings of the 2nd international conference on researching work and learning* (pp. 485–492). Calgary: Faculty of Continuing Education, University of Calgary.

Reilly, S. M., & Tamlyn, D. (2000). *Nursing 769: Contemporary issues in health care* (pp. 2–3). Calgary: Faculty of Nursing, University of Calgary.

Rogers, E. M. (1995). *Diffusion of innovations.* New York: The Free Press.

Saul, J. R. (1999). Health care at the end of the twentieth century: Confusing symptoms for systems. In M. A. Somerville (Ed.), *Do we care? Renewing Canada's commitment to health* (pp. 1–20). Montreal: McGill-Queen's University Press.

Shamian, J. (2000). On the heels of Florence Nightingale: Re-energizing hospital care. *Reflections on Nursing Leadership, First Quarter,* 24–26.

Sorrells-Jones, J. (1999). The role of the chief executive in the knowledge-intense organization of the future. *Nursing Administration Quarterly, 23*(3), 17–25.

Southon, G., & Braithwaite, J. (1998). The end of professionalism? *Social Science & Medicine, 46*(1): 23–28.

Spitzer, A. (1998). Nursing in the health care system of the postmodern world: crossroads, paradoxes and complexity. *Journal of Advanced Nursing, 28*(1), 164–171.

Storch, J. L., & Stinson, S. M. (1988). Concepts of deprofessionalization with applications to nursing. In R. White (Ed.), *Political issues in nursing: Past, present and future* (Vol. 3, pp. 33–44). Chichester, NY: John Wiley & Sons.

Sullivan, E. J. (Ed.) (1999). *Creating nursing's future.* St. Louis: Mosby.

Synder-Halpern, R. (1996). Health care system innovation: A model for practice. *Advanced Practice Nursing Quarterly, 1*(4), 12–19.

Taylor, F. (1947). *Scientific management.* New York: Harper & Row.

Toffler, A. (1980). *The third wave.* New York: William Morrow.

Epilogue

Elizabeth Thomlinson ▪ Marjorie McIntyre

In speculating about the future of Canadian nursing, students and others can identify trends that affect the profession, consider alternative futures, and challenge themselves and others to analyse how they envision nursing in this new age. Nursing is a dynamic profession that could, and should, positively affect the health of populations. As the health care profession with the greatest number of members, its relative lack of visibility until recently is a matter of concern not only for nurses, but also for society. The vast pool of knowledge and skill that resides within the profession must be tapped to change health outcomes for Canadians. The future of the profession and the health of Canadians are inextricably linked. We are facing broad societal changes that will ripple throughout every sector creating an environment unrecognizable from that which we now know.

FROM WHENCE THE FUTURE

Some of the current global and national trends that will have an impact on the health care of Canadians and on the work-life of nurses include *the information explosion, major demographic changes, the effects of climate change across the globe, advances in technology, the consumers' movement, and changes in health care delivery systems.*

These trends have been evident as the authors in this text examine their impact within each chapter and challenge readers to critically analyse why issues that have existed for years remain unresolved.

The vast amounts of information instantly available through the Internet and the growth of telehealth/telemedicine raise new questions regarding confidentiality and privacy. These changes will affect not only health care delivery, but also the education of citizens and professionals alike. Are nurses prepared and actively developing credible information for responsible distribution? Are they analyzing what is currently available or are nurses allowing others to decide what information will be available? These are questions that, as a collective, we in the profession must address.

The aging of the population within industrialized nations will have an impact on health care needs and the ability to deliver services, regardless of whether nations have socialized, mixed, or private delivery systems. The aging of the population is also applicable to those who deliver the service. As more nurses begin to consider retiring from the profession, a global shortage is evident. Work-life and workplace issues that play a role in the retention of nurses are being researched and discussed. Positive efforts that will affect the retention of nurses are not as evident. Government actions within health care systems such as the layoffs, cutbacks, right sizing, and downsizing of facilities in the early to mid 1990s continue to have an effect on the numbers of nurses available within the profession. It is questionable whether there are adequate numbers of clinical sites to educate the student nurses the system requires to be sustainable.

Another issue that needs addressing is the lack of diversity within the nursing profession. The number of aboriginal students and nurses reflects neither the number nor the nature of nurses needed to meet the complex needs of aboriginal people. Given the predicted increase in growth of First Nations communities, attention must be urgently given to attracting aboriginal students into nursing. Of equal importance is the necessity to increase the cultural, racial, and ethnic diversity within Canadian nursing to more accurately reflect the population of the country. The issue of how to attract a mix of students falls to educators and the profession at large.

The environmental and political changes within the global environment will ultimately have an even greater impact on the health of citizens. Pollution, major floods, droughts, and the increase and changes in parasites and vectors all mean that new and different disease entities will be in evidence throughout Canada. Devastating famines and poverty within the international community will ultimately affect health and health care delivery throughout the world. All of these factors raise issues with which nursing must grapple if the health of populations is to be improved.

In Canada, an increasingly enlightened public is having an impact on health and health care delivery. The need to fully inform patients regarding their health care options and the pros and cons of treatment has altered the manner in which many physicians provide information regarding risks, benefits, and options for treatment prior to the signing of treatment consent forms. Advanced directives, living wills, and consumers' rights movements, as well as questions regarding medical and nursing errors in the delivery of care, will affect practice and education. How informed are nurses regarding the legal and ethical implications of their actions?

The use of embryonic stem cells for research purposes, the genome project, and changes in treatments and materials used in organ transplantation all raise issues with which nurses must contend. Human life can be extended through the use of biotechnology and machines that continue respiration and circulation long past the time when brain function ceases. The ethical implications of biotechnical advances are vast and complex while clinical trials have raised controversial questions about human life. These advances raise an entirely different set of issues for nurses.

THE CHALLENGE

It has been suggested that nurses have waited for others to recognize their worth and the importance of the role nurses have in health promotion, disease prevention, and illness care (Porter-O'Grady, 1998). As nurses, we have often not taken the initiative to demonstrate our value, to sing our own praises. We have not addressed issues head on and we have undermined the actions of others inside and outside of the profession. An alternative viewpoint suggests that female nurses as a group are neither passive nor inactive, but that we have been socialized in particular ideologies of what it means to be a nurse and what it means to be a woman. Conservative ideologies have undermined the initiative of some women to act in direct, challenging, and powerful ways. The challenge is to disrupt discourses that promote and sustain powerlessness and to support one another in raising the profile and the esteem of the nursing profession.

The chaos that exists throughout society does not allow anyone to cling to past successes as a guide for future actions. Change is everywhere and the need to adapt is inherent in every action. It is time consuming and tiring to focus on how to reshape our actions and our entire world in the midst of heavy workloads, turmoil, and little time for reflection. However, the authors in this volume challenge us to: (a) develop a vision of the future we want for nursing; (b) tell others what we do and the value that the system receives from our actions; (c) define the conditions nurses need to provide competent, quality care; (d) build networks and relationships with other health care professionals, government leaders, and policy makers; (e) mentor other nurses, and; (f) become politically active, be cognizant of the issues, and have the data to support our positions. We owe this to nurses, to the nursing profession, and to the citizens of Canada.

REFERENCE

Porter-O'Grady, T. (1998). A glimpse over the horizon: Choosing our future. Orthopaedic Nursing, 17(2), S53-61.

Taking Action: The Mighty Pen

There are many ways of taking political action. One that has been used since time immemorial is letter writing; another is proposing resolutions. These pages feature sample letters to governmental officials, such as the Minister of Health; and sample resolutions, such as one submitted to the Canadian Nurses Association.

LETTERS TO PUBLIC OFFICIALS

Letter to the Minister of Health

Date _____

The Honourable _____, P.C., M.P. Minister of Health
House of Commons Ottawa, Ontario K1A 0A6

Dear Minister _____

The registered nurses of (name your region) are concerned that if no action is taken today, many Canadians will soon be deprived of the quality health care to which they are entitled. This will happen because there will be too few qualified registered nurses to provide the care that is needed. Seventy-five percent of health care professionals are nurses. The stark reality is that Canada faces a severe shortage. (Add an example). This is happening across Canada.

We are writing today to lend our support to the position advanced by the Canadian Nurses Association in its presentation to the House of Commons Standing Committee on Finance. Their brief, "The Quiet Crisis in Health Care," outlines a proposal that could greatly alleviate the looming crisis.

My colleagues and I would like to meet with you at the earliest opportunity to discuss our proposal. I will contact your office to set up a meeting.

Sincerely,

_____ Signature

Alternative Letter to the Minister of Health

Date _____

The Honourable _____, P.C., M.P. Minister of Health
House of Commons Ottawa, Ontario K1A 0A6

Dear Minister _____:

I would like to bring to your attention a problem that has been largely ignored by politicians, but one that Canadians will soon be facing if no measures are taken.

Seventy-five percent of health care professionals are nurses. The reality is that Canada faces a severe shortage of registered nurses with the knowledge and skills to meet the future needs of Canadians. Nurses across the country are using the term "a quiet crisis" to emphasize not only the gravity of this situation, but also the fact that this problem has gone largely unrecognized.

The good news is that there is time to act, and the nurses of Canada have put together a proposal that we believe will largely alleviate the problem.

We believe the federal government should invest in the following three key areas:

- nursing recruitment and retention;
- nursing research that improves patient care and quality of life; and,
- the dissemination and uptake of evidence to provide the best patient care.

Should you wish further information on the nursing proposal, please call me or contact the Canadian Nurses Association at 1-800-361-8404.

From The Quiet Crisis in Health Care Lobby ~ Canadian Nurses Association, September 1998

Letter to a Member of Parliament

Date _____

Name
Address

Dear Member of Parliament _____:

Last September, the Canadian Nurses Association (CNA) presented startling evidence to the House of Commons. The CNA testified that the costs of restructuring have been high, both for nurses and for their patients. The Standing Committee on Finance heard that the nursing profession is seriously affected by the increased casualisation of the workforce whereby approximately 25% of nurses are now working for multiple employers.

I am one of those nurses.

Perhaps, you will want to personalise this part by explaining how this is impacting patient care. Here is an example of what you could write:

I hold jobs for as many as three agencies at one time. In any week, I see patients in one location one day and in another the next. As challenging as this is for me, the impact of continuity of care is enormous. I am not able to conduct comprehensive assessments and to adequately implement a plan of care that involves all of the patients' needs. This is not enough time to provide the care these people deserve. The focus of my activity each day is not on the patients whom I should be caring for, but rather on constantly reorienting myself to the physical facility and how to work in this particular unit. How would you like to have a nurse care for you who does not know how to get emergency help when required?

As such, many experienced nurses are leaving the profession and many new graduates have left Canada. Those that remain, like me, are demoralized, which is why I would like to add my voice to the growing number of Canadian nurses asking that the next federal budget takes into account a nursing investment.

Sincerely,

_____ Signature

From The Quiet Crisis in Health Care. Lobby Kit. Canadian Nurses Association. September 1998

LETTERS TO THE EDITOR AND OTHER MEDIA AUTHORITIES

Write a letter to the editor of an identified newspaper or journal outlining an issue for the purpose of moving that particular issue toward resolution. If a meeting is planned with a local politician, include a news release to the local media to highlight the activities initiated for resolving an issue. The following examples have been taken from *The Quiet Crisis in Health Care.* Lobby Kit. Canadian Nurses Association. September 1998.

Date _____

Editor's Name
Name of Newspaper or Magazine
Address

Dear Editor:

I would like to draw your attention to a serious problem. Amid Canadians' increasing alarm over the quality of the health care system, the impending shortage of registered nurses has gone largely unnoticed by governments.

Seventy-five percent of health care professionals are registered nurses, and the stark reality is that Canada is facing a serious shortage. Already, in our community, the shortage is negatively affecting patient care. Canadians will soon be deprived of the care they require because there will be too few qualified nurses to provide the care they need.

Federal politicians have been saying that the next federal budget will be a health budget. The nurses of Canada are saying the next budget needs to include an investment in quality nursing care.

Sincerely,

_____ Signature

RESOLUTIONS SUBMITTED TO AN ASSOCIATION

A sample of a resolution submitted to the Canadian Nurses Association at the Annual Meeting of June 1998 follows:

RESOLUTION 5   Prescription Drugs

WHEREAS, Pharmaceuticals have an important role to play in preventing illness, promoting and maintaining health, assisting with diagnosis, controlling pain and suffering and improving quality of life;

WHEREAS, The role of pharmaceuticals in the health care system is becoming increasingly important;

WHEREAS, Between 1975 and 1994, expenditures per person (adjusted for inflation) on drugs have more than doubled — increasing from $108 to $232;

WHEREAS, For the same time period, drug expenditures as a percentage of total health spending rose from 8.7% to 12.7%;

WHEREAS, Public spending on prescription drugs pays for less than half of their cost (45%);

WHEREAS, Most provinces provide prescription drug plans for seniors and welfare recipients;

WHEREAS, Four provinces provide some coverage to all residents. However none provide first dollar coverage. The drug plans of British Columbia, Saskatchewan, Manitoba and Quebec include co-payments and/or deductibles;

WHEREAS, Twelve percent of Canadians have no insurance coverage for drugs;

WHEREAS, The National Forum on Health has recommended that the Canadian federal/provincial health insurance system move toward integration of prescription drugs as a fully funded component of publicly funded health care;

WHEREAS, Health Canada and Saskatchewan Health sponsored an invitational conference on National Approaches to Pharmacare in Saskatoon (January 1998) that examined the related issues;

WHEREAS, One of CNA's corporate objectives is to act in the public interest for Canadian nursing and nurses, providing national and international leadership in nursing and health issues;

BE IT RESOLVED THAT Promoting and facilitating the realization of the recommendation of the National Forum on Health with respect to integration of prescription drugs as a fully-funded component of publicly funded health care be designated as a priority of CNA for the next three years.

Source of data: Directions for a Pharmaceutical Policy in Canada, a Report prepared for the National Forum on Health, 1997. Submitted by the Manitoba Association of Registered Nurses.

INDEX

Note: Page numbers followed by f, t, and b indicate figures, tables, and boxed material, respectively.